THE HISTORY OF THE SOMERSET LIGHT INFANTRY
(PRINCE ALBERT'S)
1685–1914

THEOPHILUS, EARL OF HUNTINGDON
First Colonel of the Regiment, 1685-1688

THE HISTORY OF THE SOMERSET LIGHT INFANTRY (PRINCE ALBERT'S) 1685-1914

By
Major-General
SIR HENRY EVERETT, K.C.M.G., C.B.

With a Foreword by
H.R.H. THE DUKE OF YORK, K.G., K.T.
COLONEL-IN-CHIEF

WITH 17 ILLUSTRATIONS
AND 22 MAPS

First Published in 1934

PRINTED IN GREAT BRITAIN

FOREWORD

145 Piccadilly,
W.1.
March, 1934

SOME seven years ago I wrote a Foreword for the History of my Regiment in the Great War, 1914–19.

It is now my pleasure to introduce to the Regiment our History from its formation in 1685.

It gives me added gratification that the Author of this volume is a distinguished Somerset Light Infantryman—Major-General Sir Henry Everett—who, by compiling this record, has added one more service to the long series of honourable achievements he has rendered to the Regiment.

I commend this book to all past, present and future Members of the Somerset Light Infantry. It tells a tale of unbroken heroism and loyal service to King and Country for 250 years, and I am confident that the bugles of the XIII will ever sound the same clear call of duty in whatever quarter of the globe the Regiment may serve in peace or war.

Albert

Colonel-in-Chief

THE SOMERSET LIGHT INFANTRY (PRINCE ALBERT'S). [13]

The Sphinx, superscribed 'Egypt'. A Mural Crown, superscribed 'Jellalabad'.

'Gibraltar 1704-5', 'Dettingen', 'Martinique, 1809', 'Ava', 'Ghuznee, 1839', 'Affghanistan, 1839', 'Cabool, 1842', 'Sevastopol', 'South Africa, 1878-9', 'Burma, 1885-87', 'Relief of Ladysmith', 'South Africa, 1899-1902', 'Afghanistan, 1919'.

The Great War—16 Battalions.—'Le Cateau', 'Retreat from Mons', **'Marne, 1914, '18'**, **'Aisne, 1914'**, 'Armentières, 1914', **'Ypres, 1915, '17, '18'**, 'St. Julien', 'Frezenberg', 'Bellewaarde', 'Hooge, 1915', 'Loos', 'Mount Sorrel', **'Somme, 1916, '18'**, **'Albert, 1916, '18'**, 'Delville Wood', 'Guillemont', 'Flers-Courcelette', 'Morval', 'Le Transloy', 'Ancre, 1916, '18', **'Arras, 1917, '18'**, 'Vimy, 1917', 'Scarpe, 1917, '18', 'Arleux', 'Langemarck, 1917', 'Menin Road', 'Polygon Wood', 'Broodseinde', 'Poelcappelle', 'Passchendaele', **'Cambrai, 1917, '18'**, 'St. Quentin', 'Bapaume, 1918', 'Rosières', 'Avre', 'Lys', 'Hazebrouck', 'Béthune', 'Soissonnais-Ourcq', 'Drocourt-Quéant', **'Hindenburg Line'**, 'Havrincourt', 'Épéhy', 'Canal du Nord', 'Courtrai', 'Selle', 'Valenciennes', 'Sambre', 'France and Flanders, 1914-18', 'Gaza', 'El Mughar', 'Nebi Samwil', 'Jerusalem', 'Megiddo', 'Sharon', **'Palestine, 1917–18'**. 'Tigris, 1916', 'Sharqat', 'Mesopotamia, 1916–18'. 'N.W. Frontier India, 1915'.

AUTHOR'S PREFACE

WHEN the History of the Somerset Light Infantry (Prince Albert's) in the Great War was nearing completion, Lieutenant-General Sir Thomas Snow, K.C.B., K.C.M.G., then Colonel of the Regiment, did me the honour of asking me to write up the earlier records of the Regiment from 1685 to 1914. This task I felt it my duty to undertake.

The official publication of the Historical Records of the Regiments of the British Army was authorized by General Orders dated Horse Guards, 1st January 1836, and in 1848 Mr. Richard Cannon, Principal Clerk of the Adjutant-General's Office, published, under the patronage of Her Majesty Queen Victoria, the *History of the 13th Prince Albert's Light Infantry*. In 1867 Mr. Thomas Carter, of the Adjutant-General's Office, wrote and published an up-to-date edition of the History of the Regiment. This edition was not published by authority.

The present volume of the History of the Regiment is based on Cannon's and Carter's Historical Records and on the Records contained in the Digest of Services of the 1st and 2nd Battalions. I am indebted to the Officials of the Public Record Office, and to the Librarians of the British Museum, the War Office, and the Royal United Service Institution for invaluable help in collecting data for the present Edition. It is impossible to enumerate all the authorities I have consulted in compiling this volume, and I will only mention Sir John Fortescue's *History of the British Army*, which has been the mainstay of my researches for the period ending 1858.

In the spelling of Indian names the Hunterian Method as prescribed in the *Imperial Gazetteer of India*, has been followed as far as possible. The maps have been drawn by Mr. G. Sheppard, Library Clerk at the Royal United Service Institution, to whom I am much indebted.

I tender my best thanks to General Sir Walter Braithwaite, G.C.B., Colonel of the Regiment, and Lieutenant-General Sir Thomas Snow, K.C.B., K.C.M.G., for their valuable help and criticism of this work, and also to Lieut.-Colonel I. M. Smith, D.S.O., M.C., Mr. W. G. Fisher, and many other officers past and present for much valuable help and advice.

I must also express my gratitude to the Regimental History Committee, viz. Brig.-General H. C. Frith, C.B.; Colonel C. J. Troyte-Bullock, D.S.O.; Lieut.-Colonel W. H. Maud, C.M.G.; Lieut.-Colonel J. S. N. Harrison, D.S.O.; Major F. M. Kennedy, C.B.; and the officers Commanding the Home Battalion and Depôt, for their kind assistance and the patience with which they have borne my protracted efforts.

H. J. EVERETT

CONTENTS

CHAP.		PAGE
I	Formation of the Regiment, 1685—The Revolution, 1688—Declaration of the Regiment in favour of the Protestant Cause—Battle of Killiekrankie, 1689	3
II	Battle of the Boyne, 1690—Sieges of Cork and Kinsale—The Regiment in Flanders, 1692	20
III	Expedition to Camarett Bay, 1694; Bombardment of Havre, 1694—Colonel Hastings deprived of his Commission, 1695	30
IV	The War of the Spanish Succession—Campaigns in Flanders—Siege of Venloo, 1702—Siege of Liége, 1702—Expedition to Portugal, 1704—The Siege of Gibraltar, 1705	41
V	Campaigns in Spain and Portugal—The Siege of Barcelona, 1705—The Siege of San Mateo—The Regiment transformed into Dragoons, 1706—Invasion of Valencia—Relief of Barcelona—Battle of Almanza, 1707—Campaign in Catalonia—Action on the Caya, 1709	53
VI	In Garrison at Gibraltar, 1711–28—Siege of Gibraltar, 1727	73
VII	Home Service—War with France—Battle of Dettingen, 1743—Battle of Fontenoy, 1745—Campaigns in England and Scotland against Prince Charles Edward—Action of Falkirk Muir and Battle of Culloden, 1746	82
VIII	Campaign in Flanders—Battle of Val, 1747—Return to England—Designation of Regiments by Numbers, 1751—Service in Minorca, 1769–75—Return to England—The Regiment proceeds to the West Indies and returns, 1781–2	95
IX	Service in England and Ireland, 1783–90—Proceeds to the West Indies, 1791—Campaigns in St. Domingo, 1793–95—Returns Home, 1796—Service in Ireland and England—Expedition to Corunna, 1800—The Invasion of Egypt, 1801—Landing at the Bay of Aboukir—Defeat and Capitulation of the French	106
X	Service at Malta and Gibraltar, 1802–05—Return to England—Proceeds to the West Indies, 1808—Capture of Martinique, 1809—Capture of Guadaloupe, 1810	122
XI	Service in the West Indies—War with the United States—Campaigns in Canada, 1813–14—Returns Home	132

CHAP.		PAGE
XII	Service in the Channel Islands, 1815–19—The Regiment constituted a Corps of Light Infantry, 1822—Proceeds to India, 1823—Campaigns in Burma, 1824–6	141
XIII	Service in India, 1826–38	159
XIV	War in Afghanistan—The Storming of Ghazni, 1839—Occupation of Kabul—Campaign of 1840	165
XV	Sale's Brigade fights its way from Kabul to Jellalabad, 1841	181
XVI	The Siege of Jellalabad, 1841–2	186
XVII	Re-occupation of Kabul, 1842—Return to India—The Storming of the Heights of Truckee, 1845—Death of Sir Robert Sale, 1845	204
XVIII	Home Service—Presentation of Colours by H.R.H. The Prince Consort, 1846—Service in Ireland and Scotland—Proceeds to Gibraltar, 1851—Proceeds to the Crimea, 1855—The Siege of Sevastopol—Returns to Gibraltar, 1856	220
XIX	Proceeds to Cape Colony, 1856—The Indian Mutiny—The Regiment proceeds to India, 1857—Action at Azimghur, 1858—The Campaign in Oudh—Formation of the 2nd Battalion, 1858	233
XX	Early History of 2nd Battalion—Presentation of Colours by H.R.H. The Prince Consort, 1859—Proceeds to Cape Colony—Death of the Prince Consort, 1862—The 2nd Battalion proceeds to Mauritius, 1863—The 1st Battalion returns home from India, 1864—The 2nd Battalion returns Home, 1867	254
XXI	The 1st Battalion proceeds to Gibraltar, 1867 and to Malta, 1872—The 2nd Battalion in England and Ireland, 1867–77—Embarks for Malta, 1877—The 1st Battalion proceeds to Cape Colony, 1875—Marches to Pretoria, 1877	269
XXII	1st Battalion—The Campaign against Sekukini, 1878—The Zulu War, 1879—Battle of Kambula—Battle of Ulundi—The Battalion returns Home	277
XXIII	1st Battalion—Service at Home, 1879–91—Proceeds to Gibraltar, 1891—2nd Battalion at Malta, 1877—Proceeds to India, 1878—The Burmese War, 1885-6-7—Returns to India, 1887—Proceeds Home, 1894	293
XXIV	1st Battalion proceeds to India, 1893—The Mohmand Campaign, 1897—The 2nd Battalion on Home Service, 1894–9	308
XXV	2nd Battalion—South African War, 1899–1900—Battles of Spion Kop, Vaal Krantz, and Relief of Ladysmith in Natal, 1900	322
XXVI	2nd Battalion—South African War continued, 1900–02	339

CONTENTS

CHAP.		PAGE
XXVII	1st Battalion Service in India, 1899–1908—Proceeds Home—2nd Battalion Service in South Africa—Proceeds Home, 1903—Home Service, 1903–08—Proceeds to Malta, 1908—Proceeds to Tientsin and Peking, 1911—Proceeds to India, 1913—1st Battalion Home Service, 1908–14	362
	Conclusion	379
Appendix A.	Succession of Colonels	381
Appendix B.	Succession of Lieut.-Colonels	396
Appendix C.	Succession of Adjutants	397
Appendix D.	Description of Medals awarded to the Regiment	398
Appendix E.	Farewell Addresses to the Regiment in the Channel Islands, 1817, 1819	411
Appendix F.	Memorandum on the Wearing of the Sash	413
Index		419

LIST OF ILLUSTRATIONS

	FACING PAGE
Theophilus, Earl of Huntingdon, First Colonel of the Regiment, 1685–1688	*Frontispiece*
The Earl of Huntingdon's Regiment, 1686	8
Major-General Lord Mark Kerr, Colonel of the Regiment, 1725–1732	78
Pulteney's (13th) Foot, 1742	84
H.R.H. William Henry, Duke of Gloucester, K.G., Colonel of the Regiment, 1766–1767	100
Major-General Sir Henry Havelock, K.C.B.	146
Afghan Flags	174
Thirteenth, Prince Albert's Regiment of Light Infantry, 1840	178
H.R.H. The Prince Consort	202
Major-General Sir Robert Sale, G.C.B., Colonel of the Regiment, 1843–1845	218
General Sir William Maynard Gomm, G.C.B., Colonel of the Regiment, 1846–1863	220
Colours; Thirteenth, Prince Albert's Regiment of Light Infantry, 1846	222
General Lord Mark Kerr, K.C.B., Colonel of the Regiment, 1880–1900	238
Recruiting Poster, 1864	259
Major-General E. L. England, C.B., Colonel of the Regiment, 1901–1910	292
Major-General Sir Henry Hallam Parr, K.C.B., C.M.G., Colonel of the Regiment, 1910–1914	308
Major-General R. L. Payne, C.B., D.S.O., Colonel of the Regiment, 1914–19	376

THE COLOUR PLATES IN THIS REPRINT ARE PLACED AFTER THIS PAGE

xv

MAPS
(From Drawings by G. Sheppard)

	FACING PAGE
Battle of the Boyne, July 1st, 1690	24
Spain and Portugal, 1705–13	72
Dettingen, June 27th, 1743	86
Fontenoy, May 10th, 1745	90
Culloden, April 16th, 1746	94
Val or Lauffeld, July 2nd, 1747	96
Alexandria, 1801	118
Lower Egypt, 1801	120
Martinique, 1809	130
Burma, 1824–6	158
Siege of Jellalabad, 1841–2	196
N.W. Frontier of India and Afghanistan, 1839–42	208
Sevastopol, 1855	232
United Provinces, Oudh, India, 1858	252
Kambula, March 29th, 1879	286
Ulundi, July 5th, 1879	290
Zululand, 1879	292
Burma, 1885–7	304
Vaal Krantz, February 1900	332
The Relief of Ladysmith, 1900	334
Pieter's Hill, February 27th, 1900	338
South Africa, 1899–1902	360

MUSKETEER   GRENADIER   PIKEMAN

**THE EARL OF HUNTINGDON'S REGIMENT, 1686
NOW
SOMERSET LIGHT INFANTRY (PRINCE ALBERT'S)**

PULTENEY'S (13th) FOOT
1742

AFGHAN FLAGS
THE TWO OUTER FLAGS WERE CAPTURED FROM THE AFGHANS BY THE THIRTEENTH LIGHT INFANTRY AT GHAZNI, ON THE 23rd JULY, 1839, AND THE CENTRE ONE AT JELLALABAD ON APRIL 7th, 1842

THIRTEENTH, PRINCE ALBERT'S REGIMENT OF LIGHT INFANTRY
1840

QUEEN'S COLOUR

REGIMENTAL COLOUR

THIRTEENTH, PRINCE ALBERT'S REGIMENT OF LIGHT INFANTRY
1846

THE HISTORY OF THE SOMERSET LIGHT INFANTRY

(PRINCE ALBERT'S)
1685–1914

THE HISTORY OF THE SOMERSET LIGHT INFANTRY
(PRINCE ALBERT'S)
CHAPTER I
FORMATION OF REGIMENT AND EARLY HISTORY

THE origin and formation of the Regiment is inseparably bound up with that of the Standing Army of which it forms a component part. It may be said that the Regular Army dates its origin to the reigns of Charles II and James II, though a few regiments can claim a still more ancient foundation, being linked up with the Cromwellian Army, one of the most efficient armies the country has ever possessed. Had the Army of the Restoration inherited more of the virtues of the Commonwealth Army and less of the vices of the Stuart Régime, its records might have been more glorious. On the other hand, the Commonwealth Army was not content only to fight, but it must also govern. Hence arose the long-standing jealousy between Parliament and the Army; the people of England regarding a standing Army as a menace to their liberties. In spite of these drawbacks it is a remarkable fact that the great majority of the regiments raised in the seventeenth century still exist and have preserved their individuality over a period exceeding two hundred years.

On 6th February 1685 Charles II died and was succeeded by his brother, James II. This monarch was his own Commander-in-Chief, a man of strong military instincts, for he had served four campaigns under Turenne and two more with the Spaniards. Although he was a good military administrator, his talents and character were not such as to fit him to govern a kingdom.

Shortly after his accession he was menaced by two dangers. First, the landing of the Earl of Argyle in the Highlands of Scotland and secondly, the rising in the West of England headed by James, Duke of Monmouth, a natural son of the late sovereign. Both these attempts to subvert the English throne eventually failed, but the precarious position of the new king was evident to all.

The small regular Army, the foundation of which was so jealously watched by parliament and the nation, was quite inadequate for the protection of the crown and kingdom, and in consequence of the troubled state of the country, James II decided to raise several additional regiments of cavalry and infantry to meet the emergency.

At this period it was the custom when enlisting new regiments to call upon some prominent nobleman, a supporter of the throne, to raise a regiment (no doubt a relic of feudal times).

Amongst others who came forward in support of the throne at this important juncture was Theophilus, 7th Earl of Huntingdon, and to him was entrusted, by commission dated 20th June 1685, the task of raising and commanding one of the twelve new regiments of infantry. This Regiment, which was called the Earl of Huntingdon's Regiment, subsequently became known as the 13th, and now bears the title of The Somerset Light Infantry (Prince Albert's).

The effect of these augmentations and of the recall of the garrison of Tangier was that the number of regular troops in England was increased from 6,000 to nearly 20,000 men.

The Regiment was raised in the southern counties of England, and its general rendezvous was at Buckingham, where the Earl of Huntingdon established his headquarters. The Regiment consisted of ten companies commanded respectively by Colonel The Earl of Huntingdon, Lieut.-Colonel Francis Villiers, Major Charles Morgan, Captain Wolstan Dixie, Captain Hildebrand Alington, Captain John Tidcombe, Captain Thomas Skipwith, Captain Brian Turner, Captain Thomas Condon, and Captain Robert Clifford. It will be noted that the Colonel, the Lieutenant-Colonel, and the Major, in addition to their other duties also commanded companies. The other officers of the Regiment were Captain Lieutenant[1] Charnock Heron, Lieutenants William Rhodesby, John Hooks, John Frye, Michael Dunkin, Oliver Gregory, George Keyworth, Henry Walrond, Lewis Walsh, Talbott Lascells, and Ensigns Henry Anderson, Thomas Carleton, Owen Lloyd, Henry Terne, Sir John Jacob, Bart., William Staveley, Thomas Kniveton, William Delavale, Deacon Garrett, and John Orfeur. Talbott Lascells was Adjutant, John Eames, Quartermaster, Gabriel Hastings, Chaplain, and Claudius Gillart, Chirurgeon. All their commissions bore date 20th June 1685.

As a number of loyal men came readily forward to enrol themselves under the colours of the Regiment, it was speedily formed and quartered at Buckingham and Aylesbury. In the middle of July the Regiment was employed in guarding prisoners of war taken after the overthrow of Monmouth's Army at Sedgemoor.

As soon as the rebellion had been suppressed, and the Duke of Monmouth beheaded, the King assembled many of the newly raised corps on Hounslow Heath where the Earl of Huntingdon's Regiment encamped in the beginning of August.

In this year 1685, and also in the next three successive years, the camp at Hounslow Heath became a regular institution corresponding in some respects to the Aldershot of modern days. It was a training ground for the Army, and at the same time sufficiently near London for the troops in camp to overawe the inhabitants of that city; at least such was the intention of the King, but

---

[1] The Captain Lieutenant was the Lieutenant of the Colonel's Company, which the Colonel commanded only to get the pay of Captain.

subsequent events proved that the proximity of the troops to the capital imbued them with the political feelings of its citizens.

Military encampments at this time consisted almost entirely of huts. Probably the more wealthy officers, and certainly the Generals, were accommodated in tents. A hundred years before tents were common, and they came into use again less than a hundred years after the Hounslow Heath camp. In the area alloted to it each company erected its own 'baraques or hutts'. The Colonel's company was always on the right or left, next, at a space of two feet, was the Lieut.-Colonel's company, and so on. At the back of each company's row of huts was a space, usually 20 feet, dividing the company from the officers' huts. This space was known as 'the street'. At the back of the officers' huts were the camp followers' huts where liquor and foodstuffs were sold, often by soldiers themselves or soldiers' wives.

In other respects accounts of the camp at Hounslow afford interesting evidence of the interior economy of the Army of that day. Among other matters it is to be noted that a military hospital was established there with a Matron and female servants, that contracts for the supply of beer, rations, &c., for the troops were made, that orders were issued forbidding the killing of game in the Royal forests, and that instructions were issued on many other subjects which would not be thought to be out of place in the present day. The King took great delight in reviewing his troops, and in August 1685 he inspected ten battalions (including the Earl of Huntingdon's Regiment) and twenty squadrons of cavalry, when he expressed to the officers and men his approbation of the manner in which they had come forward to support the throne in the hour of danger. It is on record also that James wrote a letter to his son-in-law, William of Orange, in which he dwelt on his satisfaction at the efficiency of the troops.

In August 1685 an order was issued which settled for the time being the question of precedence, and all subsequent orders as regards precedence depend on this order. As it is important it is given in full.

'For the preventing of all questions and disputes that might arise for or concerning the ranks of the several Regiments and Companies of Foot which now or at any time hereafter shall be employed in our service and of the several officers and commanders of the same as well upon service and in the Field as in all Councils of War and other Military occasions where they are called upon to appear in their respective qualities we have thought fit to issue out these following Rules and Directions, viz.:

'That our 1st Regiment of Foot Guards take place of all the Regiments of Foot and that the Colonel be always reckoned and take place as the First Foot Colonel; that our Regiment of Foot Guards called the Coldstreamers take place next after which

Afterwards

Our Royal Regiment — — — — 1st Royal Scots.
Our Dearest Sister the Queen Dowager's Regt.
   (The Regiment of Prince George Hereditary Prince of Denmark) — — — 2nd Queen's.

ORDER OF PRECEDENCE [1685

	Afterwards
Our Holland Regiment — — — —	3rd The Buffs.
Our Dearest Consort's the Queen's Regiment	4th King's Own.
Our Royal Regiment of Fusiliers — —	7th Royal Fusiliers.
Our most dear and most entirely Beloved daughter the Princess Anne of Denmark's Regiment — — — — — —	8th Liverpool.
Our Regiment under the command of our Truly and Well beloved Henry Cromwell	9th Norfolk.
Our Regiment under the command of our Cousin and Counsellor the Earl of Bath	10th Lincoln.
Our Regiment under the command of &c. The Duke of Beaufort — — — —	11th Devon.
Our Regiment under the command of &c. The Duke of Norfolk — — — —	12th Suffolk.
Our Regiment inder the command of &c. The Earl of Huntingdon — — — —	13th Somerset Light Infantry.
Our Regiment under the command of &c. Sir Edward Hales — — — — —	14th West Yorks.
Our Regiment under the command of &c. Sir William Clifton — — — — —	15th East Yorks.

are to have precedency as they are here ranked, and all other Regiments of Foot are to take place according to their respective seniorities from the time they were raised so as that no Regiment is to lose its Precedency by the death of their Colonel and all Captains are to take place within their respective Regiments according to the dates of their commission and it is Our further Wish and Pleasure that these Our orders be signified to the Colonels of Our several Regiments of Foot and Governors of our Garrisons to be by them communicated to the respective officers under their command. Given at our court at Whitehall the 3rd day of August 1685 in the first year of our reign.

By His Majesty's Command. W. B.'

Note.—Colonel Tollemache's Regiment (afterwards the 5th Fusiliers) and Colonel Belasyse's Regiment (afterwards the 6th Warwick) were at this time in Holland serving under the Prince of Orange. This is the origin of the Regiment being 13th in order of precedence, but it was not till 1751 that the infantry of the line were officially designated by numbers, and until that year and even for years afterwards, so hard do old custioms die, Regiments were known by the names of their Colonels.

On the 31st August orders were issued for the Regiment to march to Hull. The text of the order is as follows:—

THE COMPANIES OF THE EARL OF HUNTINGDON'S AT LONDON TO MARCH TO HULL

'Our Will and Pleasure is that the Companies in our Regiment of Foot under your command now at London do march from thence according the Rout hereunto annexed, to our Garrison of Hull where they are to remain and do duty in such manner as our Governor or the Officer in Chief Commanding there shall direct. And the Officers are to take care that the soldiers behave themselves civilly and pay their landlords and all Magistrates, Justices of the Peace, etc. Given at our Court at Windsor the 31st August 1685.

By His Majesty's Command.

W. B.'

To

Our Right Trusty and Right well beloved cousin and Councillor Theophilus Earl of Huntingdon, Colonel of one of our Regiments of Foot, and in his absence, the Officers in Chief with the Companies above mentioned.

ROUT FOR THE EARL OF HUNTINGDON'S REGIMENT OF FOOT FROM LONDON TO HULL

No. of Days	Place of Lodging	Rest	Miles	Days of the Week	Days of the Month
	Waltham Abbey				
1	Waltham Cross	—	12	Friday	Sept. 4th
2	Ware	—	9	Saturday	,, 5th
3	—	Rest	—	Sunday	,, 6th
4	Royston	—	14	Monday	,, 7th
5	Huntingdon	—	—	Tuesday	,, 8th
6	—	Rest	—	Wednesday	,, 9th
7	Peterborough	—	13	Thursday	,, 10th
8	Borne	—	13	Friday	,, 11th
9	Sleaford	—	12	Saturday	,, 12th
10	—	Rest	—	Sunday	,, 13th
11	Lincoln	—	14	Monday	,, 14th
12	—	Rest	—	Tuesday	,, 15th
13	Kirton	—	15	Wednesday	,, 16th
14	Barton	—	13	Thursday	,, 17th
	Hull	—	6	Friday	,, 18th

Orders were issued on the same day to the Earl of Plymouth, Governor of the Town and Garrison of Hull, to admit the Earl of Huntingdon's Regiment and to permit the companies of the Holland Regiment to march from thence.

A little later, September 5th, an order was issued from London for Captain Charles Hatton's company to embark from Guernsey and to be incorporated into the Earl of Huntingdon's Regiment. According to the Route, the Company took 16 days exclusive of rest days to march from Portsmouth to Hull. It is probable that this company, like many others, was raised by its Captain and at the time of its enrolment was not allotted to any particular regiment.

Now that the Earl of Huntingdon's Regiment had settled down into winter quarters at Hull, it will be convenient to summarize shortly a few facts as regards its interior economy.

Establishment and Pay

Staff

	Pay per Day
	£ s. d.
The Colonel as Colonel	12 0
Lieut.-Colonel as Lieut.-Colonel	7 0
Major as Major	5 0
Chaplain	6 8
Chirurgeon 4s. and Mate 2s. 6d.	6 6
Adjutant	4 0
Quarter-Master and Marshal	4 0
Total Staff	£2 5 2

The Colonel's Company

The Colonel as Captain	8 0
Lieutenant	4 0
Ensign	3 0
Two Sergeants, 1s. 6d. each	3 0
Three Corporals, 1s. each	3 0
One Drummer	1 0
Fifty Soldiers, 8d. each	1 13 4
	£2 15 4
Nine Companies more, one commanded by the Lieut.-Colonel, one by the Major and the remainder by Captains at the same rate	£24 18 0
Total per day	£29 18 6

Per Annum £10,922 12s. 6d.

At this period the uniform of the Regiment was as follows:—

Round hats with broad brims, the brim turned up on one side, and ornamented with yellow ribands: scarlet coats, lined with yellow; yellow breeches and grey stockings; the pikemen were distinguished by white sashes tied round their waists.

Grenadiers wore caps instead of broad-brimmed hats to enable them to sling their firelocks over both shoulders with ease. These caps were first made of fur, then of cloth and afterwards assumed the shape of a mitre. They were armed with firelocks and hatchets, the latter for hewing down palisades. Grenadiers did not carry pikes.

The proportion of pikemen was about one-fifth of the strength, but the number was gradually declining owing to the invention of the bayonet.

The pike as a weapon for officers survived for some generations as the half-pike or spontoon, in the same way as the halberd[1] prolonged its life as the peculiar weapon of the sergeants.

The gorget worn as armour by pikemen survived as a badge of rank among officers long after corslet and tassets had disappeared.[2]

---

[1] The halberd was a combination of spear and battle-axe mounted on a pole, five to seven feet in length.

[2] Corslet = cuirass; tassets are thigh armour.

The sash was worn by all officers from the General down to the Sergeant whether of Horse, Foot or Dragoons. The material was generally similar to that still in vogue, the fringes, however, being in the case of commissioned officers of gold and silver. In this, as in most other details, considerable licence prevailed prior to the Revolution (1689), some officers preferring silver network, others gold, whilst others again favoured the plain crimson silk, but by degrees greater uniformity was ensured, and the use of gold and silver network became confined to the highest officers as is the case to this day.

The fashion introduced of wearing the sash over the shoulder (1857) was usual also in the seventeenth century; during the latter half of the century, however, the custom was generally to wear it round the waist. The sash was commonly tied slightly in front of the left side, although would-be dandies would often have the tassels quite in front and the sash loosely knotted in a very négligé style.

Regimental Colours[1]

The Colonel's Flag, plain yellow.
Lieut.-Colonel's, yellow with St. George's Cross edged white.
Major's, the same with a red flame.
Eldest Captain's as that of the Lieut.-Colonel's without any mark of distinction whatever.
The other Captain's flags distinct in some particulars from the others. It will be remembered that the above-mentioned Field officers also commanded companies.

Coloured drawings and detailed particulars are to be found in a finely illustrated MS. in the Royal Library at Windsor.

We are reminded by the *London Gazette* of 20th December 1685 that the activities of Colonels of Regiments were not confined to their military duties, for we read that His Majesty of His Royal Grace and Favour hath constituted the Rt. Hon. Theophilus Earl of Huntingdon, Lord Chief Justice and Justice in Eyre of all his Forests, Chaces, Parks, and Warrens on the south side of Trent, which office became vacant by the Earl of Chesterfield's surrender thereof into His Majesty's Hands.

The Regiment spent the winter of 1685–6 in garrison at Hull. During this period the only incident of which any record is forthcoming is the conduct of Captain Brian Turner, which evoked the following letter from Whitehall dated 8th January 1686 to the Earl of Huntingdon.

'My Lord,—

His Majesty has taken notice that Mr. Brian Turner, Captain in your Lordship's Regiment, has continued to absent himself from the Garrison, notwithstanding the frequent admonitions that have been given him, which being contrary to his duty and military discipline, His Majesty has commanded me

---

[1] The Colours of this period probably had not the sentimental value of the Colours of the present day; they were more in the nature of distinguishing flags, but the Colonel's Flag of the same colour as the facings of the Regiment is undoubtedly the forerunner of the Regimental Colour.

to say that he be suspended from the benefit and execution of his place of Captain.'

This letter apparently had the desired effect, for on the 29th January another letter was dispatched to the Earl of Huntingdon from Whitehall, informing him that as Captain Turner had returned to duty the suspension was cancelled.

On 13th April 1686 the Earl of Huntingdon's Regiment marched from its winter quarters at Hull to Ware and Hertford, and subsequently on 25th May to Barnett and on the following day to Hounslow Heath.

On 30th June its strength was ten companies of 50 men each. Total 500 men. The Field Officers were Colonel The Earl of Huntingdon, Lieut.-Colonel Ferdinando Hastings and Major Morgan.

During this summer there were two consecutive encampments on Hounslow Heath; the first consisted of 6,760 men and the second of 10,560 men, the Earl of Huntingdon's Regiment being included in both these concentrations.

The health of the troops in camp is the subject of an announcement in the *London Gazette* of 17th June 1686:—

'Notwithstanding the many false and scandalous reports that have been raised and spread abroad by ill men concerning the great sickness and mortality of H.M. Forces encamped on Hounslow Heath, it appears upon inquiry, that the whole number of sick and lame since the time of their Encamping hath been but 138, of which several came so thither, that only two have died, and that the rest are either cured and returned to their Colours or in a way of recovery.'

Turning to incidents at this period of regimental interest, the following notices in the *London Gazette* are inserted:—

'*25th July 1686*. Run away out of Lieutenant-Colonel Hastings' Company in the Earl of Huntingdon's Regiment, William Reyner a Welshman having upon his left foot 6 toes, and on his left hand two fingers growing together, and the little toe on his left foot always sticks out of his shoe; He is pretty tall, black hair, lean visaged, about 30 years old. Whoever gives notice of the said William Reyner at Lieutenant-Colonel Hastings' House in Downing Street, Westminster, shall have a guinea reward.'

From this announcement it may almost be inferred that the Lieut.-Colonel Hastings' company was on duty in London, although the regiment was at Hounslow at the time.

Again on 17th September 1686 the *London Gazette* records:—

'This day Edward Thornton, late soldier in the Earl of Huntingdon's Regt., was executed at Tyburn according to the sentence past upon him at the Sessions at the Old Bailey for having deserted the Colours.'

In August 1686 the Regiment left Hounslow and marched into Yorkshire and Cumberland, the Headquarters being at York with 4 companies at Carlisle, where the winter was passed.

On 23rd September 1686 orders were issued to recruit each company of the Regiment with an additional 10 men, 1 sergeant and 1 drummer, making the strength up to 60 private soldiers, 3 sergeants, 3 corporals and 2 drummers.

In February 1687 the Headquarters at York and the 4 companies at Carlisle marched to Chester. No doubt there were companies on detachment from Chester at this time, for it is on record that one company was ordered to march from Chepstow to Chester dated 14th August 1687.

The year 1687 seems to have been singularly uneventful as far as the Regiment is concerned, but among the orders issued it may be noted that soldiers were forbidden to wear bayonets off duty and officers' servants were not to be protected from arrest. During this year a company of grenadiers was added to the Regiment under the command of Christopher Viscount Hatton (not to be confused with Captain Charles Hatton, *vide* page 7). The Lieutenants of this company were Bernard Ellis and William Hawly.

The other officers of the Regiment at this period, November 1687, were:—

Captains	*Lieutenants*	*Ensigns*
Earl of Huntingdon (Colonel)	Thomas Carlton	William Delavall
	William Rhodesby	Ralph Cadworth
Ferdinando Hastings (Lieut.-Colonel)	John Hooks	Deacon Garrett
	John Frye	Henry Tern
Robert Ingram (Major)	John Sheldon	John Orefeur
Wolstan Dixie	Talbott Lascells	Ambrose Jones
John Tidcombe	Michael Dunkin	Hussey Hastings
Owen Macarty	George Comly	Joseph Byerly
Charles Hatton	George Keyworth	Thomas Kinveton
Sir John Jacob	Henry Walrond	William Callow
Thomas Comdon		
Charnock Heron		

Gabriel Hastings—Chaplain. Talbott Lascells—Adjutant. Claudius Gillart—Chirurgeon. John Eames—Quarter-Master.

The year 1688, the year of the Revolution, was a momentous one for the Stuart dynasty. The regular Army which Charles II had founded and James II had maintained, augmented and trained, was to desert the reigning sovereign, James II, and transfer its allegiance to his son-in-law, William of Orange, without striking a blow for its lord and master.

On the 6th April 1688 orders were issued for the Earl of Huntingdon's Regiment to march from Chester to Allesbury and Wendover. The march commenced on 3rd May and they reached their destination between the 16th and 18th May, the Grenadier Company, Lord Hatton's, proceeding to Southwark.

On 4th June six companies were ordered to Colebrook, via Uxbridge, and five companies to Slough, Eaton and Windsor in relief of the Holland Regiment. The Duke of Norfolk was then Constable of the Castle of Windsor.

'At this time the agitation against the Declaration of Indulgence had reached a crisis. The seven Bishops who had signed the Petition of Protest to the King were examined by the Privy Council on the 8th June. As a result of that examination they were committed to the Tower. Their journey down the river, however, was marked by such demonstrations of sympathy that James became alarmed. He ordered that the garrison of the Tower should be doubled, the Guards should stand by ready for action, and two companies from each regiment should be sent up instantly to London. Even these precautions were considered insufficient as the day of trial, 29th June, drew near. On the 27th June we therefore find Huntingdon's Regiment once again erecting "baraques or Hutts" on Hounslow Heath. The humour of the troops had been such on the day of the trial that, when it became known that the Jury would deliver their verdict on the following morning, James decided to visit the camp in order to ensure order by his presence. The verdict was known at ten o'clock and as soon as the news was received there was some cheering, although it was subdued out of respect for the King's presence. The King was then in the Earl of Feversham's tent. Hearing the noise outside he sent Feversham to find out the cause. On his return Feversham said, "It was nothing but the Soldiers rejoicing on the news of the Bishops being acquitted." "Do you call that nothing?" snapped the King, stamping his foot; then he added: "But so much the worse for them." He immediately left the camp and the pent-up enthusiasm of the troops found expression in continual cheering and drinking the health of the jury and the Bishops.'

In August 1688 orders were issued for all Governors, Lieut.-Governors and Officers of our Army of what quality soever under the degree of General officer, to forthwith repair to their respective Quarters and Garrisons and that they do not presume to absent themselves from thence without leave.

On 9th August the Regiment marched from Hounslow Heath to Plymouth and Pendennis, ten companies to the former and one company to the latter place. Plymouth was reached on 31st August and Pendennis on 6th September. At this time the Earl of Bath was Governor of the Town and Royal Citadel of Plymouth.

From Plymouth one company was sent by sea to the island of Scilly, of which Francis Godolphin was then Governor.

Later in the year, 16th October, it is on record that the companies commanded by Thomas King and Robert Lucas are to march from their present quarters (presumably Plymouth) to Ongar in the County of Essex, and again on 5th November the same two companies are ordered to march from Ongar to the Tower of London via Rumford.

The strength of the Earl of Huntingdon's Regiment at this time was 594 officers and soldiers.

On the 7th November orders were issued from Whitehall for all regiments of Foot to exchange their Matchlock Musquets for Snaphance Musquets.

Meanwhile King James II's policy of subverting the reformed religion and establishing arbitrary government filled the country with alarm, and a number of the nobility and gentry solicited William, Prince of Orange, an ardent Protestant, son-in-law of King James, to come to England with a Dutch army to aid them in opposing the measures of the Court. The Prince of Orange, after one abortive attempt, eventually set sail from Holland on 2nd November with a Dutch Army and passed the Straits of Dover.

On 4th November William landed practically unopposed at Torbay with 10,692 Foot and 3,660 Horse, and on the 8th he entered Exeter. James II, on hearing the news, concentrated 24,000 men at or near Salisbury. As has been previously related, the Earl of Huntingdon's Regiment was in garrison at Plymouth together with the Earl of Bath's Foot (now the 10th Lincoln Regiment). The members of the garrison were divided in their political views, but the Earl of Bath and Lieut.-Colonel Hastings, cousin to Lord Huntingdon, were for the Protestant cause. On hearing of William's landing they arrested Lieut.-Colonel Sir Charles Carney, of the 10th, and the following officers of the 13th viz. the Earl of Huntingdon, Captain Owen Macarty, Lieutenant W. Rhodesby and Lieutenant Talbott Lascells, who were Catholics. As nearly all the other officers and soldiers concurred in this proceeding, the Earl of Bath sent a message to William at Exeter stating he placed himself, his troops, and the fortress of Plymouth at the disposal of the Prince of Orange. The arrested officers were then released, the Earl of Huntingdon retiring to his estate.

The following is an extract of a letter from the Earl of Bath to the Prince of Orange:—

'R. Citadell, Plymouth, *27th November 1688.*
'May it please your Highnes

'I most humbly acknowledge the great honour and satisfaction I receive in your Highnes' letter of the 20th instant. I have in obedience to your Highnes' commands given Colonell Hastings his commission, who deserves extremely well for his great zeale, fidellity and prudent conduct in your service. I shall also most faithfully execute the commissions which your Highnes has been pleased to honor me with. This bearer is sent on purpose to informe your Highnes that on Saturday last, I dismissed all the popish officers and souldiers from this garrisson and confined the Earle of Huntington's person to safe custody where he still continues. On Monday morning I called all the Protestant Officers together and having caused yr Highnes' declaration to be read, I freely told them my thoughts and resolutions and desired to know theirs— They all unanimously declared their readiness to concurre with me in serving yr Highnes in yr generous great designe of defending the Protestant religion, outlands and liberties and the ancient constitutions of England soe that the R. Citadell of Plymouth is with some difficulty but without any effusion of blood secured for your Highnes' service.

* * * * *

'May it please yr Highnes, Your Highnesses most humble, most faithful and most obedient Servant

Signed BATHE'

The Prince of Orange having now no anxiety as regards his rear, marched to Salisbury, which he reached on 4th December without opposition, except for an insignificant skirmish near Wincanton. King James's Army at Salisbury either deserted to the Prince of Orange or dispersed.

In fact, on 11th December King James, having no faith in his troops, issued an order disbanding the army.

James reached London on 16th December and on the 17th part of William's army marched down St. James's Park to Whitehall. James II left England on 22nd December.

The Regiment probably took no part in William's advance on London, for in the *London Gazette* of 17th December, the quarters appointed for the Regiment were Plymouth.

The Prince of Orange promoted Lieut.-Colonel Ferdinando Hastings to the Colonelcy of the Regiment in December 1688.

The exact date of the Regiment leaving Plymouth is obscure, but it is probable that the Headquarters, less six companies, left that garrison towards the end of December 1688. This much, however, is certain: the Regiment was at Salisbury on the 8th January 1689, on which date they commenced their march into Essex and Hertfordshire, the quarters allotted to them being Chelmsford, Witham, Billaricay, Maldon, Hatfield and the two Walthams. The two companies that were at the Tower of London were ordered to rejoin the Regiment *en route* at Whitechapel on 14th January.

There were still four companies at Plymouth, and of these two companies were ordered to rejoin the headquarters at Chelmsford and two companies were ordered to march to Leicester, both these orders being dated 13th January 1689.

The stay of the Regiment in Essex was only a short one, for on the 22nd January 1689 the following orders were issued for Hastings' Regiment to march from Chelmsford and adjacent quarters as follows:—

    4 companies to Leicester.
    1 company to Montsorrell.
    2 companies to Loughborow.
    2 companies to Ashby.

As already stated, two companies were on the march from Plymouth to Leicester which completes the eleven companies of the Regiment.

Great activity in raising recruits for the Regiment may be noted at this time. Officers of Hastings' Regiment were sent to Stafford and thence to Belfast to take over 450 recruits for the Regiment and again another party of officers was sent to Ireland from Chester to take over 150 recruits.

With the addition of these reinforcements the Regiment must have been largely composed of men from Ireland and have exceeded in strength the peace establishment considerably.

On 28th March orders were issued for Hastings' Regiment to march to Berwick and places adjacent in the county of Northumberland, and they reached their destination on 27th and 28th April.

In the meantime events were occurring in Ireland and Scotland full of menace to the safety of William's throne.

James II had landed at Cork on 14th March with some hundreds of officers to organize Irish levies, while in Scotland opinion was much divided as to whether James or William should be considered the rightful sovereign. As this history is more immediately concerned with events in Scotland, a short survey of the situation there is now given.

The accession of the Prince and Princess of Orange to the throne was not accepted in Scotland with the same complacency as obtained in England.

Scotsmen as a whole were not interested in English politics, but at the same time there was a distinct cleavage between the Protestant and Catholic interests. Broadly speaking, the Lowlanders, being chiefly Presbyterians, were for King William, while the Highlanders were for King James, but even these latter were divided among themselves. The Highland chiefs were principally concerned in their own ambitions and rivalries, while the question of who was king was merely of secondary importance.

So it came about that when the Convention met in Edinburgh on 14th March, the Duke of Hamilton, a supporter of King William, was elected as President by a majority of forty. A summons was sent to the Duke of Gordon, a supporter of King James, requesting him to leave Edinburgh Castle within twenty-four hours. On the advice of the Viscount of Dundee and Lord Balcarras, Gordon sent an evasive reply, and the two former left Edinburgh to arouse the Highlands clans, and the siege or blockade of Edinburgh Castle commenced.

About 25th March a squadron of English men-of-war arrived in the Firth of Forth with three Scottish Regiments, Mackay's, Balfour's and Ramsay's, about 1,100 men on board under the command of Major-General Hugh Mackay. These regiments had been in the Dutch service.

According to the Regimental Records, Hastings' Regiment took part in the siege of Edinburgh, but in Grant's *British Battles*, where a long and popular account is given of this siege, Hastings' Regiment is not mentioned. However this may be, it is certain that as the Regiment did not reach Berwick till the end of April, they were hardly likely to be at Edinburgh before the middle of May, and therefore could only have taken part in the later stages of the siege or blockade as it may more properly be termed.

During April General Mackay left the command of the troops besieging Edinburgh Castle to Brigadier Balfour and himself proceeded to the Highlands to conduct the war against Dundee. Although Mackay was an excellent commander on the plains of Flanders, he was entirely unsuccessful in his attempts to hunt down the Highlanders; his efforts to overtake the enemy only resulted in the exhaustion of his men and horses.

At the end of May Colonel Ramsay was ordered to join Major-General Mackay with 600 men of the Scots Brigade. The Colonel commenced his march, but intimidated by the menacing attitude of the Atholl men, returned to Perth, when 100 men of Berkeley's (now 4th) Dragoons, 100 of Hastings'

Regiment, and 200 of Leven's newly raised regiment (now the 25th K.O.S.B.) were ordered to join him.

Thus reinforced Ramsay commenced his march through Athol and Badenoch for Inverness. With the aid of this detachment General Mackay expelled the clans under Viscount Dundee from the low country and compelled them to take refuge in the wilds of Lockaber. Inverness was occupied and a garrison left there consisting of Livingstone's Dragoons, Leslie's Regiment, 200 of Leven's Regiment, 100 of Hastings' Regiment and 200 Highlanders. General Mackay marched south again on 20th June with the Scots Brigade and reached Edinburgh at the beginning of July.

During the absence of General Mackay in the Highlands the surrender of Edinburgh Castle took place on 14th June, thus relieving the investing forces.

General Mackay, having scattered his troops in the low country between Aberdeen and Stirling, now learnt that the clans under Dundee at Lockaber expected to be joined by a reinforcement from Ireland, and were preparing to descend into the low country. These reinforcements only amounted to 300 men ill-armed, ill-clothed and ill-disciplined.

Mackay ordered a concentration of all available troops at Perth.

About midway between Perth and Lockaber lies the Castle of Blair near the western exit of the Pass of Killiekrankie. The situation at Castle Blair at this time is a good example of the differences among the Highland chiefs. Castle Blair was held by Stewart of Ballenach, a Jacobite, Atholl's agent and a supporter of King James. Lord Murray, a supporter of King William and son of the Marquis of Atholl, was besieging the Castle with 1,200 men. The besieged sent messages to Dundee in Lockaber, and the besiegers appealed to General Mackay at Perth for succour.

As a result of these messages Mackay from Perth and Dundee from Lockabar advanced on Castle Blair.

On 26th July Mackay, having collected some 4,000 Foot, viz. Hastings' Foot, later 13th, Leven's Foot, later 25th, Kenmare's Foot (afterwards disbanded) and the Scots Brigade in the Dutch service, viz. Mackay's, Balfour's, and Ramsay's, together with Annandale's and Belhaven's troop of horse, set out from St. Johnstown, Perth, to Dunkeld. On arrival at Dunkeld, Mackay learnt that Lord Murray, whose force of 1,200 men had dwindled to 300 men, had been obliged to raise the siege of Blair Castle on the approach of Dundee and had retired to the head of the Pass of Killiekrankie.

THE BATTLE OF KILLIEKRANKIE, JULY 27TH

General Mackay set out at daybreak from Dunkeld and after a march of 11 miles reached the entrance of the pass at 10 a.m. and rested his troops for two hours, having previously sent on 200 of Leven's men under Lawder to reinforce Murray at the exit of the pass. On Lawder reporting that the pass was clear, Mackay issued orders for the advance.

His army marched in the following order—Balfour's, Ramsay's and Kenmare's battalions first, then Belhaven's troop of horse, Mackay's battalion, and 1,200 pack animals with Hastings' Regiment and Annandale's troop as rearguard. The pass was 2 miles long, the track was rough and rocky and lay along the left bank of the River Garry, but considerably above it. The river-bed itself lay between steep and partly wooded heights.

The passage of this defile naturally occupied a considerable time, but the army formed up on the open ground at the western exit of the pass, awaiting the arrival of the baggage animals and rear-guard. Beyond this open space was some further rising ground on which the enemy, Dundee's Highlanders and Cannon's Irishmen, were posted.

General Mackay's line of battle was flanked on the left by the River Garry and on the right by some rising ground; the infantry were formed up in line three deep with intervals between half-battalions.

In the centre of the line there was a large gap behind which the Horse were formed up so that they might issue forth and, wheeling to the right and left, charge the enemy in flank should he advance to the attack. Hastings' Regiment was on the right of the line, and as was then the custom, the grenadiers company was on the outer flank with a supply of hand grenades, the musketeers forming two wings, and the pikemen standing in column in the centre. Opposite to the Regiment were the Camerons, under the fiery Sir Ewan Cameron, Lord Lochiel, and the men of Skye, under Macdonald of Sleat.

General Mackay's orders were for the army to await the enemy's attack, to reserve their fire till the enemy was within 100 paces and then to fire by successive platoons, so that there would be a continuous fire.

For two hours the armies stood facing one another, Mackay on the defensive, and Dundee uncertain whether to attack or retire.

General Mackay, to provoke the enemy, ordered his artillery, consisting of three little leather field pieces carried on pack animals, to open fire, but what follows is best described in the words of Lord Macaulay.

'It was past seven o'clock. Dundee gave the word. The Highlanders dropped their plaids. The few who were so luxurious as to wear rude socks of untanned hide spurned them away. It was long remembered in Lockaber that Lochiel took off what probably was the only pair of shoes in his clan, and charged barefoot at the head of his men. The whole line advanced firing. The enemy returned the fire and did much execution. When only a small space was left between the armies, the Highlanders suddenly flung away their firelocks, drew their broadswords, and rushed forward with a fearful yell. The Lowlanders prepared to receive the shock, but this was then a long and awkward process, and the soldiers were still fumbling with the muzzles of their guns and the handles of their bayonets when the whole flood of Macleans, Macdonalds, and Camerons came down. In two minutes the battle was lost and won. Balfour's, Ramsay's, and Mackay's Regiment broke before the onslaught. After, in vain, attempting a charge of horse (Belhaven's) who galloped off in disorder—Annandale's men followed. All was over, and the mingled torrent of red coats and tartans went racing down the valley to the gorge of Killiekrankie.

'Mackay, accompanied by one trusty servant, spurred bravely through the thickest of the claymores and targets, and reached a point from which he had a view of the field. His whole army had disappeared with the exception of some Borderers whom Leven had kept together and of Hastings' Regiment, which had poured a murderous fire into the Celtic ranks, and which still kept unbroken order. All the men who could be collected were only a few hundreds. The General made haste to lead them across the Garry, and having put that river between them and the enemy, paused for a moment to meditate on the situation.

'He marched all night. When day broke his task was more difficult than ever. Light increased the terror of his companions. Hastings' men and Leven's men still behaved themselves like soldiers. But the fugitives from Ramsay's were a mere rabble. They had flung away their muskets. The broadswords from which they had fled were ever in their eyes. Every fresh object caused a panic.

'The conquerors, however, had bought their victory dear. While they were advancing they had been much galled by the musketry of the enemy; and, even after the decisive charge, Hastings' Englishmen and some of Leven's Borderers had continued to keep up a steady fire. In this way had Hastings' Foot maintained the military reputation of the Saxon race.'

Nor does this measure of praise of Leven's and Hastings' Regiments stand alone, for in Major-General Mackay's dispatch to the Duke of Hamilton, dated 29th July, he wrote: 'There was no regiment or troop with me but behaved like the vilest cowards in nature except Hastings' (13th) and Lord Leven's (25th) whom I must praise at such a degree as I cannot but blame others.'

In Mackay's official narrative of the battle it is stated: 'I could learn of no commanding officer that misbehaved, though I confess that my Lord Leven, Colonel Hastings and their officers have distinguished themselves on this occasion above all others.' And again to Lord Melville he wrote speaking of Lord Leven: 'My Lord—Your son has behaved himself, with all his officers and soldiers, extraordinarily well, as did also Colonel Hastings with his.'

John Mackay, Esq., of Rockfield, in his life of the General published in 1836, states: 'Hastings on the right, sustained the reputation of the English Lion, but all to no purpose, so far had the panic extended.' Yet it was to some purpose, for these two corps, Leven's and Hastings', enabled the Commander-in-Chief to make good his retreat to Stirling.

The Highlanders' victory had been dearly bought, the loss of the clans in killed and wounded was much greater than that of the King's troops, and, what was worse, Viscount Dundee had been mortally wounded, which left the Highlanders leaderless in the moment of victory. Owing to this, and to the fact that the Highland clans were intent on pillaging Mackay's baggage train, that General was able to withdraw with Hastings' and Leven's Regiments across the mountains to the valley of the Tay. On the following day they reached Weems Castle, where they refreshed, and late at night Castle Drummond. On the following day they reached Stirling. According to Mackay's own account, 500 men accompanied him to Stirling, but in the account in the *London Gazette* dated Edinburgh, 30th July, 1,500 men are stated to have reached Stirling. The latter number probably included a number of stragglers who came in independently. Fortescue, commenting on this battle, writes:

'Mackay's force consisted of 5 battalions, 3 Scottish Regiments, the 13th and 25th, with 2 troops of horse. Of these, the Scotch Regiments trained in the Dutch School by competent officers should unquestionably have been the most efficient, yet all three of them broke before the charge of the Highlanders, threw down their arms and would not be rallied. The two troops of horse took to their heels and disappeared, the 25th broke, as was pardonable in such young soldiers, though they made some effort to rally. The only regiment that stood firm was the 13th, which kept up a murderous fire, and retired with perfect coolness and good order. Yet this was their first action, and Hastings, their colonel, was one of the most unscrupulous scoundrels, even in those days of universal robbery, that ever robbed a regiment. (He was cashiered for dressing his regiment in the cast clothes of another regiment.) Thus the troops that should have done best did worst, and those that might have been expected to do worst did best.'

One of the causes of the defeat of Mackay's troops at this battle was that the infantry had not time to fix the clumsy plug-bayonets into the muzzles of the muskets. Shortly afterwards these bayonets were abolished and bayonets that screwed on to the outside of the barrel substituted, which enabled the musket to be fired with the bayonet fixed, whereas formerly the musket could not be fired with the plug-bayonet fixed. In this way the musket and pike were combined into a single weapon.

The Battle of Killiecrankie was no doubt a disaster, but the results of the battle were the reverse of what might be expected. Within four days of the battle on 31st July, Mackay, undaunted by his failure, with a body of Dragoons defeated a raiding party of Highlanders at St. Johnstone and killed 120. The Highland chiefs quarrelled and many returned to their homes. On 21st August the Cameronians at Dunkeld signally defeated some 4,000 to 5,000 Highlanders. Mackay then occupied the Castle of Blair and established a chain of military forts northwards to Inverness, but the Regiment took no part in these operations.

[1689

CHAPTER II

CAMPAIGNS IN IRELAND

THE war in the Highlands was over.
Meanwhile as previously related, King James II had landed in Ireland, and with a nucleus of French troops had practically conquered the whole country with the exception of Londonderry and Enniskillen with the adjacent country.

The veteran Marshal, the Duke of Schomberg, having collected an army at Chester in August, which included a brigade of Dutch troops under the Count of Sohnes, one cavalry and three infantry regiments of French refugees (Huguenots), landed in Ireland about 20th August with about 10,000 men. He advanced to Carrickfergus which capitulated with two regiments of James II's infantry, thence to Lisburn and Loughbrickland, where he was joined by three regiments of Enniskilleners. Subsequently he advanced to Newry. Meanwhile James II had collected 20,000 men at Drogheda (10th September) and Schomberg reached Dundalk, where the army entrenched.

On 12th September it was announced from Edinburgh that the English regiments there are ordered to Ireland and later, on 10th October, that they set sail with a fair wind on 7th October; subsequently from Dundalk it was reported that Colonel Langston's Regiment of Horse, Colonel Hastings' Regiment of Foot and Colonel Heyford's Dragoons, which came from Scotland, landed at Carlingford on 9th October. On 13th October Hastings' Regiment marched towards Charlemont and on the 17th joined up with the regiments commanded by Colonel Hamilton and Colonel St. John within 5 miles of Charlemont which was being besieged. During November and possibly all through the winter the Regiment was in garrison at Clownish and Monaghan. With the approach of winter King James's army dispersed and went into winter quarters, while Schomberg retired to Belfast and fixed his headquarters at Lisburn.

The state of King William's army in Ireland during the early part of the winter was truly appalling, bad and insufficient food, want of clothing and boots, caused by the peculation of contractors, and the lack of proper shelter from wet and cold caused the soldiers to die by hundreds.

But the new King was a soldier and understood the necessities of an army. The contractors were either dismissed or punished. Clothing and boots were sent over to Ireland, and at the end of the year the *London Gazette* records that provisions were very plentiful in our quarters, beef being sold for a penny and five farthings a pound, and that most of the soldiers, that had been sick, were recovered. Moreover, it was reported that the Irish Army (King James's) was in very ill condition, and very sickly, and that many of them had deserted.

All through the winter of 1689-90 extensive preparations were made for the ensuing campaign in Ireland. Moreover, the King having no taste or inclination for the intricacies of English politics, determined to leave the government of the country to his consort, Queen Mary, and to take the field himself at the head of his army. On 14th May Charlemont, which had been closely blockaded all the winter, surrendered, and the garrison, 800 strong, were given a safe conduct to Dundalk, which lay on the frontier. Before the end of May the English force in Ulster amounted to 30,000 men. Moreover, a fleet with more troops and military stores was awaiting the arrival of King William before crossing to Ireland.

On 8th June orders were issued from headquarters, Lisburn, for the regiments of Lloyd, Babington, Cutts, Hastings, Foulkes, all the Danes both horse and foot, and the Regiments of Dutch Horse to march to-morrow or next day in order to form a camp beyond Armagh, whither the rest of the Forces were to follow.

On 4th June King William left London for Chester, he embarked on 11th June and landed at Carrickfergus on the 14th, proceeding at once to Belfast. James II, on hearing of William's landing, proceeded to the northern frontier of Leinster. William concentrated his army at Loughbrickland, where he inspected the troops and marched south on 24th June. As soon as William's advanced guard reached Dundalk, the Irish retired towards Ardee. By 27th June the whole of William's army, 36,000 strong, and well provided in every respect, was south of Dundalk.

On 30th June William's army marched in three columns towards Drogheda and the River Boyne within sight of the sea and the fleet which protected its left flank.

On approaching the Boyne King William was enabled from some rising ground to view the enemy's position, protected along the entire front by the River Boyne; on its right flank, opposite William's left, was the fortified town of Drogheda, some 2 miles from the sea; on the walls of the town floated together the flags of the Houses of Stuart and Bourbon. The enemy's left flank was protected by a bend of the river. Three miles farther upstream beyond the bend was the bridge of Slane.

King James's army occupied a strong defensive position, but it was inferior in numbers and quality, except that one-third of his force consisted of excellent French Infantry and his Irish Cavalry was good. On the other hand, the Irish Infantry and Dragoons were of inferior quality. Altogether King James mustered some 30,000 men, opposed to King William's 36,000, of which latter half were English, and the remainder Dutch, Danes, and French Huguenots.

During the afternoon King William rode along the front to reconnoitre. Within musket shot of the ford at Oldbridge he halted and dismounted for about an hour. As he was riding off the enemy opened with field pieces and the King was wounded, though not seriously.

Guns were brought up and a bombardment commenced, lasting till evening

At 8 p.m. King William held a council of war, after which the following orders were issued:

The right wing of the Foot under Lieut.-General Douglas and the right wing of the Horse under Count Schomberg,[1] son of the Duke of Schomberg, to march early towards the bridge of Slane and adjacent fords, to cross the river, and to advance on Duleek which lay on the enemy's line of retreat.

The left wing of the Horse to cross the river between the enemy's camp and Drogheda, whilst the main body of the Foot were to force their way across the River Boyne at the fords near Oldbridge and attack the enemy's centre.

Ammunition was ordered to be distributed and the troops to be ready to move at daybreak.

Every man to wear a green bough or sprig in his hat to distinguish them from the enemy, who wore white paper in their head-dresses to bring them into line with their French allies who wore white cockades. The baggage and the soldiers' greatcoats were to be left behind with a small squad from each regiment. The word that night was 'WESTMINSTER'. About midnight, King William rode with torches right along his army.

THE BATTLE OF THE BOYNE, TUESDAY, 1st JULY 1690

The account of this battle is taken from Macaulay's *History of England* and Story's *Impartial History of the Affairs of Ireland*, the latter printed in 1693.

(George Story was the chaplain to Sir Thomas Gower's Foot, afterwards the Earl of Drogheda's.)

In Story's own words: 'The day was very clear as if the sun itself had a mind to see what would happen.' In accordance with the orders, about 6 a.m. Count Schomberg, with the Horse of the Right wing, and Lieut.-General Douglas, with the Foot of the Right wing which included Trelawny's brigade, viz. the 2nd, 4th, 13th, 23rd and Erle's regiments and five six-pounders, in all some seven or eight thousand men, moved westwards towards the bridge of Slane. On the enemy perceiving this move, King James detached the greater part of the French Infantry, 5,000 men, and Sarsfield's Horse from his centre to his left flank.

Count Schomberg, on his way to the bridge of Slane, learnt that the bridge was broken down, and that there were practicable fords nearer; the right wing of King William's army was therefore deflected to the fords at Rossmare, where they crossed the river after some little opposition from O'Neil's Dragoons, O'Neil himself being mortally wounded, and formed up on the other side. After receiving some reinforcements which William had sent them, the right wing advanced with twenty-four squadrons of Horse on its right which greatly outflanked the enemy who by this time were drawn up in two lines covering the approaches to Duleek. The advance was slow owing to the boggy nature of the ground and the deep ditches which intersected the fields. But before

---

[1] Afterwards Duke of Leinster.

following the fortunes of the right wing it is more convenient to revert to what was happening in the centre and on the left.

King William, as soon as he had judged that his right wing had crossed the river, ordered the Infantry of the centre to attack at 10.15 a.m. This they did in the neighbourhood of Oldbridge, the Blue Dutch Guards being the first to cross the river on the right; when half-way over they were received with a peal of shot, but they pushed on and reached the farther bank. The Irish Foot, who were now unsupported by the French Infantry, were easily driven back, but the Irish Horse charged valiantly, but all to no purpose; a lodgement was effected on the farther bank of the river.

To the left of the Blue Dutch Guards two French Huguenot regiments, Sir John Hanmer's and Comt. Nassau's Brigades, together with the Enniskilleners, all crossed the river.

By 11 a.m. the main body was formed up on the right bank of the river while the Irish Army under Tyrconnel, Hamilton, and Antrim were holding the low hills about Dunore.

In the meantime King William himself at the head of the left wing, exclusively cavalry, prepared to cross the river near Drogheda.

For half an hour in the centre a desperate fight occurred owing to the repeated charges of the Irish Cavalry under Richard Hamilton; the veteran Duke of Schomberg was shot dead while rallying the French Huguenots. Walker, at the head of the Ulster colonists, was killed. Just at this time William came up with the left wing and his arrival, and the continued pressure of the right wing, decided the fate of the day. The Irish Horse retired fighting obstinately, though Richard Hamilton was taken prisoner, their last stand being made at Plothin Castle, 1½ miles south of Oldbridge. The Irish Foot retreated through Dunore to Duleek, which latter place Count Schomberg and Major-General Douglas were already threatening with the right wing. The battle was won, King James's army was beaten and in full retreat from Duleek towards Dublin, to which place King James galloped escorted by Sarsfield's Horse. The losses of the conquered amounted to some 1,500 men, mostly cavalry, the flower of the army. The victor's losses were but 500 men.

It can only be conjectured that Hastings' Regiment with the right wing was not very seriously engaged. They were opposed by the French Regular Infantry, but the boggy nature of the ground seems to have delayed their advance more than any action on the part of the enemy.

However that may be, the French infantry saved the situation at Duleek; the Irish army made good its retreat towards Dublin, which was further facilitated by William not pressing the pursuit energetically. He bivouacked that night at Duleek.

On the following day, 2nd July, the fortified town of Drogheda was summoned to surrender, which the Governor agreed to on condition that the garrison of 1,300 men have a safe convoy to Athlone. Of King James's army the Irish Cavalry and the French regiments reached Dublin, King James left Dublin for Waterford and subsequently embarked from Ireland for France.

The same night Tyrconnel and Lauzun, collecting their forces, evacuated Dublin.

On 3rd July the Irish Garrison of Drogheda marched towards Athlone, while King William's army proceeded to Bally Brighan and his cavalry entered Dublin.

On 5th July the army reached Finglass, 2 miles from Dublin, and on the following day King William attended service in St. Patrick's Cathedral.

On 7th and 8th July King William held a great review of his army, and though it often rained very fast, yet His Majesty sat on horseback in the midst of it, and saw each regiment march by him, inquiring the officers' names, and what other things concerning them he thought fit. The Commissaries took an exact list of all the private men, both Horse and Foot, that appeared in the ranks; and it was observable that with heat and dust, marching and other inconveniences, most people in the Army had got very sore lips, nor was His Majesty himself exempt from this inconvenience, for he had toiled and laboured as much as the best of them.

From an abstract of this list it is recorded that Colonel Hastings' Foot numbered 606 men and that neither officers nor serjeants are included in the list, nor yet those that were sick or absent, as several were, but these all marched in the ranks before the King, so that the complete number was much greater.

On 14th July King William divided his army. With one portion he marched on Waterford, and sent Major-General Douglas with another portion towards Athlone, while Brigadier Trelawny remained at Dublin with five regiments of Foot, including Hastings' Regiment, and one of Horse.

In the meantime, considerable alarm had been produced in England by the defeat off Beachy Head, the day before the Battle of the Boyne, of the combined English and Dutch Fleets under Admirals the Earl of Torrington and Evertson by the French Fleet commanded by the Count de Tourville. After this disaster, England was menaced with invasion, and a body of French troops landing on the Western coast destroyed Teignmouth, then a small village.

Among other measures to meet this new emergency King William ordered three regiments of Foot (including Hastings' Regiment), one regiment of Horse and one of Dragoons to proceed from Ireland to England. Hastings' Regiment arrived at Chester at the end of July. From Chester they marched to Abingdon via Worcester, and thence to Portsmouth via Basingstoke and Petersfield to relieve the 1st regiment of Foot Guards, arriving on 15th August.

As the French failed to follow up their naval victory the Earl of Marlborough, then commanding the troops in England, suggested to King William that an expedition should be sent from England to reduce Cork and Kinsale. This project the King approved in the following letter issued in the Queen's name:

Marie R.

'Our will and pleasure is that as soon as our fleet shall arrive at the Spithead you cause the following Regiments of Foot to embark on board the same viz.

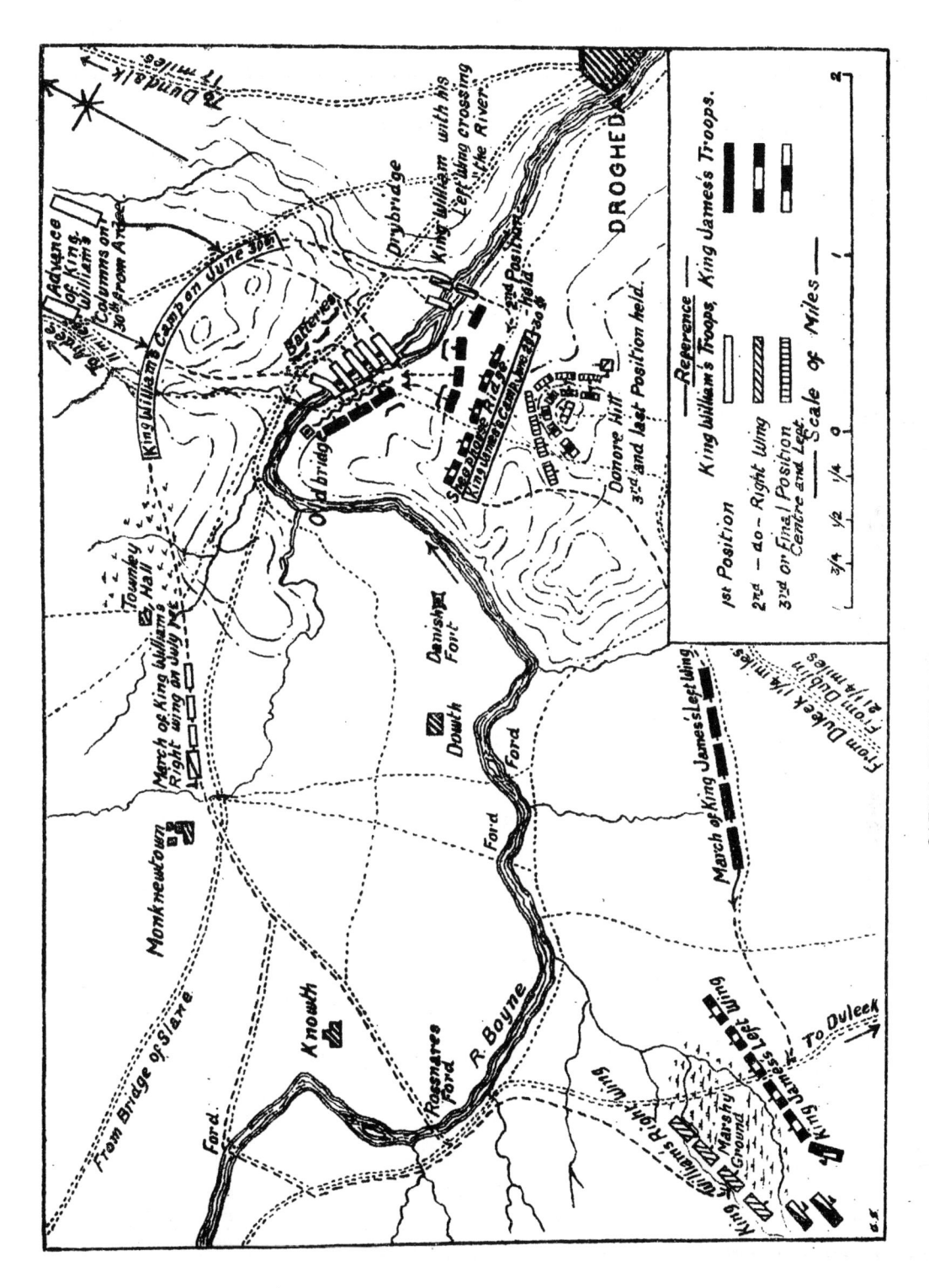

BATTLE OF THE BOYNE, JULY 1st, 1690

the Prince of Denmark's, the regiment commanded by Colonel Charles Trelawny, the Regiment of Fusiliers, the Princess of Denmark's, the Regiments commanded by Colonel Ferdinando Hastings, Colonel Hailes, Sir David Collier, and Colonel Fitzpatrick and that you go on board our fleet and take upon you the command of the said Regiments and sundry other forces as shall be added to them pursuant to such orders and directions from Us and for so doing this shall be your warrant. Given at our Court at Whitehall this 25th day of August 1690 in the 2nd year of our Reign.

By Her Majesty's Command,
NOTTINGHAM

To our Right Trusty, &c.
John Earle of Marlborough,
Our Lieut.-General of our Forces.'

THE CAPTURE OF CORK

The expedition was planned with much secrecy, and comprised, besides the troops enumerated above, a considerable number of Marines from the Fleet and a siege train.

The number of troops amounted to 5,000 or 6,000 men.

The army embarked on 30th August, but owing to adverse winds it was not till 17th September that they got to sea.

Meanwhile in Ireland King William, who was engaged in the siege of Limerick, was compelled by bad weather to raise the siege and to retire to Tipperary, and he himself went over to England, while Count Lauzun, with the French troops in King James's army, anxious for his communications with France, had, on hearing of Marlborough's expedition, embarked for that country.

Marlborough's expedition reached the entrance of Cork Harbour on 20th September and on the following day, having silenced the guns at Prince Rupert's Tower, now known as Fort Carlisle, they entered the harbour and anchored about noon.

On 23rd September the whole army disembarked at West Passage, 7 miles east of Cork, and on the same day Wurtemberg, with about 5,000 men from King William's army at Tipperary, approached the city from the north.

Wurtemberg claimed that, as a Prince of a Sovereign House, he was entitled to command above a mere Lieut.-General. Marlborough was not so easily superseded, however; although in the end he agreed to compromise. It was agreed that the Duke and he should command on alternate days. On the first day Marlborough was in command he gave orders that the word should be 'Wurtemberg'. This compliment completely won the Duke and the next day he ordered that the word should be 'Marlborough', nor did he raise any objection when he found Marlborough's genius asserting itself in council and in the field.

On 24th September Marlborough advanced $5\frac{1}{2}$ miles and took up a position close to the suburbs and within a mile of the city itself, meeting but little opposition, and at the same time Wurtemburg advanced on Shandon Castle and the surrounding hamlets; but the enemy hastily withdrew after setting fire to the buildings.

On 25th September the Admiral sent ten armed pinnaces up the river while Marlborough, accompanied by his staff, made a close reconnaissance of the city walls and forts. As a result he determined to make a breach in the Eastern wall east of South Gate, and finding that Cat Fort had been evacuated by the enemy, Hales' detachment was ordered to occupy it and a battery of siege guns was placed in position ready. Marlborough's headquarters were established in the Red Abbey.

All through the next day Marlborough's guns played on the place in the Eastern wall that it was intended to breach, and in the evening the advanced posts pressed into the suburbs, effecting a lodgement between the Fort and the South Gate.

On 27th September heavy guns were brought up the river in boats and placed in position on the right bank of the south passage and in the afternoon opened fire. The square tower of St. Finbarre's Cathedral was occupied, from which a galling fire was directed into the Fort.

On 28th September the besiegers' batteries opened fire and after some hours of battering the breach was reported practicable and every preparation was made for delivering the assault.

The plan of attack was for 1,000 of Wurtemburg's Danes to cross the north arm near where the New Custom House is now and thence to make their way across the Eastern Marsh to the breach, while at the same time 1,500 English Foot were to ford the South channel from the southern suburb to the island known as Rape Marsh. The enemy held all these marshes with strong outposts. It was dead low water between 2 and 3 p.m. and at 1 p.m. the water was sufficiently low to allow the English assaulting column to ford the river. The column consisted of Churchill's 3rd Foot; the Grenadiers of Trelawny's 4th Foot, the 7th Foot, and Hastings' 13th Foot; with two other English battalions.

The crossing of the river, though the water was up to the men's armpits, was subjected to a harassing fire from the enemy, and was accomplished with little loss. The troops quickly re-formed and drove the enemy from their entrenched posts, advancing up to the high bank forming the counterscarps, where they re-formed. While preparations were being made to make the final rush, the garrison beat a parley and the White flag was displayed upon the walls.

The garrison, consisting of seven regiments numbering 5,000 of all ranks, surrendered as prisoners of war. Fort Elizabeth was occupied by 200 English soldiers.

On 29th September Hales' Regiment was detailed to form the new garrison of Cork and the remainder of the English Army returned to their camps outside the city.

THE INVESTMENT OF KINSALE

Kinsale is about 18 miles from Cork, and after the surrender of the latter town, Marlborough lost no time in following up his success, but sent off on 29th September 300 horse and 100 dragoons under Colonel Neuhansel and Brigadier Villiers to summon the garrison and take possession of the town.

The town of Kinsale in those days was on the south side of the Harbour, protected to a certain extent by the Old Fort, whereas to-day the greater part of the town is on the north side of the Harbour, where the New Fort was then situated. Villiers arrived about 2 p.m. and duly summoned the New Fort to surrender; this the Governor, Colonel Sir Edward Scott, refused. He then made a detour of the harbour and by a rapid charge through the streets cleared the town of Kinsale, only to be held up by the garrison of the Old Fort under its commander, O'Sullivan More. Villiers demanded reinforcements. Three regiments of Foot and three guns reached him on 1st October, while Marlborough himself with the rest of the army reached the New Fort on the following day and proceeded to invest it. Hastings' Regiment formed part of the investing force in the siege of the New Fort.

Marlborough soon discovered that the New Fort could only be taken by a regular siege; his siege train was at Cork, and the roads to that place were in a deplorable condition. He therefore determined to assault the Old Fort first. The assault was successfully carried out on 3rd October when 220 of the garrison were killed and the remainder, amounting to 200 men, surrendered. On the same day trenches were opened within carbine shot of the New Fort, the plan of attack being that the English troops were to attack on the right from the north, while the Danes under Wurtemburg were to attack from the east. By 7th October the approaches were within pistol-shot of the counterscarp. On 9th October the counterscarp was crowned.

With the arrival of the siege train between the 11th and the 14th matters soon reached a climax. A mine was sprung by the English miners on the 14th and on the morning of the 15th the batteries kept up a continuous bombardment and preparations were made for a general assault, when at 1 p.m. the Governor beat a parley and demanded terms. The terms were that the garrison, 1,200 strong, were to march out the following morning with their arms and baggage and have a safe conduct to Limerick.

The spoils were 100 guns and supplies sufficient for 1,000 men for a year. The English lost 250 killed and wounded, but many more died of disease and the hospitals were crowded with sick. Hastings' Regiment is stated to have had only 462 rank and file fit for duty, 216 being reported sick. The Regiment was quartered at Cork during the winter.

When the army took the field in the spring of 1691 under General de Ginkell (afterwards Earl of Athlone) the Regiment was left in garrison at Cork, from whence they frequently sent out detachments in quest of the bands of disaffected peasantry, who prowled about the country in arms, committing every sort of depredation. On one of these occasions, when Colonel Hastings was out with 200 men of the Regiment and 500 militia, he was informed that a party of the Royal Dragoons was surrounded by a numerous body of the enemy at Drumaugh, and he instantly marched to their relief. On arriving in the vicinity of Ballycleugh, he found the hedges on both sides of the road lined with opponents; when the soldiers of the Regiment rushed into the enclosures, killed fifty of the enemy and chased the remainder some distance. On the following morning this detachment of the Regiment drove the Irish from Drumaugh and liberated the party of the Royal Dragoons at that place.

Shortly after this affair, Colonel Hastings marched out of Cork with a portion of the Regiment and some militia, and seized Drummaneer, an important post near the Blackwater.

General de Ginkell, however, with the main army was fast bringing the war to a crisis in Ireland. On 7th June Ballymore, with 1,000 prisoners, was captured, on 30th June the important fortress of Athlone was taken and on 11th July the Irish were decisively beaten at Aghrim, shortly after which Galway surrendered.

On 14th August, Ginkell reached the outskirts of Limerick and commenced the siege of that city. It may be presumed that during this period the Regiment carried out raids, but the only incident which is recorded occurred on 12th September when Captain John Orefear left Cork with a detachment of the Regiment to scour the country, and, arriving in the vicinity of Lismore, he encountered a large body of armed partisans of King James, whom he instantly attacked, killed twenty of their number on the spot, and put the remainder to flight.

The capitulation of Limerick on 3rd October brought the war in Ireland to a close.

With the conclusion of the war in Ireland the authorities woke up to the fact that the troops might require their pay. On 5th November an order was issued to Abraham Tumer, Esq., Commissary-General of the Musters, to take a Muster of all Their Majesties' forces both English and foreign now in Their Majesties' pay in Ireland, by which muster all their accounts were to be stated and satisfaction given them for their arrears of pay due to them since their first coming into the country.

On the 25th December the Regiments of Churchill, Hastings, Collyer, Earle, Brewer and Purcell set sail from Cork for England. Hastings' Regiment landed at Bristol.

The Regiment was at Salisbury on the 5th January 1692 and marched from there to Portsmouth, two companies proceeding to the Isle of Wight.

On 26th January six companies marched from Portsmouth to Winchester, two companies to Romsey, and two companies to Southampton.

On 12th February the six companies at Winchester were ordered to march, four companies to Andover, and two to Stockbridge for the assizes. On the 16th the four companies at Andover were distributed as follows: one company at Whitechurch, one at Overton and the other two at Bishops Waltham,

Wickham, Fareham and Titchfield, and one company at Stockbridge was sent to Sutton.

On the 18th February the assizes being over, the ten companies of Hastings' Foot at Winchester, Southampton, and Romsey were ordered to return to Portsmouth.

One of the consequences entailed by the accession of William and Mary to the throne of England was that this country became embroiled in the long struggle which William as Prince of Orange waged with Louis XIV of France. In the year 1691 King William and his continental allies were carrying on a campaign against the French in the Netherlands in which English troops were taking part.

Between 20th and 24th May the English Fleet defeated the French Fleet at the Battle of La Hogue, and William, judging the occasion opportune for creating a diversion on the French coast away from the operations in the Netherlands, ordered Schomberg, Duke of Leinster, to embark 14,000 men for a descent on the French coast. The troops were collected at Portsdown, Hastings' Regiment among others, the transports ready, and by 26th July all the men were on board, when they proceeded to join the fleet near Portland.

On 28th July a council of war was held on board ship, but as the naval and military commanders were unable to decide what action should be taken, the transports returned to St. Helens (Spithead).

The next information as regards the expedition is that they were at Deal on 19th August and that they set sail out of the Downs on the night of the 20th. After cruising up and down the French coast the expedition eventually reached Ostend on 1st September and the troops were disembarked the following day and encamped at Mariekerke, 4 miles from Ostend.

Leinster's army garrisoned Nieuport, Furnes, and Dunkirk and even occupied Dixmude, contact being obtained with a force sent by King William from his headquarters at Grammen. The winter approaching, King William altered his plans; the English forces at Dixmude, being relieved by Dutch troops, returned to the coast at the beginning of October, and the greater part of Leinster's army prepared to re-embark for England. On 18th October it was reported from Harwich that 25 transports with part of the English army from Ostend arrived on the 17th, and that the rest of the ships, having been separated by bad weather, were now at the Nore.

This expedition seems to have accomplished little or nothing the short time they were in Flanders; they marched and counter-marched, and the greater number, including Hastings' Foot, returned to England without encountering the enemy.

[1694

CHAPTER III

EXPEDITIONS TO THE FRENCH COAST

WHEN the Regiment returned from Flanders in the Autumn of 1692 they were quartered in the Tower Hamlets and continued in the garrison throughout the following year. The principal changes in the list of officers were that David Loches was appointed Captain, Colonel Ferdinando Hastings was promoted Brigadier-General of Foot on 2nd April (but this did not entail his giving up the Colonelcy) and on 30th December Sir J. Jacob, Bart., was appointed Lieutenant-Colonel of the Regiment and Arthur Taylor, Major. From the description in the *London Gazette* of a deserter it is recorded that Mr. Pauncefoote was the Regimental Agent.

In consequence of the bloody but honourable defeat of King William's army at Landen on the 29th July 1693 the Regiment shortly afterwards sent a draft of 150 men to Flanders to replace losses.

THE EXPEDITION TO CAMARETT BAY

In June 1694 with a view to harrying the French coast a considerable body of troops, including a mixed Battalion of Foot Guards, the 6th, 9th, 13th, 19th, and 24th Foot, together with Cutt's, Collier's, Rowe's and Coote's regiments, assembled at Portsmouth, embarked on the fleet, and on the 16th June arrived off Brest. Lord Berkeley commanded the fleet, consisting of 29 ships, and General Talmach the army.

The plan of attack was that the nine Grenadier companies, about 600 strong, under the command of Lord Cutts, were to land in front of the rest of the force and endeavour to find out whether an attack was practicable, and that each battalion should support its grenadier company.

On the 17th June the fleet anchored between Camarett Bay and Bertheaume Bay when Lord Caermarthen, the Rear-Admiral, in his galley, accompanied by Lord Cutts, Sir John Jacob and other military officers, reconnoitred Camarett Bay, and drew the fire of the shore batteries.

On the following day, after a final council of war at 7 a.m., 8 ships under Lord Caermarthen proceeded close in shore between 11 a.m. and 12 noon to engage the enemy's batteries and cover the landing of the troops. It was at once apparent that there were numerous batteries of guns, that every possible landing-place was strongly entrenched and manned by large numbers of soldiers, whilst there were some troops of cavalry in support. Caermarthen endeavoured to report this situation to the Flagship, but already the boats with the troops were on their way to land and appeared to move in great disorder.

The beach, where the landing was attempted, was but 300 yards long and flanked by powerful batteries. Nevertheless, General Talmach, with about 150 men, did get ashore and advanced to some rocks which afforded a slight amount of shelter, but all attempts to advance farther were unavailing, although he was joined by additional troops. Unfortunately the landing was made on an ebb tide. When the troops retreated they found the boats high and dry and were so heavy that they could not be launched easily or quickly. Many of the boats drew too much water to get close in shore, whilst others turned back, and it was evident that the landing was a total failure. General Talmach, mortally wounded, was with difficulty removed in a boat to the fleet, when the Earl of Macclesfield very prudently beat a retreat. Almost the entire landing-party were either killed, wounded, or taken prisoners, and of the ships that covered the landing one was sunk, while they are stated to have lost 400 men killed and wounded, so intense was the fire from the shore batteries. The following officers of the Regiment were killed: Captain A. H. Bocroix, Captain E. Thornicroft and Lieutenant Finnis. The remnant of the Grenadier company of Hastings' Regiment, with its commander, Captain David Loches, were among the prisoners taken by the enemy.

It is related of this officer that while a prisoner with his men at Nantes he gave each of his men 2d. a day besides their subsistence to prevent them taking on with the French, spending £50 in all. This amount Captain Loches endeavoured to recover some years later, but H.M. Treasury declined to reimburse him.

After this rebuff Lord Berkeley, the Admiral, decided on the following day to return to Spithead and he anchored at St. Helens on 26th June. The troops were disembarked for a few days for the benefit of their health and went into camp on St. Georges' Down, Isle of Wight.

So great was the discomfort on board ship that the Admiral thought fit to order hammocks for the soldiers.

Their stay ashore was not a long one. On 8th July they re-embarked, and on the 10th Lord Berkeley sailed up-channel to Rye, where they anchored from the 14th to the 18th. His instructions were to set sail for the coast of France and to make such attempts, or to otherwise distress and annoy the enemy as shall be thought most advisable from time to time at a Council of War.

On the latter date the fleet made for the French coast, Dieppe was bombarded on the 23rd and 24th July and half the town destroyed by fire.

On 25th July the fleet sailed for Havre, arriving on the following day and anchored as near the town as possible. Bomb vessels were placed in position, being protected by small frigates and boats manned by seamen and soldiers, as a protection against any attempt of the enemy to attack them by night. The bombardment commenced on the 27th July at 4 p.m. and continued all night, and the next morning it was reckoned that half the town and several ships in the harbour had been destroyed.

On 1st August Lord Berkeley started from Havre towards La Hogue and

Cherbourg, but as the weather was unfavourable he proceeded to St. Helens, Portsmouth, where he anchored on 6th August.

As the weather was hot and sickness on the increase it was found that ten battalions on board the fleet were too many, and on 6th August it was decided to put six battalions on shore, Hastings' Regiment remaining on board ship.

On 17th August it was decided that Berkeley with the fleet was to proceed to Dunkirk and destroy the enemy's ships there, but a storm obliged the squadron to put back to Deal on 31st August. The command of the fleet now passed to Sir Cloudesley Shovel, who on the 24th September was off the coast of Flanders when he reconnoitred Dunkirk and on 1st October attempted to bombard Calais, but owing to stormy weather little was effected, and the fleet returned to the Thames. The greater part of the Regiment now landed at Tilbury and Woolwich, while two companies landed at Portsmouth, and then marched to Norfolk and Suffolk, where they were quartered as follows :—

- 1 company at Loddon and Harlston.
- 1 ,, ,, Bungey and Halesworth.
- 1 ,, ,, Lowestoft.
- 3 companies ,, Yarmouth.
- 1 company at Norsted and Hickling.
- 1 ,, ,, Caston and Repsham.
- 1 ,, ,, Aylsham and Walsham.
- 1 ,, ,, Foulsham and Tokenham.
- 1 ,, ,, Clay and Cromer.
- 1 ,, ,, Walsingham and Holt.
- 1 ,, ,, Castle Rising and Burnham.

After some further readjustment of quarters during December, the Regiment was ordered at the end of that month to move its quarters as follows:

- 1 company to Ware.
- 1 ,, ,, Hartford.
- 1 ,, ,, Hoddesdon.
- 1 ,, ,, Bedford.
- 1 ,, ,, Hatfield.
- 2 companies ,, St. Albans.
- 1 company ,, Royston.
- 1 ,, ,, Baldock.
- 2 companies ,, Bishop Stortford.
- 1 company ,, Bickleywade.
- 1 ,, ,, Hitching and Stevenage.

During the autumn Hildebrand Jacob, Esq., was commissioned Ensign to Captain Bouchereau, and Ferdinando Richard Hastings, Esq., to be Captain of a company vice Captain Boireaux.

The establishment of the Regiment was then:—

	Officers	N.C.Os.	Drummers	Men
Regimental Staff	8			
12 Companies	36	72	24	720
1 Grenadier Co.	3	6	2	60
	47	78	26	780

Total:—47 Officers and 884 other ranks.

The numerical titles of regiments were first determined by a Board of General Officers assembled by order of William III in this year. The board further recommended that all regiments raised in future should rank from the date upon which they were placed on the English establishment. This recommendation was confirmed afterwards in 1713–15.

Notwithstanding all regiments were simply designated by their Colonel's name till about 1751.

On the 17th February 1695 orders were issued for the Regiment to march to new quarters as follows:—

1 company to Staines.
1 ,, ,, Egham.
1 ,, ,, Windsor or Eton.
2 companies ,, Colebrook.
1 company ,, Chertsey.
1 ,, ,, Ockingham.
1 ,, ,, Maidenhead.
4 companies ,, Reading.
1 company ,, Basingstoke.

It will have been noticed that at the end of December 1694 one company of the Regiment was moved to Royston.

On 23rd January 1695 a Petition of the inhabitants of Royston in the County of Hertford and Cambridge was presented to the House of Commons and read:—

'Setting forth that Captain Henry Cartwright's company of Foot belonging to Colonel Hastings' Regiment, being now quartered at Royston, demand the several sums following to be paid them weekly by the Petitioners for their subsistence over and above their Lodging and other necessaries as the Law required; viz. to the Lieutenant 17s. 6d.; every corporal 4s. 6d. and every private centinell 3s.; to the Ensign 14s., to the Sergeant 6s.; and threaten for non-payment to take the Petitioners' goods; that the Petitioners are not able to bear a grievance of this nature having formerly been great sufferers by quartering two companies of Sir John Edgeworth's Regiment from 12th January 1688 to 15th April 1689 for which the Petitioners never were paid one farthing.'

It was this Petition that led to the disgrace of Colonel Ferdinando Hastings.

In order to understand the Hastings case a short account of the pay, clothing, and subsistence of the private soldier at that time is here given.

His pay was 8d. a day or £12 3s. 4d. a year; 6d. out of the 8d. was paid direct to the soldier as subsistence money and with this sum he had to pay for his food and lodging, the prices of which were fixed by law and left the soldier no surplus. Rations were not issued except during a campaign and then only on payment.

The remaining 2d. a day or £3 0s. 10d. a year was termed gross off reckonings; out of this £3 0s. 10d. the Paymaster-General deducted 12s. and one day's pay, 8d., went to Chelsea Hospital. This left £2 8s. 2d. which was termed the 'nett off reckonings' and formed the 'Colonel's clothing fund' from which the clothing of the Regiment was purchased.

The Colonels of Regiments made money out of this fund by having fewer men on the strength of their units than were actually present on muster parades held once a month, dummy soldiers being collected for these muster parades. Again some Colonels charged their men more for their clothing than they had paid, and they even accepted bribes from contractors.

Even the soldiers' subsistence money was not safe, as instances are recorded of illegal deductions being made for medicine, agency and necessaries.

On the 8th February Tracy Pauncefoot, regimental agent, Lieutenant Turner, Colonel Hastings and Major Moncal attended the House of Commons and were examined.

The House resolved that Agent Tracy Pauncefoot, for neglecting to pay the subsistence money to the Officers and soldiers quartered at Royston, having monies in his hands to do the same, be taken into the custody of the Serjeant-at-Arms.

On the 23rd February the House of Commons inquired into a petition by William Dunston, Chaplain to the Regiment, complaining that he had not been paid his pay. The House found that the petition was untrue and dismissed it, but the Agent Pauncefoot was committed to the Tower of London for refusing to answer.

On the 26th February Colonel Hastings, Lieutenant Tremer, Lieutenant Cole, Ensign Cole, Captain Caworth and Mr. Tracy Pauncefoot were all examined by the House. On the following day the House resolved that Edward Pauncefoot, for contriving to cheat Colonel Hastings' Regiment of 500 guineas, and for giving a bribe to obtain the King's Bounty, be taken into custody of the Serjeant-at-Arms. The House referred the examination of abuses and exactions practised by the Army Agents, &c., to a committee which was to prepare a petition to be laid before H.M. the King.

On the 6th April 1695 the above committee reported to the House and the report was considered paragraph by paragraph and agreed to by the House.

'The Committee lay before Your Majesty the grievance we lie under, by some of the Officers and soldiers of the Army raising money upon the country, under pretence of subsistence; which is such a violation of the Liberty and property of your subjects that it needeth no aggravation.

'This is occasioned by the undue Practices of some of the Agents and officers the particulars of which we beg leave to lay before Your Majesty in order to the more effectual preventing the like miscarriages in the future.

1. 'Some of the Agents have detained the money due to the soldiers in their hands and make use of it to their own advantage instead of immediately applying it to the subsistence of the officers and soldiers for whom they were entrusted.

2. 'Their intolerable exactions and great extortions upon the officers and soldiers for paying money[1] by way of advance: their charging more for the discount of Tallies than they actually paid: by which fraudulent imposing upon those who serve in Your Majesty's Armies, it appeareth that, notwithstanding they have a greater pay than is given in any other part of the world, they are yet reduced to inconvenience and extremities, which ought not to be put upon those who venture their lives for the Honour and Safety of the Nation.

3. 'In particular Colonel Hastings hath compelled some officers of his Regiment to take their clothes from him at extravagant rates, by confining and threatening those who would not comply therewith: By which the authority that may be necessary to be lodged in the Colonel over the inferior officers, in some cases is misapplied and extended so as to promote a private advantage of his own, without any regard to Your Majesty's service, or the discipline of the Army.

4. 'Colonel Hastings' Agent hath presumed fraudulently to obtain 500 guineas, out of a bounty given by Your Majesty to the officers of the Regiment, under pretence of giving them as a bribe to obtain the same; to the dishonour of Your Majesty and injury to the officers thereof, and hath taken two pence per pound out of the money due to the officers and soldiers, for which deduction there being no warrant; the Colonel, whose servant the Agent is, is answerable.

5. 'Colonel Hastings' Agent hath refused or neglected to give an account of the pay due to the Captains of his Regiment and their companies, which tends apparently to defrauding the officers and soldiers.

6. 'Some of the Agents assume the liberty of making great deductions, &c., &c., under the head of contingencies, which giveth them the better opportunity of hiding their frauds and abuses which would otherwise be detected.

7. 'Colonel Hastings hath discharged an Ensign by putting another into his room, contrary to the true discipline of an army: from which the Colonels have no right to exempt themselves, to enlarge their own authority, to the prejudice of Your Majesty's service and of the officers who serve under them.

8. 'Colonel Hastings hath taken money for the recommending commands

[1] Pay and subsistence was often issued very much in arrears and then usually in 'tallies' or 'debentures', which were worth considerably less than their face value.

in his Regiment, to the great discouragement of the officers who are to serve in Your Majesty's armies, who ought to be such as deserve their commands and not such as pay for them.

'These things we most humbly present to Your Majesty in confidence of having them redressed by Your Majesty's Justice and Wisdom.

'Resolved that the above representation be presented to His Majesty by the whole House.'

As a result of this inquiry Colonel Hastings was deprived of his commission on 4th March.

It must not be inferred that Colonel Hastings and his Agent were the only people in authority who were guilty of such malpractices as have been set forth above, and it may be noted that on 23rd March the House resolved: 'That Sir John Trevor, Speaker of the House, receiving a gratuity of 1,000 guineas from the City of London, after passing the Orphans Bill, is guilty of a High Crime or Misdemeanour.'

'Sed quis custodiet ipsos Custodes?'

Some eight years later Colonel Hastings sent in a petition to the Queen praying for her royal compassion and bounty on account of his good services in Scotland and Flanders and his disablement due to long service and sickness. He was granted 'Brigadiers pay from the contingencies if there be room for it'.

On 24th March Lieut.-Colonel Sir John Jacob, Bart., was ordered to assume the Colonelcy of the Regiment. He had served in the Regiment since its formation and had distinguished himself in Scotland and Ireland.

Sir John Jacob made a pretty clean sweep of the Regimental staff, for we find that about this time or soon afterwards that Edward Rorne, Esq., was appointed Lieutenant-Colonel, Bernard Booth, Adjutant, and Duncan Campbell, Quartermaster.

In the meantime on the 19th March the Regiment had been ordered to concentrate at Staines and Ockingham and then to march as follows:

````
1 company    to Haslemere.
1    ,,      ,, Alresford.
1    ,,      ,, Alton.
1    ,,      ,, Fareham.
1    ,,      ,, Petworth.
1    ,,      ,, Midhurst.
2 companies  ,, Petersfield.
1 company    ,, Arundel.
4 companies  ,, Chichester.
````

But they were not to stay long in their new quarters for on the 8th May Sir John Jacob received orders to march his regiment from the neighbourhood of Portsmouth into the Midlands to the following stations:—

2 companies to Leicester.
1 company ,, Ashby de la Zouch.
1   ,,   ,, Oundle.
1   ,,   ,, Lutterworth.
1   ,,   ,, Harborough.
1   ,,   ,, Oakham.
1   ,,   ,, Kettering.
1   ,,   ,, Higham Ferris.
1   ,,   ,, Wellingborough.
1   ,,   ,, Hinckley
1   ,,   ,, Atherton.

On 3rd June the company at Atherton, under the command of Captain Lord Lucas, moved to Nottingham. While the Regiment was in the above quarters, orders were received to send drafts of 390 men to fill up the Regiments of Stewart, Coote, Pezar and Brudenell. These detachments on their way to the port of embarkation lost many deserters in consequence of which all the local Civil and Military Authorities received instructions to assist Sir John Jacob in apprehending the deserters.

On 29th July there was a further re-arrangement of quarters, the Regiment being split up between Towcaster, Northampton, Daventry, Higham Ferrers, and Wellingborough.

On 5th August the Regiment was concentrated and reviewed by Meinhard Duke of Schomberg and Leinster at Northampton, after which the companies were dispersed, one to each of the following places, viz. Daventry, Towcester, Oundle, Wellingborough, Banbury, Bedford, Brackley, Newport Pagnell, Stony Stratford, Buckingham, Chipping Norton, Winslow and Harborough.

On 8th September orders were issued for the four companies at Chipping Norton, Brackley, Banbury and Daventry to march to Berwick-upon-Tweed, one company from Stony Stratford to Bridlington, and the remaining eight companies to Hull.

As a result of the Duke of Schomberg's inspection, that officer was ordered by the authorities at Whitehall to reprimand severely the Colonels of Foot whose regiments he had inspected for neglecting the orders they had received for filling up their regiments, and they were further informed that they would be proceeded against with the utmost vigour, if their regiments were not filled within six weeks.

This rebuke must have seemed very hard to Sir John Jacob when it is recalled that in the preceding June he had sent drafts of 390 men to other regiments.

No further moves occurred during the year except that in December two companies from Hull marched to Berwick-upon-Tweed and Carlisle respectively.

The Officers of the Regiment at this time were:—

Officers in Sir J. Jacob's Regiment. 1695[1]

Captains	Lieutenants	Ensigns
Sir John Jacob, Bart., Col.	And. Hayes.	John Fowkes.
Edward Pearce, Lt.-Col.	Duncan Campbell.	— Chancey.
Mark Ant. de Moncal, Major.	Hen. Van Sisterfleet.	Rene Rabault.
		Alex. Dutens.
John Nanfan.	Tho. England.	Alphee Beauregard.
Phil. Griffin.	Edward Booth.	Josias Clarke.
Ralph Argyll.	George Barker.	John Hall.
David de Loches.	Isaac Scott.	William Gough.
Ferd. Ric. Hastings.	William Bury.	George Edwards.
	William Austen.	Augustin Duquerry.
Thos. Jones.	Nat. Taylor, 1st Lieut. ⎫ Gren.	Hildebrand Jacob.
Robt. Lord Lucas.	⎬	*Adjutant.* Ed. Booth.
Hen. Cartwright.	George Weston 2nd Lieut. ⎭ Coy.	*Qr. Mr.* D. Campbell.
		Chaplain. Bardsey Fisher.

Compared with the previous year, the year 1696 did not involve any extensive moves on the part of the Regiment, the only change of quarters recorded being the march of two companies from Berwick in August: one company to Morpeth and one company to Alnwick. In October the company at Morpeth proceeded to Newcastle.

As may be inferred from what has been chronicled with regard to the results of the Duke of Schomberg's inspection in the previous year, the recruiting problem was very much to the fore. The war in the Low Countries demanded large numbers of men, and the regiments on home service were constantly called upon to furnish drafts for abroad.

On 28th July Sir John Jacob was authorized to raise by Beat of Drum or *otherwise* so many Volunteers as shall be wanting to fill up the respective companies of the Regiment.

There is nothing in this order which calls for comment were it not for the interpretation of the word 'otherwise'. Very questionable methods of obtaining recruits, which can hardly be reconciled with Voluntary service, were then in vogue. As an example the following order to Sir John Jacob may be quoted:—

'Whereas by an Act passed in this present Parliament entitled an Act for the Relief of Poor Prisoners for Debt and Damages it is provided that no man being under 40 years of Age shall during this present war with France be discharged from his imprisonment or have any benefit or advantage by any means thereof unless such person or persons, do or shall before his discharge voluntarily list himself a soldier under some officer of His Majesty's Fleet or Army, or procure one able man to list himself in his place, and whereas we have received information that the persons hereunder mentioned, viz. Ralph Raditt, John Story, Percival Vipart, Thomas Grove, Henry Forster, Richard

---
[1] Ref. *Dalton's Eng. A. Lists*, Vol. IV.

Collins, and George Stevenson now prisoners for debt in Newcastle Gaol are willing to enter themselves into His Majesty's service, in the regiment of Foot under the command of Sir John Jacob, so they may have the benefit of the said Act, we do hereby permit and give leave for the said Sir John Jacob enlisting and taking into His Majesty's Service with the regiment aforesaid the abovementioned persons, or so many of them as shall appear qualified as the said Act of Parliament directs and are willing to enter or enlist themselves as aforesaid.

'Given at the Court of Whitehall, &c., &c.

18th August, 1696.'

As a matter of fact, large numbers of men were pressed, others were tricked into the King's Service after they had been made drunk by the recruiter.

In certain cases criminals condemned to death might be pardoned by accepting the King's Shilling, but it must be remembered that in those days the extreme penalty was inflicted for offences which would now be punished by imprisonment or even a fine.

In the year 1697 the war in the Low Countries was terminated by the Treaty of Ryswick and King William saw his efforts to arrest the progress of French conquests attended with complete success. Consequently all Colonels of Foot, including Sir John Jacob, were instructed to reduce the strength of their regiments as follows:—

Each company from 60 Private soldiers to 42 (servants included).
2 Serjeants.
3 Corporals.
1 Drummer,

except that the Grenadier Company will retain 3 serjeants and 2 drummers. This order was dated 4th November 1697.

The House of Commons even passed a resolution that all forces raised since September 1680 should be disbanded. This resolution was not literally carried out, but the army was reduced by 50,000 men.

Earlier in the year there had been a considerable amount of desertion in the Regiment, as an order dated 5th May directed all Magistrates, &c., to assist Sir John Jacob in recovering 'several soldiers who had run from their colours and deserted'. Nor is this surprising considering that the arrears of pay due to the Army since 1692 amounted to £1,200,000 and arrears of subsistence to a million more.

Few moves took place, and those that did occur were only those of individual companies, viz. two companies from Hull to Beverley at the end of May, who again changed quarters at the end of July to Howden, while two companies from Berwick marched to Alnwick and Morpeth at the beginning of August.

Early in 1698, viz. on 10th January, the seven companies then at Hull, Beverley, Howden, Bridlington and The Key marched as follows:—

2 companies to Berwick.
3 ,, ,, Newcastle and Gateside.
2 ,, ,, Durham.

And again in the middle of February the two companies at Durham left that place and were distributed between Stockton and Yarrow, Bishop Auckland and Hartlepool.

At the end of February Sir John Jacob received orders to march his regiment from their respective quarters to Whitehaven, and to embark and sail from thence to Dublin on board such shipping and in such divisions as the Agents of the Transports shall judge most convenient. Further, that if he found it more convenient to embark at Workington they were to proceed there.

The probable reason for sending regiments to Ireland at this time was that Parliament was clamouring for the disbandment of the Standing Army. King William adopted the expedient of a large Irish establishment in order to have a useful army at hand.

Accordingly on the 14th March we find that part of the Regiment was disposed in quarters at Workington, Dissington, Cockermouth, and Egremont, while the remainder were awaiting embarkation at Whitehaven. Soon afterwards the Regiment crossed over to Ireland. Its movements in that country are uncertain, but it is recorded in the *London Gazette* that The Lords Justice of the Kingdom of Ireland proceeded from Dublin on 27th August to review Brigadier Langston's regiment of horse, Colonel Cunningham's regiment of dragoons, and Brigadier Hanmer's, Sir John Jacob's, and Colonel Tidgcomb's regiments of foot, which are encamped near Lurgan Race.

The strength of the Regiment was further reduced this year from 13 to 11 companies and the establishment of a company exclusive of officers to 2 serjeants, 2 corporals, 1 drummer and 36 private soldiers.

If a House of Commons Resolution about this time is considered good evidence, it is probable that the garrison of Ireland amounted at the beginning of 1699 to 12,000 men distributed into twenty-six different units, while the garrison in England was but 7,000 men made up of nineteen different units.

At the beginning of the year an Act of Parliament was passed which enacted that all foreigners in the Army were to be paid off and their services were to be dispensed with from the 26th March. The officers in Sir John Jacob's Regiment thus affected were Major Moncal, Captain de Loches, Captain La Favelle, Ensign Beauregard, Ensign Du Querry and Ensign Du Tems, probably all French Huguenots. This order caused great consternation among the officers concerned, but it was probably modified, as Major Moncal was still in the Regiment at the siege of Gibraltar in 1705.

There is no record of the quarters occupied by the Regiment during their tour in Ireland from 1698 to 1701, but as that country was comparatively quiet it may be inferred that no events of any great importance affecting the Regiment occurred.

On 18th May 1700 orders were issued for the disbandment of one company in each regiment of Foot, the officers to be put on half-pay. The establishment of the ten remaining companies was raised from 36 privates to 38.

CHAPTER IV

THE WAR OF THE SPANISH SUCCESSION

BY the death of King Charles II of Spain in November 1700 the throne of Spain became vacant. The late King had left the succession to Philip, Duke of Anjou, grandson of Louis XIV of France, and naturally that monarch espoused his grandson's claim.

The combination of France and Spain, the occupation by France of the Spanish Netherlands, the capture of the Dutch garrisons in the frontier towns, and, what was more galling, the recognition by Louis XIV of the son of James II as King of England, brought England and Holland into alliance against France and Spain, and a war ensued which was to last till 1714.

On 14th June orders were issued for 12 battalions, including Sir John Jacob's, to proceed to Holland from Ireland.

The number of companies in the Regiment was raised from 10 to 13, the additional captains being John Lewis, La Favelle, William Austin and William Hyde, the number of men in each company was raised to 59. Another authority gives the number of companies as 12, including the grenadier company.

The establishment strength of the Regiment was as follows:—

	Officers	Serjts.	Drummers	Men
Regimental Staff	7			
11 Companies	30*	55	22	649
Grenadier Co.	3	6	2	59
	40	61	24	708

* The Colonel, Lieutenant-Colonel and Major held rank as Captain in addition to their Regimental Staff Rank and drew the pay of both.

The total pay of a regiment on this establishment was £14,475 5s. 10d. per annum.

Total strength 833 all ranks.

Some delay owing to contrary winds occurred in getting the expedition away from Ireland, but it is recorded that the following 10 regiments assembled at Cork Cove and embarked in 16 ships-of-war in Admiral Fairbourne's command on 26th June, viz. two of Royal Britons, Princess Anne's, Lieutenant General Stewart's, Sir Bevil Grenville's, Sir John Jacob's, Colonel How's, Sir Mathew Bridge's, Colonel Frederick Hamilton's, and Marquis Puizar's.

On 5th July they set sail from Cork, on the 10th they were off Beachy Head, on the 15th off Dover, on the 17th off Margate and on the 19th they cast anchor at Helvoetsluice in Holland.

On 20th July the troops disembarked from the warships and were transferred to Dutch ships and proceeded up the River Maes past Williamstat and

Dort and disembarked on 22nd July, when they marched into garrison at Breda, Gorum, Worcum, Geertruydenberg, Hensden and the Borsch.

On 26th September the above-named troops, under Brig.-General Ingoldsby, marched to the neighbourhood of Breda, where they arrived on the following day. On 2nd October they were reviewed by King William on Breda Heath. His Majesty passed along the line in front and rear and saw each regiment file off in single companies. He expressed himself as well satisfied with the good condition the troops were in. After the review the troops dispersed to their respective garrisons where they passed the winter.

On 25th February 1702 orders were issued to raise the strength of companies in Holland to 3 serjeants, 3 corporals, 2 drummers and 60 private soldiers, with 10 privates more for the Grenadier Company, and on 8th March an additional company was authorized for the regiments in Holland.

On 10th March the Regiment marched to Rosendael, at which place the British Infantry were encamped under Brig.-General Ingoldsby.

King William died in London in March 1702 and was succeeded by his sister-in-law, Princess Anne of Denmark, daughter of James II. About this time Colonel Sir John Jacob, Bart., being desirous of retiring from the active duties of Commanding Officer of the Regiment, obtained permission to dispose of the Colonelcy for fourteen hundred guineas to his brother-in-law, James, Earl of Barrymore, whose appointment was dated the 15th March 1702.

The Officers of the Regiment were at this time:—

Colonel, James Earl of Barrymore.
Lieut.-Colonel Moncal.
Major Jones.

Captains	Lieutenants	Ensigns
Ferdinando Hastings.	Ralph Jenkins.	Anthony Lowther.
Francis Bowes.	Boyl Smith.	Jonathan Fox.
Duncan Campbell.	Charles Booth.	Charles Paterson.
John Weston.	John Thurston.	Patrick Paterson.
George Edwardes.	Charles Moncal.	John Quinchant.
John Duncombe.	Isaac Bruce.	Mathew Draper.
William Bury.	John Lloyd.	Robert Bulman.
Thomas England.	John Stanton.	Daniell Nicholls.
William Charlton.	Benjamin Hodder.	Henry Waldron.
Thomas Hare.	Hildebrand Jacob.	Prosper Brown.
	Robert Wynne.	Thomas Brass.
	John Mohun.	Edward Booth.

Captain-Lieut. Josias Clarke was Adjutant and Lieutenant. Edward Barry was Quartermaster.

Captain F. Hastings was son of the former Colonel of that name, while Captains Lewis, La Favelle, William Austin and William Hyde mentioned on page 41 are not included.

On 20th March Ingoldsby's force of British troops marched off from their winter quarters and went into camp.

At the beginning of April Overquerque, the allied General, had assembled an army of Dutch, Prussians, Hanoverians, Hessians, Palatines, and Danes near Emrich in the Dukedom of Cleves in order to lay siege to Kayserwerth, a strong fortress on the Lower Rhine.

On 24th April the British troops marched eastwards from Rosendael via Kalfsdonck, Osterbout, Tilborg, Nerbost, Evrock and Mookherheyde and encamped between Cranenberg and Cleves on 2nd May, where they joined the covering army under the Duke of Athlone. The latter's force now consisted of 25 regiments of Foot, 40 squadrons of Horse and Dragoons, 32 cannons and 8 mortars, and amounted to 25,000 men. Overquerque, with the main body of the Allied Army, was besieging Kayserswerth with his headquarters at Emrich and covered the communications with Nimequen and Holland.

The French Army consisting of 60,000 to 70,000 men under the Duke of Burgundy was at Santen near Dusseldorf. His plan of campaign was to advance and attempt to cut off the covering army of the Allies under Athlone from its communications with Nimequen. Athlone appears to have been well aware of his perilous position, for on the 12th May, on information that the French Army was on the march, he ordered tents to be struck and the force to stand to arms. No hostile movement, however, ensued and camp was eventually re-pitched.

Nearly a month later the French Army did advance through the Forest of Cleves, and Athlone on 10th June hastily struck his camp and retired in two lines of battle towards Nimequen. All night long the march continued and at eight o'clock in the morning when they were in sight of the town of Nimequen, the enemy appeared in their rear and on both flanks with the evident intention of surrounding the Allied Army. The latter, however, showed a brave front to the enemy, retiring slowly towards the town, and about noon were safely within the outworks of the fortress. While the Allied cavalry skirmished with the enemy the army joined the Burghers in mounting 150 pieces of cannon on the walls and outworks of the town and the French were eventually driven off with the loss of 1,000 men killed and wounded and as many more deserters.

Although the allied loss is stated not to have exceeded more than 200 killed, wounded and prisoners, yet that total included a Captain of Lord Barrymore's Regiment with a detachment of 100 men. It appears that on the previous night they had been sent out into a wood as a rear-guard to discover the enemy's approach. In this wood they were severely attacked by the enemy's vanguard, the Captain and most of his command being killed. Kayserswerth surrendered on 17th June, the French Army having withdrawn.

On 2nd July the Earl of Marlborough arrived at Nimequen as Captain General of the Allies and assumed command of the army. Further reinforcements having arrived from England, the army was reorganized, and the regiments subsequently known as the 8th, 13th, 17th, and 18th Regiments of Foot were formed into a brigade under Brigadier-General Frederick Hamilton.

On 14th July Marlborough reviewed the whole army at Duckenburg.

Two days later he set out from Nimequen with 60,000 men, but in the subsequent operations he was much hampered by the refusal of the Dutch to give him a free hand.

On 26th July the army crossed the Meuse at Grave and moved south to Hamont. There was then a favourable opportunity of attacking Boufflers who lay between Peer and Bray, but the Dutch objected and the French were allowed to retire south of the River Demer. Again on 23rd August Marlborough manoeuvred the French into a false position at Hochtel, when the Dutch General Opdam hesitated to obey orders and another opportunity was lost.

Marlborough, considering it hopeless to bring the French Army to battle hampered as he was by semi-independent subordinates, determined to set about reducing the French fortresses on the Meuse. With this object in view he invested Venloo on 29th August with part of the Allied Army (including the English) whilst the remainder covered the siege.

The siege operations were under General Opdam, who had 32 battalions and 36 squadrons at his disposal. Venloo was situated on the east side of the Meuse, but it possessed a strong bridge-head on the west of the river covered by the detached fortress of St. Michael. The garrison of Venloo and its outworks comprised 6 regiments of Foot, 2 squadrons of Horse and 50 guns and mortars.

The besiegers opened two attacks, one against Fort St. Michael on the west of the river and the other against the north-east of the town; Lord Cutts, with the English, undertook the first named and Prince Nassau-Saarbruck the latter attack.

Hamilton's Brigade, viz. the 8th, 13th, 17th, and 18th Regiments, took part in the former operation. On 16th September the batteries opened, Lord Cutts having 52 guns and howitzers.

The following account is from General R. Vane's *Campaigns of King William and the Duke of Marlborough*. General Vane was in the 18th Regiment and took part in the attack.

'We carried on our approaches against Fort St. Michael by 3 attacks; our English Brigade (Hamilton's) had one of them: our Regiment (Royal Regt. of Ireland) mounted the trenches of the attack the morning before it took place. About noon there joined the 3 companies of Grenadiers that were of our attack (viz. those of the 8th, 13th and 17th Regts.) with 500 Fusiliers. At 4 o'clock the signal was given; a little before Lord Cutts called the officers together and told us, if the enemy gave way, we were to jump into their works, and follow them, let the consequences be what they might.

'On our advance the enemy gave their fire and ran, we jumped into the covered way and pursued; they made to a Ravelin which covered the curtain of the Fort and a small wooden bridge which was over a fosse by which they relieved their outward works. We drove them into the ravelin, where was a captain and 60 men; we soon dispatched most of them, the rest fled over the bridge and we, madmen like, followed still on the fosseway, under the body of the fort.

'The Port being shut, those that fled before us climbed it up, which showed us the way, for we had no choice but to carry the Fort or all perish. We climbed after them. The enemy was confounded, made but little resistance, and soon quitted the rampart and retired into the body of the Fort, where they threw down their arms and called for quarter, which we gave them and the Plunder of the Fort to the Soldiers.

'Thus were the Lord Cutts' unaccountable orders as unaccountably executed; but had not several unexpected accidents occurred in the affair, hardly a man of us would have escaped being killed, drowned, or taken.'

The Governor of the Fort, 32 officers and 225 sentinels were taken, being all that was left of 800 men. In this attack the English lost 297 killed and wounded.

A few days afterwards, viz. on 24th September, news arrived of the capture of Landau by the Germans, when the batteries of the army before Venloo were ordered to fire three volleys. The garrison and inhabitants seeing the preparations which were being made for this purpose by the besiegers, imagined that an attack upon the place by storm was intended, whereupon the magistrates begged the governor to surrender, and the town was delivered up, the garrison being allowed to march to Antwerp with their baggage and small arms.

On 29th September Prince Nassau-Saarbruck was ordered by the Earl of Marlborough to undertake the siege of Roermonde. The Regiment and Hamilton's Brigade being included in the Prince's command, they left Venloo on the 29th September and opened their trenches before Roermonde on 4th October.

On 6th October the garrison consisting of 4 French battalions and 30 guns and howitzers capitulated without waiting for an attack. During this siege the besiegers did not lose above 60 men killed and wounded.

Prince Nassau-Saarbruck's detachment having rejoined the main allied army at Suttendael, Marlborough moved south to Liège and encamped before that city on 12th October, when the French garrison of 12 battalions retired into the citadel and detached fort of Chartreuse, abandoning the city to the Allies.

Measures were then taken to lay siege to the citadel and Fort Chartreuse. After a severe bombardment the citadel was taken by storm on 23rd October, greatly due to Lord Cutts' prompt action in sending up 1,200 men as reinforcements from the ten battalions in the town, who attacked from the side of the city, much to the enemy's surprise. The English lost in this victory 534 killed and wounded. The detached Fort of La Chartreuse surrendered a few days later.

The Allied Armies then dispersed to winter quarters. The British left Liège on 3rd November and marched back to Holland, the Regiment spending the winter in garrison at Breda.

It was about this time that the Colours of Regiments were gradually reduced from one per company to three per regiment. Regiments were drawn up in three divisions, the pikemen in the centre, and the musketeers and grenadiers on each flank.

The establishment of the Forces in Holland in 1703 was as follows:—

Each Regiment of Foot: 12 Companies of 60 Privates.
                        1 Company Grenadiers, 70 privates.
In all 790 men besides Officers, N.C.Os. and Drummers.

Order of Battle, Campaign of 1703
Right Wing only

Left		Right			
1st Line		1st Line			
Foreign Regts.	Hamilton's Bde.	Withers' Bde.	*Wood's Bde.*		*Ross's Bde.*
	8th Foot.	1st Bn. 1st Guards.	1st Dragoon Guards.		1st Royal Dragoons.
	17th ,,	1st ,, Royal Scots.	5th ,,	,,	5th Dragoons.
	33rd ,,	15th Foot.	7th ,,	,,	Scots Greys.
	20th ,,	24th ,,	6th ,,	,,	A Foreign
	13th ,,	23rd ,,	3rd ,,	,,	Regt.
		9th ,,			
2nd Line		*2nd Line*			
Foreign Regts.		2nd Bn. Royal Scots.		Foreign Cavalry.	
		16th Foot.			
		2nd Bn. Cameronians.			
		21st Royal Scots Fus.			
		10th Foot.			

The Campaign opened with the siege of Bonn which Marlborough undertook with the Prussians, Hanoverians and Hessians, whilst the Dutch and English were to concentrate at Maastricht. The French in Brabant tried to overwhelm the Dutch General Overkirk near Liège before the English arrived. The French attacked on 9th May, but the Dutch withdrew towards Maastricht and were joined by the English Army on the 11th May. The French then refused battle and retired. Bonn surrendered on 15th May.

Marlborough's plan was now to capture Antwerp and Ostende. Part of his army he concentrated in the Breda district, but the greater part, including the English, moved from Maastricht towards Huy (25th May to 27th June). Marlborough then turned north and marched via Hasselt and Beeringh to Baylen, where he was on 2nd July, and to Brecht on 23rd July with a view to forcing the French lines between Antwerp and Lierre, but the Dutch Generals, being under the control of the States-General at the Hague, co-operation was impossible.

Giving up the idea of Antwerp, Marlborough left Brecht on 2nd August and turned towards Huy and arrived at Venaimont, whence he covered the siege of Huy which began on 17th August. Huy surrendered on 25th August.

Further attempts to bring the French to battle in Brabant were frustrated by the disinclination of the Dutch to co-operate. Lemburg was indeed captured on 23rd September, which completed the deliverance of Spanish Guelderland, but the French main army was not brought to battle, although Marlborough had the initiative throughout.

Shortly afterwards the army went into winter quarters.

On 16th May 1703 a treaty of alliance had been signed between England and Portugal at Lisbon. By the terms of the Treaty the Archduke Charles of Austria was proclaimed King of Spain in opposition to Louis XIV's nominee, Philip, Duke of Anjou. England and Holland were bound to provide a proportion of troops for service in Portugal, the British contingent amounting to 7,000 men. It was decided to draw these from the best regiments in the Low Countries, those selected for the expedition being the Royal Dragoons, the 2nd, 9th, 11th, 13th, 17th and 33rd Foot. These regiments proceeded to Portsmouth in the late autumn where they were made up to the strength of 13 companies of 3 serjeants, 3 corporals, 2 drummers and 55 private soldiers each. The drafts for this purpose were furnished by regiments then in Portsmouth, viz. the Royal Regiment of Fusiliers, Mordaunt's, Evans's, and Elliott's Regiments. Three pounds per man were paid by the Colonel receiving the draft to the Colonel supplying the men to enable the latter to recruit up to strength and to pay for the arms, clothes and accoutrements supplied with the men.

Nor was this the only expense incurred by the Earl of Barrymore at this time, for in a petition he made later, he prays relief for the following loss:

In November 1703 by a violent storm, a transport with three companies of the Regiment bound from Holland to Lisbon with the King of Spain on board was cast away near Helvoetsluys. About 40 men were drowned and an entire new set of arms, tents, &c., for three companies lost.

The following is a copy of Lord Barrymore's petition:—

'To the Most Honble. Sidney Earl Godolphin,
Lord High Treasurer of Great Britain.

The Memorial of the Earl of Barrymore

Sheweth

That in November 1703 by the Violent Storm, a Transport with 3 Companies of the Regiment under my command, bound from Holland to Lisbon with the King of Spain was cast away, about 40 of the Men drowned, and an Intire new Sett of Arms, Tents, and small Accoutrements for the 3 Companies lost.

That in January following upon their Arrival at Portsmouth the Regiment was compleated with Draughts from Regiments in England, and soon after their arrival in Portugal they were again compleated with Recruits from Ireland, for both which the Regiment is charged in their Accounts with £1,340 13s. 9d.

That the said charge for Recruits twice in one year exceeding the Non-effective Money of the Regiment which did not amount to above £800, the Captains are Sufferers in their personal Pay, had they been allowed full Companies; but at same time the Regiment is Respited £441 17s. and surcharged

£389 17s. 11d. for Arms and Tents furnished out of her Maj^ties Stores at Portsmouth in Lieu of those lost in the Storm at Helvoetsluys above mentioned as also £124 2s. 3d. paid Dutch Skippers for Boats to carry the Men on bord the Fleet; by means of which not only the Captains but all the Lieutenants and Ensigns Arrears of Pay for 2 years from the 24th Dec. 1703 are intirely sunk, and the Regiment still in Debt near £500.

May it therefore please your Lordship in consideration that the Non-effective Money is the only fund for Recruiting, and that 3 Companies' Arms, &c, were lost in the storm, and 3 Companies were taken Prisoners and lost their Arms going to Gibraltar to order such Releiff to this Regiment as to the Respite and the Surcharge of Arms, Tents, and Transport, as Your L^dp in Y^r Great Wisdom shall seem meet.

Signed, BARRYMORE.'

On 7th January 1704 the Archduke Charles landed at Portsmouth from Holland. On 17th January the expedition for Portugal, in all 188 ships including the transports conveying the troops, set sail from Portsmouth.

Eighteen days later most of them were back again at Spithead owing to stormy weather and it was not till 24th February that they finally departed. By 16th March all the transports had arrived at Lisbon and the troops began to disembark.

The English forces assembled in Portugal amounted to 7,000 men under General Meinhard, Duke of Schomberg. His forces consisted of:—

Harvey's Horse (2nd Dragoon Guards).
Royal Dragoons.
Portmore's Regt.
Stewart's   ,,   (9th Foot).
Stanhope's   ,,   (11th Foot).
Barrymore's   ,,   (13th Foot).
Blood's   ,,   (17th Foot).
Duncanson's   ,,   (33rd Foot).
Brudenell's   ,,
Mountjoy's   ,,

The Dutch contingent, under Lieut.-General Fagel, numbered 3,500 men, while the Portuguese force available for field and fortresses consisted of 20,000 men.

The Portuguese Count de las Galveas was the Generalissimo and he was between 80 and 90 years of age. On landing the Regiment marched up the valley of the Tagus to Abrantes. In May, owing to sickness and absolute lack of hospital arrangements, the Allied Army was much reduced in strength. At this time 12,000, including the English and Dutch, were in the Alemtejo under the veteran Count de las Galveas whose headquarters were at Estremos and 9,000 in Beira north of the Tagus, under the Marquis Das Minas.

To make matters worse the Dutch General Fagel quarrelled with the Duke of Schomberg and took his troops off to join the Marquis Das Minas in Beira. At this juncture the French Army, under the Duke of Berwick, a natural son of James II by Arabella Churchill, invaded Portugal by the valley of the Tagus from Alcantara and seized a number of Portuguese fortresses. On the 27th May two of Fagel's battalions were captured at Zarcedas while Las Galveas and Schomberg remained inactive at Estremos, but worse was to come. Portalegre, garrisoned by Portuguese and Stanhope's Regiment, was captured and later on Castel Vide on 25th June, when two Portuguese battalions and Stewart's Regiment were taken prisoners.

This ended the spring campaign; the Duke of Berwick, ill-equipped and suffering much from desertion, withdrew into Spain on 1st July. The Regiment was reviewed at Estremos on 21st July and shortly afterwards proceeded to Vimeira, having taken no active part in the campaign. Schomberg was recalled at his own request and on the 10th August was replaced by the Earl of Galway.

Early in September the Allies, including Barrymore's Foot, began to concentrate at Almeida for the autumn campaign. Most of the Spanish Army had been moved into Andalusia for the recovery of Gilbraltar, while the French Army under Berwick was at Castras in rear of Ciudad Rodrigo.

On 13th September Berwick took up a defensive position along the River Agueda. The plan of the Allies was to capture Ciudad Rodrigo. Das Minas was now General-in-Chief and his army numbered 3,000 horse and 17,000 foot. Owing to lack of bread it was some days before they could move and it was not till 7th October that they reached the Agueda.

After some exchange of artillery fire the Portuguese deemed the passage of the Agueda to be a too hazardous undertaking, and on the following day the Allies retired into Portugal where they separated into winter quarters.

Shortly before the events described above the fortress of Gibraltar had been captured from the Spaniards by a combined English and Dutch fleet under Sir George Rooke and was now held by a garrison which never exceeded 2,400 seamen and marines under Prince George of Hesse-Darmstadt. A Franco-Spanish army of about 12,000 men had been besieging the Rock since 21st August on the land side. At the beginning of December the garrison of Gibraltar had only 1,000 men fit for duty. In these circumstances Prince George appealed to the Commander-in-Chief in Portugal for help.

The Earl of Galway immediately took steps to send reinforcements to Gibraltar. The regiments selected were a battalion of the 1st and 2nd Foot Guards, Barrymore's (13th), Donegal's (35th), the Dutch Regiment of Waes, and the Portuguese Regiment of Algarve, numbering in all 2,500 men.

Barrymore's Regiment mustering 39 serjeants, 39 corporals, 26 drummers, and 650 privates embarked at Lisbon on 8th December. On 10th December the whole expedition consisting of 20 transports, escorted by the frigates *Antelope*, *Newcastle*, *Greenwich* and *Roebuck*, left the Tagus.

On 17th December when the expedition was off Cape Spartel they sighted to leeward a fleet of 22 men-of-war bearing English and Dutch colours which they deemed to be that under Vice-Admiral Leeke and Rear-Admiral Vander-Dussen. As the fleets approached one another it was observed that the men-of-war were in half-moon shape as if to encircle the transports. A private signal was made, which the men-of-war being unable to answer, instantly hoisted French colours. The danger was great with a hostile fleet so near, but the transports put out every boat and gained some way by towing, the enemy being becalmed. Presently a fresh breeze sprang up from the south-west, favoured by which most of the transports managed to escape, but one of them with three companies of Barrymore's and one company of Donegal's was captured and taken to Cadiz. On the following day the remainder, with the exception of three, which put back to Lisbon, arrived safely at Gibraltar and landed the troops to the number of 1,970 men.

The Regiment was not long at Gibraltar before they had an opportunity of distinguishing themselves. A detachment forming part of a body of troops which issued from the fortress on the night of 22nd December, forced the Spanish outposts, attacked a body of cavalry, levelled part of the hostile works, burnt many fascines and gabions and afterwards retired with little loss.

THE SIEGE OF GIBRALTAR

The Spanish and French forces before Gibraltar were commanded by the Marquis of Villadarias, a Grandee of Spain.

Towards the end of January 1705 the besiegers who, through sickness and losses, had been reduced to under 5,000 men, received reinforcements to the number of 4,000. The besiegers were now within ten paces of the Round Tower, a prominent feature of the land defences of the fortress; the batteries had completely shattered this work, the breach being wide enough for thirty men to pass abreast, and another breach in the wall on the right was also practicable.

On 2nd February a party of 50 French grenadiers made a reconnaissance on the Round Tower; they climbed the rock by the aid of hooks, but were repulsed with the loss of 2 officers and several men.

During the night of the 6th and 7th February a storming party of 600 French and Walloon Grenadiers supported by 1,000 Spaniards, the whole under the command of Thouy, silently ascended the Rock. About 300 of the grenadiers hid themselves in the clefts and hollows and at daybreak as soon as the night guard of 3 officers and 60 men had left the lesser breach and the day garrison of 1 subaltern and 30 men were the only guard, the grenadiers clambered to the extreme right of the wall, threw grenades into the post below them, and forced the subaltern and his party to retreat.

Simultaneously the bulk of the attackers, 1,300 in number, rushed at the great breach in the Round Tower, where Borr, with 240 men, was in command. He made a gallant resistance, but the grenadiers who had captured the lesser breach, which was at a higher elevation, threw grenades and large pieces of rock into the Tower, and a portion then advanced to occupy the Kings Lines in his rear. Borr therefore found himself obliged to retreat, and passing along Kings Lines, his men climbed over its parapet at the inner end and dropped into the Landport curtain a few feet below.

The French now pressed on to gain possession of the gate leading into the Fortress, but were delayed thereat by a brave stand made by Captain Fisher with only seventeen of Seymour's Marines (4th Foot).

It was at this critical moment that Lieut.-Colonel Moncal of Barrymore's Foot, having collected some 500 men principally of his own regiment, came up and charged the enemy with such spirit that they were driven back along the lines and out of the Round Tower, which was recaptured after it had been in the enemy's possession for over an hour. Captain Fisher and his men who had been captured were released.

In this gallant effort Moncal was materially assisted by Lieut.-Colonel Rivett of the 2nd Guards who, with 20 grenadiers, entered the lines from the Landport curtain below. The enemy's loss on this occasion amounted to 305 officers and men, of whom 70 were killed, 200 wounded and 35 captured. The casualties of the garrison were 27 killed and 120 wounded.

On the following day, 8th February, as Prince George of Hesse-Darmstadt, Lieut.-Colonel Moncal and other officers were standing on a new battery which had been recently constructed behind the breech in the Landport curtain, a round shot from the enemy lines fell among them, killing a Spanish officer, shattering Moncal's leg, and wounding five more.

The gallant Moncal was a French Protestant officer who had held a captaincy in the Regiment as early as 1692. Four years afterwards he was awarded a wound pension of £100 per annum.

Between the 16th and 18th February ships carrying 700 men as reinforcements arrived from Lisbon. At this time the fortifications and houses on the land front were in a deplorable state; nor is this to be wondered at, for it was computed that since the beginning of the siege 8,000 bombs and 70,000 round shot had been hurled against the fortifications, so that most of the cannon were dismounted, but by the untiring efforts of Prince George some were mounted again, whilst others were being repaired.

Rain began to fall on the 2nd March and hardly ceased for thirty days, so that the besiegers had great difficulty in keeping their trenches clear of water. On the 8th March the garrison made a sortie which cost the besiegers 65 men.

On 21st March three additional regiments arrived at Gibraltar from Lisbon.

On 1st April Admiral Sir J. Leake arrived with his squadron and attacked the French ships, taking three and driving two ashore, and about the same time several successful sorties were made by the garrison, prisoners were taken, and desertions from the enemy lines were frequent. It was evident that the enemy were preparing to raise the siege. On the 29th April the enemy began to burn their works and on the following day the bulk of their forces marched off into the interior of Spain.

On 4th May (O.S. St. George's Day) the whole garrison paraded and was reviewed by Prince George of Hesse-Darmstadt, its Commander during the siege. All the works were manned, there was a treble discharge of all the big guns, and at each discharge a *feu de joie* by the infantry. This parade was followed by fireworks from the Castle and other rejoicings.

Thus ended a siege which had lasted eight months, had cost the besiegers 12,000 men and had profited considerably to the advantage of the Allied Forces in Portugal.

CHAPTER V

CAMPAIGNS IN SPAIN AND PORTUGAL

A FEW weeks after the siege of Gibraltar was raised an expedition sailed from England under Charles Earl of Peterborough, designed either to aid the Duke of Savoy in driving the French out of Italy by making an attempt on Sicily and Naples, or to further the progress of the Archduke Charles in Spain, as should appear most advantageous for Her Majesty's service. The latter course was eventually adopted, and the expedition after calling at Lisbon arrived at Gibraltar in the beginning of August 1705. After disembarking some recently raised troops the following regiments of the garrison were embarked, viz., the Guards, Barrymore's (13th), Donegal's, Mountjoy's and some battalions of English Marines.

The troops, including two regiments of Dragoons, numbered 6,500 men, and in addition there were available for operations on shore about 2,500 Marines.

The system of command was somewhat complicated; Peterborough was Commander-in-Chief both by sea and land, Rear-Admiral Sir Cloudesley Shovel commanded the fleet, and Prince George of Darmstadt the troops. The Archduke King Charles also accompanied the expedition.

The fleet put to sea from Gibraltar on 5th August, and on the 11th anchored in Altea Bay on the coast of Valencia. Here some thousand Catalans and Valencians threw off their allegiance to King Philip, acknowledged the Archduke Charles as their Sovereign, and seized the neighbouring port of Denia.

THE SIEGE OF BARCELONA

Thus encouraged, the Earl of Peterborough undertook to attempt the siege of Barcelona, the capital of Catalonia, an undertaking of a hazardous character, as only a few years before, in 1697, it had resisted a French army of 30,000 men for eight weeks and was then only taken after the besiegers had lost 12,000 men. The fortress was now commanded by Velasco, who had 7,000 men at his disposal.

The voyage was resumed on 16th August and on the 22nd the fleet anchored three miles east of Barcelona. On the following day, the disembarkation commenced, and was accomplished without opposition. The camp was formed near the village of St. Martin, about one mile north-east of the town.

The defences of Barcelona consisted principally of a stout wall flanked at intervals by bastions and many small towers, with a ditch in front, a covered way, and a low glacis. On the south-western side of the fortress at a distance of

1,100 yards was a hill 700 feet high crowned by the small fort of Montjuich. The fort was weak and in no way served as a citadel to the fortress, nor was its capture in those days essential to the possession of Barcelona.

On the 25th the army was joined by 1,200 Miquelets and a large number of armed Spaniards, and to them was entrusted the duty of investing the fortress.

Thus the English and Dutch forces were available for offensive movements. For over a fortnight, judging by the number of councils of war that were held, the Allies hesitated whether they should attack the fortress, transfer their forces to Valencia, or even raise the siege, and embark for Italy. At length on 13th September it was decided to attack Barcelona.

The plan of attack was in the first instance to surprise and capture the Fort of Montjuich situated on that side of the camp most remote from the allied camp. In order to conceal the nature of the attack it was given out that the object of the operation was to seize a defile on the way to Valencia.

At 3 p.m. on 13th September the column, which consisted of 2,500 men under Peterborough and included Barrymore's Regiment (13th), marched off. The force was divided into two portions—viz. the advanced guard, 1,200 men under Lord Charlemont, and the reserve, 1,300 men under Stanhope. The former were to assault Montjuich, while the latter were to take post at the Covered Cross, a mile distant from Montjuich, where they could watch the San Antonio Gate of Barcelona and prevent any sortie therefrom on the rear of the assaulting column.

The night march was 12 miles long via Gracia Convent and Serja over very rough and broken ground, and at dawn when the assaulting column had reached the vicinity of Montjuich it was found that 200 men had missed their way. Nevertheless, Peterborough decided on an immediate assault. Half the assaulting column was detailed to make simultaneous attacks on the eastern and western extremities of the fort, while the remaining half was held in reserve. Peterborough and Prince George accompanied the eastern attack. The storming parties gallantly dashed up the glacis under a heavy fire and drove the enemy headlong from the outworks. The eastern party had captured a bastion and the western party a demi-bastion. Having accomplished this much they proceeded to entrench themselves. Peterborough now sent word to Stanhope to bring up the reserves.

Velasco, the Governor of Barcelona, on hearing the firing sent up a reinforcement of 200 dragoons. Between Montjuich and the town was the small fort of St. Bertran. Prince George of Darmstadt, thinking to forestall the reinforcement, conceived the idea of attacking St. Bertran. He accordingly collected some 400 men and led them towards St. Bertran, but in doing so he exposed his flank to the fire of Montjuich; several men were killed and the Prince himself was mortally wounded. This misfortune caused Charlemont, who was left in command, to desist from any further attack on St. Bertran and he retired to the outworks they had previously occupied where all was now confusion.

Meanwhile Caracioli, the Commandant of the Fort, had received his reinforcements, and parading them before the besiegers, they, with loud cries of 'Viva Carlos Tercera', pretended to lay down their arms; whereupon Colonel Allen advanced with a party of 200 English and 100 Dutch and Spaniards to the gates of the Fort. They were met by a volley of musketry, followed by a sally from the garrison who cut off their retreat. Two hundred men were taken prisoners and escorted back to Barcelona by the Dragoons who had come up as reinforcements, while the remainder fell back in confusion.

In the meantime, Peterborough, who had gone out to reconnoitre, hearing that Charlemont was unable to stop the panic, galloped up, according to the historian Richards 'in the horriblest rage that ever man was seen in', snatched Charlemont's half pike from his hand and gallantly led the troops back to the fort, the outworks of which they regained. At this juncture Stanhope came up with the reserve.

Shortly afterwards a party of Catalan Miquelets bravely assaulted and captured Fort St. Bertran. The garrison of Montjuich were now completely isolated.

On the following day, 15th September, two 7-inch mortars were brought up to bombard Montjuich and on the 17th a shell fell on the building where the powder was kept, blew it up, and killed Caracioli, the officer in command, and several others, whereupon the English advanced to the assault, when the Lieutenant-Governor, Colonel Mena, hung out a white flag, and the garrison consisting of 15 officers and 290 men surrendered. The attack on Montjuich had cost the Allies 600 officers and men.

Already on the 15th the bomb vessels of the fleet had commenced the bombardment of the south-western defences of Barcelona. On the 16th the Admiral landed 2,500 English and Dutch seamen on the beach at the foot of Montjuich hill, forming them into companies and battalions, while heavy guns and ammunition for the breaching batteries were also landed.

On 20th September ground was broken 400 yards from the escarp between St. Paul's demilune and San Antonio's bastion, and on the 24th fire was opened from eight guns and three mortars. By the 28th fifty-eight guns and mortars were in action.

Although Velasco's defence was unenterprising he inflicted a number of casualties among the seamen and trains. However, by 3rd October a large breach had been formed and preparations for the assault were made.

On 4th October Velasco was summoned to surrender, and as the Spanish Commander was in no condition to continue the struggle it was decided after negotiations that the garrison of Barcelona should march out with the honours of war on the 14th.

On the morning of that day the civilian population, who were considerably disaffected, broke out into open mutiny and attacked Velasco's troops, which resulted in that General appealing to the Allies for protection. The Allies accordingly entered the town and were joined by 2,500 men of the garrison. Eventually Velasco and 1,200 of his men were embarked on the fleet and proceeded by sea to Malaga.

On 23rd October the Archduke Charles entered the city and was proclaimed King of Spain, while the bulk of the fleet left for England.

The capture of Barcelona caused great excitement in England when the news arrived there, Queen Anne announcing great and happy successes in both Houses of Parliament on 29th November.

On occupying Barcelona the troops were billeted in empty convents and barracks, but owing to the cold and lack of comforts there was much sickness and soon nearly one-third of the British were in hospital.

MINOR OPERATIONS

As the result of the fall of Barcelona practically the whole of Catalonia declared in favour of King Charles and the Allies. In order to facilitate the supply of the troops and with a view to future operations, Peterborough sent out flying columns to the more important towns in the neighbourhood.

In December Barrymore's (13th), Donegall's (35th) and Mountjoy's Foot, together with the Royal Dragoons numbering 1,400 men under the command of Brig.-General Killigrew, were sent to garrison the town of Tortosa and if possible to support the Spanish Irregulars in Valencia where King Charles had many supporters. Barrymore's Foot (13th) was temporarily commanded by Lieut.-Colonel Edward Pearce. The Earl of Barrymore was not with his regiment at this time, and the cause of his absence is not recorded.

From Tortosa Lieut.-Colonel John Jones of Barrymore's (13th) was dispatched with 30 men of the Royal Dragoons and 1,000 Spanish Irregulars to garrison the town of San Mateo, a small but important place about 30 miles from Tortosa on the road to Valencia.

This detachment had only been there a few days when they were invested by a force of 2,500 men from Valencia under the Condé de las Torres on 27th December. When this news reached Peterborough he immediately proceeded to Tortosa and took steps to relieve the garrison.

As the Earl of Peterborough was so intimately connected with one of the most remarkable incidents in the history of the Regiment, it may not be out of place to give a short sketch of his character. Historians differ as to his abilities as a great military commander, though fame has given him a place among English soldiers of the period as second only to Marlborough. His previous military experience was chiefly at sea, but there was no exploit on this element to his credit which would lead one to suppose that he was fitted for the supreme command of an important expedition. It is recorded that the siege of Barcelona was commenced against his advice, but that when once decided on, he carried out the execution with commendable zeal. He was undoubtedly eccentric, vainglorious, and quarrelsome. He appears to have hated all foreigners, including his Allies, and he despised Charles III whom he was commissioned to place on the throne of Spain. He was romantic, addicted to pleasure and the charms of the fair sex. Yet with all these drawbacks, he had undoubted military virtues, he was popular with his subordinates, and made the best use of the irregular Spaniards under his command whom he thoroughly understood. He believed in and practised mobility, he was a master in the minor stratagems of war, and appreciated the value of the elements of secrecy and surprise in his operations. To his credit it may be said that as long as he was in charge of the campaign in Eastern Spain the arms of the Allies were consistently victorious.

THE SIEGE OF SAN MATEO

A contemporary account exists of the siege of San Mateo written in Spanish by order of the Magistracy of that town and subsequently translated into English. The following extracts hows how Colonel Jones of the Regiment came to be the Governor of the town.

'On Dec. 16th 1705 there came to the town of San Mateo an English Drum with 2 packets of letters sent from the town of La Jana by the illustrious Don John Jones an English officer and Commander of the forces of King Charles III on the frontier of Arragon and Valencia. One of these packets was for the Chief Magistrate of the town and is as follows.

'H.M. Your Sovereign Lord King Charles III whom God long preserve and prosper having been pleased to appoint me his Commander-in-Chief on the frontier of Arragon and Valencia in order to rescue his loyal subjects from the unjust dominion of the Duke of Anjou. I in pursuance of the said H.M. Commands think proper to acquaint you that I am now in the town of La Jana with a numerous force both of Horse and Foot, with intent not only to deliver that town, but all other walled towns and open places, that shall desire to be freed from the French yoke, and your town being one of the number, and head of its district, I do not question but you will give example to the rest, by acquainting me as soon as possible with your Resolution for avoiding the Calamities of a Siege, and to show you have made the better choice by putting yourself under the protection of so great and potent a Monarch as King Charles is, in whose name I offer you all the Honour, Privileges, and Immunities you have at any time enjoyed, and had granted by the Kings, H.M.'s glorious predecessors, and whereupon I promise you shall be looked upon as good and loyal subjects whom God long preserve.

Your servant,
JOHN JONES.

LA JANA
   Dec. 16, 1705.'

The Magistracy of San Mateo did not immediately comply with this request, but two days later Colonel Jones entered the town with his troops. As before related, San Mateo was besieged on the 27th, the strength of the enemy being estimated at 2,000 Horse and 4,000 Foot under the command of the Condé de las Torres. The attack was carried on vigorously and an incessant fire directed on the walls, upon which Jones erected parapets of wool sacks and other materials.

On 31st December as ammunition was running low the defenders melted their pewter pots and dishes to cast bullets and, these not proving sufficient, used the pipes of the church organ for the same purpose. Mines were laid by the attackers under the town gates, but were flooded by the garrison. Bread ran short on 7th January, but the garrison still held out, and on the 9th the besiegers were seen to be withdrawing. The operations of the relieving force under Peterborough now claim our attention.

Peterborough, with 200 Horse Royal Dragoons and 1,000 Foot (including the 13th), set out with the greatest secrecy from Tortosa on 6th January and reached Traquera by night marches on the 8th within 6 miles of the enemy's force besieging San Mateo. He also circulated exaggerated reports of his numbers and employed spies to take two copies of a letter to Colonel Jones which he arranged should fall into the hands of the enemy. The following are extracts from this letter:—

'Be sure from the first appearance of our Troops, and the first discharge of our artillery, you answer with an English Halloo; and take to the Mountains on the right with all your men. It is no matter what becomes of the town; leave it to your Mistresses. The Condé de las Torres must take to the plains, the hills on the left being almost impassable, and secured by 5 or 6000 of the Country People. . . .

'By nine or ten within an hour after you can receive this, assure yourself you will discover us on the top of the Hills, not two Cannon Shots from their camp. . . .

'Dear Jones, prove a true Dragoon, be diligent and alert, and preach this welcome doctrine to your Miquelets, "Plunder without Danger."

Your Friend
PETERBOROW.'

The spies were duly captured by the enemy, and being well schooled in the part they had to play, the strength of Peterborough's force was not diminished by the story they had to tell. Accordingly when Peterborough's men gained the top of the hill overlooking San Mateo on 9th January, the enemy's camp was seen to be in confusion, the tents were being struck and the baggage was being loaded. The sight of the Allies was sufficient to cause the enemy to retreat precipitately, harassed by the Miquelets, with the result that the greater part of the baggage and camp equipment was captured.

Thus was San Mateo relieved by a force not one-half the strength of the besieging force.

The Spanish account of the siege sums up Lieut.-Colonel Jones as follows:—

'The Governor of the place, Don John Jones, during the furious and dangerous storm of so tedious and painful a siege behaved himself like a skilful and vigilant commander, and like another Mars gave proof of his care and industry, viewing the most important posts on the walls, and providing the best Arms and Ammunition in all Parts, going continually the Rounds and giving the necessary orders, directing himself very often in firing upon the enemy, without resting, eating or scarce sleeping, either by day or night, his excessive Toil seeming to be above the strength of Man.'

In the middle of one of the bastions of San Mateo was placed a square stone with the following inscription:—

Mars Anglus Martis construxit forte Joannes Jones, Turritum hoccine Martis Opus.

which being translated by the Editor of the English edition is as follows:—

> This bastion built by Jones the British Mars
> Records his triumphs in the 'Iberian Wars.'

This distich was paraphrased by the same author in a Spanish sonnet, which in English runs thus:—

> Jones the brave English Man's Victorious name,
> Adds an eighth wonder to the list of Fame.
> This stately Bastion to his Art we owe,
> And to his Arms our safety from the Foe;
> From this one Fort so rude a storm he blows,
> As if he thundered from two mighty Towers;
> Eight bellowing Engines guard Mateo's walls,
> And rain an Iron Tempest on the Gauls;
> His dikes and Rising Mounds the rebels scare
> And all his Works confess the God of War;
> These deathless deeds in Charles' Name he wrought
> Thus wisely he advised, thus bravely fought;
> That awful Name his Martial spirit warms,
> And crowns with Conquest his resistless Arms;
> From Philip's hated Yoke he sets us free
> All, All our Glory, Jones, we owe to thee.

On another stone, which is at the entrance of the said bastion, were carved two Imperial Eagles with the following verses:—

> Carolus Austriacus decurrat Nestoris Annos
> Tertius, exclamat fida Ministra Jovis.

English Translation:—

> Let the Third Charles to Nestor's years arrive
> So sings the Bird of Jove, let Charles of Austria live.

This distich was paraphrased by the same author in a Spanish sonnet, which in English runs thus:—

> Aloft while Charles of Austria's Eagle soars
> Below the British Lyon loudly roars,
> And rends the air, and shakes the Rocky Shores
> The Bird of Jove on his Imperial wings
> Freedom and Fame to glad Iberia brings;

> From Eber to the Taijo's Golden Flood
> Her fruitful womb's enriched by Gallick blood;
> Thus Charles and Spain to Britain's Martial Sons
> Their triumphs owe, and not the least to Jones.

It is said that the enemy lost 400 men during the siege and the garrison 10 killed and 20 wounded.

On 10th January Peterborough entered San Mateo, and subsequently took up a position at Albocazar, from which he pursued the enemy with his 200 mounted troops and Spanish irregulars to Nules on the road to Valencia where he captured 200 horses.

In the meantime, on 12th January, he sent his infantry, including the (13th), over the mountains to Vinaros to recuperate.

Peterborough, not having sufficient troops to continue the pursuit of the enemy, established his headquarters at Castillon de la Plana, where he collected some 600 horses and made preparations to invade Valencia.

THE INVASION OF VALENCIA

Towards the end of the month he gave orders for the concentration of all the available troops, and among them, the 13th (Lieut.-Colonel Edward Pearce in command) was summoned from Vinaros. He rode out to meet the Regiment at Oropesa. Then followed an incident which is without parallel in the History of the British Army. The scene was a small plain near the town. On one side of the plain were some small hills behind which Peterborough caused to be paraded some 500 horses all ready accoutred concealed from the view of any one on the plain. The Earl of Peterborough and his staff took up their position. According to Fortescue, 'the Regiment marched on to the plain but 400 strong, with red coats ragged and rusty, yellow facings in tatters, yellow breeches faded and torn, shoes and stockings in holes and more often altogether wanting. The inspection over, Peterborough, after complimenting the Regiment on their gallant services, said: "I wish that I had horses and accoutrements for you to try if you could keep up your good reputation as Dragoons."'

This speech was doubtless listened to with approval, but with no expectation that it could be carried out. His lordship, however, having ordered his secretary to give the commissions, already prepared, to the officers, led them round the spur of the hill where they saw eight bodies of horse, drawn up separately, and found them all ready accoutred. Among these there were three good horses for each captain, two for each lieutenant, and one for each cornet. The field officers were given the choice of their troops, the other captains drew lots; and immediately they all mounted and marched to the quarters appointed for them. Thus within an hour Barrymore's Foot became Pearce's Dragoons.

According to the official records quoted by Cannon, it is stated that 27 officers and 660 N.C.Os. and soldiers of the 13th, then called the Earl of

Barrymore's Regiment, were formed into a corps of dragoons—but this number must have included the sick, &c.

The Earl of Barrymore, 5 other officers, 10 serjeants and 10 corporals were shortly afterwards sent back to England to recruit the Regiment (13th Foot) again.

Lord Barrymore's views regarding the changing of his Regiment of Foot into a Regiment of Dragoons may be gathered from the following extract from one of Peterborough's letters:—

'But of all her Majesty's favours, none touched me as much as her Answer to my Lord Barrymore, who made a great interest and heavy complaints, that I had ruined his regiment, taken his best officers out, and then imposed on him whom I thought fit, in the regiment he was forced to raise. The Queen made him this answer—"That she was very glad I had chosen the best officers where they could do her the best service: that they were the best judges who served with them; but, however, she had reason to believe everything I did was well done, and would change nothing."'

Peterborough now had 1,070 horsemen, including the Royals and Pearce's Dragoons; and Donegal's, Mountjoy's, Gorges' and Colberg's infantry regiments which mustered 2,000 men in addition to the Spanish Irregulars, a further 3,500 men. At the beginning of February, everything being ready, he advanced on Valencia. He came up with Arcos'[1] rear-guard consisting of 800 Irish Horse at Murviedro, the site of the ancient Saguntum, on 2nd February. This rear-guard was commanded by Mahony. Peterborough summoned Mahony to a parley and finally induced him to evacuate the pass of Murviedro without striking a blow.

On 4th February Peterborough entered the city of Valencia, Arcos retiring towards Alicante.

Shortly afterwards Peterborough, learning that 4,000 of the enemy were on the march to reinforce King Philip's troops and had already reached Fuente La Higuera, south-west of Valencia, immediately took measures with his usual secrecy and skill. A body of 800 foot and 400 cavalry set out from Valencia at night, they passed the River Xucar without being discovered, and pushing by a forced march upon the enemy's encampment, took them completely by surprise. The Spaniards were easily overpowered; 600 were made prisoners and the rest dispersed. With equal success Peterborough intercepted and captured 16 pieces of artillery which were being sent up from Alicante to reinforce Arcos. In this latter action Pearce's Dragoons are stated to have fought with great gallantry. The whole of Valencia was now clear of the enemy's troops.

BARCELONA BESIEGED AND RELIEVED

In the meantime a great danger was threatening the Allied army in Catalonia. Marshal de Tessé had been recalled from the Portuguese frontier

[1] De las Torres was superseded by Arcos in the command of King Philip's troops.

where he was opposing the Earl of Galway, and had arrived at Saragossa. After collecting an army of 12,000 men, he was joined by King Philip and together they crossed the Ebro near Lerida and invaded Catalonia. They appeared before Barcelona on 3rd April, where they were joined by an additional force of 9,000 men and 15 guns under General de Legal from Roussillon while the Count of Toulouse with a considerable fleet blockaded Barcelona on the sea front.

It was now the turn of the Allies to be besieged in Barcelona. The garrison consisted of 3,600 Regulars, English, Spanish and Dutch, and 1,500 Spanish Irregulars (Miquelets). The French army besieging Barcelona was in its turn harassed in rear by a large body of Irregular Catalans under Cifuentes.

Peterborough, on learning of this alarming invasion, set out from Valencia for Barcelona with 2,000 foot and 600 horse. (It is not recorded whether Pearce's Dragoons were included in this number.) He arrived in Cifuentes's camp on 21st April, only to hear that Montjuich had been stormed by the French. Barcelona would doubtless have fallen to the French had not the Allied fleet under Sir John Leake, of 39 English sail of the line, 13 Dutch sail of the line, besides frigates and transports, arrived off the coast of Spain on 3rd May, having just come from home waters. As they approached Barcelona, Peterborough put out to sea in a small boat, intercepted the fleet, and as Naval-Commander-in-Chief assumed command, but the Duc de Toulouse, with the French fleet, was not to be caught. They had early information of the movements of the Allied fleet, so that when Peterborough appeared before Barcelona on 8th May the French fleet had gone.

Tessé and King Philip, with the French army, were not slow in following Toulouse's example. On 11th May, leaving behind their siege train of 175 guns and 30 mortars, 3,000 barrels of powder and an immense stock of flour, together with 900 sick and wounded men, they retreated across the frontier to Perpignan, harassed by the Spanish Irregulars. So important was the relief of Barcelona considered in England that it was coupled with the victory of Ramillies as a reason for a general day of rejoicing.

PETERBOROUGH JOINS GALWAY

The road to Madrid was now open, but the Allies could not agree as to the line of advance. Peterborough was for advancing on Madrid from Valencia, the shortest route, while King Charles and his advisers favoured an advance up the valley of the Ebro to Saragossa and thence to Madrid. Eventually Peterborough proceeded by sea to Valencia with 1,200 English infantry on 28th May. He appears to have had 4,500 regular troops available for operations, including those already in Valencia.

The operations were of a local character. Peterborough sent Gorges with 1,300 Foot and 200 Horse to besiege Alicante, and Alnutt to invade Murcia, while General Wyndham with a movable column was to open the road to Madrid by the capture of Requena and Cuenca. Killigrew remained at Valencia city with five regiments.

General Wyndham's column consisted of 1,500 men, viz. the Guards, Dungannon's and Toby Caulfield's Foot, and in addition Pearce's Dragoons. They started towards the end of June. Requena, a fortified town with a strong castle on a rocky hill, defended by 600 regular troops, made a stout resistance, and as the attackers were weak in artillery, mining operations had to be undertaken. Eventually Requena was captured by Wyndham at the cost of 150 casualties. Subsequently Cuenca was taken on 5th July.

It will be recollected that the Earl of Galway, who had been conducting operations on the Portuguese frontiers since 1704, was at the beginning of 1706 opposed by Marshal de Tessé. The latter Marshal had been withdrawn to conduct the operations in Catalonia, culminating in the abortive siege of Barcelona just described. Galway at once took advantage of the weakened forces in front of him and advanced on Madrid, which he and Das Minas occupied on 27th June. Here his army rapidly crumbled away; there were soon 6,000 men in hospital, for the soldiers had given way to great excesses in which they were greatly assisted by a part of the female population, entirely, as the Spanish historians assert, out of loyalty and public spirit.

Galway, finding that the capital was demoralizing his troops, advanced to Guadalaxara, where he was in a better position to establish communications with the British forces in Valencia.

On 18th July King Charles, with two regiments of Horse and three Infantry regiments, having reached Saragossa, appealed to Peterborough in Valencia to cover his march to join Galway at Guadalaxara. Peterborough accordingly advanced to Pastrana on 4th August, 15 miles south of Guadalaxara with 400 Dragoons, including a part of Pearce's Regiment, when the King and Peterborough effected their junction with Galway.

In the meantime the Duke of Berwick had concentrated a French army 26,000 strong in the mountains north of Madrid and his cavalry entered that capital on 4th August. Moreover, the country south of the Tagus had risen in revolt and had cut Galway's communications with Portugal, and that General, having now only 14,000 men composed of English, Dutch, Portuguese, Spaniards and Neapolitans, considered it expedient to move to Chinchon south of Madrid on 11th August and a month later to Veles, where he was joined by Wyndham's column of 1,400 men, with whom were the remainder of Pearce's Dragoons.

Followed by Berwick, but unmolested, Galway then retired into Valencia, moving via Palamares, Torres, Jonfilos and Cafra to Valverde, and by 12th October he had distributed his army in winter quarters along a defensive line between Requena and Denia. Previous to this retirement Peterborough himself had been recalled and was sent on a mission to Italy.

Thus ended the campaign of 1706 in Spain, which commenced in a manner so favourable to the Allies but concluded in a general retirement to the sea. Berwick boasted that in the autumn of 1706, although no general action had been fought, no less than 10,000 prisoners had been captured.

THE 13TH FOOT RECONSTITUTED

When Pearce's Dragoons were formed the Earl of Barrymore and a small nucleus of officers and non-commissioned officers were sent back to England. They landed at Falmouth in April and marched via Tavistock, Exeter, Honiton, Salisbury and Bagshot to quarters in Knightsbridge near London and thence to Worcester via Wycombe, Bicester and Evesham. On 8th May the Earl of Barrymore received orders to recruit his regiment up to strength, £900 levy money was paid for recruiting.

Here is the order referred to:—

'ANNE R.

These are to authorize you by beat of Drum or otherwise to raise and receive so many Volontiers as shall be wanting to recruit and fill up the respective Companies of Our Regim^t of Foot under your Command for Our Service. And for the more speedy Recruiting Our said Reg^t to receive into your Custody any such able bodied men as shall be Raised and Levyed to serve as Sold^{rs} by any of our Justices of the Peace or other Magistrates or otherwise Listed in Pursuance of the Acts of Parliament for raising Recruits for Our Land Forces and Marines and for discharging out of Prison such insolvent Debtors as should serve or procure a person to serve in Our Army. And as you shall raise the said Recruits, you are to cause them to march to Our Citty of Worcester appointed for their Rendezvous. Wherein all Magistrates &c. &c. Given at Our Court at Kensington this 27th day of Aprill 1706 in the Fifth Year of Our reign.

By Her Majesties Command,
H. ST. JOHN.

To Our R^t Trusty and R^t Well-beloved Cousin James Earl of Barrymore, Colonel of One of Our Regts. of Foot.'

Such good progress was made that by 7th October the thirteen companies had been reconstituted, when they were quartered as follows:—

5 companies at Worcester.
1 company ,, Pershore.
1   ,,   ,, Evesham.
1   ,,   ,, Tewkesbury.
1   ,,   ,, Upton.
1   ,,   ,, Anliester (?).
1   ,,   ,, Droitwich.
1   ,,   ,, Bewdley.
1   ,,   ,, Broomsgrove.

In December the Regiment marched to Hull, the headquarters, and six companies being quartered in that town; when two companies were sent to Richmond, three to Ripon, one to Bedal Masham, and one to Midlam (?).

It is now necessary to revert to the fortunes of Pearce's Dragoons.

THE CAMPAIGN OF ALMANZA

Although during the winter of 1706–07 Galway received substantial reinforcements from England, King Charles withdrew the bulk of the Spanish troops for service elsewhere. Notwithstanding this disadvantage Galway determined on an advance to Madrid, and at the beginning of April he began to concentrate between Elda and Xativa. In order to safeguard Valencia against hostile incursions during his absence, he moved into Murcia and destroyed or captured the enemy's magazines at Yeda and Caudete. He then proceeded to lay siege to the Castle of Vilena, but he then heard that Berwick had been reinforced and was barring the road to Madrid with 25,000 men, of whom half were French troops, Galway's army at this time being only 16,000 strong, consisting of 4,800 English and 8,000 Portuguese, the balance being made up of Dutch, Huguenots and Germans.

In spite of this disparity in numbers, Galway determined to raise the siege of Vilena and to advance against Berwick, who had drawn up his army outside the small town of Almanza. On the night of 24th April the Allies camped at Caudete and at daybreak on the 25th they marched in four columns towards Almanza, 8 miles distant. At noon they debouched on to the plain, and after a short halt they formed up in two lines, the bulk of the infantry in the centre, but some of the infantry battalions were interpolated between the Horse on the wings. The Portuguese Horse were on the right, and the English and Dutch Dragoons on the left. The Allies were tired after a long march, the French were fresh and ready. It is noteworthy that the French army was commanded by an Englishman, the Duke of Berwick, a natural son of James II, and the Allied army was commanded by a Frenchman, the Earl of Galway, a Huguenot, and the son of the Marquis De Ruvigny.

The Duke of Berwick's army was also formed up in two lines, the infantry in the centre, the Spanish Horse on the right and the French Horse on the left. The right rested on high ground extending towards Montalegre, the left rested on a hill overlooking the road to Valencia.

At 3 p.m. the Allies advanced to the attack. On the left Carpenter's Brigade of Horse comprising Carpenter's (3rd Light Dragoons), Essex's (4th Light Dragoons), and Guiscard's Dragoons; together with Killigrew's Brigade comprising Harvey's Horse (2nd Dragoon Gds.), Pearce's Dragoons (effective strength 273 of all ranks), Peterborough's Dragoons, and Killigrew's Dragoons (8th Hussars) were opposed to the Spanish Horse under Popoli. The attack was in echelon of brigades from the left. Carpenter's brigade was at first driven back, but the Spanish cavalry being fired at in flank by Wade's Infantry Brigade (17th and 33rd Foot) wavered, when Killigrew's Brigade (including Pearce's Dragoons) charged and drove the enemy back with considerable slaughter.

In the centre Erle, with Macartney's Infantry Brigade and Frisheim's Dutch and Huguenots, attacked Vincentillo's Spanish and La Badie's French infantry with great boldness, and being supported by Shrimpton with Breton's English and German Brigade, Dohna's Dutch, and Lislemarais' Huguenots, they drove the enemy back on to their second line.

Meanwhile on the right Das Minas' Portuguese Horse should have attacked the French Horse opposite to them, but they did not move, whereupon D'Avaray's French Horse charged the Allied infantry under Erle and Shrimpton in the centre in flank and rear, which caused the latter to cease their pursuit of the French infantry and to fight for their own safety.

Berwick now sent St. Gilles' French Horse to attack the Portuguese Horse, but these latter, with the exception of a few squadrons under Das Minas, galloped off the field of battle, and their example was followed by the second line both horse and foot, though some Portuguese battalions stood firm for a time.

Although on the left the battle was more equal, Galway, who had been wounded in the face, was obliged to retire from the field, when Tyrawley took his place. Killigrew, charging at the head of his brigade, had been first wounded and then killed, the Commanding Officers of Essex's, Carpenter's, and Peterborough's Dragoons were also killed, while Pearce was wounded at the head of his regiment and De Loches, his Lieut.-Colonel, was killed.

At this juncture Berwick sent 9 French battalions from his second line against Wade's Brigade, reinforced by Stewart's (9th Foot) from the second line, and at the same time a powerful array of fresh squadrons made a final charge on the shattered English and Dutch troops. The Allied left wing, undaunted but greatly fatigued, were obliged to give way, and Tyrawley was forced to retreat.

In the centre there had been hand to hand fighting between the Allied foot and the French cavalry by whom they were surrounded, but Shrimpton managed to rally 2,000 men, the remains of 5 English, 3 Huguenot, 3 Portuguese and 2 Dutch regiments, when they made their way in the direction of Caudete for a distance of 8 miles pursued by a numerous body of horse, led by D'Asfeld. Shrimpton took up a position for the night, but in the morning finding himself surrounded and without food or ammunition he surrendered.

The Allied left, to the number of 3,500, alone retired from the field in good order and proceeded to Ontiniente, some 22 miles distant.

Such was the disastrous battle of Almanza. The Allies lost 4,000 killed and wounded and 3,000 prisoners, 2 Portuguese guns and a number of Regimental Colours and Standards. Some 1,500 stragglers, chiefly infantry, managed to rejoin Galway some days after the battle.

The French loss was estimated at 6,000 killed and wounded, and so severely were they handled that Berwick did not move for five days after the battle.

Pearce's Dragoons lost in officers:—

Killed: Lieut.-Colonel De Loches, Cornet Holmes, Cornet Caudley and Quarter Master Sturgess.

Wounded and prisoners: Lieutenant Fitsgerald and Cornet Barry.

THE CAMPAIGN IN CATALONIA

After this disaster Galway marched to Alcira, on the Xucar, on the 26th and stopped there six days, and having left a garrison of 800 foot in that place under Stewart, and sent 700 foot under Campbell to Xativa, he set out with all his mounted troops, including Pearce's Dragoons, for the Ebro. He reached Murviedro on the 5th and Tortosa on the 19th May. This city was then entirely on the left bank of the Ebro. Galway threw up defences on the right bank opposite the town and garrisoned the works with 500 men and a number of field guns.

On 23rd May Berwick arrived before the defences and on the 25th he assaulted the works but was repulsed with loss. On 29th May D'Asfeld came up with Berwick's siege train from Valencia, while the latter with 10,000 men marched to Caspe, 60 miles higher up the Ebro. In the meantime D'Asfeld captured the works on the right bank of the Ebro after a brave resistance, and then retired to Valencia.

The Allied Horse under Carpenter were now holding the line of the Ebro from Tortosa to Mequinenza.

On 14th June Berwick crossed the Ebro with 6,600 Horse and 5,400 Foot at Caspe and marched to Ballover on the Cinca, only to find that Galway with 4,000 Horse was holding the line of that river with his left on Mequinenza; thus time was gained to organize fresh forces for the defence of Catalonia.

However, on 1st July, the French succeeded in crossing the Cinca at Estiche and Fraga, when Galway fell back to Lerida, and as the heat had by then become very great, Berwick placed his army in cantonments and gave the Allies a period of rest.

Hostilities were not resumed till October, by which time Galway had concentrated 4,800 Horse, 7,600 Foot, 2,200 Miquelets and 20 guns at Tarraga. Total—14,600 men, of whom 3,100 were English.

Already in the middle of September Lerida had been invested by the French, the Bourbon army then numbering 6,600 Horse and 16,300 Foot; of this total 17,200 were French and 5,700 Spanish. The Allied garrison of Lerida consisted of 1,800 Regulars and 600 Miquelets under Prince Henry.

On 2nd October the French commenced the attack, and on the 14th the garrison evacuated the town and withdrew to the citadel, where they were forced to capitulate on 10th November, the remnants of the garrison, 600 men, joining Galway at Cervera.

Thus ended the campaign. The Allies went into winter quarters at Reuss and Tarragona, with a strong garrison at Tortosa.

From a return of British troops in Catalonia in November 1707, the strength of Pearce's Dragoons is given as 192 men.

It is now necessary to follow the fortunes of Barrymore's Foot, who at the beginning of 1707 were occupying quarters in the north of England.

On the 23rd of February 1707 Barrymore was ordered to march four companies to Winchester, two to Andover and one each to Waltham, Stockbridge, Havant, Fareham, Odiham, Alton, and Alresford. Whilst on the march to their stations, the dispositions were changed and the quarters finally assigned to the Regiment were as follows:—Headquarters and five companies at Winchester, four companies at Salisbury and four companies at Wilton.

On 16th April fresh orders were received and Barrymore was instructed by the Secretary-at-War to march his regiment to Southampton, thence to cross over into the Isle of Wight and to be prepared to embark for service in Portugal or Spain.

No sooner was it assembled in the Isle of Wight than the orders for embarkation were cancelled.

On 19th May seven companies were ordered to cross over to Lymington, and thence to march to quarters as follows: two companies to Blandford, one to Wimborne, one to Christchurch, one to Ringwood, one to Downton, and one to Fordingbridge; the remaining six companies remaining in the Isle of Wight.

On 8th June five of the companies on the mainland marched to Winchester and two to Stockbridge, and a month later the two latter companies marched to Alresford. Finally, on 17th July Barrymore again received orders to embark for Portugal as soon as transport was available, but they remained till the spring of the following year in the above stations.

In this year the Union of Scotland with England having taken place, the Cross of St. Andrew was placed on the colours of the English regiments in addition to the Red Cross of St. George, previously displayed, thus forming the combination known as the Union or Union Flag. As the Lieut.-Colonel's flag had previously borne the Cross of St. George, his colour became the Union Flag.

A small 'Union' was introduced into the upper corner nearest the staff of the Colonel's Flag which had a plain yellow groundwork corresponding to the colour of the facings, and also showed the Colonel's armorial bearings, or any device he might fancy.

The Colours were provided by the Colonel of the Regiment out of his means.

THE CAMPAIGN ON THE PORTUGUESE FRONTIER

According to the *Life of Sir John Leake*, by Stephen Martin-Leake, Admiral Leake, on the 7th March 1708, made sail down the Channel with his squadron and nine sail of transports, having on board Barrymore's and Paston's Regiments, consisting of about 1,500 men. On 27th March they arrived at Lisbon. With these reinforcements the English Army in Portugal consisted of 2 brigades of English troops, the one commanded by General Montandre comprising Pearce's (5th), Newton's (20th), Sankey's (39th) and Paston's

Regiment; the other, commanded by General Sankey, comprising Barrymore's (13th), Stanwix's and Galway's Regiments (Spanish).

The English Division was commanded by the Earl of Galway, who had been transferred to the Portuguese frontier from Catalonia.

On arrival in Portugal Barrymore's Regiment (13th) marched to the Alemtejo and was subsequently encamped between Elvas and Campo Mayor with the army commanded by the Marquis of Fronteira.

The campaign on this front was extremely uneventful ; it consisted of a few marches and reviews, and never soared above the sacking of a village or the capture of a convoy. The best that can be said of the operations is that the enemy, commanded by the Marquis De Bay, did not think fit to hazard an engagement.

In the early summer of 1708 a draft of 3 officers and 62 men was sent to join the Regiment in Portugal. By the autumn of that year the infantry regiments in that country had become so reduced in strength, that strong recruiting parties were sent from each to England and they landed on 1st November. The party sent by Barrymore's consisted of Colonel Moncal (brother of the defender of Gibraltar), Major Duncomb, Captains Bower, Charleton, Mohun, Clarke, and Edwardes; Lieutenants Hodder, Fitzgerald, and Honeywood; Ensigns Bullman, Patterson, Brasse, and Brown, together with 14 serjeants and 6 corporals.

Although the system which obliged regiments on active service to send so considerable a proportion of officers home, for the purpose of obtaining recruits and sending out drafts to fill up the depleted ranks, seems open to criticism, it has to be remembered that England was maintaining a very large army in the field in proportion to her population and that recruits were with each year of the war becoming more difficult to obtain. With so many different corps all seeking men—besides the quota required by the Navy—each regiment abroad was obliged to look after its own interests in the matter of recruiting and it was a case of help yourself or God help you.

PEARCE'S DRAGOONS

It will be remembered that Pearce's Dragoons spent the winter in Catalonia after the campaign of Almanza and the subsequent retreat north of the Ebro. As they had become much more reduced in strength, and fresh forces having arrived in Spain, it was decided to send Pearce's Dragoons and other war-worn corps back to England to recruit.

Colonel Pearce and what was left of his regiment arrived at Falmouth in May 1708, when they proceeded via Exeter to London, and thence on 26th July to Aylesbury.

Here at Aylesbury, the Regiment began to re-form. It was reduced from the Spanish establishment of eight troops to the home establishment of six troops. The two superfluous troops commanded by Captains Dutem and Rogers, together with all surplus N.C.Os. of the remaining six troops, were transferred to Lieut.-General Echlyer's Regiment of Dragoons, and joined that

ACTION ON THE CAYA

corps at York, where it had arrived in September 1708 from Ireland. Pearce was ordered to recruit his regiment up to the strength of the Irish establishment in order to take the place of Echlyer in Ireland. In November Newbury was appointed as headquarters and all men recruited were drafted to that place.

ACTION ON THE CAYA

In the spring of 1709 the Anglo-Portuguese army concentrated at Campo Mayor was under the command of the Marquis De Fronteira and consisted of 3,000 Portuguese Horse, 9,200 Portuguese Foot, and 2,800 English Foot, the latter being under the command of the Earl of Galway. The enemy, under the command of the Marquis De Bay, numbered 5,000 Horse and 10,000 Foot, all Spaniards.

On 23rd April Galway was encamped at Cancan, about a league from Elvas. On the 25th he reached the Caya, 3 leagues from Elvas and 2 leagues from the enemy, who lay on the left of Badajos.

On 3rd May the Marquis De Bay, having posted his infantry at Atalaya del Rey, advanced with his cavalry to the plain of Gudina on the left bank of the River Caya, about 3 miles from Aronches, where Fronteira was encamped.

Fronteira, contrary to Galway's opinion, decided to cross the river and attack. On 7th May, having bridged the river, Fronteira sent all his horse, Montandre's Brigade (Newton's 20th, Sankey's 39th and Paston's Regiment) and 5 guns across to attack the enemy's cavalry which was drawn up on the plain opposite.

The Allied force was drawn up with the foot in the centre and the cavalry on the wings. About noon Fronteira opened fire with his artillery, when the Spanish Horse charged the Portuguese cavalry on the right wing and immediately put them to flight and captured the guns. The Marquis De Bay next turned his attention to Montandre's Brigade, who firmly repulsed three charges and then retired in good order up the left bank of the river to Aronches.

Galway had in the meantime sent Sankey's Brigade (Barrymore's 13th, Stanwix and Galway's Regiment) across the river in support with the intention of recapturing the guns and covering Montandre's retreat.

Barrymore's (13th) were in front, and charged the Spaniards with distinguished gallantry; the other two regiments of the brigade also displayed great bravery, and the three corps overthrew the leading columns of the opposing army, and recaptured the guns. Encouraged by this success, they pressed forward and became exposed to the attack of superior numbers, when the Portuguese cavalry of the left wing were ordered to support them, but instead of obeying their orders they galloped to the rear. Thus forsaken, the three regiments were surrounded by a host of opponents, and only a few officers and men were able to cut their passage through their numerous adversaries; the remainder were forced to surrender as prisoners of war; but Montandre's Brigade was enabled to reach Aronches in safety. On 9th May the Allies withdrew to Elvas.

In this action each side lost 500 killed and wounded, whilst the Allies lost 80 officers and 900 men as prisoners. The Regiment's loss was particularly severe; besides those killed and wounded, the Earl of Barrymore, four captains, eight lieutenants, eight ensigns, three volunteers, and between two and three hundred non-commissioned officers and men were taken prisoners.

It ceased to exist as a unit for the remainder of the campaign of that year, but meanwhile Colonel Moncal's recruiting party in England had already raised 120 men for the Regiment. It is interesting to note that a return, dated 19th July 1709, of officers absent from the Regiment in Portugal, gives the names of all Colonel Moncal's party, mentioned previously and in addition, the following:—

Names	Cause of Absence
Captain Hastings	A child.
„ Bowes	} Came over since last action.
„ Charleton	
„ Edwardes	
Lieut. Maxwell	A child.
„ Booth	A child.

It will be seen that at this time there were three children on the roll of officers; this was a device quite usual until long afterwards, by which the Authorities made provision for the families of deserving officers who had been killed on service, without burdening the Army Estimate with the cost of pensions. As might be expected the system was open to abuse, and persons with more influence than merit sometimes obtained a commission for their offspring and deprived the infant of the pay which it was too young to earn and too innocent to claim.

There is one more entry in this history as regards Pearce's Dragoons. By the end of February 1709 so good was the progress of recruiting that the Regiment was so far completed that the troops were distributed as follows: two at Wantage, two at Bampton, and two at Burford. During the spring of 1709 the headquarters were moved to Faringdon, thence to Cirencester, and finally to Chesterfield; those at Wantage were moved to Abingdon. On the 16th June Pearce (who had been gazetted Brigadier-General since his return from Spain) was ordered to assemble his regiment at Whitehaven in order to cross into Ireland. In this country it remained till the Peace of Utrecht, 1713, when, with numerous other Dragoon Regiments, it was disbanded.

In sharp contrast to the romantic origin of Pearce's Dragoons, no details of its disbandment, except the bare fact, can be found. It existed for seven years under the same commanding officer, Edward Pearce, and fought with great distinction under Peterborough and Galway. It may be here mentioned that Peterborough's Dragoons was formed about the same time as Pearce's, but this regiment was made up of detachments of different infantry regiments in Spain, an example that has been followed in more recent years by the formation of Mounted Infantry Regiments for special campaigns.

To Barrymore's Foot, subsequently (the 13th Foot) belongs the unique honour in the British Army of serving in the same campaign both as a Foot and a Horse Regiment, an honour that will always be remembered in the annals of the old Regiment.

After the Battle of Caya the efforts of Colonel Moncal's recruiting party were rewarded with greater success, for between the 3rd of October 1709 and the 23rd April 1710 no less than 24 officers and 380 men left England to join the Regiment in Portugal. Owing to the great victories achieved by Marlborough and the number of French prisoners that were captured, it was not long before the Earl of Barrymore, his officers, and other ranks captured at the Caya, were exchanged and the Regiment was reconstituted in Portugal for the campaign of 1710.

That campaign is chiefly remarkable for the great successes gained by General Stanhope at Almenara and Saragossa and his subsequent advance to Madrid from Catalonia and Aragon. Several English colours and standards, taken in the Battle of Almanza, were found hung up in the chapel of the Lady De Atocha and restored to the English General.

On the Portuguese frontier, however, where the Regiment was engaged, Galway was hampered by the Portuguese Government, who refused to allow him to advance. Consequently nothing was achieved, when much might have been done, to complete Stanhope's success. In fact, that General was obliged to retreat into Aragon at the end of the year. Galway left Portugal for England in October.

The campaign of 1711 was equally uneventful on the Portuguese Frontier, and towards the end of the year all the English troops were withdrawn from Portugal to Gibraltar and Minorca, the Regiment proceeding to Gibraltar, where it remained in garrison.

A suspension of hostilities was agreed to at Utrecht in August 1712, and in the following month all the English troops left Spain.

By the Peace of Utrecht in 1713 Gibraltar was added to Great Britain. Pearce's (5th), Barrymore's (13th) and Newson's (25th) Regiments were detailed to compose the garrison of Gibraltar, and into them were drafted the men of the junior regiments serving in Portugal; the latter regiments were disbanded as being in excess of peace requirements.

The establishment of the Regiment at Gibraltar was:—

Staff: 1 Colonel, 1 Lieut.-Colonel, 1 Major, 1 Adjutant, 1 Qr.-Master, 1 Chaplain, 1 Surgeon, 1 Surgeon's mate.

Twelve companies each of 1 Captain, 1 Lieutenant, 1 Ensign, 2 Serjeants, 2 Corporals, 2 Drummers, and 32 men 'including 2 men for the widdows' (whatever their duties may have been).

The Grenadier company included in the twelve had 3 additional men. The total strength of the Regiment was 500 Rank and File.

Brig.-General Thomas Stanwix was Governor of Gibraltar, which was stated by Major-General Pearce in 1712 to be at the best but an indifferent town with not above one house in twenty standing.

SPAIN AND PORTUGAL, 1705-13

CHAPTER VI

IN GARRISON AT GIBRALTAR

THE Regiment was in garrison at Gibraltar from 1711 to 1728, 17 years, a long period, but by no means uncommon in the eighteenth century. To make matters worse, conditions of life in the garrison were almost unbearable. To the rank and file, although a small bounty was given to induce them to serve in the colonies, it meant, in fact, perpetual exile. Very few who went to Gibraltar from Spain ever saw their homes again. As an illustration of the disgraceful neglect by the authorities of the troops in the garrison a petition was drawn up and signed on 3rd December 1713 by all the officers present of the three regiments then quartered in Gibraltar and sent to Whitehall. The following is a summary of 'A Representation of the Hardships the Garrison of Gibraltar lies under:'

1. That the Jews, Genoese and Greeks get the best homes because they can afford to pay a high premium and rent to the Governor which the English inhabitants cannot afford.

2. That the Commanding Officers of the three Regiments are forbidden by the Lieutenant-Governor to make contracts for fresh provisions. The Lieutenant-Governor reserving to himself this right.

3. That all boats that come in or go out with wine or provisions have to pay duty to the Lieutenant-Governor, and that consequently the officers and soldiers have to pay an enhanced price.

4. That no officer is allowed to go on board to buy at first hand, but must purchase through the suttlers at exorbitant rates.

5. That no Guard Room (except the Main Guard) is proof against rain, and there are no guard beds in any of the guard rooms.

6. That several Guards have no cover at all.

7. That no Fire or Candle is allowed in any of the Guards.

8. That the Jews bring in Brass money from Barbary and take in exchange all the Spanish money they can get, making 500 per cent.

9. That no coals are allowed to the garrison, nor can coal or wood be purchased, consequently officers and soldiers are unable to cook the rations allowed by Her Majesty.

10. That the Lieutenant-Governor and Town Major confine men without acquainting Commanding Officers, keep them in prison for 80 or 90 days on bread and water, where they lose the use of their limbs and their clothes rot. When the men are released without trial or punishment the Lieutenant-Governor demands their pay for the time of their confinement, which it is estimated exceeds the pay allowed to the Lieutenant-Governor by Her Majesty.

11. That Colonel Jones, commanding Lord Barrymore's Regiment, having sent in a petition from one of his men representing the miserable condition he was reduced to by long confinement, was told by the Lieutenant-Governor that no one except himself had anything to do with the Provosts, nor would he allow any petitions to be forwarded to Commanding Officers.

12. That soldiers confined by officers in the Guard Room are often set at liberty by the Lieutenant-Governor without any explanation whatever.

13. That non-commissioned officers and men who have been encouraged to take their discharge in Gibraltar are unable to get houses owing to the exorbitant rents, they have accordingly left Gibraltar and their places have been taken by Jews and strangers.

14. That houses, which have been applied for by officers and refused, have subsequently been let to Jews and Genoese.

15. That the price of provisions in the market is exorbitant owing to taxation by the Lieutenant-Governor.

16. That the Spaniards keep a guard to prevent provisions coming into Gibraltar and at the same time smuggle out tobacco.

17. That a number of soldiers have been killed or hurt by the falling in of houses, due to the necessary repairs not having been carried out.

The Earl of Portmore, Governor of Gibraltar, then on leave in England, received the following letter in reply:—

'Whitehall, *9th March*, *1714*

My Lord,

The proceedings of the officers of the three Regiments which compose the Garrison at Gibraltar have been taken in consideration by Her Majesty, who, being offended by the mutinous manner in which they have represented their Grievances has thought fit to direct that the three Commanding Officers of those Regiments be suspended, and that both they, and all the rest of the Officers who signed the Representation be very severely reprimanded for their behaviour in taking a method, which, supposing every article of their complaints to be just and reasonable, is so contrary to all military order, and so inconsistent with the preservation of good discipline among Her Majesty's Troops. I have likewise signified the Queen's Pleasure to the Secretary-at-War upon this subject, who will confer with Your Lordship about putting Her Majesty's orders in execution.

The Queen has thought fit to refer the consideration of the complaints themselves to a Committee of the Lords of her Privy Council, wherefore your Lordship will please to put the Original Representation into the hands of one of the Clerks of the Council, that my Lord President may be acquainted with it.

My Lord,
Your Lordship's most
obedient humble servant,
Bolingbroke.'

Although the breach of discipline on the part of the officers must be condemned, it is hoped that the Committee of the Lords of Her Majesty's Privy Council were able to effect some amelioration in the conditions of service in the garrison of Gibraltar. As a further instance of regimental life at this period, the proceedings of a Board of General Officers held in London on the 24th March 1714, record the case of Captain Charlton.

'May it please Your Majesty.

In obedience to Your Majesty's Commands, the General Officers have examined into the complaint of Capt. William Charlton of the Earl of Barrymore's Regt. of Foot in Garrison at Gibraltar setting forth that after twenty-two years' faithful service in which he had suffered much by wounds received, he was by a Combination of Officers, in many instances made uneasy to the end that he might be obliged to quit his command; and particularly that he was confined for several months together for only striking the Paymaster who had denied him the accounts and subsistence of his Company, and for the same brought to trial before a Court Martial, upon which a sentence was imposed upon him derogatory to his Honour, and contrary to the Fact alleged against him. That the Officers failing in their design in that Prosecution, he was again imprisoned, and Crimes sought for with diligence wherewith to accuse him. Under the Terror whereof, and for Regaining his Liberty, he submitted to a Resignation of his Company, and now prays Relief.

Whereupon the General Officers do most humbly report to Your Majesty that they find Capt. Charlton to have been dealt with in a very arbitrary manner and that being confined and tried as set forth, and sentenced to ask pardon of the Paymaster whom he struck; Colonel Godly the President, by his own single authority, imposed a form of words upon him not required by the Court. And that at last the Complainant being again imprisoned upon very slight pretences and threatened with fresh severities, he was, under the Terror thereof, compelled to a Resignation of his Company at an Under-Value; all which fully appearing, the Board is unanimously of opinion that the said Resignation ought no way to bind the said Capt. Charlton; and therefore humbly offers that Your Majesty be pleased to continue him in the Command of the said Company, and that he be accounted with for the Pay thereof, and for his own Pay as Captain for the time past, provided he return the money he received with Interest for the time he has had the same in his hands.

Which is

PORTMORE   JOS. SABINE
N. SANKEY   G. KELBURN
GEO. CARPENTER   GEO. WADE
S. DAVENPORT   JOHN HOBART.'
THO. WHETHAM

On the 28th July 1715 the Earl of Barrymore was succeeded in the command of the 13th by Colonel Stanhope Cotton, who had served in Brig.-General Bowle's Regiment which was disbanded at the peace. Colonel Cotton had to pay heavily for this honour, as Lord Barrymore included in the price £3,500 as a debt for clothing, and £2,362 'lost by an Agent'.

According to the Regimental Records, Colonel Cotton was a first-rate Commanding Officer, and the Regiment was as much distinguished for its excellent conduct in time of peace, as it had been for gallantry in action during the war.

About this time George I instituted periodical inspections by General Officers and a uniform system of drill.

Below will be found a nominal roll of the Officers in the Regiment in 1715:—

Colonel Cotton's Regiment of Foot

Name	Rank
[1] Stanhope Cotton	Colonel and Captain
Francis Bowes	Lieut.-Colonel and Captain
[2] Ferdinand Richard Hastings	Major and Captain
Mark Antonio Moncale	Captain
John Duncomb	,,
John Lloyd	,,
Thomas England	,,
William Carlton	,,
William Knypes	,,
Benjamin Hodder	,,
Moses Moreau	,,
Edmund Webb	,,
Ralph Jenkins	Capt.-Lieutenant
Patrick Paterson	Lieutenant
Isaac Bruse	,,
Charles Booth	,,
Robert Bullman	,,
Hildebrand Jacob	,,
Edward Barry	,,
Charles Moncale	,,
Adam Enos	,,
Stephen Bateman	,,
Daniel Pecquer	,,
— Quinchant	,,
George Walsh	,,
David Barry	Ensign
James Charleton	,,
Henry Waldron	,,
Robert Fielding	,,

[1] Commandant of Gibraltar 1716–19.
[2] Son of Brig.-General Ferdinando Hastings, former Colonel.

Name	Rank
Edward Windus	Ensign
Charles Lieving	,,
Thomas Williams	,,
John Hadzor	,,
Jonathan Fox	,,
Daniel Nicholas	Lieutenant
James Barry	,,
David Barry	Chaplain
Matthew Draper	Adjutant
John Lloyd	Quartermaster
John Hadzor	Surgeon

In 1716 Colonel Cotton was appointed Lieutenant-Governor of Gibraltar as set forth in the following letter:—

'GEORGE R.

Stanhope Cotton, Esq.
Lieutenant-Governor of Gibraltar.

George By the Grace of God, King of Great Britain France and Ireland, Defender of the Faith, &c. To Our Trusty and Welbeloved Stanhope Cotton, Esq. Greeting: We reposing particular Trust and Confidence in your Loyalty Courage and Experience, do by these presents Constitute and appoint you to be Lieutenant-Governor of the City and Garrison of Gibraltar; hereby giving and Granting unto you full power and authority to execute and perform all things to the place of Lieutenant-Governor belonging or appertaining and We do hereby Command all the Officers and Soldiers of the said City and Garrison to Obey you as Lieutenant-Governor of the same: and you are to observe and follow such orders and Directions from time to time as you shall receive from Us, Our Governor of the said City and Garrison of Gibraltar, or any your Superior Officer, according to the Rules and Discipline of Warr, in pursuance of the Trust We hereby repose in you. Given at Our Court at — the Tenth day of August 1716, in the Third year of Our Reign.

By His Majestyes Command

J. CRAGGS.'

In 1718 the Regimental Chaplain, David Barry, appears to have got into trouble with his Colonel as is shown by the following report of a Meeting of General Officers:—

(W.O. 71/5) PROCEEDINGS OF GENERAL OFFICERS   1718

At a Meeting of the General Officers Wednesday the 3rd of December 1718

The Petitions of Chaplain Barry being again considered the following Reports to His Majesty were agreed to and signed.

'May it Please Your Majesty

In Obedience to Your Majesty's Commands to Examine into the Memorial of Mr. David Barry Chaplain to the Regiment of Foot under the Command of Col. Stanhope Cotton in Gibraltar, wherein he complains of hard Usage received by him in that Garrison; The General Officers have Examined into the same and do most humble Offer it to Your Majesty as their Opinion that he may have Your Majesty's leave to Exchange with some other Chaplain, according as he has requested, if Your Majesty shall be so pleased, there appearing to be a very great misunderstanding between him and his said Colonel.

But they submit the same in all Humility to Your Majesty

W. Evans	Geo. Carpenter
Geo. Wade	Geo. Macartney
Hump. Gore	Jos. Sabine.

Horse Guards,
3rd December 1718.'

In 1720 the Spanish fortress of Ceuta, on the opposite shore of the Straits of Gibraltar, was being besieged by the Moors. The Marquis de Leda assembled a large force in Gibraltar Bay ostensibly to relieve Ceuta but secretly to take Gibraltar, which at that time was only garrisoned by three weak infantry regiments, viz. the 5th, 13th and 20th, with only two field officers in the fortress. Moreover, there were only 14 days' supplies in the garrison. At this juncture Colonel Kane, the Governor of Minorca, was sent to Gibraltar with 500 men from that island, and he brought with him a welcome supply of provisions and ammunition. After Colonel Kane's arrival the Spaniards thought fit to desist from any attempts on Gibraltar.

On the arrival of Colonel Kane he assumed the appointment of Lieutenant-Governor of the Fortress in the place of Colonel Cotton.

In 1725 Colonel Richard Kane, Lieutenant-Governor of Gibraltar, having represented that the arms of the three Regiments of Foot in Garrison, viz. Pearce's, Egerton's and Cotton's, were 'old and much decayed', the Board of Ordnance were ordered to issue complete sets of Firelocks and Bayonets, the Regiments to pay at the rate of £1 4s. 6d. per musket and 2s. for each bayonet.

After commanding the 13th upwards of twelve years Colonel Cotton died on the 7th December 1725, when King George I conferred the Colonelcy upon Brig.-General Lord Mark Kerr, from the 29th Regiment.

It is interesting as showing how the troops were fed in those days, to insert the copy of a document penned by the chief storekeeper at Gibraltar dated 3rd August 1726:—

'Every Monday morning the Regiments receive all their provisions except bread, except in the winter time when one regiment is served in the afternoon by reason of the days being short, and they take it in turns in being first served. The biskett taking up more time, it is served out every Tuesday morning, and when soft bread is issued it is every fourth day, except to officers every second day.' (Regimental Records 5th Fusiliers.)

MAJOR-GENERAL LORD MARK KERR
Colonel of the Regiment, 1725-1732

Other details are that oil was issuable in lieu of butter or cheese, viz. one pint oil instead of 1 lb. butter or 2 lb. cheese. Rice was issued as an alternative to pease or oatmeal.

The weekly ration seems to have been 7 lb. of biscuit or bread, 2½ lb. beef, 1 lb. pork, 4 pints of pease, 3 pints of oatmeal, 6 oz. butter, 8 oz. cheese.

The loss of Gibraltar in 1704 was naturally still a sore subject to the Spanish people, and on the prospect of England being involved in a continental war in 1726 the Spanish Monarch resolved to commence hostilities with Great Britain, by a determined effort to recover possession of that coveted fortress at the entrance of the Mediterranean. So it came about that the Regiment had another opportunity of partaking in a second successful defence of Gibraltar.

THE SIEGE OF GIBRALTAR, 1727

The first hostile act was the arrest of Colonel Dunbar at Malaga in the previous December, carrying dispatches from England to Gibraltar. He was cast into the common gaol and was not released till a month later.

In January all the Spanish militia in Malaga were called out and ordered to proceed to San Roque. In addition most of the garrison of Cadiz, with brass cannon from that port, and guns from Algeciras were being concentrated opposite Gibraltar, while 3,000 peasants were engaged in making huts and fascines.

On 14th January Admiral Sir Charles Wager with six ships arrived from England having on board three companies of Anstruther's (26th), eight companies of Disney's (29th) and six companies of Newton's (39th).

By the middle of February the Spanish army, commanded by the Count de las Torras, numbered nearly 20,000 men, and on the 22nd the Spaniards broke ground by commencing a battery on the western beach on neutral ground which drew forth a remonstrance from General Clayton, at that time Lieutenant-Governor. Las Torras sent a defiant reply, to which Clayton replied by opening fire from the guns at the Old Mole and Willis's batteries.

On the night of 22nd February General Spinola, with five battalions, a brigade of engineers and 1,000 workmen, opened the first parallel running from the Devil's Tower on the eastern beach along the base of the Rock to the inundation, and at daybreak next morning opened a heavy fire. Thereupon Admiral Wager sent two ships round to the east of the Rock to enfilade the Spanish trenches, which they did effectually, especially as 2,000 Spaniards had advanced close up to the face of the Rock from the top of which the garrison threw down grenades and stones, while the ships did such good execution by their fire that the Spaniards were forced to retreat with heavy losses.

Eventually Las Torras threw up a powerful battery of 10 guns to command the anchorage, and the ships had to return to the west side of the Rock.

The enemy now directed their attack against the North Front from the extremity of the Old Mole to Willis's battery. Numerous guns and mortars were mounted, the first parallel was completed on 25th February and the second on 3rd March. By 10th March the batteries were approached within 100 paces of the Rock, and on the 15th a battery was unmasked within 100 paces of Landport Gate.

On 7th April the *Torbay* came in, bringing a welcome reinforcement of Colonel Middleton's (25th) and six companies of Colonel Hayes' Regiment (34th). Very wet weather now set in, and the Spanish trenches became inundated, and much of their work destroyed.

On 21st April the *Solebay*, with four transports from Minorca, arrived, having on board 27 officers and 485 men. And on 1st May three ships arrived from England, having on board Lord Portmore, the Governor of Gibraltar, Lord Mark Kerr, Colonel (13th), a battalion of the 1st Regiment of the Guards, and Colonel Clayton's Regiment (14th), besides numerous senior officers. The ten companies of the Guards were each commanded by a colonel.

The strength of the garrison was now 5,481 of all ranks. The 13th, or Lord Mark Kerr's Regiment, numbering 434. In the ensuing week the enemy opened fire with four gigantic batteries of brass guns which continued for 14 days; 700 shot per hour were thrown into the fortress from 92 guns and 72 mortars.

To oppose this bombardment the garrison had 60 guns, 21 on the Grand Battery, 23 on the Old Mole, 9 at Willis's and 5 at the side of the Moorish Castle. Of the 60 guns 23 were dismounted by hostile fire in 7 days.

By 20th May the enemy's artillery, owing to rapid firing, became gradually ineffective, until at length only 19 guns were in play. The garrison repaired the breaches and mounted 13 new guns, as well as 100 mortars. The Spanish artillery ammunition had become nearly exhausted, and owing to the impossible state of the roads no reinforcements could reach their camp. It was represented to Las Torras that unless the army was reinforced by 25,000 men Gibraltar could not be taken.

By the end of May the guns of the garrison had gained complete ascendency over the besiegers, and on 3rd June the Earl of Portmore opened a general bombardment with 100 guns and numerous mortars, with the result that in a few days not a single gun replied. The Spanish trenches had been completely destroyed; moreover, sickness was rife in their camp.

On 23rd June a courier arrived at San Roque from Madrid with dispatches for the Count de Las Torras and a letter for the Earl of Portmore announcing that preliminaries of peace had been signed, and that a suspension of hostilities was to take place.

The losses of the garrison amounted to 5 officers killed and wounded; rank and file killed 69, wounded 207, died of wounds or sickness 49. Total 361. Deserted 17. The losses of the 13th were 7 men killed, 26 wounded and 3 died of wounds. The Spanish losses were 57 officers killed and wounded. Rank and file killed 346. Wounded 1,119. Deserted 875. Died of sickness or invalided, over 5,000.

This siege of Gibraltar consisted mainly of artillery duels. At no time were the garrison in serious straits, as the British command of the sea was at all times secure.

The following document shows the names of the officers of the Regiment at this time:

(State Paper Dom. Military Entry Book 179) 1727

COMMISSIONS ISSUED OUT FOR THE OFFICERS IN LORD MARK KERR'S REGIMENT OF FOOT DATED AT KENSINGTON 20TH JUNE 1727

Field Officers and Captains	Lieutenants	Ensigns
[1] Ld. Mark Kerr, Colonel and Captain.	James Charlton, Captain-Lieutenant.	Edwd. Scott.
Wm. Hargrave, Lieut.-Colonel and Captain.	Thos. Cokayne.	Edwd. Hopson.
	Thos. Williams.	Robt. Lejonquiere.
Moses Moreau, Major and Captain.	Thomas Lister.	Geo. Hamilton.
	Chris. Legard.	Wm. Burnet.
Mark Anth. Moncal, Captain.	Daniel Nicholas.	Boteler Hutchinson.
	Robt. Bullman.	George Kerr.
Benjn. Hodder.	Beaumont Perkyns.	Geo. Mackenzie.
Ralph Jenkins.	Alex. Cummins.	Robt. Pearce.
James Cunningham.	Thos. Cardiffe.	John Farie.
David Barry.	Saml. Becher.	Henry Trepsack.
James Stewart.	Robt. Fielding.	
Richard Husbands.		
Charles Walker.		
Jean Jenvre Quinchant.		

Staff Officers
Edward Austin, Quarter Master
Thomas Cokayne, Adjutant
Thomas Spateman, Chaplain
John Hadzor, Surgeon

The Regiment was only relieved from duty at Gibraltar in the spring of 1728, and returning to England after an absence of upwards of twenty years, landed at Portsmouth on 1st May.

[1] Lord Mark Kerr was promoted Major-General 24th June 1727.

CHAPTER VII

DETTINGEN, FONTENOY, AND CULLODEN

SOON after arrival at Portsmouth the Regiment was ordered to march to Shrewsbury, the chief halting-places being Andover, Hungerford and Faringdon, but subsequent instructions assigned Worcester as their station. In January 1729, six companies of the 13th proceeded on detachment as follows: one company to Bromsgrove, one company to Kidderminster, two companies to Bewdley, two companies to Evesham. On 25th December of this year Lord Mark Kerr was appointed Governor of the Fort of Sheerness in the Isle of Sheppey in the County of Kent *vice* Henry Withers, Esq., deceased, but this appointment did not necessitate his relinquishing command of the Regiment.

Orders were issued on 22nd June 1730 for Lieut.-General Thomas Whetham's Regiment (12th) and Lord Mark Kerr's Regiment (13th) to march from their present quarters to Windsor Forest with intent to employ the non-commissioned officers and private men of both corps in mending the roads and avenues in the said forest which were then greatly in need of repair. While engaged in this task the Regiment was reviewed by His Majesty King George II, as described in the following notice from the *London Gazette* of 18th July:—

'Windsor Castle, *18th July*.

This morning Their Majesties accompanied by His Royal Highness the Prince of Wales, the Duke, the Princess Royal, and their Royal Highnesses the Princesses, and attended by a great number of Lords and Ladies, and several General Officers went to Wingfield Plain in the Great Forest three miles from hence, where Lieut.-General Whetham's Regiment (12th) and Lord Mark Kerr's Regiment (13th) passed in Review before His Majesty; they performed the Manual Exercise, Evolutions and Firings with so much exactness, that His Majesty was pleased to express his entire satisfaction thereat, as also with the good appearance they made.'

After completing their road-mending work in Windsor Forest the Regiment proceeded to Bristol, and in October five companies proceeded from Bristol to Portsmouth to relieve six companies of Brig.-General Fielding's Invalids who had been sent to Jersey to suppress disorders there.

In February 1731 the Regiment sent a detachment of one officer and 40 men from Bristol to Aberystwith in Cardiganshire to relieve a detachment of the Royal Welch Fusiliers. In May of the same year, the companies on garrison duty at Portsmouth having rejoined, the whole Regiment, less the detachment at Aberystwith, marched from Bristol to Berwick, where they came under the orders of Lieut.-General Wade. The Aberystwith detachment rejoined the Regiment in August.

In May 1732 Lord Mark Kerr was transferred to the 11th Dragoons, and was succeeded in the colonelcy of the 13th by Colonel John Middleton from the 25th Regiment.

From 1731 to 1739 the Regiment was quartered in Scotland or on the border and the details of their movements are extremely vague. In 1734 and 1735 they were in and around Edinburgh; in 1736 their quarters are described as being in North Britain 'near the Highlands'.

Colonel John Middleton died on the 4th May 1739, and the colonelcy remained vacant two months, when it was conferred on the 5th July on Colonel Henry Pulteney from Major of the 2nd (Coldstream) Foot Guards.

In May 1739, three companies of the Regiment proceeded from Edinburgh to Berwick, to be followed by the remainder of the Regiment as soon as relieved by another regiment. In June the establishment of the Regiment was raised by 11 men per company or 110 men altogether, which raised the strength to 815 of all ranks. On 23rd October war was declared against Spain.

In December of this year orders were issued for the inspection of the arms of all regiments at home, with the result that 399 muskets which the Regiment had brought back from Gibraltar were condemned as unserviceable.

In January 1740, the Regiment being relieved by Major-General Howard's Regiment, proceeded from Berwick to Carlisle and in the ensuing summer they marched south and encamped in Windsor Forest, where they were brigaded with two regiments of Horse, three of Dragoons, and three of Foot under Lieut.-General Honeywood. On 12th October the Emperor Charles VI of Germany died, when the succession to the throne was disputed by his daughter Maria Theresa, as Queen of Hungary and Bohemia, backed by England and Holland, against the Elector of Bavaria, supported by the French Monarch.

In this year Parliament called for and printed a return of the officers of the Army. The next list was not published till 1754, from which date they have been published regularly and are known as the Army Lists.

The Officers of the Regiment at this time were:—

Colonel Henry Pulteney. Lieut.-Colonel Moses Moreau.
Major James Cunningham. Captain-Lieutenant Thomas Williams.

Captains	Lieutenants	Ensigns
James Stuart.	Thomas Lister.	Richard Hargrave.
Charles Walker.	Daniel Nicholas.	George Middleton.
John Quinchart.	Christopher Legard.	William Jones.
James Charleton.	Samuel Beecher.	Peter Lyons.
Thomas Cockayne.	John Hadzor.	Charles Maitland.
Robert Bullman.	Edward Scott.	James Haliburton.
— Maule.	John Farie.	Gilbert Gray.
	David Robert de la Jonquire.	John Crawford.
	William Burnet.	John O'Carroll.
	George Mackenzie.	

On the prospect of Great Britain being involved in hostilities on the Continent, the 13th were placed under orders to embark for foreign service, and in July 1741 they pitched their tents on Lexden Heath, Essex, where three regiments of horse, four of dragoons, and seven of foot were encamped, and held in readiness to proceed to the seat of war.

In the spring of 1742 Colonel Pulteney was promoted to be Brigadier-General and was ordered to serve with his Regiment under the orders of Field-Marshal the Earl of Stair and Lieut.-General Honeywood. The Earl of Stair, 70 years of age, was in chief command of the expedition which numbered 16,000 British troops, of whom 5,000 came from the Colchester camp, including the 13th. They landed at Ostend during May in driblets and proceeded to quarters in Bruges and Ghent. The Earl of Stair urged an immediate attack on Dunkirk, but the Austrians would not agree, and King George being lukewarm and nominally at peace with France, the opportunity was lost, when the winter came on and put a stop to all movements.

WAR WITH FRANCE

On the 31st March 1743 war was declared against France, but before that date the Allies in Flanders had already commenced to march eastwards, the British troops being sadly in need of officers, many of whom had gone home on leave.

At this time there were 50,000 French troops on the Moselle. The French army in Flanders was available either to join their comrades on the Moselle or to proceed to South Germany should the Allies cross the Rhine south of Cologne.

Eventually Stair, commanding the British contingent including the 13th, was ordered to occupy the Heights of Mainz and to command the junction of the Rhine and Main. The Allies crossed the Rhine at Newidt, 18 miles above Bonn.

By May the forces of England, Hanover and Austria were assembled on the north bank of the Main. Their position extended from the Rhine to Aschaffenburg facing south, a bridge of boats being kept ready at Frankfort. Opposed to them was a French army of 70,000 men under Marshal Noailles, who had taken up a position near Spires on the Upper Rhine.

On 3rd June the Allies commenced to cross the Main. Two days later the Earl of Stair learnt that Noailles was advancing from Darmstadt to Frankfort; the former offered battle, but Noailles declined, whereupon Stair re-crossed the Main to the right bank.

On 19th June King George arrived from Hanover and took over command of the army which was concentrated near Aschaffenburg, where there was a bridge over the Main. Shortly afterwards Noailles advanced, seized the southern end of the bridge at Aschaffenburg and threw two bridges over the river at Seligenstadt lower down. On 26th June King George, becoming alarmed as regards his supplies, decided to retreat along the right bank of the river to Hanau that night. Noailles was prepared for this move and had stationed batteries on the left bank to harass the Allies during their march.

THE BATTLE OF DETTINGEN

At 1 a.m. on 27th June, Noailles ordered Count Grammont to cross the Main with 28,000 men at Seligenstadt and take up a position facing east by the village of Dettingen on a little brook running down from the Spessart Hills. Meanwhile Noailles returned to the opposite bank of the Main to direct operations against King George's flank and rear. The Allies moved off at 4 a.m. in the following order of march: British Cavalry, Austrian Cavalry, British Infantry, Austrian Infantry, Rear-Guard, British Guards, choicest of German Infantry, and Hanoverian Cavalry. On arrival at Klein Ostheim at 7 a.m., the Allies were obliged to file by a single road. The cavalry were halted for an hour, and news was received that Grammont was obstructing their path at Dettingen. The French artillery on the left bank of the river began to play on the columns of the Allies, and as the baggage train was massed between the 1st and 2nd Divisions of the column of route the confusion became very great, and what was worse the Allied artillery being far in rear, an hour elapsed before any effective reply could be made to the French fire. In the plain between Klein Ostheim and Dettingen there stood a wood, which being secured by the cavalry, eventually afforded a sufficient protection for the baggage train, and it became possible to form up the Allied Line of Battle. About noon Grammont, tired of waiting on the north side of Dettingen, had injudiciously advanced beyond the ravine to a fresh position, and to the Allies he appeared to be threatening their right flank.

By this time King George's Line of Battle was formed in two lines :—

1st Line. On the left within 200 yards of the river the 33rd Foot and on their right in succession the 21st Fusiliers, 23rd Fusiliers, 12th Foot, 11th Foot, 8th Foot and 13th Foot. On the right of the 13th stood an Austrian Brigade and then in succession, the Blues, Life Guards, 6th Dragoons and Royal Dragoons.

2nd Line. From left to right 20th Foot, 32nd Foot, 37th Foot, 31st Foot and the Buffs. On their right the 7th Dragoon Guards, King's Dragoon Guards, 4th and 7th Dragoons and Scots Greys.

Opposite to them the French were drawn up in two lines, with a reserve in 3rd Line, the infantry in the centre and the cavalry on the flanks.

The French Household Cavalry on the French right were opposed to the 33rd Foot on the Allied left. As soon as General Clayton, who commanded the Allied left, saw this, he ordered up the 3rd Dragoons to fill the gap between the 33rd Foot and the river.

The British line now advanced, King George himself waving his sword and urging the troops on, but the nature of the ground was boggy, and frequent halts to redress the line necessitated a slow advance. Meanwhile the French batteries on the other side of the river were raining destruction on the 3rd Dragoons and the battalions on the left. When the British Infantry opened an irregular fire along their front, King George's horse took fright and ignominiously bolted, carrying His Majesty to the rear. However, he shortly afterwards returned, dismounted and continued to cheer his troops on.

The French Infantry of the Guard on Grammont's right centre now advanced, and opened a disorderly fire, but the British line, cheered on by the Earl of Stair, who gave orders not to fire till the colour of the eyes of the enemy could be distinguished, replied with continuous volleys by platoons. This so staggered the French Guards that they fell back in disorder in rear of their Horse, who in turn advanced against the British left, where they were met by the 3rd Dragoons, the 33rd Foot and 21st and 23rd Fusiliers. The Dragoons made a famous charge, and the infantry manfully standing their ground, the French Horse fell back after a desperate encounter.

This was but a prelude to a severe cavalry action. The British Infantry on the left were in danger of being broken up. King George transferred cavalry from his right to his left flank. First of all the 1st and 7th Dragoons, followed by the Blues, and later the 4th and 6th Dragoons and two regiments of Austrian Dragoons arrived, and after repeated charges compelled the French Household Cavalry to retire.

A feeble attack on the British right was repulsed, while the French Infantry could make no progress under the steady British fire. When suddenly the French Black Musketeers broke away from the French right and galloped madly between the opposing lines of infantry to attack the British right, they were attacked in turn in front and flank by British and Austrians and cut to pieces. A general advance of the Allied line now took place, and the French Infantry, not relishing the prospect of a charge, retreated, and made for the bridges over the Main at Seligenstadt, when they were charged by the Allied Cavalry, which completed their confusion. The victory was not followed up, as Noailles had some 25,000 men on the left bank of the Main who had not been engaged, and King George was only too thankful to have escaped from the trap which had been set for him.

The French losses were 5,000 men killed, wounded and prisoners. The Allies lost about half that number, the British share being 265 killed and 561 wounded and prisoners. The loss of the 13th was 21 rank and file killed; Ensigns Ogilbie and Gray, 1 drummer and 29 rank and file wounded.

This was the last action in which a King of England commanded the army in person.

On the day following the action, the Allies marched to Hanau, where they were joined by 12,000 Hanoverians and Hessians, and remained there several weeks. On 27th August the Allied Army crossed the Rhine above Mainz and marched south to Worms and Speyer, which latter place they reached on 25th September. After halting a few days they retraced their steps and were back at Mainz on 11th October, when they went into winter quarters, the British proceeding to Flanders.

DETTINGEN, JUNE 27th, 1743

Most important changes took place this year as regards the Regimental Colours. The warrant of 1743 is accordingly given in full:—

Warrant of 1743

'The Union Colour is the first stand of Colours in all Regiments, royal or not, except the Foot Guards.

No Colonel to put his arms, crest, device or livery in any part of the appointments of his Regiment.

The first colours of every marching Regiment of Foot is to be the Great Union; the second colours is to be the colour of the facing of the Regiment, with the Union in the upper canton. In the centre of each colour is to be painted in gold Roman figures, the number of the rank of the Regiment, within a wreath of roses and thistles on one stalk except those regiments which are allowed to wear royal devices or antient badges; the number of their rank is to be painted toward the upper corner; the length of the pike and colours to be of the same size as those of the Foot Guards; the cord and tassels of all colours to be crimson and gold.'

The principle laid down in the first paragraph of this warrant completely altered the existing order of things, the old Colonel's and Lieutenant-Colonel's colours in Infantry Regiments disappeared and of the two new ones which took their places, the first (afterwards called the King's Colour) bore the 'Union' throughout, the second the regimental facings and had a small Union in the upper corner nearest the staff. But the most important change lay in the fact that the regimental number was to appear in the centre of both standards, the first occasion of its display upon any part of the regimental equipment.

In May 1744 the Regiment again took the field, and served the campaign of that year under Field-Marshal Wade. The Allies were concentrated close to Brussels and numbered 55,000, while the French had 80,000 between the Scheldt and Sambre under the command of Marshal Saxe. In June the latter advanced and occupied Ypres and Fort Knock, thus threatening the British lines of communication with the coast. Tournai was at this time held by the Allies. In July Saxe advanced and entrenched his army between Menin and Courtrai. The Allies in their turn advanced and crossed the Scheldt. It seemed as if a general action would take place, but owing to divided counsels and want of horses for the artillery nothing was done. August passed and September came, and finally in October the Allies retired into winter quarters. Marshal Wade, sick and disappointed, resigned his command.

In June of this year the establishment of the Regiment was raised to twelve companies, each consisting of 3 serjeants, 3 corporals, 2 drummers and 70 privates, besides officers.

FONTENOY

The Regiment again took part in the Campaign of 1745 when the Allied Army was commanded by the Duke of Cumberland, a prince of the Royal blood, and, young though he was, far more likely to ensure the co-operation of the Allies than a more experienced General. He concentrated his army at Brussels on the 2nd May and marched south the following day. His object was to relieve Tournai, which Marshal Saxe had already invested. On 9th May Cumberland reached Brissod in sight of Saxe's army.

The intermediate ground was broken up by small woods and enclosures, beyond which an open plain sloped upwards to the village of Fontenoy, the centre of Saxe's position. Cumberland halted for the night, fixing his headquarters at Maubray, $1\frac{1}{2}$ miles south-east of the French camp.

Early on the morning of 10th May the Allied advanced guard cleared the French posts out of the woods and enclosures on his front, and Cumberland was enabled to reconnoitre the French position. Its right rested on the Scheldt at Antoin, thence eastwards to the village of Fontenoy, the centre of the position, while the left rested on the Forest of Barry. The whole position including Fontenoy was fortified by entrenchments and redoubts, of which latter the Redoubt D'Eu in front of the Forest of Barry protected Saxe's left flank. The space between Fontenoy and the Forest of Barry was held by nine battalions in the 1st Line and eleven in the 2nd Line, and the flower of the French army. Cumberland decided to attack the following day; he had 50,000 men half of whom were British. The Austrians were to attack the French right, the Dutch the French centre including Fontenoy, and the British the French left between Fontenoy and the Forest of Barry.

At 2 a.m. on the 11th May the British advanced, the cavalry leading. Vezon, a village in front of the Forest of Barry, was soon cleared and the British infantry deployed. On the right was Ingoldsby's Brigade consisting of the 12th, 13th, 42nd and a Hanoverian battalion with 3 six-pounders. Their task was to assault the Redoubt D'Eu. On their left, from right to left in succession, were the 1st Guards, Coldstreams, 1st, 21st, 31st, 8th, 25th, 33rd and 19th in 1st Line, and in 2nd Line from right to left, The Buffs, 23rd, 32nd, 11th, 28th, 34th and 20th and some Hanoverian battalions on the extreme left.

When all was ready the Dutch and Austrians advanced against Fontenoy and Antoin and the intervening ground, but being received with a murderous fire in their front and from some guns on the farther bank of the Scheldt, they fell back behind cover and could not be induced to advance again. The battle thus resolved itself into a duel between the British and French to the east of the village of Fontenoy.

Ingoldsby on the right, mistaking his instructions, hesitated to attack the Redoubt D'Eu. He found the redoubt to be a formidable work, in fact, as a contemporary chronicler remarked, 'the Brigadier smelt too long at the physic to have any inclination to swallow it'. It is only fair to state that Ingoldsby was wounded and had to be taken off the field. Notwithstanding this untoward incident, Cumberland placed himself in front of the British line, now joined by Ingoldsby's brigade. The whole line, with drums beating and shouldered arms, deliberately advanced across the open space of half a mile which separated them from the enemy. Great gaps in their ranks were caused by artillery fire in their front, and on each flank from Fontenoy and the Redoubt D'Eu, and as the advance continued the guns on the flanks took the ranks in reverse; still they closed up the gaps, but the front became narrower, and the ground they had marched over became dotted with killed and wounded.

It was not till they were within 30 yards of the French line that the British levelled their muskets and volleys rang out from end to end of the line, two battalions loading while the Third fired. It is said that 19 officers and 600 men of the French and Swiss Guards fell at the first discharge. The 1st French line was crushed and broken. Marshal Saxe now sent up reinforcements, but they in turn were swept aside by the murderous fire of the British, who had now advanced some 300 yards into the heart of the French camp. The British columns were now repeatedly charged by French cavalry from the rear of the Forest of Barry, and although these charges were repulsed with heavy loss it gave time to the French infantry to re-form. Waldeck, with the Dutch, undertook to make another attack on Fontenoy, while Cumberland again advanced, and this time he was opposed by the Irish Brigade of six battalions and numerous artillery. Although some progress was made, Cumberland, owing to the failure of the Dutch on his flank and his own heavy losses, was compelled to retire. The retreat was made in good order, three battalions of the Guards and one battalion of Hanoverians forming the rear-guard. The retreat was made good to Ath, where the army encamped under the guns of that fortress.

Of the 15,000 English and Hanoverian Infantry nearly 6,000 were killed and wounded. The losses of the 13th were Captain Queenchant, 2 serjeants and 35 privates killed, Captain-Lieut. D. Nicholas, Lieuts. W. Jones and S. Edhouse, 2 serjeants and 39 men wounded, and 10 missing. The French loss in killed and wounded was fully 10,000 men.

Marshal Saxe, in a report sent by him to the French Minister of War, comments on this battle as follows:—

'I question much whether there are many of our Generals who dare undertake to pass a plain with a body of infantry before a numerous cavalry, and flatter himself he could hold his ground for several hours with 15 or 20 battalions in the middle of an army, as did the English at Fontenoy, without any charge being made to shake them, or make them throw away their fire. This is what we have all seen, but self-love makes us unwilling to speak of it, because we are well aware it is beyond our imitation.'

Leaving Ath on 16th May, Cumberland retired to Lessines and subsequently crossed the Dender to cover Brussels. Tournai fell into the hands of the French army, whose strength was double that of the Allies. On 16th September the 13th were present at a review of the army at Vilvorde to the north of Brussels.

While the army was in Flanders, Prince Charles Edward, eldest son of the Pretender, landed in Scotland on 25th July, and being joined by several clans, asserted his father's pretensions to the throne. He reached Perth on 4th September and Edinburgh on the 17th, though Edinburgh Castle was held by the King's troops. He utterly defeated Cope at Prestonpans on the 21st.

CAMPAIGNS IN ENGLAND AND SCOTLAND

In consequence of this invasion, orders were sent to Flanders to send ten battalions home, of whom three were Guards. The 13th was one of the battalions, and after landing at Blackwall on 23rd September they proceeded to join Marshal Wade's force at Doncaster, and thence proceeded to Newcastle-on-Tyne, where were assembled on 29th October the 13th, 27th and 34th Foot, the 2nd and 3rd Dragoon Guards and the 8th Dragoons, besides militia and volunteer corps, in all 14,000 men and 20 guns. Frantic endeavours had been made to raise new regiments and among these a Mr. Oglethorpe in Yorkshire had raised a regiment of Foxhunters whom he converted into Hussars. Prince Charles Edward marched south from Edinburgh on 31st October with 5,000 men, and laid siege to Carlisle on 8th November. Wade, at Newcastle, was in an excellent position to relieve Carlisle and frustrate the whole expedition, but he advanced too late, was impeded by a fall of snow, and hearing of the fall of Carlisle on 13th November retreated to Newcastle.

In Wright's *England under the House of Hanover* this inglorious manœuvre is thus described:—

> Horse, Foot and Dragoons from lost Flanders they call,
> With Hessians and Danes, and the Devil and all;
> And hunters and rangers led by Oglethorpe;
> And the Church at the tail of the Bishop of York.
> And pray who so fit to lead forth this parade,
> As the babe of Tangier, my old grandmother Wade
> Whose cunning's so quick, but whose motions so slow,
> That the rebels marched on, while he stuck in the snow.

Prince Charles Edward, marching south from Carlisle on 20th November, crossed the Ribble at Preston on the 27th; he then proceeded to Wigan and Manchester, and eventually reached Derby on 5th December.

Cumberland, who had been recalled from Flanders, thinking that the rebels would proceed to Wales, had marched from Lichfield to Stone with 8,000 men. Thus on 5th December there were no troops between Derby and London to impede Charles's further progress. There was a panic in London, business was suspended, the shops were closed, and the Bank of England only escaped disaster by making its payments in sixpences. Meanwhile Wade's force including the 13th had moved south via Durham, Darlington and Richmond to cover Yorkshire. On the 28th they were at Persbridge, and a few days later they occupied Wetherby and turned south to Ferry bridge. The rebels, however, hearing that a French force had landed at Montrose, hesitated to advance farther and commenced to retreat on 6th December. Cumberland made great efforts to catch the rebels up and engaged their rear-guard at Penrith on 18th December, but Wade made no attempt to intercept them. Charles crossed the Esk on 20th December and six days later reached Glasgow. Wade reached Newcastle on 20th December.

FONTENOY, MAY 10th, 1745

From Newcastle the 13th and other regiments marched to Edinburgh. General Hawley, a strict disciplinarian, was in command of the force consisting of 12 battalions of Foot and 4 regiments of Dragoons. He had artillery, but no gunners, and the infantry were in a deplorable state, hardly fit for service.

In the meantime on 3rd January Prince Charles Edward left Glasgow for Stirling, where he was joined by the French who had landed at Montrose. His strength was now 9,000 men, and he proceeded to lay siege to Stirling Castle with the battering guns the French had brought with them.

Hawley's task was to raise the siege of Stirling Castle. He accordingly moved his force to Falkirk, where they were concentrated on 16th January. Charles Edward, hearing of his approach, moved his force to Bannockburn and drew up his troops on the famous battlefield. As Hawley refused to move, Charles Edward decided to attack on the 17th January.

ACTION OF FALKIRK MUIR

Charles led his army to the south of the English camp and then advanced towards it over Falkirk Muir. Hawley was temporarily absent from his command, but messages were sent to him and he galloped up without his hat; placing himself at the head of three regiments of Dragoons, he made for the top of Falkirk Muir, ordering the Foot to follow with fixed bayonets. The rebels reached the high ground first, and Hawley had to form his line of battle on lower ground in the following order: 1st Line: Glasgow Militia, 8th, 34th, 13th, 1st, 14th and 48th. 2nd Line: 27th, 37th, 36th, 4th, Battereau's Foot and 3rd Foot. The cavalry were on the right and the left was covered by a morass. The numbers on each side were about 9,000 men. Hawley ordered the Dragoons to attack, but the Highlanders, awaiting their charge with great coolness, poured in an effective volley which so disconcerted the 13th and 14th Dragoons that they galloped off the field of battle; the 9th Dragoons showed more firmness, but they also became involved in the flight. The Highlanders then attacked the infantry, who, blinded by a violent storm of wind and rain, fired an irregular volley, and, with the exception of two regiments (4th and 48th), who stood firm, retired and fled. The 4th and 48th repulsed the left wing of the rebel army, and later in the day were joined by the 14th, 1st and 3rd Regiments, who with the 9th Dragoons covered the retreat.

This disgraceful action is the more surprising because many of the regiments were the same who had fought gallantly at Dettingen and Fontenoy and many officers had sacrificed themselves to stay the rout. In those days the terror inspired by the Highlanders' charge was a factor to be reckoned with. The English Army lost all its camp equipment and 7 guns, but their losses in men were extremely small, namely 280 killed, wounded and missing, of which the 13th lost 14. The rebel loss was about 100 killed and wounded. Hawley then retreated to Linlithgow and Edinburgh.

BATTLE OF CULLODEN

The Duke of Cumberland had by this time arrived in Edinburgh, and he at once took stern measures to restore discipline in the Army. Adequate reinforcements having arrived, he set forth on 31st January for Falkirk with 12 battalions, 2 regiments of Dragoons and several companies of loyal Highlanders, when the young Chevalier raised the siege of Stirling and made a precipitate retreat towards Inverness. The 13th, whose strength at this time was 639 of all ranks, took part in the pursuit of the rebel clans, but a halt had to be made at Perth on 17th February in consequence of the severity of the weather, but this delay was utilized in practising the troops in special training against the Highlanders' tactics. On the 20th February the march was resumed, and at the beginning of March the troops reached Aberdeen, where they were detained by heavy rain and snowstorms. The fleet, while securing the supplies for the army, were enabled to prevent supplies reaching the enemy. Meanwhile on 18th February Charles Edward had occupied Inverness, and one of his detachments had even captured Fort Augustus, held by three companies of the 6th Foot, but Fort William and Blair Castle resisted all attempts to capture them.

It was not till 8th April that the Duke of Cumberland was able to advance, and having crossed the Spey on the 12th, he reached Nairn on the 14th, and established contact with the rebel army. Charles Edward was then at Culloden House about 9 miles from Nairn. His troops, to the number of 5,000, were dispirited and starving. On the 15th he drew up his force in order of battle, but Cumberland refused to engage and gave his men a day's rest. On the evening of the 15th Charles Edward conceived the idea of attacking Cumberland that night, but though the troops were set in motion the enterprise miscarried. Between 4 a.m. and 5 a.m. on the 16th Cumberland advanced from Nairn; the infantry were in three columns and the guns were behind the right column. After proceeding 8 miles, intelligence was received that advanced parties of the rebels were in front, whereupon Cumberland formed his troops in line of battle, their strength being about 10,000 men, of whom the 13th numbered 374 of all ranks.

1st Line, left to right—Earl of Albemarle:—
    4th, 37th, 21st, 14th, 34th Royal Scots.
2nd Line, left to right—General Hulse:—
    27th, 8th, 48th, 25th, 20th, 36th, 3rd.
3rd Line, left to right—Brig.-General Mordaunt:—
    Battereau's Regt., 13th.

The guns were distributed in pairs in the intervals between the battalions in the first line. The cavalry, under General Hawley, were on the left.

The rebels were formed in two lines, their right resting on some straggling park walls and huts, and the left extending towards Culloden House.

As soon as the English army was formed up the Duke addressed his men saying: 'Now I don't suppose that there are any men here who are disinclined to fight, but if there be, I beg them in God's name to go, for I would rather face the Highlanders with 1,000 resolute men at my back than with 10,000 half-hearted.' The men answered this speech with cheers.

As a distance of 500 yards still separated the opposing armies, the English army advanced at about 1 p.m. and in doing so they left behind a morass which covered their right flank; the 13th were ordered up from the reserve to take post on the right of the 1st Foot or Royal Scots while Kingston's Horse and 60 of Cobham's Dragoons covered their flank. Hawley and the Dragoons were sent to break down the enclosures on the enemy's right and at 10 a.m. the rebels opened the action with a discharge of artillery, to which the English guns replied with such effect that Charles's guns were soon silenced.

The right and centre of the Highlanders, unable to endure the grape, rushed forward, swept round the left of the British line upon the flank and rear of the 4th and 27th; and for a short time threw them into confusion, but at every other point they were speedily driven back by a crushing fire. The 4th and 27th rallied and were now turning their bayonets to good account against claymore and target. Hawley had by this time broken through the enclosures on the right and turned 4 guns on Charles's 2nd Line.

On the English right where Cumberland had placed himself he thus describes the action in his dispatches:—

'They (the rebels) then came rushing on in their wild manner, and upon the right, where I had placed myself, imagining the greatest push would be there, they came down three several times within a hundred yards of our men, firing their pistols and brandishing their swords, but the Royals and Pulteney's (13th) hardly took their firelocks from their shoulders, so that after those faint attempts, they made off, and the little squadrons on our right were sent to pursue them.'

The cavalry on the English left also charged and the whole rebel line now gave way and fled in confusion. Their loss amounted to 1,000 killed and 500 prisoners on the field of battle, but they were pursued for several miles with great slaughter and the loss of all their artillery. The English loss was barely 300 killed and wounded of whom two-thirds belonged to the 4th and 27th. The 13th had no casualties. Cumberland entered Inverness at 4 p.m. that day. The victory was decisive, the rebellion was crushed and all hope of a Stuart restoration was over. The Young Pretender, after enduring great privations, eventually escaped to France, but his adherents were hunted up and down the country and ruthlessly dealt with.

King George II, on hearing the news of this victory, wrote as follows to the Duke of Cumberland: 'I desire that you may give my hearty thanks to the brave officers and soldiers, who fought so gloriously at the late battle, and assure them no less of my real esteem, than of my constant favour and attention'; to which the Duke added on reading it out to the troops: 'You, gentlemen, have resisted an attack, which I believe no troops on earth could have withstood but yourselves; the enemy indeed fought like furies, and you my fellow soldiers have behaved like so many heroes'.

The city of London were equally appreciative. The Lord Mayor sent the sum of £4,000 sterling to be given to the N.C.Os. and the soldiers who fought at the Battle of Culloden. The Duke of Cumberland ordered that the debts of the men should be a first charge against this gift. The share of Pulteney's Regiment (13th) amounted to £276 13s. 4d.

Soon after the Battle of Culloden Mordaunt's Brigade, the 2nd Battalion Royal Scots, with the 13th and 25th, were ordered to march to Perth to relieve the Hessians (under orders for Flanders) and arrived about 14th May. In the beginning of August the 8th, 13th and 25th Regiments marched to Burntisland and embarked for Flanders, after being re-equipped and recruited. The recruits were mostly obtained from a newly formed regiment, 'Gower's', at Gloucester. Their height was not under 5 feet 5 inches and their age from 17 to 30. Not more than 2 guineas and 1 crown was paid for each. The men were medically examined for fear of sores or ruptures, and a certificate of character was obtained from the Commanding Officer.

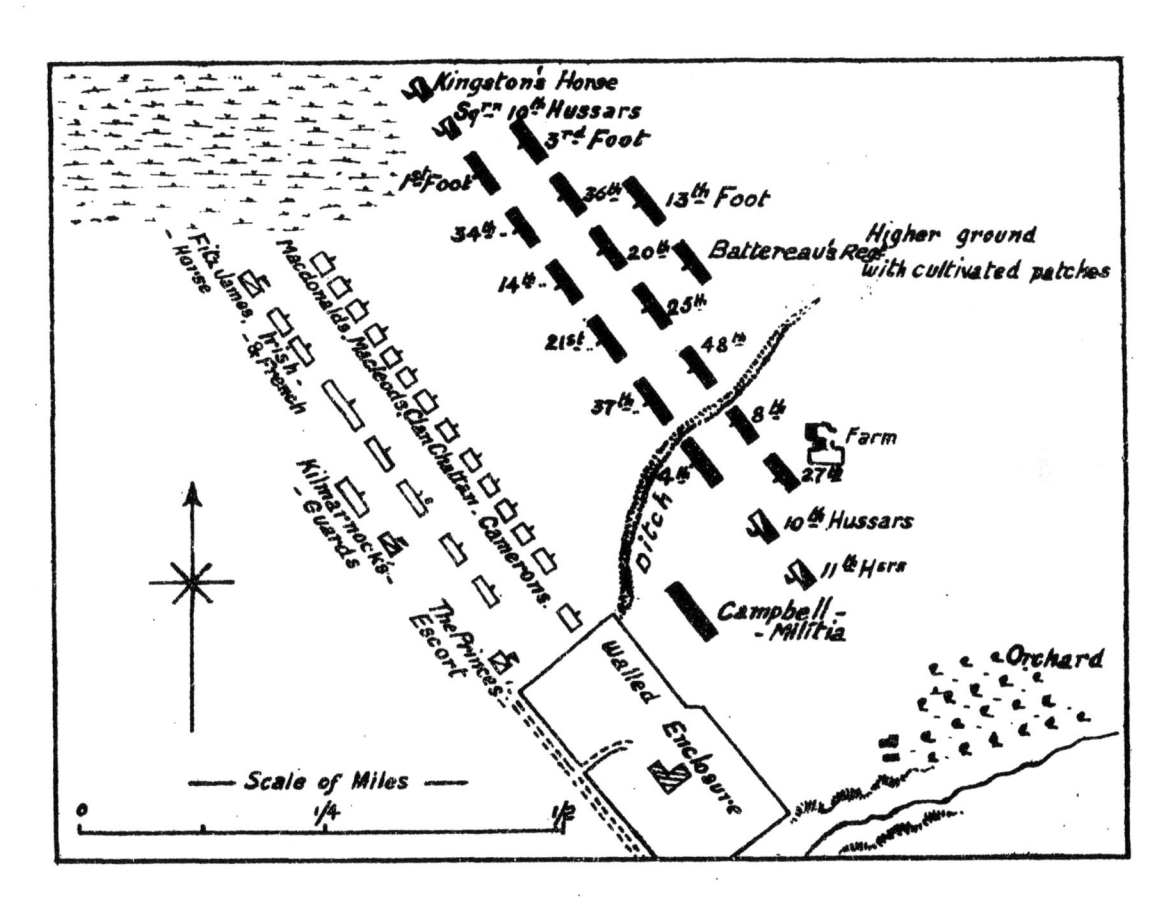

CULLODEN, APRIL 16th, 1746

CHAPTER VIII

FLANDERS AND MINORCA

IN the early autumn of 1746 the British troops in Holland consisted of 3 Regiments of Dragoons and 7 Regiments of Infantry (including the 13th), the whole force being under the command of Sir John Ligonier. This contingent formed part of an Allied Force amounting to 80,000 men under the command of Prince Charles of Lorraine, who was opposed by a French army of 120,000 men under Marshal Saxe in the vicinity of Liège.

On 9th October the 13th reached Maestricht just in time to hear that the French were assuming the offensive. They accordingly marched on the following day with the 26th Regiment to join the main army and arrived on the battlefield on the morning of 11th October, where a desperate engagement was taking place for the possession of the villages of Liers, Varou and Roucoux. The 13th and 26th, under Brig.-General Houghton, took up a position in the vicinity of Roucoux to cover the retreat which was successfully accomplished. The Meuse was crossed the following day in the neighbourhood of Maestricht. Although the Allies lost 5,000 men on this occasion and the British 350, it is not recorded that the 13th had any casualties.

The Regiment was subsequently employed in the province of Limburg, and passed the winter in quarters near the Dutch frontier.

In the spring of 1747 the Regiment took the field again and formed part of the army under the command of His Royal Highness the Duke of Cumberland (the British Contingent had been increased to 12 Foot Regiments and 4 Horse Regiments). The 13th, with the 25th and 37th Regiments, were brigaded under the command of Brig.-General Price and formed part of the 3rd Corps. The strength of the Regiment in April was 33 officers, 30 serjeants, 20 drummers, 662 rank and file fit for duty, 8 sick present and 19 sick in hospital, total 689. After encamping for a short period near the banks of the Scheldt, it was employed in operations on the Great Nethe and on the Demer.

On the 1st July the opposing armies confronted each other between Tongres and Maestricht, and the 13th, 25th and 37th Regiments, with Freudeman's Hanoverians and a portion of artillery, occupied the village of Val on the left of the line of battle, situated about a league from Maestricht, and on the south of the road from that place to Tongres. The day was passed in cannonading and skirmishing, and the troops lay all night on their arms.

THE BATTLE OF VAL

Early on the morning of 2nd July, the French infantry descended the hills and advanced in a grand column of upwards of sixty battalions against the village of Val, where the above-mentioned troops including the 13th were formed to oppose their powerful enemy. The Duke of Cumberland galloped to that part of the field to encourage the soldiers to a determined resistance, and to be ready to support them as circumstances might require. About ten o'clock the French artillery opened a heavy fire, and the second shot killed the Duke of Cumberland's German aide-de-camp, Baron Ziggesaer. Under the cover of this cannonade, the leading brigade of the French column attacked the village. The British battalions stood firm, repulsing their adversaries with severe loss. As the discomfited regiments retired, a second line of combatants advanced to storm the village, but they in like manner were met and overthrown, the 13th and other corps at that point remaining triumphant at their post. Two further attacks were likewise repulsed, but Marshal Saxe, the French Commander, appeared determined to carry this point, and his superior numbers enabling him to continue to send forward fresh troops, he eventually gained possession of the village, but the 13th and other regiments brigaded with it, being reinforced by four additional battalions, returned to the charge and recovered the ground in gallant style. For four hours the struggle went on, the village being taken and retaken four times. Eventually the left wing of the army being in danger of being outflanked, the Duke of Cumberland ordered a retirement across the Meuse to Heer, a little to the east of Maestricht, which was effected in good order.

The Duke of Cumberland in his dispatch to Chesterfield on this battle stated:

'Was I to commend any particular corps of horse or foot, it would be doing injustice to the rest, for though some have had more occasions than others, yet there is not a squadron or battalion of His Majesty's Royal or Electoral troops which has not charged and beat the enemy two or three times, and I appeal to the judgment of both our Allys as well as the enemy whether any troops could have done more, or whether there are many who would have done as much.'

The losses of the 13th in this battle were:—

Killed: Lieutenant Haddock and 29 men.

Wounded: Captain Stafford, Ensigns Naylor and John Hollyday and 83 men.

Missing: 57 men.

The Duke of Cumberland, in his dispatch to Lord Chesterfield, further states:—

'As we are in great want of Field Officers . . . both the Field Officers of Douglas's (32nd) are killed, may Major Legard of Pulteney's (13th) be made Lt.-Colonel to Douglas's . . . may Capt. Crauford, Major of Brigade, and eldest Captain of Pulteneys succeed Major Legard. . . . I must do every one of these gentlemen the justice to say, they have each of them, exerted themselves in the late action, and are the eldest in their respective corps.'

Early in November the 3rd, 13th, 32nd and 36th Regiments were ordered to proceed to Willemstadt to embark for England. On arrival in England six companies of the Regiment were quartered in Maidstone, the remaining companies being split up in detachments on the coast line to prevent smuggling.

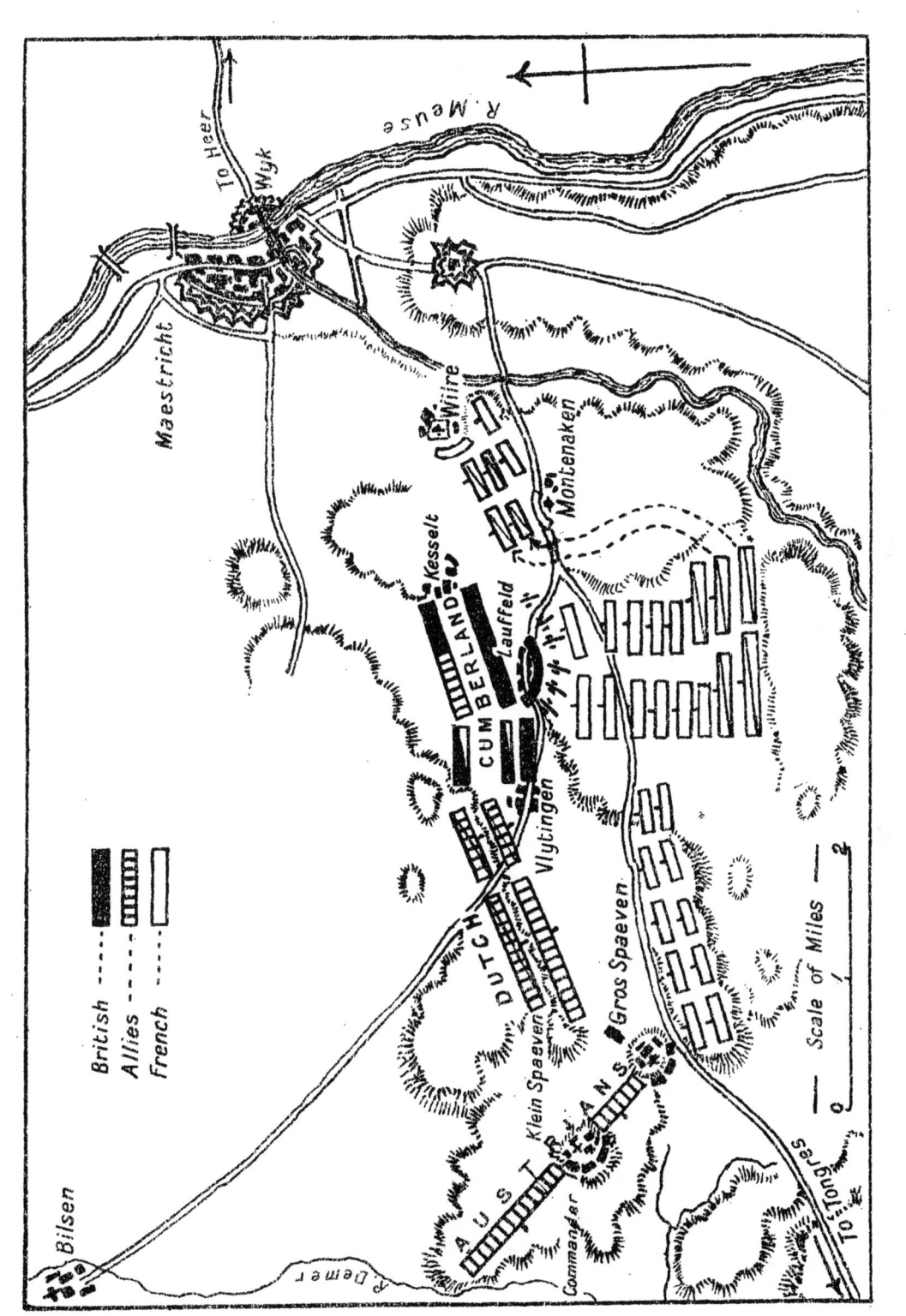

VAL OR LAUFELD, JULY 2nd, 1747

Here is a small item regarding dress in the Army from the *Gentleman's Magazine*, 1747. When the Duke of Cumberland returned from Holland 'he wished officers of the Army to leave off ruffles and himself set the example'.

Peace with France was concluded in 1748 by the treaty of Aix-la-Chapelle. As a consequence two companies of the 13th were disbanded. The instructions issued for this purpose directed that each N.C.O. and Private take his clothes, belt and knapsack and to be paid 3s. for his sword, which was to be delivered into H.M. Stores. Each man to have 14 days' subsistence to carry him home, and a pass if they desire the same.

In November 1749 the Adjutant-General issued the following instructions to the Clothing Board which are of general interest:—

No Colonel to put his Arms, Crest, Device or Livery on any part of the appointments of his Regiment.

No part of the clothing or ornaments of the Regiment to be altered but by His Majesty's or His Royal Highness the Duke's permission.

The Drummers of all Regiments except Royal Regiments are to be clothed with the colour of the facings of their Regiment, lined, faced and labelled with Red, and laced in such manner as the Colonel shall think fit for distinction sake, the lace being of the Colours of that on the soldiers' coats.

The front of the Grenadier caps to be the same colour as the facing of the Regiment with G.R. embroidered on it. The number of the Regiment may be in figures on the back part of the cap.

The Bells of Arms to have G.R. and the number of the Regiment under it, painted on a ground of the same colour as the facing of the Regiment.

The Drums to be painted in the same.

The Camp Colours to be the colour of the facing of the Regiment with the Rank of the Regiment upon them.

Previous to 1749 Colonels of Regiments had been in the habit of hiring bandsmen, but in this year bandsmen were enlisted as soldiers and placed under military discipline, but the main expense of supporting the band rested entirely on the officers.

The band instruments of about this time were: Drums (made of brass), hautbois, clarinets, French horns, bassoons, trumpets, cymbals, tabors and fifes, the latter introduced by the Duke of Cumberland. Light Infantry companies usually, but not always, had bugle horns.

By the Royal Warrant of the 1st July 1751 for ensuring uniformity in the clothing, standards, and colours and regulating the number and rank of regiments, the facings of the 13th were directed to be philemot (feuille morte) yellow.

The first, or King's Colour, was the Great Union; the second or Regimental Colour was of philemot yellow silk with the Union in the upper canton; in the centre of the Colour was the number of the Regiment in gold Roman figures within a wreath of roses and thistles on the same stalk.

Dimensions of colours, 6 feet 2 inches square.

Length of pike (spear and ferrule included), 9 feet 10 inches.
Length of the cords and tassels, 3 feet, each tassel 4 inches.
The cords and tassels of both colours were crimson and gold.
The length of the spear head was 4 inches.

It was customary to hand over disused colours to the Colonel of the Regiment when he provided new ones.

Little is known of the movements of the Regiment about this period except that from 1751 to 1753 they were in Scotland.

Interesting accounts of Courts Martial at this period exemplify the severity of their sentences.

On the 24th day of July at the camp of Fort George a General Court Martial was held for the trial of two deserters of the Regiment, viz. John McFarlane and William Thompson, both of the 13th. They were both found guilty and sentenced to death.

The minute of confirmation reads as follows:—

'I do approve of the Proceedings of the Court Martial and confirm the Sentence thereof in part, that is to say, as John McFarlane and William Thompson seem equally guilty, I order him of the two to be shot dead upon the Inst. who shall throw the lowest die. The Commanding Officer to be present and see the strictest justice done on this occasion.

Given at Edinburgh this 3rd day of August 1751.

GEO. CHURCHILL

To Lt.-Col. Crauford
Or Officer Commanding
Lt.-Gen. Pulteney's Regiment.'

By the General's Command,
Jas. Stewart, Aid-de-Camp

It is not recorded which of the two suffered the extreme penalty.

Again at Linlithgow on the 10th October 1752, a General Court Martial was held to hear an appeal of a prisoner, John Robinson, of Captain W. Jones's company in the 13th, accused of absenting himself from his Party when at the 'Roads'; and found guilty and sentenced to receive 600 lashes. Prisoner says he was not so long absent (2 or 3 days) as is recorded.

SENTENCE OF THE COURT

'The Court having considered the aforesaid sentence together with the Examinations taken before the Regimental Court Martial, as also what the prisoner had to say against the aforesaid sentence, is of opinion that the appeal is groundless and vexatious, and therefore affirm the said sentence, and because the same is groundless, they adjudge the appellant to Receive Four Hundred Lashes.'

(The sentence was confirmed)

In October 1753 the Regiment proceeded from Scotland to England, and were quartered as follows: six companies at Chichester and four companies at Lewes with numerous detachments in the villages on and near the sea coast for the purpose of 'aiding and assisting the civil magistrates and officers of the Revenue in preventing the Owlers and Smugglers from Running of goods, and in apprehending the said Owlers and Smugglers and seizing their goods'.

A month or so later the Regiment was relieved of these duties and proceeded to Salisbury, where they were concentrated in that city and in the neighbouring villages.

In this year regiments were designated by their numbers for the first time, but some time elapsed before the Colonel's name was finally discarded.

In April 1754 the 13th proceeded from Salisbury to Portsmouth and embarked for Gibraltar. Very detailed instructions as regards the conduct of the troops on board ship were issued to the officers commanding the 13th Regiment on this occasion which are too long to insert here, but they vary very little from the instructions contained in the King's Regulations on this subject 150 years later. The Regiment remained at Gibraltar till 1762. Very few records of the life of the Regiment during this period exist and these are mostly of a trivial character. In December 1756 orders were issued for the re-arming of the Regiment, the old arms being completely worn out.

The arms issued were as follows:—

730 Firelocks with iron ram rods.
730 Bayonets.
730 Cartouch Boxes with straps.

At the termination of the 'Seven Years' War' in 1762 the Regiment returned to England.

An Inspection Return of the Regiment at this period, 1764, contains the following items:—

Officers. 'A fine corps. Made a good appearance and saluted well.'
N.C.Os. 'Very good and well dressed.'
Men. 'A very fine body—some of them rather advanced in age.' (N.B.—Two had over 35 years' service.)
Exercises. 'The Manual in good time. Evolutions, very well. Manœuvre, very good. Through the whole, great steadiness in Officers and Men.'
Firings. 'Exceeding good.'
Arms. 'Good.'
Accoutrements. 'Good, clean and well put on—Buff colour.'
Cloathing. 'Good and compleat.'
Recruits. 'Very good.'
Accounts. 'Regularly kept.'
Complaints. 'None.'
Gaiters. 'White and black.'

'An exceeding fine regiment—a great size, well disciplined and fit for service.

Signed CHAS. JEFFERYS, M.G.'

In June 1766, His Royal Highness, William Henry, Duke of Gloucester,

K.G., was appointed Colonel of the Regiment in succession to General the Honourable Henry Pulteney, who resigned. This latter officer had been in command of the Regiment for twenty-seven years, attaining in succession the ranks of Brigadier-General, Major-General, Lieutenant-General and General. It is probable that during this period the Colonel of the Regiment on attaining high rank ceased to take an active part in the command of the Regiment, as War Office letters were addressed to the Colonel by name or to the Lieutenant-Colonel Commanding.

In March 1767 instructions were issued to Colonel Clinton to the effect that the King would review the 12th and 13th Regiments in June, 'that the Marching, Manual and common Firings are to be performed as usual, that after the Common Firings are over, His Majesty leaves it to you to direct such Manœuvres with the two Regiments to be performed, as you shall think proper, not restraining you to those that are transmitted'. The Review of the 12th and 13th Foot took place in Hyde Park on 5th June, when the King, the Queen, and a numerous assemblage of distinguished persons were present. The King was pleased to express his high approbation of the appearance and discipline of the two regiments.

In December the Duke of Gloucester was promoted to the rank of Major-General, and appointed Colonel of the 3rd Foot (Scots Fusiliers) Guards; at the same time the Colonelcy of the 13th was conferred on Major-General the Honourable James Murray, from Colonel-Commandant the 60th Regiment.

In this year the numbers of the Regiment appeared for the first time on the Regimental buttons.

In May 1768 the 13th were quartered at Chatham. On the 12th of that month they were inspected by Major-General George Casey. His inspection report is as follows. The report is given in full.

RETURN OF THE ARMS

	Halberts	Drums	Firelocks	Bayonets	Cartridge Boxes
Good	—	18	—	—	—
Bad	27	—	432	432	432

When received—at Gibraltar in June 1757.

RETURN OF ACCOUTREMENTS

	Colours	Sergeants' Sashes	Grenadiers' Swords	Waist-belts	Pouches with Shoulder-belts	Slings
Good	2	27	55	432	432	432

Pioneers

	Axes	Swords	Aprons
Good	9	9	9

Also Grenadier Match Cases 48.

H.R.H. WILLIAM HENRY, DUKE OF GLOUCESTER, K.G.
Colonel of the Regiment, 1766-1767

FIELD RETURN
Total Effectives

Colonel	Lt.-Colonel	Major	Captains	Lieutenants
1	1	1	7	10

Ensigns or 2nd Lieutenants	Chaplain	Adjutant	Quartermaster
9	1	1	1

Surgeon	Mate	Sergeants	Corporals	Drummers and Fifers	Privates
1	1	27	27	20	404

Wanting to complete—1 private.

REMARKS

Officers. Properly armed. Uniforms good—faced with yellow. Silver embroidered button holes. White waistcoats and Breeches plain. Epaulettes and laced Hatts.

Non-Commissioned Officers. Appeared well and properly dressed.

Men. In general young and of a good size, but there are some few old and others low. The whole perfectly dressed, well appointed and very steady under arms.

Manual Exercise. Very well performed—with great steadiness and attention.

Firing. Very close and regular.

1st. Retreated by files from the centre of Grand Divisions—formed the battalion to the front.
2nd. Formed 4 columns by half companies—formed the battalion.
3rd. Retreated from the right of Grand Divisions by Files—formed the battalion to the front.
4th. Advanced from the right of companies by the Indian File—formed the battalion.
5th. Retreated by Files from the Centre and Wings—formed the battalion to the front.
6th. Changed the front of the battalion to the right and to left.
7th. Retreated from the left of Grand Divisions—formed battalion to the front.
8th. Obliqued from the centre and formed 2 deep—obliqued from the flanks—formed battalion.
9th. Retreated from the centre of the battalion—formed battalion to the front.
10th. Formed a column from the centre by companies—advanced charged to the front and flanks—formed the battalion.
11th. Formed a column from the right company at half distance—formed the oblong square—reduced it and formed the battalion.

12th. Formed two lines from the right-hand companies of Grand Divisions—retreated—fired—and formed the Line—fired a volley—ranks opened—officers saluted, &c.

All which performed with the greatest steadiness and attention.

Arms. Complete in numbers, but all bad.

Accoutrements. Complete and very good.

Clothing. Tight, clean and well fitted—white waistcoats and Breeches—Grenadiers and Drummers have furr caps with white plated Fronts.

Recruits. 75 since last Review—some of them low but very young.

Gaiters. Black leather with white garters and very well fitted.

Complaints. The allowance of Ammunition not sufficient for the exercise and discipline of the Regiment.

Accounts. Settled to 24th June 1767.

A fine Regiment and fitt for immediate service.

signed G. CASEY,
Major-General

Shortly after this inspection the Regiment moved to Dover, and on the 3rd August they formed a Guard of Honour of one Captain and 50 men on the occasion of the landing of the King of Denmark.

From Dover the Regiment moved to Ireland, but remained in that country only a few months, embarking on 10th March 1769 on H.M.S. *Hero* at Cork and proceeded to Minorca, where they arrived on 31st March, and were quartered at St. Phillips, Mahon. Grievances regarding pay and the difficulty of the rate of exchange are set forth in the following copy of a letter from the Governor of Minorca, Lieut.-Governor Johnston, to Lord Barrington, dated 9th October 1769:

'The Commanding Officers of His Majesty's 3rd, 11th, 13th, 25th and 67th Regiments, now in garrison in the island of Minorca, beg leave to remind your Excellency of the distress the Captains are almost continually put to in raising money for the subsistance of their companies, owing to the shamefull disappointment they constantly meet with at the time the Regimental Pay Masters are (from the King's orders and the constant custom of the Army) entitled to expect the whole pay for the Non-Commissioned and Private(s) of the several Regiments. It is true that the Pay Master General in the island offers to supply them with Spanish money, which were they to accept of would naturally have the consequence of raising the Exchange; as they suppose the Pay Master General would in that case draw bills upon England, and of course would be a considerable loss to all the Officers of the Garrison who would be obliged to receive their subsistence at this advanced Exchange; but moreover as three shillings in every 36 is stopt from the men for purposes unknown to the Regiment, but as part of it is said to go for the Remittance of their pay, we humbly conceive the unaccountable mismanagement that appears in this affair, is a grievance, that neither the King, his Commander-in-Chief, or his Ministers are acquainted with; and as it is well known to your Excellency that what we complain of is not an occasional grievance, but one that has oppressed the garrison here ever since the arrival of His Majesty's Forces in 1763.

Signed by the Commanding
Officers of the Regiments
mentioned.
DAVID OGILVY,
Lieut.-Colonel 13th Regiment'

In September 1770 Lieut.-Governor Johnstone received the following orders as regards Dress from the War Office:—

'The Epaulettes are to be discontinued on the future clothing of the 13th Regiment.'

'That all the Corps may appear in their Dress with as much Uniformity as possible, the King will have no white Knee Tops.'

A possible explanation of this order is that up to this period the black gaiters worn by the infantry had reached above the knees, being tied below the knee with, sometimes, a white garter. It was probably the custom in some regiments to adopt gaiters which were black below the garter and white above the garter to coincide with the white pantaloons then commonly worn.

In 1771 on 22nd March, the Regiment was inspected by His Excellency Lieut.-General Mostyn, Governor of Minorca. His report contains little of interest, except that the arms are reported as unserviceable, otherwise a very good battalion and fit for service.

In 1773 the distribution of Quarters of the 13th Regiment in Minorca was as follows:—

6 companies at Cuidella.
3   ,,   ,, Alioure.
1   ,,   ,, Fort Fornelles.

In September 1775 orders were issued for the 13th Regiment to proceed to England, being relieved in Minorca by a battalion of Hanoverians. The Regiment arrived in England in February 1776 and was stationed at Wells until May, when they proceeded to Plymouth.

On 5th June 1777 the Regiment was inspected at Plymouth by the Honourable Major-General Parker. The following are extracts from his report:—

'*Drummers and Fifers.* Beat and played well. The Boys who were additional Fifers were clothed like the Soldiers. Some of them very young.

General Observations. The Regiment is extremely fit for immediate service, was well dressed, but some of the pouches hung rather too low. The Grenadiers Company is an exceedingly good one, and so is that of the Light Infantry. The front rank of the Battalion is tall, and the recruits of last year much improved. The Light Infantry company was drawn up three deep being cramped for Room, and was posted on the left of the battalion and marched by in the Rear. The Ensigns bearing the Colours with a Captain between them, marched at the head of the 3rd Grand Division, advanced before the others. All the Manœuvres were performed quick and well, some with great Rapidity, but the ground on which the Battalion acted was rather confined. The slow march was little more than 60 paces in a minute, the quick about 90. There was besides a redoubled time which was very proper. When the battalion halted the Ranks were generally very well dressed, and the men stood fast at once without shuffling or padding, and all the Intervals were commonly well preserved, and the Wheelings Regular and Straight. In short the Regiment went through the whole of the business extremely well. There were under Arms in the battalion, Rank and File 331. In the Field besides, who did not fall in, exclusive of Recruits, 9 Pioneers, and 12 Private soldiers acting as Musicians and Fifers.

The Officers all mess together and live in perfect Harmony.

signed GEO. LANE PARKER,
Major-General'

This report is notable for the mention of a Light Infantry company for the first time. As a matter of fact, orders were issued for the adoption of one Light Infantry company to every regiment of infantry in 1770, but as the Regiment was abroad at the time it is possible that the orders were not then carried into effect. The report also infers that there was a Regimental Mess. The origin of the Officers' Mess is somewhat obscure, but judging from the practice in continental armies it seems to have been essentially an English institution.

As an instance of the slow promotion and advanced age of some of the officers Colonel David Ogilvy, Lieutenant-Colonel of the 13th Regiment of Foot, sent the following memorial in 1778 to the Right Honourable Charles Jenkinson, His Majesty's Secretary-at-War:—

'Humbly sheweth

That your Memorialist has served as a Commissioned officer in His Majesty's 13th Regiment of Foot eight and thirty years, is an older officer than many of His Majesty's Lieutenant Generals, and was wounded at the Battle of Dettingen under the command of His Late Majesty King George the second.

That he served all the Campaigns in Flanders under the command of His Royal Highness the Late Duke of Cumberland.

That he was at the Battles of Fontenoy, Roucoux, Laffeldt and Culloden.

Your memorialist therefore Humbly Prays you to move His Majesty that in consideration of his Long and Faithfull services, and having paid a very great price for his Lieutenant Colonelcy His Majesty will be graciously pleased to deem your Memorialist not unworthy to be appointed to a Regiment.

Which is humbly submitted.'

In September 1778 the 13th were encamped near Plymouth with four battalions of Militia under Lieut.-General the Honourable George Lane Parker. The Regiment proceeded to Rye in June 1779 and was inspected there on 12th July by Major-General Sloper. There is nothing of interest in his report. In November the 13th marched to Canterbury.

In June 1780 the Regiment was stationed at Waterdown Camp, in August at that of Dorking, and in October proceeded to Hilsea, where they were inspected by Major-General Morris on 10th October.

On the 14th November the 13th, consisting of 31 officers, 30 serjeants, 22 drummers and 708 rank and file, under the command of Brevet Colonel David Ogilvy, embarked at Portsmouth for the Leeward Colonies, to augment the force stationed there, and to prevent the re-capture of the French West India Islands which had been taken by the British.

Shortly after the arrival of the Regiment in the West Indies, a treaty of peace was concluded in 1781, in consequence of the recognition of the independence of the United States by Great Britain. This circumstance occasioned the 13th to return to England in 1782. On its arrival it was stationed at Frome.

In the autumn of 1782 the 13th Regiment was for the first time connected with the County of Somerset as set forth in the following letter:

'GEORGE R.

Whereas We have been pleased to direct that our 13th Regiment of Foot under your Command shall take the County Name of the 1st Somersetshire Regiment, and be considered attached to that County. These are to authorize you by Beat of Drum or otherwise to raise so many men in the County of Somerset, in our Kingdom of Great Britain, as are or shall be wanting to recruit and fill up the respective Companies of Our said Regiment to the numbers allowed on the Establishment. And all Magistrates &c. And for so doing this Our Order shall be and continue in force from the date hereof until the 25th day of March next.

Given &c. &c. this 11th day of October 1782, in the 22nd year of Our reign.

By H.M.C.
GEO. YONGE

To Jas. Murray, Esq., L.G.'

The army was reduced in 1783, when the Regiment was placed upon a peace establishment.

CHAPTER IX

WEST INDIES AND EGYPT

IN May 1783 the Regiment proceeded from Frome to Taunton, and in June to Plymouth, where it embarked on the 11th November 1783 for Ireland, under the command of Lieut.-Colonel Thomas Coppinger Moyle. At this period it only mustered 1 Lieut.-Colonel, 3 Captains, 4 Lieutenants, 2 Ensigns, 3 Staff, 8 Serjeants, 6 Drummers and 117 Rank and File, being 272 privates under the reduced establishment. Twenty-three women and children accompanied the Regiment. They landed in Ireland on 28th November and were placed on the Irish Establishment.

On the 5th June 1784 the Regiment was inspected at Cork by Major-General Sir Henry Calder.

The following items of the Inspection Report are of interest:—

'*Officers.* Made a good appearance. Properly armed. Saluted well. Uniforms agreeable to His Majesty's regulations.

Men. Of a good size. Young and well made. Clean under arms. Well dressed. Attentive. Hats well cocked, and black spatterdashes according to order.

Arms. In good order. Twenty-three bayonets and 392 cartridge boxes wanting.

Recruits. 168 enlisted since last Review.

Orderly books. Inspected their Regimental Standing Orders, &c., &c.

This Regiment made a good appearance in the field for their numbers, being mostly recruits, which are very good and well set up.

They have a Band of Musick.'

The above is the first mention of the Regimental Standing Orders.

From Cork the Regiment moved to Dublin, where they were inspected by Major-General Edward Stopford on 6th July 1785.

There is little of interest in the Report except—'Recruits. 127 enlisted since last Review of which 1 dead, 3 discharged, 22 deserted, 65 in the Ranks, and 36 unfit for the Ranks. This Regiment makes a very good appearance and is fit for service.'

In the following year, 1786, the Regiment was inspected at Dublin on the 10th May by General O'Hara.

The concluding paragraph of his Report reads as follows: 'This Regiment performed their movements not very correct, nor their intervals properly preserved. The cloathing of a bad colour.'

In 1787 the Regiment moved to Armagh, where they were inspected by

Major-General Paterson on 11th June. His concluding remarks are as follows: 'A remarkable fine Body of Men.'

In 1788 the Regiment was back again in Dublin when it was inspected by Major-General Lyon on the 16th August.

Among the items of his Report the following are noted:—

'*Men.* Light infantry in half gaiters.

Arms. 27 firelocks, 75 bayonets wanting.

Accoutrements. 47 waist-belts, 3 pouches, 11 shoulder belts, 73 slings, 3 axes, 2 saws, 2 aprons wanting.

Recruits. Enlisted since last Review 190, of which—Dead 5, Deserted 61, Discharged and not recommended 11, Fit for the ranks, 59, Not fit 54, of which 3 bad. The remainder good. Stout. Young and well made. Wanting to complete the Regiment 31. Many of the recruits not fitted with cloth spatterdashes.

Orderly and Regimental books. Certified by the Commanding Officer that all His Majesty's Orders received by the Regiment are inserted in the Regimental Orderly Books and that all the Officers have a copy of the Regimental Standing Orders.

General Remarks. This Regiment made a very good appearance and is in the way of being made, and, I have no doubt, through the diligence and attention of the officers, will soon become as fine a Regiment as most in His Majesty's Service.'

According to the Warrant by the Lord Lieutenant General and Governor General of Ireland, dated 27th May 1788, the establishment of the Regiment was:—

Staff. 1 colonel and captain, 1 lieutenant-colonel and captain, 1 major and captain, 1 chaplain, 1 adjutant, 1 quartermaster, 1 surgeon, 1 mate. Other officers: 7 captains, 12 lieutenants, including captain-lieutenant, 8 ensigns.

Rank and File. 22 serjeants, 30 corporals, 12 drummers and fifers, 370 private men. Total 469.

The total annual cost in pay and allowances was £11,174 3s.

On the 13th May 1789 the Regiment was reviewed at Dublin by Major-General James Paterson, but as this officer died during his Reviewing Circuit the Returns contain no Remarks.

On the 5th June 1789 General the Honourable James Murray was removed to the 21st, or Royal North British Fusiliers, and His Majesty conferred the colonelcy of the 13th on Major-General George Ainslie, from the Lieut.-Colonelcy of the 15th Light Dragoons.

In 1790 the Regiment received orders to hold itself in readiness for foreign service. A Revolution had taken place in France, and Great Britain was on the eve of being engaged in a contest to arrest the progress of the doctrines of liberty and equality, which threatened Europe with anarchy.

These doctrines naturally spread to the French West India Islands, and their mischievous tendency being soon experienced among the black population, the British Government deemed it necessary to augment their military power in that part of the world.

The Regiment, which was augmented to 30 officers, 32 serjeants, 22 drummers and 690 rank and file, under the command of Lieut.-Colonel John Francis Cradock, embarked on the transports *Dover* and *Sheerness* at Monkstown near Cork on the 15th July, but remained in the harbour until October following, when it proceeded to the Windward and Leeward Colonies, and arrived at Barbados in November.

The Regimental stores, women and children proceeded in the transport *Lord Mulgrave*.

The Colonel of the Regiment, Major-General George Ainslie, did not proceed with the Regiment.

In January 1791 the Regiment moved from Barbados to Jamaica. During that month 324 men were drafted from the 13th to other corps serving in the West Indies, which reduced the Regiment to 426 non-commissioned officers and men. During 1791 and 1792 the situation in the French Settlements in St. Domingo (afterwards the Black Republic of Hayti), one of the largest and most fertile of the West India Islands, was going from bad to worse. The negroes had revolted and the island became the scene of massacres and devastation, so much so that the French planters invoked the aid of British troops and even transferred their allegiance to the British crown in order to recover their estates from their former slaves. But before describing the operations in which the Regiment took part it is of interest to note that in 1791 the field officers of all regiments were required to wear epaulettes, thus causing a distinction in their dress. Officers of Grenadiers wore a grenade embroidered on the epaulette and those of Light Infantry a bugle horn. The idea of the Bugle Horn was probably borrowed from the Hessian Jagers.

In 1792 no fewer than nineteen Battalions of British Infantry were either in the West Indies or on their way there as a security against the rising of the coloured population.

The forces at the disposal of the French Republican authorities were certainly formidable. There had recently arrived from France 6,000 chosen troops of the National Army, while the local troops consisted of a militia numbering 14,000 to 15,000 effectives. This was in addition to those freed slaves who sided with the French.

In 1793 the British troops commenced operations in the French Settlement of St. Domingo. On 9th September of that year the 13th, consisting of 25 officers, 21 serjeants, 12 drummers and 305 rank and file, together with the flank companies of the 49th and 4 guns, under the command of Lieut-Colonel John Whitelocke of the 13th, embarked from Jamaica in four frigates and smaller craft under Commodore Ford and set sail. On 19th September they arrived at Jeremie, where they were well received, the garrison siding with the British.

The salient features of the eastern half of the island of St. Domingo are two great promontories enclosing a bay 100 miles broad. In the centre of the bay is the important harbour of Port au Prince, at the extremity of the northern promontory is Cape St. Nicholas, and at the extremity of the southern promontory is Cape Tiburon. Jeremie is some 30 miles north-east of Tiburon.

On 22nd September the Grenadier Company of the 13th was sent by sea to Cape St. Nicholas and took possession of the mole, while Irois, quite close to Tiburon, was occupied by another detachment. On 3rd October Whitelocke proceeded by sea to Tiburon, but owing to the want of co-operation by the French settlers under Duval, the attack failed, and Whitelocke returned to Jeremie with the loss of 20 men.

On 31st January 1794 Lieut.-Colonel Whitelocke started on a second attempt to capture Cape Tiburon. On the evening of 2nd February the squadron approached the shore where about 650 blacks and 200 mulattoes and whites were formed to oppose the landing. A few broadsides from the frigates soon cleared the beach, when the flank companies of the 13th, 20th and 49th, under Major Brent Spencer of the 13th (afterwards General Sir Brent Spencer, G.C.B.), quitted the ships. As the boats approached the shore, a line of opponents commenced a sharp fire of musketry; but the soldiers leaped upon the beach, charged with the bayonet, killed and wounded a number of blacks and mulattoes, and took possession of a house which was well situated for protecting the disembarkation of the whole of the detachment. At daylight on the following morning, the 13th and 20th Regiments landed with a party of Marines and of the British Legion, and there found all the forts evacuated; 22 pieces of heavy ordnance, 3 field pieces, and a magazine full of every description of ammunition was left by the enemy, of whom about 50 were killed and wounded, and 150 were made prisoners.

On this occasion the Regiment had two privates killed, Captain the Honourable Charles Colville (afterwards General the Honourable Charles Colville, G.C.B., so distinguished in the Peninsula), Lieutenant George Kinnaird Dana, Volunteer Dolphin, and 2 privates wounded. The conduct of Major Spencer of the 13th and of the officers and soldiers of the flank companies was commended in Lieut.-Colonel Whitelocke's dispatch.

This important post was placed under the charge of Lieutenant Robert Baskerville of the 13th, who had under his orders 50 men of his own regiment, the colonial levies, and Jean Kino's corps from Irois.

The following incident in connexion with the defence of Tiburon is taken from Colonel Jackson's Military Anecdotes:—

'During this period the fort of Cape Tiburon was invested and repeatedly attacked by the brigands. Its small garrison, consisting of about 30 men of the 13th Regiment and some colonial troops, as often beat them back. Being at length too much weakened to withstand such incessant attacks, they found means during a temporary suspension to withdraw from their fort, and save themselves; and placing their wounded in the centre, endeavoured to reach the adjoining fort of Jeremie. Amongst the wounded was Lieut. Baskerville of the 13th Regiment, too much disabled to accompany them. Knowing well the fatal consequences of the arrival of the enemy, he was determined not to fall into their hands and carried his remedy in his bosom.

The final departure of the companies from the fort was the moment chosen by this noble youth to act the part of a Roman and escape the vengeance of his merciless foes.'

On the 18th February the flank companies of the 13th, 20th and 49th were engaged in the storming of the fortified post of L'Acul on the northern coast of St. Domingo. Part of the force designed for this service proceeded by water, and the remainder by land; the whole under the command of Lieut.-Colonel Whitelocke. Contrary winds prevented the troops in transports taking part in the attack, but the other division captured the fort in gallant style; the soldiers climbing the hill, exposed to a heavy fire of grape and musketry, and their progress impeded by felled trees placed in all directions. After obtaining possession of the fort, two officers and 13 men were killed by the explosion of a magazine. The only loss sustained by the 13th was one private killed, one serjeant and one private wounded. Major Spencer again distinguished himself, and his conduct was highly commended.

On 16th April Rigaud, a mulatto, with 2,000 men attacked the fort of Tiburon, then commanded by Captain Handyman of the 13th, and it is probable that some of the Regiment formed its garrison. At 6 a.m. after three hours' fighting the magazine exploded, disabling the gunners and dismounting the guns, yet the garrison after two hours more fighting repulsed the enemy, who left 170 dead on the field. The British loss was 28 killed and 109 wounded.

On 31st May the flank companies of the Regiment formed part of an expedition of 1,600 men under Brig.-General Whyte for the reduction of Port au Prince. The capture of that town and Port Bizzeton was accomplished in four days with little loss, but a malignant fever broke out in the town soon afterwards, and the British lost 40 officers and 600 soldiers by disease within two months of its surrender.

In this expedition Lieut.-Colonel Whitelocke performed the duties of Quarter-Master-General, and Major Spencer that of Deputy-Quarter-Master-General. They both distinguished themselves, in fact Major Spencer commanded the troops who captured Fort Bizzeton, and their conduct was commended in the strongest terms in Brig.-General Whyte's dispatch.

On 7th June the enemy made a second attempt on the British post at Tiburon, then commanded by Captain Bradshaw of the 13th, who was assisted by the guns of the *Success* frigate in the harbour. The attack was commenced by a general discharge of firearms about midnight and lasted for several hours. Bradshaw's men, being well under cover, reserved their fire, and the enemy thinking they had inflicted severe loss, attempted to storm the fort about 6 a.m. in the morning. The consequences were fatal to them. Captain Bradshaw allowed them to approach within a short distance of the walls, when he opened so tremendous a fire both from artillery and small arms, that they were compelled to retreat in great confusion. A sortie was then made by the garrison, who killed many in the pursuit.

About this time Lieut.-Colonel Whitelocke of the 13th was sent home by Brig.-General Whyte with dispatches. Until the arrival of Brig.-General Whyte, Lieut.-Colonel Whitelocke had been in command of the troops in St. Domingo. He seems to have addressed a letter of thanks to the officers who served under him, as will appear from the following letter from Lieut.-Colonel Spencer, a copy of which is preserved in the Public Record Office:—

W.O. 1/59 (Copy)   'Port au Prince, St. Domingo,
June 8th 1794.

Sir,

Being favor'd with your letter expressing your thanks for the conduct of the Officers who have had the Honor to serve in St. Domingo under your Command, we return you our warm and cordial thanks for the handsome manner you have expressed your approbation of our Conduct, and with real Esteem and Sincerity beg leave to express our feelings on the present occasion.

We congratulate you Sir on the possession of so valuable a Colony with so little loss, and considering the smallness of the Force, the unavoidable sickness of the Troops, the number of Places necessary to be defended, and the Enemies of all kinds to be encountered, we can ascribe our success to your Conduct and Vigilence alone, and sorry as we are to lose you, we entertain a Hope that your active and zealous Services in this Country will meet with the regard they merit, and we are convinced they will be honor'd with his Majesty's fullest approbation.

We have only one word more to add; that as we have always served with Unanimity, and confident of success hitherto, we trust that hereafter we may meet again, and again serve under the Command of an Officer who carries with him such universal approbation, and so well earn'd Applause.

I have the Honor to be,
Sir,
(In the name of the Army who served
under your Command in St. Domingo),
Your most obliged & very humble
Servant,

(signed) Brent Spencer,
Lieut.-Col.

Lieut.-Col. Whitelock
Port au Prince.'

Later on in the year on 5th December, Captain James Grant of the 13th was in command of the garrison of Fort Bizzeton consisting of 120 men.

Between four and five o'clock in the morning three columns of the enemy, amounting to about 2,000 men, approached the fort in great silence, and arrived under the works before they were discovered; but the garrison was under arms, and repulsed the assailants, driving them before the works with severe loss.

Major-General Sir Adam Williamson, K.B., stated in his dispatch of 20th December: 'Captain Grant and his two lieutenants—Lieut. Hamilton of the 22nd Regiment and Lieut. Cluner of the Royals—merit every attention that can be shown them. They were all three severely wounded early in the attack, but tied up their wounds and continued to defend the post. It has been a very gallant defence and does them great honour.'

At the end of the year 1794 the strength of the Regiment was only 182 and by August 1795 there were only sixty men present and fit for duty. Under these conditions it is not surprising that there is no mention of the Regiment in the guerrilla warfare which was continually going on, with the possible exception of the activities of Major Bradshaw of the 13th, who commanded the garrison at St. Marc.

In August such men of the Regiment who still survived were drafted to other regiments remaining in the West Indies, while the officers and non-commissioned officers returned to England.

It is uncertain where the skeleton of the Regiment went to on arrival in England, but it is probable that they proceeded to Bath, as they were certainly there at the beginning of February in the following year, 1796. On 30th March the transport *Theodosia* arrived at Spithead from the West Indies with the colours of the Regiment and 38 non-commissioned officers under the command of Captain Lowry. This detachment marched to Bath to rejoin the Regiment. The Regiment remained at Bath till the end of August, when they proceeded to Taunton.

In the spring of 1797 the 13th embarked at Bristol for Ireland and were placed on the Irish Establishment. The headquarters of the Regiment were at Wexford. It is fortunate for this history that beginning in 1796 and continuing till 1806 many of the routine orders of the Regiment were preserved by Lieut.-Colonel Colville and subsequently presented to the 1st Battalion in 1913 by Viscount Colville of Culross.

The year 1798 was notable in Ireland as the year of the rebellion. It does not appear that the Regiment was seriously engaged, being weak in numbers, although among the casualties in the Battle of Vinegar Hill on the 21st June 1798 Lieutenant Baines of the 13th Foot is shown as killed. It was not employed in the campaign against the French troops who had landed in Ireland, which came to an end towards the end of July with the surrender of the enemy.

From Colville's orders it is recorded that in June the Regiment was at Waterford, and that at the beginning of November they marched to Cashel.

The following order dated 6th October is of interest:—

'The Commanding Officer is sorry to observe that such is the inattention in the officers to the standing orders on the subject of dress, that any two appearing together can hardly be supposed to belong to the same corps, which is the less excusable, as the dress itself is so well adapted to the convenience of every one. From this day every officer is positively forbidden to wear when in uniform any other Pantaloons than of the light pepper and salt mixture adopted by their own choice in August last, plain and without edging of any other colour.

Round Hats are not on any account to be worn with uniform and the Cocked Hats are to be worn in a smart officer like manner with the Cock to the front, but inclined over the left eye. The Quartermaster will at any time show the pattern for the Pantaloons.'

The 13th spent the year 1799 at Cashel. On the 30th July they were reviewed by the Lord-Lieutenant. The Regimental order dealing with the inspection is as follows:—

'The Commanding Officer is happy to inform the Regiment that His Excellency, Marquis Cornwallis, Lord-Lieutenant, was pleased to express his satisfaction at their steadiness, cleanliness and general good appearance at the inspection this day.'

On 27th August of this year a British Army under Abercromby had made a successful landing after severe fighting in Holland.

This event is reflected in Regimental Orders as follows:—

8th September. 'In consequence of the glorious success of His Majesty's Army in Holland, the Regiment will fire 3 vollies this day immediately after Divine Service.'

On 3rd November it is recorded that 1 subaltern (Lieutenant Wood), 2 serjeants, 2 corporals, and 20 privates are to proceed to Waterford to take charge of a party of convicts to sail to Martinique.

In the early part of 1800 the establishment was completed by volunteers from the Irish Militia and was as follows:—

1 Colonel and Captain.	1 Lieut.-Colonel and Captain.
1 Lieut.-Col. with a Company.	1 Major and Captain.
1 Major with a Company.	9 Captains.
1 Captain-Lieutenant.	25 Lieutenants.
10 Ensigns.	1 Chaplain.
1 Adjutant.	1 Quartermaster.
1 Surgeon.	2 Mates.
2 Staff Serjeants.	60 Serjeants.
60 Corporals.	30 Drummers and Fifers.
540 Privates.	

Total 748.

On the 1st March the Regiment was at Kinsale and on the 3rd they embarked for England, after leaving behind 1 Field Officer, Lieut.-Colonel Colville, 1 Captain, 2 Subalterns, 4 serjeants, 1 drummer and 12 old soldiers to bring in volunteers from the Irish Militia.

The 13th arrived at Spithead on the 31st March under the command of Lieut.-Colonel Lawrence Bradshaw. On arrival they were quartered at Silver Hill barracks, where they were inspected by Major-General Charles Henry Somerset. His report is as follows:—

W.O. 27/83   'Tunbridge Wells,
April 30th 1800.

Sir,

I have the Honor herewith to transmit to you an Inspection Return of the 13th Regiment of Infantry together with Returns of the Arms, Ammunition, Cloathing and Accoutrements of that Regiment. I should have transmitted a general Inspection Return of this Regiment specifying the Age and Size of every man, but Lieut.-Colonel Colville has not yet been able to make an exact one. The Regiment having been a month on board Ship and being compos'd of Drafts from numberless different Regiments of Irish Militia. I am happy however, Sir, in being able to state to you that they are a very fine body of young men, that they have behav'd extremely orderly and well since they have been at Silver hill and that I have found them infinitely better in their Field Exercise than I had any Reason to expect—had they Arms and Accoutrements I have but little Doubt but in a fortnight or three weeks they would be perfectly fit for Service—but I leave you, Sir, to judge how great a Drawback the Want of those Articles must be, when I state to you that of 658 Rank and File that I saw in the Field yesterday only 217 had Arms. Indeed I must take the Liberty of urging this point in the strongest Manner as it is impossible that either this Regiment or the second Battalion of the Royals can be brought forward if their Arms are not sent to them. Lieut.-Colonel Colville informs me that the Colonel (Lieut.-General Ainslie) was applied to for Accoutrements early in February last but none are arriv'd. The Cloathing is getting forward, but it is the Cloathing for 1800. The old men of the Regiment (about 250) only having been supplied with the Cloathing of 1799. The Commanding Officer proposes to allow the Men that came from the Militia[1] Off Reckonings from the Day of their joining respectively to the 4th of June next. The Regimental Books are all properly kept—but the old Men of the Regiment (250) only have their Accounts settled. The Volunteers from the Militia Regiments not having been able to settle their Accounts either of Bounty or Pay from the Absence of the Paymaster. He however arriv'd this Day and I hope all their accounts will be settled by the 14th of May.

*   *   *   *   *   *   *   *   *   *

                                          I have the Honour, &c.,
                                          Charles Henry Somerset,
                                                  M.-General.

Lieut.-General Hulse, &c., &c.'

W.O. 27/83
Letter from Major-General Charles Henry Somerset to Lieut.-General Hulse, dated Tunbridge Wells, *14th May 1800*

*   *   *   *   *   *   *   *   *

'I have scarcely anything to add to my last Report on this (13th) Regiment

---

[1] 'Off reckonings' were the amounts deducted from a man's pay to form the Colonel's Clothing Fund.

as they have not received either Arms or Accoutrements, without which they can make no Progress in the Field. The Men I have the pleasure to say have behav'd uniformly extremely well and Lieut.-Colonel Colville's attention and Assiduity is unremitting.'

* * * * * * * * *

On 22nd May the Regiment marched to Netley. Spain having united with France in the war against Great Britain, an attack on the ports of that country was projected by the British Government. The 13th, mustering 51 officers, 40 serjeants, 20 drummers and fifers and 792 rank and file, embarked in the *Duke of York* transport on 31st July and sailed early in August with the expedition under Lieut.-General Sir James Pulteney to the Bay of Corunna. His force included sixteen battalions of infantry and amounted to 13,000 men, besides a naval squadron under Sir John Warren.

They appeared before Ferrol on 25th August, and commenced disembarking in the evening; by 5 a.m. on the 26th they were all ashore.

After reconnoitring the land defences, Pulteney came to the conclusion that the capture of the fortress by a *coup de main* was impossible. In the operations the British casualties were: Killed, 1 officer and 16 rank and file; Wounded, 4 officers and 64 rank and file. The 13th had no casualties. He accordingly re-embarked the whole of the troops and proceeded to Vigo and thence to Gibraltar, where he arrived on 19th September, to find that General Sir Ralph Abercromby had arrived a week previously with 10,000 men from Minorca. It was then decided to attack Cadiz and the joint forces appeared before that city on 4th October. The Governor of Cadiz was summoned to surrender. He refused, and Abercromby, having ascertained that plague was ravaging the city at the time, decided to return to Gibraltar. After many conflicting instructions from home, orders were received to send the greater part of the force to Egypt.

Egypt at this time was held by a veteran French Army styled the 'Army of the East' who, under the command of General Buonaparte, had conquered that country, but its renowned commander had since returned to France.

The 13th, commanded by Lieut.-Colonel Bradshaw, was one of the regiments selected for this enterprise. After experiencing much severe weather, the fleet arrived at Malta at the end of November, when the army went ashore. After recruiting the health of the troops, the army re-embarked on 20th December. The strength was now 16,000 N.C.Os. and men fit for duty of whom only 700 or 800 were cavalry and artillery. The Regiment numbered 47 officers, 40 serjeants, 22 drummers and 716 rank and file, 56 of whom were sick.

The fleet and transports proceeded to Marmorice Bay in Asiatic Turkey, 40 miles north of Rhodes, where they assembled on the 29th and 30th of December.

The whole of January and part of February 1801 was spent in Marmorice Bay, but Sir Ralph Abercromby was not idle, the troops were continually practised in embarking in boats and disembarking on the beach; while boats were being procured for this purpose, horses for the cavalry and a plan of co-operation was being arranged with the Turks.

On the 22nd February the fleet and transports again put to sea, and arriving off Alexandria on the 1st March, bore down at sunset into the Bay of Aboukir. Owing to unfavourable weather, and other obstructions, the landing of the army could not be effected until a week afterwards.

At this time the French Army in Egypt consisted of about 27,000 men under General Menou. Of these 8,000 were in Cairo, while Friant commanded about 2,000 men at Alexandria and with these he marched to Aboukir to oppose the landing.

The British Infantry were brigaded in six brigades, the 13th with the 8th, 18th and 90th Regiments, forming the 2nd Brigade under Major-General Cradock. Major-General Moore, better known afterwards as Sir John Moore, commanded the Reserve, and to him was entrusted the task of commanding the assaulting troops who consisted of the Reserve, the Guards Brigade, the Royals and 54th Regiment.[1]

On the morning of the 8th March 150 boats, laden with soldiers, rowed for the beach which was commanded by low sandhills held by the French troops. As the British approached the shore, they were assailed by a tempest of bullets, which cut furrows in the surface of the water. A few boats were struck and began to sink; others stopped to save the men, and a momentary check ensued; but pressing onward with increased ardour through the storm of grape and musketry, the rowers forced their boats aground. The soldiers instantly leaped on shore, formed as they advanced, and rushing up the sandhills, charged with the bayonet, and thrust back the opposing forces. A sharp combat then ensued. The 13th and the remaining troops disembarked during the action, and the French were driven from their position with the loss of 300 men, 8 pieces of cannon and many horses. The British losses were 31 officers and 621 men killed, wounded and missing. Before nightfall the British had advanced about 2 miles and halted for the night. Thus was the first step of the desired object accomplished; and this landing on the coast of Egypt will ever rank among the proud achievements of the British Army.

The British position faced west on a narrow strip of land 3,000 to 4,000 yards wide with the sea on the right and the salt lake of Madieh on the left. At the western extremity of this strip of land some 10 miles distant was Alexandria, the immediate objective of the British Army.

Friant now drew in all his detachments and was also joined on the following morning by General Lanusse, which brought up his force to 5,000 men with 21 guns.

On the 9th, 10th and 11th the British remained halted while the stores were being landed.

On the 12th the army advanced about 4 miles, the French cavalry retiring before them and disclosing the enemy in a position known as the Roman Camp.

---

[1] The 2nd Battalion of the 40th (2nd Somerset) Regiment, who took part in these operations, was commanded by Lieut.-Colonel Brent Spencer, who left the 13th in 1794 on appointment as Lieut.-Colonel of the 115th Regiment.

Abercromby, having decided to attack the following day, bivouacked about 1½ miles from the enemy.

At 6.30 a.m. on the 13th the British advanced in three parallel columns; Moore with the Reserve forming the right column, Cradock's Brigade (including the 13th), Coote's Brigade, and the Guards Brigade the centre column, and Cavan's, Stuart's and Doyle's Brigade, plus a battalion of Marines, the left column.

The 90th and 92nd Regiments formed the advanced guards respectively of the centre and left columns.

These two battalions pressing too far in advance led Friant to suppose that they were unsupported, the centre column being hidden by some rising ground. Friant, leaving 1,800 men to contain Moore's column, decided to attack the 90th and the left column. The French cavalry charged the 90th, who were deploying from column into line. The 90th successfully resisted the charge, enabling Cradock to deploy the remainder of his brigade, the 13th, 18th and 8th. As the French infantry now came up the British centre and left columns became heavily engaged, but Moore on the right and Cradock in the centre gradually hurled back the enemy, the former occupying the Roman Camp, when the enemy began to retreat in the direction of Alexandria, and took up a position on the heights of Nicopolis. Abercromby decided to attack this position by turning both flanks. Some success attended the left attack, but the centre suffered heavily from artillery fire. Abercromby finding the enemy's position stronger than he expected, and night coming on, he broke off the action and occupied the position captured from the enemy in the morning. The French lost in this action about 500 and the British 1,300 killed and wounded.

The losses of the Regiment were Captain Anthony Chester, one serjeant, and 15 rank and file killed; Captains John Beaver Brown and Andrew Copland; Lieutenants Thomas Dolphin, Thomas Serle, Richard Buller Handcock and John Peck; Ensigns Richard Huron, Alexander Andrews and George O'Malley, three serjeants and 97 rank and file wounded. Lieutenant Dolphin and three men subsequently died from their wounds.

In general orders issued on 13th March it was stated:—

'The Commander-in-Chief has the greatest satisfaction in thanking the troops for their soldierlike and intrepid conduct in the affair of yesterday. He feels it incumbent on him to express his most perfect satisfaction with the steady and gallant behaviour of Major-General Cradock's brigade.'

Major-General Cradock (afterwards General Lord Howden, G.C.B.) formerly commanded the 13th in the West Indies.

After the action Abercromby entrenched himself in the position, the right being covered by the natural bastion of the Roman Camp. The reserve, under Moore, held the right, the Guards and Coote's brigade the centre, and Cradock's brigade the left, which was thrown back to the head of Lake Madieh. In the 2nd Line from right to left were Stuart's, Doyle's, Finch's and Cavan's brigades.

On 18th March the Castle of Aboukir in rear of the British lines surrendered with its garrison of 200 Frenchmen. On 19th March General Menou having arrived in the French lines from Cairo with reinforcements took over the command from Friant. He now had 10,000 men, including 1,400 cavalry and 46 guns. The British sick already amounted to 2,400 men.

General Menou attacked the British position on 21st March, making a feint on the British left where Cradock's brigade, including the 13th, were posted; the real attack developed against the British right. A desperate encounter ensued, and it was only after the most severe fighting that the French were finally repulsed with the loss of 1,800 men killed, wounded and prisoners. The British losses were 73 officers and 1,400 men killed and wounded. The 13th were not engaged. This action is better known as the Battle of Alexandria.

Sir Ralph Abercromby was wounded during the action and died a few days afterwards, much regretted by the Army. He was succeeded by Lieut.-General (afterwards Lord) Hutchinson.

The French army now withdrew within the lines of Alexandria.

The greater part of the British army, reinforced by 4,000 Turks on the 25th, was now available for operations farther afield. The siege of Rosetta was undertaken and an advance made to Cairo, but Coote with 6,000 men was left in front of Alexandria. Among his troops were the 13th, now reduced to 32 officers, 39 serjeants, 13 drummers, and 404 rank and file fit for duty. Sick present, 157. Sick at Aboukir and on board ship, 75. Sick, Mediterranean, 34. On command, 28. Total 698.

In April 1801 Lieut.-Colonel Bradshaw left the Regiment for England, on sick leave from the 24th of that month, when the command of the Regiment devolved upon Colonel the Honourable Charles Colville.

Rosetta was captured on 6th April and Fort St. Julian, its principal work, surrendered on the 19th, after which the main army advanced on Cairo which resulted in the surrender of all the French troops in Egypt with the exception of those at Alexandria on 27th June.

A few glimpses of regimental life during this time may be culled from the Regimental Orders.

'11th May. Such few officers as have adopted mustachoes are desired to discontinue them as they carry an appearance not only of affected singularity but of want of cleanliness.

'17th May. As some officers notwithstanding the orders of the 30th of last month continue to keep their asses within the Encampment forgetting perhaps, as well as the order, the serious disturbance they are at night, to several of their Brother Officers now dangerously ill; it is the C.O.'s order that the Serjeant of the Rear Guard and a couple of file patrols the encampment twice during the night and drive out by the Barriers in front all asses which he may find loose or tied up in the streets of the encampment.'

On 3rd July the Regiment moved to Rosetta and on the 19th the following Regimental Order was issued:—

'It being the Commanding Officer's intention to communicate to the

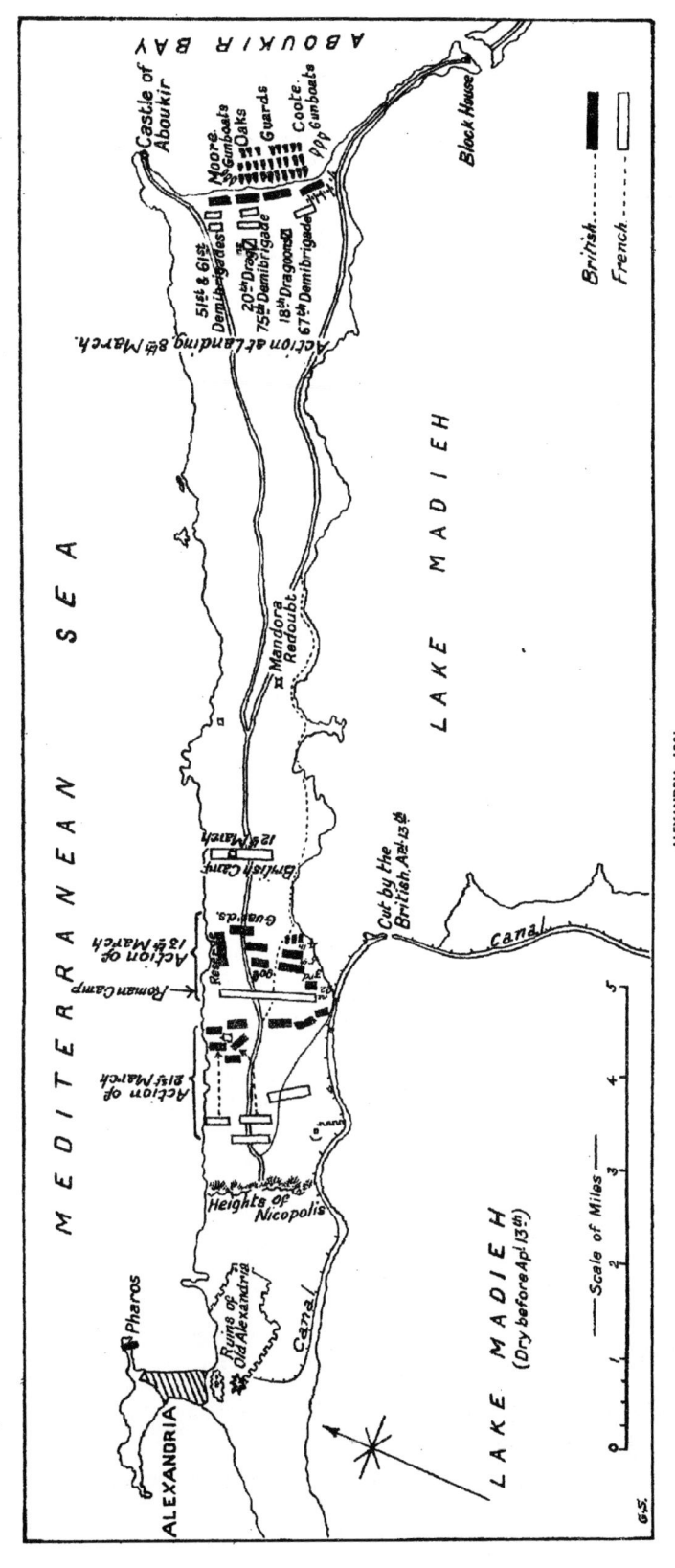

ALEXANDRIA, 1801

Regiment at Evening Parade a General Order from H.R.H. The Duke of York, Captain General, expressive of His Majesty's Most Gracious Approval of the Conduct of His Army in Egypt; he desires as numerous an attendance of officers and men as possible dressed in the cleanest and most uniform manner. He is sorry to say that General Oakes at the inspection this morning remarked that altho Sunday there were many men with dirty shirts. Out of respect to the occasion of our Assemblage this Evening the Commanding Officer pardons all prisoners at present in Regimental Confinement.'

The General Order referred to above was as follows:—

'Lieut.-General Hutchinson has received His Majesty's orders which are hereto annexed, to return the generals, officers, and soldiers of the army, his thanks for the brilliant services that they have rendered to their country, and for the manner in which they have sustained and increased the honour of the British name, and the glory of the British arms.

'You landed in Egypt to attack an enemy your superior in number, provided with a formidable body of cavalry and artillery, accustomed to the climate, flushed with former victory, and animated by a consciousness of hard and well-earned renown.

'Notwithstanding these advantages, you have constantly seen a warlike and veteran army fly before you; and you are now in possession of the capital. Such are the effects of good order, discipline, and obedience, without which courage itself must be unavailing, and success can be but momentary.

'Such are the incitements which ought to induce you to persevere in a contest that has led you to victory, acquired you the applause of your Sovereign, the thanks of Parliament, and the gratitude of your country.

'To such authorities it would be superfluous for me to add my testimony, but be assured that your services and conduct have made the deepest impression on my heart, and never can be eradicated from my memory.

'During the course of this arduous undertaking, you have suffered some privations, which you have borne with the firmness of men and the spirit of soldiers. On such painful occasions no man has ever felt more forcibly than I have done; but you yourselves must know, that they are the natural consequences and effects of war which no human procedure could obviate. Every exertion has been made to diminish their extent and duration, but they have now ceased, and I hope, are never likely to return.

'Nothing now remains to terminate your glorious career but the final expulsion of the French from Egypt, an event which your country anticipates; and a service which to such troops as you can neither be difficult or doubtful.'

The French who surrendered at Cairo were sent back to France in accordance with the terms of the capitulation, and the main body of the British army was now free to prosecute the siege of Alexandria. Hutchinson accordingly concentrated 16,000 men in August for the reduction of that town. The 13th accordingly proceeded from Rosetta to Alexandria and formed part of Brig.-General Doyle's brigade, the other Regiments being the 30th and 44th. The strength of the 13th was now 39 officers, 41 serjeants, 20 drummers. Rank and file fit for duty, 514. Sick present, 27. Sick absent, 92. On command, 2. Total 635. On 2nd September Menou, at Alexandria, capitulated and the campaign was over.

The British soldiers received the thanks of Parliament and their Sovereign's approbation of the heroic conduct which had been displayed by them.

The Grand Seignior established the Order of Knighthood of the Crescent, of which the general officers were made members; large gold medals were presented to the field officers, and smaller ones, of the same pattern, were awarded to the captains and subalterns, which they were permitted by the King to wear.

As a further proof of the estimation in which the Sultan held these services, he ordered a palace to be built at Constantinople for the future residence of the British Ambassador. The following officers of the 13th received the Turkish Medal:—

Lieut.-Colonels
Lawrence Bradshaw.
Hon. Charles Colville.

Majors
Edward Scott (Lieut.-Colonel).
G. Kinnaird Dana (Lieut.-Colonel).

Francis Weller.
William Belford.
John Beaver Brown.
A. W. Young.

Captains
John O'Neil Bayley.
Arthur Wilkinson.
Francis William Schyler.
John Staunton (Capt.-Lieutenant).

Thomas Serle.
Caesar Colclough.
James Wood.
George Innes.
James Blake.
Richard Huron.
Alexander Andrews.
William Trench.
Alexander Patterson.
George Thornhill.

Lieutenants
Hyacinth Daly.
Richard Butler Handcock.
John Peck.
James Kearney Brown.
Patrick Hering.
George O'Malley.
Eyre Trench.
John Dunn.
Richard M. West.

Soden Davys.
Brinley Purefoy.
James Galbraith.
Edward Sheridan.
Peter Shanrey.

Ensigns
John Richardson.
Richard Church.
James Fitzsimons O'Reilly.
John Curtice.

Adjutant—George Parsons.
Surgeon—William Patterson.

Quartermaster—Edward Murray.
Assistant Surgeons—James M'Guire and Francis Coal.

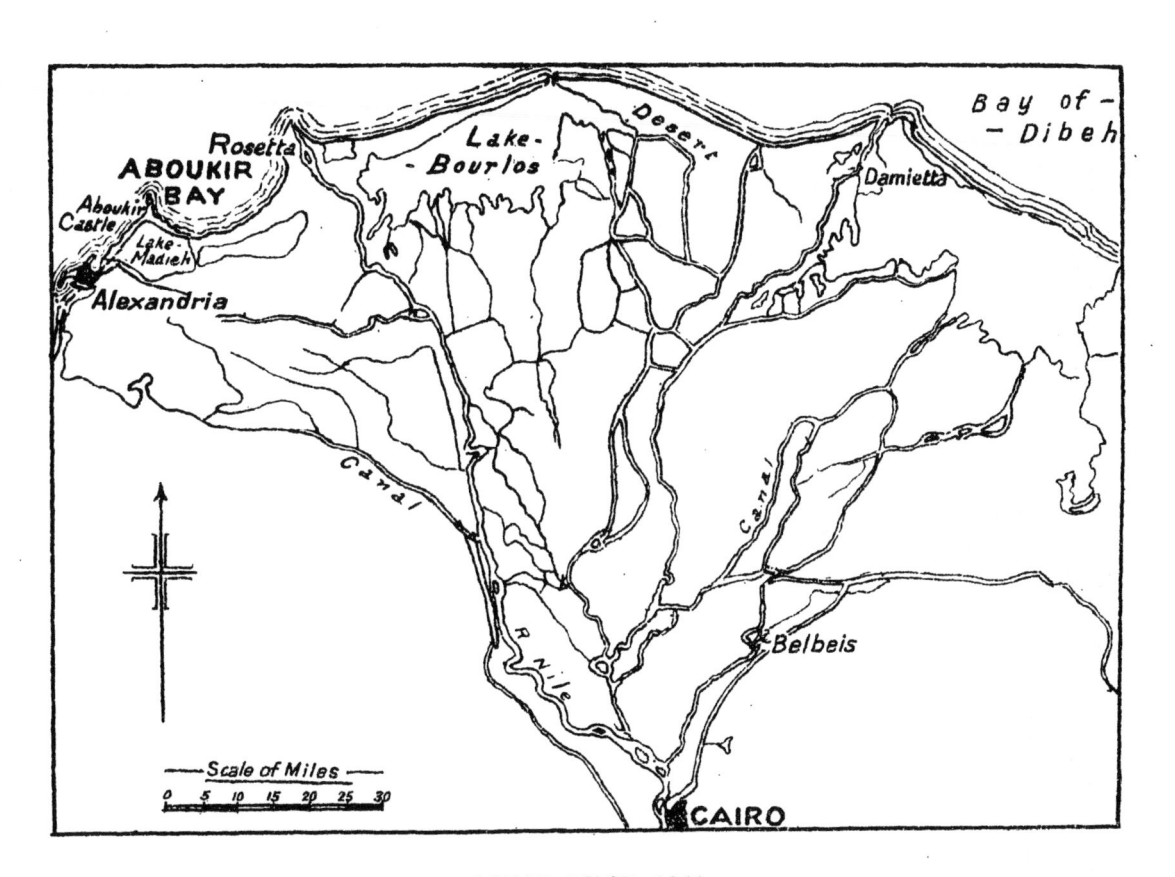

LOWER EGYPT, 1801

To commemorate this campaign 'The Sphinx' and the word 'EGYPT' were placed under the central wreath of the Regimental Colour. It may also be noted here that towards the end of the century the Regimental number appeared on a heart-shaped shield on the Colour.

The Union of Great Britain and Ireland in 1801 necessitated a considerable alteration in the Colours. The Union Flag itself received an additional cross, that of St. Patrick being added to the two already displayed upon it. The Shamrock was introduced into the Union wreath.

The result of this successful and memorable campaign was the Treaty of Peace signed at Amiens on the 27th March 1802, and the restoration of Egypt to the Ottoman dominions.

The Regiment remained in Alexandria, being quartered in barracks near Fort Cretin, till January 1802, when they embarked for Malta, arriving in Valetta on 11th February.

CHAPTER X

MARTINIQUE AND GUADALOUPE

ON arrival at Malta the Regiment was quartered in Floriana barracks. There is nothing worth recording during their stay in the Fortress of Malta excepting that in July 1803 a rather important change was made in the dress of non-commissioned officers. The use of epaulettes and shoulder-knots was discontinued and replaced by chevrons on the right arm.

In 1803 the Regiment—consisting of 23 officers, 31 serjeants, 22 drummers, and 586 rank and file, under the command of Brevet Lieut.-Colonel George Kinnaird Dana, embarked for Gibraltar, at Valetta, Malta, on the 3rd of March, to relieve the 2nd Battalion of the Royal Regiment from garrison duty at that fortress, where it arrived on the 28th of that month. On the 3rd May England declared war on France, but the tide of war did not at that time involve the garrison in the Mediterranean.

Upon the decease of General Ainslie, in the summer of 1804, King George III conferred the colonelcy of the 13th upon Lieut.-General Alexander Campbell (from the 7th West India Regiment, which was disbanded in 1802) by commission dated the 11th July 1804.

The Regiment was inspected by General Sir Thomas Trigge on the 12th April.

The only items in his report which are of interest are that the Colours were in bad order, as were also the great coats, and serjeants' swords, and sashes, while the drummers were deficient of swords and caps—otherwise the report is a good one.

While the Regiment was stationed at Gibraltar, a fever of a very fatal character broke out in the town and garrison, and during October, November, and December the Regiment lost four officers (Lieutenants Alexander Patterson, James Kearney Brown, Trevor Hull and Joseph Massey) and 122 non-commissioned officers and men.

The epidemic is referred to in a report made by the Governor of Gibraltar, the Hon. General Fox, dated 11th January 1805.

'*Secret and Confidential*

SIR,

I have the honor to inclose for His Royal Highness the Commander-in-Chief's information a Report of the Board of public health, which I mentioned in my letter of the 25th Ultimo my intention of forming.

. . . .

I must at the same time say that the British Regiments in General, particularly the Commanding Officers of Regiments and Officers (from everything that I can learn) have shewn the most Manly example of attending to their Sick both Comrades and Men, and never forsaking them tho' in the most desperate Situation, which I really believe was one great cause of the Mortality among the Troops being less than among the Inhabitants.

It is but justice to say, that amongst the Officers no one has been (by what I hear) more forward or has shewn a better example, than Lt.-Col. Colville of the 13th Regiment.

W. E. Fox.'

There are several orders relating to this epidemic in Regimental Orders, but the most curious is that published on 18th February 1805.

'It appearing that the men's hair is falling off very fast (most probably the effect of the late Fever), the Quarter-Master will issue a sufficiency of Rum and Oil to be well mixed in equal parts, and which under the direction of a non-commissioned officer of a Squad is to be well rubbed into the Roots of the men's hair every day until further orders.'

Although Great Britain had been at war with France since May 1803, it was not till 12th December 1804 that Spain, pressed by Napoleon, formally declared war on England, and in consequence instituted a blockade of the fortress on the land side, and established a large camp at St. Roch which had the effect of keeping the English on the alert. Preparations were made at Algeciras for assembling a large flotilla of galliots, gun-sloops and flat-bottomed vessels completely armed, and it was even rumoured that a considerable body of French troops was on the road to join the Spanish forces for a siege of the fortress. This latter threat did not materialize, as Napoleon had a more ambitious scheme in hand, namely the invasion of England itself.

It does not appear that any active operations took place on the land front of Gibraltar between the English and the Spaniards, but it is recorded that on 6th March 1805 at about 2 a.m. in the morning a party of Spaniards raided a guard of the 13th commanded by Lieutenant Hancock, who afterwards achieved some fame in the American War, and carried off that officer and one man of the Guard as prisoners. The Spanish commander however, General Cartaneos, immediately ordered the release of the captives.

There was doubtless an understanding between the opposing forces that there should be no hostilities between the land forces.

It will be remembered that the year 1805 was remarkable for the naval campaign between the English and combined French and Spanish fleets which culminated in the victory of Trafalgar on 21st October of that year. Ships of the Royal Navy were constantly coming into Gibraltar to refit, and in fact H.M.S. *Victory* with the body of Nelson on board was towed into the port by H.M.S. *Neptune* on 28th October.

The following sentences by Court Martial reflect the scale of punishments at this period:—

Pte. D. Hayley, 13th Regiment—9th February 1805—abusing and striking an officer—300 lashes.

Pte. T. Cloghessey, 13th Regiment—3rd June 1805—assault with intent to ravish—700 lashes.

In November 1805 the Regiment was relieved from garrison duty at Gibraltar and embarked for England in the transports *Freelove*, *Eliza Anderson*, *Pretty Lass* and *Tiber*. On board the latter were three companies, under Captain Thomas Serle, consisting of 6 officers, 7 serjeants, 4 drummers, 117 rank and file, 8 women and 6 children—148 in all, exclusive of the crew. These would probably have all perished had it not been for the extraordinary gallantry of Pte. Patrick Cloghessey of the 13th, on the occasion of a fire breaking out on the morning of the 7th December. This originated in the lower hold, from the negligence of the steward, who went down with a candle without a lantern to draw off spirits. The fire first communicated with the spirits thus drawn off, and afterwards with the bread bags. It was spreading with rapidity in the direction of the magazine, when the above-named soldier, with great coolness and bravery, saved the vessel and the lives of his fellow passengers at the imminent hazard of his own. Wrapping himself up in a wet blanket, he leaped at once into the hold, and rolling himself in the fire, succeeded in checking the progress of the conflagration. Assisted by others, who, following his idea, tied together their blankets and damped them, the flames were at length extinguished.

Major-General Harry Calvert, Adjutant-General, upon receiving the report of this extraordinary act of heroism,—by desire of the Duke of York —brought the subject before the Secretary-at-War, and in his official communication, stated that 'the reward which naturally presented itself to the Commander-in-Chief as most adapted to the essential service which the man performed was promotion; but as on inquiring, it appears that his education and character will not justify his obtaining military preferment, His Royal Highness is induced to recommend that he may receive such pecuniary recompense as may be judged proper by the Secretary-at-War'.

In reply to this representation, an allowance of twenty guineas was authorized to be paid to Private Cloghessey, whose description was as follows: 5 feet 7 inches high, 30 years of age, fresh complexion, round visage, grey eyes, dark brown hair; was born in the County of Mayo, in the Parish of Two-More, Ireland, and by trade a cooper, but cannot read or write.

It was unfortunate that his moral conduct was not equal to his gallant conduct; though it is to be hoped that Patrick Cloghessey was not the same individual as T. Cloghessey who was sentenced to 700 lashes on the previous 3rd June. However that may be, the record of such a noble and gallant act deserves a prominent place in the history of the Regiment.

Another adventure was to happen to the *Tiber*. The convoy for the transports, formed by the *Sirius* frigate and H.M.S. *Polyphemus* was entirely dispersed in a gale of wind off Brest on the evening of the 11th of December. The several vessels also encountered imminent dangers from lee-shores and the enemy's fleet, by which latter the *Tiber* transport was captured on the 14th of that month in 47·9 N. Lat., 9 W. Long. By great good luck, the *Tiber* escaped the same night and reached Portsmouth on 24th December without losing a man. The whole Regiment, consisting of 25 officers, 40 serjeants, 22 drummers and 466 rank and file, under the command of Brevet Lieut.-Colonel Edward Scott, were stationed at Portsmouth for a few days, and then proceeded to Winchester, which they reached on 15th January, and a few days later sent a detachment to Southampton.

The following Regimental Order dated 21st January 1806 mentions for the first time the existence of a bandmaster.

'Serjt. Hurst, Master of the Band, having returned from sick furlough, Serjt. Irwin will on the 25th inst. be again mustered as private conformably to the terms upon which he was appointed to hold the rank of serjeant.'

At the end of February seven companies proceeded to Andover, two to Stockbridge, and one to Whitchurch, but on the 12th of March they were again concentrated at Winchester and on the 18th the Regiment began its march to Weymouth via Salisbury, Blandford and Dorchester. Whilst on this march the following regimental order describes the compliments to be paid by one corps to another at this period. March 20th. 'When two corps meet upon a road, the Junior halts and salutes the Senior, except when one only has Colours, when that so distinguished, is to receive the compliments.'

On arrival at Weymouth the regiments were inspected by Brig.-General MacFarlane, but there are no details of this inspection.

The old-established custom of the married women doing the laundry work of the Regiment may be detected in a Regimental Order dated 27th March 1806.

'While there are other more deserving Women ready to do the work, Mrs. Gravin, living with a man of the name of Kenny, who would have been drummed out of the Garrison of Gibraltar, had she not secreted herself, is not to be employed to wash for the men.'

At the end of April a parliamentary election took place at Weymouth in consequence of which it is recorded that the Regiment marched to Wimborne via Dorchester and Blandford, and was absent from Weymouth from 22nd April to 7th May.

On 10th June the Regiment changed its quarters and proceeded to Winchester via Blandford and again on 29th July they proceeded to Ringwood, where they were inspected by Major-General Warde on 30th July.

The following are interesting extracts from his report:

Men. '80 English—6 Scotch—485 Irish—2 Foreign—chiefly comprised between the ages of 35 and 25, size between 5 ft. 9 in. and 5 ft. 4 in. and under—22 men of 20 years' service, and 10 of 15 years' service. The greater part (320) of 7 years' service. 47 Recruits, generally pretty good. The Regt., a Serviceable body of men. They have discharged 33, and 67 have joined since last inspected.'

'The clothing due since 1803 has not been received and there are no saddles for the Bât horses.' *General Observations*. 'The interior economy of this Regt. is under good regulations, and the Messes properly attended to.—They have an unusual proportion of sick, nearly all Venereal and unable to procure a hospital at Ringwood. They have been chiefly commanded by Colonel The Honble. Charles Colville, who is vigilant in his Duty, but has a troublesome people to command; have some unknown people amongst them who encourage dissatisfaction, and letters have been written to the Irish Militia to advise against joining them. I believe this to have been anterior to my addressing them, as I have heard nothing of an unpleasant nature since, but it is highly desirable that they should be satisfied as to the Clothing due, to prevent any excuse for any disorder which might arise.

GEO. WARDE, M.-Gen.'

At the beginning of August the British Government contemplated sending an expedition against the Spanish possessions in South America, and the following regiments were concentrated at Portsmouth; the 1st and 3rd/1st Guards, the 13th, 40th, 45th, 52nd, 62nd, 87th and 8 companies of the 95th under the command of Lieut.-General Simcoe. They actually embarked, but the idea was given up, and in September the Regiment marched to Dover and subsequently to Deal.

On the 18th April 1807 the Regiment was inspected at Deal by Major-General Spencer, but no record of his report now exists.

On the 4th May the 13th, consisting of 26 officers, 33 serjeants, 17 drummers, and 549 rank and file, under the command of Lieut.-Colonel (afterwards Lord) Keane, left Deal for Ramsgate, where it embarked on the following day for Ireland, and landing at Monkstown on the 23rd May, marched from thence to Middleton Barracks, and afterwards to Cahir, where they were ordered to complete their establishment by recruiting volunteers from the Irish Militia.

On the 10th November 1807 the Regiment, consisting of 22 officers, 31 serjeants, 17 drummers, and 668 rank and file, embarked at Cork Harbour for Portsmouth, under the command of Brevet-Colonel the Honourable Charles Colville. Five officers, 5 serjeants, and 143 rank and file embarked at Monkstown on the 22nd December following, under Major Francis Weller, who had remained at Fermoy to receive volunteers.

On the 26th January 1808 the Regiment, consisting of 37 officers, 35 serjeants, 18 drummers, and 830 rank and file, under the command of Colonel the Honourable Charles Colville, embarked for the West Indies, but did not leave Spithead till 8th February. On the 26th March they landed at Bermuda.

The Regiment was inspected by Brig.-General John Hodgson on the 3rd of May. In his report the following remarks are of interest:—

'There are many ill-disciplined and unformed Volunteers from the Irish Militia.'

Officers. 'Many of the subalterns are young and unformed'. *Non-Commissioned officers.* 'Some of the old ones good, the generality of those from the Irish Militia very indifferent.'

General Remarks. 'I have every reason to think this Regt. will in the course of a few months be very serviceable and well disciplined. At present the Volunteers from the Irish Militia require much attention, the system, in which they have been instructed, being extremely erroneous. The great coats are in good order, and the clothing in wear is for the year 1807. The Commanding Officer appears zealous and attentive to the discipline of the Regt.'

Among minor details connected with the Regiment's stay in Bermuda, the following may be noted:—

There was no money in Bermuda to pay the troops, and it was found necessary to send the Paymaster, Samuel Cooper, to Nova Scotia in July to obtain cash.

On the 10th September Lieutenant Edward Tronson, 5 officers and 25 rank and file joined from England.

On the 29th of the same month the general order of the 20th July 1808, dispensing with pig-tails in the Army was received from the Horse Guards. This must have been a veritable boon as the following particulars regarding the dressing of the hair in the Army show. They are from Luard's *History of the Dress of the British Soldier*.

'The wig also felt the influence of the French Revolution: it had been gradually diminishing in size during the last half-century, and the practice of frizzing, plastering and powdering the hair till it was uglier than a wig came into fashion. The poor soldiers, who had always been compelled to follow fashion, however ugly, and unfit for military purposes, were not yet released from the torture of hair-dressing; stiff curls were worn on each side, and a long tail behind, the whole plastered and powdered. The officers, perhaps, could afford pomatum; but the privates used the end of a tallow candle to keep this wonderful head-dress in regulation order.'

The health of the Regiment was anything but good, as twenty-eight men were reported as having died in the autumn.

The West India Islands belonging to France, which had been restored to that country in 1802, had not been molested since the recommencement of hostilities in 1803. It was decided in 1808 to capture the French Island of Martinique, and for this purpose an expedition was assembled at Carlisle Bay, Barbados. The land forces consisted of 10,000 men under Lieut.-General George Beckwith, and the Navy of 44 vessels under Rear-Admiral Sir Alexander Cochrane, K.B.

The 13th, mustering 35 officers, 37 serjeants, 18 drummers and 748 rank and file, embarked at St. George's, Bermuda, on the 22nd November under Colonel the Honourable Charles Colville and proceeded to Barbados to take part in the expedition.

The following general instructions to officers commanding regiments illustrate the general conditions under which the expedition took place:—

(C.O. 318/35) = (Colonial Office Papers) 1808 and 1809

GENERAL ORDERS, RELATIVE TO THE EXPEDITION AGAINST MARTINIQUE 1808, 1809

'Headquarters, Barbados,
18th December 1808

The Corps at the several Stations now under Orders to embark, or which shall hereafter receive Orders to embark upon actual Service are to be in the lightest marching Order, not exceeding one spare Shirt, a second pair of Shoes, Razor, Soap, Comb and Brush each Man, in the inside of the Great Coat or Blanket, as may be preferred by the Field Officer Commanding; and the Men are to wear such proportion of Woollens as they may be possessed of, whether Drawers, Woollen Trousers or Pantaloons, and Cloth half gaiters, or Breeches and Cloth whole Gaiters, Canteens and Haversacks, Sixty Rounds of Ball Cartridge, forty of which in their Pouches and five Flints a Man. If from experience any Field Officer Commanding a Corps can venture to lessen the proportion of Necessaries specified in this Order, he may do so, but must not increase it.

When Corps proceed to a Rendezvous they will move in full marching Order. This order respects the ultimate movement against the Enemy.

The Troops are to land with three Days' Biscuit, three Days' Pork and one Day's Rum. The Meat to be dressed either previous or subsequent to embarkation according to local circumstances in the judgment of the Senior Officer and on a consultation with the Senior Naval Officer, and every Company or Division not exceeding Sixty Men to have two Breakers[1] to carry Rum, Companies exceeding Seventy Men to have three Breakers.

The King's Pioneers to embark with the Corps to which they are attached, but after a landing are to be disposable for General Service, to be regulated by the Quarter-Master-General, Troops in the Field not being entitled to Pioneers.

Where Corps amount to Four hundred Men or embark from separate Stations, they are to be allowed a small Vessel of Forty or Fifty Tons.

Where Corps are weaker, and two embark from the same Station, they are to be allowed a Vessel of the foregoing description between them.

Extra Necessaries, Officers' Baggage of the lightest description, other Comforts, but limited in extent, to be conveyed in these Vessels, which will also have on board an extra proportion of Musquet Ball Cartridges, where they

---

[1] A 'breaker' is a small flat water cask used in boats for emergencies.

can be procured; when not, a proportion of Musquet Ball, and they will be distinguished by a Red Broad Pendant, at the Main Top Mast Head with the number of the Regiment in White.

These Vessels will be directed to keep as close as circumstances admit, to the Corps to which they belong, with a view to an early intercourse, and it is recommended to the Field Officer Commanding a Corps to put his Horse on board this Vessel. A Steady Non-Commissioned Officer and three good Soldiers to be in each of these Vessels to take care of the Baggage and Effects.

The utmost care to be taken of the Provisions with which the Troops land, as they cannot be replaced without great detriment to the Service; and during the early Operations, the Officers must necessarily carry whatever they require of Food and Clothing, sharing with the Troops in all Privations, and animating them by their example.'

Martinique was garrisoned by 2,400 French Regulars and 2,500 Militia, while there were about 290 guns mounted in the batteries.

On the 28th January 1809 the fleet left Carlisle Bay and arrived off Martinique in two days. The 13th, consisting of 35 officers, 36 serjeants, 18 drummers and 840 rank and file, under the command of Lieut.-Colonel John Keane, formed with the 8th and 1st West India Regiment, the 2nd Brigade, under Brig.-General the Hon. Charles Colville. On the 30th the troops landed in two Divisions on opposite sides of the island, the 1st Division, consisting of the 1st Brigade, 2nd Brigade, and Reserve, under Lieut.-General Sir George Prevost, landed at Roberts Bay; and the 2nd Division, consisting of the 3rd, 4th and 5th Brigades, under Major-General Maitland, landed near St. Luce and Point Salomon.

The landings were unopposed. The first Division, after a night march of seven miles through a difficult country, took up a position on the Great Lizard River; on the 1st February it engaged the enemy on Morne Bruneau and on the days following upon the heights of Sourier. In both cases the enemy were driven back. The 2nd Division was equally successful; and by 5th February, eight days after leaving Barbados, Fort Desaix (or Fort Bourbon) was invested; these operations being effected notwithstanding heavy rains and most unfavourable weather, in which the troops bore every species of privation in a manner worthy of their character as British soldiers. The siege of Fort Desaix was prosecuted with vigour. It was bombarded on the 19th February and on the 24th the Governor, General Villaret, surrendered, the French 26th and 82nd Regiments becoming prisoners, and delivering up their arms and eagles. As a token of respect General Villaret and his aides-de-camp were returned to France. The remainder of the garrison were held prisoners until exchanged.

The total French prisoners amounted to 155 officers and 2,000 men. The total British casualties on this occasion amounted to 550 killed, wounded, and missing. The loss of the 13th was only 2 killed and 4 wounded. The part taken by the 13th in this expedition is commemorated by the honor 'MARTINIQUE' being inscribed on the Regimental Colour. Brig.-General Colville and Lieut.-General Keane both received gold medals, which were alike except in size, the larger one being confined to the general officers, including brigadiers.

Among others, Brig.-Gen. Colville and the Field Officers of the 13th were mentioned in Sir George Prevost's dispatch dated 26th February.

After the receipt of Sir George Beckwith's dispatches in London, a reply was sent from Downing Street dated 13th April 1809, of which the following is an extract :—

'The Rapidity with which this Conquest has been effected and the inconsiderable loss with which it has been accomplished is a satisfactory Proof to His Majesty not only of the Zeal and Valour which has animated and Distinguished his Troops, but of the excellent arrangement with which the Operations were planned and the Attacks conducted as well as of the cordial spirit of Co-operation which has so honorably pervaded and united the Military and Naval Services.

His Majesty commands me to express his full approbation of your Conduct, and of the Zealous and Gallant Behaviour of all the Officers and Soldiers under your Orders, and to desire you will convey to them the just sense His Majesty entertains of the honor they have reflected on His Majesty's Arms, and the service they have rendered their Country.'

After the capture of Martinique the 13th constituted part of its garrison, the other regiments being the 3rd Battalion 60th, the 63rd and the 4th West India Regiment. In July a detachment left behind in Bermuda of 2 officers, 2 serjeants, 1 drummer and 34 rank and file, under Lieutenant Henry Moore, rejoined the Regiment and in October a draft of 250 volunteers from the English Militia arrived.

Among the English Militia who joined the 13th Regiment in Martinique were some from the Somerset Militia Units. The following copy of a letter from Colonel Keane to Colonel Earl Poulett, Lord-Lieutenant of the County, is of special interest. It is taken from 'Memoranda of the 1st Somerset Regiment of Militia', collected by Lieutenant W. H. Chorley. The MS. is in the Museum of the Somerset Archaeological Society at the Castle, Taunton.

'Martinique, *Apl. 6, 1810*

Colonel Earl Poulett
My Lord,—

I feel great pleasure in having it in my power to inform your Lordship that we have lost very few of the Somerset men.

It is but justice to them to add that a finer or more respectable set of men never were seen.

Their conduct has been highly creditable and deserves the greatest praise. A very great acquisition indeed they have been to us.

Should we be so fortunate as to see Old England again it will give me sincere gratification to renew the friendship that exists with the 1st Somerset.

(Sgd.) J. Keane,
Lt.-Colonel, 13th Infantry.'

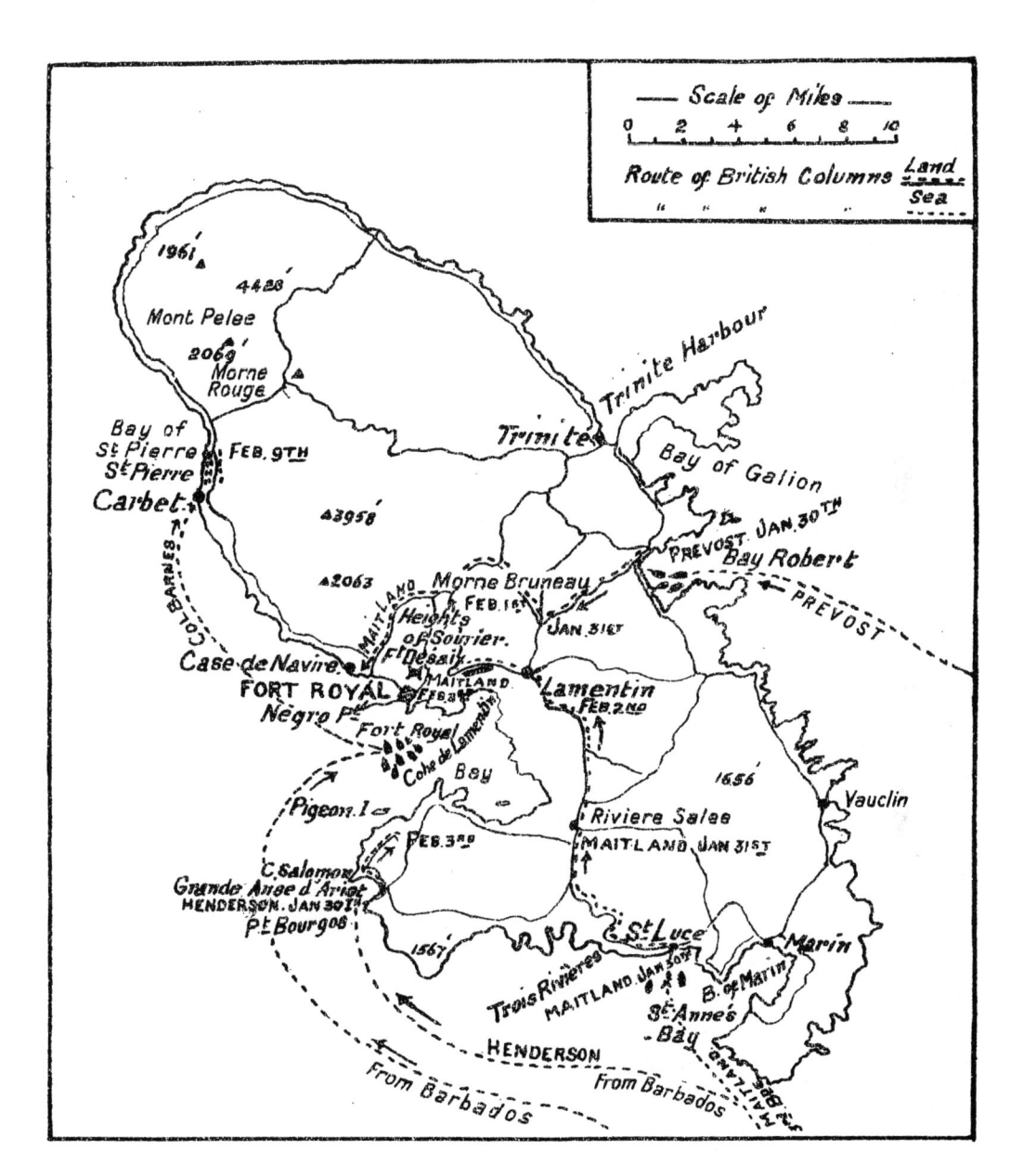

MARTINIQUE, 1809

On the 10th October 1809 the Regiment was inspected by Sir George Beckwith. There is little of interest in his report except to mention that the Regiment had many sick.

On the 21st January 1810 a strong detachment of the Regiment, consisting of 20 officers, 23 serjeants, 5 drummers, and 403 rank and file, under Captain John Staunton, embarked from Martinique and sailed to Prince Rupert's, Dominica, where it joined the expedition against Guadaloupe, under the orders of Lieut.-General Beckwith, and formed part of the 4th Brigade under Brig.-General Skinner, in the 1st Division commanded by Major-General Heslop. This brigade was composed of three battalions, viz. the battalion formed by the Detachment of the 13th, the 63rd Regiment with 200 of the York Light Infantry Volunteers, and the 4th West India Regiment. The expedition, which consisted of two Divisions, sailed from Dominica on the 26th January, landed at St. Mary's in Capesterre on the 28th, and took an active part in the operations by which the French troops, to the number of 3,000, in the island of Guadaloupe were forced to surrender on the 5th February. The total British casualties were 52 killed and 250 wounded, the 13th losing one man killed and five wounded.

Immediately after the capture of the island, the Detachment rejoined the Regiment under the command of Lieut.-Colonel Keane at Martinique.

CHAPTER XI

WAR ON THE CANADIAN BORDER

IN February 1810 a general order was issued from the Horse Guards by which the ranks of officers were to be distinguished by epaulettes and badges. It may be briefly summarized as follows:—

1. All Field Officers are to wear two epaulettes.
2. The Epaulettes of a Colonel to have a Crown and a Star on the strap, a Lieut.-Colonel's a Crown and a Major's a Star.
3. The Epaulettes of the Grenadiers to have a Grenade on the strap and those of the Light Infantry a Bugle Horn, below the Device pointed out in the preceding paragraph.
4. Captains and Subaltern Officers are to wear one epaulette on the right shoulder, excepting those belonging to the Flank companies.
5. Captains and Subaltern Officers of the Flank companies are to wear a Wing on each shoulder with a Grenade or Bugle Horn on the strap according as they belong to the Grenadiers or Light Infantry.
6. The Epaulettes or Wings worn by Field Officers and Captains, to be of Bullion, those by Subaltern Officers of Fringe.
7. Adjutants and Quarter-Masters are to wear Epaulettes or Wings of the same description as those of the Subaltern Officers. The Adjutant in addition to the Epaulette on the right shoulder is to wear on the left, a strap the same as that of the Epaulette.
8. Paymasters, Surgeons and Assistant Surgeons, who compose the Civil Staff of Regiments are not to wear either Epaulettes or Wings. They are to substitute a Waist belt instead of the Shoulder belt at present worn, and are not to wear a sash.

The 13th Regiment was inspected on the 19th May 1810.
Below are extracts from the Report:—

'The Battalion under Arms consisted of 2 Field Officers, 7 Captains, 15 Lieutenants and 3 Ensigns, 3 Staff, 19 Drummers and 611 rank and file.

The Regiment was commanded by Lieut.-Colonel Keane and performed its Manœuvres with a Precision and correctness highly creditable to the Commanding Officer.

The Officers were extremely well disposed and attentive to their Duty.

The Arms, Accoutrements and Clothing in very good order, the latter now in wear is for the year 1809, that for the present year is ready to be delivered.

The Paymaster's Accompts for the Quarter ending 24th March 1810 have been made up and sent home. The Explanation given by the Paymaster of the reasons of this delay not being perfectly satisfactory a fuller Statement will be forwarded by the first opportunity.

Perfect Regularity and cleanliness prevail in their Hospital and the Patients are satisfied with their treatment.

The Hospital fund remaining in the Paymaster's Hands amounts to £340 7s. 7½d.

The Barracks are in the worst state of repair and reported to be incapable of lasting beyond the Hurricane Season.'

(Endorsed) Inspection Report.
13th Regiment,
Martinique,
19th May 1810.
Without signature.

Major-General the Honourable Charles Colville, who had been serving as Brigadier, was promoted to the rank of Major-General on the 25th July 1810.

During the years 1811 and 1812 the 13th remained at Martinique.

On the 4th of May 1811 the Regiment was inspected by His Excellency The Honble. Major-General Brodrick. A short extract from the report reads as follows:—

'The Regiment was commanded by Lt.-Colonel Keane, to whose uniform exertions it is indebted for its present high state of Discipline in every Point.

His Majesty's Regulations are in every Respect complied with and the Officers and Non-commissioned Officers well instructed and active in their Duty. The men in general are stout and healthy.

The Clothing in Wear is for the year 1810 and still good.'

* * * * * * * * *

On 29th May 1812 the 13th were inspected by Major-General Charles Wale. His report contains so much detailed information about the Regiment that it is reproduced in full.

(W.O. 27/106) — Inspection Returns.
(*Inspected by His Excy. Majr.-Genl. Charles Wale*)
(*Martinique*)

'Fort Royal, *May 29th 1812*

(Holograph)
SIR,—

Herewith I have the honor to annex the Half-yearly Inspection Return of the 13th Regiment foot, and to make the following Confidential Report.

Brevet Lieut. Colonel Weller has been in command of this Regt. during the whole of the period since last Inspection. This Officer is active and zealous in the discharge of his duties as Commanding Officer, living in the quarters of his Regiment and employing most of his time in promoting its discipline, and by following the line of conduct of his Predecessor Colonel Keane has succeeded in preserving the health of his men, and keeping his Regiment constantly in a state fit for active service, always turning out more men, in comparison of its strength, than any Regt. in the command, and generally mustering as strong on Parade as they could possibly be expected to do were they in England.

Lieut.-Colonel Weller is well supported by his second-in-command, Major Hancock, a steady and intelligent Officer, who with the Captain's and senior Officers exert themselves to maintain Discipline and interior economy. Their uniforms and appointments are according to the King's Regulations, and each officer is in possession of the book of Field Exercise and Movements.

The Junior Officers appear to have profited by the example of the Seniors. There is, however, one exception in Lieut. Gunning, whom I have to report as unfit for Service.

. . . .

(further *re* this officer who has weak intellect and drinks—suggests he retire upon half-pay as he 'occupies the constant attention of others to keep him out of mischief'.)

The Adjutant, Ensign John Kemble, has joined about five months. This Officer appears active and willing, is well liked in the Regt. and by the attention he seems inclined to pay to his duty, will, I make no doubt, improve himself and be able to instruct others; at present he himself requires instruction.

The Quarter-Masters' Department has been discovered to have been badly conducted.

In the absence of Qr. Master Murray the duty was performed by Lieut. Tronson, whose conduct has already undergone an investigation before a General Court-Martial which suspended him from Rank and Pay for six months, but it appears that the irregularities existed before his time and under Qr. Master Murray, who having been since ordered to join, that his conduct may be investigated, I shall refrain from making any further comment, than observing that the Weights and Measures proved to have been deficient have been destroyed agreeable to General orders, and the new ones marked by the Commissariat in presence of the Commanding Officer, the acting Qr. Master and the Pay-Serjeants of Companies, leaving no room for similar frauds. And in justice to the Commanding Officer I must observe, that as nothing led him to suspect anything of the kind, he did not examine the Weights and Measures, but the instant their incorrectness began to be surmised, he used every means of discovering the iniquity and that most effectually.

Since Lieut. Tronson's suspension, Ensign Wright has done the duty of Qr. Master with satisfaction to the Commanding Officer and the Regt. in General.

Captain Gillman, acting as Pay Master for Mr. Cooper, keeps his books with much order and regularity.

The Non-commissioned Officers are active and intelligent, and appear to contribute much to the discipline and good economy of the Regt. They are in possession of the printed copy of the abstracts of the Rules and Regulations respecting drill and Field Exercise.

The Drummers are perfect in the Beats of the Drum and competent to their duty.

The Musicians are all trained to the Ranks and the number is limited to the King's Regulations.

The Privates form a fine body of active young men, of a good size, clean, healthy and of a soldier-like appearance. They are in general well conducted, indeed as much so as can be expected, considering the situation of their Barracks, being hutted in an open Country uncircumscribed by wall or bounds, consequently where all depends upon the effect of discipline upon the minds of the men.

There is no man kept upon the strength of the Regiment, who is not clothed and does not do duty as a soldier.

The Interior Economy is well regulated; the Officers careful and attentive to the comfort of their men, inspecting their Messes, seeing their Breakfasts and dinners served at the stated hours in a neat and comfortable manner. Fresh meat twice a week, the Messes well supplied with vegetables. The Bread, which has been furnished by the Contractor, has been of a very good quality. The Serjeants Mess separately from the Privates.

The Officers Mess together at the rate of three Dollars and their rations per week.

The Regimental Books and those of the Companies are kept in a neat and regular manner and according to the established Regulations of the 12th Augt. 1811, as set forth in page 292. Every man signs his account. The Companies are paid by their respective Captains or Commanding Officers, who personally settle with their men. They are all complete in Necessaries, nor do I perceive any charge but what is reasonable.

I examined each Company separately, also the men in Hospital as to any complaints they might have to make. One man only preferr'd a claim, Michl. Melville, a private, for £21 6s. 9d. pay due him whilst sick and absent from the Regt.—this claim I referr'd to a Court-Martial, the decision of which was, that he was not entitled to such pay, being returned as a Deserter during that period, not having returned at the expiration of his Furlough or brought any certificate of ill health during his absence. Moreover he was present on Parade at the former half yearly inspection and tho' called upon by me to come forward if any of the Company had any complaint, he did not then prefer any.

The Decision of the Court-Martial is left with the Battn. as a record.

Forty-six Recruits and two transfers from other Regts. have joined since last inspection, and doing duty in the Ranks. They are all able-bodied, serviceable men.

There is no man I can propose to be discharged as unfit for service.

Tho' the Regt. can go through its field exercise and movements with alertness and celerity, I must say, its formations admit of much greater precision. This, in a great measure, may be owing to a change in the Commandg. Officer and the Adjutant, and are only inaccuracies, such as may be easily corrected when the Adjutant himself becomes thoroughly master of the duties of his department. I, however, by no means wish it to be understood, that the Regt. is not equal to every duty they may be called upon to perform or that is essentially necessary in the Field.

I have not discovered any irregularity in the Proceedings of the Regimental Courts-Martial—the frequency of Punishment is much to be regretted but the crimes speak the necessity of the measure, and till very lately there has been no accommodation for Solitary confinement, but that being now established I have by circular letters to the Commanding Officers strongly urged the adoption of that punishment, in preference to that of flogging, for such crimes as are not in their nature so disgraceful to the perpetrator as to evince an hardened dereliction of all sense of shame.

The Regimental Hospital is well conducted in every respect, the utmost attention is paid to the comfort of the Sick, the diet and refreshments have no other limits than the discretion of the Medical Department, the Wards are large and well aired and always kept very clean.

The Surgeon and his assistant attentive to their duty, and I can suggest no improvement for the comfort of the Sick, but a Gallery to be added to the Windward side of the Hospital.

The Hospital saving up to the 24th of April last, amounting to £41 3s. 5½d. Stg., has been paid into the hands of Assistant Commissary Somerville.

The number of Sick has always been very small in proportion to the strength of the Regt.

The Clothing that was due the 25th of Dec. last is now in wear; it only arrived in this Country the 13th of Febry. and taking some time to alter, has been only lately in wear. The Regt. is complete in Great Coats, which are in a serviceable state, and in good preservation for the time they have been in wear.

The Accoutrements are complete and in good order, as also the other appointments.

The Colours of the Regiment are in conformity to the King's Regulations.

The Ammunition is completed to 60 Rounds of Ball Cartridges per man, all good, part kept in the Pouches and part in the Regtal. Store, at hand for immediate service.

The Arms are clean and in perfect order, regularly marked with the number of the Regt., the letter and number of the Company.

There is a school in the Regiment, which is now regulated in conformity to last General Orders upon that head.

For want of a Chaplain in the Garrison, the Regiment is assembled every Sunday Morng. and prayers read by the Commanding Officer; the like service is performed in the Hospital by the Surgeon or his assistant.'

I have the honor to be, Sir,
Your most obt. Sert.,
CHAS. WALE
M.-General

P.S. This report begun in May, owing to sickness was not finished till this 23rd June 1812.

Lt.-Genl. Sir Geo. Beckwith, K.B.
Commander of the Forces.

(W.O. 27/106) — (Inspection Returns)

FIELD RETURN OF HIS MAJESTY'S THIRTEENTH REGIMENT OF INFANTRY WHEREOF GENERAL ALEXANDER CAMPBELL IS COLONEL, AT PRESENT COMMANDED BY LIEUT.-COLONEL WELLER

Bouillie Heights, Martinique, *25th May 1812.*

(Inspected by His Excellency Major-General Charles Wale, 25th May 1812).

	Serjeants	Corporals	Drummers	Privates
English	22	17	12	210
Scotch	2	—	—	1
Irish	29	31	8	388
Foreigners	—	—	—	1
	53	48	20	600

Age	Serjeants	Corporals	Drummers	Privates
Of 55 and upwards	—	—	—	3
,, 50 ,, ,,	4	—	—	5
,, 45 ,, ,,	—	—	—	8
,, 40 ,, ,,	3	3	—	18
,, 35 ,, ,,	8	3	—	52
,, 30 ,, ,,	11	9	3	114
,, 25 ,, ,,	16	17	1	175
,, 20 ,, ,,	11	16	5	208
,, 18 ,, ,,	—	—	3	13
Under	—	—	8	4
Total	53	48	20	600

On the 15th of February 1813 General Campbell was removed to the 32nd Regiment, and was succeeded in the Colonelcy of the 13th by Lieut.-General Edward Morrison, from Colonel-Commandant in the 60th.

Meanwhile the measures adopted by the Government to counteract the decrees of Napoleon, designed for the destruction of the commerce of Great Britain, had involved England in war with the United States of America, and the frontiers of Canada had become the theatre of conflict, to which the 13th were directed to repair. The Regiment, consisting of 37 officers, 46 serjeants, 16 drummers, and 641 rank and file, under the command of Lieut.-Colonel William Williams,[1] accordingly embarked at Fort Royal, Martinique on the

---

[1] This officer had a most distinguished career in the Peninsula in the 60th Rifles and exchanged into the 13th with Lieut.-Colonel Keane in 1812.

2nd May 1813, reached Halifax on 1st June, and after a stay there of ten days left for Quebec, where they arrived on 28th June. From Quebec they proceeded in steam boats and *bateaux* to Montreal.

At this period of the war the United States' Army had invaded Upper Canada in force, and the British Commander in order to create a diversion resolved to threaten the American Settlements on Lake Champlain from Lower Canada. For this purpose 9 officers and 181 other ranks of the 13th crossed the St. Lawrence in boats on the 24th and 25th July and proceeded up the Richelieu River, which connects Lake Champlain with the St. Lawrence, to the Isle Aux Noix, a fortified post 10 miles from the above Lake. There they joined the expedition being formed under the command of Lieut.-Colonel John Murray, C.B.; Lieut.-Colonel Williams of the 13th being Second-in-Command.

Murray now had at his disposal 900 men of the 13th, 100th and 103rd Regiments, two sloops, three gunboats and a number of *bateaux*, and with these he crossed Lake Champlain 29th July and attacked Plattsburg. The garrison of that post to the number 1,200 militia ran away without firing a shot. The British destroyed the arsenal, blockhouse, commissary buildings, and store at Plattsburg after taking away whatever they could. The barracks at Saranac, capable of holding 4,000 men, were also destroyed. Other posts on the shores of Lake Champlain, viz. Swanton, Burlington, and Champlain, were treated in a similar way, and the flotilla returned to Isle Aux Noix on 3rd August.

Lieut.-Colonel Murray in his dispatch stated: 'I experienced very great benefit from the military knowledge and zeal of Lt.-Colonel Williams, 13th Regt. (Second-in-Command). I have to report in the highest Terms of Approbation, the discipline, regularity and cheerful conduct of the whole of the troops and feel fully confident that had an opportunity offered their courage would have been equally conspicuous.'

After this expedition the 13th Regiment relieved the 100th Regiment in the garrisons of St. John's and Isle Aux Noix. There were available for the defence of Lower Canada during the winter of 1813-14, 3 troops of the 19th Dragoons, 2 companies R.A. 10th Royal Veteran Regiment, the 13th Regiment, the 103rd Regiment, 6 companies Canadian Fencibles, De Mearon's Regiment, 4 companies of Voltigeurs, besides 6 battalions of embodied militia.

At the beginning of 1914, when Lieut.-Colonel Williams of the 13th was in charge of the advanced posts on the River Richelieu, Major-General Wilkinson, the American Commander, concentrated a considerable force for the invasion of Lower Canada. The British forces, consisting of the 13th and 49th Regiments, the Canadian Voltigeurs, a troop of the 19th Light Dragoons, and a field train, were assembled at St. John's and its vicinity under the command of Colonel Sir Sidney Beckwith, who proceeded to dislodge a body of Americans, who had taken post at Philipstown in the seigniory of St. Armand. The enemy, however, did not await an attack, but retreated across the ice on Lake Champlain.

Later in the spring Wilkinson, having concentrated 4,000 men, proceeded to invade Lower Canada. On 30th March the American Light Troops entered Odell Town, followed by three brigades of infantry, a squadron of cavalry and 11 guns; they drove in the British picquets and attacked the post at Burton Ville held by two companies of Canadian troops who gave them such a warm reception that the American forces turned aside to attack the post at La Cole Mill on the river of that name, a tributary of the Richelieu River, which was held by a small force under Major Handcock of the 13th.

The garrison included Captain Blake's company of the 13th, a detachment of the Frontier Light Infantry under Captain Ritter, 70 marines and 4 gunners. The mill was a stone building on the American side of the river, and covered the approaches to a bridge which connected the mill with a blockhouse on the other bank.

The Americans, about 2 p.m., having driven in the picquets and gained possession of a wood where they established a battery among the trees, opened a sharp fire on the post, and detached a portion of their force to cross La Cole River higher up and cut off Handcock's retreat. Soon after the two flank companies of the 13th, under Captains Ellard and Holgate, arrived at the blockhouse from the Isle Aux Noix. Handcock now ordered these two companies to cross the river and charge the enemy's guns. They did so in gallant style, but were driven back by greatly superior numbers, Captain Ellard being severely wounded. Further reinforcements now arrived, viz. the Grenadier Company of the Canadian Fencibles and a company of Voltigeurs from Burton Ville. Captain Blake now made a further charge with four companies on the hostile artillery. He drove the American gunners from their guns but was unable to retain his position and eventually retired on to La Cole Mill. At this juncture two British gunboats came up the Richelieu River and opened fire on the American troops. Eventually at 6 p.m. the American General, being unable to make any impression on the little garrison, desisted from his attack and retired, having lost 144 killed, wounded and missing. The chief losses of the British fell on the 13th, who lost 13 rank and file killed; Captain Henry Ellard, Ensign John Whiteford, 2 serjeants and 46 rank and file wounded.

Major Richard Butler Handcock, and the officers and soldiers who had so nobly defended this post, were thanked for their conduct by the Commander of the Forces, Lieut.-General Sir George Prevost.

At Wilkinson's court-martial the American artillery commander stated: 'The conduct of the enemy that day was distinguished by desperate bravery. As an instance one company made a charge on our artillery, and at the same instant, received its fire and that of two brigades of infantry.'

Sir George Prevost, the Commander-in-Chief, mentioned in General orders his most entire approbation of the 'judgment, zeal, and unwearied assiduity displayed by Lt.-Colonel Williams in his arrangement of the defence of the important posts placed under his immediate command.'

The Regiment continued to hold posts on the Richelieu River during the summer, but were not seriously engaged. In September 1814 it appears from a field return that they garrisoned posts at St. John's, Isle Aux Noix, La Cole and L'Acadie, their strength being 40 officers, 43 serjeants, 15 drummers and 556 rank and file.

In April 1814 the long war with France came to an end for the time being, which enabled the British Government to send large numbers of troops to America, who were employed principally on the Atlantic seaboard and on the shores of the Gulf of Mexico. The war with America continued into 1815, but the Regiment was not seriously engaged. Peace was made with America early in the year, and in March, Napoleon having escaped from Elba, as many troops as possible were hurried back to Europe; among them were the 13th, who proceeded down the St. Lawrence and embarked in transports at the Three Rivers on the 4th June under Brevet Lieut.-Colonel Francis Weller and sailed for Portsmouth, where they arrived on 24th July too late for the Waterloo Campaign.

CHAPTER XII

CAMPAIGNS IN BURMA

ON the 24th July 1815 the Regiment embarked at Portsmouth for service in Ireland, but was afterwards ordered to disembark, and in August proceeded to Jersey under the command of Lieut.-Colonel Sir William Williams, who had been recently created a K.C.B. in recognition of his services in the Peninsula and North America.

In January 1816 an order was received for the reduction of the Regiment to ten companies of sixty rank and file each.

On the 24th May 1817 new colours, having thereon the 'SPHINX' with the battle honours 'EGYPT' and 'MARTINIQUE', were presented to the Regiment on the parade in Fort Regent Square, Jersey. These were consecrated by the Rev. George Lawrence, acting garrison chaplain, who delivered a very appropriate address on this interesting occasion. About this time a minor change was made in the Regimental Colours; the heart-shaped shield carrying the regimental number was abolished, and replaced by a girdle of silk having inscribed upon it the county title of the Regiment. Within the girdle on red silk was the regimental number, thus 13 Regt.

The Regiment was inspected by Major-General H. M. Gordon on the 29th May.

Items of interest in this report read as follows:—

'Captain and Brevet Major Baron Moncrief is reported to speak bad english (*sic*), being a french (*sic*) man; he is about to be placed on half pay.'

Privates 'are a tolerable good body of men, with a general appearance of health and cleanliness and of the standard annexed to the Return'.

'The officers mess together, and the mess established upon a system of economy, that enables the Subaltern Officer to belong to it.'

'A book is kept for the Registry of the Marriage of the soldiers, and of the Baptism of their children.'

'The proportion of sick is rather large occasioned by Ophthalmia; but the mortality is not at all considerable.'

'The Vaccine Inoculation has been introduced; and no man has been kept on the sick list for slight and equivocal complaints.'

'The Regimental School has great attention paid to it. The Commanding Officer and Chaplain have a favorable opinion of the Talents and correctness of conduct of the Serjeant Schoolmaster, and of the progress of the children.'

In June of the same year the establishment was augmented to 907 officers and other ranks.

After two years in Jersey, during which time the conduct of the 13th, on all occasions, procured for the corps the respect and esteem of the inhabitants and civil authorities of the island, the Regiment embarked in August and proceeded to the neighbouring islands of Guernsey and Alderney. Before leaving Jersey a numerous public meeting of the inhabitants and functionaries of the parish of St. Helier expressed the high sense they entertained of the distinguished merits of the corps, which was communicated to the commanding officer, Colonel Sir William Williams, K.C.B., by the principal Constable of St. Helier.

The States of the island also passed an Act setting forth their estimation of the discipline and orderly behaviour of the Regiment, which was communicated to the Commanding Officer by His Excellency the Lieutenant-Governor, Major-General Hugh Mackay Gordon.

This Act of the States, and Colonel Sir William Williams's reply are contained in Appendix E.

On the 17th October 1817 the 13th (or 1st Somerset) Regiment of Infantry was inspected by Colonel Anthony Walsh. There is nothing in his report which calls for special mention, and the same remark applies to the next inspection in May 1818 when the Regiment was inspected by Major-General H. Bayly.

In October 1818 the establishment was reduced to 746 officers and other ranks.

In May 1819 the Regiment was again inspected by Major-General H. Bayly and the following items of his report are of interest:—

'Lieut.-Colonel Sir William Williams remained in command till the 8th of November, when upon his going away on leave of absence the Command devolved to the Regimental Major, Lieut.-Colonel Handcock. The exact system of steady discipline adopted by Lieut.-Colonel Sir William Williams, and rendered familiar to the men by his indefatigable exertions, has been strictly and zealously followed by Lieut.-Colonel Handcock. The Regiment is well versed in Field Exercises and follows punctually the Regulations of His Majesty for the Army.'

Firing with Ball. 'I have attended this practice which has taken place frequently, and found the men fire extremely well.'

Sword Exercise. 'Practised constantly by the Regiment. The officer, Lieut. Fenton, who was ordered to England last year by His Royal Highness the Commander-in-Chief, has been indefatigable in his Instructions, and the Officers and Non-commissioned Officers equally zealous in learning the exercise.'

'The Regimental School was formed in 1812.'

In consequence of this inspection, 3 serjeants, 2 corporals and 43 privates were ordered to be discharged as being unfit for service.

While quartered at Guernsey the Regiment fully maintained its reputation for good conduct, as may be seen in the letter dated 4th May 1819 from 'The Bailiff of Guernsey'. This letter and Lieut.-Colonel R. B. Handcock's reply are contained in Appendix E.

During May and June 1819 the Regiment embarked by detachments for Portsmouth, but their stay there was not of long duration, as in September they proceeded by sea to Scotland, and landing at Leith, marched from thence to Stirling Castle, with detachments to Dumbarton Castle, Paisley, Callander, and Bucklyvie.

After a year in these quarters the 13th marched to Edinburgh Castle in September 1820, and towards the end of October to Port Patrick, where it embarked for Ireland landing at Donaghadee, and marching from thence to Dublin, with detachments to Stranorlar, Carndonagh, Greencastle, Buncrana, Rathmelton, and Letterkenny.

After occupying these stations ten months, the Regiment called in its detachments, marched to Richmond Barracks, Dublin, and arrived there on the 21st of September 1821.

From Dublin the Regiment embarked on the 18th July 1822, for England, and two days after landing at Liverpool, orders were received from the Horse Guards for it to embark for Greenock, proceed thence to Edinburgh, and do duty there during the visit of King George IV to Scotland.

The 13th arrived at Edinburgh on the 31st July and the 1st August; it had the honour of mounting guard over the royal person when the King visited that city, and Captain Ellard, who commanded the guard of honour assembled to receive His Majesty on landing at Leith on the 14th August, obtained the brevet rank of Major.

After the King's departure, the Regiment embarked for Chatham, where it arrived on the 21st, 23rd and 24th September.

In October orders were received to make preparations for service in India. The establishment was increased, and additional serjeants, one for every 20 effective rank and file, sanctioned, but not to take effect until arrival in India, when transfers from other corps would take effect. Unserviceable arms were not replaced, but the whole Regiment was to be rearmed on arrival in India with arms of the India pattern used in the Company's service.

A recruiting company, consisting of 1 captain, 2 lieutenants, 8 serjeants and 8 corporals, was allowed on the establishment of the 13th Foot. This company was the forerunner of the depôt; it did not leave England and was quartered in the first instance at Chatham.

The married officers had to make the necessary arrangement with the captains of the transports for the accommodation of their wives and children.

Prior to embarkation, on Christmas Day 1822 the 13th were constituted a corps of Light Infantry.

The official letters and orders on the subject are set forth below:—

(W.O. 3/72)

1822

'H. Guards,
15th. Novr. 1822

Sir,—

I have had the honor to receive and lay before H.R.H. The Com^r· in Chief your Letter of the 13th Inst., and Enclosure, and in reply am directed to signify to you, that, in compliance with your wishes, and under all the Circumstances stated, H.R.H. will recommend to His Majesty that the 13th Regt. of Foot may be Clothed, Armed, and Equipped as Light Infantry from the 25th December next.

I have &c.
JOHN MACDONALD,
D.A.G.

General Morrison,
   Colonel 13th Foot
      &c. &c. &c.,
         77 Baker Street.'

at
(War Office) (General Orders, Circulars, Letters &c.)

'*Most humbly submitted to His Majesty*

That the 13th Regiment be clothed, equipped and trained as a Light Infantry Regiment from 25th December next.'

app^d.
G. R.

16th November 1822'

(W. O. 3/72)

1822

'H. Guards,
   28th Nov^r· 1822

SIR,—

In reference to my Communication of the 15th Inst. I have now, by the Com^r· in Chief's Command, the honor to signify to you, that His Majesty has been pleased to approve of the 13th Regt. of foot, being formed into a Corps of Light Infantry from the 25th December next.

In order to prevent as far as practicable any expence being occasioned to the Public, or to the Colonel, H.R.H. has been pleased to direct that the Alterations, conformable to the Patterns prescribed for Light Infantry, in respect to Appointments, shall not take place, until those at present in possession of the Corps are considered unfit for further Service.

I have the honor &c.
JOHN MACDONALD,
D.A.G.

General Morrison,
   Colonel of the 13th Regt. of Foot
      &c. &c. &c.'

It would be interesting to know why the 13th was constituted a Light Infantry Regiment. It is evident from Horse Guards letters dated 15th November 1822, that the initiative came from the Regiment through its Colonel, General Morrison, as shown in the phrase 'in compliance with your wishes', but the further words 'and under all the circumstances stated' are tantalizing, and there is no record of the letter in which these circumstances are stated.

The most probable explanation is that Lieut.-Colonel Williams, an old officer of the 60th Rifles, who exchanged into the 13th in 1812, was instrumental in bringing this change about. Lieut.-Colonel Lewis Butler, the Historian of the 60th Rifles, states that 'as a commander of Light troops in the field Sir W. Williams has never been excelled', referring to his services in the 60th Rifles during the Peninsular War. When in command of the 13th in the American War it is fairly certain that he practised the Regiment in Light Infantry drill and tactics as being particularly suitable for forest warfare. Williams relinquished the appointment of Lieut.-Colonel Commanding in 1821, only a year before the title of the regiment was changed. It would seem highly probable that he induced General Morrison to bring to the notice of the authorities the claims of the Regiment to be considered a Light Infantry Corps.

On the 1st and 3rd of January 1823 the 13th embarked at Gravesend on board the *General Kyd* and *Kent* Indiamen under Lieut.-Colonel M'Creagh and Major Robert Henry Sale and landed in May and June at Calcutta, where the Regiment received 620 volunteers from corps about to return to England.

Among the officers of the Regiment who embarked in these transports, and there were many who achieved distinction afterwards, there were two of outstanding merit. The one was Major Robert Sale who in 1795, at the early age of fourteen, had the honour of carrying his Sovereign's colours as ensign in the 36th Regiment. On the 8th January 1798 he exchanged into the 12th Regiment, with which regiment he served in five campaigns, and on the 28th June 1821 he exchanged into the 13th Regiment. Known as 'Fighting Bob', Sale was a brilliant leader of men, ever in the forefront of the battle, and his personal bravery remarkable; it is no wonder that his officers and men served him with a devotion that sheds lustre on the period of Sale's service in the Regiment.

The other was Henry Havelock, who obtained his commission in 1815 in the Rifle Brigade, and after a period of half-pay in the 21st Regiment was transferred to the 13th in 1822. He had seen no active service, but he was a student of the art of War and a deeply religious man. He combined in his personality the attributes of scholar, soldier, saint. For twenty years, except for brief intervals on the staff, he served as a regimental officer, honoured and respected by all. His subsequent career, and especially the prominent part he took in the Indian Mutiny, gained for him an undying reputation in the history of the British Army. On the voyage to India he was not idle. He started classes in Hindustani, having taken, previous to embarkation, some lessons in that language from a Doctor Gilchrist.

It was owing to a friendship he made on the voyage to India that Havelock turned his thoughts to religion. His mother had always been intensely religious, but Havelock at the time he left for India treated religion in much the same way as the average man does. His friendship with Lieutenant James Gardner, of the 13th, altered his outlook completely. Gardner was a deeply religious, but very unassuming man, but it was he who roused Havelock's enthusiasm for religious matters.

Havelock had to contend with a lot of opposition within the Regiment and but for the staunch support of Sale he and his 'Saints' would probably have had a poor time. This opposition arose or was intensified after Havelock became a Baptist. When some complaints were made to Sale, he is reported to have said: 'I know nothing about Baptists, but I know I wish the whole regiment were Baptists, for their names are never on the defaulters' roll, and they are never in the congee house.'

On arrival in India the Regiment was quartered at Fort William, and it was here that Havelock first assembled men of the Regiment for religious instruction.

THE BURMESE WAR, 1824-6

Shortly after the arrival of the Regiment in India relations with the King of Ava became strained. For many years the Burmese Officers in the country adjacent to British Territory had been guilty of acts of aggression, which at length became of so outrageous a character as to render it necessary to call upon the Court of Ava for an explanation. No answer was given; but after overcoming several petty tribes by which the kingdom was surrounded, the King made preparations for invading British territory at that time under the jurisdiction of the East India Company.

Hitherto all hostilities with the Burmese had taken place on the land frontier in the neighbourhood of Chittagong and Manipur with very unsatisfactory results. It was now determined to invade Burma from the sea and as a preliminary to capture the important town of Rangoon on the River Irrawaddy 30 miles from the sea. Accordingly a joint naval and military expedition was ordered to assemble at Port Cornwallis in the Andaman Islands under the command of Brig.-General Sir Archibald Campbell and Commodore Grant.

The military forces consisted of two contingents; the one from Bengal comprised the 13th Light Infantry, strength 727, the 38th Regiment, Detachment 40th Bengal Indian Infantry and 360 European Artillery, under the command of Lieut.-Colonel Michael M'Creagh, C.B., of the 13th, now appointed Brigadier-General; the other from Madras of the 41st Regiment, 102nd Regiment, 1st Battalion Pioneers, the 3rd, 7th, 8th, 9th and 10th, Madras Infantry and 560 Madras Fortress Artillery, the whole under the command of Brig.-General Maclean. The total strength was about 11,000 men with 42 guns. No land transport was provided and supplies were reduced to a minimum, as it was expected that the troops could live on the country. The following officers of the Regiment served on the staff:—

Lieutenant H. Havelock, D.A.A.G.; Captain H. Waterman, D.A.Q.M.G.; Lieutenant G. W. Malim, Brigade Major.

The command of the Regiment devolved on Major Robert Sale.

The 13th Light Infantry embarked at Calcutta on 5th April 1824 and by the 2nd May the whole expedition was concentrated at Port Cornwallis.

From this port three companies of the 13th, with a detachment of the 40th Bengal Indian Infantry under Brig.-General M'Creagh, was sent to subjugate the island of Cheduba on the Aracan Coast.

MAJOR-GENERAL SIR HENRY HAVELOCK, K.C.B.

The main body of the expedition, however, set out for Rangoon and anchored within the bar of Rangoon River, 15 miles from the town on 10th May. On the following day the fleet proceeded upstream, and having silenced the enemy's batteries anchored off the town.

Detachments of the 13th, 38th and 41st Regiments were now landed to cover the disembarkation. The 13th, under Major Sale, landed in the town at the river gate, the 38th above it and the 41st below it. There was no resistance; the inhabitants quitting the town and taking refuge in the surrounding jungles.

The attack had been a complete surprise. Major Sale, on advancing up the main street, was instrumental in saving some six Europeans, missionaries and merchants who had been threatened with torture and death by the 'Barbarians', as Havelock describes the Burmese in his book, *Three Campaigns in Ava*.

The first night on shore, the European troops, attracted by visions of loot on seeing in the distance the Great Golden Pagoda of Shwe-da-gon, chanced upon a brandy store left by a European merchant. Most of them got drunk and started looting. Half the town was burnt down, and the other half only saved by the exertions of the sailors from the fleet.

On 12th May the remainder of the troops were disembarked. During the ensuing fortnight the town, which was about half a mile square, was placed in a state of defence, as was also the Great Pagoda about $2\frac{1}{2}$ miles to the north of the town, which was garrisoned by the 13th and 38th Regiments.

The Burmese were by no means a despicable enemy; furnished with fire-arms and well versed in all the wiles of jungle warfare, they were adepts in entrenching themselves and erecting barricades. The jungles surrounding the British posts swarmed with these Burmese warriors, who kept up a continuous sniping on the British garrisons.

The headquarters of the 13th Light Infantry were in a temple close to the Great Pagoda. In a large apartment of this temple was a huge image of Buddha. The Regimental Colours rested on the arms of this Buddha, and it was the regimental jest to introduce visitors to 'The New Ensign'. Near by in a chapel of the Great Pagoda Havelock established his religious services. Marshman thus describes this chapel:—

'It was a side chapel with little figures of Buddha in the usual sitting posture arranged around the room. An oil lamp had been placed in the lap of each figure and the pious soldiers of the 13th were standing up around Havelock, singing a Christian hymn amidst these idolatrous surroundings. It would be difficult to picture to the mind a more delightful or romantic episode in this scene of warfare and desolation.'

THE EXPEDITION TO CHEDUBA

Before proceeding with the operations in the main theatre it is necessary to give some account of Brig.-General M'Creagh's detachment which had been dispatched from Port Cornwallis for the reduction of Cheduba.

The expedition, escorted by H.M.S. *Slaney* under Captain Mitchell, concentrated off the island of Cheduba on the night of the 12th May, but it was not till the 14th that the landing party, consisting of 200 of the 13th Light Infantry and 100 of the 20th Indian Infantry, as many as the boats would hold, made for the shore and a small outpost at the entrance to a creek was easily captured, but when the flotilla had proceeded up the creek about half a mile, the enemy were discovered lining a trench on the northern bank, who opened with musketry fire and flights of arrows. The boats made for the shore, and although the bank was steep, two or three parties of the 13th were soon on the top, and after a few minutes' firing, were reinforced by the rest of the troops, when the enemy fled, leaving upwards of 20 killed and many wounded.

An advance was then made into the town, the troops advancing along the main street. When near the end of it about one-quarter of a mile from the gate, a formidable stockade, 12 to 20 feet high in the shape of a square with sides 200 yards long, barred the way. This stockade was strongly held by the enemy who opened fire from several 6-pounders and other cannon.

May 15th and 16th were occupied in landing some howitzers, and two 9-pounders on ships' carriages, while the troops constructed trenches and emplacements for the guns. On the morning of the 17th, all being ready, feints were made against the enemy's left, and as soon as their attention had been drawn to that quarter, the British guns opened fire on the gateway on the enemy's right. After a short bombardment the assaulting column, led by Major Thornhill's company of the 13th, advanced and after a brief struggle were soon in possession of the enemy's stronghold.

On 19th May a reconnoitring party, under Captain Aitken of the 13th, succeeded in capturing the Rajah, who was concealed with some of his followers in the jungles near by. The enemy lost about 300 killed and wounded in these operations. Out of a total British casualty list of 3 killed and 41 wounded, the 13th lost 3 rank and file killed and 2 officers (Captain and Bt.-Major G. Thornhill and Ensign J. Kershaw) and 18 rank and file wounded.

Among those mentioned in Brig.-General M'Creagh's dispatch were Major Thornhill and Lieutenant Malim of the 13th.

After leaving Lieut.-Colonel Hampton and the detachment of the 20th Indian Infantry as a garrison, M'Creagh with the 13th re-embarked on 3rd June and arrived at Rangoon on 11th June.

OPERATIONS OF MAIN BODY

The position of the British troops in Rangoon was not an enviable one; having no land transport, an advance was out of the question, added to which the monsoon had set in and large numbers were already in hospital.

Sir Archibald Campbell, rightly judging that a passive defence of the ground already won would be injurious to the morale of his army, decided on engaging the enemy whenever possible in the vicinity of Rangoon. Accordingly on 28th May he moved out on an extended reconnaissance with two companies of the 13th under Major Dennie, two companies of the 38th, 400 Indian soldiers and a light gun and a howitzer. After advancing 7 miles through the jungle the artillery, which were man-handled, became so exhausted that it was decided to send them back escorted by the Indian Infantry. The European companies continued to advance for another mile when they debouched on to an open valley of paddy fields on the far side of which there were two villages about 2 miles distant defended by 4,000 to 5,000 Burmese. The advance was by echelon of companies, left flank leading. When close to the villages a heavy fire was opened from two stockades in their front cleverly hidden. Sir A. Campbell, leaving the right company of the 13th to engage the enemy in front, moved round the enemy's right with the two companies of the 38th under Major Evans, and Major Dennie's company of the 13th. These three companies moved to the assault with great gallantry, and after ten minutes' fighting the companies of the 38th captured the first stockade, and the company of the 13th the second stockade. The enemy left 300 dead on the ground. Lieutenant Alexander Howard of the 13th, who behaved with great gallantry, was killed, while one bugler and nine rank and file of the Regiment were wounded.

The death of this officer was thus described by Havelock:—

'Lieutenant Alexander Howard, who was a volunteer for the day, and had been seen cheering on the men with very distinguished gallantry, unluckily rushed upon an angle where the Burmese, pent like rats in a corner, were struggling desperately to escape from the British bayonet. As he pushed on, sabre in hand, three balls struck him on the side, and at the same time a Burmese speared him in the back. Dennie tells me he found him expiring, his sabre yet clenched in his hand, fallen and lying over a dead Burman, in whose skull was a frightful gash.'

Marshman says:—

'Howard's remains were interred the same evening, in a corner of the enclosure of one of the pagodas. As he lay before the door, it was proposed to strip and reattire the body. Havelock pointed to his gory side, and said, "You can affix no brighter ornament than that to the body of a brave soldier; had we but his own good sword and the spear of his enemy, his obsequies would be complete."'

After the action the column returned to Rangoon. On June 3rd an unsuccessful attempt was made to capture the enemy's stronghold of Kemmendyne about 2 miles higher up the river. The 13th were not engaged on this occasion.

In order to counteract this set-back, Sir A. Campbell set out with 3,000 men, four 18-pounders, four mortars and some field-pieces on the 10th June to attack Kemmendyne, while two divisions of the naval forces flanked the advance on the side of the river. As soon as the enemy's position was located, the following dispositions were made: the 41st and 102nd were to attack in front, while two advanced companies of the 13th, under Major Robert Sale, and 2 companies of the 38th were to move round to the rear of the stockades which formed the enemy's position. The movements were well timed and the attacks simultaneous, the artillery taking part in the frontal attack. Sir A. Campbell thus describes the attack: 'A very spirited and successful attack was made on the other side of the stockade by the advanced companies of the 13th and 38th Regiments, who by assisting each other up the face of the stockade (at least 10 feet high) entered about the same time as the Party by the breach, putting every man to death who opposed their entrance, and it affords me pleasure to state that the first man who appeared on the Top of the work was I believe Major Sale of His Majesty's 13th Light Infantry.'

The Burmese lost 150 killed, while the British casualties were 32, of which the 13th had one man killed, Lieutenant J. Petry and 10 rank and file wounded.

After this success, the column advanced about a mile, and at four o'clock in the afternoon found that the enemy had taken up another position fortified by stockades. Batteries were erected during the night, and the artillery opened a heavy fire at daylight, when the Burmese forsook their works and fled.

On the 1st July numerous columns of the enemy were seen in front of the British position when four companies of the 13th were ordered to make a reconnaissance under the command of Major Dennie; they discovered the enemy on the plains of Kumaroot 5 miles distant from the Great Pagoda, and after a slight engagement returned to camp having lost two men wounded.

On the 5th July the Regiment was again engaged when Bt. Captain Knox Barrett was wounded, losing an arm, while 16 rank and file were also wounded.

On the 8th July an operation of a more serious nature was undertaken. Generals MacBean and McCreagh with 250 men of the 13th, 250 of the 38th, 250 of the 89th, 250 of the 102nd and a detachment 7th Madras Indian Infantry with Artillery were to proceed by land to Kumaroot on the Hlaing River, while Sir Archibald Campbell with 300 men of the 41st and the 17th Madras Native Infantry proceeded by water, the naval escort on this occasion being commanded by Captain Marryat, the well-known novelist.

The land attack was led by the 13th under Major Sale, followed by the artillery and other infantry regiments. The 13th, which led on that day, advanced in perfect silence, the 38th loudly cheering, both in the most perfect order. On approaching the stockades, scaling ladders were ordered to the front, and as soon as the ladders were fixed the 13th and 38th stormed the works in the most gallant manner. In the mêleé which ensued the following incident occurred and is described by Havelock as follows:—

'Here a singular combat took place. A Burman chief singled out a soldier of the 13th. He aimed a blow at his head. Major Sale, who was near, interposing his own sabre, parried the cut. He, in his turn, made a cut at the Chief. The blow caused the Burman to stagger, but the Major's sabre shivered like glass to the very hilt. Instantly closing with his enemy, he wrested from him his broad gilded weapon and striking the Barbarian with his full force below the ribs, nearly severed his body into two portions.'

Several other stockades were also carried in the same brilliant manner, while numbers of the enemy were intercepted fleeing from the attacks made by the river contingent. 800 of the enemy were killed on this occasion, and 39 pieces of artillery, 40 swivels and 300 muskets captured. Among the spoils were seven golden chattahs,[1] a quantity of silver dishes and plates, and the Commander-in-Chief's bed. Soomba Wongee, Second Minister of State and Commander-in-Chief of the Army, was killed in this action.

Sir Archibald Campbell in his dispatch declared that 'nothing could have been more brilliant and successful. He (Brig.-General McBean) took by assault seven stockades with most rapid succession' .... 'The Brigadier-General assures me the ardour of the column was irresistible and speaks highly of the able aid he received from Brig.-General M'Creagh; he also reports favourably upon the judicious and gallant style in which Majors Sale and Frith of the 13th and 38th Regiments, led the troops under their respective command.'

Captain John Johnson of the 13th was severely wounded on this occasion, while one serjeant was killed and seven rank and file wounded.

This success caused the Burmese troops to remove to a greater distance, where they were favoured by the difficult character of the country. The British forces accordingly enjoyed comparative quiet for some time, and this was the more necessary owing to the heavy rains, the extensive inundations and the lack of supplies for an advance. In addition each of the European regiments had 200 to 300 men in hospital.

On the 22nd September a river expedition set out from Kemmendyne escorted by the *Satellite*. The troops consisted of 2 officers and 67 other ranks from each of the European Regiments, including the 13th. Major Sale was in command of the landing parties. Almost 2 miles above Pagoda point five stockades were located, two on the right bank and three on the left bank. Landing parties were sent ashore and the stockades carried by storm, the enemy dispersing after a slight resistance. On 23rd September, a further advance of 12 to 15 miles was made without opposition, and the following day, after advancing a further 5 miles, three stockades were located and carried. There were no casualties among the troops.

On 7th October some detachments of Indian Infantry had suffered a reverse in the neighbourhood of Keghloo, and to avenge this defeat Sir A. Campbell sent out on 9th October, 420 rank and file of the European Regiments and 350 men of the 28th and 30th Madras Regiments and 3 guns, the whole under the command of Brig.-General M. M'Creagh, to attack the enemy at Keghloo. At 7 a.m. on the 10th they reached the Toodoghee stockades where a detachment of Madras troops was left, and the march resumed to within a mile of the enemy's stockades at sunset. After halting for the night they advanced to attack in the morning, but found the position evacuated. A further advance was made the following day with the hope of engaging the enemy, but in this M'Creagh was disappointed as the Burmese would not stand. He accordingly returned to the neighbourhood of Rangoon on the 14th October. Major Sale and Captain Aitken of the 13th were both mentioned in General M'Creagh's dispatch.

Sickness, which had been very bad during the month of October, began to

[1] The umbrellas of the native chiefs. The size of the umbrella appears to have marked the rank of the chief.

diminish in November, and it was just as well, as a veteran chief, named Maha Bandoola, had been appointed Commander of the Burmese forces. He had succeeded in collecting an army of 50,000 foot, a body of 700 Cassay horse, and 300 pieces of artillery. The guns were mostly carried by elephants, while of the infantry 35,000 had muskets, and the rest swords and spears.

The following are extracts from Sir Archibald's Campbell's dispatch of the operations that ensued:—

'Their haughty leader had insolently declared his intention of leading us in Captive Chains to grace the triumph of the Golden Monarch, but it has pleased God to expose the vanity of his idle threats, and crown the heroic efforts of my gallant little Army with a most complete and signal victory.'

. . . .

'In the afternoon of the 1st Dec. I observed an opportunity of attacking the enemy's left to advantage and ordered Major Sale with 400 men from the 13th Light Infantry and 18th Madras Infantry, under Major Dennie of the former and Captain Ross of the latter corps, to move forward to the point I had selected, and I never witnessed a more dashing charge than was made on this occasion by His Majesty's 13th, while the 18th Madras Infantry followed their example with a spirit that did them honour; carrying all opposition before them, they burst through the Intrenchments, carrying dismay and terror into the Enemy's ranks, great numbers of whom were slain, and the party returned loaded with Arms, Standards, and other Trophies.'

This victory was followed by a decisive triumph over the left wing of the Burmese Army on the 5th of December, on which occasion 245 rank and file of the Regiment under Major Dennie formed part of the first column of attack under Major Sale. The following is the account given by Sir Archibald Campbell in his dispatch:—

'The enemy having apparently completed his left wing with its full complement of Artillery and warlike stores, I determined to attack that part of his Line early on the morning of the 5th.

'Two columns of attack were formed, agreeably to orders I had issued the preceding evening, composed of details from the different Regiments of the Army. The first consisting of 1,100 I placed under the Orders of that gallant Officer, Major Sale, and directed him to attack and penetrate the centre of the Enemy's Line; the other consisting of 600 men I entrusted to Major Walker of the 3rd Madras Light Infantry, with orders to attack their left which had approached to within a few hundred yards of Rangoon. At 7 o'clock both columns moved forward to the point of attack: both were led to my perfect satisfaction, and both succeeded with a degree of ease their intrepid and undaunted conduct undoubtedly deserved, and I directed Lieut. Archibald, with a Troop of the Right Hon[ble] the Governor General's Body Guard, which had been landed the preceding evening to follow the column under Major Sale and take advantage of any opportunity which might offer, to charge.

'The Enemy was defeated and dispersed in every direction and the Body Guard gallantly charging over the broken and swampy ground completed their terror and dismay: The Cassay Horse fled mixed with the retreating Infantry, and all their Artillery, Stores, and reserve Depôt which had cost them so much toil and labour to get up with a great quantity of small Arms, Gilt Chattahs, Standards and other Trophies fell into our hands. Never was Victory more complete or more decided!! and never was the triumph of Discipline and valour over the disjointed efforts of irregular Courage and infinitely Superior Numbers more conspicuous!! Majors Dennie and Thornhill of the 13th Light Infantry and Major Gore of the 29th were distinguished by the Steadiness with which they led their men, but it is with deep regret I have to state the loss we have sustained in the death of Major Walker, one of India's best and bravest Soldiers.

. . . .

(On the 7th inst. the right and centre of the Enemy were defeated.)
'Our loss in killed and wounded, although severe will not, I am sure, be considered great for the important service we have had the honour to perform.

'Of my troops I cannot say enough, their Valour was only equalled by the cheerful patience with which they bore long and painful privations. My Europeans fought like Britons, and proved themselves worthy of the Country that gave them birth, and I trust I do the gallant Sepoys justice when I say that never did Troops more strive to obtain the palm of honor than they to rival their European Comrades in every thing that marks the steady, true and daring Soldier.'

* * * * * * * * *

The losses of the 13th Light Infantry during these operations were:—
Killed: B^t. Captain and Lieut. Henry O'Shea, 1 serjeant, 3 rank and file.
Wounded: Captain Clark, severely; Ensign J. Blackwell, slightly; Ensign R. W. Crooker, severely; 1 serjeant, 20 rank and file.

Notwithstanding these reverses the Burmese Chieftain Maha Bandoola was by no means at the end of his resources. He rallied his troops, called up reinforcements, and took up another position which he fortified with great skill, and in addition managed to introduce emissaries into Rangoon itself who set fire to the town in several places. One quarter of the town was destroyed before the fire was got under.

On 15th December Sir Archibald Campbell again attacked the Burmese. Two columns were sent out; the Right column, consisting of 200 of the 13th Light Infantry and 300 of the 18th and 24th Madras Infantry with a field gun, a detachment of the Body Guard, the whole under Brig.-General Cotton, were to make a détour round the enemy's left, and if possible to gain the rear of his position at Kokien, the other column in two divisions, under Lieut.-Colonel Miles of the 89th and Major Evans of the 38th, were to attack in front. These attacks were well timed and carried out simultaneously. The 13th met with a very determined resistance. Their Commanding Officer, Major Sale, received a severe wound in his head; he was succeeded by Major Dennie who was wounded in the hand, but who continued at the head of the Regiment till the action was over. After a desperate struggle the Burmese fled, leaving their camp standing, with all their baggage, and a great quantity of arms and ammunition.

Sir A. Campbell in his dispatch thus refers to Major Sale:—

'In the list of wounded will be seen, with regret, the name of Major Sale, of His Majesty's 13th Light Infantry, an officer whose gallantry has been most conspicuous on every occasion since our arrival at Rangoon. I am happy to say that his wound, though severe, is not dangerous, and I trust that his valuable services will not long remain unavailable.'

The total British casualties in this action were 132 killed and wounded. Of these the 13th had 62 as follows:—

Killed: Lieutenants William Darby, John Petry, and James Jones, 2 serjeants and 7 rank and file.

Wounded: Major R. H. Sale, severely not dangerously; Major W. H. Dennie, slightly; Captain and Bt. Major G. Thornhill, severely; Captain James McPherson, severely; Lieutenant M. Fenton, slightly; Lieutenant R. Pattison, severely; Ensign N. Wilkinson, slightly; Ensign T. Blackwell, slightly; 2 serjeants and 40 rank and file.

These successes connected with the efforts of the Royal Navy had cleared the neighbourhood of Rangoon of the enemy to such an extent that the inhabitants returned to the town, the market was opened, and some indeed enlisted in the transport for boat service. The maritime provinces of Mergui, Tavoy, Yeb and Martaban had also been captured.

THE EXPEDITION TO BASSEIN

In February 1825 the 13th, under Major Dennie, with the 38th and 12th Indian Infantry, the whole under the command of Major Sale, were dispatched by sea to occupy Bassein, in the south-western part of the ancient kingdom of Pegu, constituting part of the Burmese empire. The Regiment embarked on this service on the 10th February, and after a tedious passage, arrived on the evening of the 24th, off Pagoda Point, Great Negrais. An attempt was made to negotiate with the enemy, but as the flag of truce was fired on, the fleet weighed anchor and entered the river on the 26th, when 150 men of the 13th, 50 of the 38th and 100 of the 12th Madras Infantry, covered by the guns of H.M.S. *Larne* and H. C. Cruiser *Mercury*, landed and captured the enemy's fort at the entrance.

The troops afterwards re-embarked and proceeded upstream. The expedition reached Narputtah on 1st March and anchored off Bassein on the 3rd of that month, which had been set on fire and abandoned by the Burmese. That same evening the troops were disembarked and occupied some good houses, that had escaped the conflagration, in the vicinity of the principal pagoda. Many of the inhabitants were induced to return to the town and soon more or less normal relations were established. On the 13th of March Major Dennie made a reconnaissance up the Bassein River. He was afterwards joined by another party under Major Sale, and together they proceeded to Lamina, 120 miles up-river, meeting with little opposition. The expedition returned to Bassein on the 23rd, having had two men wounded.

As all opposition in the province of Bassein had ceased the 13th embarked for Rangoon at the end of April and arrived at that port on 2nd May. On the 2nd June Major Sale was promoted Lieutenant-Colonel.

OPERATIONS OF MAIN BODY

During the absence of the 13th at Bassein the main army under Lieut.-General Sir Archibald Campbell had advanced up the valley of the Irrawaddy to Prome, 150 miles above Rangoon.

During August the Regiment embarked from Rangoon for Prome. From a statement dated 18 August 1825 there were present fit for duty *at Prome* 2 captains, 5 subalterns, 11 serjeants, 5 drummers and 162 rank and file; *at Rangoon*, or on their way to Prome, 2 captains, 5 subalterns, 1 assistant surgeon, 9 serjeants, 7 drummers and 120 rank and file. While the Regiment was at Prome the following incident occurred. One night an outpost was heavily attacked by the enemy; some men of another corps were ordered by Sir A. Campbell to support it. Unfortunately owing to some carouse they were not in a fit state to do so. On this being reported to the Commander-in-Chief he exclaimed: 'Then call out Havelock's saints, they are always sober and can be depended on, and Havelock himself is always ready.' Needless to say the enemy were at once repulsed.

In October overtures of peace were made by the Burmese, but they came to nothing, and when in the middle of November the Burmese defeated three bodies of Indian Infantry it became evident that further hostilities were imminent. In fact, 60,000 Burmese advanced to surround the 6,000 British and Indian troops at Prome.

In the following operations the 13th were brigaded with the 38th, under the command of Lieut.-Colonel Sale. On 1st December Sir A. Campbell, leaving four regiments of Indian Infantry for the defence of Prome, advanced with the remainder to attack the enemy's position at Simbike, 11 miles northeast of Prome. The army advanced in two columns, the right column, under Brig.-General Cotton (afterwards General Sir Willoughby Cotton, G.C.B., K.C.H.), advanced up the left bank of the river and the left column, including the 13th, under the immediate command of the Commander-in-Chief, up the right bank of the river. Cotton's column were involved in the assault on Simbike which they carried in gallant style in less than ten minutes. The whole force advanced that day to Ze-ouke, having covered 20 miles. On the following day, 2nd December, the advance was continued and the enemy located on the fortified ridge of Napadee. Arriving in the vicinity of the position the British artillery commenced a sharp cannonade; Brig.-General Elrington's troops then drove the enemy from the jungle, six companies of the 87th carried the posts at the bottom of the ridge, and the Burmese were driven from the valley to the principal works on the hills, which appeared very formidable. The heights could only be ascended by a narrow road, commanded by artillery, and defended by stockades crowded with men armed with muskets. As soon as the artillery had made an impression on the works the 13th and 38th Regiments sprang forward, rushed into them, and overcoming all opposition with the bayonet, drove the Burmese from hill to hill, over precipices that were only accessible by a narrow stair, until the whole position, nearly 3 miles in length, was captured. Lieut.-Colonel Sale and Major Thornhill of the 13th were both mentioned in Sir A. Campbell's dispatch. On the 5th December the enemy's right wing was driven back, and the army of Ava, forced from its position by the determined attacks of British soldiers, sought safety in flight. The Anglo-Indian Army continued to advance and on the 19th December reached Meaday and on the 27th they were within 4 miles of Melloone and 140 miles from Prome. The advance was much facilitated by the waterway of the Irrawaddy which even at Melloone is 600 yards wide. Negotiations for peace which had been initiated as early as 3rd December were now in progress, but as the sequel shows, they only served as an excuse to the enemy for gaining time wherewith to organize further resistance.

The Anglo-Indian Army remained halted in front of Melloone till 18th January 1826, the date stipulated for the signing of peace. As the conditions of peace had not been fulfilled, Sir Archibald Campbell resumed hostilities on the 19th, by opening a cannonade at 11 a.m. from a battery of 20 guns on the left bank of the river on the enemy's position on the right bank. Meanwhile the troops intended for the assault were embarking in the boats of His Majesty's ships and of the Flotilla at a point above their encampment. The 13th and 38th, under Lieut.-Colonel Sale, were to assault the enemy's position near its south-eastern angle. The remaining troops, under Brig.-General Cotton, were to cross above Melloone and after carrying some outworks to attack the northern face.

Although the whole of the boats pushed off together from the left bank, the strength of the current and a strong breeze from the north carried Lieut.-Colonel Sale's brigade to the given point of attack before the other columns could possibly reach the opposite shore. Lieut.-Colonel Sale was unfortunately wounded in his boat, but the units of his brigade having landed and formed with admirable regularity under the command of Major Frith of the 38th, rushed on to the attack with their usual intrepidity, and were in a short time complete masters of the work. Major Frith himself was wounded, but was succeeded in command of the brigade by Major Thornhill of the 13th.

When Brig.-General Cotton saw the success of the 13th and 38th Regiments, he detached Lieut.-Colonel Blair's brigade to cut off the retreat of the enemy, which was done with great effect.

Sir A. Campbell refers to Major Thornhill in his dispatch as follows: 'Major Thornhill of His Majesty's 13th Light Infantry was the third on whom the accident of war bestowed the perilous distinction of leading these troops; and he conducted their movements to the close of the affair in a style worthy of his predecessors in command.'

Concerning the two regiments, the Commander-in-Chief wrote: 'The conduct of His Majesty's 13th and 38th Regiments during the advance and their gallantry in the storm far exceed all that I can write in their Praise. I sincerely hope that I shall not long be deprived of the services of two brave Commanders.'

The loss of the Regiment was one man killed; Lieut.-Colonel Sale and 3 men wounded. The total British casualties were 9 killed and 44 wounded.

After this action the advance on the Burmese capital was continued. Considering that the Anglo-Indian Army was over 300 miles from Rangoon the available fighting force seemed dangerously weak; it numbered but 1,300 men of all ranks, when once more they engaged the enemy on the open fields near Pagahm Mew on 9th February.

On this day the 13th went into action 216 strong and led the night attack in their usual gallant style. Havelock states that they charged in extended order on this occasion and having defeated the enemy pursued so far that the Commander-in-Chief caused them to be recalled and concentrated by sound of bugle. As the Burmese were still threatening in large numbers, the moment seemed critical, but Sir Archibald Campbell, having reached a small eminence, confidently asserted to one of his staff, 'I have here the 13th and the Body Guard. The whole Burmese Army shall not drive me from this hill.' Nor was his confidence misplaced. The action was renewed and soon the enemy were fleeing in disorder. The 13th had one man killed, Captain Edward T. Tronson and 6 men wounded.

After this fight the advance was continued on Ummerapoora, the capital, situated upon the shores of a romantic lake; and when within four days' march of that city at Yandaboo the King of Ava sent the ratified treaty, agreed to pay the expenses of the war, and gave up a considerable portion of his territory. Havelock was one of the British representatives to proceed to Ava to receive the ratification of the treaty.

On the conclusion of this campaign the following statements appeared in General Orders:—

'While the Governor-General enumerates with sentiments of unfeigned admiration, the 13th, 38th, 41st, 89th, 47th, 1st (or Royals), 87th and 45th Regiments, the Honourable Company's Madras European Regiment, and the Bengal and Madras European Artillery, as the European troops who have had the honour of establishing the renown of the British arms in a new and distant region, His Lordship in Council feels that higher and more justly merited praise cannot be bestowed on those brave troops than that, amidst the barbarous hosts whom they have fought and conquered, they have eminently displayed the virtues, and sustained the character, of the British soldier.'

.   .   .   .

'The frequent mention in the public dispatches of the gallantry and zeal of Lieut.-Colonel Sale deservedly marks that officer as one who has established peculiar claims to the distinguished notice of His Lordship in Council.'

Among other officers mentioned in General Orders the following may be noted, viz. Brig.-General M'Creagh.

In the same orders it was announced that medals, bearing a suitable device, would be distributed to the Indian troops employed; and when the general medal for the several campaigns in India was awarded to the British troops twenty-five years afterwards, a bar inscribed 'Ava' was granted.

It will easily be believed that in 1851 there would be but few survivors to claim this medal. Fortunately the medal rolls have been preserved in the Public Record Office and they contain the names of fifteen officers and eighty-six other ranks. These medal rolls will be found in Appendix D.

Lieut.-Colonel Sale and Majors Dennie and Thornhill were rewarded with the honour of being constituted Companions of the Order of the Bath.

The following General Order is the authority for the Battle-honour 'Ava' being borne on the Regimental Colour.

at
War Office) General Orders &c.

Most humbly submitted to His Majesty

13th. Foot

That the Regiments named in the Margin be permitted to bear on their Colors and Appointments, in addition to any other Badges or Devices which may have heretofore been granted to those Regiments the Word

'AVA'

in commemoration of their Services during the late Burmese War.
                                                        approv'd
                                                              G. R.

6th December 1826.

Communicated on 19th Decr 1826 to the Colonels or Com^{ed} Officers and to the War Office.

All ranks were awarded a donation of six months' Full or Field rate of Batta for those who had served twelve months or more in Burma. Those who had served less than twelve months got three months' Full or Field rate of Batta.

The Regiment embarked in boats from Yandaboo on the 7th March and arrived at Rangoon on the 22nd of that month.

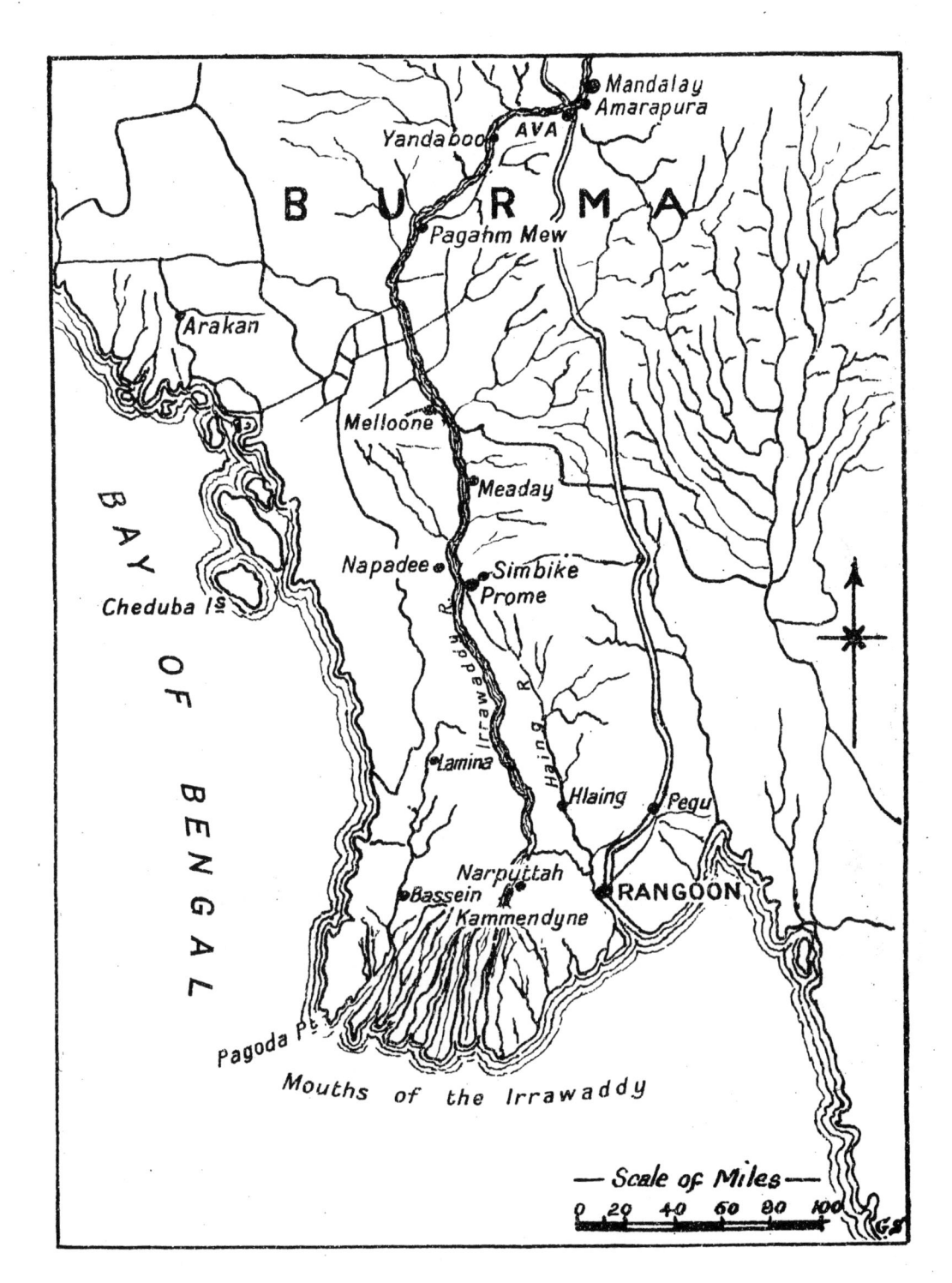

BURMA, 1824-6

CHAPTER XIII

SERVICE IN INDIA

THE 13th Light Infantry set sail from Rangoon in the transports *Almorah* and *Aurora* on the 26th and 28th March respectively and reached Calcutta in the middle of April 1826. After remaining there a few days, they proceeded to Berhampore where they were stationed till November.

On the 15th of that month they commenced their march to Dinapore, and arrived there on the 3rd January 1827, and remained in that station till December 1831.

During their stay at Dinapore a few glimpses of Regimental life may be gleaned from the inspection reports. The chief items in the inspection report of 1829 were that the number of courts martial, fifty-one, was considered excessive, and that many of the sentences consisted of solitary confinement, at that time considered to be irregular and contrary to instructions issued in 1823. The commanding officer was blamed for the state of the military prisons at Dinapore, and was informed that Colonel McCreagh, at that time enjoying a superior command, would be recalled, should the military prisoners continue to escape.

The Regiment was inspected by Brig.-General A. Knox commanding the Dinapore Division on the 6th December 1830. He reported the Regiment to be in good order. Other items in his report are as follows:—

'Lieut.-Colonel Sale discharges his important duties with zeal and ability.

'Captain Tronson's wound in his leg prevents his marching; he is often confined with it, and Lieut.-Colonel Sale considers him unfit for active service.

'Brevet Captain Keir has never joined the Regiment. (He was at that time in the Nizam's service.)

'A well-regulated System is established, and the interior arrangement duly attended to.'

To show the heavy mortality among the troops in India at this period, the Church register of St. Luke's, Dinapore, shows that the Regiment lost during their stay of four years 448 of all ranks, including women and children.

In 1831 Havelock, who in March 1827 had been appointed Adjutant of the King's Depôt at Chinsurah, rejoined the Regiment. He at once resumed the religious instruction of the men and soon had a congregation of fifty to sixty.

In the year 1831 Standing Orders of the Regiment were 'framed and revised under the directions of Lieut.-Colonel Sale, C.B.' These Standing Orders are interesting because they relate to rules for the issue of medals and stripes for good service. Thus—

A gold medal for 20 years' service.

Silver medals for 7 years' and 14 years' service.

Stripes. 'Two stripes of Lance after 5 years and one for 3 years. Worn round the sleeves and a little above the facings.'

The Standing Orders also show that the Canteen profits were divided into 16 shares, which were distributed as follows:—

2 shares for the Regimental School, to provide education and books.
1 share to form a fund for the benefit of the widows of the Regiment.
2 shares for the orphans of the Regiment.
3 shares for the men's library.
2 shares for the purpose of assisting the men and women of the Regiment in defraying the charges incurred in removing their things from one station to another.
2 shares to form a fund for granting donations to old and disabled soldiers of the Regiment on discharge.
4 shares to form a general fund for contingencies.

In December 1831 the Regiment commenced its march to Agra and arrived in that station early in January 1832. On the 14th of that month it was inspected by Major-General Sir Sandford Whittingham. The following items of his report are of interest:—

'The 13th Light Infantry is one of the finest corps I have seen in India; and its very high state of discipline does great credit to the zeal and ability of its commanding officer, Lieut.-Colonel Sale. The new system of Defaulter Book, as directed in the Horse Guards Memorandum of the 24th June 1830, and G.O. of the 14th October of the same year, has been partly commenced on in this Regiment.

'I had an opportunity in the course of the movements of the Battalion as Light Infantry in extended order to form a favourable judgment of the abilities of the Officers Commanding Companies.'

Havelock's religious activities have been perpetuated in Agra; for at the present day there is a chapel there known as the Havelock Baptist Chapel on which is inscribed:—

'This Chapel was removed to the present site and rebuilt A.D. 1873 to provide better accommodation for the congregation, and likewise to perpetuate the memory of Sir Henry Havelock, Bart., C.B., who with the men of H.M. 13th Regiment built the first Baptist Chapel in Agra A.D. 1832'.

> He was every inch a soldier
> And every inch a Christian.

During this year, 1832, two companies of the Regiment escorted the Governor-General on a visit to the Ranee of Gwalior, who made an inspection and review of the force, when she expressed her pleasure at their appearance, and gave a present of rupees to the extent of five or ten shillings per man.

In 1833 the inspection report of Brig.-General Richards discloses the fact that the Regiment was commanded by Major Dennie. Among General Richard's observations the following may be noted:—

'A well-regulated Discipline is established.

'Captain Tronson from the effects of a wound in his leg is unfit for Active Service.

'Lieut. Malin who left England on 26th July 1830 to join the headquarters of the Regiment via New South Wales has never been heard of since that period. (As a matter of fact this officer was wrecked and returned to England.)

'The arms generally are not in a serviceable state, but clean and regularly marked.

'As far as I can judge, Officers Commanding Companies have no proper control over their companies, as men confined for being drunk, &c, are not brought before the officer, but are confined by Non-Commissioned Officers, and taken before the Commanding Officer the next morning. The Punishment awarded is entered in the Books kept in the Adjutant's office, the Company Officer being left in ignorance apparently of the whole transaction.

'The Guard Report is signed by a Serjeant and not by the Officer commanding the Guard.'

The following note by the Adjutant-General follows:—

'The Officer commanding this Regiment will be peremptorily ordered to model his Interior System strictly according to the General Orders and Regulations of the Army, and in no respect whatever to presume to deviate therefrom.

'Very unsatisfactory.

J. M.
A.-G.'

On the 7th January 1834 the Regiment was inspected by Major-General the Hon. John Ramsay, Lieut.-Colonel Dennie being in command. The Reports contain the following commendation:—

'The appearance of His Majesty's 13th Regt. of Light Infantry on Parade, the way in which the Regt. manœuvred both as a Battalion and Light Infantry and the thorough manner in which both officers and men appeared to have been instructed, called for my entire approbation, and the Regiment fully maintained its former character for proficiency in the practice at the Target. I saw a Captain and a Subaltern manœuvre the Regiment which they did to my satisfaction.'

On the other hand, the Inspecting Officer considered the number of Courts Martial excessive, and he blamed Lieut.-Colonel Dennie, who was in temporary command, for deviating from the system established by Lieut.-Colonel Sale, with whom, it appears, he was not on good terms.

Other criticisms of interest are:—

'Major Johnson—the only field officer present is qualified in other respects, but is certainly very slow in taking up points in the field, from, I think, timidity on Horseback.

'The Talents and acquirements of the Adjutant cannot be surpassed by any Adjutant in the Service. He is now in Arrest (*sic*) and the duty is performed by Lieut. Keating.

'Lieut. Foulston is not fit for the duties of a Light Corps, he is 58 years of age, and has been much on the sick list since last Inspection.

'Captain Stehelin from physical infirmity is not considered capable of Active Service.'

In 1835 Havelock was appointed Adjutant of the 13th and his influence with his Commanding Officer soon made itself felt. Chapels were erected near the Regimental barracks both for the Church of England and the Baptists (Havelock belonging to the latter denomination). A temperance society was started, of which it is stated that Colonel Sale and Captain Chadwick were members, and a Coffee Room built as a counter-attraction to the Canteen.

The Regiment was again inspected by Major-General the Hon. J. Ramsay at Agra on 7th December 1835. The following are extracts from his report:—

'I inspected His Majesty's 13th Light Infantry at Agra, and cannot speak too highly of the excellent discipline and high order in which I found His Majesty's 13th Light Infantry, and it fully equals what from my former experience I expected to find it.

'I saw it go through its different movements with the greatest correctness and precision, and it appeared to me to be well grounded in the Light Infantry Drill. I am sorry to have to report so many Courts Martial which proceeded from habitual drunkenness. Drunk on duty, and selling various articles of clothing are the chief crimes for which they have been brought forward, but I trust, the examples that have been made, and the certainty of punishment for their crimes, will prevent a repetition of them for the future.

'The greatest unanimity seems to prevail among the officers of the Regiment.

'The Ball practice was very good.

'Lieuts. Wade and Keating are well calculated for Adjutants and will make good ones.

'No deviations in Dress are allowed.'

Major Johnson is again reported as a bad horseman. Lieutenant Foulston's health is stated to have improved and that officer is reported to be still active though old.

Colonel Sale reports that he has known Lieutenant Stehelin for upwards of ten years and always considered him incapable of any Active Service.

Shortly after this inspection the Regiment left Agra and marched to Kurnaul where they arrived in January 1836.

In February 1837 two companies, consisting of 9 officers, 13 serjeants, 6 drummers and 193 rank and file, under the command of Captain Nicholas Chadwick, were selected to accompany the Commander-in-Chief, General Sir

Henry Fane, G.C.B., on a visit to the Ruler of the Sikhs, Maharajah Runjeet Singh, at Lahore, the chief city of his dominions. After a toilsome journey Sir Henry arrived there on the 10th of March, and was greeted by a grand display of Oriental magnificence. The British troops of all arms, which accompanied him, were reviewed, on the 17th March, by the Maharajah, who expressed great admiration of their appearance and discipline and, in a general order published immediately after the review, it was stated: 'The Commander-in-Chief has much pleasure in communicating to the officers, non-commissioned officers, and soldiers of the escort, that their appearance and steadiness under arms this morning met with much approbation, and their performance of the various movements will leave in the Punjaub a very favourable impression of their discipline.'

Very valuable presents were made to the officers of the escort, and the Maharajah also gave eleven thousand rupees (£1,100) to be distributed among the non-commissioned officers and soldiers.

After remaining about seven weeks at the Sikh capital, the Commander-in-Chief commenced his journey back to the British dominions, and the officers and soldiers of the 13th Light Infantry rejoined the Regiment at Kurnaul, towards the end of April.

The inspection report for this year by Brig.-General A. Duncan contains the following remarks:—

'Major Johnson is qualified for command, but Colonel Sale represents that Major Tronson has not made himself sufficiently acquainted with the Drill Regulations.

. . . .

'The 13th Light Infantry is in a highly efficient state, remarkably steady under Arms, and correct in Field Movements.

'The Temperance Society established in the Regiment by Colonel Sale has been joined by 274 Persons.'

On the 5th June 1838 the Regiment was again inspected by Major-General A. Duncan commanding the Sirhind Division. The following extracts are of interest:—

'H.M. 13th Light Infantry is in a highly efficient state, steady under Arms and correct in the performance of Field Movements.

'Courts Martial continue to be numerous, but they appear all to be held on the same set of men for habitual drunkenness.

'The hearing of Majors Johnson and Tronson is stated by Colonel Sale to be impaired and both are bad horsemen.

'Private Owen Kileen, No. 9 Company, complained that he had been made to pay the full price of a new musket and that the one he broke was not given to him; he claims the broken Musket as his own property or some remuneration for it; the Commander-in-Chief's decision is solicited upon this point.'

During July, August, and September of this year the Regiment suffered considerably from cholera and fever, but in the latter month the health of the men improved.

In 1838 Havelock was promoted Captain without purchase. He was then 43 years of age and had seen twenty-three years' service. In his correspondence with his friends Havelock used frequently to parody one of Byron's couplets as follows:—

> Nought's permanent among the human race,
> Except that Havelock ne'er will get that place!

CHAPTER XIV

WAR IN AFGHANISTAN

DURING the years 1837 and 1838 events occurred which were fraught with momentous consequences.

A Persian army encouraged by the Russians was besieging Herat on the border of Afghanistan, while the court of Persia claimed an extensive portion of that kingdom, apparently with the intention to menace the safety of the British Dominions in the East Indies. Shah Shoojah, a dethroned monarch of Afghanistan, was living in exile in the Punjaub. Runjeet Singh, the great ruler of the Sikhs, and a firm ally of the British, had been attacked by Dost Mahomed Khan, the dominant Afghan chief. These circumstances led to the conclusion of a tripartite treaty between the British, Runjeet Singh, and Shah Shoojah, for the purpose of restoring the dethroned Monarch; and to effect this, an Anglo-Indian force was to be assembled, which was named the 'Army of the Indus'.

The force was to consist of one brigade artillery, one brigade cavalry, and five brigades of infantry, distributed into two divisions, one commanded by Sir Willoughby Cotton and the other commanded by Major-General A. Duncan.

In addition a Bombay contingent, consisting of one brigade cavalry, one brigade artillery and one brigade infantry, was to proceed to Karachi under Sir John Keane,[1] a former officer of the Regiment, while Shah Shoojah, helped by British Officers, raised an irregular corps of 5,000 to 6,000 Indian troops.

On the 8th November the 13th Light Infantry, who had been selected to form part of the force, began their march from Kurnaul to Ferozepore and arrived at that station on 26th November, where the Bengal troops were being assembled.

Havelock in commenting on their concentration writes: 'A force has never been brought together in any country in a manner more creditable and soldier-like, than was the Bengal portion of the Army of the Indus.'

Whilst this concentration was going on, news arrived that the Persians had raised the siege of Herat. The Commander-in-Chief, General Sir Henry Fane, then decided that the Army might be reduced in strength and he did so by the unusual method of casting lots which brigades should go forward. The

---

[1] He was an Officer of the Regiment 'from 1803 to 1812.' He became Lieutenant-Colonel in the 13th Regiment on the 20th August 1803. Joined the Regiment at Gibraltar early in 1804, returned home with it in 1805 and served several years in Ireland. He accompanied the Regiment to Bermuda as junior Lieutenant-Colonel and commanded the Regiment at the reduction of Martinique in 1809. Appointed Brevet-Colonel in January 1812 when he was transferred to the 60th Regiment.

lot fell on the 1st (to which the 13th belonged), the 2nd, and 4th Infantry Brigades; the 3rd and 5th Infantry Brigades to be left behind.

Havelock comments as follows on this proceeding:—

'It sent forth to the labours of the campaigns the 13th Light Infantry, then as ever zealous indeed and full of alacrity, but even at Ferozepore shattered by disease; the spirit of its soldiers willing, but unequal to the task; whilst it doomed to inactivity the Buffs, one of the most effective corps in India.'

Such is the impartial testimony of an officer of the Regiment.

The historian Kaye adds: 'No one would now regret the chance which sent Sale and Dennie into Afghanistan and associated the name of the 13th Light Infantry with some of the most illustrious incidents of the war.'

Before the Army of the Indus set forth on the campaign a series of durbars, entertainments and reviews took place in conjunction with the Sikh Army under the redoubtable Maharajah Runjeet Singh, 'The Lion of the Punjaub', which were conducted with great magnificence. One of these reviews is described by Havelock as follows: 'Under cover of the cloud of skirmishers composed of the whole of the 13th Light Infantry in extension, which the two native regiments of the brigade supported, battalions, regiments, troops, and batteries now broke into column, and regained their original line, and then in long and splendid array the whole force defiled in open column past the astonished and delighted Maharajah.' It is noteworthy that on this occasion the troops of Runjeet Singh were manœuvred by French officers, who were their instructors.

At this time the River Sutlej formed roughly the north-western boundary of British India. The Punjaub dominated by the Sikhs was outwardly friendly to the British, but the Chiefs were jealous of the power of the British, while the Khyber Pass, the direct line of advance to Kabul, had even then an evil reputation. Moreover, as has been already mentioned, a contingent from Bombay was to co-operate in the invasion of Afghanistan advancing from the sea up the valley of the Indus.

In these circumstances it was decided that the Army of the Indus should march down the left bank of the Sutlej to where it joins the Indus and effect its junction with the Bombay contingent at Sukkur, cross the Indus, proceed to Quetta by the Bolan Pass and thence on to Kandahar and Kabul, a distance of 1,500 miles as against 450 miles via Peshawur and the Khyber Pass.

Nor was the length of the line of advance the only disadvantage. The country through which the army was to march was practically unknown, having only been traversed by a few European travellers and British political officers, and its capability of feeding an army a matter of conjecture. Moreover, the attitude of the Ameers of Scinde and the Khan of Kelat through whose territory the march was to be made, was extremely doubtful, while it was confidently expected that little or no opposition would be offered by the Afghans, a contingency which was belied by subsequent events.

In consequence of the reduction of the army Sir Henry Fane, the Commander-in-Chief, gave up the command to Sir John Keane, though he accompanied the Bengal contingent to Sukkur on his way to England. The Bengal contingent was commanded by Sir Willoughby Cotton, K.C.B., K.C.H., who selected Havelock as his A.D.C. The 1st Brigade, consisting of the 13th L.I., 16th and 48th Native Infantry Regiments, was commanded by Colonel Robert Henry Sale, C.B., and the 2nd Brigade temporarily by Lieut.-Colonel William Henry Dennie, C.B., in the absence of Major-General Nott.

The officers of the Regiment who were present with the Regiment at the commencement of the campaign were Major Edward T. Tronson, commanding the Regiment; Captains George Fothergill, William Sutherland, James Kershaw, Robert Pattison, John George Dalhousie Taylor, and Horatio Nelson Vigors; Lieutenants Arthur Philip Savage Wilkinson, James H. Fenwick, John Foulston, Peter Raymond Jennings, Philip D'Ormieux Von Streng, Alexander Essex Frederick Holcombe, George King, Rollo Gillespie Burslem, Frederick Holder, William Alexander Sinclair, Hon. Emilius J. W. Forester, Thomas Oxley, and David Rattray; Ensigns Edward King, George Mein and Richard Edward Frere; Paymaster Harry Carew; Adjutant Hamlet C. Wade; Assistant Surgeons John Robertson, M.D., and George West Barnes, M.D. In addition Captain Tristram Charnley Squire was Major of Brigade, Lieutenant John Stewart Wood A.D.C. to Sale, and Ensign George Wade A.D.C. to Dennie.

The strength of the army at Ferozepore exclusive of Shah Shoojah's contingent was 9,500 fighting men accompanied by 40,000 followers and a transport column of 30,000 camels.

On 2nd December Shah Shookah's native levies, under Major-General Simpson, commenced their march, followed on the 10th by the British in five columns at one day's interval in the following order—Sappers and Miners, Cavalry Brigade, 1st, 2nd and 4th Infantry Brigades.

On 29th December. Headquarters reached Bahawulpore and the army closed up.

On 1st January 1839 the march was resumed. Khanpur was reached on 8th January and the borders of Scinde crossed on the 14th. Towards the end of December Sir John Keane, with the Bombay contingent, had landed at the mouth of the Indus. Between 11th January and 17th: Shah Shoojah's contingent crossed the Indus in boats at Goth Amil and marched to Shikarpore, while on the 24th the main army reached Rohri opposite Sukkur and came in sight of the Indus which at that place was over half a mile broad. Between Rohri and Sukkur and 800 yards from Rohri the rocky island fortress of Bukkur divided the river into two parts. It was at this spot that the Commander-in-Chief determined to build a bridge of boats. After some lengthy negotiations with Meer Roostem, the ruler of Khyrpore, that chief handed over to the British the island of Bukkur on 28th January, and to mark the occasion the 13th L.I. furnished a guard of honour to that chief. The assembling of the bridge of boats was at once commenced.

Meanwhile Sir John Keane had arrived at Jerrak, two marches south of Hyderabad. He found the Ameers of Scinde disposed to dispute his further advance. Consequently Sir Willoughby Cotton, with the cavalry and 1st and 2nd Infantry Brigades, marched south on 30th January from Rohri towards Hyderabad, and after having accomplished 60 miles of his march, he received news that the Ameers had given in, and would allow the Bombay contingent to advance, much to the disappointment of the troops, for it was reported that in Hyderabad there was treasure amounting to over eight crores of rupees. After halting a few days Sir Willoughby Cotton returned with his force to Rohri, and commenced crossing the Indus, which was completed by 18th February. The Bengal contingent then marched to Shikarpore where Headquarters were established on the 20th.

The distance between Shikarpore and Dadeer, the eastern entrance of the Bolan pass, is 170 miles, of which the Desert of Usted forms the greater part.

On 22nd February the march was resumed, Shah Shoojah's troops now forming the rear contingent of the Bengal Army. The 1st (Sale's) Brigade reached Dadeer on 14th March after sixteen marches, but the losses in camels had been enormous, and as there were only supplies for one month left, the followers were placed on half-rations.

The Bolan Pass, 60 miles long, is a narrow rocky defile commanded by heights on either side, at that time of year covered by snow and without a trace of vegetation, but water was to be had in plenty from the stream which traverses its entire length. The local tribesmen were ever on the watch to cut off stragglers and raid the baggage columns.

On 16th March the passage of the Bolan Pass was commenced, and on the very first day the dhooly bearers of the 13th deserted in a body, leaving forty sick men, but were pursued and brought back. Many camels perished from want of fodder. Six days were occupied in traversing the Pass, during which the column constantly crossed and re-crossed the stream. Havelock describes the following scene which was probably typical of this portion of the march:—

'The pass of Beebee Nanee was seen to peculiar advantage this morning at the moment at which the 13th passed it. They halted a few moments to close up the rear of the column after crossing the nullah, and then advanced by bugle signal which rang out amidst the caverns and lofty peaks. They formed, during their short pause of rest, finely grouped figures in the mountain picture and these soldiers with their shoes off and trousers tucked up to the knees after fording, their bronzed countenances, and drenched and faded uniforms, recalled those ideas of active service which a long period of inactivity had banished.'

On the 22nd the 1st (Sale's) Brigade emerged from the Pass and reached Sar-i-ab, 10 miles south of Quetta, and by the 26th there were assembled at the latter place the cavalry, the 1st Brigade, and Headquarters. One-third of the camels had been lost, there were practically no local supplies to be obtained, and there remained but ten days' rations for the troops and two days' grain for the horses. Kandahar was 150 miles distant, and Shikarpore, the nearest depôt for supplies, was 200 miles in rear. The troops were placed on half-rations and the followers on quarter-rations.

Nor was the scarcity of supplies the only source of anxiety to the Commander-in-Chief. The local tribesmen were continually harassing the line of march. On 31st March some Kalsur freebooters raided about forty camels. Five companies of the 13th and a troop of cavalry were sent in pursuit, but failed to come up with the raiders, though a couple of days later the cavalry in a skirmish killed and captured a few of them.

On 6th April Sir John Keane, with the Bombay contingent, reached Quetta, when Sir Willoughby Cotton resumed command of the 1st Division, and General Nott that of the 2nd Brigade, consequently Lieut.-Colonel Dennie reverted to the command of the Regiment.

On 7th April General Nott, with the 2nd Brigade, being left as garrison of Quetta, the army proceeded on its march to Kandahar, at first through the vale of Shawl, then descending the picturesque height of Kotul into the Valley of Pesheen; the army arrived at the foot of the Khojak Pass on the 14th. It took seven days to cross this Pass as the guns had to be man-handled over many parts of the track. Moreover, water was extremely scarce, the loss in camels and horses continued to increase, and it was not till the 23rd, when the army reached the banks of the Dooree, that the sufferings to man and beast from thirst ceased. Since leaving India, it is stated, no less than 20,000 camels perished.

The rulers of Western Afghanistan on the approach of the British Army fled in dismay from Kandahar; some indeed surrendered, but the majority disappeared to await a better opportunity of harassing the invaders. On 26th April Shah Shoojah and the British troops entered Kandahar without opposition. The Bengal contingent had marched 1,000 miles in 137 days.

Kandahar was a walled city 6,000 yards in circumference, the walls, 33 feet high, and flanked by sixty-two towers, were capable of offering a strong defence, but the inhabitants, though not disposed to welcome Shah Shoojah, received him politely.

The troops encamped outside the town on grassy meadows, provisions were fairly plentiful, markets were opened, and a considerable trade, especially in horses, of which the army was in great need, ensued.

On 4th May the Bombay brigade reached Kandahar and the army was complete. On the 8th the troops were reviewed by Shah Shoojah. On 12th May Brig.-General Sale, with two companies of the 13th, one squadron Bengal Light Cavalry, the 16th Native Infantry and 1,000 men of Shah Shoojah's contingent, set out against the fort of Girishk, 70 miles to the westward, which he occupied without opposition on the 15th, and towards the end of the month returned to Kandahar.

On 27th May Shah Shoojah held a public reception of the British Officers, at which every general officer presented him with twenty-five gold mohurs, every field officer five, and every captain and subaltern one gold mohur. It will occasion no surprise to learn that these sums had been previously doled out to the officers from the British Treasure Chest.

The health of the army at Kandahar was indifferent, fever, dysentery and jaundice being especially prevalent. On 4th June the fighting men, exclusive of sick, numbered 8,802, of whom the 13th accounted for 451.

The greater part of June was spent at Kandahar in making preparations for the advance on Kabul. No serious hostilities occurred, but any one who ventured beyond the line of outposts did so at his own risk, some officers were murdered, and it is related that a party of the 13th, who had been tempted to drive their animals and cattle too far to graze, were set upon and several of them wounded.

At length on 27th June everything was ready for the advance. A garrison of all arms being left in Kandahar, the army advanced on Ghazni in three columns at one day's interval: First column—Headquarters, Horse Artillery, 2 Brigades Cavalry, 1st (Sale's) Brigade Infantry, Camel Battery and 4th Local Horse; Second column—4th Brigade Infantry and Shah Shoojah's troops; Third column, Bombay Brigade Infantry, Poona Horse, and Bombay Artillery. The total strength of the Anglo-Indian Army was 7,800 troops; Shah Shoojah's numbered 2,000, and in addition there were 2,000 friendly Afghans. The siege train was left behind in Kandahar. The marches were made chiefly at night. On the 30th June the advance entered into the valley of the Tarnuk River and then proceeding up the right bank of that river, traversed the country of the Western Ghilzees and finally on 20th July arrived at Nanee, 11 miles from Ghazni. It was now ascertained that Ghazni, a fortress estimated by the Afghans to be well-nigh impregnable except by protracted siege operations, was garrisoned by 3,000 men under Prince Mahomed Hyder Khan, was well provided with stores, and in addition was surrounded by a wall 60 feet high and a wet ditch, thus rendering an assault by escalade impossible, while mining could be only undertaken at the gates. All the gates with the exception of the Kabul Gate had been bricked up.

THE STORMING OF GHAZNI

On 21st July Sir John Keane advanced from Nanee on Ghazni in five columns, the cavalry being on the right and the artillery in the centre. As soon as the skirmishers penetrated the gardens outside the walls, fire was opened by the enemy, which was replied to by the Camel Battery and some guns of the Bombay artillery. After an artillery duel of about an hour, during which Sale's Brigade advanced towards the ramparts of the southern face, the halt was sounded.

It was then decided to break off the engagement, and to march round the eastern face of the fortress, and to take up a position on the northern side opposite the Kabul Gate.

Accordingly at 4 p.m. the encircling movement began, the cavalry being on the right to protect the columns against the Ghilzee horsemen hovering in the neighbouring hills, and the infantry on the left nearest to the fortress.

The march continued well into the night, and it was not till the early hours of the morning that the troops took up their positions. The 1st Division, including Sale's Brigade, after ascending a lofty range of hills and descending into the plain on the other side, found themselves opposite the citadel and the north-western face of the fortress facing south. Shah Shoojah's troops were on the extreme left and next to them the cavalry and Bombay Infantry Brigade. In the centre were the artillery.

When dawn broke on the 22nd the baggage and supply columns were still far in rear, and it took the whole day to assemble them, and it was not till a late hour that the troops got their rations.

Havelock recounts the following anecdote of a soldier of the 13th:—

'A medical officer of the 13th reproved a sick soldier for want of care of his health on account of the manifest effect produced on his wasted frame by exposure to cold during this night—The man said in his defence, "Why, sir, what could I do? The black fellows set down my dhooly in the dark on the top of that mountain, and as I did not know how near the enemy might be, I was obliged to leap out, and take my arms, and stand sentry over myself the whole night."'

A new species of outpost duty.

During the day a company of the Regiment, under Captain William Sutherland, accompanied Captain Thomson, Bengal Engineers, on a reconnaissance of the fortress and lost one man killed and two wounded, and about 2 p.m. a considerable body of Afghan horsemen attacked the left rear of the British position but were speedily put to flight by the Shah Shoojah's troops and the British Cavalry.

In the light of the reconnaissance Sir John Keane now issued his orders for the assault which may be summarized as follows:—

The artillery to move at midnight and take up the positions allotted to them, they will be accompanied by the sappers and miners and six companies of native infantry as a support to the Engineers and escort to the guns.

The storming party will be under the command of Brigadier Sale, C.B., and will be composed as follows:—

'An advance' to consist of the light companies of H.M. 2nd and 17th Regiments, and of the European Regiment, and of a flank company of H.M. 13th L.I., the whole under the command of Lieut.-Colonel Dennie, C.B.

The main column will consist of H.M. 2nd Regiment, and the European Regiment, with the remainder of H.M. 13th L.I., formed as skirmishers on the flanks.

The whole of the storming party to be in position by 2 a.m.

The skirmishing line of the 13th to move forward at 2.30 a.m. to cover the front, and keep down any fire which may be opened on the Engineers who are to blow in the Kabul Gate.

Three companies of native infantry will march at midnight to the gardens on the southern face of the fortress and at 3 a.m. open fire to distract the fire of the garrison.

The remaining Infantry will form the reserve under Major-General Sir Willoughby Cotton.

One Regiment of Cavalry to move to the southern face of the fortress to cut off the retreat of the enemy. The remainder of the Cavalry to act as a corps of observation on the Kabul road.

The night was favourable; the wind blew in strong gusts from the east, so that the movements of the guns and troops were inaudible.

The operations were well timed. At about 3.30 a.m. the artillery and skirmishers of the 13th opened fire on the Kabul Gate and neighbouring ramparts; the Engineers, carrying 900 lb. of powder in twelve large bags, crept noiselessly up to the Kabul Gate, and the assaulting column was following slowly behind. The roll of musketry fire from the feint attack on the southern face could be distinctly heard. The Afghans, in anticipation of a general escalade, had manned all the ramparts.

Scarcely had day begun to break, when, after an explosion barely audible beyond the head of the column amidst the sighing of the boisterous wind, and the rattle of the cannonade, a pillar of black smoke was seen to rise, and then after a pause the bugle sound to advance was distinctly recognized. The Engineers had done their work boldly, prudently and skilfully. Immediately after the explosion a party of the 13th, under Lieutenant Peter Jennings, moved up with the Engineer officer to see if the operation had been attended with success, and having verified the fact that the Gate was blown in, the Advance was sounded, upon which the storming column under Lieut.-Colonel Dennie surged forward to the Gate, closely followed by Brigadier Sale with the main column.

Unfortunately at this juncture Brigadier Sale chanced to meet in the dim light of the morning an Engineer officer named Peat, evidently half-dazed and suffering from the effects of the explosion, and inquired of him whether the breach was feasible. The reply was that although the Gate was blown in, the passage was choked by the débris and that the storming party was unable to force an entrance. Sale considered that the advance under these circumstances would entail certain destruction, and ordered the retreat to be sounded. A few moments later he met another Engineer officer who told him that Dennie, with the storming party, had already won his way through the Gate, whereupon Sale recognizing his mistake gave orders for the Advance to be sounded, and the main column at once resumed its march. In Carter's *Records of the Regiment* it is stated that a certain Bugler Wilson of the 13th sounded the 'advance double' on his own initiative on this occasion. No corroboration of this statement can be found, and it is thought best to rely on Havelock's account who was an eye-witness.[1]

---

[1] There is a photograph of Bugler Wilson in the *Light Bob Gazette* of September 1912. He left his medals to Lord Cheylesmore. Old Wilson had some half-dozen extra clasps attached to his Jellalabad ribbon, which he had minted to his own order. An officer of the Regiment at the time gave the following account of Bugler Wilson to Major R. S. Clarke many years after:—

'I remember him well. He was the best bugler I ever heard. He had a small, short, shrill, brass Light Infantry bugle, but could be heard at any distance as distinguished in tone to other buglers. He was General Sale's bugler! Bugler Wilson's son was serving in the Regiment in 1877, the fourth generation of his family, his grandfather and great-grandfather having served in it as well.'

As a considerable gap existed between Dennie's and Sale's column, Sale and his men, on entering the fortress, were met by Afghans trying to get out of the Gate in rear of Dennie's column. A desperate encounter took place.

Sale himself, as had been his wont in the Burmese War, now became engaged in a personal combat with an Afghan who cut him down, and had it not been for the timely assistance of Captain Kershaw of the Regiment, matters might have gone badly with him.

Once inside the fortress the Afghan resistance was gradually overcome, and the Commander-in-Chief, Sir John Keane, gave orders that the Citadel should be attacked. The 13th and 17th Regiments, who were led by Brigadier Sale notwithstanding his wound, took part in this attack and in a few minutes, amidst general cheering from the troops, the colours of these Regiments were seen to be waving and flapping on the ramparts of the Citadel. Havelock narrates that the first standard to be planted was the regimental colour of the 13th Light Infantry, carried on that occasion by Ensign R. E. Frere.

Among the trophies captured by the Regiment in the storming of Ghazni were two small Afghan flags. In 1846 Lieut.-Colonel Squire of the Regiment gave the following account of their capture:—

'They were captured in a Redoubt at Ghazni by a party of the 13th, under Captain Wilkinson, who had been ordered to cut off the retreat of the enemy at that time escaping over the walls in great numbers by means of ropes fastened inside. This party in meeting with some resistance in their progress round the fortress suddenly found themselves in front of the Redoubt alluded to, from which the enemy were then firing; the men, however, undismayed, advanced and forced the outer door. The enemy now finding themselves assailed by the British both from the Fortress (which at this time had been captured) and by the party under the walls, ceased firing. The men had now reached the second door and rushed in, headed by Serjeant Smith, where, after mounting a narrow staircase (up which there was only room for one man to ascend at a time), they found themselves in the presence of the enemy, 75 of whom, with their Chief, Mahomed Khan, were made prisoners on the spot. The Colours were seized by Serjeant Smith, who for this gallant act was promoted to the rank of Colour-Serjeant on the first opportunity. In a short time after, Captain Wilkinson had arrived from a distant part of the field with the remainder of the party, where they had been engaged, and marched the whole of the prisoners up to Brigadier Sale's tent. The loss of the party in the encounter was, I am happy to say, trifling, owing no doubt to the fact of the enemy's attention being drawn towards the fortress.'

These two flags, together with another, captured subsequently at Jellalabad, were eventually presented to Her Majesty Queen Victoria, and by her handed over to Chelsea Hospital, who surrendered them to the Regiment about 1890, and they are now at the Depôt, Taunton.

Mahomed Hyder Khan, son of Dost Mahomed Khan, was among the captured. His sword, a valuable Persian blade which had been left in the

Zenana, was found by a soldier of the 13th, and made over to Brigadier Sale, who passed it on to the Commander-in-Chief.

The success of the victors was complete, their total losses amounting to 17 killed; and 18 officers and 147 other ranks wounded. The Regiment lost one killed and 20 wounded. Over 500 Afghans were killed, and 1,600 captured. Upwards of 1,000 horses, 300 camels, a large number of mules, and vast quantities of arms and stores of all kinds were captured, the fortress of Ghazni having been provisioned for a lengthy siege.

When the Afghan horsemen, who had assembled in the neighbourhood of Ghazni, learnt the fate of the fortress, they abandoned their camp equipage and baggage and fled towards Kabul.

The following are extracts from General Orders by H.E. Lieut.-General Sir John Keane, Commander-in-Chief, Army of the Indus, Headquarters, Ghazni, 23rd July:—

'Lieut.-General Sir John Keane most heartily congratulates the army which he has the honour to command on the signal triumph they have obtained in the capture by storm of the strong and important fortress of Ghazni. H.E. feels he can hardly do justice to the gallantry of the troops.

. . . .

'The advance under Lieut.-Colonel Dennie of H.M. 13th, consisting of the Light companies of H.M. 2nd and 17th and of the Bengal European Regiment with one company of H.M. 13th, and the leading column consisting of H.M. 2nd or Queen's under Major Carruthers, and the Bengal European Regiment under Lieut.-Colonel Orchard, followed by H.M. 13th L.I. as they collected from the duty of skirmishing which they were directed to begin with, and by H.M. 17th under Lieut.-Colonel Croker.

'To all these officers and gallant soldiers under their orders, His Excellency's best thanks are tendered; and in particular he feels deeply indebted to Brigadier Sale for the manner in which he conducted the arduous duty entrusted to him in command of the storming party. H.E. will not fail to bring it to the notice of his Lordship the Governor-General; and he trusts that the wound which Brigadier Sale has received is not of that severe nature long to deprive the army of his services. Brigadier Sale reports that Captain Kershaw of H.M. 13th Light Infantry rendered important assistance to him and the service in the storming.

'The Commander-in-Chief feels, and in which feeling he is sure he will be joined by the troops comprising the army of the Indus, that after the long and harassing marches they have made and the privations they have endured, the glorious achievement and the brilliant manner in which the troops have met and conquered their enemy, rewards them for it all. H.E. will only add, no army that has ever been engaged in a campaign deserves more credit than that which he has the honour to command, for patient, orderly, and cool conduct under all circumstances, and Sir John Keane is proud to have the opportunity of thus publicly acknowledging it.'

In Sir John Keane's dispatch of 24th July to Lord Auckland, the Governor-General, the following allusion is made to Brigadier Sale:—

'To Brigadier Sale, I feel deeply indebted for the gallant and soldierlike manner in which he conducted the responsible and arduous duty entrusted to him in command of the Storming party, and for the arrangements he made in the Citadel, immediately after taking possession of it. The sabre wound which he received in the face, did not prevent his continuing to direct his column until everything was secure, and I am happy in the opportunity of bringing to your Lordship's notice the excellent conduct of Brigadier Sale on this occasion.'

Colonel Dennie and Major Tronson of the 13th are also mentioned.

The dispatch containing Sir John Keane's account of the Storming of Ghazni evoked the following encomium from Lord Auckland:—

'The Storm of Ghazni is a great military achievement, which must ever rank among the most brilliant of the many triumphs which have signalized the exploits of our Armies in the East, and it must be a subject of heartfelt congratulation to your Excellency that a conquest marked by so signal a combination of judgement, science, discipline, and valour, and by so inconsiderable a loss of life to the troops under your command, should have been gained under your personal superintendence and directions.'

Dost Mahomed, at Kabul, on hearing of the capture of Ghazni, sent an envoy to Sir John Keane to treat for peace, but the negotiations coming to nothing, that Chief advanced to Ughandee and took up a position for the defence of the capital.

On 30th July Sir John Keane, after leaving a garrison in Ghazni, commenced his march to Kabul, the Bengal Division with the 13th L.I. leading. On 3rd August the army reached Sheikhabad, and on the 5th Ughandee, to find that Dost Mahomed had been deserted by his army, and had fled, accompanied by a select body of cavalry, abandoning his artillery amounting to 23 guns.

On 6th August Shah Shoojah and the British Army appeared before the walls of Kabul, and on the following day that monarch entered his capital without opposition after an exile of thirty years.

Thus after a march of 1,500 miles the conquest of a kingdom was achieved by British skill and enterprise, with trifling loss, and the army pitched its tents in a rich valley near the capital.

Meanwhile Colonel Wade with an independent force had been advancing from the Punjaub and had captured Ali Musjid in the Khyber Pass. On 3rd September he arrived at Kabul, bringing with him Prince Timour the heir-apparent, and establishing direct communications with India.

On 17th September a Durbar was held, followed by a race-meeting lasting five days. In fact, the troops settled down to the ordinary life of an Indian Cantonment. The political officers, who had accompanied the army, and who had to be consulted on every possible occasion, now assumed complete control.

It was assumed that Afghanistan could be held by a comparatively small force. The Bombay column commenced its march to India via Kandahar and the Bolan Pass, and in October Sir John Keane, with the troops destined for Bengal, set out for the Khyber Pass, accompanied as far as Jellalabad by Shah Shoojah and his court.

The 13th Light Infantry, the 35th Native Infantry and 3 guns of the 6th Light Field Battery moved into the Bala Hissar, the citadel of Kabul, and formed its garrison, under the command of Brigadier Dennie with Lieutenant H. C. Wade of the 13th as Brigade Major. Kandahar, Ghazni and Jellalabad were also held by British troops, the command of the troops in Afghanistan devolving on Sir Willoughby Cotton after the departure of Sir John Keane. Sir Robert Sale commanded in Eastern Afghanistan, Headquarters Kabul, and General Nott in Western Afghanistan, Headquarters Kandahar. Subsequently the 13th Light Infantry and other units engaged were rewarded with the royal authority to bear on the Regimental Colour the words 'Affghanistan' and *Ghuznee*' in consideration of the good conduct of those Corps during the Campaign in Afghanistan in 1839, and of the gallantry displayed by them at the Storm and Capture of Ghazni on the 23rd July in that year.

An order of merit was instituted by the Shah, called the Order of the 'Dooranee Empire', the decorations of which were conferred on the general and field officers; and Her Majesty was graciously pleased to grant permission to Sir Robert Sale to accept and wear the insignia of the first class, and Brevet Major James Kershaw and Adjutant Hamlet C. Wade, of the Regiment, the insignia of the third class of the Order. Brigadier W. H. Dennie was also awarded the insignia of the third class, but he refused to accept it, on the grounds that at the capture of Ghazni he was commanding a mixed force and therefore entitled to a higher class than third. It is impossible to deny that Dennie was hardly treated on that occasion.

Colonel Robert Henry Sale was advanced to the rank of Major-General and was appointed a Knight Commander of the Most Honourable Military Order of the Bath, Major Edward T. Tronson was promoted to the rank of Lieutenant-Colonel in the Army, and Captain James Kershaw to that of Major, for their services in the campaign; the promotions taking place from the 23rd July 1839, the date of the capture of Ghazni.

A medal was given by the restored monarch to the officers and soldiers present at the storming of that fortress, which Her Majesty Queen Victoria authorized them to receive and wear. The officers of the 13th who received this medal were:—

Brigadier Sir Robert Henry Sale, K.C.B.

Brigadier William Henry Dennie, C.B.

Major Edward T. Tronson, Major Tristram Charnley Squire.

Captains George Fothergill, William Sutherland, James Kershaw, Robert Pattison, John George Dalhousie Taylor, Horatio Nelson Vigors, Henry Havelock.

Lieutenants Arthur Philip Savage Wilkinson, James H. Fenwick, John

Foulston, Peter Raymond Jennings, Philip D'Ormieux Von Streng, Alexander Essex Frederick Holcombe, George King, Rollo Gillespie Burslem, John Stewart Wood, Frederick Holder, William Alexander Sinclair, Hon. Emilius J. W. Forester, Thomas Oxley, David Rattray.

Ensigns Edward King, George Mein, Richard Edward Frere, George Wade.

Paymaster Harry Carew, Adjutant Hamlet C. Wade.

Assistant Surgeons John Robertson, M.D., George West Barnes, M.D.

The Governor-General of India in General Orders dated 18th November 1839 congratulated the Army on the result of the Campaign and alluded to officers of the Regiment as follows:—

'Brigadier Sale, C.B., already honourably distinguished in the Annals of Indian warfare, who commanded the Storming Party at Ghazni. Lieut.-Colonel Dennie, C.B., who led the advance on the same occasion.'

The winter of 1839-40 was an unusually severe one, and the troops in Kabul (6,000 feet above sea-level) suffered accordingly.

Late in the year 1839 the 13th Light Infantry were inspected by Brigadier Dennie, C.B., as Major-General Sir Willoughby Cotton was unable to leave Jellalabad owing to the impassable nature of the roads. In this report two privates of the Regiment were recommended for the restoration of their service forfeited by desertion, having subsequently performed good and gallant service. They were Private Rogers, who lost an arm at the Storm of Ghazni, and Private Kay, whose conduct was reported as being good in quarters and in the field.

The monthly Court Martial Returns show that from 12th June 1839 to 30th January 1840 there was one General, one Garrison, and thirty Regimental Courts Martial. The number of lashes awarded was 2,500, and the amount inflicted 1,877. Sir Willoughby Cotton considered the number of lashes excessive but attributed it to the fact that the Regiment was most of the time before the enemy in the field.

The inspection reports for the year 1840 show that the clothing of the Regiment was worn out, none having been issued since 1838, but that their field equipment was in good order. The Regiment lost, since leaving Ferozepore at the end of 1838, two captains, four serjeants, six corporals, four buglers and ninety-seven privates; of these the following died at Kabul—two captains, four serjeants, four corporals, two buglers and forty-six privates.

Brigadier Dennie complained that the Regiment was chiefly recruited from Ireland and recommended an admixture of Englishmen, as they offered, from their habits and education, a better field for the selection of Non-commissioned officers.

The Adjutant-General annotated this complaint as follows: 'The Brigadier ought to know that, notwithstanding his objections, by far the larger proportion of the Non-commissioned officers of the Army is Irish.'

Regimental life in Kabul during the winter of 1839-40 and the summer of 1840 may be described as similar to that in an Indian cantonment. Officers and men indulged in skating, cricket, racing and other sports. The post from India was fairly regular, and the wives of some of the officers were able to join their husbands, while much-needed drafts helped to replenish the ranks. Sir William Macnaghten, the British Minister and Envoy at the Court of Kabul, was optimistic on the prospects of the occupation of the country, but as a matter of fact Shah Shoojah was far from popular, and his authority only extended to places occupied by Anglo-Indian troops, and when Dost Mahomed, who after the occupation of Kabul had fled to Bokhara, escaped from that place on 17th July and was reported as advancing on Bameean, many discontented Afghan chiefs rallied to his standard and it was found necessary for the British to take the field again.

THE AUTUMN CAMPAIGN IN 1840

Early in September Brigadier Dennie, with the 35th Native Infantry and some guns, was dispatched to reinforce the post at Bameean, now threatened by Dost Mahomed with some 6,000 men. On 17th September he came up with the enemy and entirely defeated him. For this gallant action Brigadier Dennie and his troops were very highly commended by Major-General Sir Willoughby Cotton, the Commander-in-Chief, but Dost Mahomed was still at large and commanded a considerable following.

On 23rd September Sir Robert Sale, with the 13th not quite 400 strong, under Lieut.-Colonel Tronson, two companies of the 27th Native Infantry, two companies of the 37th Native Infantry, two squadrons 2nd Bengal Light Cavalry, 3 guns, and the 2nd Regiment of Shah Shoojah's Horse, left Kabul and marched northwards via Jerbon, Karrabagh and Robat to Charekar, which he reached on the 29th. On arriving at the latter place he learnt that Ali Khan, a refractory chief, was in position at Tootumdurra commanding the Ghoreband Pass. Moving forward at 8 a.m., the cavalry being in advance, Sale determined on attacking. The village of Tootumdurra commanded the entrance to the Pass and was flanked on either side by small detached forts.

While one company of the 37th Native Infantry, a party of Shah Shoojah's 2nd Cavalry and two 6-pounders attacked the forts on the left, and two companies of the 13th, under Lieutenant Holkham, aided by artillery, attacked the forts on the right, the main body, consisting of the remainder of the 13th, two companies of the 27th Native Infantry and the light company of the 37th Native Infantry, advanced on the village. All three attacks were completely successful, and the enemy fled. The loss of the 13th was limited to two privates wounded, one mortally.

On the 3rd October the Regiment was more seriously engaged. While in camp at Charekar, Sale learnt that several rebel chieftains were holding some forts at Julgar about 16 miles distant. Sending his cavalry forward at 1 a.m., he instructed them to surround the forts until such time as the infantry and artillery could come up. This they succeeded in doing. The 13th arrived at 10 a.m., followed later by some of the artillery, but the mortars did not arrive till 4 p.m. As time was pressing it was deemed inadvisable to wait for the heavy ordnance, and after a short bombardment, a storming party under Lieut.-Colonel Tronson of the 13th, consisting of five companies of that Regiment under Brevet Major Kershaw, and detachments of the 27th and 37th Native Regiments, advanced to the assault. The scaling ladders, hastily improvised from the poles used in carrying the litters for the sick, unfortunately proved too short, and although the troops acted with great gallantry and Brevet Major Kershaw, Lieutenant and Adjutant Wood, Lieutenants Edward King and George Wade at one time attained the crest of the breach, the assault was repulsed. Serjt.-Major Airey and fourteen men of the Regiment were killed, and Lieutenant and Adjutant Wood, three serjeants, two corporals and twelve privates were wounded. Serjeant Hurst of the 13th, unable to move from his wounds, was carried off by Lieutenant King; and a sepoy was in like manner conveyed to the rear, under a most terrific fire, by Private Thomas Robinson of the Regiment.

It was subsequently determined to renew the attack, when it might be made by a combined movement with better chance of success, but the Afghans, notwithstanding the precautions taken to intercept them, succeeded in escaping from the fort before 7 p.m., at which hour the British took possession, and measures were taken for its destruction.

Major-General Sir Willoughby Cotton in forwarding to the Government of India Sir Robert Sale's dispatch on this action comments as follows:—

'Although the attack was unfortunately not successful the conduct of the storming party, consisting of the Detachment of H.M. 13th Light Infantry under Brevet Major Kershaw, and the detachments of the 27th and 37th Regiments of Native Infantry, the whole under the command of Brevet Lieut.-Colonel Tronson of Her Majesty's 13th Light Infantry, appears to have been characterized by the most determined bravery and steady courage.'

The 13th came again in contact with the enemy on the 19th October at Babookoosghur, when they were attacked in camp at night, but experienced little loss, and on the 21st took part in the capture of the town of Khandurrah. On 2nd November Sale learnt that Dost Mahomed was at Purwan, north-east of Charekar, on the right bank of the Ghoreband; he accordingly broke up his camp, and advanced on the enemy's position. The advanced guard consisted of four companies of the 13th, the two flank companies of the 37th Native Infantry, one company of the 27th Native Infantry, 2 guns, two squadrons of the 2nd Light Cavalry and 200 of Anderson's Horse, the whole under the command of Colonel Salter, while Sale followed with the main body. The strength of the enemy was estimated at 500 horse and 3,500 foot. On nearing the enemy's position the 2nd Cavalry moved to the right and Anderson's Horse to the left of the Afghans; the infantry and guns being about a mile in rear, when suddenly a body of 200 Afghan horsemen charged the 2nd Cavalry, who broke and fled. Notwithstanding, the infantry, supported by the guns, continued to advance, when the enemy retired in a leisurely manner.

This action was an undoubted success for the enemy, but it had a curious sequel. Dost Mahomed on the following day, accompanied by a single retainer, delivered himself up to the British authorities in Kabul. The purpose of the campaign having been accomplished, Sale's column returned to Kabul on 8th November.

On 12th November Dost Mahomed Khan, under a strong escort, started for India, and at the same time Sir Willoughby Cotton proceeded to that country, when the command in Afghanistan devolved temporarily on Sir Robert Sale.

In December Shah Shoojah and the Court proceeded to Jellalabad for the winter.

CHAPTER XV

FROM KABUL TO JELLALABAD

THE year 1841 in Kabul commenced in calm and peace; it was destined to end in disaster and dishonour.

The envoy, Sir William Macnaghten, was optimistic as to the future; he had succeeded in obtaining possession of the person of Dost Mahomed, his most formidable opponent, and by transporting him to India he thought that by judicious administration the country would settle down.

There were not wanting, however, indications that Afghanistan was seething with discontent beneath the surface, for the rule of Shah Shoojah was extremely unpopular, and possible only because it was upheld by British bayonets, nor is it too much to say that the invaders were cordially hated.

Shelton's Brigade, including the 44th Regiment, had reached Jellalabad from India early in January, and on 1st February Sir Willoughby Cotton informed the Commander-in-Chief in India that there was no reason why the 13th Light Infantry, three battalions of Native Infantry and two batteries, who had been nearly three years on active service, should not return to India.

Sir Willoughby Cotton was relieved of the chief command in Afghanistan about the same time, and was succeeded by General Elphinstone; a most unfortunate appointment, as this officer, a most gallant gentleman, was crippled with gout, and plainly incapable of exercising his command efficiently. He arrived in Kabul towards the end of April.

Ensign Stapylton joined the Regiment at this time. He was afterwards Lieut.-General E. G. Chetwynd-Stapylton, who died in 1915 at the age of 92, and he has left on record a most interesting diary. He left Gravesend with a detachment of ninety men of the 13th on the 8th November 1839, sailed round the Cape of Good Hope and arrived at Calcutta on 21st July 1840; he then proceeded by boat to Cawnpore, and from thence marched to Kabul via Meerut, Ferozepore, Peshawar, and Jellalabad, arriving at his destination on 21st April 1841; a journey of seventeen months, which well illustrates the length of time it took in those days to send out reinforcements from England to the seat of war.

The summer of 1841 passed peacefully enough in Eastern Afghanistan. Shelton's Brigade had arrived in Kabul on 10th June, and it was expected that Sale's Brigade would shortly return to India.

With the approach of autumn, the country between Kabul and Jellalabad became very disturbed. Perhaps the immediate cause was the cutting down of the subsidies paid to local chiefs for keeping the peace along the line of communications with India. This in itself should not have proved serious had it not been for the fact that there was friction between the Civil and Military authorities, due entirely to the extraordinary system of command that obtained. The military authorities were completely under the control of the political department. The Envoy, Sir William Macnaghten, described by the Duke of Wellington as 'The gentleman employed to command the Army', not only ordered operations in the field, but did so entirely without any regard to military considerations and in this respect he was faithfully imitated by all his subordinates. No force could take the field unless it was accompanied by a political officer. The only general in Afghanistan to make a stand against this system, was General Nott, commanding at Kandahar, and he incurred the displeasure not only of the Envoy but also of the Government of India.

The new Commander-in-Chief in Afghanistan, General Elphinstone, infirm in body, and suffering from disease, was a military chief after the Envoy's own heart; he could be calculated on to do what he was told, and not to cause trouble.

Again many of the political officers were but junior officers, but lately Majors and Captains in the Indian Army, and it was these officers that the Commanders in the Field had to consult on every possible occasion. They took the credit when the operations were successful, and laid the blame on the soldiers when they failed.

It is no wonder that such a system destroyed the initiative of the Generals, caused general dissatisfaction among the officers, and gradually undermined the reliance of the rank and file in the leadership of their superiors.

On 9th October Lieut.-Colonel Monteith, with the 35th Native Infantry and 2 guns, proceeded to Bootkhak, 9 miles from Kabul at the entrance of the Khoord Kabul Pass. On the night of the 10th they were heavily attacked and suffered severe losses. Consequently Sir Robert Sale, with the 13th Light Infantry, nearly 800 strong, four companies sappers and miners, 2 guns of Abbott's battery, and some cavalry, were sent to Bootkhak on the 11th and joined forces the same evening.

On 12th October Sale, taking with him the 35th Native Infantry, besides his own troops, proceeded at daybreak to force the Khoord Kabul Pass. They were strenuously opposed by the enemy, who were concealed in large numbers among the rocks on the almost precipitous faces of the Pass, and who had constructed a breastwork in the centre of the defile which they allowed the advance guard almost to reach before they showed themselves. Suddenly a tremendous fire was opened on the head of the column, when General Sale was wounded severely in the ankle. The command then devolved on Colonel Dennie, who lost no time in clearing the heights commanding the Pass, and the whole force eventually arrived at Khoord Kabul. Dennie on this occasion spoke with admiration of 'the fearless manner in which the men of the 13th, chiefly young soldiers, ascended the heights nearly perpendicular under the sharp fire of the insurgents'. The whole force had fifty casualties, those of the 13th amounting to three killed and twenty-four wounded. Among the wounded, in addition to Sale, were Captain H. C. Wade, Major of Brigade, Lieutenant G. Mein, and

Ensign Oakes. Lieutenant Mein was dangerously wounded in the head, and was subsequently sent back to Kabul.

After the action Sale, leaving the 35th Native Infantry at Khoord Kabul, returned to Bootkhak with the remainder of his force. The enemy having now evacuated the Khoord Kabul Pass, Sale's force remained at Bootkhak from the 13th to the 20th October, during which time they were constantly harassed by night attacks, called by the enemy 'Shub Khoon' (night slaughter), which caused some loss and might have been much greater had not Sale prohibited night firing by which the position of the defences could be detected by the enemy. The troops were ordered to rely on the bayonet alone.

On 20th October Sale, having been reinforced by the 37th Native Infantry, a regiment of the Shah's cavalry, a Mountain train, and the remainder of Abbott's battery, marched to Khoord Kabul without opposition.

Sale now had under his command the 13th, the 35th and 37th Native Infantry Regiments, Sappers and Miners under Captain G. Broadfoot, Mountain train under Captain Backhouse, one troop 2nd Cavalry, one squadron 5th Bengal Cavalry, one Battery Artillery under Captain Abbott, and 200 Irregular Cavalry. Captain H. C. Wade of the 13th, was Major of Brigade, Captain Henry Havelock of the 13th, Aide-de-Camp to Sale, and Captain Macgregor political officer. The enemy were reported to be concentrating at Tezin and the whole country between Kabul and Jellalabad was in a state of insurrection.

On 22nd October Sale marched to Tezin (17 miles), though not without opposition; the advance guard, which included Lieutenant King's and Lieutenant Rattray's companies of the 13th drove the enemy from some heights and pursuing too far, had to retire. Lieutenant King, a promising young officer, who fell at the head of his company while gallantly charging the enemy, was killed, and Lieutenant R. E. Frere was wounded. In addition three privates were killed and nine rank and file wounded. At Tezin a welcome supply of two days' forage was found. On the following day Sale made dispositions to attack a neighbouring fort when the Ghilzai Chief sent in a proposal to Macgregor to tender his submission and begging that the stronghold might be spared. Negotiations were opened and continued till the 25th, when Macgregor agreed to restore the old scale of subsidy to the Chiefs and the fort was spared on hostages being given.

This is a typical example of the interference by a political officer in the military operations. To Sale's credit it may be noted that he issued the following order: 'Though the enemy have given hostages it would be both imprudent and unsafe in us to relax our vigilance.'

On 26th October the 37th Native Infantry, three companies Sappers and Miners and half the Mountain Train were sent back to Kabar Jabar on the way to Kabul owing to the want of transport. It may be mentioned that the camels had been dying thirty or forty a day, owing to lack of forage. Sale, with the remainder of his force, in accordance with orders from Kabul, continued his march eastwards towards Gandamak. On the 26th he reached Seh Baba, the rear-guard being attacked but not seriously. On the 27th he marched to

Kuttur Sung, when the rear-guard was in action all day, being aided by Captain Wilkinson's company of the 13th, who held the summit of the Pass near Bareek-Aab. On the 28th the column gained Peribagh in the Jagdalak Pass.

On 29th October the enemy were found in force at the Jagdalak Pass. The first three miles entailed a steep climb upwards and after attaining the summit a gradual decline to Gandamak. Excellent dispositions were made by the advance guard in capturing the heights at the summit of the Pass, and it is stated that Serjeant Thomas Hoban of the 13th, in command of a party of six men, mounted the highest point of the Pass, and took possession of it from the enemy, and again, with a similar number, captured a breastwork from a party of Afghans thrice his strength. It was quite otherwise with the rear-guard, which consisted of two companies of the 13th, two companies of 35th Native Infantry, Lieutenant Dawes and 2 guns, and one company of the Sappers and Miners. They were heavily attacked before they left camp and thrown into confusion and saved only by the efforts of some British officers and a gallant stand made by Broadfoot's sappers until reinforcements arrived from the main body, when the march was continued in security. In this action a gallant officer, Captain Wyndham of the 35th Native Infantry, seeing a soldier of the 13th badly wounded, got off his pony and placed the disabled soldier on it. As the Captain was himself lame, he could not keep pace with the men who were hurrying up the steep slope and stony gully, and was killed.

It seems that the main body, owing to the easy success of the advance guard, pushed on too far on attaining the summit of the Pass and did not wait for the rear-guard to close up. The blame must be attached either to Sale or to Dennie. Sale it may be observed was, owing to his wound, still being carried in a dhooly. The rear-guard reached Surkhab, the halting-place at nightfall. The total British casualties amounted to 120. One British officer was killed. The 13th lost four men killed, three officers, Lieutenants P. R. Jennings, A. E. F. Holcombe, David Rattray and forty-two men wounded. In addition seventy camels were lost. Lieut.-Colonel Dennie, Captains Wilkinson, Havelock, Wade (Brigade Major) and Fenwick were specially mentioned in Major-General Sir Robert Sale's dispatch.

On 30th October Sale's force reached Gandamak, then a cantonment, which was garrisoned by Shah Shoojah's troops consisting of one regiment of cavalry, one regiment of Infantry (Khyberis) and 200 Irregulars under British officers.

On 4th November Sale's grass cutters were attacked by Afghans from the Mammoo Khel, a fort belonging to Afzul Khan Urzebegi. This Afghan Chief had been prominent in the disturbances in Kabul and had returned to Mammoo Khel to raise the country against the British. Macgregor sent him a request to appear in person at Sale's camp, presumably to explain the attack.

On 5th November Sale marched out of Gandamak against the fort of Mammoo Khel which he captured, and returned to Gandamak on the following day, when he received the news that a formidable insurrection had broken out in Kabul and that Sir Alexander Burnes, the Envoy's Assistant, had been killed. He also received an order from Sir William Macnaghten to return with his force to Kabul provided he could arrange for the security of his sick, wounded and baggage without endangering his force.

Sale, after consulting his officers, decided he could not obey Macnaghten's order. His main reasons were that he was encumbered with 300 wounded, and consequently that there was only sufficient transport for one day's rations, and two days' expenditure of ammunition. He suggested that the Kabul force should retire on Jellalabad. It will be noted that the order recalling Sale to Kabul emanated from the Envoy and not from Elphinstone, the Commander-in-Chief. It may also be recorded that General Nott, then at Kandahar, was summoned to Kabul, but he was unable to comply.

It is a moot point whether Sale could have returned, and if so, whether he could have saved the Kabul force. Herbert Edwardes says there were at least two men with Sale's Brigade who would have made all the difference, one, Havelock, who would have recalled the discipline and spirit of poor Elphinstone's subordinates, if mortal man could do it, and the other George Broadfoot, who in the last resort would have dared to supply the army with a leader.

Sale decided to proceed to Jellalabad, but on the 10th November most of his camel and pony drivers deserted, so it was decided to leave the camp, equipage and officers' baggage with Shah Shoojah's troops at Gandamak. At noon on 11th November Sale started for Jellalabad and marched to Futtehabad, 14 miles, but in the meantime the cantonment at Gandamak was attacked, the Shah's troops went over bodily to the enemy, but the infantry battalion of Khyberis stood by their European officers, and following Sale, rejoined his column.

On 12th November Sale marched to Jellalabad, but the rear-guard under Dennie was heavily attacked. A running skirmish, which lasted some miles, brought out the fine qualities of the troops and ended in the complete discomfiture of the enemy. Dennie placed the cavalry in ambush, brought up his infantry to attack, advanced firing, and then wheeled about as if in panic. The enemy pursued to the open space where the cavalry were free to act when the latter charged with great effect.

The very night of Sale's arrival at Jellalabad the cantonments were burnt presumably by the enemy and most of the inhabitants fled.

CHAPTER XVI

THE SIEGE OF JELLALABAD

THE town of Jellalabad (meaning the abode of splendour) was in form an irregular quadrilateral surrounded by a wall 2,300 yards in length with thirty-three bastions, but the fortifications were in a ruinous condition, and outside them, there were numerous walled gardens, mosques and ruined forts, giving excellent cover to the enemy. North, east, and west of the town at a distance of 500 yards there were the ruins of an old wall, on which the sand had accumulated so as to form a line of low heights, and to the south-west of the town and one quarter-mile distant was a collection of rocks afterwards called Pipers Hill owing to the fact that the enemy used to dance there to the tune of a bagpipe.

It was decided to occupy the town and not the citadel alone, as giving more freedom of action. The only troops outside the town were the Khyberies, who occupied the Mission compound. The troops had but two days' supplies.

The force at Sale's disposal consisted of the 13th Light Infantry, 700 strong, armed with unserviceable flint muskets which had recently been condemned by a Committee, but not withdrawn, although there were a large number of serviceable muskets in store at Kabul to replace them; the 35th Native Infantry, 750 strong; Broadfoot's Sappers, strength 150; 40 of the Shah's Infantry, one squadron 5th Bengal Cavalry, 130 strong, under Captain Oldfield, one rissalah Shah Shoojah's irregulars, 90 sabres. The artillery consisted of five 9-pounders, one 24-pounder, three 3-pounders, two 8-inch and three $5\frac{1}{2}$-inch mortars, under Captains Abbott and Backhouse. The troops had 120 rounds per musket, while gun ammunition was plentiful.

The enemy, strength about 6,000, at once closed in round the town, especially on the side of Piper's Hill, so on the 14th Sale ordered a sally. 300 men of the 13th, 300 of the 35th, 100 sappers and 2 guns, the whole under Lieut.-Colonel Monteith, attacked Piper's Hill, stormed the heights and then returned, the enemy losing 200 killed. In the meantime the Khyberies had been attacked in the Mission compound, and were forced to retire, but the squadron of 5th Cavalry relieved the situation by a successful charge.

As a result of this action the enemy kept at a respectful distance and the inhabitants of the neighbouring villages brought in supplies, so that provisions for a month on half-rations were soon collected.

The first duty of the garrison was to place the fortifications in an efficient state of defence, and it was fortunate that a very able Engineer officer, Captain Broadfoot, was available. He put his whole mind into the work, and soon all the troops available were busily engaged in demolishing the ruinous forts and old walls, filling up ravines, destroying gardens, cutting down groves, raising the parapets to six or seven feet high, repairing and widening the ramparts, extending the bastions, retrenching three of the gates, covering the fourth with an outwork, and excavating a ditch 10 feet in depth, and 12 feet in width round the whole of the walls. No one was allowed to be idle, officers as well as men taking their hand with spade or shovel. On this duty the 13th were conspicuous for their alacrity and indefatigable perseverance. Broadfoot, who was no admirer of Sale's, nor indeed of his troops when he compares them with his own sappers and miners, wrote a few days before: 'In spite of what has happened (referring to certain rear-guard actions), a finer brigade than Sale now has I would not desire to see.'

The officers of the 13th occupied the King's palace, while the men were quartered in numerous buildings outside the harem wall to the west.

A fortnight of comparative quiet now ensued, which enabled the garrison to remedy the worst defects of the defences, but on the 27th November the enemy again approached the town and occupied a fort 2 miles west of Jellalabad, when the inhabitants ceased bringing in supplies. Two days later the enemy occupied all the commanding ground outside the town, including Piper's Hill, and sent their skirmishers continually nearer the town, so that the working parties had to cease work.

On 1st December Sale determined to make another sally, and this time Dennie was in command. The 13th supplied 300 men, the 35th Native Infantry 300, while the sappers and miners, the cavalry and 2 guns also took part. At 1 p.m. they issued from the main gate and made straight for the enemy, who were commanded by Azeez Khan. The infantry carried the hills at the point of the bayonet in fine style, while the cavalry completed the defeat of the enemy by repeated charges. Serjeant Hoban again distinguished himself by twice defeating opponents in single combat. The enemy lost 150 men, while there were no casualties on the British side. After this brilliant action the garrison was left unmolested for six weeks and the villagers again brought in supplies.

Every garrison in Afghanistan, including Kabul, Kandahar, Ghazni, and Charekar, was now closely blockaded, communication with India and Kabul was very irregular, while rumours of disaster from the latter place kept coming in.

On 17th December Sale heard that arrangements had been made for the capitulation of the garrison of Kabul, and that they were to be allowed to evacuate Afghanistan unmolested, but under conditions by no means honourable to the British name.

Christmas Day was celebrated in Jellalabad by Divine Service, and even by Christmas dinners, but there were strange forebodings as regards the fate of their comrades in Kabul, and when on 2nd January news was received that Sir William Macnaghten had been treacherously murdered by the Afghans on 23rd December whilst engaged in making arrangements with Akbar Khan for the withdrawal of the troops, it seemed as if some appalling disaster was at hand.

On Boxing Day, 1841, twenty-five troopers from Tora Baz Khan, Chief of Lalpoora (who was friendly to Britain), arrived at Jellalabad, each trooper carrying 1,000 Rs. in his saddle bag. This was a useful addition to the garrison's treasure chest.

On 9th January a letter was received by Macgregor dated Kabul 29th December 1841. The important part is as follows: 'It having been found necessary to conclude an agreement, founded on that of the late Sir W. H. Macnaghten, for the evacuation of Afghanistan by our troops we have the honour to request that you will intimate to the officer commanding at Jellalabad, our wish that the troops now at that place should return to India, commencing their march immediately after the receipt of this letter.' This letter was signed by Major Pottinger, who had succeeded Macnaghten as Envoy, and also by Major-General Elphinstone.

On the same day a reply was sent informing the authorities at Kabul that Akbar Khan had sent a proclamation to all the local Chiefs to intercept and destroy the force at Jellalabad, and that in these circumstances Sale and Macgregor have deemed it their duty to await a further communication from Kabul, which they desire may point out the security which may be given for their safe march to Peshawar. Seaton, a Captain in the 35th Native Infantry, tells us in his book, *Cadet to Colonel*, that when Sale's determination was made known—to hold Jellalabad until the Kabul force arrived—it gave universal satisfaction, and their confidence in their commander was greater than ever.

On 11th January Sale wrote to the Commander-in-Chief in India stating his opinion, that, in the absence of all instructions from India, he is not bound by the convention made under duress, and that he intends to remain at Jellalabad as long as provisions and ammunition hold out. On the same day Sale heard from Peshawar that Colonel Wild's Brigade was unable to advance to Jellalabad, and from Kabul that the guns and ammunition had been surrendered and that the army was completely in the hands of the enemy.

On 12th January news was received from the Kabul force to say that they were not allowed to proceed by the Khoord Kabul Pass, and that they had been detained for two days at Bootkhak.

On 13th January the worst anticipations of the garrison of Jellalabad were fulfilled. This is Havelock's description:—

'About 2 p.m. on the 13th January some officers were assembled on the roof of the loftiest house in Jellalabad. One of them espied a single horseman riding towards our walls. As he got nearer it was distinctly seen that he wore European clothes and was mounted on a travel-hacked yaboo, which he was urging on with all the speed of which it yet remained master. A signal was made to him by some one on the walls which he answered by waving a private soldier's forage cap over his head. The Kabul Gate was thrown open, and several officers rushing out, received and recognized in the traveller, who dismounted, the first and it is to be feared the last fugitive of the ill-fated force at Kabul, Dr. Brydon.'

The arrival of Dr. Brydon at Jellalabad has been immortalized by Lady Butler's famous picture, 'The Remnants of an Army'.

He was the sole survivor of an army of 4,500 fighting men and 12,000 followers to reach Jellalabad, though there were about 100 captives, including women and children, in the hands of the enemy.

Stapylton writes in his diary:

'On that night, however, a large lanthorn was suspended over the Kabul Gate, and the Colours of the Regiment by day, our bugles sounded the advance every half-hour during the night for the ensuing week to attract the attention of any who might have escaped and feared to approach the fort not knowing if it was occupied by friends or foes, all however without success.'

The cavalry sallied out along the Kabul road, and although they discovered the mutilated bodies of four of Brydon's companions about 4 miles out, not a living soul was seen.

After the arrival of Dr. Brydon all the Afghans were turned out of Jellalabad, including Captain Ferris's Jezailchees, who had always been loyal. Arrangements were made to arm the camp followers with pikes. The pike-making was left to Captain Abbott, but there was not sufficient material to make pikes for all.

It may not be out of place in a regimental history to give some account of this catastrophe, especially as some officers and men of the 13th were involved in it, not to mention Lady Sale, a brave and heroic woman, Mrs. Sturt, her daughter, and other women and children of the Regiment.

As has been already stated, the insurrection at Kabul broke out on 2nd November. There were at that time in Kabul Major Kershaw, Lieutenant Hobhouse and eleven men of the Regiment fit for duty; Lieutenant Mein wounded and a number of men in hospital.

As early as 6th November Elphinstone recommended making terms with the enemy. The garrison were mainly stationed in the cantonments, but there was a detachment in the Bala Hissar. The site of the cantonments was ill chosen and hardly capable of being defended. General Elphinstone was a sick man and his staff, with one or two exceptions, incapable. Shelton, the most senior officer, though a brave man, was a pessimist who hated Macnaghten and despised Elphinstone. The operations were characterized by indecision and want of energy, and consequently the morale of the troops steadily deteriorated. Although the troops achieved some measure of success on 13th November at Kabul, on the same day a battalion of Gurkhas were cut to pieces at Charekar. On 13th December the British troops evacuated the Bala Hissar, and negotiations were entered upon for evacuating the country. Even the treacherous murder of the Envoy on 23rd December failed to arouse any energy among the military commanders, and the negotiations for evacuation were continued. In accordance with the terms of the capitulation which guaranteed a safe conduct the army left Kabul on 6th January, in deep snow and bitter cold. At the end of the first day's march, discipline and order disappeared. The enemy hovered round cutting off stragglers and attacking the troops where occasion offered. There were no tents or shelters of any kind. In the first two days over 500 soldiers and 2,500 followers were killed, and half the force were frostbitten or wounded. On the second day out from Kabul Lady Sale was wounded in the arm by a bullet, but she made light of her injuries and never lost heart. As the wretched army slowly made its way through the passes they were attacked day and night by the treacherous Afghans. Two women of the Regiment, Mrs. Cunningham and Mrs. Stoker, disappeared and were never heard of again, though the latter's son was saved. On the 11th January there was not a single Indian foot soldier left in the whole force, only 150 of the 44th, 50 of the 5th Cavalry and 16 artillery men.

On the 13th the last stand was made at Gandamak when 18 officers and 50 men were killed. Among these officers was Lieutenant Hobhouse of the 13th. Major Kershaw of the Regiment was killed earlier in the retreat.

Lady Macnaghten, Lady Sale and other ladies and children were handed over to Akbar Khan during the retreat, while from time to time other officers, including Elphinstone and Shelton, Pottinger, Lawrence, and Colin Mackenzie, were handed over as hostages. Altogether there were from 80 to 100 British captives, including Lieutenant Mein of the 13th, in the hands of the enemy.

Many gallant deeds by individuals and groups of officers and men might be recorded during this disastrous retreat. It will suffice to mention one which concerns an officer of the Regiment. The account is taken from a speech delivered by Sir Robert Peel in the House of Commons on the 20th February 1843:—

'Lieutenant Sturt (son-in-law of Sir Robert and Lady Sale) had nearly cleared the defile (Khoord Kabul) when he received his wound, and would have been left on the ground to be hacked to pieces by the Ghazies, who followed in the rear to complete the slaughter, but for the generous intrepidity of Lieutenant Mein of Her Majesty's 13th Light Infantry, who, on learning what had befallen him, went back to his succour, and stood by him for several minutes, at the imminent risk of his own life, vainly entreating aid from the passers-by. He was at length joined by Serjeant Deane of the Sappers, with whose assistance he dragged his friend, on a quilt, through the remainder of the Pass, when he succeeded in mounting him on a miserable pony, and conducted him in safety to the camp, where the unfortunate officer lingered till the following morning, and was the only man of the whole force who received Christian burial. Lieutenant Mein was himself suffering from a dangerous wound in the head received in the previous October, and his heroic disregard of self, and fidelity to his friend in the hour of danger, are well deserving of a record in the annals of British valour and virtue; I think, Sir, it is but just that the name of Lieutenant Mein should be mentioned with honour in the House of Commons, and I do not regret having noticed this circumstance, as it has called forth so generous and general an expression of sympathy and approval.'

The majority of the captives were taken to Buddee-abad, about 35 miles from Jellalabad, where they remained till after the defeat of Akbar Khan by Sale on the 7th April.

Commenting on this disaster Havelock wrote:—

'This has rendered our task a difficult one, but I trust we look its asperities in the face like soldiers. We can no longer trust our Afghan Irregulars and are getting rid of them. We must by God's help strive to defend an extensive enceinte, of which the parapets are not simply cannon-proof, with an insufficient supply of ammunition which can last only by being husbanded, and only two, not strong regiments of infantry, one European, and the other native, a good artillery and 200 horse. We have full six weeks' provisions, but forage for about three weeks longer. We have embodied our camp followers already to upwards of a thousand, and are arming them with muskets, jezails, swords, spears and even stones for the defence of the walls. Akbar Khan has been at Lughman and is now at Tigree raising followers. I think we can, by God's Blessing, if besieged with guns, protract our defence full forty days. We are resolved on every effort to save for Government Jellalabad and eastern Afghanistan. If it cannot then relieve us, we sink, but we shall, I trust, die like soldiers.'

On the Sunday after Dr. Brydon's arrival the whole force assembled for Divine Service in one of the open squares of the Citadel, when Havelock read the Church Service, but substituted for the Psalms of the day the 46th Psalm, 'God is our refuge and strength, a very present help in trouble. Therefore will we not fear though the earth be removed.'

At this time Broadfoot urged Sale to evacuate Jellalabad and fight his way through the Khyber to Peshawar, but the latter refused to entertain the idea, partly because he doubted his ability to do so with much prospect of success, and partly because he would thereby sever his connexion with the captives with whom he was in communication.

On 19th January Brigadier Wild, with a brigade from Peshawar, was repulsed in an attempt to relieve the garrison of Ali Musjid in the Khyber Pass, and on the 24th that garrison was withdrawn to Peshawar. The troops at that station were suffering severely from sickness, and what is worse, were mutinous, so far had the demoralization entailed by the disaster to the army in Afghanistan spread. Save only in Jellalabad was discipline maintained and the troops in good heart, yet there were some croakers even in that garrison.

On 26th January Sale, despairing of obtaining aid from India, convened a Council of War. Letters were produced from the Government of India:—

1. Detailing the military arrangements for the support of Jellalabad, and if possible to advance there, but forbidding any forward move.

2. A letter indicating the intention of the Government to retire from Afghanistan.

3. Letters from Peshawar stating that they were unable to relieve Jellalabad.

4. Letter from Captain Pottinger at Buddee-abad saying that Akbar Khan would befriend the British if Dost Mahomed was released.

5. Private letter from Shah Shoojah at Kabul, endeavouring to exculpate himself from any share in the disasters to the Kabul force, professing friendship, and asking what Sale's intentions were.

The Council were naturally indignant at the letters received from the Government of India, who seemed unwilling or unable to render prompt assistance, so it was resolved by the Council that an attempt should be made to negotiate with Shah Shoojah at Kabul in whose employ the garrison nominally were.

Accordingly it was resolved to send a letter to Shah Shoojah stating that it was impossible for the Jellalabad garrison to retire to India without his permission and that in consequence of the bad faith and treachery shown by the Afghans as regards the Kabul force no reliance could be placed on their professions. As a preliminary to withdrawal it was stipulated that Akbar Khan and his force should retire to Kabul, that certain princes of the Royal blood should be given up as hostages, and that the garrison should be provided with the necessary transport.

The sending of this letter was opposed by Broadfoot and Oldfield and also by Havelock, who was not a member of the Council.

The letter was sent and the answer came on 8th February and said: 'If you are sincere in your offers let all the chief gentlemen set their seals.'

Sale now suggested an additional stipulation that all the captives, sick and wounded in the hands of the enemy should be given up on the arrival of the force at Peshawar.

But by this time Sale and others had come round to Broadfoot's way of thinking, and it was resolved to have no more negotiations with the enemy.

On the 30th January a foraging party succeeded in capturing 175 bullocks. On the following day the cavalry made a raid on the enemy's flocks and drove off 734 sheep.

On 13th February intelligence was received that General Pollock had arrived at Peshawar invested with full military and political powers in Afghanistan. On the following day Sale informed Pollock that the strength of the garrison was 2,263 of all ranks fit for duty and 195 unfit; of these the 13th had 719 fit and 30 unfit, that the health of the troops was good, but medicines were scarce, that the British had full supplies for 70 days, and the natives half-rations for that period, further that they had twenty-five days' forage.

On 15th February Akbar Khan crossed the river and took up a position 10 miles from the town with a force of 2,000 men (which was being augmented day by day), and he had patrols and vedettes covering all the country round.

February 19th was a memorable day. Sale and Havelock narrowly escaped being killed. They were in a house together when a severe shock of earthquake occurred, and they just got out in time. The parapets which had been built with so much labour were cast down, several bastions were injured, the guard houses were destroyed, a third of the town was demolished, a considerable gap appeared in the rampart of a curtain in the Peshawar face, while the Kabul Gate was reduced to a shapeless mass of ruins.

Shocks continued without intermission with frightful violence. A dense cloud of dust arising from the town and neighbouring villages obscured the sky. A confused rumbling sound was heard, wildly mingling with the crash of falling houses and the outcries of the inhabitants. During the next six weeks over one hundred further shocks were registered.

Captain Broadfoot observed, 'Now is the time for Akbar Khan', but the earthquakes were no respecters of the contending forces; besieged and besiegers suffered alike, the villages and forts in the Jellalabad valley were shaken to the ground, many of the inhabitants were killed, and ruin and destruction reigned everywhere.

Nothing daunted, the garrison, with that unconquerable spirit of perseverance for which the troops had already been distinguished, started to repair the works, and by the end of the month, the defences were tolerably secure. In Major Broadfoot's Note on the Defensive Works in Jellalabad, prepared by order of Major-General Sir Robert Sale, dated 16th April 1842, the following paragraph alludes to the services of the 13th:—

'It will be seen that the largest parties were furnished by H.M.'s 13th Light Infantry, and I know not how adequately to express my sense of the services of this admirable body of men; though having little more than every other night in bed they laboured for months, day after day, officers and men, with a cheerfulness and energy not to be surpassed.'

On 26th February Akbar Khan pitched his camp about 2 miles off on the Kabul side, and a few days later a large body of infantry with some cavalry entrenched themselves about the same distance on the Peshawar side—Jellalabad was now strictly blockaded.

Sale's chief anxiety at this time was the possibility that the enemy might, by utilizing the guns and ammunition taken from the Kabul force, eventually make such breaches in the defences as to make an assault feasible, and this danger was enhanced by the scarcity of ball ammunition.

Strict measures were taken to husband ball ammunition. Stapylton narrates that all pewter basins and mugs, as well as the enemy's bullets, were collected for melting down and recasting, while the officers armed themselves with sporting rifles and shot-guns.

On 7th March a letter was received from Kabul demanding the evacuation of Jellalabad. The messengers were referred to Major-General Pollock at Peshawar as commanding the forces in Afghanistan. News was also received of the capitulation of the garrison of Ghazni after a protracted siege.

It was reported by spies that the enemy were attempting to mine the fort at the north-west angle, so at daybreak on 11th March a sortie was made with 600 infantry, 200 sappers and the cavalry under Dennie to examine the ground, but no mines were discovered, the enemy's works were destroyed, and about 100 Afghans killed with little loss to the garrison.

On the 17th news was received that Pollock was delayed, and asking if the garrison could hold out till the end of March. A reply in the affirmative was given, but orders were issued to destroy all the camels in order to conserve forage for the artillery and cavalry horses.

On 24th March it is recorded that the Major-General was highly gratified this morning by the spirited manner in which a detachment of H.M. 13th under Captain Fenwick, and of the Sappers and Miners under Lieutenant Orr, the whole led by Major Broadfoot, drove the enemy in confusion, and with loss from a work attached to the north-western wall, which they had temporarily taken possession of upon our working and foraging parties retiring. One man of the 13th and two sappers were killed on this occasion while Captain Broadfoot was wounded.

There was yet another sortie on the 1st April made by 200 men of the 13th, 200 of the 35th Native Infantry and the Cavalry in order to secure sheep and goats. It was entirely successful, about 500 head being captured. It is interesting to record the good feeling shown by the 35th Native Infantry to the 13th on this occasion. The former regiment declined to take their share of the captured animals and gave them up to the 13th as they said that meat was far less necessary to them than to the Europeans.

In this and other skirmishes Captains Pattison and Fenwick, Lieutenants George Wade and John William Cox are mentioned in dispatches as having distinguished themselves. No doubt the garrison was in splendid fettle at this time. Macgregor writes on the 1st April: 'Our troops of all arms are in the highest pluck, and they seem never so happy as when fighting with the enemy.'

On the 5th April there were strong rumours that the force under Major-General Pollock, C.B., had experienced reverses in the Khyber, and had retraced its steps to Peshawar, and these rumours were rather confirmed on the following day when Akbar's guns thundered out a salute, it is said, in honour of the event.

Yet there were other reports to the effect that a revolution had broken out at Kabul, that the Ghazies had been defeated in the Khyber, and that Akbar Khan was about to hasten to the capital.

Sale felt that a crisis had arisen and he summoned a Council of War. The Council was of opinion that if Pollock had been defeated, his advance might be facilitated and the blockade raised by a successful action, or if Akbar was really about to proceed to Kabul now was the time to deal him a deadly blow.

The decision to make a sortie on the 7th April was also influenced by the fact that there was very little ammunition left, being only sufficient to repel one determined attack by the enemy.

THE ACTION OF 7TH APRIL

Sale, once determined to fight, was no believer in half-measures. Every available man was to take part, except strong detachments in charge of each of the gates, while the walls were to be manned by the camp followers. Captain Pattison of the 13th was to take command of the reduced garrison. There were to be three columns of attack: the left column the 35th Native Infantry, less one company, under Lieut.-Colonel Monteith; the centre column the 13th Light Infantry mustering 500 bayonets, less one company, under Colonel Dennie; the right column, one company 13th Light Infantry, one company 35th Native Infantry, and a detachment of the Sappers and Miners, under Captain Havelock of the 13th. No. 6 Light Field Battery was to support the attack, while the Cavalry, under Captain Oldfield, were held in readiness to act as required.

Akbar Khan's camp, 3 miles distant, was flanked on the right flank by a fort and on the left flank by the Kabul River. The strength of the enemy was about 6,000 men. Between the enemy's position and Jellalabad was an old fort held by the enemy's outposts. On the previous evening Sale had carefully pointed out the lines of advance to each of the column commanders, and in accordance with his orders Dennie's column should have passed 300 yards to the left of it.

At daybreak on the 7th April the troops marched out of Jellalabad and, after having been formed up, the columns, covered by a line of skirmishers, advanced towards the enemy's position.

Unfortunately the centre column, under Dennie, failed to keep its true direction and had edged in towards the ruined fort, and coming within range of its defenders, naturally became engaged. Sale, hearing the firing, galloped up, ordered one company of the 13th to clamber through a gap in the wall, which they did, but found an inner wall loopholed which there was no getting over, except with scaling ladders. It was here that the gallant Dennie lost his life. Backhouse narrates: 'There must have been some strange work going on here, the 13th putting their muskets in through the loopholes firing in, while the enemy were in the same manner firing out at them. The rascals inside pulled one of the 13th muskets in, and the 13th, in exchange, pulled one of theirs out, which proved to be one of the late 44th.' Sale ordered up some guns but, finding them useless against the solid masonry, eventually ordered the advance to proceed. In the meantime the right column, under Havelock, had got somewhat in advance, and the enemy taking advantage of this, at once charged with their cavalry, but Havelock in no wise disconcerted promptly formed square and beat off the hostile horsemen. Sale then gave his orders for a general advance which may be described in his own words.

'The artillery advanced at the gallop, and directed a heavy fire upon the Afghan centre, whilst two of the columns of infantry penetrated the line near the same point, and the third forced back its left from its support on the river, into the stream of which some of his horse and foot were driven. The Afghans made repeated attempts to check our advance by a smart fire of musketry, by throwing forward heavy bodies of horse, which twice threatened the detachments of foot under Captain Havelock, and by opening upon us three guns from a battery screened by a garden wall, and said to have been served under the personal superintendence of the Sirdar. But in a short time they were dislodged from every point of their position, their cannon taken, and their camp involved in a general conflagration. The battle was over—and the enemy in full retreat in the direction of Lughman by about 7 a.m. We have made ourselves masters of two cavalry standards, recaptured four guns lost by the Kabul and Gandamak forces, the restoration of which, to our government, is matter of much honest exultation among our troops, seized and destroyed a great quantity of material and ordnance stores, and burnt the whole of the enemy's tents. In short the defeat of Mahomed Akbar in open field, by the troops which he had boasted of blockading, has been complete and signal. The field of battle was strewed with the bodies of men and horses, and the richness of the trappings of some of the latter seemed to attest that persons of distinction had been among the casualties.'

By nightfall there was not an Afghan within 8 miles of Jellalabad. The British losses were 14 killed and 66 wounded. The Regiment had Colonel Dennie killed and Lieutenant Jennings and Assistant-Surgeon Barnes wounded, 8 privates killed and 31 rank and file wounded. Colonel Dennie was mortally wounded in the attack on the 'patched-up fort'. Mr. Gleig, in his book *Sale's Brigade in Afghanistan*, says:

'A ball entered his side, passing through the sword-belt; and he bent forward upon his horse. Lieutenant and Adjutant Wood instantly rode up to him, and expressed the hope that his hurt was not serious. But it was more than serious—it was fatal. A couple of orderlies, by Lieutenant Wood's direction, turned his horse's head homewards, and leading it by the bridle, endeavoured to guide him to the town. But he never reached it alive.'

Armourer-Serjeant Henry Ulyett of the 13th captured Mahomed Akbar's standard, which he took from a cavalry soldier whom he killed, and he subsequently received the medal and annuity of £20 for 'distinguished conduct.' This standard with the two flags captured at Ghazni is now at the Depôt of The Somerset Light Infantry at Taunton.

Captain Havelock is thus alluded to in Sale's dispatch: 'The able and judicious manner in which Captain Havelock moved the force under his command, which acted on a line sufficiently distant to render its manœuvres independent of any immediate control demands my particular and especial commendation.'

Captain Wilkinson of the 13th, who succeeded Dennie in command of the centre column, and Captain Hamlet C. Wade (Brigade Major) were highly commended in Major-General Sir Robert Sale's dispatch, in which it was also stated 'that Lieutenant and Adjutant Wood, H.M. 13th Light Infantry, made a dash at one of the enemy, and in cutting him down, his charger was so severely injured as to have been since destroyed.' Captain Havelock reports in the most favourable manner the gallant conduct, throughout the day, of Lieutenant Cox, H.M. 13th Light Infantry, and he was the first of the party, which captured them, to seize two of the enemy's guns.

Towards the conclusion of the engagement a sally was made from the Kabul Gate by Lieutenant George Wade of the Regiment into the fort before

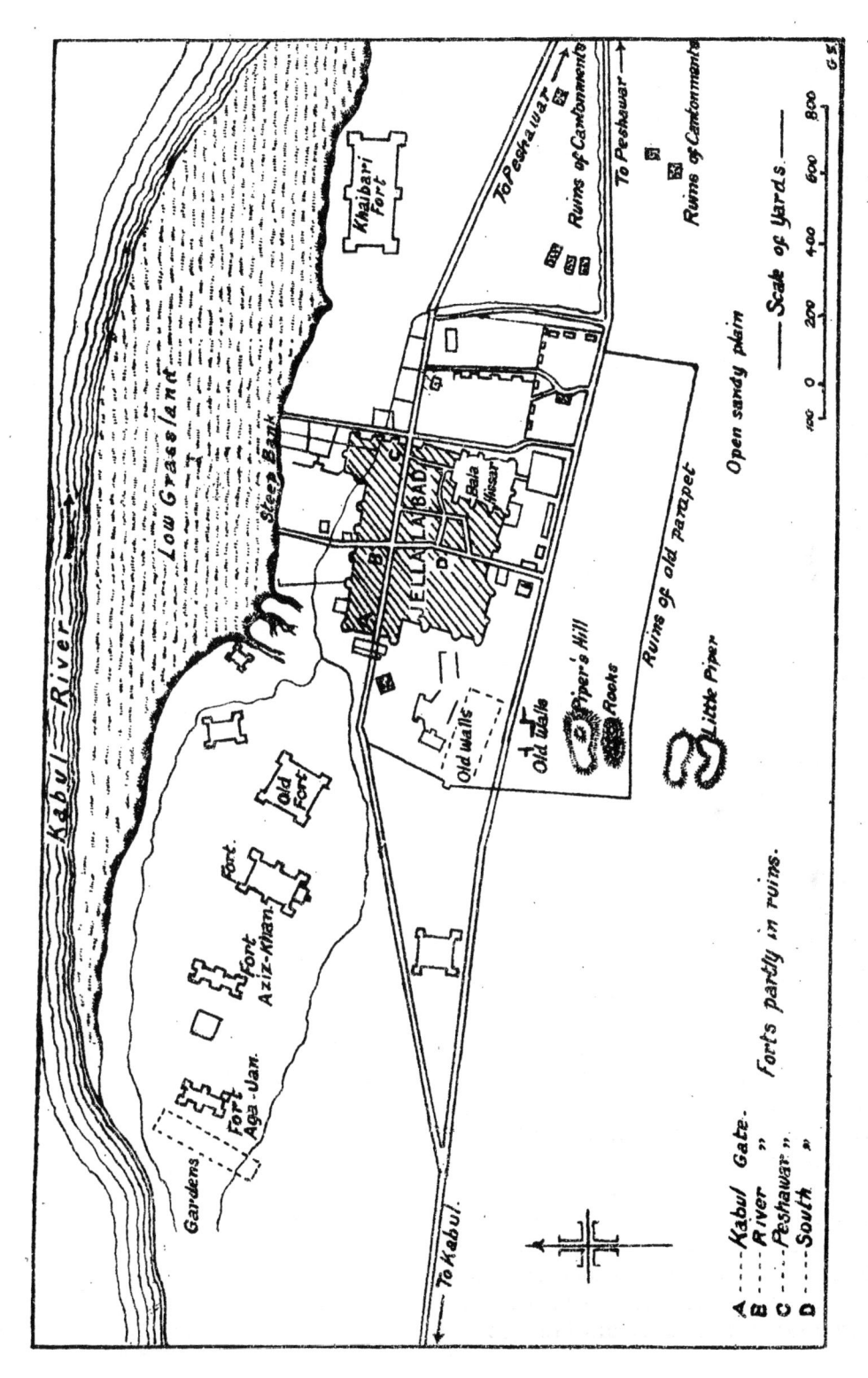

SIEGE OF JELLALABAD, 1841-2

which Colonel Dennie had fallen, when it was observed that the enemy were abandoning it. It was set on fire and some of the defenders were bayoneted.

A few words about Dennie. He joined the 22nd Foot in 1800 at the age of fifteen and exchanged into the 13th as Major in 1821, and thus had forty-two years' service. Sir Robert Peel in his speech in the House of Commons of 20th February 1843, when a vote of thanks was accorded to the officers and troops employed in Afghanistan, thus alludes to Colonel Dennie:—

'That victory (7th April) would have been the cause of almost unqualified rejoicing if it had not been purchased at the cost of the life of one of the most noble and gallant spirits, whose actions have ever added brilliance to their country's military renown. Need I mention the name of the lamented Colonel Dennie? With his accustomed valour—a valour which was unquenchable—he led the British troops against the enemy. The attack which he headed was successful, but he fell in the conflict; and a spirit as gallant as his own has offered to his family and his friends that which he thinks—and justly thinks—the highest consolation that can be afforded them. "True it is," he says, "he has lost his life, but he lost his life on the field of battle, and in the hour of victory." Such is the consolation which Sir Robert Sale offered to his bereaved family and friends. I wish it had been possible—but it was not—that the dying moments of Colonel Dennie could have been consoled, as I believe they would have been by the knowledge that on account of the former valour and intrepidity he had displayed—he having no other interest or influence than that just interest and influence which such courage and devotion ought always to command—the Queen of England had signified her personal wish that Colonel Dennie should be appointed one of her Aides-de-Camp. I sincerely wish that Colonel Dennie could have been made acquainted with this fact.'

It is gratifying to be able to state that Colonel Dennie's appointment as Aide-de-Camp to the Queen was known in the Regiment about a week previous to his death. There are tablets to his memory in St. Peter's Church, Fort William, Calcutta, and also in Carisbrook Church, Isle of Wight.

After the action of 7th April, the local chiefs made their submission, and plentiful supplies came in to the market established outside the walls.

On 9th April news was received that General Pollock had been successful in forcing the Khyber Pass and that he would be in Jellalabad in a few days. On the 15th he was at Alee Bogham, 7 miles off; on the 16th he marched to Jellalabad, when his troops were met by the band of the 13th, who played them in to the tune of the old Jacobite air, 'Oh! but ye've been lang o' coming.'

So ended the memorable siege of Jellalabad, not particularly remarkable like many other sieges for the privations and heavy losses of the defenders, but rather for the fact that Sale and his troops had upheld the honour of the British Army for five months in a hostile country surrounded by a treacherous enemy where their comrades in arms had met with unparalleled disaster.

Major-General Pollock reported in his dispatch of the 19th April 1842 as follows:—

"I have had an opportunity of inspecting the works thrown up, for their protection by the indefatigable exertions of Sir Robert Sale's force, and my surprise at their strength and extent has been only equalled by my admiration of the excellent arrangements which must have pervaded all departments, since, after a siege (by greatly superior numbers) of upwards of five months' duration, I find the garrison in excellent health and spirits, and in an admirable state of discipline, with a good supply of ammunition, ready and anxious to take the field, and most willing to advance on Kabul.'

The insurrection in Kabul had had a paralysing effect on the Government of India, and it was not till 30th January when the Governor-General, Lord Auckland, received the news of the disaster to the Kabul Army that measures were taken to send Pollock to Peshawar with 10,000 men. Lord Ellenborough, who succeeded Lord Auckland as Governor-General at the end of February, had to deal with this crisis, and though he disapproved of the policy of penetration into Afghanistan, he recognized the necessity for relieving or evacuating the garrisons still in Afghanistan, viz. Kandahar and Jellalabad. The idea of exacting retribution for the treachery of the Afghans was then far from his mind. With some misgivings he sanctioned the advance of Pollock's division through the Khyber Pass.

Great was the relief and joy with which the news of Pollock's and Sale's victories was received throughout all India and especially by the Governor-General who felt that an enormous load of responsibility had been lifted from his shoulders. He felt that Sale and his men had saved the prestige of the Government and the reputation of the Army. Europeans said that now again they could look a native in the face.

It was in these circumstances that Lord Ellenborough issued that well-known notification which conferred on Sale's brigade the honourable title of the 'Illustrious Garrison'.

It is as follows; and is dated Benares 21st April:—

'The Governor-General feels assured that every subject of the British Government will peruse with the deepest interest and satisfaction the report he now communicates of the entire defeat of the Afghan troops, under Mahomed Akbar Khan, by the garrison of Jellalabad.

'That illustrious garrison, which by its constancy in enduring privations, and by its valour in action, has already obtained for itself the sympathy and respect of every true soldier, has now, sallying forth from its walls, under the command of its gallant leader, Major-General Sir Robert Sale, thoroughly beaten in open field an enemy of more than three times its number, taken the standards of its boasted cavalry, destroyed their camp, and recaptured four guns, which, under circumstances which can never occur again, had during the last winter fallen into their hands.

'The Governor-General cordially congratulates the Army upon the return of victory to its ranks. He is convinced that there, as in all former times, it will be found, while, as at Jellalabad, the European and native troops mutually supporting each other and evincing equal discipline and valour, are led into action by officers in whom they justly confide.

'The Governor-General directs that the substance of this notification, and of Major-General Sir Robert Sale's report, be carefully made known to all troops, and that a salute of twenty-one guns be fired at every principal station of the Army.'

On 30th April Lord Ellenborough issued a congratulatory order to Major-General Pollock and his troops and concluded with the following paragraph:—

'The Governor-General taking into consideration the many great privations to which the troops composing the garrison of Jellalabad were exposed during the blockade of that place, and the noble fortitude with which all such privations were borne, as well as the various losses the troops sustained is pleased to direct that a donation of six months' batta be made to all the officers, non-commissioned officers, and privates, European and Native, who composed the garrison of Jellalabad on April 7th, 1842.'

Sir William Casement, military member of Council in Calcutta, adds his testimony as follows:—

'Your Lordship's orders of the 21st and 30th April announcing the victory of the Illustrious Garrison of Jellalabad, and their consequent rewards, will be perused by every soldier throughout India with feelings of pride and gratitude, and will add more to the real strength of the Army than would be effected by an augmentation of 10,000 men.'

Sir Robert Sale's report of the transactions in which the garrison of Jellalabad had been engaged gives the following interesting particulars:—

'From the time that the brigade threw itself into Jellalabad the native troops have been on half, and the followers on quarter rations, and for many weeks they have been able to obtain little or nothing in the bazaars to eke out their scanty provision. I will not mention, as a privation, the European troops from the same period having been without their allowance of spirits, because I verily believe this circumstance, and their constant employment have contributed to keep them in the highest health and the most remarkable state of discipline. Crime has been almost unknown among them, but they have felt severely, although they have never murmured, the diminution of their quantity of animal food, and the total want of ghee, flour, tea, coffee and sugar: these may seem small matters to those who read them at a distance, but they are serious reductions in the scale of comfort of the hard-working and fighting soldier in Asia. The troops have also been greatly in arrears of pay, besides their severe duties in heat and cold, wind and rain, on the guards of the gates and bastions. The troops, officers and men, British and Hindostanee, of every arm, remained fully accoutred on their alarm posts every night from the 1st March to the 7th of April. The losses of officers and men, in carriage and cattle, camp equipage and baggage, between Kabul and Jellalabad, were heavy; and their expenditure during the siege and blockade, in obtaining articles of mere subsistence and necessity, has been exorbitant.

'It is gratifying to me to forward the opinion of my second-in-command, Lieut.-Colonel Monteith, C.B., placed on record without solicitation, of the merits of the 13th Light Infantry, of which corps I am proud to be a member. I must express my gratitude to Providence for having placed so gallant and devoted a force under my command; in every way it has exceeded my most sanguine expectations, and I beg leave in the strongest manner, to solicit the interposition of Major-General Pollock, C.B., who has nobly laboured and fought to relieve it from its critical position in the midst of a hostile empire, in now committing it to the protection and favour of the Right Honourable the Governor-General in Council and through him to the Court of Directors and our Sovereign.'

Lieut.-Colonel Monteith stated in his report:—

'As doing but due justice on this occasion to Her Majesty's 13th Light Infantry might be looked upon as a highly coloured record of the merits of your Regiment, and seeing that no such partial bias can possibly be supposed to guide my feelings in the estimate I have formed of their deserts, I have pleasure in sincerely declaring, that their conduct, throughout the painful and perilous position in which we have so long been placed, has been such as fully to deserve the applause and admiration of their country, and the confidence and best consideration of our well-beloved Sovereign.

'On our throwing ourselves, on the 12th of November last, into the old and ruined town of Jellalabad, without money, without food, and almost without protection, with a nation of highly excited and barbarous enemies in arms against us, our situation seemed as hopeless a one as British troops were ever called upon to confront; notwithstanding which, the enemy was twice attacked within twenty days, and on both occasions defeated with signal success.

'You, yourself, will doubtless detail the works performed by the Regiment; let it then be only my province, who have witnessed their exertions, almost hourly during a period of four months, to record, that their devoted perseverance and cheerfulness amidst all the gloom that surrounded them, after the destruction of their comrades of the Kabul force, could not have been surpassed by any troops in the world; and that after months of extreme toil, when an earthquake, such as man is not often in the habit of experiencing, in a moment left scarcely a vestige of their labour standing; their flying as they did with redoubled zeal to the work, and completing it in ten days (so that on the arrival of the enemy before Jellalabad, they declared that the calamity which had befallen the valley arose from nothing but English witchcraft, it being the only place that had escaped uninjured), was what none but British soldiers could have performed, and what no price could have purchased, for it was the labour of the heart, work of all others most deserving of distinction and reward.'

The defence of Jellalabad, situated amid scenery of wild and savage grandeur, against an undisciplined but desperate enemy, who used his rude implements of war with deadly precision, will ever excite the highest admiration, and the British nation owes a lasting debt of gratitude to Major-General Sir Robert Sale, and the gallant band of heroes composing the garrison. These successes, contrasting so forcibly with the unforeseen disaster at Kabul, which partook more of the character of a hideous dream than of stern reality, may well make the 13th refer with honest pride to the part they bore in these achievements.

On the 16th of June 1842, the Queen was graciously pleased to appoint Colonel Sir Robert Henry Sale (serving with the rank of Major-General in Afghanistan) to be a Knight Grand Cross of the Most Honourable Military Order of the Bath.

Major Edward T. Tronson was promoted to the rank of Lieutenant-Colonel, in succession to Lieut.-Colonel Dennie, and Captain Robert Pattison was advanced to the majority—Lieut.-Colonel Tronson retired on full pay on the 2nd August following, and was succeeded by Major Squire, Captain John Taylor being promoted to the vacant rank of major.

The distinguished conduct of the Regiment was fully appreciated, and Her Majesty alluded to the defence of Jellalabad in her most gracious speech on proroguing Parliament on the 12th August 1842:—

'Although I have had deeply to lament the reverses which have befallen a division of the Army to the westward of the Indus, yet I have the satisfaction of reflecting that the gallant defence of the city of Jellalabad, crowned by a decisive victory in the field, has eminently proved the courage and discipline of the European and Native troops, and the skill and fortitude of their distinguished commander.'

On the 26th of August, the pleasure of Her Majesty was officially announced in the *London Gazette*, and a letter of the same date and purport was, by direction of His Grace the Commander-in-Chief, addressed from the Horse Guards by the Adjutant-General (Lieut.-General Sir John Macdonald, K.C.B.) to the officer commanding the 13th Light Infantry:—

'War Office, *26th August 1842*.

'In consideration of the distinguished gallantry displayed by the 13th Light Infantry during the campaigns in the Burmese empire and in Afghanistan, Her Majesty has been graciously pleased to approve of that Regiment assuming the title of the 13th or **Prince Albert's Regiment of Light Infantry**; and its facings being changed from yellow to blue.

'Her Majesty has also been pleased to authorize the 13th Regiment of Light Infantry to bear on its colours and appointments a Mural Crown, superscribed Jellalabad, as a memorial of the fortitude, perseverance, and enterprise, evinced by that Regiment and the several corps which served during the blockade of Jellalabad.

'Her Majesty has been likewise pleased to permit the 13th Regiment to receive and wear a silver medal, which has been directed by the Governor-General of India to be distributed to every officer, non-commissioned officer, and private, European and Native—who belonged to the garrison of Jellalabad on the 7th April 1842—such medals to bear on one side a Mural Crown superscribed Jellalabad, and on the other side, April 7th, 1842.'

The riband of this medal is popularly known as the 'Rainbow'. This is a misnomer. Lord Ellenborough stated that it represents the colours of the Eastern sky, when the sun rises without a cloud, crimson fading into yellow, and yellow into blue.

This medal was granted to the following officers of the Regiment:—

Lieut.-Colonels
Colonel Sir Robert Sale, G.C.B.
„ William H. Dennie, C.B.[1]

Major
Robert Pattison.

Captains

Henry Havelock.
Arthur P. S. Wilkinson.
Hamlet C. Wade.

James H. Fenwick.
Peter R. Jennings.

Lieutenants

Alec E. F. Holcombe.
George King.
John S. Wood (Adjutant).
Wm. A. Sinclair.
Hon. E. J. W. Forester.
David Rattray.
Richard E. Frere.
George Wade.

John Wm. Cox.
William Williams.
Fred Van Straubenzee.
Thos. B. Speedy.
J. Francis Scott.
G. Chetwynd Stapylton.
Robt. S. Parker.

Ensigns

Arthur Oakes.

George Talbot.

Surgeon Jno. Robertson, M.D.

Asst. Surg. G. W. Barnes, M.D.

[1] The following interesting circumstance was related by Lord Fitzgerald and Vesey in the House of Lords in his speech on the 20th February 1843, regarding the vote of thanks for the operations in Afghanistan. The Adjutant-General of the Army in India, by the Command of Lord Ellenborough, transmitted to the aged mother of Colonel Dennie that medal which her son would have worn, had he happily survived. In replying to the letter which accompanies this token, Mrs. Dennie beautifully said that 'she accepted it with pleasure and with pride, for she had a right to feel a pride in her son's life, and in his death'. Lord Fitzgerald added, that it was impossible to read that passage without honouring the lady, and even more deeply lamenting the fate of the son of whom she had so justly and truly written.

H.R.H. THE PRINCE CONSORT

It is not surprising that some confusion exists on the subject of the medals issued in this campaign.

The original Jellalabad medal was struck in the Indian Mint by the order of Lord Ellenborough so that he might present the medals to the Illustrious Garrison on their return to India, and the riband of their medal is known as the 'Rainbow riband'.

After the return of the Regiment to England in 1845 a new Jellalabad medal was issued, but the riband was changed to red and blue.—

As many officers and other ranks had left the Regiment then, they did not receive the new medal.

It was the intention of the Home Authorities that the Jellalabad medal should have a red and blue riband, and that the Ghuznee and Kabul medals should retain the Rainbow riband.

Although all records testify to Sale's valour and show that he was a gallant leader of men, some contemporary writers are inclined to throw doubts on his power of initiative, and to belittle his actions as an independent commander.

These writers draw their conclusions chiefly from the criticisms made by Major Broadfoot who commanded the detachment of Sappers and Miners during the siege, and who was highly spoken of by Major Havelock.

Great stress is also laid on the way in which Sale voted at the Council of War held on 26th January 1842, when his opinion was opposed by Broadfoot and Oldfield; Havelock also, though not a member of the Council, was known to have agreed with the latter.

In considering Major Broadfoot's criticisms, it must be remembered that, although he was a man of outstanding character, he was a very junior officer at the time, and intensely jealous of the deeds of his own corps, so jealous indeed that he did not hesitate to belittle those of other corps. He did not get on well with Sale, who had on one occasion reprimanded him, and he was obsessed with the idea that everybody and every thing connected with the campaign was wrong.

As regards Sale's vote at the Council of War. Without doubt his constant intercourse with the Political Agents may have had some effect on his military instincts; and his constant fear of shortage of ball ammunition probably caused him to take a somewhat pessimistic appreciation of the situation.

In considering these questions, the reader might well refer to the account of the siege as narrated in *Cadet to Colonel*, by Major-General Sir Thomas Seaton, K.C.B., who was, during the siege, a Captain in the 35th Native Infantry. Sir Thomas Seaton in this account makes out that Sale was the real hero of the siege, and extols his tactics as being the best suited to the occasion.

CHAPTER XVII

KABUL REOCCUPIED. THE HEIGHTS OF TRUCKEE. DEATH OF SALE

ONE of the first results of Akbar's defeat on 7th April at Jellalabad was that he removed most of the prisoners from Buddee-abad on 11th April and after many wanderings they settled down once more towards the end of May at Noor Mahommed in the neighbourhood of Kabul.

It may be mentioned that, while the prisoners were at Buddee-abad, Sale was in constant communication with Lady Sale and the officers there and he managed to send them clothes and other necessaries of life.

It is difficult to surmise the exact purpose Akbar Khan had in keeping the prisoners so close to Jellalabad, but Captain Seaton in his book, *From Cadet to Colonel*, relates the following story:—

'Shortly after Akbar's Camp appeared in sight it was whispered about in garrison that Akbar intended to bring Lady Sale, then a prisoner in his hands, before the walls, and to put her to torture within sight, and so compel Sale to surrender.

'Every day, when the men were at their dinner, Sale used to make a turn on the ramparts ostensibly to have a quiet look round at the progress of our works, but in reality I believe to ponder on the desperate situation of his wife and daughter and debate with himself the possibility of effecting their rescue. We knew that they were well off and had hitherto been kindly treated and were in Akbar's fort in Lughman not many miles off. One day Sale in going his rounds came and stood over the South Gate, where I was on duty, and as I had enjoyed the privilege of great intimacy with him and Lady Sale at Kabul I went out and joined him. Our conversation naturally took the direction of his thoughts. I ventured to mention this report, and asked him what he would do if the report should prove true, and Akbar put his threat into execution. Turning towards me his face pale and stern, but quivering with deep emotion, he replied, "I will have every gun turned on her; my old bones shall be buried beneath the ruins of the fort here, but I will never surrender."

'I believe I am not the only one to whom he expressed this determination. Could Lady Sale have heard it her heart would have bounded with pride, for the heroine was worthy of the hero.'

Had the Government of India been able to obtain possession of the prisoners in Afghanistan it is probable that they would have withdrawn Pollock and Nott with their forces from Jellalabad and Kandahar respectively to India, so hateful was the idea of any further campaign. In fact on 29th April Sir Jasper Nicolls, the Commander-in-Chief in India, instructed Pollock to withdraw to Peshawar, but advised delay having regard to the safety of the prisoners and the possibility of inflicting defeat on the Afghans.

Pollock, who was in favour of a forward movement to Kabul in order to avenge the annihilation of Elphinstone's force, was only too glad to avail himself of the Commander-in-Chief's advice. He concentrated his army round Jellalabad, and at the beginning of May it amounted to 15,000 fighting men and consisted of one cavalry brigade of six regiments, four infantry brigades, of which the 1st or Garrison Brigade consisted of the 13th Light Infantry, the 35th Native Infantry and Broadfoot's Sappers and Miners, and five batteries of artillery.

June came and it was now decided that neither Pollock nor Nott could withdraw till October. Meanwhile fever and dysentery increased to an enormous extent and the hospitals were full. Beyond a punitive expedition into the Shinwari Valley in July no active operations took place. On the 6th August the 1st or Garrison Brigade started for Fatehabad on the Kabul road for change of air; so sickly were the troops that it took them three days to accomplish 19 miles and on the first day the 13th lost four men from heat apoplexy.

THE REOCCUPATION OF KABUL

On 20th August Pollock received orders to advance on Kabul, while Nott at Kandahar was also to converge on the capital. According to Seaton, this order cleared the hospitals better than all the doctors, so eager were the troops to avenge the destruction of the Kabul Army.

The army was to concentrate at Gandamak. Sale and his brigade arrived there on 3rd September, where the troops were organized in two divisions, the 1st Division commanded by Sir Robert Sale and the 2nd Division by Major-General McCaskill. Captain Havelock was appointed D.A.A.G. to the 1st Division, while to show that the Government of India had learnt a lesson no political officer accompanied the army.

On the 7th September the army advanced, the 1st Division leading, followed on the next day by the 2nd Division.

On the 8th September as the 1st Division approached the hills commanding the Jagdalak Pass, the enemy were discovered on the summits of an amphitheatre facing the left of the road. Columns of attack were formed, the leading troops being the 13th, under Captain Wilkinson in the centre, and the 9th Foot and Broadfoot's Sappers and Miners on either flank. A deep gully separated the opposing forces. The artillery having opened fire, the infantry descended into the ravine and up the opposite heights. Nothing could withstand their progress. It was typical of Sale that although he was a divisional commander, he placed himself, sword in hand, at the head of his old regiment, and cheered his men on, while the men, maddened by the sight of the skeletons of Elphinstone's force which they had passed by on their approach march, followed in gallant style. The enemy were quickly driven from two successive positions. The victory was complete and it was to a great extent achieved by the brave men of the old Jellalabad garrison. General Pollock in his report states: 'Seldom have soldiers had a more arduous task to perform, and never was an undertaking of the kind surpassed in execution.' The total casualties were 64 of all ranks killed and wounded. Major-General Sir Robert Sale was again among the wounded. The other casualties of the Regiment were one private killed and two serjeants and twelve privates wounded.

The advance towards Kabul was then continued, the 1st Division reaching Tezin on the 11th, where a halt was made to allow the 2nd Division to close up. On the evening of the 12th a picquet of Broadfoot's sappers holding a commanding position was vigorously attacked by the enemy, and its defenders were getting the worst of it, when a company of their old comrades, the 13th Light Infantry, came to their assistance and the Afghans were dispersed. The road from Tezin to Khoord Kabul is through a succession of lofty hills, called Huft Kotal, or Eight Hills. Dispositions for the attack on the Huft Kotal Pass, strongly held by Akbar Khan and his army, were made on the evening of the 12th, and the force moved off on the following morning.

The day commenced auspiciously with a successful cavalry charge against the Afghan horsemen. The leading regiments in the attack on the hills commanding the pass were the British Regiments the 13th Light Infantry on the right, the 9th in the centre and 31st Foot on the left. Slowly and steadily they ascended the steep slopes, driving the enemy before them, and then over successive ridges they drove the enemy by bayonet charges from their positions, until the summit of the Huft Kotal was gained, when three cheers were given by the victors, and the Afghans fled leaving 2 guns and 3 standards in the hands of the conquerors. The company of the Regiment, under Lieutenant W. A. Sinclair, especially distinguished itself on this occasion, while Serjeant Hoban again bore a conspicuous part; when his company was detached to reinforce the Ghoorka Sappers, who were overpowered and driven from the heights, he was the first to mount the hill in the face of a heavy fire from the enemy. The total British casualties were 32 killed and 132 wounded. The 13th lost one man killed and five wounded. The enemy was completely defeated and his losses were heavy.

Pollock, in a private letter describing this fight, says: 'I think no officer could possibly have had finer regiments under his command than I have, and to them do I owe all my success which as far as I am able to judge, has been so far complete.'

On 14th September the army reached Bootkhak; on the 15th they encamped on the race-course at Kabul, no further organized resistance being offered, in fact the city was almost deserted. On the following day the Bala Hissar was occupied, and the British Flag hoisted, when the guns thundered out a royal salute, the troops, consisting of the Grenadier companies of each corps, presented arms, and the National Anthem was played, after which three hearty cheers were given.

On 17th September Nott's army arrived within 4 miles of Kabul.

Although on arrival at Kabul some few of the prisoners in the hands of the enemy had been released, the great majority, including Lady Sale, Mrs. Sturt, and Lieutenant Mein of the 13th, had already been dispatched by Akbar Khan on 25th August to Bameean in the rugged range of the Hindu Khush, with a view to their being sent into Turkestan. They arrived at Bameean on 3rd September, where they halted till the 16th. As news gradually leaked through of the advance of the British armies on Kabul, their gaoler, Saleh Mahomed Khan, thinking to ingratiate himself with the British, offered to take them back to Kabul, if he could be assured of a sufficient ransom. This the captives readily promised. Saleh Mahomed Khan even offered to arm the few British soldiers among the captives. So demoralized were they that they refused to take arms, even though Lady Sale said, 'You had better give me one and I will lead the party'. On the following day they thought better of it, and when the party set out for Kabul most of them were armed.

As soon as Pollock arrived at Kabul, he dispatched his military secretary, Sir Richmond Shakespear, with 600 horsemen towards Bameean to obtain the release of the prisoners, and afterwards thinking that Shakespear might want support, he sent an order to Nott as being nearer to Bameean to send a brigade in support. Nott declined to obey the order, as he deemed the expedition to be fraught with danger, so Pollock turned to Sale, and that officer, having no qualms on the subject, joyfully accepted, and set off with a brigade including part of the 13th on the 18th September. It was the eve of his sixtieth birthday.

Meanwhile the captives on their return towards Kabul had been met by Sir Richmond Shakespear on the afternoon of the 17th at the foot of the Kaloo Pass. On the 18th they reached Gundundewar, and on the 19th they reached Tarkhana, where they heard that Sale was close at hand with a brigade.

On 20th September Sale, who was then at Urghandee, continued his march and, leaving his infantry at the pass near Kote Ashruffee, pushed on at the head of the 3rd Dragoons. Not many miles had been accomplished when Sir Robert Sale and the 3rd Dragoons met the party of captives and their escort. There was an affecting meeting between Sir Robert and Lady Sale, and then the whole party turned towards Kabul. What happened now is best described in Lady Sale's own words:—

'On proceeding to where the infantry were posted, they cheered all the captives as they passed, and the men of the 13th pressed forward to welcome us individually, most of the men had a little word of hearty congratulation to offer, each in his own style, on the restoration of his Colonel's wife and daughter, and then my highly wrought feelings found the desired relief; and I could scarcely speak to thank the soldiers for their sympathy, whilst the long-withheld tears now found their course. On arriving at the Camp, Captain Backhouse fired a royal salute from his mountain train guns; and not only our old friends, but all the officers in the party, came to offer congratulations, and welcome our return from captivity.'

On the following day Sale's Brigade marched through Killa Kazee to Kabul, and on arrival at the Camp at Siah Sung, the captives were greeted with another salute of twenty-one guns.

Lady Sale's journal of the events at Kabul after 7th November 1842, the subsequent evacuation of that city, the disastrous retreat, and the story of the captivity of most of the survivors, is a historic document, which at the time caused an enormous sensation in India and England. It is well worth perusing even now.

Sir Robert Peel thus alludes to Lady Sale in his speech of 23rd February 1843 in the House of Commons:—

'We are now acknowledging military services; but I never should excuse myself if in mentioning the name of Sir Robert Sale, I did not record my admiration of the character of a woman who has shed lustre on her sex. Lady Sale his wife. (Loud cheering.) The names of Sir Robert and Lady Sale will be familiar words with the people of this country. (Cheers.) I hold in my hand a memorandum of events which occurred in the neighbourhood of Kabul, from the 7th November, written by Lady Sale, and a document more truly indicative of a high, a generous, and a gallant spirit I never read.' (Cheers.)

As winter was approaching, and supplies limited, it was considered unadvisable to delay too long in Kabul, but in order to exact some just retribution for the treachery of the Afghans, Pollock caused the great covered bazaar, the mosque in which the Envoy's head had been displayed, and the houses of the Chiefs principally concerned in the rising to be burnt down.

On 12th October the army set out on its return to India, Sale's division leading, followed at intervals of one day by McCaskill's and Nott's divisions. The Regiment lost by death this night a very promising young officer, Lieutenant Scott.

There is little to record in the return march beyond a few skirmishes with the Afghans. The 13th Light Infantry reached Jellalabad on 22nd October and halted there a few days, during which time the fortifications were levelled to the ground. On the south face of the fortress was a large bastion, close to which was an open space which had been converted into a burial ground; here the remains of Colonel Dennie, with many other gallant soldiers, were laid and the Engineer Officer in mining the bastion, caused the whole mass to be thrown by the explosion over the grave, thus leaving a lasting monument over them, and what was of still greater importance, effectually preventing the bodies being disturbed by the Afghans.

On 26th October the march to India was resumed. The passage of the Khyber entailed some fighting, though not of a very serious kind, the chief losses being sustained by McCaskill's Division. The fort at Musjid was destroyed, and on 4th November the 13th were at Peshawar.

The Governor-General, Lord Ellenborough, directed that the army in its march through the Punjaub to British territory at Ferozepore should be preceded by the Jellalabad garrison, so that they might make a triumphal entry into the British Provinces by themselves. The Regiment reached Nowshera on the 11th November, Rawal Pindi on the 17th, where Lieutenant Frere, who had previously distinguished himself in the campaign, died, the Jhelum was crossed on 27th November, and the Ravee on 10th December.

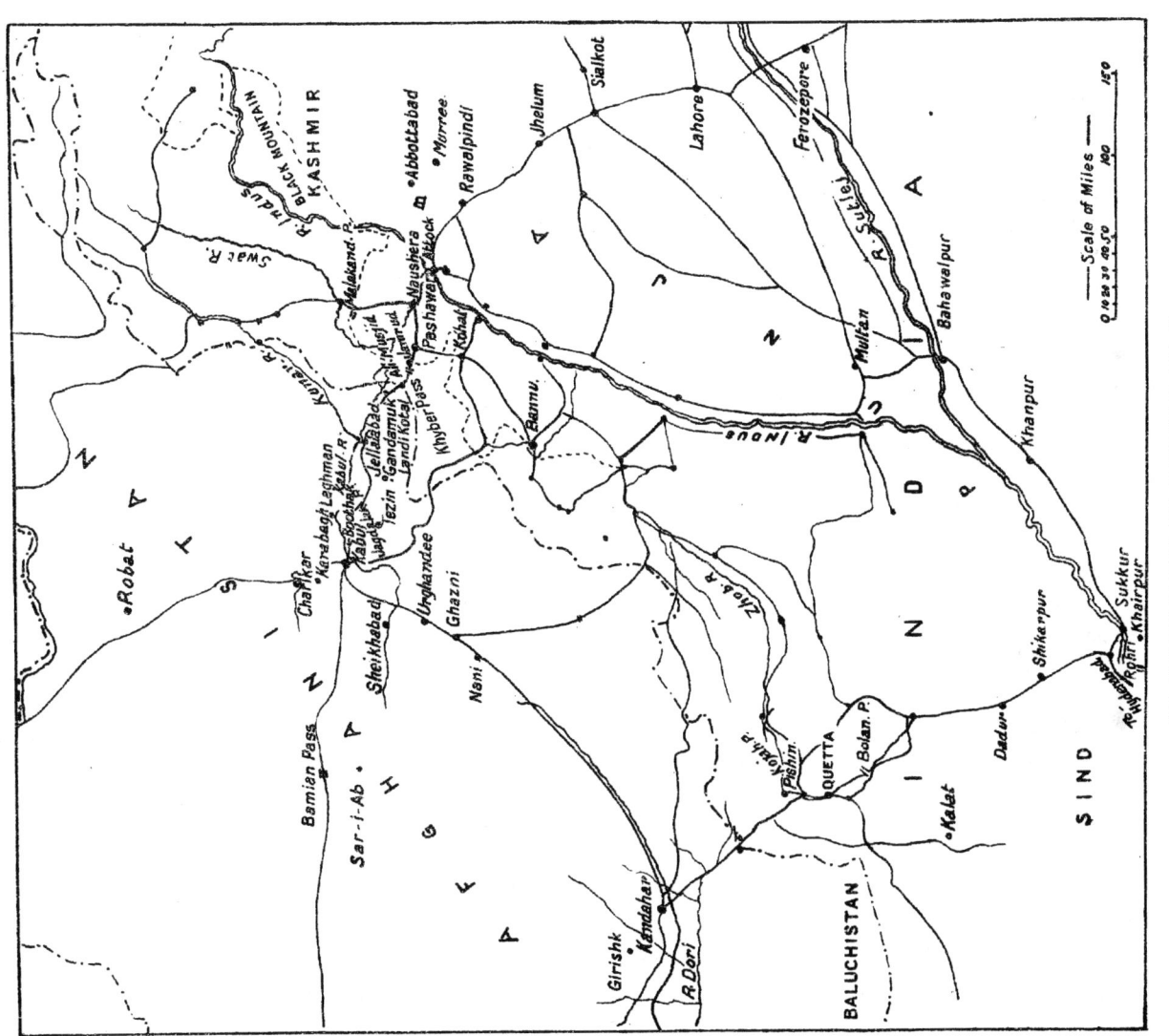

N.W. FRONTIER OF INDIA AND AFGHANISTAN, 1839-42

On the 14th December the Jellalabad garrison reached the right bank of the Sutlej, where they were met by two of the Governor-General's aides-de-camp, who presented the troops with the Jellalabad medal, so that they might wear them on their entry into Ferozepore.

On the 17th December Sir Robert Sale led the Jellalabad garrison across the bridge of boats gaily dressed with flags and streamers. At the opposite side was erected a triumphal arch, where they were met by Lord Ellenborough. The road to the camp was about 6 miles long; for the first 3 miles a sort of street was formed for the troops to pass through by placing elephants decked in their gayest trappings at intervals of about twenty paces, the remainder of the road was lined by the Army of Reserve encamped at Ferozepore, who presented arms as they passed, the bands playing the National Anthem.

These honours were rendered agreeably to the concluding paragraph of the General Order by the Right Honourable the Governor-General in India, dated Allahabad 30th of April 1842, which stated that: 'The Governor-General will request His Excellency the Commander-in-Chief of the Army to give instructions, in due time, that the several corps comprising the garrison of Jellalabad may, on their return to India, be received at all the stations on their route to their cantonments by all the troops at such stations, in review order, with presented arms.'

The same evening the officers of the Jellalabad garrison were entertained at a magnificent banquet given by the Governor-General.

The Regiment received the Queen's permission to bear on its colour and appointments the word 'CABOOL 1842' to commemorate its important services. On Major Pattisson was conferred the brevet rank of Lieutenant-Colonel; while Captains Havelock, Wilkinson, Wade and Fenwick were promoted to the brevet of major.

The following officers received the silver medal for CABOOL:—

Colonel Sir Robert Sale, G.C.B.

Captains

Major Henry Havelock.
," Arthur Wilkinson.
," Hamlet C. Wade.
," James Fenwick.

Captain Peter Jennings.
," Alex. E. F. Holcombe.
," George King.

Lieutenants

John S Wood, Adjutant.
William A. Sinclair.
Hon. Emilius J. Forester.
David Rattray.
Richard E. Frere.
George Wade.
John W. Cox.

Fred. Van Straubenzee.
Thomas B. Speedy.
J. Francis P. Scott.
G. G. C. Stapylton.
Robert S. Parker.
Arthur Oakes.
George Tablot.

Surgeon J. Robertson, M.D.

Asst. Surgeon George Barnes, M.D.

As regards the total casualties sustained by the Regiment during the Afghan War, it may be noted that the Regiment erected a Memorial in Canterbury Cathedral on which is inscribed the following words:—

'Whilst serving in Afghanistan between the years 1838 and 1842, either from the fatigues of service or in action with the enemy, these perished of the 13th Prince Albert's Light Infantry—Lieut.-Colonel Wm. H. Dennie, C.B., A.D.C., Brevet Major James Kershaw, Captains George Fothergill and Wm. Sutherland, Lieutenants Edward King, Richard Edward Frere, John Byron Hobhouse, and I. P. C. Scott, Sergt.-Major Airey, 12 serjeants, 11 corporals, 3 buglers, and 264 privates.

'Also shortly after their return from the country—Major J. G. D. Taylor, Captain William A. Sinclair and Assistant Surgeon G. W. Barnes.

'To the memory of the above their surviving brothers in arms of the same Regiment have caused this tablet to be erected.'

During the march to Ferozepore the non-commissioned officers and men of the 35th Native Infantry had arranged that after their arrival at that station the non-commissioned officers and men of the 13th Light Infantry should dine with them as their guests. The invitation was conveyed in the following letter:—

'To the Non-commissioned Officers and Privates of Prince Albert's Light Infantry—

'Friends and Fellow Comrades, permit me, in the name of the Native Officers and men of the 35th Native Infantry to request the favour of your partaking of a dinner, which it is our wish to provide, to evince our appreciation of the kindness and cordial good will all of you have shown towards us throughout the dangers and difficulties we have together encountered during the campaign.

'We trust the mutual good feeling will ever remain undiminished in our future intercourse, and we pray that you may be happy and live many years.

(signed) MANICK SING,
Sabadar-Major 35th Native Infantry'

The Regimental Serjeant-Major of the 13th then addressed a letter to Lieutenant and Adjutant Wood of the 13th expressive of the wish of the non-commissioned officers and men of the Regiment to testify their feelings of regard for their comrades in arms of the 35th Bengal Native Infantry before they separated at Ferozepore.

The letter continued:—

'As the Government have so amply provided for commemorating their services, it might not be inappropriate to offer them an entertainment, as also a silver attar-dan, and therefore trust you will procure the sanction of the commanding officer, for the attainment of our object, by applying to the officer in command of that corps for permission of their acceptance of this small token of acknowledgment of our gratitude for their conduct towards us during the siege of Jellalabad, and of our admiration of the manner in which they so cheerfully endured every privation, and joined hand in hand with us in meeting the enemies of our country during an eventful campaign of four years' duration, and it is our fervent prayer that they may long live to enjoy the honours conveyed on them by our Gracious Sovereign.

'It is more particularly gratifying to us to learn at this moment that this gallant corps has been beforehand with us in offering an entertainment, which has been accepted with feelings of much pride and gratification, and no length of time can suffice to erase from our remembrance conduct so generous and noble.

(signed) G. MUNROWA,
Serjeant-Major 13th or Prince Albert's Light Infantry'

There is a long account of these festivities which took place at Ferozepore in Seaton's *From Cadet to Colonel*. The 35th Native Infantry left nothing undone to make the dinner to the 13th a success, they took all the guards of the 13th on the day of the banquet. The fare included roast beef, mutton, fowls, plum pudding, oranges, almonds and raisins, while each man was provided with a bottle of beer and an extra ration of rum. The 35th even provided dhoolies for those who might be incapacitated, but history relates that these were not required.

In due course the 13th gave a return dinner in native style and presented the 35th with the piece of plate mentioned above to be kept in perpetual remembrance of their friends the soldiers of the 13th. At the side of the attar-dan is a shield supported by a soldier of the 13th and a sepoy of the 35th, and on the shield is an inscription in Persian and Hindi containing the history of the piece of plate.

The 35th Native Infantry were disbanded during the Indian Mutiny, but the piece of plate remained in the hands of the officers till 1863, when it passed into the care of Major-General Sir Thomas Seaton, K.C.B.

On 31st December there was a grand review at Ferozepore in which 40,000 troops with 100 guns took part.

On 16th January 1843 the Regiment marched from Ferozepore and arrived at Ludhiana on 23rd January, where the troops in garrison were drawn up to receive and present arms to the Regiment as forming part of the Garrison of Jellalabad. On 5th February they reached Mubarakpur and were joined by four officers and 150 recruits. The Regiment was inspected at Mubarakpur by Major-General J. W. Fast on 6th February 1843. His report contains the following observations:—

'Sir Robert Sale, the regular Commander, is highly qualified to command. He states however as follows: Lt.-Colonel Squire is qualified. Brevet Lt.-Colonel Pattisson is not—Major Vigors—from his long absence from the Regiment, and previous bad health cannot be formed an opinion of yet.'

The Commanding Officer's remarks on the officers are:—

'Lieut.-Colonel Squire is worn out in the service.

'Capt. Stehelin, who was left at Karnal, when the Regiment took the field in 1838, is unfit for active service, and who has not been able to join the Regiment since, being still absent on such leave, is quite worn out.

'Thirty men are recommended for discharge as being unfit.

'229 Recruits have joined the Regiment since the last inspection.

'The arms are clean but worn out. New arms are required

'The Colours are worn out. New ones are required.'

'GENERAL REMARKS

'This Regiment has but just returned from an Active Service of more than four (4) years' duration in Afghanistan, and its efficiency is in no degree impaired and it could at this moment take the Field—being in every respect qualified for doing so.

'The Field movements of the Regiment both Light and Heavy—under the personal direction of Major-General Sir Robert Sale, G.C.B., the Lieut.-Colonel of the Regiment—and subsequently under several of the Officers indiscriminately called upon for that duty—were performed with the greatest precision and celerity—and this upon ground that the Corps had never seen—until drawn up upon it for the purpose of being inspected—and which presented Inequalities and ravines—and was calculated to test the general drill and field movement discipline of a Corps to a considerable degree.

'The Interior Economy of the Regiment reflects the greatest Credit upon Major-General Sir Robert Sale, G.C.B., Commanding the Corps, and upon the Officers who have so ably supported him in the performance of their respective duties. The results of which has been to place the Regiment in the distinguished and highly honourable position it now holds.

'The Kits of the men are in some slight articles (with reference to regulations) deficient—as was to be expected—after the Service the Regiment has gone through—but not in anything that is really essential when in the Field and in an Active Campaign—and such deficiencies as have unavoidably happened during the Service the Corps has so long been on—are now rapidly replacing.

'The Hospital arrangements were most satisfactory and complete—so far as being in Tents admitted, and the Surgeon, D^{ctr} Robertson, was spoken of in the highest and most approbationary manner by Sir Robert Sale.

'Previous to the Field Movements of the Regiment the Company Drill was performed by Officers Commanding or having present charge of Companies.

'Their Light Infantry Movements under Sir Robert Sale, G.C.B., commanding the Regiment—comprising The Attack carrying a Bridge and defile. A Line of position by the whole Reg^t with adequate supports formed—Retiring from the Bridge with coverings well executed—some change of position and front, as Light Infantry with Lines of Skirmishers advanced, retired and relieved. The subsequent Line or heavy movements were by three (3) Captains and three (3) Lieutenants. The Serjeants and Corporals of Companies were examined by the Inspecting General—as to their knowledge of the duties of their situations.

'The Marching past in Review—in both times was admirable and the wheelings as though a solid Wall moved round—so firm, collected and compact, was each Company as it wheeled. The time was most correct, in both ordinary and quick.

J. W. Fast—Major-General,
Inspecting Officer'

'The mode adopted by Sir Robert Sale, G.C.B., for preventing damp or Water from entering the Muskett Barrel is very neat in appearance and perfect in obtaining the end required—as it preserves the charge uninjured though the Muskett should by chance be under water even.

'Captain and Brevet Major Havelock of this Regiment—as a Mounted Officer—evinced great activity and intelligence in the Field Movements—and is I am informed—in all respects a very valuable Officer.

'Major-General Sir Robert Sale, G.C.B., Commanding the Regiment, is one of the most active Men of his length of Service I have seen—and has his energies unimpaired—notwithstanding his long residence in India and a more complete Officer on a Parade I have not met with—nor a Regiment in better order at every point, than the one under His Command.

J. W. Fast, Major-General,
Inspecting Officer'

'It is due to the Regiment to mention that it was inspected the day following its arrival at Mubarakpore from Ferozepore so that no previous preparations for Inspection had or could be made by drills or parades and opportunities for drills could scarcely have existed during the time it was Blockaded in Jellalabad by the Afghans—or during the subsequent Operations of General Pollock's Army—of which it formed a part and scarcely any opportunity after re-entering Hindostan. This therefore proves the original drill and discipline of the Corps to have been sound and well conducted and attended to.

J. W. Fast, Major-General,
Inspectg. Officer'

On 9th March the 13th proceeded to Kasaulie in the Simla hills where they were employed in building barracks, cutting out and repairing roads—here Havelock, having returned to regimental duty, resumed his religious Services with the men of the 13th. Havelock had now twenty-eight years' service and was 48 years of age. He was in a hopeless position as he could not afford to purchase his majority in the Regiment. He had shortly before written to General Smith (afterwards Sir Harry Smith) as follows: 'Now in a word I will tell you what I want. I desire not to have to starve on 400 rupees a month when I return to the provinces, and to have some better employment than looking at the shirts and stockings of No. 4 company of the 13th, though they *did* pitch it into Akbar Khan's horse in such good style in the hour of need.' Many an ambitious young officer of the present day might deliver himself of similar sentiments. Havelock remained with the Regiment until October when he was appointed Persian Interpreter to the Commander-in-Chief, and never rejoined the Regiment.

On 14th April the Regiment received another draft of four officers and 94 men. On 23rd July the Regiment was inspected by Major-General J. W. Fast. His general observations contain the following: 'The Regiment is in the best possible order, and its Commander, Major-General Sir Robert Sale, G.C.B., is remarkably active, and a most attentive and intelligent officer in every respect.'

Stapylton tells us that on 24th July, a dinner-party consisting of some of the officers of the 9th Foot, 1st Europeans, and residents of Kasaulie dined at the 13th mess to celebrate the anniversary of the capture of Ghazni.

On 24th October the Regiment marched from Kasaulie to Loodianah, which they reached on 6th November. At this place percussion muskets were issued to the Regiment for the first time, the old flint arms being returned to store. The march was then continued to Ferozepore and they arrived at that station on the 15th. After a halt of ten days the Regiment embarked in boats on the Sutlej and proceeding down-stream reached Sukkur on 20th December. Here Sale took over temporary command of the station.

On 3rd December General Edward Morrison, the Colonel of the Regiment, died. He had held the command since 1813, a period of thirty years; surely a record!

The Colonelcy of the Regiment was now conferred on Sir Robert Sale by Her Majesty the Queen, and early in 1844 Sir Robert and Lady Sale proceeded home on leave. They were received by Her Majesty the Queen at Windsor Castle, who kindly expressed her gratification at seeing them and settled from her civil list a pension of £500 per annum on Lady Sale, with remainder to Sale should he survive her.

Public receptions and honours were paid everywhere to Sir Robert and Lady Sale, notably at Londonderry and Southampton. On the 29th March Sale was appointed Quartermaster-General to the Queen's forces serving in India, and he returned to that country early in 1845.

Sir Robert Sale's place as Lieutenant-Colonel commanding the Regiment was filled by Lieut.-Colonel Tristram C. Squire, who joined the Regiment at Sukkur on 13th January 1844, with a draft of officers and men from England; Major Horatio Nelson Vigors was promoted to the rank of Lieutenant-Colonel; and Captain R. M. Meredith succeeded to the majority.

On the 29th May the Regiment was inspected by Major-General Simpson commanding in Upper Scinde. Under the heading 'General Observations' he remarks: 'This is a very fine and effective Regiment. In the course of my inspection, I have remarked nothing calling for animadversion. Everything seems strictly in conformity with the Regulations of the Service, and the Corps fit for a continuance of active and immediate Service.'

In June the Regiment was utilized in suppressing the mutiny of the 64th Bengal Native Infantry, who had been brought down to Sukkur from Shikarpur. They were disarmed and thirty or forty of the ringleaders arrested.

During September the 13th moved from Sukkur, by wings, *en route* to Karachi, the left wing on the 4th and the Headquarters division on the 24th. The former arrived at Karachi on 21st September and the latter on 8th October. During this march the Regiment suffered severely from malaria, having two to three hundred in hospital daily. The Regiment was now under orders for England, and as was the custom in those days, volunteers were called for service in corps serving in India. Four hundred and forty-six responded to the call, and were left temporarily at Karachi.

The Regiment embarked at Karachi for Bombay on board the Honourable East India Company's steamers, *Pluto* and *Sesostris*, on the 4th December and disembarked at Bombay in the afternoon of the 8th, being received by the Governor and military authorities of the Presidency; the guard of honour presenting arms as the Regiment passed, and the band striking up 'See the conquering hero comes'. While stationed at Bombay, the Regiment had the misfortune to lose Captain William Alexander Sinclair, who had served throughout the campaigns in Afghanistan; he died of cholera after an illness of a few hours; the soldiers, however, continued generally healthy.

On the 20th March 1845 the Headquarters division of the 13th embarked in the freight ship, *Cornwall*, at Colaba, Bombay, under the command of Lieut.-Colonel Squire, and the second division in the freight ship, *Boyne*, on the same day under Lieut.-Colonel Vigors. The right wing disembarked at Gravesend on the 28th July, and the second division arrived there on the 8th August, from whence it proceeded to Walmer Barracks, in order to join the Headquarters, which had marched thither from Chatham.

Before following the fortunes of the 13th in other countries there were two events of outstanding interest in India which claim our attention.

The one is the gallantry and heroic conduct of a part of the volunteers left behind, and the other is the death of Sir Robert Sale.

THE STORMING OF THE HEIGHTS OF TRUCKEE

It has been mentioned before that 446 of the rank and file of the Regiment volunteered for service in regiments remaining in India. Of these 192 volunteered for the 39th Regiment, which was then stationed at Dinapore in Bengal. In order to reach their destination they had a long march to make. Sir Charles Napier, a great soldier and administrator, was then Governor of Scinde, and he happened to be in Karachi when the Regiment left for Bombay, and, as he was about to proceed up country, he formed the volunteers of the 13th destined for the 39th Regiment into a separate unit, and they formed part of his escort. They proceeded in the first instance to Larkana about 50 miles south-west of Sukkur. Early in 1845 Captain Beatson, with a mixed force, was engaged in hunting out nests of robbers in the Baluchistan Hills, and in order to give him some assistance Napier sent his camel corps and the volunteers of the 13th, also mounted on camels, to Beatson at Shore who was to proceed by the Goojroo defiles to the Murrow plain, and to seize the northern entrance to Trukkee. What followed is best described in Sir William Napier's account of the action taken from his book, *The Administration of Scinde*.

'In the course of the operations on the 8th March 1845, the troops having entered a short way into the defile, a serjeant and 16 men of the 13th volunteers got on the wrong side of what appeared to be a small chasm and went against a height crowned by the enemy, where the chasm suddenly deepened so as to be impassable. The Company from which the serjeant had separated was on the other side, and his officer seeing how strong the hillmen were on the rock, made signs to retire, which the serjeant mistook for a signal to attack, and with inexpressible intrepidity scaled the precipitous height. The robbers waited concealed behind a breastwork until eleven of the 13th came up, and then, being seventy in number, closed on them. All the eleven had medals, some had three, and in that dire moment proved that their courage at Jellalabad had not been exaggerated by fame. A desperate encounter took place. Six of the 13th were killed, and the others, being wounded, were pushed over the edge of the steep slope of the hill, but this did not happen till seventeen of the enemy and their commander had been killed.

'There is a custom with the hillmen, that when a great champion dies in battle, his comrades, after stripping his body, tie a red or green thread round his right or left wrist according to the greatness of his exploit—the red being the most honourable. Here those brave warriors stripped the British dead, and cast the bodies over; but with this testimony of their own chivalric sense of honour and the greatness of the fallen soldiers' courage—each body had a red thread on both wrists! Thus fell Sale's veterans, and he as if ashamed of having yielded them precedence on the road to death, soon after took his glorious place beside them in the grave. Honoured be his and their names!'

This exploit called forth the following letters from His Excellency Sir Charles Napier and His Grace the Duke of Wellington:—

'Sukkur, *30th March 1845*

Sir,—

It will gratify you, and be just to some brave men, who volunteered from the 13th for your regiment, to send to you a copy of my letter to the Commander-in-Chief, relative to a gallant action performed by them on the 8th instant.

The whole of the volunteers for your regiment have behaved admirably during the five months they have been serving under my own immediate observation; they have shown themselves worthy of the regiment they have left, and of that which is under your command.

I have &c.

C. J. Napier, Major-General,
Governor of Scinde

Officer Commanding
H.M. 39th Regiment.'

'Camp Sukkur
25th *March 1845*

Sir,—

It is with regret I have to say that, misled by the report of Captain Beatson, I stated that the six soldiers, who on the 8th instant, fell on the heights of Truckee, were killed in consequence of their own imprudence. This was incorrect and unjust. They acted in obedience to their orders, and died in the fullness of glory, worthy of the brightest names in our military annals. The enclosed return, received from the orderly room, is more eloquent than anything I can say. I am convinced that one who has so often witnessed the gallantry of soldiers, will not read unmoved this proud but distressing record of heroism and death.

The survivors of those, who reached the top, merit the honour to have their names laid before His Grace the Duke of Wellington, and it would be very grateful to their feelings if your Excellency would do this. They are men of excellent character; most of them had two, and some three medals. The bold Sepoy of the Camel Corps is highly praised by them for his courageous conduct.

Hoping that some mark of approbation may be bestowed on these admirable soldiers, I have &c.

C. J. Napier, Major-General
Governor of Scinde

His Excellency
General Sir Hugh Gough, Bart., G.C.B.,
Commander-in-Chief in India.'

Nominal Roll of the Serjeant's Party of a Detachment of Her Majesty's 39th Volunteers, which stormed the Hill at Truckee on the 8th March 1845

Serjeant John Power. Reached the summit of the hill and was slightly wounded.

Corporal Thomas Waters. Did not quite reach the summit of the hill. Three medals.

Corporal John Kenny. Did not quite reach the summit of the hill. Three medals.

Private John Action. Reached the top, killed three of the enemy, and was then killed himself. Two medals.

Private Robert Adair. Reached the top, killed two of the enemy and was then killed himself. Two medals.

Private Hugh Dunlap. Reached the top, killed two of the enemy, and was then killed himself.

Private Patrick Fulton. Reached the summit of the hill, and was killed. Two medals.

Private Samuel Lowrie. Reached the top, killed the Commander of the enemy and another man, and was then killed himself. Two medals.

Private William Lovelace. Reached the top, and was killed.

Private Anthony Burke. Reached the top, killed three of the enemy (shot one, bayoneted another), broke his musket on the head of the third. Two medals.

[1] Private John Maloney. Reached the top, bayoneted two of the enemy, saved Burke and Rohan's lives, and was severely wounded. Three medals.

Private Bartholomew Rohan. Reached the top, bayoneted one of the enemy, and was severely wounded. Two medals.

Private George Campbell. Reached the top, and killed two of the enemy.

Private Philip Fay. Did not quite reach the summit. Two medals.

Private Mark Davis. Did not quite reach the summit. Two medals.

Private Charles Hawthorn. Did not quite reach the summit. Two medals.

Camel Corps. Ruinzan Aheer. Did not quite reach the summit.

'Horse Guards, *12th June 1845*

Sir,—

I have the honour to receive your letter of the 15th April, with a letter and its accompanying return from Major-General Sir Charles Napier setting forth the conspicuous gallantry of a party of volunteers of the 13th Light Infantry to the 39th Regiment, in storming the almost inaccessible hill position of Truckee, occupied by a strong force of the Mountain Desert Robbers; and having laid these papers before the Commander-in-Chief, I am instructed to request that you will cause the expression of his highest approbation to be conveyed to such of these brave men as have survived the attack; and that you will further be pleased to recommend them specially to the notice and protection of the commanding officer of the 39th Regiment, and ascertain and report for His Grace's information whether the serjeant is qualified to hold a commission in His Majesty's service.

The Duke of Wellington deeply laments the loss of those who fell on this memorable occasion.

I have &c.

Fitzroy Somerset

To General Sir Hugh Gough, Bart., G.C.B.,
 Commander-in-Chief in India.'

This gallant feat of arms is finely described in the poem entitled 'The Red Thread of Honour', by Sir Francis Hastings Doyle.

THE DEATH OF SIR ROBERT SALE

During the cold weather of 1845–6 the Sikhs had invaded the British provinces bordering on the Sutlej and laid siege to Ferozepore. Sir Hugh Gough, the Commander-in-Chief, hastily assembled an army for its relief. Among his staff were three Jellalabad heroes, Sir Robert Sale, Quarter-Master-

---

[1] John Maloney was wounded with his own bayonet, after he had driven through a Baloochee, for the latter unfixed it, drew it out of his own body, stabbed Maloney and fell dead.

MAJOR-GENERAL SIR ROBERT SALE, G.C.B.
Colonel of the Regiment, 1843-1845

General; Lieut.-Colonel Henry Havelock, and Major Broadfoot. At the first encounter, at the battle of Mudkee on 18th December 1845, Sir Robert Sale had his left thigh so dreadfully shattered by a grape-shot wound that he died on 21st December. Major Broadfoot was killed at the Battle of Ferozeshah on 21st December. They were buried in the cantonment cemetery at Ferozepore on 26th December, and were laid to rest in adjacent graves in the presence of the Governor-General, Sir Henry Hardinge; the Commander-in-Chief, Sir Hugh Gough, and their staffs. Sir Robert Sale was 64 years of age, had over fifty years' service, forty of which had been spent in the East and had only been three years and one month in England during his active service. Of Sale it may be said that he was essentially a fighting man, ever in the van he had been wounded five times. In his earlier campaigns, especially in Burmah, he had justly earned the sobriquet of 'Fighting Bob'. His ambition was to lead his men into action, knowing full well that where he went they would follow. Like the knights of old, he sought out personal encounters with the enemy. Even as a Brigadier commanding the main assaulting column at Ghazni he became involved in a personal combat with an Afghan. On the 7th April 1842 at Jellalabad when Dennie's advance was threatened by an outpost of the enemy on his flank, Seaton tells us, 'Sale's blood was up' and he ordered Dennie to attack; and again on 8th September 1842, as a divisional commander, he led his old regiment into action. As Quarter-Master-General to the Army at the Battle of Mudkee when mortally wounded, he appears to have been well in the forefront of battle. These incidents in his later career testify to the fact that he never lost the fire of youth. From his portrait he must have been a fine-looking man. Major-General Fast's description of him three years before his death is probably correct: 'Sir Robert Sale is one of the most active men of his length of service I have seen, and his energies unimpaired notwithstanding his long residence in India, and a more complete officer on parade I have not met with.'

Undoubtedly the Regiment owes to Sale a large measure of the fame it has acquired, the royal facings on its uniform and the royal title of 'Prince Albert's'. His name will always be cherished and revered in the Regiment as 'The Hero of Jellalabad'. Lord Ripon in the House of Lords alluded to his loss as follows: 'One of the most distinguished men in that or any other army fell in that battle. Who does not know the name of Sir Robert Sale? Who can forget the services he has rendered to his country and his sovereign?' In like manner Sir Robert Peel, speaking in the House of Commons, said: 'It is mournful, Sir, that we should have to deplore the loss in the same conflict of two gallant men so devoted to their country's service as Sir Robert Sale and Major Broadfoot.'

CHAPTER XVIII

HOME SERVICE. THE SIEGE OF SEVASTOPOL

LIEUT.-GENERAL SIR WILLIAM MAYNARD GOMM, K.C.B., was appointed Colonel of the 13th on the 10th March 1846 in succession to Sir Robert Sale. Sir William Gomm was a most distinguished officer, having served throughout the Peninsular War, and as Quarter-Master-General of the 5th Division was present at Quatre Bras and Waterloo. At the time of his appointment to the 13th he was Governor and Commander-in-Chief of Mauritius. Subsequently in 1851 he was appointed Commander-in-Chief in India and held that appointment till 1855.

The inspection of the 13th at the end of 1845 called forth the severe censure of the Commander-in-Chief, His Grace the Duke of Wellington. The Commanding Officer, Lieut.-Colonel Squire, was informed that should the Regiment continue not to profit by the superior advantages it enjoyed in its present quarters at Walmer, it would be moved to quarters under the immediate eye of a General Officer.

On the 4th March 1846 Lieut.-Colonel Squire applied to the Horse Guards for permission for the Regiment to wear the Jellalabad medal suspended from a Ribbon of Crimson with Black edges in memory of Colonel Sir Robert Sale. This request was refused on the grounds that no portion of the Army had ever been permitted to wear permanently any emblem of mourning for a subject.

The Regiment proceeded from Walmer to Portsmouth on the 27th April 1846, and were quartered in the Cambridge barracks. Previous to the march of the 13th, a high testimonial of their conduct, while at Walmer, was received from the Mayor and Magistrates of Deal.

In May the Regiment was inspected by Major-General Sir H. Pakenham, who reported as follows:—

'The 13th Light Infantry is complete to the Establishment and in very advanced discipline, and by the end of the season will be in perfect order.

'Some disappointment in the material has prevented the new light trowsers being yet taken into wear; that will shortly be done.

'The books, barracks, and interior economy are all regular, and there is an excellent school.

'The men have no confidence in the Savings Bank, having had above £1,500 among them on landing, there is not one depositor.'

On Thursday the 13th of August, the Regiment had the gratification of

GENERAL SIR WILLIAM MAYNARD GOMM, G.C.B.
Colonel of the Regiment, 1846-1863

being presented with new Colours by His Royal Highness Prince Albert on Southsea Common.

The account of this interesting ceremony is taken from the *United Service Gazette* of 15th August 1846.

'His Royal Highness Prince Albert, wearing a Field-Marshal's uniform, came over from Osborne House in the Royal yacht, accompanied by Colonel Wylde and a small retinue, all in uniform, and landed at the King's Stairs in the Dockyard, at about a quarter to four o'clock. The Commander-in-Chief, Admiral Sir Charles Ogle, Bart., the Lieut.-Governor, Major-General the Honourable Sir Hercules Pakenham, K.C.B., and a brilliant staff of officers of both services, received His Royal Highness on landing, who immediately entered General Pakenham's carriage, and was driven to the field, escorted by General Pakenham and staff on horseback, receiving the shouts of welcome from the immense concourse of spectators, who lined the road as he passed. Soon after three o'clock the Regiment took up its position on Southsea Common, in line, at open order, with the old Colours in the centre. On his arrival the Prince was received with the customary honours. The Regiment then formed three sides of a hollow square, the company told off as a guard for the new colours remaining in the centre of the open face. The Prince having alighted from the carriage, mounted his charger (which together with five other beautiful animals, came down from the Royal Mews to the George Hotel last night), rode along the line both inside and out, inspecting the troops, as they covered the ground, after which the Prince dismounted and entered the hollow square, accompanied by General Pakenham, Sir Charles Ogle, and staff, and stood uncovered while the Rev. C. R. Gleig, Chaplain-General to the Forces, consecrated the Colours, which, after this ceremony, were handed to the Prince by Lieut.-Colonel C. T. Van Straubenzee and Major Meredith. The Prince then handed them to the two senior ensigns (J. D. Longden and Melville Browne), who received them kneeling, and continued in that position while His Royal Highness addressed them in a brief but most spirited and soldierly manner, enjoining them to preserve their Colours, never allow them to be captured, but to emulate the conduct exhibited by the departed hero, Sir Robert Sale, whose absence was the only alloy to the gratification he felt in performing the august ceremony of the day. His Royal Highness, in the course of his address, passed some high and well-deserved encomiums on Colonel Squire and the 13th Regiment, to which that gallant veteran replied: "I beg most respectfully to return my most sincere thanks for the distinguished honour your Royal Highness has just conferred upon this corps in the presentation of new Colours and for the highly flattering manner in which your Royal Highness has been pleased to mention my name, in connexion with its services in India, and also for the gratifying encomiums which you have passed on our late honoured and respected commanders, Sir Robert Sale and Colonel Dennie. Your Highness may be assured that your gracious condescension will ever be esteemed by all ranks in the Regiment as the greatest stimulant to the loyal and faithful discharge of their duty under whatever circumstances of trial they may hereafter be placed, in supporting the honour and interest of our beloved Queen and country. God save the Queen.'

His Highness seemed much gratified with the sentiments of the gallant Colonel, and having bowed, retired with General Pakenham and Sir Charles Ogle, and remounted his charger. The sides of the square, which were wheeled up, then wheeled back and the Regiment formed line. The new Colours were now trooped, followed by the guard in charge, the band playing 'The Grenadiers' slow march.

On arrival at the left of the line, the Colours were carried, and the officers took post in front of the line, one rank of the guard marching between the ranks of the line, and the other rank in rear of the rear rank. On arrival at the place where the old Colours were stationed, the new Colours took up their place, whilst the old ones were paraded up the remaining portion of the line, the trooping still proceeding, and were then delivered over to the escort on the right of the line; their military existence, as standards of the Regiment, then ceasing.

The ceremony having terminated, the Prince re-entered the carriage of General Pakenham, and, accompanied by Admiral Sir Charles Ogle, Bart., and escorted by General Pakenham and staff, returned to the dockyard, whence he embarked for Osborne House, under salutes from the ships in harbour, the Platform battery, and the *Contest, Columbine,* and *Sardinian* corvettes at Spithead. A magnificent entertainment was given in honour of the event in the evening, by the officers of the 13th, at the King's Rooms, Southsea beach.

In the following October the Regiment was again inspected by Major-General the Hon. Sir H. Pakenham.

His general observations are as follows:—

'The 13th Light Infantry is in good order as to interior economy, but requires some bracing up in field movements, particularly the Light Exercises.

'The men are a fine, active, well-conditioned body and will soon make a fine Corps.

'The whole of the Regiment estimate most highly the Honour conferred upon them by His Royal Highness Prince Albert presenting their new Colours. This feeling, if judiciously managed, will always produce a salutary effect.

'The general conduct of the Corps has been regular and satisfactory. The Regiment only requires 15 men to complete.'

On the 3rd November 1846 Lieut.-Colonel Squire retired from the Service, and Lieut.-Colonel A. A. T. Cunninghame succeeded to the command of the Regiment; in the following month he exchanged with Captain and Lieut.-Colonel Charles Stuart of the Grenadier Guards.

On the 12th and 13th January 1847 the Regiment proceeded in two divisions from Portsmouth to Ireland and arrived at Dublin on the 16th of that month. His Royal Highness Prince George of Cambridge, K.G., was in command, and he inspected the Regiment in April.

His general observations were as follows:—

'It is with extreme regret that I cannot make so favourable a report of the 13th Light Infantry as I could have wished and this Corps is decidedly in many respects in a most deficient state. The drill of the Regiment is not good, the men badly set up, and not half drilled, their carriage slovenly and equally deficient in the performance of their Garrison duties. There is much crime, particularly that of desertion, and the selling of necessaries, also stealing from their comrades. The men do not appear satisfied or contented and though no actual complaints were made on parade they all said on going around their messes in their barrack rooms that they were not sufficiently fed. I made every inquiry on the subject, but could not discover that they were differently fed from any other corps in this Garrison. I attribute the want of smartness and exactness in this Corps in a great measure to the very indifferent body of Non-Commissioned Officers and should hope to see a great improvement in them ere long. Lieut.-Colonel Stuart having but lately assumed the command, I trust that with the zeal he evinces, and with a due degree of firmness, though mildness, he will be enabled to correct much that is at present defective. In justice to this corps I must add that in consequence of the very high price of provisions the soldier at this moment is worse off than at any other period for many years past.

'A regimental library existing in this corps, I have desired that it may be gradually done away with.'

Towards the end of September the Regiment proceeded to Birr and on 22nd October it was inspected by Major-General Sir Guy Campbell, Bart., C.B., Commanding the Athlone District. His general observations are as follows:—

'Lieut.-Colonel Stuart appears to be a good commanding officer, and very attentive to the well-being of the corps. The appearance of the 13th Light Infantry at my inspection was very soldierlike, and the field movements performed in good style. The Regiment is composed of very young men, but the material is excellent. I had every reason to be satisfied with all I saw.'

On the 18th April 1848, the Regiment marched from Birr to Newry, and during July it proceeded to Belfast where the headquarters were stationed, with detachments of one company each at Carrickfergus, Armagh, and Downpatrick. On 11th October the Regiment was inspected by Major-General Bainbrigge.

Extracts from his general observations are as follows:—

'This is a beautiful regiment well drilled and well conducted.'

. . . .

'I enclose the copy of a regimental order dated Dublin, 8th April 1847, granting exemptions from certain duties to good-conduct men, and placing them in three classes. I have directed that Her Majesty's Regulations may be strictly followed.

'I also found it necessary to cancel some other Regimental orders, viz. the keeping of the last year's clothing, and obliging the men to wear it on certain occasions, and the having Squad bags to carry clothing &c. on the march and obliging the soldier to pay for the carriage. Also an order directing that no man of the Regiment is to be called upon to lift a package of more than 400 lbs. weight. Also an order requiring all Recruits to attend school until dismissed from drill, and an order requiring all non-commissioned officers under the rank of serjeant to attend school. . . .

'It was painful to me to object to measures which had been adopted by so zealous and well intentioned an officer as Lieut.-Colonel Stuart, and still more painful to report what I have done, but I feel that it is impossible to judge of the state of the Regiment unless I mentioned all these particulars. . . .

'The school of the Regiment is exceedingly well conducted; shirts for the soldiers are turned out at a cheaper rate made by the children, than they can be bought for, and of better materials and better workmanship.

'The Serjeants' Mess is very well conducted and on a most respectable footing; I enclose a copy of the Rules. I remarked one word in it which I have noted, viz. the word "gentlemanly" which I considered applied to officers and not to non-commissioned officers, who are not in the situation of "gentlemen". I have not required the word to be altered as Lieut.-Colonel Stuart said he feared it would hurt the feelings of the non-commissioned officers to alter it.'

In commenting on this inspection report and others made during the time that Lieut.-Colonel Stuart commanded the Regiment there can be no doubt that that officer was far ahead of his times. Many of the reforms he instituted were a little later firmly established in the Army. This applied particularly to Regimental Libraries and Schools, and with regard to the Serjeants' mess, it may now be said that the epithet 'gentlemanly' correctly describes the conduct of a well-regulated Serjeants' Mess.

No change was made in the stations of the Regiment during 1849. Major-General Bainbrigge again inspected them on the 15th May and 1st October of that year.

On the former occasion he made the following general observations:—

'The Regiment appears to be in very good order and fit for any service, and has decidedly improved in every respect since the last half-year's inspection. . . .

'It is the custom with the Regiments in this district to fire Ball at target practice with unfixed bayonets, thereby showing better practice than with fixed bayonets; I have however directed that the Ball firing may be practised with fixed as well as with unfixed bayonets.'

On the latter occasion among his general observations are the following:—

'Although I should be very sorry to lose this Regiment from my Headquarters, yet I feel it a duty to say that a change of quarters would be desirable, the men seem to have got too intimate with the women both at Belfast and

Carrickfergus. Women have been known to carry off soldiers from Carrickfergus in a car; taking them to Belfast and keeping them there for several days. There is a good deal of absence from tattoo and staying out at nights; 53 Courts Martial and 10 desertions since last Inspection. The Regiment however is well drilled and in good order and, the Commanding Officer, Lieut.-Colonel Stuart, has taken the greatest pains. In consequence of having a good exercise field, the men are pretty well instructed in Light Infantry movements. . . .

'I have effectually carried out the Queen's Regulations on the subject of haircutting with all corps in this district, which I had great difficulty in doing before. The men had been so long accustomed to wear the hair at the top of the head long, and combed down on one side, and plastered with grease, that the orders requiring it to be cut short, were almost considered obsolete, and then the practice of cutting the hair close on going into cells and prisons and gaols, caused short hair to be looked upon as a mark of infamy.

'The school of this Regiment is particularly well conducted, Mrs. Stuart, the wife of Lieut.-Colonel Stuart, taking a great interest in it, and visiting it herself very often.'

It will be remembered that all ranks of the Regiment during the Afghan campaigns had earned three medals viz. the Ghuznee, Jellalabad, and Kabul medals. Previous to those campaigns medals had not been generally issued to the British service, except in the case of the Waterloo campaign and even in that case they were the personal gift of the Prince Regent.

When the veterans of the Peninsular War and of the other campaigns during the Napoleonic struggle learnt that troops employed on the Indian frontier had earned three medals in the course of three years, a considerable agitation was started in England that the services of these veterans should be duly recognized. The Duke of Wellington at first strongly opposed this proposal, but eventually he had to give in, and on the 12th February 1850 a General Order was published awarding the Army General Service Medal to all those who took part in the Napoleonic Wars. The medal has no less than 28 clasps; of these clasps the 13th were entitled to those of 'Martinique', 'Guadaloupe' and 'Egypt'.

It might be supposed that in 1850 there would be but few survivors to claim this medal. It is very gratifying, however, to record that the numbers of the 13th then alive and claiming the medal were in the case of

Martinique	67
Guadaloupe	58
Egypt	23

A copy of the medal rolls now at the War Office is contained in Appendix D.

On the 26th of April 1850 the headquarters and four companies under the command of Lieut.-Colonel Charles Stuart embarked at Belfast for Scotland, and arrived at Fort George, Inverness, three days afterwards, and was followed shortly by the remainder of the Regiment.

On 15th May the Regiment was inspected by Major-General H. J. Riddell, K.H. There is nothing of special interest in his report.

On the 11th November three companies proceeded to Dundee and three to Perth, the headquarters, with four companies being moved on the 14th of that month to Stirling, where on the 21st November they were again inspected by Major-General H. J. Riddell, K.H. His report contains little of interest, but the Commander-in-Chief's remarks contain the following:—

'According to the tenor of this report all would seem to be right in this Regiment, but the Commander-in-Chief cannot consider any corps as in a satisfactory state in which there is so much crime, and in which 67 trials have taken place within six months, and that too in an enclosed Fort where there could be no external incitement, or temptation, or irregularity.'

In March 1851 the Regiment again received orders for foreign service, and proceeded by railway, in detachments, to Winchester, where they were collected and stationed.

On the 24th May the headquarters and six companies mustering 24 officers and 578 Non-commissioned officers and men, embarked under the command of Lieut.-Colonel Stuart in the freight ship *Herefordshire*, for Gibraltar, where they arrived on the 5th June and were quartered in the Casemate barracks of that fortress. The Depôt companies, under Major Holcombe, proceeded from Winchester to Gosport.

The Regiment was inspected at Gibraltar by Major-General Sir Robert Gardiner on 3rd July and 13th October, but there is nothing of special interest in his reports.

In May 1852 the Depôt moved from Gosport to Jersey. The Regiment remained at Gibraltar and was inspected by Lieut.-General Sir Robert Gardiner on 10th May and 11th October. The reports were good and the Commander-in-Chief's remarks are as follows: 'Very satisfactory in all respects and the C.-in-C. is glad to find that a large reduction has taken place in the number of trials since last inspection.'

In May 1853 the Depôt moved from Jersey to Fermoy and later on in December to Clonmel. Major-General R. C. Mansel inspected the Depôt at Fermoy on 7th October and reported that this Depôt is composed of a fine body of stout men in a high state of order and discipline, and is well managed by Major Holcombe.

The Regiment was inspected at Gibraltar on 10th October 1853 by Lieut.-General Sir R. Gardiner. His report is a satisfactory one. He reported the proportion of Courts Martial as one to every 33 men.

In 1854 during March and April a portion of the garrison of Gibraltar received orders to join the expedition in the Black Sea; England and France having joined Turkey in the war against Russia. One hundred and thirty-seven volunteers of the 13th Light Infantry were transferred to the 30th, 44th and 55th Regiments. Soon after the regiment was augmented to twelve companies consisting of 67 serjeants, 25 drummers and 1,200 rank and file.

The Regiment was inspected by Lieut.-General Sir Robert Gardiner on 15th May. He reported a considerable decrease in the number of Courts Martial, and that the Regimental Savings Bank deposits had increased from £256 in 1851 to £1,256 in 1854 and the number of depositors in the same period from 26 to 120.

The Depôt at Clonmel was inspected on 5th May by Major-General John McDonald. His report is a good one. Major Burslem and the officers are reported as active and intelligent and on the whole the Depôt is in good order. At this time there was one company at Wexford and a subaltern's party at Cashel.

On 8th November the Regiment was again inspected at Gibraltar by Lieut.-General Sir Robert Gardiner. The returns show an average of one Court Martial to every 218 men, as against one to every 33 men in the previous year.

On the 22nd December Colonel Charles Stuart (who had been promoted to the brevet rank of Colonel on the 20th June 1854) retired on half-pay in consequence of ill health and was succeeded by Colonel Lord Mark Kerr from the 20th Regiment. Lord Mark had been asking the Horse Guards for months previously for the command of a battalion or an appointment on the staff in the Crimea, and he was just about to proceed to the Black Sea on his own account when he was gazetted to the 13th. He arrived at Gibraltar on the 18th January, 1855. According to his journal, he formed a favourable opinion of the discipline of the Regiment, though their drill did not please him. He reports the band and bugles as very good, and the Adjutant and Quartermaster as very good at blundering, but hopes to replace them by really good officers.

On the 15th February Major Burslem and the Depôt companies, strength 6 officers and 289 men, arrived from Ireland in Her Majesty's ship *Caesar* and the transport *Scindia*.

Lord Mark Kerr made every effort to get the Regiment sent to the Crimea; he even wrote to Lord Raglan, the Commander-in-Chief, and enlisted the support of Delane of *The Times*, who published an article signed 'Instans' on 7th May in support of Lord Mark's ambitions.

On 24th May as the Regiment was returning to barracks from the Queen's birthday parade on the North Front, Lord Mark received a message that the Governor, Sir Robert Gardiner, wished to see him when he was informed that the Regiment was to proceed at once to the Crimea. The news was received by great cheering from the men. No transport was available till 5th June, but the intervening days were spent in practising with the new Minié Rifle on the North Front. Unfortunately there were only 100 available. At length on 7th June the Regiment, strength 30 officers and 858 other ranks, embarked on the steam transport *Robert Lowe*.

The following garrison order was issued by Lieut.-General Sir Robert Gardiner, G.C.B., on the Regiment quitting Gibraltar:—

'The Governor, while expressing his regret at the departure of the 13th Regiment from the garrison, congratulates them on being called to a field of duty in which it is the ardent wish and first ambition of every officer and soldier in Her Majesty's Army to serve.

'The Crimea has been the field of some of England's most glorious triumphs, attended with trials and endurance of privation which have raised the character of the British soldier no less than the victories of our Army have added to England's military renown.

'The 13th know well, from the records of their past success, what it is to defend a town—and the remembrances associated with Jellalabad's defence —whether in the hour of combat or under the incidental privations of service, will animate them with a zeal and ardour that will know neither peace nor abatement till their Colours are planted on the walls of Sevastopol.

'It only remains for the Governor to wish them, as he does heartily, farewell; and to assure Lord Mark Kerr, the officers, non-commissioned officers and men of the 13th, how sincerely he wishes them every honour of the service with individual success, health and happiness.'

THE CRIMEAN WAR

The Regiment was now augmented to 16 companies, 8 companies consisting of 1,000 rank and file in the field; 4 companies as a reserve at Malta, and 4 companies as a depôt in Ireland. The entire strength was directed to be 109 serjeants, 41 drummers, 2,000 rank and file.

This augmentation occasioned an additional Lieutenant-Colonel to be added to the Regiment, and Major Alexander Essex F. Holcombe was promoted to that rank, his commission bearing date 26th June 1855.

Brevet Lieut.-Colonel John Stewart Wood became the senior Major, and Captain and Brevet Major Peter Raymond Jennings was appointed to the vacant majority. He retired in August and was succeeded by Brevet Major George King.

The steam transport, *Robert Lowe*, proved to be a slow boat. Malta was reached on the 18th, Constantinople on the 24th, and Balaclava on the 29th when the Regiment was greeted with the news of the death of Lord Raglan, the British Commander-in-Chief.

It may be remembered here that when the Regiment arrived in the Crimea, the war in that theatre had already been going on for nearly ten months and the siege of Sevastopol was entering upon its final stages, while the scandalous deficiencies in the medical and transport services had been largely remedied.

The Regiment disembarked on 30th June and were quartered near the village of Kadikoi, being attached to the 4th Division. For the first two months the Regiment was employed on working parties at the base at Balaclava, and it suffered severely from sickness, the average number of men in hospital in July and August was 143, and the deaths 62, chiefly from cholera.

On 13th August General Orders announced a new organization of the army. The 13th were posted to the 1st Division commanded by Lord Rokeby, of which the Guards formed one brigade, and the 9th, 13th, 31st and 2nd Battalion the Rifle Brigade the other brigade, under Brig.-General Ridley.

At midnight on the 16th August news arrived that an attack by the Russian relieving force on the Tchernaya was imminent. The Regiment marched off at once and arrived at the rendezvous, a height beyond the Marine Camp and overlooking the Mackensie farm, half an hour before daybreak. A fine view of the battle was obtainable. At first the Russians forced the passage of the Tchernaya, driving in the Sardinian and French outposts, but ultimately they were driven back with heavy losses. The 13th were not engaged.

On 21st August there was another alarm, the Regiment again marched out to No. 4 Redoubt, their old camp. The Russians came down into the plain on the other side of the Tchernaya, but on seeing the French Imperial Guard ready for them, they retired.

On 6th September in the evening a portion of the Regiment went into the trenches for the first time. Lord Mark relates that some of the men had never had an Enfield rifle in their hands before. On the evening of the 6th they were in reserve, but on the 7th they moved up to the advanced trenches, when they lost 11 men wounded. On these two days a terrific bombardment was directed on the Russian defences by the Allies.

September 8th was the day selected for the grand attack on the Malakoff and Redan. The 1st Division was in Reserve, the Guards Brigade in the 1st Line and the 2nd Brigade in the 2nd Line. The French captured the Malakoff, but the English troops, although they got into the Redan several times, failed to hold it. On the following day, 9th September, it was found that the Redan was unoccupied, that Sevastopol had been evacuated by the Russians, and that all their ships of war had been sunk in the harbour. So the siege of Sevastopol was over. In the final attack the French losses were computed at 7,567, the English losses at 2,271 and the Russian losses at over 12,000. A General Order in the evening congratulated the Army on the result of the siege.

Sunday, 4th October, was celebrated as a day of Thanksgiving for Victory.

Although the siege of Sevastopol was over, the Allies still confronted the Russian Army on the line of the Tchernaya, but owing to rain and snow and the advent of winter, field operations were wellnigh impossible.

Lord Mark Kerr, in his journal, gives an interesting insight into the daily life of the Army, his quarrels with the A.Q.M.G. of the 1st Division, whom he refers to as 'a mixture of red tape and obstruction'. He also relates how on one occasion he rode into Sevastopol, of course without stirrups, which made the Frenchmen stare; how he twisted his moustache into long points, *à la* Napoleon III, which caused the French soldiers to make remarks which however were not uncomplimentary ones.

Once or twice a week the officers had a mess dinner but, as a rule, they observed the usual custom of regiments on service of having their meals by twos and threes in their own tents. On Christmas Day 1855 there was the usual Church parade service, the ground was white with snow, the sun shone brilliantly and the men's Christmas dinners were followed by games. The officers all dined together at 5.30 p.m.

On 31st January 1856, Lord Rokeby, commanding the 1st Division, made his inspection of the Regiment, which went off very well.

During January and February the docks, forts, and defences of Sevastopol were destroyed by the Allies. Occasional field days were held, when the 13th acted as Light troops, leading the advance, and covering the retreat.

On Sunday, 24th February, the British Army, about 20,000 men, were formed up in contiguous columns on the Col. de Balaclava, when Sir William Codrington, the British Commander-in-Chief, inspected the line, accompanied by a large staff, after which the troops marched past in half-distance columns, when the following incident occurred which is best described in Lord Mark Kerr's own words:—

'Besides the question of my stirrups, there has been a more important one, concerning ourselves as light infantry marching past at the trail; or like ordinary battalions, with fixed bayonets and shouldered arms. I have struggled hard to do on the Division Field days as I do on my own parade, that is, march past with trailed arms. On this day, as I am nearing the saluting point, one of the Staff gallops up to me and I am ordered to fix bayonets and shoulder. I am very much put out, and I astonish my Staff friend by shouting out "fix fiddlesticks"; the men laugh and fix bayonets accordingly.'

On 29th February an Armistice was signed suspending hostilities till 31st March. Peace was proclaimed in Paris on 30th March, and announced in the Crimea on 2nd April by artillery salutes.

On 17th April there were grand reviews of the French and English armies, the former in the morning, the latter in the afternoon, when the Russian, as well as the English and French generals were present.

Medals and other distinctions were conferred on the victorious troops, and the following officers of the Regiment received the Crimean Medal, with the clasp for Sevastopol (bestowed likewise on the men generally), together with that granted by the Sultan of Turkey to the allied forces:—

Lieut.-Colonels	Majors
Lord Mark Kerr.	John S. Wood.
Alex. E. F. Holcombe.	George King.

Captains

John William Cox (Bt. Major).	Robert Gosling.
George Henry Tyler.	G. Fitzgerald King.
Hugh Maurice Jones.	Edward Boyd.
Robert Peel.	Arthur Bainbrigge.
Fred. Van Straubenzee.	Charles P. Long.
R. Blackall Montgomery.	John Aug. Fuller.

Lieutenants

S. L. Douglas Willan.
Jos. Angerstein Rowley.
Conwallis H. Chichester.
Geo. Henry Cobham.
Henry Lewis Fitzgerald.
John Fred. Everett.
Henry Edward Hall.

Philip E. Victor Gilbert.
Jos. Priestley Miller.
William Haslett.
Henry Gillett.
William Williams.
Richard N. Clayton.

Paymaster B. C. M'Naughten.
Adjutant Hon. Jas. C. Dormer.
Quarter-Master Thos. Hoban.

Surgeon Daniel P. Barry, M.D.
Asst.-Surgeon W. Brown, M.D.

Major Wood (who had been serving since March 1854 as Major of Brigade, and from August as Assistant-Adjutant-General to the Army in the East) was promoted to the Brevet Rank of Lieutenant-Colonel and was made a Companion of the Bath. He was also awarded the 4th Class of the Turkish Order of the Medjidie, and with Major King and Captain Tyler received the Imperial Order of the 5th Class of the Legion of Honour.

The 5th Class of the Medjidie was likewise conferred on Colonel Lord Mark Kerr, Lieut.-Colonel Holcombe, Major King, Brevet Major Cox, Captains Hugh Maurice Jones, Van Straubenzee, Montgomery, Long and Lieutenant Cobham.

The following N.C.O's. and men of the Regiment were selected to receive the French War Medal:—

1. Serjt. James Godwin, senior Serjeant with the Regiment in the trenches during the bombardment from 6th September to the 8th, in command of a party in a rifle pit near second Boyau, right attack where he did good service.

2. Pte. Valentine Corry, good conduct in the trenches, and good service in the rifle pits, second Boyau, during the night of 7th September 1855.

3. Corporal Edward Tallman, severely wounded in the advanced parallel night attack, 7th September.

4. Serjt. T. Coogren, good conduct when in charge of a detached party in the rifle pits on the night of 7th September 1855, during the bombardment.

5. Pte. Frederick Stokes severely wounded.

The name of Pte. Lechie also appears in the Regimental Record, but there is no mention of his name in the Official list.

The word 'Sevastopol' was also authorized by Royal authority to be emblazoned on the regimental Colour of the 13th, Prince Albert's Light Infantry, in commemoration of the services performed before that place.

During the period the Regiment was in the Crimea it received in reinforcements 13 officers and 192 N.C.O's. and men, while the wastage amounted to 87 N.C.O's. and men killed or died of disease, and invalided home 7 officers and 141 N.C.O's. and men.

During the winter of 1855–6 Bt. Major Cox and Captain C. P. Long were attached to the Land Transport Corps; Captain G. F. King was D.A.A.G. at Scutari.

Soon after peace was signed the Army in the Crimea was broken up. On the 24th May, the Queen's birthday, the 13th embarked at Balaclava on the transport *Khersonese* for Gibraltar. Two years previously the Regiment left England for Gibraltar on the Queen's birthday, and in the previous year they received orders at Gibraltar to proceed to the Crimea on that day.

On 26th May Constantinople was passed, and on the 31st the Regiment reached Malta, and on 7th June Gibraltar, after exactly one year's absence.

The Depôt companies had meanwhile remained in Ireland, but were moved from Clonmel to Templemore in May 1855, and to Cork, for embarkation for Colchester in November 1856.

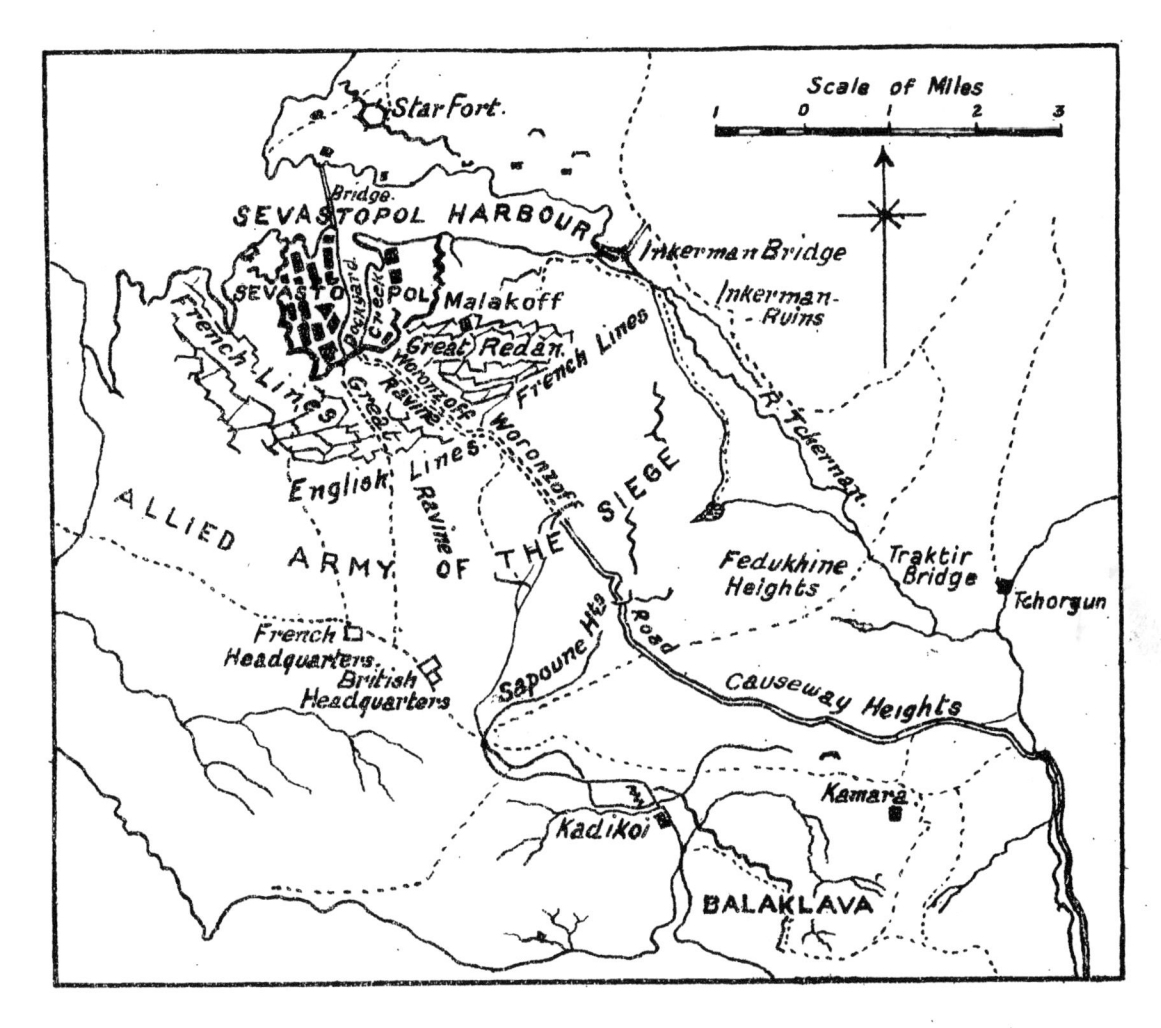

SEVASTOPOL, 1855

[1856

CHAPTER XIX

THE INDIAN MUTINY

ON arrival at Gibraltar on 7th June 1856 the Regiment was encamped at the North Front, and was joined by the Depôt companies from Malta on the 20th.

On 24th July, orders were received for the 13th and 89th Regiments to proceed to the Cape of Good Hope. The 13th, seven companies and headquarters, embarked in the steam transport *Imperatriz* on 7th August, and the remaining company in the steam transport *Cleopatra* on the following day. Madeira was reached on the 10th August, and Ascension Island on the 28th, where the transports remained four days.

The *Imperatriz* called at Simon's Bay, Cape of Good Hope, on the 19th September and then proceeded to Port Elizabeth, Algoa Bay, where the Regiment disembarked.

The ostensible reason for sending troops to South Africa was that a Kaffir war was imminent, but this was far from being actually the case, as Lord Mark Kerr states in his journal that the Kaffirs were starving and in no condition to fight.

After disembarkation the Regiment marched by detachments to Grahamstown where the headquarters arrived on 10th October; one company was stationed at Hawood's Post.

The South African summer of 1856–7 was usefully spent in training the battalion, road-making, and the development of soldiers' gardens.

Lord Mark Kerr also instituted a weekly examination of the junior officers in history, strategy, tactics, and geography. The principal sport consisted in mounted paper-chases, Lord Mark himself being one of the hardest riders.

The Indian Mutiny had broken out in May 1857, but the news of it and the demand for reinforcements did not reach South Africa till the beginning of August. There were some 10,000 British troops in South Africa at the time, and in the absence of telegraphic communications, Sir George Grey, the Governor-General, and Lieut.-General Sir James Jackson, the Commander-in-Chief, had to use their own discretion as to the number of troops to be sent.

Lord Mark Kerr lost no time in advancing the claims of his regiment. After some disappointment he was finally rewarded by receiving orders to prepare for embarkation on 20th August. The headquarters of the Regiment with 500 N.C.O's. and men started its march for Port Elizabeth on 22nd August, Captain Tyler with 237 other ranks being left at Grahamstown.

The march from Grahamstown to Port Elizabeth, a distance of nearly 100 miles, was covered in four days, amid heavy rains and over a hilly country.

On arrival at the sea coast, it was found that the steamship *Madras* would only hold 400 men, so Major Cox and 100 men were left behind to bring on the rest of the battalion left at Grahamstown.

The headquarters wing embarked on 30th August and proceeded to sea, reached Mauritius on 10th September, Point de Galle, Ceylon, on the 25th, and Calcutta on the 1st of October.

The military situation in India was indeed serious, for although Delhi had been captured, Outram and Havelock, after bringing relief to the Residency at Lucknow, were themselves besieged there. The greater part of Bengal and Oude was in a very disturbed state, and the line of communications from Calcutta to Cawnpore was by no means secure. Sir Colin Campbell, the Commander-in-Chief, was at Calcutta busily engaged in organizing the reinforcements arriving from China and South Africa for the relief of Lucknow.

The right wing of the Regiment, strength 23 Officers and 403 other ranks, disembarked on 3rd October and were quartered in certain public buildings set apart for the troops.

Lord Mark, ever anxious for the health of his men and being convinced that a large meat meal in the tropics in the middle of the day was bad for the liver, postponed the dinner hour till late in the afternoon, and he did this gradually by putting back the hand of the guard-room clock ten minutes every day, thus anticipating, though for a different reason, the present system of summer time.

It had been Sir Colin Campbell's intention to entrust to Lord Mark Kerr the command of a column of all arms to disarm the mutineers of the 32nd Native Infantry Regiment in the Raneegunge district, and Lord Mark went to see the Commander-in-Chief on the subject on 13th October, when he mentioned to the Chief that his men were not yet provided with spare soles and heels for their boots. This intelligence was evidently displeasing to Sir Colin Campbell, for on the following day Lord Mark learnt that he had been superseded in the command of the column by Colonel Barker, R.A.; but worse was to follow, for on the 15th, when the headquarters wing of the Regiment was entraining, Lord Canning, the Governor-General, and Sir Colin Campbell came to the station to see them off—Sir Colin greeted Lord Mark with a smile, but the latter passed the Commander-in-Chief without looking at him, and later on when Sir Colin engaged him in conversation, the only replies he made were 'Yes' and 'No'. Lord Mark admits in his journal that he was 'most imprudent', and the sequel shows it.

The troops reached Raniganj the same day; Colonel Barker arrived on the following day, the 16th, and took command of the column which consisted of the Wing of the 13th, a battery of artillery, two companies of the Madras Rifles and a troop of the Bengal Yeomanry Cavalry, altogether about 1,000 strong.

It was originally intended that the column should march to Sooruy to disarm the 32nd Native Infantry, but this was rendered unnecessary as on the 22nd the greater part of the 32nd marched into Raniganj and laid down their arms.

On the 26th October the column commenced its march to the North-West Provinces. On the 28th two companies of the Regiment, under Captain

H. M. Jones, with the Yeomanry Cavalry were detached in pursuit of some mutinous sepoys of the 32nd, thus leaving Lord Mark with three companies barely sufficient to provide an escort for the guns. At the end of the day's march Sir Colin Campbell with his staff overtook the column, when he sent for Lord Mark and asked him courteously enough how his regiment was getting on. Lord Mark replied 'I cannot tell how it is, for I see very little of it. . . .' 'I've got no wing here, only an escort for artillery.'

Sir Colin explained that he had to put Colonel Barker in command as being the senior officer, and that he did not wish to hurt any one's feelings. Lord Mark maintained that Colonel Barker was a Captain in the same camp at Sevastopol when he commanded a regiment, and that Sir Colin had promised him the command of the column at Calcutta. They parted and Sir Colin proceeded on his journey, but it was the common belief among the officers of the Regiment that the Regiment lost their chance of taking part in the final relief of Lucknow in consequence.

Colonel Barker's column continued its march and on 23rd November reached Benares, and on the 30th Allahabad, where the news was announced of the death of Sir Henry Havelock at Lucknow on the 24th November. It will be recalled that this officer had once been Adjutant of the Regiment, and had fought in its ranks in the Burmese and Afghan Wars. Since then he had added many laurels to his fame, but notably in the early days of the Mutiny he had fought his way with a small column from Allahabad to Cawnpore, too late indeed to prevent the horrible massacre at that place, but he established communications with Lucknow and somewhat later, Outram and he relieved the garrison of the Residency at that place, only to be besieged there in their turn.

On 18th November Sir Colin Campbell relieved Lucknow and evacuated that place on the 22nd. On his way to Cawnpore Havelock had died worn out by the effects of the campaign.

Lord Mark states in his journal that he was in hopes that Havelock might have seen his old regiment at Lucknow, but it was not to be.

The chances of high command came to Havelock too late perhaps to prove his ability as a great general, but like Gordon he captured the imagination of the English-speaking world both in Europe and America as being a great soldier and a devout Christian. His statue may be seen in Trafalgar Square.

Sir Colin Campbell had returned to Cawnpore after evacuating the garrison at Lucknow, owing to the attacks on the former place by a fresh body of mutineers from Gwalior. He finally defeated the enemy on 6th December, but the news of the fighting at Cawnpore was extremely disconcerting to Lord Mark and the Regiment. Lord Mark was all for going on, orders or no orders, but Colonel Barker would not budge. On the 6th December the ladies and wounded from Lucknow came into Allahabad, and on the 7th orders at last arrived for a further advance. On the 8th December the column reached Fatehpur, where a halt was made. On the 11th, in consequence of further orders, Colonel Barker's column left the main road and marched on a punitive expedition to Koth, a village on the River Jumna, which was captured on the

13th, and on the succeeding days further villages. Finally the column returned to Fatehpur on the 17th.

On the 18th the march was resumed to Cawnpore, and on the 21st, the headquarters of the 13th joined Sir Colin Campbell's army there. Lord Mark again urged the Commander-in-Chief to allow the Regiment to proceed with the Army to Lucknow, but he was told he must wait for the rest of the Regiment to rejoin.

Meanwhile, the portion of the Regiment which had been left at the Cape was collected at Port Elizabeth. The left wing consisted of 9 officers and 252 men, under Major Cox, and embarked in H.M.S. *Megeara* on 6th November, while Captain Tyler's company embarked a few days afterwards in the ship *Trafalgar*. These ships arrived in Calcutta on the 18th and 19th January 1857.

The Depôt companies quitted Colchester for Pembroke Dock in September 1857, and in December returned to Fermoy, where they remained during 1858.

The headquarters and 3 companies of the Regiment spent Christmas at Cawnpore, and early in the New Year received orders to proceed to Allahabad as escort to 23 captured guns and about 200 sick and wounded men. They reached Fatehpur on 8th January and Allahabad on the 14th. On the 17th the two companies which had been detached under Major Jones rejoined headquarters.

On the 4th February Lord Canning, the Governor-General, arrived at Allahabad and on the following day there was a levée when the officers of the Regiment were presented by Lord Mark.

On the 8th February the Commander-in-Chief, Sir Colin Campbell, arrived at Allahabad to confer with the Governor-General. The 13th furnished a guard of honour, and in the afternoon Lord Mark had another interview with the Chief. The former tells us in his journal that he spoke to Sir Colin for half an hour more strongly, he suspects, than the latter is accustomed to hear, urging the claims of the Regiment to proceed to the front and concludes: 'I tell him I have claims for my service and family, and that I have the blood of Wellington, Napier, Marlborough, and Schomberg.'

It was of no avail; the Commander-in-Chief would not give way.

On the 10th February the band which had been with the left wing arrived at Allahabad.

It is now necessary to revert to the fortunes of the left wing, who immediately after disembarkation on 19th January proceeded to Benares, reaching that station on 9th February.

On the 18th February the left wing, with 100 men of the Madras Rifles, marched to Azimghur about 8 miles north of Benares. Here a small column was formed under Major Cox, consisting of the above-mentioned troops, a few Native Cavalry, with two guns manned by a party from the 13th, who had been trained as gunners.

Various small parties of the enemy having been reported in the vicinity, the column set out on the 24th February and made a tour of the district without meeting any opposition.

On the 7th March the column returned to Azimghur, and on the 13th they marched still further north into the Gorakhpur district to reinforce the 'Sarun Field Force' under Brigadier Rowcroft, and actually joined his headquarters at Amorah on 26th March.

The left wing of the Regiment had been relieved at Azimghur by a portion of the 37th Regiment and a detachment of artillery. In the meantime Sir Colin Campbell had finally defeated the rebels at Lucknow on 21st March, but a large part of the rebel army had previously dispersed over the surrounding country. Among the Chieftains of this Army was one Koer Singh, a man of considerable military ability, who had under his command some of the best infantry regiments of the Sepoy army. He made off south-eastwards in the direction of Azimghur with a view to crossing the Ganges into the Tirhut country, where he had great influence.

Colonel Milman of the 37th Regiment had marched out 30 miles from Azimghur to engage Koer Singh, but instead of arresting the rebel progress, he was himself defeated and had to retire to Azimghur with the loss of his baggage, where on 25th March he was closely invested. The presence of a large hostile force variously estimated at 4,000 to 8,000 men within three marches of Benares, a large city on the line of communications with Calcutta, was evidently a situation fraught with some peril to the main army operating in Oudh, while Milman's position was extremely critical.

AZIMGHUR

The news of this disaster reached Allahabad on 27th March. In the afternoon of the same day, Colonel Birch, Military Secretary to Lord Canning, went to Lord Mark Kerr, and inquired of him 'How soon can your regiment start for Azimghur?' 'In a couple of hours' was Lord Mark's prompt reply, and at 7.30 p.m. they started off for Benares, the headquarters with the companies commanded by Captain H. M. Jones, Captain E. Boyd, and Lieutenant V. Gilbert proceeding by bullock dak, while the band and Captain W. H. Jones's company proceeded by steamer. The headquarters companies arrived at Benares on the 29th, but the steamer with Captain W. H. Jones's detachment did not arrive till the 31st. At Benares Lord Mark learnt that Sir E. Lugard had been dispatched from Lucknow with a strong force of all arms to Azimghur, and that in accordance with Sir Colin Campbell's orders, Lord Mark was not to engage the enemy till Lugard's arrival.

Lord Mark's column, consisting of the 2nd Dragoon Guards (Bays), 2 officers and 55 men; Royal Artillery two 6-pounder guns, two $5\frac{1}{2}$-inch mortars, 1 officer and 17 men, and the 13th Light Infantry, 19 officers and 372 men, left Benares at 10 p.m. on 2nd April with a large convoy of supplies and ammunition for the garrison of Azimghur. The column reached Sursana within 10 miles of Azimghur at 8 a.m. on 5th April.

At this place Lord Mark received urgent messages from Colonel Dames who had relieved Colonel Milman in command at Azimghur to advance at once and informing him that the enemy had been reinforced by 2,000 Sepoys and 2 guns.

In view of Sir Colin Campbell's instructions and the necessity of collecting his convoy, 312 carts, 11 elephants, and 20 camels, Lord Mark deferred his further advance till 4 a.m. on the 6th. At that hour there was a bright moon and Lord Mark rode ahead with a reconnoitring party of the Bays.

At 6 a.m. the enemy were observed to be occupying a mango tope and buildings to the left of the road, and also the banked ditches of the fields on the right of the road.

Lord Mark then halted the head of his column to allow the transport to close up. At about 8 a.m. Captain Boyd's company advanced rapidly on the right of the road in skirmishing order with the Cavalry on their right and slightly in rear in order to turn the left of the enemy's position. Boyd succeeded in his task and drove the enemy in his front to a second line of ditches. But by this time a heavy fire came from the mango tope and buildings on the left of the road, and, what was more serious, the enemy opened fire from some enclosures in rear of the column. Captain H. Jones's company, Lieutenant Everett's and Lieutenant Gilbert's companies threw out skirmishers to the left of the road and were soon hotly engaged, while Lieutenant Hall, who had been sent with a subdivision to support Captain Boyd, was soon dangerously wounded.

The two guns under Lieutenant Robertson had opened fire on the enemy opposing Boyd's company. The firing continued for some time without producing any effect on the enemy's position.

The position was somewhat serious. At this juncture Lord Mark learnt that his convoy had not only retired some distance but the drivers had bolted, so he sent Lieutenant Stewart of the 13th, an excellent officer and horseman, with 25 of the Bays to the rear to endeavour to re-establish order. At this time the enemy's reserves, drawn up in quarter-columns, could be seen in rear of their skirmishing lines on both flanks of Lord Mark Kerr's column, while some bodies of the enemy had got in between the rear-guard and the main body.

Lord Mark, although advised at this time to abandon his convoy, sent word to Major Tyler commanding the rear-guard to hold his own, determined to force his way to Azimghur, and then with the aid of the Madras Rifles to return to the relief of the convoy.

After an ineffectual attempt to bring the howitzers into action, Lord Mark continued the bombardment of the buildings on his left front, setting fire to them, and eventually effected a breach which the infantry succeeded in enlarging only to find another wall in rear. After a further bombardment, the enemy evacuated the buildings and the whole line advanced—a hill of dead bodies inside covered the ground to a height of three feet. Lieutenant Ormsby, commanding the Bays, joining the pursuit, the whole line advanced; the skirmishers thrown back on the left, wheeled rapidly up and the fight was over. It was now ten o'clock.

To return to the rear-guard, the enemy had seized a high embankment crossing the road. It was necessary to dislodge them, and Captain Wilson Jones of the 13th, a most gallant young man, led his company to the attack,

COLONEL LORD MARK KERR, C.B.
afterwards
GENERAL LORD MARK KERR, K.C.B.
Colonel of the Regiment, 1880-1900

driving off the enemy from their position, but in doing so this officer was killed. The drivers of the convoy, seeing the enemy retreating, returned to their bullocks, and thus the convoy was enabled to follow the main body on the way to Azimghur about 2 miles distant. The elephants carrying the tents had bolted altogether, and some five or six carts were burnt including the orderly room cart which contained the Regimental Records.

The further advance of the Regiment was continued with scarcely any opposition. On arriving at the bridge over the River Taptee leading to the entrenchments of Azimghur, Lord Mark sent a request to Colonel Dames, commanding the garrison, for assistance in bringing in the convoy. Two companies of the 37th and Madras Rifles were sent and proved of service.

At the bridge there was firing from the high ground at the other side of the nullah, but this soon died out owing to the fire of two guns from the fort and some skirmishers of the 13th. On entering the entrenchments at Azimghur the 13th were accommodated in small half-ruined houses.

Lord Mark Kerr concludes his dispatch on this engagement of which the above is a summary as follows:—

'I am thankful to say that all the officers under my command behaved with daring courage and resolution; non-commissioned officers and private soldiers the same. I owe my best thanks to Lieutenant the Hon. James Dormer, staff officer of my force, and to Ensign Yardley, my orderly officer, who both behaved with great coolness under heavy fire. To Lieut.-Colonel Longden and Mr. Venables, who accompanied me throughout the day, I am most deeply thankful for their cordial and constant advice and assistance. Major Tyler speaks of invaluable assistance from Quartermaster Hoban, 13th, in many difficulties and dangers with the convoy.'

The losses of the 13th in this action were Captain Wilson Jones and seven privates killed. Lieutenant Edward Hall (dangerously) and one serjeant, and thirty-two men wounded, four dangerously and twenty-nine severely.

The enemy left on the ground 250 dead, while 60 wounded were brought into the British lines.

Serjeant W. Napier and Private Patrick Carlin of the 13th were granted the 'Victoria Cross' for their gallant conduct on the 6th April.

Serjeant Napier for defending and finally rescuing Private Benjamin Milnes of the Regiment when severely wounded on baggage guard. He remained with the latter at the hazard of his life, when surrounded by Sepoys, bandaged his wounds under fire, and then carried him in safety to the convoy.

Private Carlin for having rescued a wounded Naick, of the 4th Madras Rifles, on the field of battle, after killing with the Naick's sword a mutineer sepoy, who fired at him while bearing off his wounded comrade on his shoulder.

Lord Mark Kerr issued the following orders to the Troops after the fight:—

7th April 1858. 'The Commanding Officer congratulates the 2nd Dragoon Guards, Royal Artillery, and Headquarters 13th Light Infantry, on the result of their action of yesterday. It shows what the power of discipline over numbers is. For two hours our small force—500 combatants protecting a convoy two miles in length—was completely surrounded by probably 10,000 of the enemy, in a position of great strength, on our direct line of advance. After two hours of courageous endurance, discipline, which enables brave men to bide their time, carried the day, and the 10,000 fled, pell-mell, in utter rout. Lord Mark Kerr tells Major Tyler, Lieutenant Ormsby, 2nd Dragoon Guards, and Lieutenant Robertson, Royal Artillery and the officers, Non-commissioned officers and soldiers of each arm, that their steady obedience to orders, and bravery, have won, at this Azimghur, a battle, which has not often been fought. Let them remember that it was no noisy enthusiasm which has done this, but courage—strengthened by discipline—that has given them the power to thrash an enemy in a strong position—probably twenty times their number and hidden in an ambuscade; excited too by their defeat of a British force only a few days ago. Let them remember these things, and that any odds are nothing against a disciplined English Army.'

The following is an extract from Regimental Orders of the same date:—

'The Commanding Officer has congratulated the Regiment along with the Cavalry and Artillery on their hard-won battle. He wants to remind them that looting and discipline cannot exist together. Looting tends to relax discipline. A regiment of good looters will never fight against odds of ten to one. Do nothing without orders. If you take a town and are given permission to loot, so be it; but otherwise looting and thieving are the same thing. Honesty and courage go hand in hand with discipline, and these are the qualities which, by God's blessing, win battles and make soldiers contented and happy.'

The bodies of Captain Wilson Jones and eleven soldiers were buried in the public gardens, Lord Mark Kerr reading the funeral service over the graves of those of the Church of England, and Lieutenant the Hon. James C. Dormer over the Roman Catholics. A handsome stone cross, twelve feet in height, has since been erected on the spot by the officers of the Regiment.

The Right Honourable Earl Canning, the Governor-General in India, expressed his sense of the relief of the Garrison of Azimghur in the following terms:—

'Allahabad, *13th April 1858*

Dear Lord Mark Kerr,—

I received your first report of your success, written on the 6th instant, with great satisfaction damped only by the sad loss which your fine Regiment has so unhappily, but unavoidably sustained.

I have now seen your fuller and more detailed account of the whole affair. It is most clearly and simply given.

I congratulate you upon the success with which you met and broke through a formidable opposition. Gallantry and skilful arrangement were both needed in the circumstances in which you found yourself, and officers and men have shown unmistakably that neither were wanting.

It has been a matter of regret to me that the 13th have, hitherto, had so little share in active operations; and I am proportionately rejoiced that upon the first occasion offering, the Corps should so greatly have distinguished itself.'

I am &c,
CANNING.

Colonel Lord Mark Kerr,
Azimghur.'

MINOR OPERATIONS

The entrenchments at Azimghur occupied by the British forces were outside the town which was still strongly held by the enemy.

On 8th April, in consequence of a message received from Colonel Cumberlege commanding a convoy approaching Azimghur to the effect that he was in difficulties, Lord Mark Kerr set out at 4 p.m. with 150 of the 13th, 100 of the 37th, the troop of the 2nd Dragoon Guards (The Bays) and 2 guns under Lieutenant Walsh, R.A., and proceeded 10 miles on the Ghazipur road and halted. The following day at 9 a.m. they were joined by Colonel Cumberlege who had with him detachments of the 10th, 37th, and 97th Regiments, some Madras Rifles, and the 6th Madras Cavalry.

The return march to Azimghur was commenced at 4 p.m.; Advanced Guard and Madras Cavalry, followed by 100 of the 13th, then the guns, and then the rest of the infantry with the exception of the detachment of the 97th, the Madras Rifles, and Bays, who formed the rear-guard. No opposition was encountered until close to Azimghur, when the enemy issued from the town in large numbers, but offered no serious opposition, except on reaching the bridge, when a heavy fire was opened from some high ground on the left. Their fire was soon silenced by the British skirmishing line, and the force crossed the river, only one man of the 13th being severely wounded.

The whole ground outside the entrenchments, occupied by the 13th and the Cavalry, was more or less under fire, and there was occasional firing, to which the sentries had orders not to reply. The enemy meanwhile were busily engaged in making breastworks in anticipation of an attack, but the British garrison remained inactive in accordance with the Commander-in-Chief's instructions to await the arrival of Sir E. Lugard's column.

On the morning of the 14th April Koer Singh, with the greater part of his troops, evacuated Azimghur, when the British Commandant, Colonel Dames, ordered Colonel Cumberlege to march in pursuit with the headquarters of the 13th, 2 guns and the 6th Madras Cavalry and to prevent them crossing the River Ganges. According to Lord Mark, Colonel Cumberlege was 'a good man but mighty slow'. On the 15th the column reached Mau, having lost touch with the enemy, 30 miles from Azimghur, where they were joined by Major Carr and some Madras Rifles from Ghazipur, and remained halted. On 17th April news was received from Azimghur that the enemy had attacked the entrenchments but that on the arrival of Colonel E. Lugard's force, the enemy had fled.

Later in the day orders were received for Colonel Cumberlege's column to join in the pursuit. Accordingly at 2 a.m. on the 18th the column set out south-east for Bulliah on the Ganges, which they reached on the 21st and remained there till the 26th, when Colonel Cumberlege received orders from Sir E. Lugard to send Lord Mark Kerr with the 13th, 2 guns and the Madras Cavalry to Sinia Ghat on the Ganges. The detachment marched at 2 a.m. on the 27th and reached Sinia Ghat at 10 a.m. on the 28th, a distance of 31 miles (notwithstanding very heavy rains at night). In the course of the day Lord Mark's column crossed the Ganges in boats and joined Sir E. Lugard's advanced guard, consisting of the 84th Regiment, some Royal and Bengal Artillery and Sikhs.

On the 29th orders were received for Lord Mark to re-cross the Ganges with the 13th and 2 guns and proceed by forced marches to Gorakhpur which the rebels were threatening from the Nepaul jungles. The detachment having crossed the Ganges, marched at 6 p.m. on the 30th, met Sir E. Lugard and his force early in the morning of 1st May, proceeding to Sinia Ghat and reached Bulliah, 27 miles, at sunrise.

The march was continued to Chilgur, Russorah, and Mau which they reached on 5th May, and were met by Lieutenant Adair with the Colours, band, and baggage, which had been left behind at Azimghur. On 7th May the column crossed the Deera Ghat of the Gogra, and on the 11th marched into Gorakhpur.

It is now necessary to review the fortunes of the left wing of the Regiment under Major Cox. On 17th March they were at Almorah, 70 miles west of Gorakhpur, and formed part of the 'Sarun Field Force' under Brigadier Rowcroft.

On 17th April this force was engaged with the enemy near the village of Belwah. After a very harassing day, and much exposure to intense heat, the mutineers were dispersed with a loss of between 200 and 300 men, together with a 6-pounder gun. The Bengal Yeomanry Cavalry had two killed and fifteen wounded, while the 13th lost two men wounded.

Brigadier Rowcroft, commanding the force, in his dispatches, acknowledged the services rendered on this occasion by Major Cox and the left wing under his command.

On the 25th April the force was again engaged upon nearly the same ground, their camp having been attacked by three columns of the enemy, estimated at 4,000 men with 4 guns. This attack, however, was repulsed with trifling loss.

The 'Sarun Field Force' marched on the 27th April to Captaingunge and on the 29th, a body of the enemy having assembled in the town of Nugger, 6 miles distant, a column under Major Cox was sent out to deal with them. Brigadier Rowcroft, in forwarding the accompanying dispatch from Major Cox, reported that the expedition had been ably and successfully carried out, and that the officers and men of all arms had behaved admirably, with great zeal and gallantry.

The following is Major Cox's report:—

'Camp, Captaingunge, *30th April 1858*

Sir,—

Authentic information having yesterday morning been received that a body of the enemy, about a thousand strong (half of them being Sepoys) were posted at and about the town of Nugger, seven miles from our camp, I have the honour to report that, in compliance with your orders, I started to dislodge them at one p.m. with the following force. Left Wing 13th Light Infantry; 5 officers and 151 men under Command of Capt. Kerr, 13th Light Infantry. Pearl's Naval Brigade—5 officers and 91 men with two 12-pounders, and 24-pounder rocket under Lieut. Grant, R.N. Bengal Yeomanry Cavalry—9 officers and 58 men under command of Capt. Jenkins, Bengal Yeomanry Cavalry. Gorucknath Regiment of Ghurkhas—11 officers and 281 men, in charge of Capt. Barclay, 68th Native Infantry. Sikhs of the Bengal Police battalion—1 officer and 46 men under Lieut. Burton, H.E.I. Company's Service.

The intelligence procured from villagers on the road corroborated our information, both as to numbers and position of the enemy, and on approaching we found them in occupation of the town and partially ruined fort of Nugger which is situated at the extremity of a dense bamboo jungle, about two miles in length, the jungle being bordered by a large lake with swampy ground about it; on the further extremity of the town there are thick groves of trees, which as well as the bamboo jungle, were occupied by the enemy. By making a slight detour, we kept the jungle about half a mile on our right as we advanced, covered by a flanking party of the 13th, and the Sikhs, who skirmished with the enemy, and kept them back until the column came opposite the town and fort. I then halted and wheeled into line to the right, while I directed the two guns and rocket to take up a position on a slight rise of ground, five hundred yards from the town, and sent the Cavalry round beyond the grove, to intercept any force that might escape in that direction.

The guns and rocket, under Lieut. Grant, R.N., then opened with precision and effect, and after about forty shells and rockets had been thrown, the enemy's fire began to slacken.

I then sent orders for the guns to cease firing, directed Capt. Kerr's company of the 13th, and the Sikhs to clear the groves beyond the town, wheel to their right, and enter from that side, while the remainder of the Naval column, gallantly led by Lieut. Pym, Royal Marine Light Infantry, and the Ghurkas by Captain Barclay, having arrived within a hundred yards, we made a simultaneous advance on the town and fort which was completely successful; the enemy were driven through the town and fort, some of them being killed in houses which they ineffectually attempted to defend, and were pursued for a considerable distance into the swamps and jungle, leaving 40 or 50 dead on the field.

As soon as we had got possession of the town, I sent orders for the Cavalry to pass round to the rear, and endeavour to intercept the enemy in their retreat; this was promptly done by Capt. Jenkins, but the extremely unfavourable nature of the ground prevented him from cutting off many of the fugitives.

Four standards were captured during the day, two of them being handsome silk colours; we also found a quantity of powder and ammunition, and a large number of baggage animals with other property.

The conduct of the whole of the troops was excellent, and they were ably and gallantly led by their respective commanding officers.

Mr. Wingfield (the Civil Commissioner) accompanied me during the action, and I feel much indebted for the valuable and accurate information he afforded me; he was also good enough to convey my orders to the Cavalry, and guide them to the position I wished them to take up.

Lieut. Leet, 13th Light Infantry, acted as staff officer on the occasion, to my entire satisfaction.

I beg to enclose a return of casualties, which I am glad to say are not of a serious nature.

J. W. Cox,
Major, 13th Light Infantry

To
Brigadier Rowcroft, Commanding Field Force.'

The casualties in the Regiment on the 29th of April were limited to one serjeant and one private wounded.

On the 8th May the left wing marched to Bustee where straw sheds for the men were constructed during the summer.

Much to the annoyance of Lord Mark, Brigadier Rowcroft ordered two companies of the right wing at Gorakhpur to reinforce the left wing at Bustee on the 18th and 28th May respectively.

Lord Mark tells us in his journal that there was a certain rebel chief, Mohammed Hussein, who was the *bête noir* of the Brigadier, and who was one day in front, and the next day in rear of fidgety old Rowcroft, who bothered his troops in consequence.

At the beginning of June, a force consisting of two squadrons of cavalry, a detachment of Pearl's Naval Brigade with 2 guns, a detachment of Artillery with 2 guns, 200 men of the 13th Light Infantry under Major Cox, marched towards Bhansee in pursuit of a large body of the enemy. After occupying that place they continued their march and on 9th June came in contact with the enemy, whom they defeated with a loss of about 40 killed. The column had one killed and four wounded, two men of the 13th being amongst the latter.

Brigadier Rowcroft, in his dispatch transmitting Major Cox's report of the same, said:—

'I beg to express my best thanks to Major Cox, and my full satisfaction with the careful manner my instructions were carried out, and the judgment and ability shown by Major Cox in carrying out the service confided to him.

'The officers and troops of all arms went through their fatigue at this hot and most trying season of the year with their usual cheerfulness and readiness.'

The Column returned to Bustee on the 11th June.

On the 18th of that month 150 men of the Regiment, under Captain Van Straubenzee, formed part of a column commanded by Colonel Byng of the 6th Madras Light Cavalry, which attacked and drove the enemy from Hurryah, 18 miles from Bustee.

On this occasion Lieutenant Rowley of the 13th acted as orderly officer to Colonel Byng and with Captain Van Straubenzee, Lieutenants Everett and Wroughton, and the men of the 13th, were favourably mentioned in dispatches. One hundred men of the regiment under Capt. Kerr, with some native troops, were subsequently stationed as an outpost at Hurryah.

In the middle of July Lieutenant the Hon. J. C. Dormer relinquished the appointment of Adjutant to take up the post of A.D.C. to the Commander-in-Chief. Lieutenant W. Knox Leet was appointed Adjutant in his place.

Active operations practically ceased during July and August owing to the rains, but towards the end of August, Major Cox led a column from Bustee for the relief of Hurryah. The following is Major Cox's report of this operation:—

'Camp Debreheah, *1st September 1858*

Sir,—

I have the honour to report for the information of Brigadier Rowcroft, commanding Gorakhpur district, that the rebels who attacked Hurryah on the 29th ult., having retreated towards this place, on the arrival of the reinforcements under my command, I marched here this morning with the following troops—

Bengal Yeomanry Cavalry—4 officers and 45 men under Lieut. De Hoxar.

6th Madras L.I.—1 European officer, 1 native officer, and 46 men under Capt. Vine.

Naval Brigade—2 officers and 20 men, two 12-pounder Howitzers (mountain Train) under Commodore Turnour, R.N.

13th Light Infantry—4 officers and 175 men under Capt. Rowley.

27th Madras N.I.—1 European officer, 1 native officer and 41 men under Capt. Garrard.

Sikh Levy—1 native officer and 47 men.

On our approach to Debreheah the enemy's infantry at once retired, covered by their cavalry, which consisted of 50 well-mounted men. I pushed on in pursuit for eight miles, during which 25 of them were cut up by our cavalry, and as by this time men and horses were much exhausted from marching sixteen miles over very bad roads, and across a country in many places under water, as soon as the enemy were quite clear from our front, I took up a position for my camp about a mile in advance of Debreheah.

After a few hours, however, the rebels returned in considerably increased numbers, being then about 1,000 strong with 3 guns; they extended nearly two miles on our front, and threatened our flanks; at the same time a party of several hundreds took up a position behind some large embankments on our right, from which they kept up a heavy fire upon our advanced picquets.

As the number here continued to increase, I took down a company of the 13th Light Infantry under Capt. Rowley, and a mountain train howitzer under Capt. Turnour, R.N. about 10 a.m., and joined them to a party of Native Infantry under Capt. Garrard, and 30 of the Bengal Yeomanry Cavalry under Lieut. De Hoxar; we then charged them with the bayonet, drove them from that position, and again pursued them for a considerable distance, after which they gradually retired from along our whole front. I then returned to camp with the party.

The infantry opposed to us seemed to be all rebel Sepoys, and the whole force was of a superior description to any I have met in the district; they used Minié ammunition, and some of them greased cartridges.

The enemy's loss during the day is reported to be 90 killed and wounded. The troops all behaved very gallantly, and their cheerful and willing advance, having been marching and fighting for twelve hours over a wet country, and wet from rain, is most praiseworthy.

I have &c.,
J. W. Cox,
Major, 13th Light Infantry
To Brigade Major, Bustee, Commanding Field Detachment.'

Although Lord Mark's relations with his Brigadier were always strained, he paid a visit to Bustee at the end of September, inspected the wing of the Regiment there and afterwards returned to Gorakhpur.

On 9th October Lord Mark received orders from Brigadier Rowcroft to march with 100 of the Regiment and the band to Kullulabad on the road to Bustee and to stop there. He replied that unless he got orders to the contrary, he would march straight through to Bustee. He accordingly marched on the 10th, reached Kullulabad on the 11th, and Bustee on the 12th.

The greater part of the Regiment were now concentrated for the first time since leaving South Africa.

On 23rd October a detachment of 100 men of the 13th, under Captains Melville Brown and Boyd, started for Bhansee where 2,000 rebels were reported, but the report turned out to be false, and the detachment was employed elsewhere.

On the 25th October a detachment marched from Bustee, under Lord Mark Kerr, with orders from Brigadier Rowcroft to reinforce the outposts at Hurryah and to expel 800 of the enemy from the open village of Jugdespore, about 8 miles off on the borders of the jungle. The following dispatch is the report of the operations, and it shows how bad the information was on which the column had to act. The Commander-in-Chief on receiving Lord Mark's report, praised highly the conduct of the expedition and the behaviour of the troops; but censured the intelligence system obtaining in Brigadier Rowcroft's brigade. The following is Lord Mark Kerr's dispatch, taken from Carter's Historical Records—

'Hurryah, *27th Oct. 1858*

Sir,—
I have the honour to report for the information of Brigadier Rowcroft that in accordance with orders received through you, to defeat and pursue the rebels at Jugdespore, and having been joined late at night by the detachment under Capt. Garrard from Almorah, I marched yesterday upon Jugdespore, and as day broke advanced on the place with the following troops:—

65 Sabres. Royal Yeomanry Cavalry.
92 Sabres. Madras Cavalry.
2 twelve-pounder howitzers, 1 rocket, 56 men Naval Brigade.
256 bayonets. 13th Light Infantry.
52 bayonets 27th Madras N.I. and Sikhs.
21 Police Levy.

Having been informed that Jugdespore was a village with one pucka house in it, I was surprised to find it a regular fortification, a parallelogram, about 200 yds. by 150 yds., with a deep ditch, bastions at angles, and in other places, and filled with loopholed buildings of different heights and descriptions.

Capt. Condy, 27th Madras N.I., has succeeded in improvising a plan of the fort, which will be ready, I hope, by the time the casualty list arrives from Almorah, to be enclosed with this report.

Our advanced guard drove in the enemy's pickets and Ram Bux's force, said to consist of 500 men and 2 guns, and after a reconnaissance, in which I could discover no entrance, and stationing bodies of cavalry so as to intercept fugitives, we moved on and shelled the place on the north side, and then on the west side, and silenced to a great extent the fire of the gingals and musketry which came from every building. Observing crowds of armed men, horse and foot, apparently escaped from the fort, but since proved to be Ram Bux's force, driven in by our advance, and who had remained hid in topes on the north side, hitherto making their way through the topes in the direction of the ford over the Munowa, I gave chase with cavalry, guns and infantry; but these topes around the fort were thick and frequent, and the enemy soon became unseen. I therefore resolved, having given a severe lesson to the enemy, and being unable to find any entrance to the fort, and from the great loss an assault would entail, to march back to Hurryah, but we were now, on our return, met by so sharp a fire that it would not have been prudent to leave the place behind us without a further lesson, and perhaps attempt at capture. I had before shelled it on the north and west side.

I now tried it on the south and part of the east sides, making a feint with a strong party of infantry on the west side, and hoping to enter by the south; but on consideration I decided that I was not warranted in making an assault, and had recalled, with the object of allowing the evacuation of the fort, about half our cavalry from the further side of the fort; and when no effect was produced by this on the rebel fire, I was just giving orders to retire from our right, along the rear, towards the road to Hurryah, when at the edge of the topes to the west, appeared large bodies of cavalry and infantry, and from their rear came the booming of Mohammed Hussein's nine-pounders, arrived at this juncture from Bourgaon, on the borders of the jungle to the north.

There was no talk now of an assault, equally none of moving off by the road by which we had advanced in the morning.

One hundred skirmishers of the 13th and one twelve-pounder howitzer supported by cavalry, were thrown out to protect our flank and our elephants and ammunition camels. I had brought 25 elephants to carry the party which had arrived in the night from Almorah; and I sent Capt. Condy with an escort of cavalry to sound the ford over the Almorah, from which there is a road leading to Hurryah by the other bank. He performed this service with great dispatch, bringing back word that the ford was practicable for guns, and we turned off in direct echelon from the left—guns alternately and infantry by companies—and succeeded in making the passage good without loss and securing the road, or rather the track intersected by wet ditches, and in many places difficult for the guns and camels, which leads to Hurryah.

Ram Bux's force and two guns driven across the river early in the day, and unseen at first by us, now strongly reinforced from Raneepore and Cassepore, opened fire upon us, and the fire of Mohammed Hussein's guns from the other bank also came crashing through the topes, through which at first our route lay; but protected by the two companies of the 13th and our guns, the ammunition of which was reported as nearly expended some time before leaving the other bank, the retreat was conducted with as much regularity and discipline, under a burning sun, and after some thirteen hours out, without even the refreshment of a drop of water, as on parade, withdrawing our guns, and as their ammunition became expended, relieving the skirmishers. The retreat was effected in the same order. The enemy, whose cavalry far exceeded ours in numbers, and who used it in constant attempts to harass our skirmishers throughout the day, but taking care to keep out of reach of our cavalry, keeping up an intermittent fire upon us from the opposite bank and on our rear.

After three or four hours they gave up the attempt to molest us, and on arriving at the point where the road to Almorah branches off, I sent back the detachment to that place, and arrived without loss at Hurryah at 4 p.m.

The enemy's strength must have been at least eight times greater than ours, and our men had been out, for sixteen hours without, as I have said, breakfast or any other refreshment, and I trust that though we did not take the fort, to attempt which, with our guns, would have been to disobey the order of His Excellency the Commander-in-Chief, and to have incurred a heavy loss of life, the Brigadier and H.E. Lord Clyde will commend the steady gallantry of the troops under my command, who succeeded in making good a retreat under such circumstances. Our casualty list enclosed shows 18 men wounded, which, as the majority are slight wounds, is not excessive.'

.   .   .   .

Lord Mark after mentioning various officers on his staff and in other units, concludes his dispatch as follows:—

'Of Capt. Peel's (13th) daring and good management throughout and in command of the rear-guard in the retreat, I cannot speak too highly; and I feel, I hope, a just pride in saying the same of every officer, non-commissioned officer, and soldier of my Regiment, who acted on this occasion as if each felt that the glorious reputation of this Regiment was in his keeping, and whose example, with that of the Naval Brigade, was emulated by all. I beg to thank Asst. Surgeon Longhurst (13th) in medical charge, for his untiring zeal and courageous attention to the wounded throughout the day.

signed, MARK KERR,
Colonel Commanding Detached Field Force

To the Major of Brigade.'

A few days after this action the enemy evacuated Jugdespore. On the same day two companies of the Regiment were engaged with the enemy at Bhaupore, for which service Captain Melville Brown, who commanded, received the brevet rank of Major.

A *Special Gazette* of the 28th September nominated Lord Mark Kerr a Companion of the Order of the Bath. Subsequently he received the £100 pension for 'distinguished services'.

On 5th November the Queen's Proclamation arrived, by which Her Majesty the Queen assumed the direct rule of the country and the East India Company's rule came to an end. The troops at Hurryah were paraded, when a *feu de joie* and three cheers for Her Majesty were given. The proclamation did not come into force till 1st January 1859.

On 26th November Major Tyler, with 20 officers and 418 men of the Regiment, took part in a successful engagement with the enemy at Domereagunge, and again on 3rd December they took part in a further action in that locality.

On 6th December Lord Mark Kerr, with the Regimental headquarters, marched from Hurryah to Domereagunge, 13 miles, and joined the headquarters of the Brigade there. He now found himself in actual command of nine companies of his Regiment amounting to 700 men. These companies he reorganized as three battalions in single rank under Major Tyler and Captains H. M. Jones and R. Peel respectively. Rowcroft's Brigade was now under the direct orders of Sir Hope Grant and on the 7th marched to Jutwah. On the 17th the Brigade had orders to march to Toolsepore, as soon as the heavy guns arrived. They set out on the 20th and on the 23rd were within striking distance of Toolsepore, which was covered by a rebel force under Bala Rao and Mohammed Hussein. Line of battle was formed, the Bengal Yeomanry Cavalry being on the right, and then in succession from right to left, the 13th, Cadell's battery, Brasyer's Sikhs, Naval Brigade, Madras Infantry and Cavalry.

Lord Mark's objective was a village on the left centre of the enemy's line. After some delay the Brigadier ordered the line to advance at 1 p.m. Lord

Mark, finding that the village outflanked his troops considerably, advanced covered by two companies, one in skirmishing order, the other in support on the right flank in echelon of sections to that flank. When the skirmishers arrived within fifty paces, having been reinforced by half of the supporting company, Lieutenant Gilbert, who was in command, ordered his men to fix bayonets, and with his subaltern, Lieutenant Sanderson, attached from the Bengal Infantry, carried the place in gallant style, bayoneting or shooting between 30 and 40 gunners, and taking one 6-pounder brass gun with limber complete. Most of the defenders of the village retreated; but one sepoy, close to Lieutenant Gilbert, shot himself dead sooner than retire.

By the time the Regiment came up, though immediately afterwards, the whole village had been abandoned.

On clearing the left flank of the village, a large rebel force of cavalry and infantry was discovered, said to be the troops of the Ranee of Toolsepore, and estimated at between 3,000 and 4,000 men with one gun, some thousand yards to the right front of the British.

Lord Mark Kerr threw out skirmishers to cover his right flank, and keep the enemy at a distance. The 13th advanced in direct echelon from the left, with a view to closing with the enemy, but at this juncture the Brigadier came up, and decided to leave the enemy alone, and ordered an advance on Toolsepore, which was found to be in flames and deserted.

The 13th lost four men wounded on this occasion. On the following day Lord Mark noted in his journal: 'We were to have pursued but do not; no one knows where the enemy is.'

On Christmas Day Sir Hope Grant arrived and at once ordered the column, with the exception of the 53rd, who were to remain at Toolsepore, to march off to the eastwards, 'in the hopes of catching the enemy'. On the 26th the column reached Jutwah, and here Lord Mark met Captain Garnet Wolseley, A.Q.M.G. to Sir Hope Grant commanding the Oudh Division.

Lord Wolseley, in *The Story of a Soldier's Life*, gives the following account of this interview:—

'We then had a small column operating in the Gorakpore district under a stupid Brigadier. His movements were so slow that the force he commanded was commonly known as the "Hackery Brigade". The only British troops with him was a battalion of Somerset L.I. under a remarkable man, Colonel Lord Mark Kerr. He was able but flighty, and amongst other peculiarities he entertained a sovereign contempt for his Brigadier, who was a weak old Indian fossil entirely unaccustomed to the control or management of British soldiers, and absolutely unfit for any independent command on active service. The two men had no idea in common, and their temperaments differed as much as the climate of Iceland from that of the Gold Coast. Numerous misunderstandings arose between them, until at last Lord Mark telegraphed to know if he might put his Brigadier under arrest!

'Sir Hope Grant sent this Brigadier orders to take Toolsepore, but he completely failed in the attempt as Lord Mark would give him no effective help. Sir Hope then ordered the Brigade to join him, and I was sent out some miles to meet it. When I saw the dust of its column in the distance I halted to let the advanced guard come up. The first figure I made out was a man on horseback without a hat but with a white umbrella over his head. He carried in his hand a light infantry shako, and he rode without stirrups. His horse was a good one, and he sat it like one who was no stranger to the saddle. I had often seen him during our year's stay in the Crimea, and had there heard amusing stories about him. He was eccentric by nature, and wished the world to remark upon his eccentricities. He was a very well-read man, full of talent and had his regiment in first-rate order, though he ruled it as an absolute monarch, and was consequently often "in hot water" with the military authorities.

'Subsequently I came to know him well; to admire his talents, to forget his peculiarities, and to like him for the goodness of his heart. Taking it all together, this "Hackery Brigade" on the march was a curious sight and amused me and others intensely.'

The 13th, having joined Sir Hope Grant's force, marched northwards to the borders of the Nepaul jungles, and even advanced into Nepaul, but the enemy dispersed.

On 3rd January 1859, the 13th and Cadell's battery, under Brigadier Rowcroft, were left on the frontier and Sir Hope Grant marched off with the rest of the force.

On the 13th February 1859 the field force was broken up and the 13th returned to Gorakhpur.

On the 15th February a wing of the Regiment, under Lieut.-Colonel King, proceeded towards the Nepaul frontier and returned across the River Gunduk in pursuit of rebels, reaching their camping ground 5 miles beyond the river at 5 a.m. the next day. The same evening they marched another 16 miles and after a short halt 14 miles more, without coming up with the enemy.

Some weeks later they marched into the Terai and took part in a small action on 25th March, and on the 28th March they were engaged in an attack in the Nepaul hills. Two parties of the Regiment, one under the command of Captain Peel, and the other under Lieutenant Gilbert, ascended the hills to reinforce the 3rd Sikhs under Captain Rennie, and the 27th Panjaubees under Captain Stafford—a most arduous duty owing to the steepness of the ground. Both parties were thanked and mentioned in dispatches. The enemy made good their retreat over the first range of hills, leaving their horses, elephants, &c., in the jungles, many throwing away their arms, while others, more daring, were killed in action. After some short stay in the Terai, the wing marched to Bustee, where it arrived in May, and was quartered in the temporary barracks at that station.

As the Battle Honours for the Indian Mutiny were limited to 'DELHI',

'LUCKNOW', and 'CENTRAL INDIA', no additional battle honour was gained for the Regimental Colour, but the 13th performed an essential service towards the suppression of that terrible outbreak, and materially aided in preserving British supremacy in the East.

In recognition of the services performed during the Mutiny, Colonel Lord Mark Kerr and Major J. W. Cox were awarded the C.B., while the latter and Major G. H. Tyler were promoted to the rank of Brevet Lieutenant-Colonel. Captains H. M. Jones, W. H. Kerr, F. Van Straubenzee, and Melville Brown received the brevet rank of Major.

The following officers received the Indian Mutiny Medal which was bestowed on the soldiers generally:—

Colonel and Lieut.-Colonel Lord Mark Kerr.

Lieut.-Colonel George King.

Major and Bt. Lieut.-Colonel John William Cox. Major and Bt. Lieut.-Colonel George Henry Tyler.

Captain and Bt. Major H. M. Jones, Captain Robert Peel, Captain and Bt. Major W. H. Kerr, Captain F. Straubenzee, Captain W. H. Jones (killed in action), Captain C. F. King, Captain and Bt. Major Melville Brown, Captain E. Boyd, Captain G. S. Twynam, Captain J. R. Turnbull, Captain J. B. Rowley.

Lieutenants Hon. J. C. Dormer, H. L. FitzGerald, J. F. Everett, R. N. Clayton, H. E. Hall, P. E. V. Gilbert, W. Haslett, H. Gillett, W. Williams, J. C. Connington, H. A. C. Wroughton, A. S. Adair, D. Stewart, J. F. James, F. W. Ruck, W. Cox, C. E. Palmer, E. L. England and T. Yardley.

Paymaster D. C. M'Naughten, Adjutant W. Knox Leet, Quartermaster T. Hoban, Surgeon P. H. E. Cross, Asst.-Surgeons A. E. T. Longhurst, C. J. Kirwin.

The total effective strength of the Regiment on the 1st January 1858 was 765 of all ranks and on the 1st December of the same year it was 916 of all ranks. Drafts from England during this period amounted to 323 of all ranks, thus the wastage due to deaths and invaliding amounted to 172, a very moderate figure considering the tropical nature of the climate.

The Regiment had the bad luck to be employed on subsidiary operations principally in the neighbourhood of the Nepaul hills. This has been attributed by some to the unfortunate relations which existed between Lord Mark Kerr and the Commander-in-Chief, but it is probable that as the Regiment arrived from South Africa in two detachments at an interval of two and a half months, it was found more convenient to leave the headquarters of the Regiment on the line of communications until the left wing arrived; and when it did arrive in the country, the major operations in the neighbourhood of Lucknow were in full swing, while the guerrilla warfare, which ensued, necessitated the dispatch of small columns in all directions.

It must be said in all fairness to Lord Mark that when he was in sole charge of the operations, as at Azimghur, he conducted them with skill and ability.

A perusal of his journal will show that he studied the efficiency and well-

Divisions of Agra
1. Meerut Division. 4. Allahabad Divn.
2. Agra   "   5. Benares   "
3. Bareilly "   6. Gorakhpur "
7. Kumaun Division.
Divisions of Oudh
8. Lucknow Div.   9. Fyzabad Div.

HIMALAYA MOUNTAINS

NEPAUL

UNITED PROVINCES

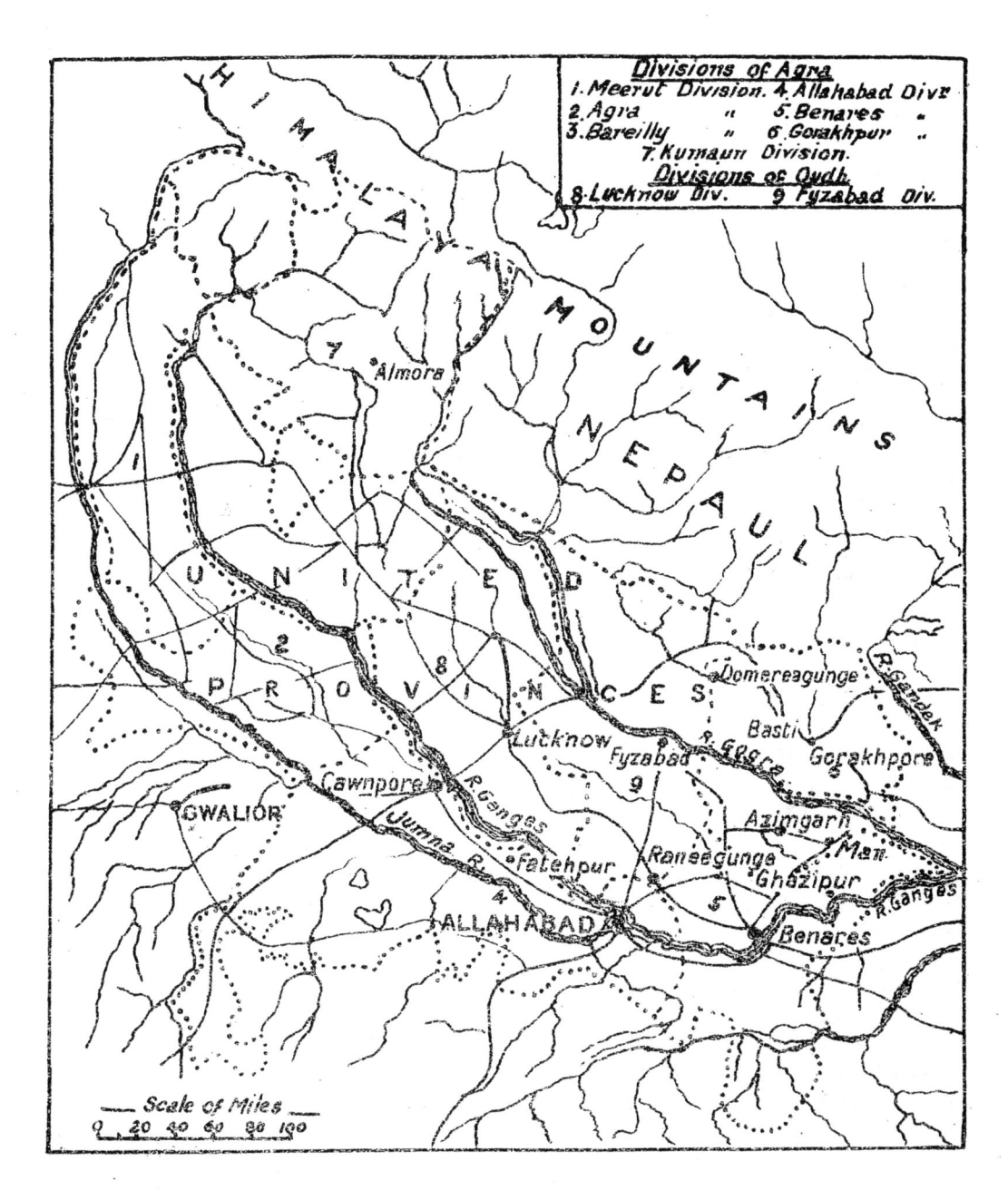

Almora
Domereagunge
R. Gandek
Basti
R. Gogra
Lucknow
Fyzabad
Gorakhpore
Cawnpore
R. Ganges
GWALIOR
Jumna R.
Azimgarh
Man
Fatehpur
Raneegunge
Ghazipur
ALLAHABAD
Benares
R. Ganges

Scale of Miles
0 20 40 60 80 100

UNITED PROVINCES, OUDH, INDIA, 1858

being of his men, and that he thoroughly realized the necessity of night marching in a hot climate, which enabled the Regiment to make forced marches with little effort.

The year 1858, apart from the campaign in India, was also a notable one for the Regiment in that in the beginning of the year the 2nd Battalion was raised. Major and Brevet Colonel Arthur Horne was promoted from the 21st Foot to be its Lieutenant-Colonel. Brevet Lieut.-Colonels Thomas Faunce, from the St. Helena Regiment, and the Hon A. Murray Cathcart, from half-pay, were appointed the Majors. The two former by commission dated 8th January and the latter dated 9th January.

The 2nd Battalion on formation was stationed at Winchester.

In 1858 the size of the new Colours was reduced from 6 feet to 4 feet in the fly and from 5 feet 6 inches to 4 feet 6 inches on the pole. The old Spearhead was abolished and replaced with a gilt lion and crown, the crest of England.

The Colours of the 2nd Battalion were identical in design to that of the 1st Battalion, except for the title 'II. Batt.' immediately underneath the wreath.

CHAPTER XX

2ND BATTALION

AS stated in the last chapter, the 2nd Battalion was raised at Winchester, and its formation commenced on the 27th February 1858. On the 19th April the establishment was raised from eight to twelve companies. The Commanding Officer, Lieut.-Colonel Horne, joined in July.

The Battalion was remarkably fortunate both in the number and class of the recruits, of whom the majority were from the agricultural districts, and comparatively few from the large towns.

The Battalion having been inspected on the 25th October by Major-General Sir James Yorke Scarlett, K.C.B., who expressed the highest approval of its appearance and efficiency, orders were received for the Battalion to be held in readiness to proceed to join the Camp at Aldershot, there to form part of the 1st Brigade under Major-General Lord William Paulet, C.B. The Battalion left Winchester on the 19th November 1858 and the same day joined the 1st Brigade at Aldershot. Recruiting for the Battalion ceased in the beginning of December and on the 15th of that month H.R.H. the Duke of Cambridge, Commander-in-Chief, reviewed the Battalion, and expressed his extreme approbation to Colonel Woods, C.B., A.A.G., of its readiness under arms, and the soldierlike appearance of the men.

In 1857 a curious omission was made in the Dress Regulations issued in that year. The 13th were omitted from the list of Regiments privileged to wear distinctive badges, and the Regiment was ordered to revert to the simple bugle above the number on the chako and forage cap, which was distinctly contrary to Her Majesty's command that a Mural Crown superscribed JELLALABAD should be worn on the Colours and appointments of the Regiment. Lord Mark Kerr at once appealed but was unsuccessful. Colonel Horne, through the interest of Sir William Gomm, was more fortunate, and the privilege was restored by Horse Guards letter dated 24th January 1859.

The Colours for the Battalion having been received from the War Office, the presentation by His Royal Highness the Prince Consort took place on the 21st February 1859. The following description is taken from the Records of the 2nd Battalion:—

'Among a range of hills six miles from the Camp at Aldershot, and near the village of Blackwater, was found a spot which formed a natural amphitheatre. On the sloping sides were drawn up in close column three brigades of Infantry with their artillery and train in the intervals. At each flank of the horse-shoe-shaped elevation, which formed the amphitheatre, a brigade of Cavalry in two divisions was drawn up, inclining towards the centre, at an obtuse angle. The Gentlemen Cadets from Sandhurst College were formed two deep on each inner flank of the Cavalry. On the level ground between the two sides the 2nd Battalion 13th Light Infantry was drawn up in line with two companies on each flank wheeled a little forward. In front of the centre of the Battalion was a 9-pounder gun and in front of the gun and a little in advance of the Gentlemen Cadets was the Prince Consort and his staff with the Rev. J. R. Gleig, Chaplain-General, who consecrated the Colours.

'Brevet Lieut.-Colonel the Hon. A. M. Cathcart and Brevet Major W. H. Carr handed the Colours to His Royal Highness, who presented them respectively to Ensigns William Moffett and Lloyd P. Jenkins, who received them kneeling. The Prince then addressed Colonel Horne who replied, thanking His Royal Highness for the honour he had conferred on the battalion.

'The whole division, having marched past in quick time, returned to Camp.'

A printed copy of the programme on this day was drawn up by Colonel J. Stuart Wood, C.B., A.A.G., an old and distinguished officer of the Regiment who had been adjutant of the 1st Battalion at the time of Jellalabad.

On 11th February 1859 Brevet Lieut.-Colonel Faunce, the senior major, retired on full pay, and was succeeded by Captain and Brevet Major H. M. Jones from the 1st Battalion.

On the 23rd February the 2nd Battalion, consisting of 23 officers, 44 serjeants, 12 drummers and 796 rank and file, under the command of Colonel A. Horne, moved from the North Camp, Aldershot, proceeded by rail from Farnborough to Portsmouth, and embarked in the steam troopship *Himalaya* for the Cape of Good Hope, arriving at Algoa Bay on the 7th April. From thence the Battalion marched to Grahamstown where it arrived on the 18th April.

On the embarkation of the 2nd Battalion the Depôt companies of that battalion proceeded to Ireland and formed part of the Depôt battalion at Fermoy.

1st BATTALION

During 1859 and 1860 the headquarters of the 1st Battalion remained at Gorakhpur, three companies being on detachment at Azimghur and one at Jaunpur. On 20th April the women and children of the Battalion who had been left at the Cape rejoined headquarters at Gorakhpur where they were all accommodated in a big serai. Lord Mark tells us in his journal, that it was very like having the command of another battalion.

July 28th was celebrated in India as a Thanksgiving Day for Peace and the Suppression of the Mutiny. The Regiment attended Divine Service.

Four companies of the Battalion, under the command of Captain Bainbrigge, marched on the 22nd November to Segowlie towards the Nepaul frontier, with a view to intercepting rebels who were supposed to be proceeding in that direction. They remained encamped at that place for two months, when they were recalled, and rejoined the headquarters at Gorakhpur.

Mess dress was introduced into the Army by Horse Guards Circular dated 9th June 1859 which is as follows:—

'H.R.H. the General Commanding-in-Chief is pleased to permit the Shell Jacket to be worn at Regimental Messes on all ordinary occasions by officers when not on duty.'

Previous to 1859 full-dress uniform was the official Mess dress; the shell jacket was not a new garment, it was the undress uniform worn on ordinary parades and was worn buttoned up. It seems that Commanding Officers introduced waistcoats with the result that a variety of patterns existed in the Army. Tradition has it that Lord Mark introduced the high waistcoat, as worn by the mounted arms, in the 1st Battalion, and it was not till 1874 that the Dress Regulations of the Army laid down a universal type of mess dress for the Army, though for many years after the high waistcoat continued to be worn in the Regiment.

2ND BATTALION

The 2nd Battalion remained at Grahamstown during nearly the whole of 1859. They were inspected by Lieut.-General R. N. Wynyard, C.B., commanding the Forces in South Africa, in September, and his report, which was very favourable, evoked the following comments from H.R.H. the Duke of Cambridge in the following year:—

'The steady soldierlike appearance which this young battalion is assuming is a source of great pleasure to the General Commanding-in-Chief, who feels confident from the material of which it is composed, that it will arrive ere long at a complete state of efficiency.'

Towards the end of 1859 orders were received for the Battalion to relieve the 1st Battalion 2nd Foot at King William's Town, who were proceeding to China. Accordingly on 26th December detachments consisting of 4 officers and 150 men were sent to relieve the outposts of the 2nd Foot at Fort Glamorgan, Fort Jackson, Tamasha Port and Lyne Drift in British Kaffraria, and on 27th January 1860 the headquarters followed, arriving at King William's Town on 31st January after leaving a sufficient number at Grahamstown and Fort Brown until the arrival of the 2nd Battalion 10th Foot from England. By the 9th April the whole Battalion was concentrated at King William's Town with the exception of the outposts first mentioned.

In August 1860 Prince Alfred, son of Queen Victoria, paid a visit to South Africa, and on the 13th of that month he visited King William's Town when the Battalion furnished a Guard of Honour under Captain Grimston with the Regimental Colour and Band at Government House. The Battalion lined both sides of Smith Street from the Buffalo River to Government House, and as the Prince approached, each man presented arms in succession. The whole of the troops on this occasion were under the command of Colonel Horne, commanding the Battalion. On the evening of the following day His Royal Highness did the officers of the 2nd Battalion the honour of dining with them, accompanied by his Staff.

Colonel Horne started a temperance society in the Battalion, allotted them a separate room in barracks and soon had 250 members. The proceeds of this institute were spent on furthering games and sports in the Battalion, while one day a week was set aside as a whole holiday for this purpose.

Later in the year a serious native rebellion took place in New Zealand, and in consequence orders were received on 6th November for the 2nd Battalion to be held in readiness to embark at East London for New Zealand, but their services were not required. It is, however, interesting to record that the 2nd Battalion was selected for active service out of a number of old regiments then stationed in the Colony.

1st BATTALION

In February 1861 the 1st Battalion, from Gorakhpur and Azimghur, marched to Gonda in Oudh, being relieved by the 20th Regiment. On 9th October Lord Mark Kerr, who had been absent on leave for eighteen months, rejoined the Regiment. On 16th November the Battalion commenced its march for Morar, Gwalior; Lucknow was reached on the 25th. On the 27th they halted for a few minutes at the Alum Bagh, and paid their respects at Havelock's grave, the soldiers removing their helmets.

On the 30th they entered Cawnpore and halted there till 5th December, when the march was resumed. The Jumna was crossed on the 7th at Calpee, and on the 21st the Battalion marched into Morar cantonments and encamped. On the 24th they occupied the barracks vacated by the 27th Regiment, who were to proceed to Gonda. Christmas Day was celebrated in the usual manner, but on the following day Lord Mark, in addressing the men on parade, told them that cheering the Commanding Officer was a humbug and common to all battalions in the Army, and that they were not to do it again.

On 11th January 1862 the news of the death of the Prince Consort, Prince Albert, was received. Lord Mark Kerr notes in his diary: 'I feel that we could spare a dozen Palmerstons and Russells much easier. The nation will now appreciate his enormous merit and ability as they have not hitherto sufficiently done.' Subsequently Lord Mark Kerr tells us that the Officers all subscribed handsomely to the Albert Memorial. Notwithstanding that the Battalion was in India, it was the first regiment to subscribe.

On 17th January a draft from England joined the Battalion. Lord Mark Kerr tells us in his diary that on 5th and 7th April, the 6th being a Sunday, the Anniversary Games in honour of Azimghur and Jellalabad were held. This is the first recorded mention of the Regimental Annual Sports.

S.L.I.—17

On 12th April the invalids for Kasaulie and home left by train. Lord Mark comments as follows: 'They should have gone two months ago, as the hot journey now kills some, and half-kills many. I have been doing my best to get this villainous and thoughtless system altered.'

At the beginning of July cholera broke out in the garrison, when there were a few cases first in K Company, and later in three other companies of the Regiment, who were promptly sent out of cantonments to camp. At the end of July the whole Battalion was under canvas, but the epidemic continued notwithstanding that the camps were frequently changed. Among those who died was Bandmaster MacPherson. The following Regimental Order refers to his death:—

'The Lieutenant-Colonel calls the attention of the non-commissioned officers and men to the loss the Regiment has sustained in the late Bandmaster, and to his career. By his own exertions and strict performance of duty he rose to a position of independence, and if his life had been spared, would have soon become an officer, for which rank no man living was more qualified. For his sense of duty, education, and high feeling, made him a gentleman.

'Lord Mark reminds all ranks that Bandmaster MacPherson joined the Regiment as a boy, in which his father was a private soldier, and that his proficiency was the result of education in the regimental school alone.

'His early death is a cause of deep sorrow to the Commanding Officer, but his loss will prove a gain, if it should cause others to remember and imitate the bright example which is his legacy to us all.'

The epidemic continued till the end of September, when the Battalion returned to cantonments, but they had sustained the loss of 37 non-commissioned officers and men from cholera. In addition fever was rife in the Battalion owing to exposure in camp in the rainy season; the average daily sick in November was 121.

In October Lord Mark Kerr was given the command of the Delhi brigade, and was succeeded in command of the Battalion by Lieut.-Colonel King.

On 22nd December 1862 the 1st Battalion, having been relieved by the 81st Regiment, moved by marches and rail to Dum Dum via Agra, arriving at its destination on 21st January 1863. On 31st March one company proceeded to Barrackpore, and on 10th April three more companies proceeded to that station.

On 5th October two companies from Headquarters at Dum Dum and one company from detachment at Barrackpore proceeded to Fort William, Calcutta, and were followed on 8th October by the headquarters and four companies from Dum Dum, in relief of the 43rd Light Infantry, who proceeded to New Zealand.

Major-General Philip McPherson, C.B., was appointed Colonel of the 13th, Prince Albert's Light Infantry, on the 15th August 1863, in succession to General Sir William Maynard Gomm, G.C.B., who was removed to the Coldstream Guards.

V. R.

2nd BATTALION 13th
PRINCE ALBERT'S REGIMENT
OF LIGHT INFANTRY.

REQUIRED
FOR THE ABOVE BATTALION,
A FEW INTELLIGENT YOUNG MEN OF GOOD APPEARANCE & ACTIVE FIGURE.

The history of the 13th Light Infantry is so well known in the annals of our countrys' glory, that it would be needless to describe, at any length, the varied scenes, climes, and countries in which, by its gallantry and devoted bravery, it has added to the stability and welfare of the British Empire, "on which the sun never sets."

Under the burning Sun, and on the sandy deserts of the **Land** of the **Egyptians**, in the tropical climate of the **Carribean Sea**, where the Emerald waves roll o'er the golden sands and glittering coral reefs of the **Isle of Martinique**; in the "Indian Hemisphere," that **Koh-i-noor** of England's Crown, in **Ava, Afghanistan, Ghuznee, Jellalabad,** and **Cabul**; in the glorious **CRIMEAN Campaign**; and at a later date serving a second time in India, avenging the fell cruelties of the murderous Sepoys; have waved in victorious triumph the Battle Flags of this Renowned Regiment!!!

HONOURS, PROMOTIONS, REWARDS, & IMMENSE SUMS OF PRIZE MONEY FELL TO THE LOT OF THESE HEROES.

THE SPHINX!!

Emblem of that land where those wonders of all ages, the stupendous Pyramids, raise their undecaying summits to the arch of Heaven.

THE MURAL CROWN!!

Awarded (as in the days of ancient Rome) for deeds of valour, and acts of undying fame, at the heroic defence of the City of **Jellalabad**, a marvel of bravery that sheds a lustre even on the name of Briton!!!

With other mottoes and Badges of victorious combat, and emblazoned on the Banners of the Regiment, sparkling like jewels in the sun as the breeze gently fans the silken folds.

TO PERPETUATE ITS FAME TO FUTURE GENERATIONS, HER MAJESTY, THE QUEEN HAS BEEN PLEASED TO BESTOW ON THE CORPS THE PROUD TITLE OF

PRINCE ALBERT'S REGIMENT of Lt. Inft.

And in the presence of assembled thousands, His Royal Highness, the **Prince Consort** presented to the **2nd Battalion** the Colours under which they have now the honour to serve, as a mark of the estimation in which the 2nd Battalion 13th Light Infantry is held. Her Majesty, during the past month, has granted a Commission to the Serjeant Major of the Corps.

From the salubrity of the climate and its even temperature, in addition to the advantages of increased allowances, the Isle of France or Mauritius has been selected as the Station for a few years of the Battalion. It will be recollected that this Isle of the Eastern Ocean is celebrated as the scene of the romantic and interesting narrative of the lives of **Paul** and **Virginie**, and their sad and untimely end.

N.B.—It is advisable that Volunteers for this Battalion should present themselves for Enlistment without delay, as the few present vacancies will be rapidly filled, and thus may be lost an opportunity for travel and observation of the striking scenes of foreign life seldom offered to the aspiring Soldier.

Fermoy, March, 1864.

GOD SAVE THE QUEEN.

WILLIAM LINDSEY, ARMY PRINTER, KING STREET, FERMOY.

RECRUITING POSTER, 1864

2ND BATTALION

On 28th August 1863 Major William Lawes Peto retired on half-pay, and was succeeded by Major A. A. Dick. Early in 1863 the 2nd Battalion, who had been stationed at King William's Town since January 1860, received orders to proceed to Mauritius, but before leaving the Commanding Officer received a letter of appreciation of the good conduct of the Battalion from the Mayor and inhabitants of King William's Town. The General Officer Commanding the Forces in Cape Colony, in his farewell order, also recorded his high opinion of the efficiency of the Battalion, and there can be no doubt that under Colonel Horne the Battalion was in very good order.

The Battalion embarked at East London on board the *Himalaya* on 30th March, and sailed the following day for Mauritius, where they disembarked on 9th April. Colonel Horne was in command and the strength of the Battalion was 25 officers, 44 serjeants, 20 buglers and 730 other ranks.

The men suffered considerably from ophthalmia, which had been contracted in South Africa, during their first year at Mauritius. All attempts to stop the epidemic having failed, it was determined to invalid those suffering from the disease, and in February 1864, 102 men were invalided home. This proved entirely satisfactory and the epidemic was entirely eradicated. It is not out of place to insert here a recruiting poster issued at the Depôt, Fermoy, to attract recruits for the Battalion to replace this wastage.

In June 1864 the Battalion was ordered to find the outposts on the island when the General Officer Commanding took the opportunity of publishing the following order:—

'On the occasion of the move of the 2nd Battalion 13th Light Infantry to take Outpost duty, the Major-General has a peculiar gratification in signifying to the officers and men of this distinguished corps the high approval of their conduct during the time they have been under his immediate observation. Comparing their conduct by the unerring test of Court Martial Records and Defaulter Sheets with that of the other troops in the Command, the Major-General feels it to be only a justice to the 2/13th Light Infantry, to hold them up as an example worthy of all imitation.

'The 13th Light Infantry have shown that under good discipline British soldiers are to be trusted as steady men, and that no Commanding Officer has now a right to urge as an excuse for the drunkenness of the men, that it is a vice of the Army, and that it cannot be eradicated.

'The 13th Light Infantry have shown the contrary.

'During the last eight months with an average strength of 701 men there have only been 27 men tried by Court Martial, while for minor offences the account is likewise highly gratifying.

The efficiency of the Regiment on parade contrasts strongly with that of other corps, and demands on that account record and acknowledgement by the Major-General.

'Whilst only seven men were absent from the inspection parade as "under punishment" the smallness of the casualties in "sick" and "on duty" equally attracted the Major-General's observation and approval.

'It will be a pleasing duty of the Major-General to make mention of these facts so much to the credit of Colonel Horne and his officers, in a special report to His Royal Highness, Field-Marshal Commanding-in-Chief, and he trusts the 13th Light Infantry will ever have a pride in maintaining the high character they at present enjoy.

By command, W. STRATTON, Colonel D.Q.M.G.'

At the next inspection in November 1864, the Major-General Commanding had again occasion to remark on the pre-eminent superiority of the 2nd Battalion 13th Light Infantry over the other troops in good conduct.

In 1865 the Battalion sustained a great loss in the death of Colonel Horne. He died after a few days' illness on the 3rd January.

It was under his able guidance that the Battalion attained a high state of discipline and efficiency. He was buried, as he himself requested, at Mahebourg, Mauritius, where he had spent some of his early days in the 12th Foot.

A monument which was raised by the officers stands over his grave in the cemetery of that place.

Major P. Macdonald was gazetted Lieutenant-Colonel of the Battalion on the 19th December.

1st BATTALION

On 13th January 1864 the headquarters and right wing of the 1st Battalion, under the command of Brevet Lieut.-Colonel Cox, C.B., embarked on board the freight ship *Newcastle* for England. The left wing, under Brevet Lieut.-Colonel D. D. Muter, embarked for the same destination in the *Shannon* on the 15th. The Battalion was reduced to 36 serjeants, 19 buglers, and 530 rank and file, having given 206 volunteers to regiments remaining in India.

Prior to the departure of the Battalion the following general order was issued by the Commander-in-Chief in India:—

'On the departure from India of Her Majesty's 1st Battalion 13th (Prince Albert's) Regiment of Light Infantry, the Commander-in-Chief in India deems it due to the Regiment to notice in general orders, the good service which the headquarters wing with the force detailed in the margin under Colonel Lord Mark Kerr, C.B., performed in 1858 in relieving the Fort of Azimghur, held by a British garrison, and closely invested by the rebel leader, Koer Singh.

	Officers	R. and F.
2nd Dn. Gds.	2	55
Royal Artillery	1	17
2 six-pounders		
2 5½-inch mortars		

'The relieving force, embarrassed by a very large convoy of supplies, was attacked by greatly overpowering numbers, but gallantly forced its way through the enemy into the fort.

'The wing of the 1st Battalion, 13th Regiment, in performing this important service, sustained a loss of two officers and forty men killed and wounded.

'During the time that the Regiment has served under Sir Hugh Rose, His Excellency has had reason to be much pleased with its discipline and efficiency.

By order signed E. HAYTHORNE,
Adjutant-General.'

Lieut.-General Philip Spencer Stanhope was appointed to the colonelcy of the Regiment on the 3rd February 1864, in succession to Major-General M'Pherson, deceased.

The *Shannon* arrived at Gravesend on the 22nd and the *Newcastle* on the 30th April 1864, when they proceeded to Dover and were quartered for the first two months in the citadel.

Lord Mark Kerr rejoined the Battalion on the 17th July, having relinquished the command of the Delhi Brigade.

Almost the first thing Lord Mark did was to get the Battalion moved from the Citadel to the Western Heights barracks, then occupied by the 78th, who were about to leave, and whose place was to be taken by the 37th. In this project he was strenuously opposed by General Dalzell commanding the district, and Brigadier Ellice. On 1st August there was a parade on the Western Heights when the 13th, the 78th, and the two Generals were present. From Lord Mark's account of what happened, it appears that he repeated his request to move the Battalion to the Western Heights barracks on parade, alleging that it had been the general custom at Dover for new arrivals to occupy the worst barracks, i.e. the Citadel. This statement Colonel Walker, the A.Q.M.G., denied. Lord Mark repeated his statement and asked permission of General Dalzell to ride up the hill to see the Staff Officer of the Royal Engineers to corroborate his assertion. General Dalzell reluctantly gave leave, but said that it was useless, as the 37th would march into the good barracks on their arrival on the 5th August. Lord Mark, very angry, then turned away to mount his horse, but finding his horse-holder looking the other way, threw his shako at the horse, which being startled nearly pulled the orderly over. Lord Mark, however, caught his horse, hastily mounted and, to the astonishment of the two Generals and the troops, galloped up to the barracks, leaving his shako on the ground. He was fortunate in finding the Royal Engineer Staff Officer in, who said that Lord Mark was right, and at the latter's request put it down on paper. This paper Lord Mark on his return to the parade showed to the two Generals, who read it and said nothing. Lord Mark, however, won his point, for on 3rd August general orders announced that the 13th were to go into the Western Heights barracks and the 37th into the Citadel. It will be remembered that the 37th were relieved by Lord Mark and the 13th at Azimghur in 1858, and this incident about the barracks caused some ill feeling between the regiments, which was, however, quickly allayed by their respective commanding officers.

On 27th August the Battalion was detailed to find a Guard of Honour for the Duke of Saxe-Coburg who was to arrive at Dover by steamer. As the hour of the Duke's arrival was uncertain the Guard of Honour was warned to stand by till further orders. Lord Mark, from his vantage-point on the Western Heights, was the first to see the steamer conveying the Duke approach. He immediately sent off the Guard of Honour, galloped down to the landing-stage, ordered the artillery to fire a salute, and himself received the Duke on landing. The two Generals arrived late, having only learnt of the Duke's arrival on hearing the artillery salute. It may be surmised that Lord Mark derived particular satisfaction from this incident.

Lord Mark Kerr lost no time in getting the Battalion into shape; he found that Light Infantry drill had deteriorated, that the Savings Bank was not so well patronized as in India, and that interior economy was slack. He at once set to work to remedy these defects, and converted the ground in front of the barracks into terraces, and planted them with trees and shrubs.

On 7th October H.R.H. the Duke of Cambridge arrived on inspection duty, when he was received at the station by a Guard of Honour furnished by the Battalion, and on the following day there was a field day, concluded by a march past in which the garrisons of Dover and Shorncliffe took part.

The Colours of the 1st Battalion after eighteen years' service, including two campaigns, were at this time completely worn out. They had been presented by the Prince Consort, and for that reason the Battalion was loth to part with them, but Lord Mark, recognizing the necessity of replacing them, approached Her Majesty the Queen, and asked as a special favour that one of her sons might be desired to present new ones. Her Majesty graciously acceded to the request and on October 28th H.R.H. Prince Alfred arrived at Dover and was met at the station by Major-General the Hon. Arthur Dalzell commanding the South-Eastern district, Brig.-General Ellice, Lord Mark Kerr, and the staff of the district and garrison.

Prince Alfred, who was dressed in the uniform of the Royal Navy with the insignia of the Garter, attended by Major Cowell and Lieutenant Haig, Royal Engineers, rode on to the parade ground and was received with a Royal Salute.

The troops of the garrison were drawn up as follows, namely—13th Light Infantry in line, with the 37th and a wing of the 73rd Regiment and Royal Artillery in columns of grand divisions on each flank facing inwards. After His Royal Highness had ridden down the line of the 13th, three sides of a square were formed, by wheeling forward the outer companies of the Regiment.

The ceremony of consecrating the Colours was then commenced by a hymn, admirably sung by the band. The Rev. G. R. Gleig, M.A., Chaplain-General to the Forces, who had performed the ceremony of consecration in 1846, assisted by the two Chaplains of the garrison, the Rev. T. Coney, M.A., and the Rev. J. Y. Barton, then read the consecration service, after which the new Colours were given to the Prince by Colonel Lord Mark Kerr, and were presented by him to Ensigns Middleton and Barker, who received them kneeling.

His Royal Highness in presenting the Colours said he had great pleasure in delivering these new Colours to a regiment which bore the name of his lamented father, and the more so as his father had been the last to present Colours to the Regiment. He felt satisfied that the Colours which he now presented by the desire of the Queen, would be borne always with the same gallantry as those which had been so often in peril and nobly defended.

Colonel Lord Mark Kerr, C.B., then replied as follows:—

'After thanking your Royal Highness for the gracious words which you have spoken to us, I wish to offer, through your Royal Highness, the loyal and earnest thanks of the officers, non-commissioned officers, and private soldiers, of the Battalion under my command, to Her Majesty the Queen, for Her Majesty's gracious condescension in having desired your Royal Highness to do us the distinguished honour of presenting us with these Colours. It has not been our wish to make a great display on this occasion, nor to celebrate it with the customary ball-giving and feasting, for we have felt it to be no ordinary one. All of us remember with feelings of love and devotion, that when this ceremony was last performed, those old Colours were given to us by that illustrious and gifted Prince, your Royal Highness's father, whose name we have such pride in bearing, and whose loss has since been felt with such a deep sense of its irreparable nature, as has perhaps never before occurred in English history. And those old Colours have passed with some honour and renown through two wars, and have seen arduous and dangerous service. On one occasion, certainly, during the Indian Mutiny, they were exposed to greater peril than probably ever before befel the Colours of a British Regiment in India, for the reserve being called to the front, the sacred emblems were entrusted to the custody of the band alone, the Regiment being enveloped by an ambuscade as cleverly laid, and with more overpowering odds against it than was the case when Hannibal entrapped and took captive the Roman Army under the Consul Flaminius by the Thrasymene lake. And speaking of this incident in the Indian Mutiny War, and going back to older times, there are some names not on these Colours, your Royal Highness, which I could fain hope at some time to see there. There was a battle nearly two centuries ago, when there was a gallant English Regiment which stood resolute and unwavering, and amidst surrounding panic and disaster protected the retreat of the Royal Commander-in-Chief[1] (*sic*). The battle so eloquently described by the late Lord Macaulay, was Killiecrankie, and the Regiment was the 13th. And it has been the peculiar lot of the 13th to stand thus in great measure alone on several occasions. It was thus at Killiecrankie, and it was the same during the American War in 1813; it was so at Jellalabad, and it was so on the occasion to which I have referred during the war of the Indian Mutiny. And now I trust that I have not wearied your Royal Highness with these details of ourselves, and I will conclude by expressing a confident hope, that the discipline and the conduct of the 13th Prince Albert's Light Infantry will be always such

[1] General Mackay commanded the troops at Killiecrankie.

as to ensure, in future wars, an equally glorious career to these Colours which we have just received from your Royal Highness; and further I will say that I have no doubt but that your Royal Highness's gracious presence and words to-day will live in the minds of soldiers of all ranks in this Regiment, and that the memory of Prince Alfred will be the fruitful source, if the occasion arises, of deeds worthy of the Victoria Cross.'

The 13th then re-formed line, and the new Colours were trooped and marched along the ranks of the Battalion, preceded by the band and followed by an escort. On arriving at the centre of the line, the exchange of Colours was effected, the new ones taking part as the standards of the corps, and the old ones proceeded with the escort to the right of the line, after reaching which, with the escort and the band playing 'Auld Lang Syne', they were marched along receiving the parting compliment of presented arms from the Regiment which had so long defended them.

His Royal Highness then took post at the flagstaff and the whole of the troops, preceded by the 13th, marched past in grand divisions, and proceeded to their respective quarters. The Prince, attended by Major Cowell, Lieutenant Haig, the Major-General, Brigadier-General and Staff, afterwards rode to the mess room of the Regiment, where he honoured the officers with his company at luncheon. In the evening the Prince left by special steamer for Ostend. There was a ball at the Officers' Mess to celebrate the occasion. The old Colours were afterwards deposited in Wells Cathedral.

On 21st February 1865 the 1st Battalion left Dover by rail for Aldershot and was quartered in the west block of the permanent barracks.

In February the Depôt was removed from Fermoy to Templemore, and in December to Newry.

It is now necessary to refer to a subject which is of considerable interest to the Regiment. Shortly after the 1st Battalion arrived at Aldershot, the General Officer Commanding, Sir John Pennefather, noticed that the serjeants of the Battalion wore their sashes over the left shoulder and tied on the right side in the same way as the officers, and ordered the discontinuance of the practice. Lord Mark Kerr was on leave at the time, but on the 1st March, he had an interview with H.R.H. the Duke of Cambridge at the Horse Guards. The following is Lord Mark's account of the interview in his journal:—

'I speak to the Duke of Cambridge about the serjeants' sashes of the 13th which had been worn since Culloden—where they distinguished themselves greatly—by the Duke of Cumberland's orders, on the same side as the officers wear theirs. This distinction and tradition, which is much prized by the Regiment, has now been rudely ordered, in my absence, to be discontinued by Sir John Pennefather, commanding at Aldershot; and I point out to H.R.H. the advisability of its restoration, but I shall have to write about it from Aldershot before it can be done.'

On 28th March Lord Mark wrote to the Horse Guards. No copy of his letter can be found, but the following is the reply:—

'Horse Guards, *3rd April 1865*

Sir,—

Referring to Lord Mark Kerr's letter, dated 28th ult. I am directed by the Field-Marshal Commander-in-Chief to request that you will be pleased to intimate to His Lordship that His Royal Highness, having taken into consideration the length of time the custom of wearing the Sash on the right side by the Serjeants of the 13th Light Infantry has existed, is pleased to approve of the practice being continued in that regiment.

I have &c.

J. Yorke Scarlett, A.G.

Lt.-Gen. Sir John Pennefather, K.C.B.,
Commanding at Aldershot.'

This ruling has since been embodied in the King's Regulations, and the privilege is naturally very highly prized by the Serjeants of the Regiment.

Further details on the custom of wearing the sash tied on the right side will be found in Appendix F.

During the drill season of 1865, Lord Mark fully maintained the reputation of the Battalion in Light Infantry movements, though these manœuvres did not altogether find favour with the authorities. On one occasion Sir John Pennefather said to Lord Mark: 'You have ruined my field day entirely by sending out your skirmishers so far to the front. I never send mine out more than 20 paces in front of the line.' Lord Mark Kerr commented in his journal: 'and this from a General who was in the Crimea, and is now commanding the Camp of Instruction'. Later in the season at another field day when the Duke of Cambridge was present, and the 13th skirmished in front of the division, H.R.H. afterwards told Sir John Pennefather and the officers commanding how pleased he was at the improvement in the Aldershot skirmishing!

On Christmas Day 1865 Lord Mark visited the Serjeants' and soldiers' dinners for the last time, when he was received with a great deal of cheering, which on previous occasions he had forbidden. In an appropriate parting order, in which, after referring to the eleven eventful years he had commanded the Regiment, and to the deeds already related, his Lordship continued:—

'In the meantime he leaves the Regiment in whose welfare he has taken so deep an interest—whose life, indeed, has been his life—with feelings of pain, the description of which in words would sound like exaggeration, and in saying farewell, he thanks officers, non-commissioned officers, and private soldiers for the cheerful and willing obedience which they have at all times shown him.

'Lord Mark Kerr feels confident that discipline, courage and endurance (as he told them on a memorable occasion some years ago) qualities which have already gained the Regiment so much renown, will be its constant characteristics, and will always make the 13th Prince Albert's Light Infantry eminent amongst soldiers.'

Brevet Colonel MacBean succeeded Lord Mark Kerr in the command of the 1st Battalion. Major Peter Macdonald was promoted to the rank of Lieutenant-Colonel in the Regiment on the 19th December, which gave him the command of the 2nd Battalion, to the vacant majority of which Captain and Brevet Major Frederick Van Straubenzee succeeded.

On 26th and 27th May 1866 seven companies of the Battalion proceeded by rail to Portsmouth and proceeded thence by ship to Devonport and were followed a few days afterwards by the Headquarters and the remaining companies. The Battalion remained quartered in the Raglan barracks till the 1st September, when they proceeded to Ireland in H.M. Troopship *Tamar* and were quartered at Cork, with six companies on detachment at Kinsale, Bundon, Bantry, Skibbereen and Ballincollig. Prior to embarkation the following order was issued by the General Officer Commanding:—

'Devonport, *31st August 1866*

'The Major-General, the Hon[ble] Sir A. A. Spencer, K.C.B., in taking leave of the officers, non-commissioned officers and men of the 13th Prince Albert's Light Infantry, wishes them every success, wherever they may go.

'The Major-General considers the 1st Battalion of the 13th Prince Albert's Light Infantry to be in every respect one of the best corps he ever had the honour of having under his command.'

An event of some interest took place in the Barrack Square at Cork on the 16th October. The Battalion, under command of Colonel MacBean, was drawn up in line. The flank companies having been wheeled inwards, the band and bugles formed facing the Colours. The Battalion was thus drawn up for the purpose of receiving a handsome bugle, about to be presented by Captain Hoban, late quartermaster, on his retirement from the service. Captain Hoban advanced towards the Colours and addressing the officers and men, handed the bugle to Colonel MacBean who, in the name of the Regiment, thanked Captain Hoban for his exceedingly handsome present and assured him that the gift would always be highly valued of the officers and men of the Regiment in memory of an officer who had so often distinguished himself in the field, and rendered valuable service to his Queen and country.

The silver bugle is beautifully ornamented, and bears on it the names of the several engagements in which the Regiment has taken part. The inscription is as follows: 'Presented to the 13th Prince Albert's Light Infantry by Captain T. Hoban, on his leaving the Regiment, after having served upwards of thirty-five years. August 1866.'

Captain Hoban joined as a boy in 1831, and was promoted to an ensigncy on the 12th January 1855, and became quartermaster of the Regiment on 25th May 1855. He served with the Army of the Indus during the campaigns in Afghanistan in the years 1838, 1839, 1840, 1841, and 1842, with great gallantry. He was present at the storming of Ghazni in July 1839, and the forts of Tootumdurra and Julgar, in the Kohistan, in 1840; was present at the several engagements in forcing the passes from Kabul to Jellalabad, in 1841, and in defence of the latter fortress in 1841 and 1842; engaged in the general actions, Jellalabad 7th April 1842; Jugdulluck 8th September 1842; Tezin, 13th September and the recapture of Kabul, 15th September 1842. He was present at the siege and fall of Sevastopol, 8th September 1855. He was engaged in the suppression of the Indian Mutiny; present at the action of Azimghur 6th April 1858, and subsequent operations in that district; present in the action at Jugdespore 26th October, and Toolsepore, 23rd December 1858. He was highly complimented by Sir Robert Sale in 1841 for his conduct in the field and mentioned in Colonel Lord Mark Kerr's dispatch of 6th April 1858, after the action of Azimghur. Captain Hoban was slightly wounded in the shoulder on 3rd October 1840. He was in possession of the following medals: Medal for the storming of Ghazni, 23rd July 1839; Medal for the defence and general action at Jellalabad, 7th April 1842; Medal for the recapture of Kabul, 15th September 1842; Medal and clasp for the siege and fall of Sevastopol; Turkish War Medal; Medal for the suppression of the Mutiny in India; and Medal for meritorious conduct.

The above account is taken from the *Army and Navy Gazette* of 27th October 1866.

The headquarters of the Battalion were moved from Cork to Kinsale on the 29th October, and another company detached to Clonakilty.

The Battalion remained in the south of Ireland during the Fenian excitement and was during the whole of that time broken up into various detachments; the headquarters for many months consisting of only one company with the Band and Bugles.

On 14th May 1867 orders were received for the formation of the Depôt and the establishment of the Battalion was increased as follows:—

Ten Service companies numbering 33 officers, 50 serjeants, 40 corporals, 21 boys, and 640 privates.

Two Depôt companies numbering 6 officers, 10 serjeants, 10 corporals, 4 boys, and 100 privates.

On 30th May 1867 the headquarters were ordered into Cork that the Battalion might be concentrated previous to embarkation for Gibraltar.

2ND BATTALION

On 12th July 1866 the 2nd Battalion, who had been stationed for upwards of two years on outpost duty, returned to Line Barracks, Port Louis, Mauritius.

Early in the year 1867, after a long drought and excessive heat, fever of an intermittent type presented itself in the leeward districts of the island and daily increased in intensity until about the end of February when it was pronounced epidemic. The Battalion suffered severely, and the hospital accommodation being insufficient, 200 of the fever patients were sent to the quarantine station at Cannonier Point, but notwithstanding this, the hospital was still crowded and many, who were ill in barracks, could not be admitted, consequently it was decided to move the Battalion to Flacq Island on 1st April.

Here the men were encamped, and unfortunately many circumstances combined to add to their suffering.

All supplies had to be imported from Port Louis, and owing to bad weather regular rations were frequently interrupted, so that fever continued to increase to such an extent that very few, either officers or men, were free from it. The women and children were especially in a deplorable condition, all sick, and no nourishing diet to be procured. At last, when fever began to abate, dysentery of a most malignant type attacked the camp. On 23rd May the Battalion returned to Port Louis preparatory to embarkation for England, having lost by death during the few weeks they had been on Flacq Island, 15 men, 1 woman and 14 children.

On 7th June the Battalion embarked for England on board H.M.S. *Himalaya*.

Prior to embarkation the Major-General commanding at Mauritius issued the following general order:—

'On taking leave of the 2nd Battalion, 13th Light Infantry, the Major-General Commanding has much pleasure in recording the general exemplary conduct of the Battalion and desires to congratulate Lieut.-Colonel Macdonald on the very orderly and well-disposed corps, that is about to embark for home, under his command.

'The Major-General further begs to communicate to the Battalion his wishes for their recovery and welfare after the unprecedented sickness that has prevailed in the most virulent form at Mauritius during the present year and from which the corps, he regrets to say, has suffered considerably.

By command,

Signed G. H. L. MILLMAN,
Lieut.-Col. A.A. and Q.M.G.'

CHAPTER XXI

SERVICE AT HOME AND ABROAD

1st BATTALION

THE various detachments of the 1st Battalion having joined the headquarters at Cork between the 1st and 4th June 1867, the Battalion consisting of ten companies, strength 27 officers, 44 serjeants, 38 corporals and 593 other ranks, embarked on board H.M.Troopship *Simoon* on the 15th of the month and proceeded to Gibraltar, where they disembarked on the 20th and marched to the North Front, where they remained under canvas until 9th July, when they moved to Windmill Hill Barracks.

Gibraltar at this period was a pleasant enough station for the officers, who were able to enjoy during the winter two days a week with the Calpe Hounds, occasional race meetings, and rough shooting in Spain and Morocco, but soldiering was practically limited to Guard duties, the number of nights of bed being as low as two to three.

In October 1868 the Battalion moved from Windmill Hill Barracks to South Barracks, where they remained till the 12th March 1870, after which they occupied the Grand Casement Barracks till the 11th April 1871 when they moved to the Europa and Windmill Hill Barracks. There is little of interest to record during the Battalion's stay at Gibraltar, the establishment varied almost from year to year. On the 1st April 1870 it was as low as 27 officers and 558 other ranks, though in the following August it was raised to 30 officers and 608 other ranks. Their long stay at Gibraltar came to an end on 17th February 1872, when the Battalion, under the command of Colonel MacBean, embarked for Malta on H.M.S. *Jumna* and disembarked at Valetta five days later.

Prior to leaving Gibraltar the Major-General Commanding issued the following order:—

'In bidding farewell to Colonel MacBean and the 1st Battalion 13th Light Infantry, the Major-General desires to assure them of his sincere regret at losing from his Brigade a Battalion so admirably disciplined and so ably commanded. He has so often had the pleasure of recording, in reports to his superiors, his high opinion of its efficiency, and the excellence of its conduct both on and off duty, that he has little to add now but to express his full appreciation of the unanimity and good feeling which has prevailed so generally among the Regiments now about to separate, and in which, the 13th, as the one longest in the garrison, may fairly be said to have set the example.

'The Major-General wishes the Battalion health and prosperity in its new station, and wherever else its services may be required.
By order of Major-General Bisset, C.B.,
Signed Clifford Parson,
Major, Brigade Major.'

When the 1st Battalion left Ireland in 1867 the two Depôt companies of the Battalion were quartered at Shorncliffe, where they remained till March 1869, when under the command of Captain W. Knox Leet they proceeded to Winchester and were attached to the 7th (Rifle) Depôt Battalion. In the following March 1870 this Depôt Battalion was dismembered, and the two Depôt companies of the 13th Light Infantry under the command of Captain T. A. Cary proceeded to Aldershot, where they were attached to the 2nd Battalion of the Regiment, and accompanied that battalion in its subsequent moves.

The 1st Battalion on arrival at Malta occupied the Floriana Barracks, where it remained rather more than a year, until in April 1873 it moved over to the Cottonera district on the other side of the Grand Harbour.

In April 1873 Colonel W. Forbes MacBean, who had commanded the Battalion since 1865, was appointed to the command of a Brigade depôt and was succeeded by Lieut.-Colonel R. B. Montgomery on July 13th.

Colonel MacBean was an officer of exceptional merit, who had throughout the period of command maintained a high order of efficiency in the Battalion, and had renewed the original system of infantry organization under which the Captains were made to feel that they really commanded their companies, while the adjutant, quartermaster, and serjeant-major were relegated to their proper sphere on the regimental staff. In this connexion it is interesting to note that in 1872 Lieutenant H. Hallam Parr, an officer destined to achieve considerable distinction in the Army, was appointed adjutant by Colonel MacBean, and became thoroughly imbued with his commanding officer's ideas, but soon after Lieut.-Colonel Montgomery took over command, finding that his new commanding officer had little sympathy with Colonel MacBean's system of command, he resigned his appointment as adjutant, a bold step for a junior officer to take, but characteristic of his high sense of duty.

On the 4th April 1874 an interesting ceremony took place on the Floriana parade, Valetta. In the presence of the Infantry Brigade commanded by Lieut.-General Sir Francis Seymour, Bart., C.B., Lieutenant James Guillet Westaway was presented by H.E. Lieut.-General Sir C. T. Van Straubenzee, K.C.B., commanding the Troops in the island of Malta and its dependencies, with the Humane Society's Silver Medal and Testimonial for 'having on the 8th July 1872, jumped into the River Liffey at Dublin, Ireland, to the relief of a boy who was in danger of drowning, and whose life he saved', which decoration he was authorized to wear on his right breast.

On the 3rd December 1874, the 1st Battalion, under the command of Lieut.-Colonel R. B. Montgomery, strength 22 officers, 46 serjeants, 38 corporals, 14 buglers and 598 privates, embarked on board H.M.S. *Himalaya* for conveyance to the Cape of Good Hope and Natal.

2ND BATTALION

It is now necessary to revert to the fortunes of the 2nd Battalion. As related in the last chapter, the Battalion embarked at Mauritius for England on 7th June 1867. They disembarked at Portland on 25th July, the headquarter wing being stationed at Verne Citadel, and four companies at Weymouth. On the following day the Depôt companies joined from Shorncliffe and were incorporated in the Battalion.

After a stay of rather more than a year at Portland and Weymouth, the 2nd Battalion was relieved by the 51st Light Infantry, and embarked on 17th September in H.M.S. *Simoon* for Gosport, where it disembarked, and was quartered as follows:—

Fort Grange	H.Q. and four companies
Fort Rowner	six companies
Fort Gomer	Detachment

On the 28th October Lieut.-Colonel Thomas Maunsell, late of the 32nd, 28th, and 75th Regiments, was appointed from the Half-Pay List and assumed command *vice* Lieut.-Colonel P. Macdonald exchanged to Half-Pay.

The distribution of the Battalion was slightly altered in the early part of 1869, one officer and 23 men proceeding to Fort Fareham on 1st February, and three officers and 70 men to Marchwood on 3rd March.

In June the Battalion moved from Gosport to Aldershot by march route via Bishops Waltham, arriving on the 5th, and was encamped at Rushmoor Bottom, where they remained till 14th September, when they moved into the West Infantry barracks.

The two Depôt companies of the 1st Battalion arrived at Aldershot from Winchester on 1st March 1870 and were attached to the 2nd Battalion.

The year 1870 is noteworthy as marking the inauguration of the Annual Regimental Dinner in London which has continued with few exceptions ever since. It was held on 4th July at Willis' Rooms. The price of the tickets was 35s. each. The following were present:—

Major-General the Lord Mark Kerr, C.B., presiding; Lieut.-Colonel A. P. C. E. Somerset, K. R. Murchison, Esq., Captain E. Boyd, Major the Hon. J. C. Dormer, Lieut.-Colonel J. Maunsell, Lieut.-Colonel W. H. Kerr, Major C. P. Long, Captain A. McG. Denny, F. Lynch, Esq., J. J. Ross, Esq., P. C. Caldwell, Esq., N. Sauley, Esq., F. W. S. Stanhope, Esq., Major R. Douglas, Colonel H. A. Wade, C.B., Major R. B. Montgomery, Leigh Smith, Esq., P. O'Kelly, Esq., Captain A. S. Adair, Captain J. Busby, J. M. Read, Esq., and Lieut.-Colonel J. F. Everett, who acted as Honorary Secretary.

On the 7th October 1870 the 2nd Battalion, with the Depôt companies of the 1st Battalion, moved from Aldershot to Pembroke Dock, detachments being furnished as follows: Hubberston Fort, Popton Point, South Hook and Defensible barracks.

The following letter from the Horse Guards containing a report from

Lieut.-General the Hon. Sir James Yorke Scarlett, G.C.B., on the conduct of the Battalion is here placed on record:—

'Horse Guards, S.W.
11th October 1870

Sir,—

I am instructed by the Field-Marshal Commanding-in-Chief to inform you that His Royal Highness has received with much satisfaction from the Lieut.-General Commanding at Aldershot the following report on the 2nd Battalion 13th L.I. on their departure from the Camp for Pembroke Dock, viz. "The conduct of the Battalion, since its arrival here in June 1869, has given me every satisfaction, and that, by the regularity and good order in which their departure was effected, they maintained to the last the good opinion I had formed of the Corps."

His Royal Highness wishes the foregoing to be communicated to the Officer Commanding the Battalion.

I have &c.
Signed J. Hope Grant, Q.M.G.'

About this time a new badge was designed and approved for the Glengarry Cap. The badge was an imitation of the ornaments worn on the appointments of officers and men with the number '13' superimposed.

On the 31st August 1871 the Battalion gave 150 volunteers to the 44th Regiment, which was proceeding to India.

The 2nd Battalion, accompanied by the Depôt companies of the 1st Battalion, embarked at Pembroke Dock on the 27th September on board H.M.S. *Orantes* for conveyance to Kingstown, Ireland, proceeding on arrival to Kilkenny, from which station detachments were furnished to the following towns—Waterford, Clonmel, Duncannon, Dungarvon, and Carrick-on-Suir.

On the 31st May 1872, 55 transfers were received from the 43rd Light Infantry, and later on in September 33 men were transferred from the 2nd Battalion to that regiment.

On the 2nd July the Battalion, with the Depôt companies of the 1st Battalion, proceeded from Kilkenny to Dublin and took up quarters in the Royal Barracks with a detachment at the Curragh Camp.

In July of this year sanction was given for the rank and file to wear a badge consisting of a bugle with mural crown on the collars of their tunics and frocks, instead of the regimental device on the buttons, which latter were replaced by those of a universal pattern.

In 1873 the Depôt of the 13th (Prince Albert's) Regiment of Light Infantry was constituted at Taunton, and styled the 36th Brigade Depôt, the 1st and 2nd Somerset Regiments of Militia being affiliated to the Regiment. The Depôt companies of the 1st Battalion, owing probably to the want of barrack accommodation at Taunton, still continued to accompany the 2nd Battalion, who moved on the 8th July from Dublin to Newry, detachments being found at Armagh, Drogheda and Monaghan.

Prior to leaving Dublin two companies of the Battalion on the night of 7th June were on duty in aid of the Civil Power on the occasion of a great fire in Thomas Street, and had to act in clearing the streets of a riotous mob who assembled in great numbers and stoned the military. The officer in command and many of the men were severely injured. The military arrangements and conduct of the troops on this occasion were commended by His Royal Highness the Commander-in-Chief.

In consequence of the anticipated Orange Riots at Belfast on the 12th July, the Drogheda detachment proceeded direct to Belfast on the 9th and remained there till the 23rd, while six companies of the Battalion from Newry and Armagh were concentrated at Belfast from the 9th to 15th July.

On the 15th October the Battalion sent 50 men as volunteers to the 83rd Regiment, then serving in India.

It was notified in a letter dated Horse Guards, 9th October, that black ball tufts would replace the green plumes hitherto worn in the shakos of the 13th Light Infantry on the issue of new shakos to the Regiment in April 1874.

On the 3rd July 1874 the Battalion, with the Depôt companies of the 1st Battalion, moved from Newry to Belfast. Prior to leaving Newry Lieut.-Colonel Maunsell received an appreciative letter from Mr. William Henry, Chairman of the Newry Town Commissioners, expressing their thanks for services rendered in suppressing fires, and also for the interest shown in the local charities.

On the 4th January 1875 the Martini-Henry Rifle was issued to the Battalion in replacement of the Snider Rifle, and in the following September valise equipment was issued. On the 31st March, the Battalion and Depôt companies of the 1st Battalion attached embarked at Belfast on board H.M.S. *Simoon* for conveyance to Glasgow, from which station detachments were furnished at Maryhill Barracks and at Stirling.

Bt. Colonel T. Maunsell was placed on half-pay on the 24th March, and was succeeded in the command by Major Arthur Bainbrigge.

On 20th October 22 men were transferred as volunteers to the 33rd Regiment, then serving in India.

On the 7th August 1876 the Battalion, with Depôt companies attached, embarked on board H.M.S. *Orontes en route* for Aldershot, but on the evening of the 8th the ship's engines broke down, and the voyage was continued under sail to Holyhead, where the Battalion disembarked and proceeded by rail to Aldershot, where they were quartered in the West Infantry Barracks, and remained there till the 27th July 1877, when they proceeded to Portsmouth and embarked on board H.M.S. *Crocodile* for conveyance to Malta, where they occupied quarters at Fort Ricasoli with companies detached at Zabbar, Salvatore, and Lazaretto.

1st BATTALION

The 1st Battalion arrived at Table Bay, Cape of Good Hope, on the 5th January 1875, disembarked on the 7th and were encamped on the Grand Parade at Cape Town, where they were joined by a draft of 3 officers, 1 N.C.O. and 132 men from England and by 52 volunteers of the 86th Regiment.

The engines of H.M.S. *Himalaya* having broken down, the Battalion was ordered to proceed to its ultimate destination by half-battalions in H.M.S. *Simoon*.

On the 15th January the right half-battalion, strength 2 Field Officers, 3 captains, 7 subalterns, 3 staff, 26 serjeants, 19 corporals, 9 buglers and 384 privates, under the command of Lieut.-Colonel R. B. Montgomery, embarked, and arrived at Durban (Port Natal) on the 22nd, but owing to bad weather the disembarkation could not be completed before the 25th. On the 27th, after leaving a detachment of one officer and 36 N.C.Os. and men at Durban, the half-battalion marched for Pietermaritzburg, arriving there on the 30th, where they were joined by 15 volunteers from the 75th Regiment.

The left half-battalion while waiting at Cape Town were called out to assist in extinguishing bush fires on the 9th and 10th January in the vicinity of the town, for which they received the thanks of the Town Council and a cheque for £50 as some compensation for the damage done to their uniforms. Ultimately the half-battalion, strength 1 Field Officer, 3 captains, 5 subalterns, 1 staff, 19 serjeants, 18 corporals, 5 buglers and 378 privates, under the command of Major A. Bainbrigge, embarked on the 30th January and disembarked at East London on 5th February. There they left a detachment of 2 officers and 52 N.C.Os. and men and marched for King William's Town, where they arrived on the 9th and were joined by 14 volunteers from the 75th Regiment.

The two wings of the Battalion remained in their respective stations during the whole of 1875, but at the end of the year orders were received for the left half-battalion at King William's Town to rejoin headquarters in Natal. On the 31st December they marched for East London, arriving there on the 2nd January 1876, and embarked the same day on board the steamer *Anglian* for Durban, arriving there on the 3rd. They disembarked on the 4th and marched for Fort Napier, Maritzburg, on the 7th, arriving there on the 10th. As there was no barrack accommodation the troops went under canvas. Maritzburg afforded a good deal of sport; besides rough shooting there was hunting, Captain Dudley Persse showing quite good sport with a pack which at one time amounted to 22 couples.

The year 1876 passed quietly enough, but in December Sir Theophilus Shepstone, K.C.M.G., Secretary for Native Affairs, was dispatched as Her Majesty's Special Commissioner to Pretoria, the capital of the Transvaal, to negotiate with that Republic respecting matters concerning the internal policy of that country, and under certain exigencies and conditions he had power to annex the Transvaal to the British Crown. For this latter purpose a contingent of the troops stationed in Natal was placed at his disposal, but in the first instance Sir T. Shepstone with his staff, among whom was Captain James, 13th Light Infantry, acting as Military Secretary, proceeded alone to Pretoria, accompanied by an escort of 20 Natal Mounted Police.

The contingents placed at the disposal of the Special Commissioner were the 1st Battalion 13th Light Infantry, 2 guns, 11th Battery Royal Artillery, a detachment 7th Company R.E. and one troop of the Natal Mounted Police, the whole under the command of Colonel Pearson of the Buffs.

The detachment of the Regiment stationed at Durban was relieved by the Buffs, while one captain was to remain at Pietermaritzburg in charge of all details.

In order that the 13th might be nearer the possible scene of action, they were ordered to proceed to Newcastle, a distance of 200 miles, and within 36 miles of the Transvaal border. They marched there in two detachments. The first, consisting of headquarters and five companies, started on 2nd March and arrived on March 21st, the second, of three companies, reached Newcastle on the 28th March. The Jellalabad Sports were held on 7th April. The tug-of-war on this occasion was across a stream, necessitating the losers being dragged through the water.

On the 11th April dispatches were received from the Special Commissioner requesting that the contingent placed at his disposal should be sent across the frontier without delay, but owing to the difficulty in procuring transport it was not till the 17th April that the contingent started, and then only with flying column equipment. On the 18th they reached Coldstream and the following day crossed the frontier. At Coldstream they were met by the Commissioner of the Wakkerstroom district, a Mr. Whitehead, who drove up in a Scotch cart bearing the Union Jack, and who assured the officer in command that there would be no opposition, for up till then it was doubtful how the British troops would be received. Private McToy, the author of the *13th Regiment in South Africa*, tells how there was quite a ceremony when the troops crossed the frontier. The troops presented arms, the Colours were lowered, and the band played 'God save the Queen', while the reception of the troops by the Boers left nothing to be desired. Nevertheless, in their march to Pretoria all military precautions were taken, as from time to time reports of intended opposition by the Doppers (Boers) kept coming in. Marches amounting to 96 miles brought the column to the Vaal River where there was an unusually large number of Boers, all armed, assembled to meet them, but they gave the troops a hearty welcome. Standerton and Heidelberg were reached and passed in turn, until on 2nd May the column halted at Erasmus Farm, 7 miles from Pretoria.

May 3rd was spent in making preparations for the public entry into Pretoria, then little more than a large village of poor houses; accoutrements and appointments were burnished up and the best uniforms produced.

Early on 4th May the march to Pretoria was resumed, and McToy tells us that the road to Pretoria was lined with carriages laden with the fair sex, and thousands on foot (surely an exaggeration) who gave the troops a hearty welcome. On reaching the Poort, the entrance to the town between two precipitous hills, the band struck up the 'Alliance March', and a little later the Administrator and Officials of Government met the column, when Colonel Weatherby, the Resident and Chief of the 'Mutual Defence Association', called for three cheers, which was heartily responded to; after which the troops went into camp.

The conduct of the march of the column from Natal to Pretoria called forth the following eulogies from the authorities:—

His Excellency the Administrator in a letter to Colonel Pearson, 'The Buffs', dated 10th May 1877, states:—

'I beg you to be kind enough to convey my personal thanks and acknowledgements to Lieut.-Colonel Montgomery and the officers and men of the Force under your command for the exemplary manner in which the policy of Her Majesty's Government has been supported by them during their arduous march as shown by your report.'

And later on the following General Order dated 20th August 1877, issued by H.E. Lieut.-General Sir A. A. Cunynghame, K.C.B., commanding Troops South Africa, dated 20th August 1877:—

'The Secretary of State for the Colonies having transmitted to the Secretary of State for War an extract from a dispatch received from the Administrator of the Government of the Transvaal reporting the good physical condition of the Troops and their exemplary conduct since their arrival at Pretoria; the same has been laid before H.R.H. the Field-Marshal Commanding-in-Chief who has been pleased to consider it to be highly satisfactory and most creditable to all concerned.'

May 24th, the birthday of Her Majesty the Queen, was the day selected for the official ceremony of hoisting the British flag over the Transvaal. For this purpose General Sir A. Cunynghame, accompanied by his A.D.C., Lieutenant Coghill, 24th Regiment, had arrived in Pretoria, whilst large numbers of Boers with their families had been invited to Pretoria to be present. Unfortunately the day turned out to be miserably wet, and the ceremony was postponed till the following day when the troops were formed up on the race-course facing south, in the presence of the Administrator and General Officer Commanding, their staffs, and a large concourse of people. The Union Jack was hoisted, the troops presented arms, and the guns thundered a salute which was followed by general cheering, and a march past of the troops.

Shortly afterwards Colonel Pearson returned to Natal, being replaced by Colonel Montgomery as Commandant in the Transvaal.

In August one company of the 13th Light Infantry was sent on detachment to Standerton on the lines of communication with Natal.

In December, in consequence of the threatening attitude assumed by Cetewayo, the Zulu King, three companies of the Regiment over 300 strong, under the command of Major Gilbert, 2 guns of the 11th Battery, R.A., and a detachment of Mounted Infantry were dispatched from Pretoria to Utrecht, then garrisoned by three companies of the 80th Regiment under Major Tucker. The column started on 12th December and reached Utrecht on 27th December, after a march of 220 miles. During the stay of this detachment at Utrecht they were employed in building a good fort, and establishing store accommodation. The trouble with the Zulus having been temporarily settled, the three companies of the 13th, being relieved by the 90th Light Infantry, left Utrecht on the 12th March 1878 and returned to Pretoria on 28th March.

CHAPTER XXII

CAMPAIGNS IN THE TRANSVAAL AND ZULULAND

THE CAMPAIGN AGAINST SEKUKINI

EARLY in April 1878 when Sekukini, a notable Chief in the North-East Transvaal, instigated by Cetewayo, King of the Zulus, began to give trouble to the local farmers, English and Dutch, who lived in those remote parts, one company of the 13th, under Captain Persse, was sent to Middelburg and two companies, under Major England and Captain Cox, were sent to Lydenburg, where they arrived on the 23rd and 30th April respectively. Although the presence of the troops in some way alleviated the situation, it did not prevent the purloining of cattle and the burning of deserted homesteads by the native tribes. In fact, the situation got gradually worse; Sekukini was in open revolt, he made raids on isolated posts, and finally on 7th August he surprised the Diamond Fields Horse, 83 strong, on the Dwars River, who lost 52 horses and 48 oxen.

On 13th August Colonel Rowlands, V.C., C.B., was appointed to command the troops in the Transvaal. The 80th Regiment were ordered to relieve the 13th at Pretoria, Lydenburg, Middelburg and Standerton, the latter to take the field against Sekukini.

Accordingly on 28th August Rowlands, with a force of all arms including five companies of the 13th commanded by Lieut.-Colonel P. E. V. Gilbert, who had lately taken over the command from Lieut.-Colonel R. B. Montgomery, started for the front. He proceeded down the valley of the Eland River into that of the Oliphant River. On 8th September he crossed the Oliphant River and on the 11th reached Fort Weeber, where he was joined by Major England's two companies from Lydenburg. The latter officer had built a fort called Fort England for the protection of Lydenburg, and its garrison had successfully cleared the neighbouring country of the enemy. It is very difficult to follow the distribution of the Battalion at this period, but it is certain that not more than half the Battalion was available for active operations, the remainder were garrisoning forts commanding the approaches to the Lulu Mountains where Sekukini's stronghold was situated. Captain Waddy's company erected and garrisoned Fort Oliphant, Captain Persse's company was in Mapoch's district with the Diamond Field Horse. Captain Thurlow's company was distributed between Forts Faugh-a-Ballagh and Mamelube at the entrance of the Steelpoort Valley, in which valley Captain Cox's company had in the previous month been smartly engaged with the enemy. Then again there was Fort Burghers, the nearest of all to Sekukini's town, garrisoned by three companies of the Regiment.

The plan of operations was to garrison the forts built on the Western slopes of the Lulu Mountains, so as to threaten the enemy from that side, while with the remainder of the force an attack was to be made along the eastern slope, and if possible to destroy Sekukini's stronghold.

Rowlands himself arrived at Fort Burghers at the junction of the Steelpoort and Speckboom valleys on 19th September.

The command of the detaining force was given to Major England, 13th Light Infantry. He had at his disposal at—

Fort Mamelube—Captain Thurlow with 50 men of the 13th and 40 Mounted Volunteers;

Fort Oliphant—Captain Waddy with 100 men of the 13th, one 4-pounder Krupp gun and 40 mounted Volunteers;

Fort Faugh-a-Ballagh—Lieutenant Pollock with 50 men of the 13th, one 4-pounder Krupp gun, 20 Mounted Volunteers and 100 natives.

It was not till 3rd October that Rowlands was in a position to advance from Fort Burghers. After leaving garrisons in Forts Weeber and Burghers, he set out with a strong force of mounted men, viz. 338 men of the Frontier Light Horse and Mounted Infantry, two companies (130 strong) of the 13th and 2 Krupp guns towards Sekukini town, 25 miles distant. The column had only advanced about 4 miles when firing commenced, there was little or no water to be obtained, the country was rocky and covered with thick bush. The difficulties of the terrain were more formidable than the resistance of the enemy, and at the end of the day only 8 miles had been covered. A further advance of 9 miles was made on the 4th October, but the conditions did not improve, the weather was very hot, and there was no grazing for the animals. The troops went into bivouac at the base of a chain of almost insurmountable hills. About 8 p.m. the enemy were perceived stealing down the hills in great numbers; the 13th occupied the front, Major Russell with the Mounted Infantry on the right, and Colonel Buller with the Frontier Light Horse on the left. The hostile attack was easily repulsed, but a good many slaughter oxen were lost owing to a stampede.

On the 5th the march was resumed, after a successful attack on the enemy's positions, but little progress could be made owing to the scarcity of water.

On the 6th Rowlands, unable to close with the enemy, lacking water and forage for the animals, decided to give up the expedition and retire to Fort Burghers. This he accomplished successfully on the 7th October, though the loss in horses, mules and oxen was considerable. Meanwhile the garrisons of the forts under Major England were not seriously menaced, though at Forts Mamelube and Faugh-a-Ballagh some desultory fighting took place, and an ox-cart convoy from the latter fort to Fort Weeber was attacked and two of the escort, Corporal Meneary and Private Doherty, were wounded.

Colonel Rowlands being unable to effect anything against the enemy's positions in the Lulu Mountains, now turned his attention north and eastwards. Three companies of the Regiment were dispatched to the Speckboom Valley, where they built Fort Jellalabad, and the mounted troops pushed eastwards to the Mariep Goldfields, where they captured some cattle.

At this juncture four companies of the 80th arrived as reinforcements, viz. one company at Middelburg, one company at Fort Weeber, one company at Fort Oliphant relieving Captain Waddy's company and one company at Lydenburg. This enabled Rowlands to concentrate four companies of the 13th under Lieut.-Colonel Gilbert and he determined to make another excursion into the Steelpoort Valley.

On 24th October the columns, strength 1,200 of all arms, set off and on the second day reached the Umsoct Valley; there they found the enemy in position on some precipitous hills beyond the stream. The Mounted troops and three companies of the Regiment under Captains Cox, Waddy, and Otway forded the stream, extended, and advanced to the attack; only the infantry could ascend the rocky hills, and when they reached the top the enemy had vanished, but they were located later on at Tolyana Stradt, and it was determined to attack them on the following day.

THE ACTION OF TOLYANA STADT

At 4.30 a.m. on 27th October the force preceded by the mounted troops advanced on Tolyana Stadt. The artillery came into action at 1,200 yards and at once shelled the houses, which the enemy evacuated. A little later they could be seen ascending two gigantic masses of rock immediately in rear, the approach to which was interrupted by dongas. The Swazies (friendly natives) and Raafs Mounted Corps, supported by Captain Otway's company of the 13th, moved rapidly northwards to make a detour round the principal spur of the mountain, the Frontier Light Horse and Mounted Infantry protected the left flank. Meanwhile the Rustenberg contingent (Boers) and the three remaining companies of the 13th under Lieut.-Colonel Gilbert occupied Tolyana Stadt and then proceeded to attack the hills behind, supported by the fire of the guns. Slowly the infantry forced their way to the top, only to find a still higher hill commanding the position they had captured. Leaving one company, Captain Waddy and Lieutenant Payne, to hold the position won, the other two companies were directed to attack the enemy's new position, but by this time the Swazies and Captain Otway's company had effected a lodgment on the enemy's flank, so that it was subjected to a crossfire. The result was not long left in doubt. A ringing cheer from the attacking troops proclaimed that the position had been captured and that the enemy were in full retreat. The guns then got into play among a retreating mob of 600 men and did some execution. The British loss on this occasion was 11 men wounded, including 7 of the 13th, of whom Colour-Serjt. Pegg died the next day.

Colonel Rowlands afterwards issued the following order:—

'The Commandant desires to express his satisfaction at the conduct of all who took part in the attack on Tolyana Stadt yesterday morning.

'The direct attack made by the main body, three companies 13th Light Infantry and the Rustenberg Contingent, was well and successfully carried out.

'The repeated efforts of the enemy in large numbers to occupy sluits and threaten the left and left rear were completely checked by the Officers commanding the Mounted Infantry and the Frontier Light Horse.

'The party which was directed to attack the enemy from the left rear of his position, viz.—one company 13th Light Infantry and Swazies, made a difficult flank march through the thick bush with rapidity, and succeeded in crowning the ridge with fortunately little opposition. This movement was well supported by Raaf's Corps.

'The Commandant congratulates the forces engaged upon the small number of casualties which took place, considering the great natural strength and intricate character of the enemy's position; but he regrets the death of Colour-Serjeant Pegg, 1st Battalion 13th Light Infantry, who died from the effects of a wound, and in whom the 1st Battalion 13th Light Infantry has lost a brave fellow and a valuable non-commissioned officer. The Commandant sympathizes with the wounded in their patient sufferings.'

The officers of the Regiment present at this action were Lieut.-Colonel P. E. V. Gilbert, Major E. L. England, Captains Persse and Otway, Lieutenants Fownes, Waddy, Bradshaw (Adjutant), Poynton, Walsh (Mounted Infantry), Clarke, Williams, Payne, and Allen—Captain Evans and Lieutenant Levinge were at Fort Burghers, while Captain Cox and Lieutenant Wilbraham were with the transport 4 miles distant from the scene of action.

Other officers detailed in charge of forts were Captain Evans, Lieutenant Thurlow and Lieutenant Pollock. A full list of all the officers at the front is not available. Soon after this action, owing to the threatening state of affairs in Zululand, orders were issued to Colonel Rowlands to suspend operations on the northern frontier of the Transvaal, and to withdraw the greater part of his forces to the Zulu border.

In November the headquarters of the 13th with four companies, the Mounted Infantry, and Nicholson's guns were constituted into a Flying Column under Lieut.-Colonel Gilbert, and moved South via Lydenburg to Lake Chrissie, where they arrived on 17th November. Meanwhile the left half-battalion under Major England had been concentrated at Middelburg, and from thence had marched to Lake Chrissie, so that the whole Battalion was assembled there at the end of November.

On 3rd December the march was resumed to Derby, where the column was split up, one column making for the Pongolo River and the other for the Intombi River, but the former river was found to be impassable owing to heavy rains, and consequently it was found necessary to reunite the columns, and the whole force marched on to Utrecht, where it arrived on 22nd December and formed part of Colonel Wood's column.

As the 13th marched into Utrecht they were welcomed by the 90th, a young regiment just out from home, smartly turned out in good uniforms and white helmets. In strong contrast to the 90th, the 13th, although a fine lot of hard-bitten, muscular veterans, presented a strange appearance. Their uniforms were in rags, and patched with cloth of different colours, some had no boots, their helmets of the old Indian pattern were covered with old shirts to keep the cotton-wool on the bamboo frame, and their belts and rifles dirtied to order. These two regiments were destined to fight side by side in the approaching Zulu War.

THE ZULU WAR

It is not necessary to go into the events or the causes which led to the war with the Zulu nation. It may suffice to say that they were of long standing, and did not admit of being settled in a peaceful way owing mainly to the fact that the Zulus were a warrior race, with a complete military organization, bound together by an iron discipline, and ruled by a cruel and despotic king, Cetewayo. The Boers had a wholesome respect for their fighting powers: the English had yet to learn by bitter experience, that the prowess of the Zulus was far superior to that of the Kaffirs in the Cape Colony or the natives of the northern Transvaal, the native races they had hitherto dealt with.

The military forces at the disposal of Cetewayo were estimated to number 40,000 men organized into impis or regiments, varying in strength, from 4,000 to 1,000 men. They were well supplied with firearms, including a few breechloaders, but fortunately they were not proficient in their use. They relied chiefly on the assegai, a short spear, which could either be thrown from a distance or used as a dagger in hand-to-hand combats. Their mobility was extraordinary, and they could cross rivers in flood by forming a human bridge, linking themselves to one another till the river was spanned, and then the main body would walk over on the shoulders of this living bridge; some few would be drowned in the process, but this was taken as a matter of course.

Zululand was bounded on the south-east by the sea where there is no natural harbour, on the south-west by Natal, and on the north by the Transvaal. The northern face was comparatively open, but the south-western face was mountainous, broken, and covered with forests.

Lord Chelmsford, the Commander-in-Chief, had organized five separate columns for the campaign with the object of securing Natal and the Transvaal from invasion, spread over a front of over 200 miles with very bad lateral communications.

No. 1 Column was concentrated at the Lower Tugela Drift near the sea coast, No. 2 Column at the Middle Tugela Drift, No. 3 Column at Rorke's Drift, No. 4 Column at Utrecht, and No. 5 Column at Luneberg.

An ultimatum had been delivered to Cetewayo which was due to expire on 11th January 1879, when it was intended to cross the frontier with No. 1 Column under Colonel Pearson, No. 3 Column under Colonel Glyn, and No. 4 Column under Colonel Wood. Nos. 2 and 5 Columns were to act on the defensive.

The troops at the disposal of Colonel Wood were the 13th, the 90th, 4 guns, the Frontier Light Horse under Lieut.-Colonel Buller, the Mounted

Infantry and a corps of natives termed Wood's Irregulars. Previous to the arrival of the 13th at Utrecht, Wood had established an advanced depôt at Baltee Spruit, 20 miles south of Utrecht, and thither on 26th December one company of the 13th and one of the 90th were sent with a convoy.

The main body of the column marched to Baltee Spruit on 3rd January 1879. Leaving two companies of the 13th and 2 guns at Baltee Spruit, Wood advanced with the remainder of the column to the Blood River, but it was so swollen by heavy rains that it was impossible to cross. Camp was established at Conference Hill opposite Bemba's Kop. On the 6th January the column crossed the river and encamped at Bemba's Kop. On the 10th January at 2 p.m. Wood started with 2 guns, six companies of the 13th, six companies of the 90th, the Frontier Light Horse and Wood's Irregulars and marched 9 miles down the left bank of the Blood River, and then halted for the night.

At 2 a.m. on the following morning Wood set out towards Rorke's Drift with the Frontier Light Horse, 2 guns, 24 marksmen from the two infantry regiments carried in mule wagons, and Wood's Irregulars. The remainder of the force under Lieut.-Colonel Gilbert followed in support for 9 miles. At 9 a.m. Wood met Lord Chelmsford on the Nkonjene hill 12 miles from Rorke's Drift, and after an interview retraced his steps and with his whole column was back at Bemba's Kop on the morning of the 13th.

On the 18th January Wood marched eastwards to the Sand River, when the Irregulars had a slight skirmish on the far side of the White Umvolosi River. On the 20th the column proceeded to the above-named river, when the Zulu Chief Tinta submitted and was sent with all his people into Utrecht. Large numbers of Zulus, however, were observed on the Zungi Range.

After constructing a fort on the White Umvolosi as a store depôt with a garrison of one company of the 13th, one company of the 90th and 2 guns, the remainder of the force set out on 22nd January in three columns for the Zungi Mountain. No. 1 Column, under Buller, consisting of the F.L.H., the Dutch contingent, and 2 guns, was to ascend the White Umvolosi River, and make for the west end of the mountain. No. 2 Column, the 90th and Wood's Irregulars, was to attack the mountain 3 miles to the east of No. 1 Column. No. 3 Column, consisting of the 13th under Gilbert, left camp later and after a march of 12 miles halted beneath the south-east extremity of the mountain. Nos. 1 and 2 Columns reached the top of the mountain unopposed, and proceeding eastwards could see about 4,000 Zulus on the north-west slopes of the Inhlobana Mountain. During this evening gun-fire could be heard in the direction of Isandhlwana, 50 miles distant. On the 24th Wood, leaving the 90th and 2 guns to follow the wagon track with the baggage, went to the right with the 13th and some 40 burghers, when they soon came under fire, but finding the ground too bad for guns turned north to a hill where the 90th and transport had halted. He found the 90th and Frontier Light Horse advancing against the Zulus holding a strongly defended kraal at Zungi Nek. The enemy's position was soon cleared, but the success could not be followed up, much to the disgust of the troops, as a dispatch conveyed by Private J.

Dixon of the 13th from Baltee Spruit, 24 miles distant, was received by Wood informing him of the disaster at Isandhlwana. He decided to retire at once and reached the fort on the White Umvolosi at 7 a.m. on the 25th.

The news from No. 3, the centre column, was indeed alarming. On the 11th January the centre column, with whom was Lord Chelmsford, crossed the Tugela at Rorke's Drift, and on the 20th, leaving a garrison at the drift, marched to Isandhlwana. On the 21st a strong reconnaissance was made by the Mounted troops and natives under Dartnell, when large numbers of Zulus were seen. This reconnoitring party Lord Chelmsford determined to support, and on the morning of the 22nd he himself left Isandhlwana with a force of all arms. During his absence the camp at Isandhlwana was attacked by 14,000 Zulus and after some hours of severe fighting was completely wiped out, only a few individuals escaping.

In this disastrous engagement 52 officers and 806 other ranks were killed, no quarter being given by the enemy.

The garrison at Rorke's Drift was also attacked, but after a most gallant defence they beat off the enemy. Chelmsford, with the remainder of the column, got back to Rorke's Drift on the following day.

Thus within a fortnight of the opening of the campaign a British column had been signally defeated by the enemy, some 800 Martini Henry rifles, 400,000 rounds of ammunition, 2 guns and the whole of the transport, equipment, and supplies of No. 3 Column had been captured; Pearson, with No. 1 Column, advancing from the Lower Tugela, was closely blockaded at Etchowe, and the remaining troops on the Natal and Transvaal border were everywhere thrown on the defensive, for grave fears were entertained that the Zulus would invade British territory. Moreover, the morale of the British forces had received a severe blow. The resumption of the offensive was out of the question till reinforcements should arrive from England, a matter of some months. Luckily for the British the Zulus, who had lost some 1,400 men at Isandhlwana and Rorke's Drift, did not immediately follow up their victory, and thus some breathing space was allowed for reorganizing the forces at Lord Chelmsford's disposal.

To return to No. 4 Column, Colonel Wood retired from his advanced position on the White Umvolosi and on 31st January reached Kambula Hill on the slopes of Ngabaka Hawane Mountain, where he selected a strong position and proceeded to place it in a state of defence.

Outpost duty was particularly heavy. One officer relates that he did not average more than four hours' sleep per night, the 'Austrian patrol' being the worst. Patrols consisted of one officer, six soldiers and four natives each and were sent out at night about one mile to cover all the approaches to the laager. If attacked the patrol fired a volley to alarm the camp, and got back as best it could.

Kambula covered the approaches to Utrecht, from which it was 30 miles distant. About half-way to Utrecht a fortified post was established at Baltee Spruit garrisoned by two companies of infantry to ensure the safety of the convoys bringing up supplies. The supply of fuel was a difficulty, woodcutting parties being sent out daily to Ngabaka Hawane Mountain to cut and collect fuel, and for this purpose a fortified post was established about the middle of February. Meanwhile the mounted troops were not idle; Buller made repeated reconnaissances, notably on the 1st, 5th, 10th and 15th February, when a certain number of cattle were captured. Towards the end of February certain Boers in the Transvaal began to give trouble, which necessitated Colonel Rowlands and his staff repairing to Pretoria, when the troops of No. 5 Column at Luneberg and Derby were placed under Colonel Wood.

At the end of February and beginning of March the force at Kambula was augmented by various mounted corps, viz: Raaf's Rangers, Weatherby's Border Horse, Schermbrucker's Mounted Riflemen, and Russell's Mounted Infantry. Communications with Utrecht were uninterrupted and supplies kept coming in daily.

On 12th March a detachment of the 80th on the Intombi River, 5 miles from Luneberg, were heavily attacked and lost 2 officers and 60 men. Just previously to this action Uhamee, half-brother to Cetewayo, with 700 followers, surrendered to Colonel Tucker at Derby. They were sent on to Kambula and thence to Utrecht.

On 26th March Colonel Wood received instructions to make a diversion to aid the force marching from the Lower Tugela for the relief of Etchowe.

On the 27th Buller, with 400 Mounted Troops and 300 natives, marched for the south-eastern end of the Inhlobane Mountain, while Russell with 250 mounted men and a battalion of Wood's Irregulars made for the western extremity of the Mountain, Colonel Wood with his staff joining the latter column.

On the 28th, after some fighting, both columns reached the top of the mountain. From the top of the mountain a Zulu army estimated at 20,000 men could be seen approaching from the south-east, the direction from which Buller had approached the mountain, and consequently he had great difficulty in withdrawing, the only line of retreat being down a most precipitous path when all the horses had to be led. Weatherby's detachment was cut to pieces, all except 50 of Wood's Irregulars deserted, while the total loss in Europeans amounted to 92 killed and 7 wounded; of the former 12 were officers. The 13th took no part in this engagement, but Major William K. Leet of the 13th commanded a battalion of Wood's Irregulars. He was awarded the Victoria Cross for his gallant conduct on the 28th March 1879 in rescuing from the Zulus Lieutenant A. M. Smith of the Frontier Light Horse during the retreat from Inhlobane. Lieutenant Smith, whilst on foot, his horse having been shot, was closely pursued by the Zulus, and would have been killed, had not Major Leet taken him upon his horse, and rode with him under fire to a place of safety.

Another account of this gallant deed is as follows:—

'Major Leet of our Regiment behaved splendidly. He was at the time dead lame from a sprain incurred a few days previously. His horse was shot under him and he caught a pack horse carrying ammunition boxes, which he cut off with his knife. This horse was also shot under him. He then managed to get hold of a third, without a bridle, when he saw a lieutenant in the Frontier Light Horse on foot just about to shoot himself, as two or three others had done. Leet took the youth up behind him, and they rode down the breakneck hill together.'

Late at night the mounted troops returned to Kambula. Meanwhile the news of the disaster and approach of a large Zulu army became known to the troops on Kambula Hill about 1 p.m., when Lieut.-Colonel Gilbert of the 13th, the officer in command, with commendable zeal turned out all the troops to strengthen the defences, by banking up the earth up to the axles of the wagons forming the perimeter of the laagers, and strengthening the parapets with sandbags, knapsacks, &c.

THE BATTLE OF KAMBULA

The morning of 29th March was miserably wet, and in accordance with custom a wood-cutting party consisting this day of two companies of the 13th had gone out early to cut and collect wood on the mountain-side about 5 miles from camp. At 10 a.m. Wood received information from a native that the Zulu army intended to attack about 1 p.m., and at 11 a.m., seeing the Zulu army advancing in 5 columns from Zungi Mountain, he recalled the wood-cutting parties, who got back just in time for the action. At 12.45 p.m., dinner being over, the troops repaired to their posts, and the tents were struck. This latter proceeding is stated to have caused the Zulus to think that the British contemplated retreating.

The British position at Kambula was situated on a spur running south-west from the Ngabaka Hawane Mountain; it consisted of a main laager, a redoubt 280 yards to the east of the main laager situated on a knoll some 20 feet higher than the main laager, and a cattle laager in rear which was connected with the redoubt by a trench.

The garrison of the redoubt consisted of Captain Evans' and Lieutenant Fownes' companies of the 13th, one company of the 90th, and 2 guns, the whole under the command of Major Leet of the 13th.

The cattle laager was garrisoned by Captain Cox's company of the 13th, but the rear face rested on a ravine which afforded a considerable amount of cover to an enemy, and moreover could not be covered by the fire of the main laager and redoubt.

The main laager was held by the remaining companies of the 13th and 90th, and within its confines were the mounted troops, hospital and stores.

The guns, Major Tremlett's battery, were in the open between the main laager and the redoubt. The Zulu method of attack can be best described by comparing it to a bullock's head, the horns of which represent the flanks, the head, the main body, in rear of which are the reserves. Between the main body and the reserves are the carriers of food, mats and supplies. If the attack developed, the horns would encircle the enemy, making escape wellnigh impossible.

To return to the manœuvres of the Zulu army, the direction of their advance due west was at first uncertain as to its objective. It was feared that they might move on towards Utrecht without attacking the camp, but all doubts were soon set at rest, when the right wing, still three miles distant, circled to the north of the Kambula position and the left wing to the south.

At 1.30 p.m. Wood sent out Colonels Buller and Russell with 100 mounted men to meet the right wing of the Zulu army and, if possible, to tempt the Zulus into making a premature attack. In their object they were entirely successful, the Zulus advanced boldly, Buller's men retiring fighting in front of them into the main laager. When the Zulus came within 300 yards of the laager, they were received by a murderous fire from the 90th, the guns and the garrison of the redoubt, which checked the advance, and indeed caused them to retire to some rocky ground north-east of the laager.

At about 2.15 p.m. the centre and left Zulu attacks developed; the left attack on the west face of the main laager and the centre attack on the south face of the position where the broken ground south and south-west of the cattle laager afforded a considerable amount of cover. Notwithstanding a vigorous defence of the cattle laager by Captain Cox's company of the 13th, this company, after suffering somewhat heavy losses, was forced back and ultimately withdrawn into the main laager. The cattle laager now became a vantage-point for the enemy to renew their attacks on the main position, but all their attempts were frustrated by the fire of the infantry and guns holding the main position.

Wood now determined to make a counter-attack against the enemy sheltering in the broken ground in rear of the cattle laager, and he sent out two companies of the 90th under Major Hackett to effect this. The counter-attack was successful in driving the enemy back, but as they came under a severe flanking fire from a ridge to the west, they could not maintain their advanced position, and Wood withdrew them.

At 5.30 p.m. the Zulu attack slackened when Captains Thurlow's and Waddy's companies of the 13th and one company of the 90th were sent out to clear the cattle laager and the broken ground in its rear, and here they did great execution among the retreating Zulus. At the same time the mounted men issued forth and pursued the enemy for 7 miles till darkness, and the worn-out condition of their horses, owing to the gruelling they had received on the previous day, obliged them to desist.

Such are the main features of the Battle of Kambula. The Zulu loss was estimated at 2,000 men, the British loss amounted to 18 non-commissioned officers and men killed, 8 officers and 57 other ranks wounded. The casualties of the 13th were 6 N.C.Os. and men killed, 2 officers, Captains Cox and Persse, and 24 N.C.Os. and men wounded; of the latter two subsequently died of their wounds.

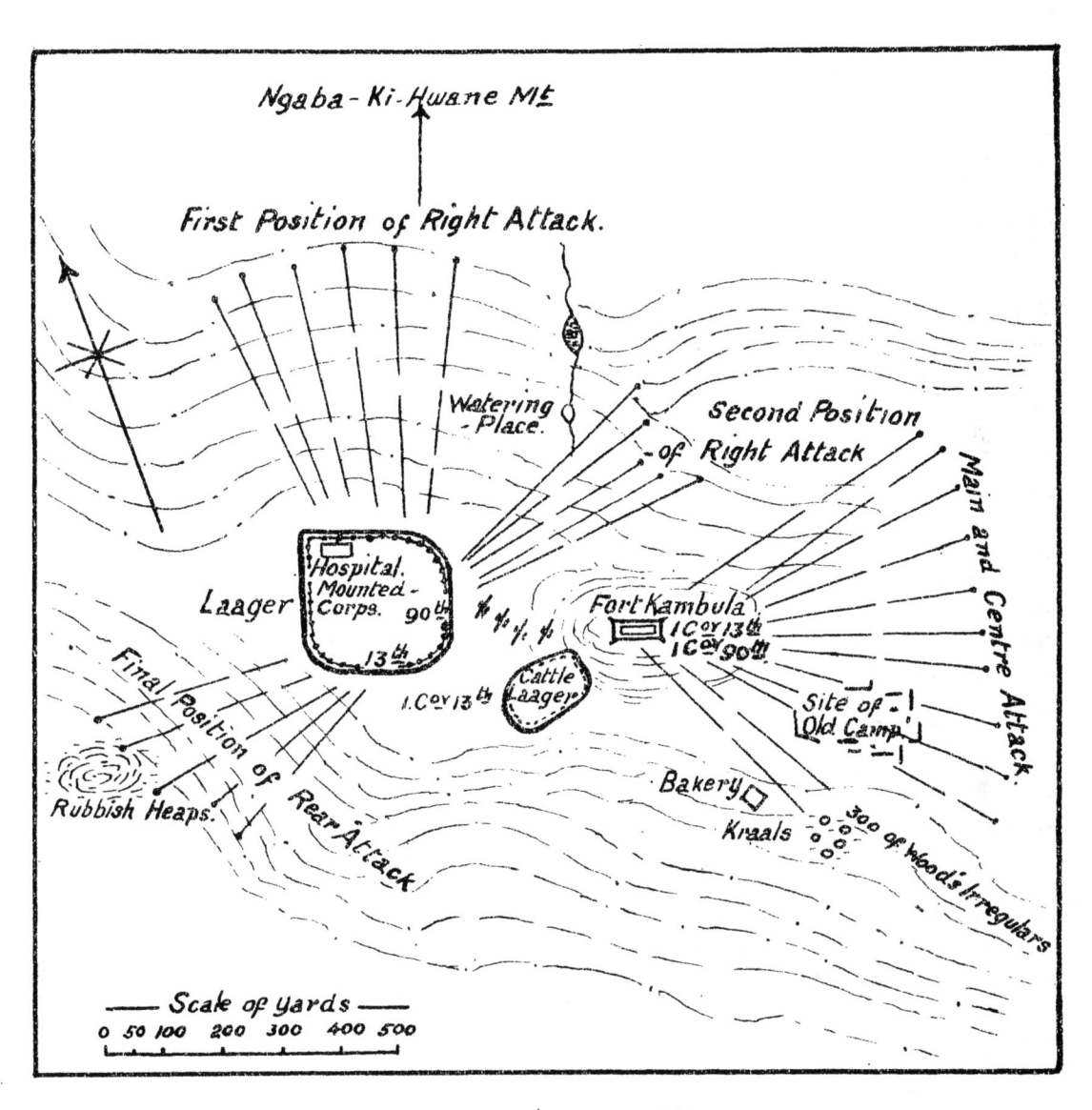

KAMBULA, MARCH 29th, 1879

The brief hold of the cattle laager by the Zulus was their solitary success during the day. In all other respects Wood's Column by its decisive defeat of the enemy, not only retrieved the repulse of the previous day, but to a great extent avenged the disaster at Isandhlwana, proved to the Zulus that they were no longer invincible, and conferred on Wood's Column a sense of superiority which they maintained during the rest of the campaign.

The officers of the Regiment present at Kambula were Lieut.-Colonel Gilbert, Majors England and Leet, Captains Cox, Persse, Kinloch, Evans, Thurlow, Waddy, Lieutenants Fownes, Gallwey, Clarke, Townshend, Poynton, Walsh, Levinge, Wilbraham, Williams, Pollock, Payne, 2nd Lieutenants Lovett and West and Asst. Paymaster Gleig, A.P.D.

The strength of the Regiment present at Kambula was 527 of all ranks.

Among the gallant deeds recorded in this action the following may be noted:—

Private W. Grosvenor, 13th Light Infantry, who, when his company was ordered to retire from the cattle laager, remained behind to assist Serjeant A. Fricker of the same Regiment, who was wounded, and thus lost his own life.

Private Albert Page, 13th Light Infantry, who crossed under heavy fire from the main laager and brought in one wounded native from the cattle laager, receiving a distinguished conduct medal in recognition of this service.

Colonel Wood issued the following order on the 30th March: 'Officer Commanding Column desires to thank soldiers of all ranks for their behaviour yesterday, which enabled us to gain such a complete victory.'

Subsequently the Secretary of State for War referred to this victory in a dispatch as follows:—

'Having received telegraphic intelligence of the successes gained by His Lordship and Colonel Wood respectively, I have the honour to express to you the general satisfaction with which the news has been received in this country. I rejoice to note that the repulse of the enemy on both occasions was complete and decisive. I have received Her Majesty's commands to communicate to you and the forces under your command a gracious message of congratulation.'

March 30th and 31st were spent in burying the dead, 785 Zulus being buried within 300 yards of the laager. The Zulus had completely evacuated the neighbourhood of Kambula immediately after the action.

On 2nd April a British Force marching from the Lower Tugela to relieve Etchowe defeated the Zulus at Ginghilovo. The garrison at Etchowe were subsequently withdrawn to the Tugela.

On 14th April a new position was taken up at Kambula; while the redoubt was still held, the main entrenched camp was moved 600 to 700 yards to the west.

Reinforcements having reached South Africa by this time, a new rearrangement of the forces was carried out. No. 1 Column on the Lower Tugela, now augmented to two Brigades of Infantry and other arms, became the 1st Division.

Wood's Column, which included the 80th Regiment at Utrecht, was constituted an independent flying column. The remaining troops in Northern Natal, consisting of a Brigade of Infantry and other arms, constituted the 2nd Division under Major-General Newdigate.

On the 21st April Lieut.-Colonel Gilbert was compelled through ill health to return home, and the command of the Battalion devolved on Major E. L. England.

Owing to the increasing difficulty of obtaining fuel one company of the 13th and one company of the 90th were sent with 28 wagons to Potgieter's farm on the Pivan River, where coal could be obtained from an outcrop. A stone laager was built there, but its garrison was shortly afterwards relieved by two companies of the 4th King's Own from Utrecht.

On 22nd April Major-General Newdigate and his staff arrived on a visit of inspection, in the course of which the alarm was practised, and the position examined.

On 30th April Buller, with the mounted troops, started for Bemba's Kop and examined the country as far as Mumhla Hill without meeting with the enemy.

Lord Chelmsford and his staff, attached to whom was the ill-fated Prince Imperial, visited Kambula on 3rd May. On the following day all arrangements for a sudden alarm were again practised and the troops inspected.

On the 5th May Wood's Column marched south 10 miles to Sengonyama Hill, where they remained halted for a week.

On 12th May a further advance was made to Wolfe's Hill, whilst on the march the column was practised in preparing for sudden attack, the wagons moving in such a way that as fast as they marched they completed a laager. By this method two laagers in echelon were formed in thirty-five minutes whilst the troops covered the operation.

On 25th May the column marched south to Mumhla Hill and a few days later five companies of the 80th from Conference Hill and Doornberg and Owen's Battery of four gatlings from Landsman's Drift joined the column.

At the end of the month Wood's Column consisted of 1/13th, five companies 80th, 90th, 11/7 Battery R.A. with 4 guns, 10/7 Battery R.A. with 4 gatlings, No. 5 Company R.E., 740 mounted men and 700 natives, with supplies for six weeks.

On 1st June the column marched south and encamped at midday on the right bank of the Umyanyene River. Here it came into contact with the 2nd Division with whom was the Commander-in-Chief, Lord Chelmsford, who had advanced from Landsman's Drift. It was on this day that the Prince Imperial lost his life in an insignificant skirmish, but that unfortunate occurrence is no part of our history.

On 3rd June the 2nd Division, preceded by Wood's Flying Column, moved to the Ityotyosi River, Wood's Column camping on the far side of the river. On the 4th the 2nd Division crossed the Ityotyosi and Wood's Column moved to the far bank of the Nondweni River. On the following day Wood advanced a further 6 miles to Matyanhlope Hill, while the 2nd Division constructed Fort Newdigate as a Supply Depôt.

On the night of 6th June a serious incident occurred. An alarm was given in the 2nd Division when a young battalion opened fire on the outposts and on a company of Royal Engineers detached in a small laager, wounding several men. A few days later an account of this panic was read out to all the troops, when Brigadier Wood congratulated the Flying Column on having had no occurrences of this nature.

On the 7th June the Flying Column, leaving in position Buller's mounted troops, retraced its steps to Fort Newdigate. Here it was joined by two squadrons 17th Lancers, one squadron 1st King's Dragoon Guards, and four companies of the 1st Battalion 24th, and formed the escort of all the empty wagons belonging to the Flying Column and 2nd Division returning to Natal for further supplies. On the 8th they set out for the Blood River, reaching Kopje Allein on the 9th, Conference Hill and Landsman's Drift on the 10th. By the 12th June the whole convoy of 660 wagons being collected, they left the Blood River on their return journey on the 13th and camped on Itelezi Hill. On the 16th they were back again on the Nondweni River. Sir Evelyn Wood tells us in his *Memoirs* that as the bands of the 13th and 90th Light Infantry passed the 2nd Division camp they played with fine sarcasm 'Wait for the Wagon'. The Flying Column then resumed its place of honour at the head of the Army.

On 18th June the combined forces of the 2nd Division and the Flying Column resumed their advance through a most difficult country, the Flying Column leading. The first day's march brought them to the upper waters of the Upoko River where Fort Marshall was established. On the 19th they reached the Ibabanango Spruit and a few miles farther on Fort Evelyn was constructed on the 22nd. The advance was necessarily very slow, owing to the rugged nature of the country and the necessity of establishing fortified posts on the line of communications. Finally on the 27th they reached Entonjaneni Hill, 16 miles from Ulundi, the Zulu King's headquarters. That monarch now sent envoys to treat for peace, the negotiations lasting several days, and at the same time Sir Garnet Wolseley, who had arrived in Natal to take over from Lord Chelmsford, assumed command by telegram.

A large depôt was established on Entonjaneni Hill, a most prominent feature of the landscape, and a suitable guard being left in charge, the remaining troops with ten days' rations commenced their advance to Ulundi on 30th June, and on 1st July reached the White Umvolosi River, on the far bank of which large numbers of Zulus could be seen. The following day was spent in establishing a laager and clearing away the bush, five companies of the 1st Battalion 24th and one company of the Royal Engineers being detailed as garrison.

On 3rd July Lord Chelmsford received the following telegram from Sir Garnet Wolseley dated Durban, 1st July:—

'If compelled to fall back, retire on 1st Division via Kwamagwasa and St. Paul's Mission Station, bringing with you the troops and stores from Fort Evelyn; in case of falling back order its garrison to retire to Fort Marshall.

Wish you to unite your force with the 1st Division as I strongly object to the present plan of operations with two forces acting independently of each other, and without possibility of acting in concert.'

This order meant that Lord Chelmsford was to change his line of communications from Upper Natal to the sea coast and that he was to combine with the 1st Division, then on the Lower Tugela. This same day Buller, with the mounted troops, had made a reconnaissance in force across the White Umvolosi. He had encountered 5,000 Zulus, and negotiations had been broken off. Meanwhile Sir Garnet Wolseley had proceeded by sea to Port Durnford, but was unable to land owing to bad weather.

It is obvious that Lord Chelmsford could not at once march to join the 1st Division leaving an unbeaten army on his flank. He therefore decided to cross the White Umvolosi and, if possible, engage the enemy, and in this he was not disappointed.

THE BATTLE OF ULUNDI

The previous evening Brigadier Wood held a parade of the Flying Column. A square four deep was formed preparing for cavalry. It was explained that in this formation the column would meet the enemy on the morrow. The Brigadier then addressed the men and concluded with the following words: 'Obey your officers; be particular in firing volleys; fire low, and to-morrow night I can promise you, if you stand shoulder to shoulder, back to back, we are the victors.'

At 5 a.m. on 5th July the British force, carrying two days' supplies, preceded by the mounted troops under Colonel Buller, commenced crossing the Umvolosi River. By 7.30 a.m. the mounted men had reached the open country and covered the advance of the main body formed up in a hollow rectangle 150 yards wide and 300 to 400 yards long; the front side consisted of five companies of the 80th, the right flank of eight companies of the 13th under Major England and four companies of the 58th, the left flank of eight companies of the 90th and four companies of the 94th, the rear of two companies of the 94th and two companies of the 2nd Battalion 21st. The guns and gatlings, 14 all told, were distributed in pairs at the angles and at intervals in the sides. The ammunition and tool carts, the bearer company and Natal Pioneers occupied the centre of the rectangle.

The mounted troops, numbering 800 men, included the 17th Lancers, one squadron of 1st Dragoon Guards, besides the Colonial Corps belonging to the Flying Column.

The general direction of the advance was towards the north-east. After passing the Nodwengu kraal, Lord Chelmsford ordered the force to wheel half-right and take up a position on some advantageous ground previously reported on by Lieut.-Colonel Buller. At 8.30 a.m. the force halted facing Ulundi, which lay due east about a mile and a half distant.

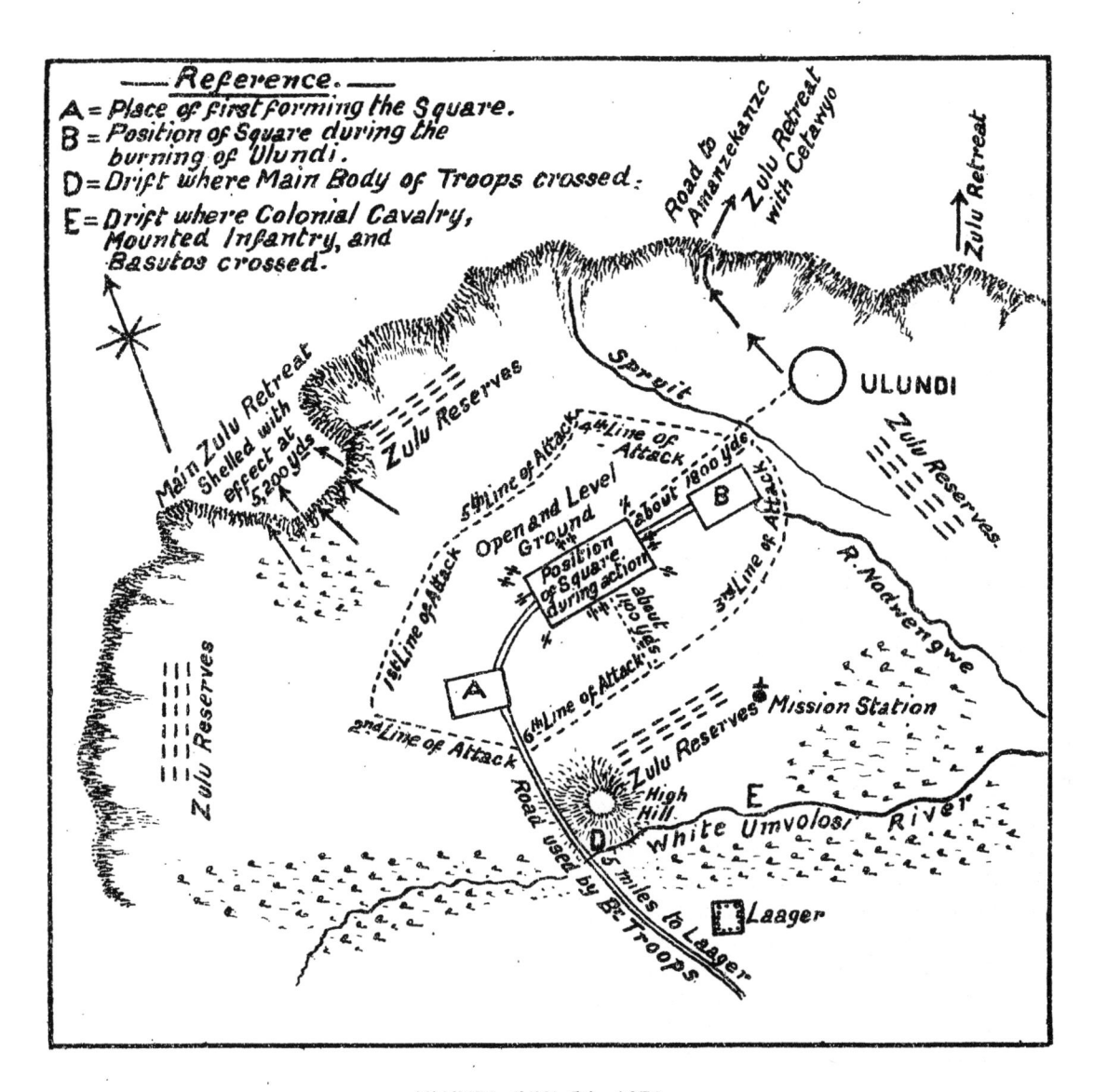

ULUNDI, JULY 5th, 1879

The Zulus who had been assembling on the neighbouring heights soon after the British got clear of the bush now began to advance from all sides and at 8.45 a.m. came into contact with the mounted men of the Flying Column in front and on the right flank, who now retired within the rectangle. At 9 a.m. the artillery opened fire with good effect, but the Zulus still continued to advance, converging on the square as they did so, but the steady fire of the infantry and artillery was too much for them; in no quarter did they approach nearer than 30 yards, and they found an impenetrable wall of fire from whichever side they approached. Their movements lacked the cohesion and dash they had displayed at Kambula, while the reserves never came into action at all. At 9.25 a.m. Lord Chelmsford, seeing that the enemy were losing heart, ordered the 17th Lancers to emerge from the rear side of the rectangle and to charge the enemy, and this they did with deadly effect. Buller and his mounted men, issuing from the front of the rectangle, joined in the pursuit when the rout became general. The great kraal of Ulundi was burnt by the mounted men.

After the wounded had been cared for, the troops of the Flying Column and 2nd Division, still in the same formation, moved about a mile nearer Ulundi and halted on the banks of the 'Mbilane stream. After a rest here the force commenced its return march at 2 p.m. to their camp on the Umvolosi River, the band of the 13th, the only one present, playing the 'Royal Alliance March'. They reached camp at 4 p.m.

The total British losses in this action were 12 killed and 88 wounded; of these the 13th lost 2 N.C.Os. and men killed and one officer, Lieutenant Pardoe, and 9 N.C.Os. and men wounded. Lieutenant Pardoe, badly wounded in the thigh, died of his wounds a few days later on 14th July. The Zulu loss was estimated at 1,500 out of a total strength of 20,000.

By this action the military power of Cetewayo was completely broken, the Zulu warriors dispersed to their kraals, while the King took refuge in flight.

The officers of the Regiment present at this engagement were Major England, Captains Evans, Kinloch, Thurlow, Waddy and Otway, Lieutenants Fownes, Gallwey, Clarke, Poynton, Walsh, Levinge, Wilbraham, Williams, Pollock, Payne, Allen, Pardoe, West and Hillas. Lieutenant Lovett was left sick in camp on the Umvolosi River.

The strength of the Regiment at Ulundi was 24 officers and 587 other ranks.

The following are extracts from Lord Chelmsford's dispatch of 6th July:—

'The Lieutenant-General commanding desires to place on record his hearty appreciation of the gallantry and steadiness displayed by all ranks of the forces under his command during the Battle of Ulundi. The fine discipline of all corps was beyond all praise, and mainly contributed to the defeat of the enemy being so rapidly accomplished. . . .

'The Lieutenant-General has had much pleasure to bring to the notice of the Secretary of State for War the excellent behaviour of the troops, and he feels sure that the good service rendered will be fully appreciated.'

On the 5th July the 2nd Division and the Flying Column marched back to the Entonjaneni Heights, the former camping on the top of the hill, while the Flying Column remained below. On the following day the Flying Column rejoined the 2nd Division. Orders were now received from Sir Garnet Wolseley for the Flying Column to join the 1st Division in the coastal district and to march via Kwamagwasa and St. Paul's Mission Station, while the 2nd Division with all the wounded were to return to Fort Newdigate.

No movements were possible on the 7th and 8th owing to heavy rain, accompanied by a bitterly cold wind. On the 9th the Flying Column marched 3 miles towards Kwamagwasa, which they did not reach till the 11th; in the meantime Lord Chelmsford, who had resigned his command, joined Wood's Column.

After halting on the 12th, the march to St. Paul's was resumed on the 13th, and they reached that station on the 15th, Sir Garnet Wolseley and his staff arriving the same evening. Pipe-clay was here issued to the troops for the first time since the commencement of operations, in preparation for the inspection of the troops by Sir Garnet Wolseley which was held on the 16th.

The Flying Column was now broken up. On the 18th Brigadier Wood and Colonel Buller left for England on medical certificate. The former records in his book, *From Midshipman to Field-Marshal*, the following account of his departure:—

'On the 18th July I left the Flying Column, and their shout "God speed you" made my eyes moisten. We had served together one Battalion eight months, and the other for eighteen months. Much of the time had been fraught with anxiety; the good-bye of these men, of whom it was commonly said "I worked their souls out", and whom I had necessarily treated with the sternest discipline, was such that I have never forgotten.'

The 13th were now for a few days employed on improving communications, but on 1st August, their further services being no longer required, they set out for Natal and reached Durban on the 16th, where they embarked on H.M.S. *Euphrates* for England, reaching Devonport on the 19th September after a service in South Africa of nearly five years.

In recognition of the services of the Battalion during the South African campaigns, the following distinctions and promotions were granted:—

Lieut.-Colonel P. E. V. Gilbert	Companion of the Bath
Major E. L. England	Brevet Lieut.-Colonelcy
Captains Cox and Persse	Brevet Majority
Captain Parr	Companion of St. Michael and St. George

The latter was Assistant Military Secretary to Sir Bartle Frere, the Governor of the Cape Colony. The South African War Medal with clasps 1878–79 was issued to all the troops engaged, and the battle honour 'South Africa 1878–79' added to the Regimental Colour.

MAJOR-GENERAL E. L. ENGLAND, C.B.
Colonel of the Regiment, 1901-1910

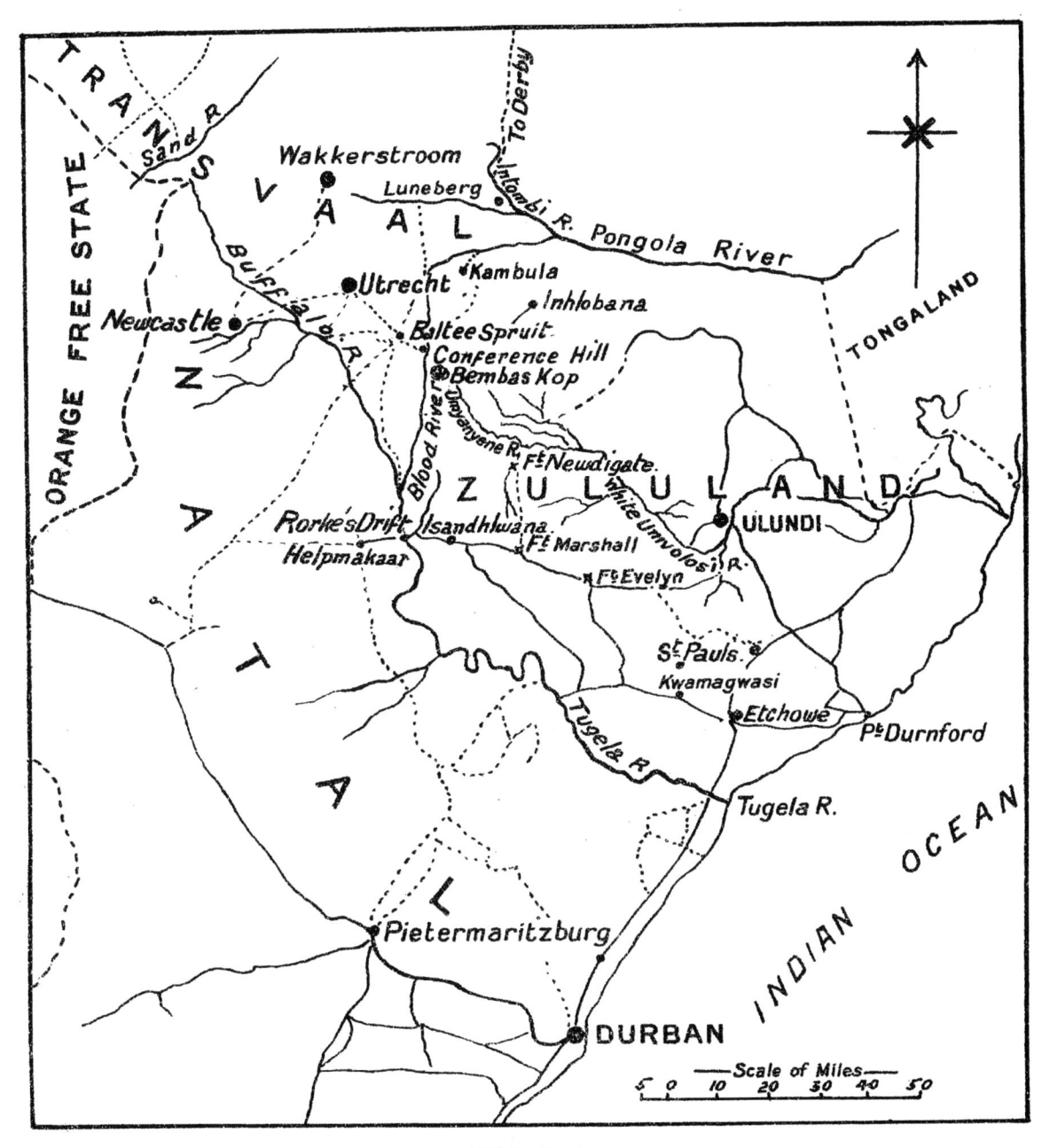

ZULULAND, 1879

CHAPTER XXIII

SERVICE AT HOME AND ABROAD. THE BURMESE WAR, 1885-6-7

1st BATTALION

IN the last chapter it was recorded that the 1st Battalion arrived at Devonport on the 19th September 1879, when they were quartered in the Raglan Barracks. On the 1st October the Depôt companies of both battalions, under the command of Brevet Major R. P. Ethelston, joined the Battalion from Newport, Monmouth.

On the 3rd December 1880 Lieut.-Colonel E. L. England, having been promoted in succession to Lieut.-Colonel W. E. Brown (retired on half-pay), took command, having exchanged from the 2nd Battalion with Lieut.-Colonel P. E. V. Gilbert.

The Battalion was inspected on the 19th July 1880 and subsequently the following observations were issued:—

'Horse Guards, War Office,
28th October 1880.

The Battalion and Depôt attached appears to His Royal Highness to be in a most creditable state of efficiency in every respect reflecting much credit on Lieut.-Colonel England who was in temporary command.'

In 1881 the Territorial system was introduced. The Regiment became definitely associated with the County of Somerset, the 1st and 2nd Somerset Militia Battalions became the 3rd and 4th Battalions of the Regiment, while the title was changed from Prince Albert's (13th Light Infantry) to Prince Albert's (Somersetshire Light Infantry). The change was by no means popular as it practically abolished the Regimental Number '13' which had been in vogue for over one hundred years since the days when regiments were known by the names of their Colonels; thus an old link with the past disappeared, but the advantages of the new system, not then fully recognized, have since been fully justified.

Certain changes were also introduced in the Colours. The small Union in the left-hand top corner of the Regimental Colour was abolished. The first or Royal Colour to bear in the centre the territorial description, and the Royal or other title within the whole, surmounted by the Imperial Crown.

In accordance with the Territorial system the Depôt of the Regiment was moved to Taunton. On the 1st August the Depôt companies of both regular battalions, each of a strength of one major or captain, one subaltern, four serjeants, five corporals, one bugler and twenty privates, proceeded from

Devonport to Taunton, where they came under the command of Colonel R. B. Montgomery, commanding the 13th Regimental District.

On the 17th October orders were received for the Battalion to proceed to Ireland. On the 18th one company, under Captain Stanhope, and 40 N.C.Os. and men left for Dublin by contract steamer, and from thence by rail to the Curragh Camp, arriving on the 20th. Major Allfrey, with Lieutenants Lovett and Hills, proceeded at the same time.

The headquarters, with six companies strength, as under, left Devonport in H.M.S. *Assistance* on the 19th, arrived at Kingstown on the 22nd, and proceeded by rail to the Curragh on the 23rd: viz. 3 Field Officers, 4 Captains, 12 Subalterns, 3 Staff, 28 Serjeants, 30 Corporals, 12 Buglers and 331 Privates.

On the 2nd November the remaining company and attached men under Captain Thurlow, strength 1 Captain, 2 Subalterns, 10 Serjeants, 5 Corporals, 4 Buglers and 124 Privates, embarked in H.M.S. *Assistance* for passage to Kingstown *en route* to join headquarters at the Curragh, where they arrived on 5th November.

The following letter was received from Major-General Pakenham, commanding the Western District, on the occasion of departure of the Battalion from Devonport:—

'I was sorry on my return last night to find your Regiment had gone before I could say Good-bye, which I now do with, I can assure you, great regret. During the two years that I have had the pleasure of numbering you in my brigade I have had every reason to be pleased with your Battalion in every respect; a better behaved or more contented one, it would be hard to find. I should so much like to have said this on parade, but only heard of your move for the first time on Wednesday. Would you kindly convey to your officers and men my great regret at losing them and my wishes for their future.'

During the winter of 1881-2 and the summer of the latter year Ireland was in a rather disturbed state, which necessitated many detachments being found by the Battalion; the principal ones were stationed at Naas, Ballina, Ballinrobe and Athenry, and it was not till the beginning of August that the whole Battalion was again concentrated at Dublin, to which garrison the headquarters and five companies had moved from the Curragh on the 30th January 1882.

On 12th August 3 corporals and 55 privates, and on the 19th 30 privates, rejoined the Colours from the Army Reserve.

An old link with the past history of the Regiment was revived when Horse Guards letter No. 1470, dated 20th September 1882, notified that Her Majesty had been pleased to approve of the Somersetshire Light Infantry being permitted to wear on its Colours the word 'Dettingen' in commemoration of the battle fought at that place on the 27th June 1743.

In the following year 1883 the Battalion moved to the North of Ireland. On the 18th July Major Ethelston, with 36 other ranks, proceeded to Ballyshannon to relieve a detachment of the 2nd Battalion Royal Inniskilling Fusiliers, and on the 14th August the headquarters and six companies, under the command of Lieut.-Colonel E. L. England, proceeded to Enniskillen in relief of the 2nd Battalion Royal Inniskilling Fusiliers, while Captain Stanhope and 'M' Company proceeded to Belturbet in relief of a detachment of that regiment. The total strength of the Battalion at this time was 571 of all ranks. Detachments at Belturbet and Ballyshannon continued to be found till the beginning of May 1884, when they were withdrawn, but at the same time three companies were sent to Londonderry.

In the summer of 1884 the Government decided on an expedition to relieve General Gordon, at that time holding Khartoum, invested by the forces of the Mahdi.

Among the troops taking part in this expedition was a Regiment of Mounted Infantry. Captain H. A. Walsh, late Adjutant of the 1st Battalion, was selected to command a company in this regiment, while Lieutenant T. D'O. Snow, with 27 rank and file of the 1st Battalion, formed a section in 'D' Company commanded by Captain Pigott, 21st Hussars. Colour-Serjeant Hathaway of the 1st Battalion was selected as Colour-Serjeant of this company.

The above details, after concentrating at Aldershot, embarked at Portsmouth in the hired Troopship *Ghoorka* on 27th August for Egypt.

The Mounted Infantry on arrival in Egypt were mounted on camels and later formed part of the Camel Corps, which was sent across the desert from Korti to Metemmeh, when it was heard that Khartoum was hard pressed.

The force had hard fighting at Abu Klea on 17th January 1885, and near Metemmeh on 19th January, in which latter action Lieutenant Snow and Private Nicholson were severely wounded.

When it was found that Khartoum had been taken and that Gordon had been killed the force was withdrawn. The Mounted Infantry remained on the Upper Nile during the spring, but during the summer the regiment was disbanded and the detachment rejoined the 1st Battalion at Birr on 6th August. Captain Walsh was dangerously and Private Palmer severely wounded during these operations.

Lieut.-Colonel T. A. Cary, commanding the 1st Battalion, received a letter from Lieut.-Colonel Barrow, who had succeeded to the command of the Mounted Infantry, in which the latter spoke very highly of the behaviour of the detachment, adding that they had fully maintained the reputation of the Somersetshire Light Infantry.

During the trooping season of 1884–5, two large drafts with a total strength of 260 of all ranks were dispatched from the 1st Battalion to the 2nd Battalion at Rangoon.

On the 23rd June 1885 Lieut.-Colonel T. A. Cary, having been appointed to command a battalion, joined the Battalion in succession to Colonel E. L. England, who retired, having completed five years in command.

On the 19th September the Battalion, consisting of 20 officers and 554 other ranks, under the command of Colonel T. A. Cary, proceeded from Enniskillen and Londonderry to Birr. Prior to the departure of the Battalion the Town Commissioners of Enniskillen passed a resolution showing their appreciation of the good conduct of the Battalion during their stay in that town. The commanding officer sent a suitable reply of thanks.

Although a complete list of the Adjutants of the Regiment will be found in Appendix C, special mention must here be made of Lieutenant T. D'O. Snow, appointed Adjutant on 30th December 1885. This officer, afterwards Lieut.-General Sir Thomas Snow, K.C.B., K.C.M.G., served with great distinction as a Divisional and Corps Commander during the Great War, and subsequently was Colonel of the Regiment.

On 1st February 1886 Colonel T. A. Cary presented the Soudan War Medal with two clasps, 'Abu Klea' and 'Nile' 1884–5, to the members of the detachment who had served in that campaign.

On 12th October the Battalion left Birr for Colchester, embarking at Kingstown in H.M.S. *Assistance* the same day and disembarked at Harwich on the 15th, proceeding the same evening to Colchester in relief of the 1st Battalion Bedford Regiment. At this station they came under the command of Major-General Sir Evelyn Wood, V.C., K.C.B.

On the 29th March 1887, the eighth anniversary of Kambula, Sir Evelyn Wood invited all those who had served under him in South Africa to dinner at his residence, Scarletts; about 5 officers and 80 N.C.Os. and men were present at the dinner.

On 1st May Colonel T. A. Cary, having completed his term of command, was succeeded by Colonel I. S. Allfrey.

On 21st June Queen Victoria's Jubilee day was celebrated. All the troops in garrison paraded on the Abbey field when a *feu de joie* was fired, followed by a march past.

On the 1st May 1889 Colonel I. S. Allfrey, having completed his term of command, was succeeded by Lieut.-Colonel G. H. A. Kinloch.

On the 26th July the Battalion, consisting of 19 officers and 769 other ranks, under the command of Lieut.-Colonel Kinloch, moved to Aldershot in relief of the 2nd Battalion Connaught Rangers and was quartered in the North Camp.

On 12th May 1890 a detachment under the command of Major Fownes attended the Unveiling of the Prince Consort's statue in Windsor Park, detachments of all regiments of which the late Prince Consort was Colonel being present.

On 19th May the following letter was received from Horse Guards relative to the troops who took part in the Unveiling Ceremony.

'SIR,—
I have the honour by desire of the Commander-in-Chief to acquaint you that H.R.H. has received the Queen's command to convey to the troops employed on the occasion of the Unveiling of the statue erected in commemoration of H.R.H. the late Prince Consort in Windsor Park on Monday the 12th inst. Her Majesty's satisfaction at the appearance of the Detachments and Regiments present at this interesting ceremony.

signed W. LASCELLES, A.A.G. for A.G.'

On 8th November 1890 Lieut.-Colonel G. H. A. Kinloch retired on retired pay and was succeeded by Colonel H. Hallam Parr, C.M.G., A.D.C., from half-pay. This officer had joined the Regiment as a subaltern at Aldershot twenty-five years before and for a short time had been Adjutant of the 1st Battalion. From 1877 to 1882 he was employed in various capacities on the Staff in South Africa. In 1882 he proceeded to Egypt and was appointed Commandant of the Mounted Infantry, but being wounded early in the Tel-el-Kebir campaign he was invalided home. After his return to Egypt in October 1882 he served in various appointments, seeing much active service. In 1885 he was appointed Adjutant-General of the Egyptian Army, which appointment he held till 1888. Previous to assuming command of the 1st Battalion he held the appointment of A.A.G. Southern Command with Headquarters at Portsmouth.

Commencing on the 7th July 1891, the Battalion marched from Aldershot via Chobham and Hounslow to Kingston Vale in order to take part in lining the streets of London on the occasion of the visit of H.I.M. the German Emperor, and afterwards to take part in a grand review at Wimbledon before the same august visitor. The Battalion returned to Aldershot by march route on the 15th of the same month.

On the 10th November the Battalion, consisting of 24 officers and 695 other ranks, under the command of Major H. H. Thurlow, embarked from Portsmouth in H.M. Troopship *Orontes* for conveyance to Gibraltar, which latter station they reached on the 18th November. The Battalion was quartered on arrival in the Town Range Barracks and North Front.

On the 13th August 1892 Lieutenant and Quartermaster F. W. Tremlett died from dysentery, after serving in the Battalion for twenty years. He had served with credit through every rank, but he will probably be best remembered as a typical serjeant-major, smart in appearance, strict in his duties, and endowed with a decisive word of command.

On the 28th January 1893 the Battalion moved from Town Range Barracks and the North Front to the South Barracks.

On the occasion of Her Majesty's birthday in this year Colonel Hallam Parr was appointed a Companion of the Most Honourable Order of the Bath.

2ND BATTALION

The fortunes of the 2nd Battalion now claim our attention. In a preceding chapter it is recorded that the 2nd Battalion arrived in Malta on 6th August 1877. They remained in that island till 21st February 1878, when they embarked for India in H.M.S. *Jumna* and arrived at Bombay on 14th March, and then proceeded by rail to Bellary, arriving at that station on 22nd March.

Lieut.-Colonel A. Bainbrigge retired on pension on 23rd January 1878 and was succeeded in the command by Major and Bt. Lieut.-Colonel W. E. Brown.

On the 19th December the left wing of the Battalion proceeded from Bellary to Bangalore.

In the following year, 1879, the whole Battalion changed stations, moving to Kamptee on 23rd December.

Lieut.-Colonel W. E. Brown retired on half-pay on the 8th May 1880. Major and Bt. Lieut.-Colonel E. L. England was gazetted to the command in his place, but he exchanged with Lieut.-Colonel V. Gilbert, C.B., who joined for duty on 19th January 1881.

In September 1881, cholera having broken out in the barracks, the whole Battalion went under canvas on the 7th of that month, and remained in camp till the 20th October when, all symptoms of illness having disappeared, the Battalion returned to barracks.

On the 1st November four companies proceeded to Secunderabad and remained there till the 3rd February 1882, when they rejoined headquarters at Kamptee.

On 1st May 1883 Lieut.-Colonel P. V. Gilbert retired and was succeeded by Lieut.-Colonel W. Knox Leet, V.C. In the autumn of this year cholera again broke out in the Regiment when they went into camp for six weeks. On the 5th and 6th December the Battalion left Kamptee by half-battalions and proceeded to Madras and embarked on the Indian Government steamer *Clive* on 15th December *en route* for Burma, arriving at and disembarking 'E' Company under Major Madden at Port Blair, Andaman Islands, on the 19th and reaching Rangoon on the 22nd.

The garrison of Lower Burma at this time consisted of two British Infantry Regiments, five Indian Infantry Regiments, besides Artillery, Sappers, and Miners, numbering altogether 2,035 Europeans and 3,284 Indians, the whole under the command of Major-General Buck.

Thayetmyo on the Irrawaddy and Toungoo on the Sittang River were the two most northerly posts of the British Garrison. Upper Burma with its capital at Mandalay was ruled by King Theebaw.

THE BURMESE WAR, 1885-6-7

In the autumn of 1885 relations between King Theebaw and the Government of India became so strained that the latter mobilized a fresh division in India which concentrated in Lower Burma at the beginning of November under Major-General Prendergast, who then assumed command of all the troops in Burma.

The primary object of the campaign was to occupy Mandalay and dethrone King Theebaw, and this was accomplished with extraordinary ease. Prendergast, with the troops from India, crossed the frontier on 15th November and proceeded up the Irrawaddy by water; Minhla, 40 miles north of Thayetmyo, was occupied on the 17th and Mandalay itself on 28th November, when King Theebaw surrendered. On 1st December a proclamation was issued announcing the surrender, dethronement, and deportation of King Theebaw and notifying that the civil and military administration of the country was vested in Major-General Prendergast pending instructions from the Queen Empress.

After the capture of Mandalay and the removal of King Theebaw and his queen to India, the country was quite peaceful for a time as the Burmans thought the British would just 'make proud' and then depart again, but when they realized the troops intended to stay, trouble began. The Burmese authorities ceased to function in the administration of the country, their soldiers were allowed to go home with their arms, and self-styled princes raised standards in different districts and gathered a following. To cope with them, posts in small entrenched forts had to be established all over the country. Apart from the main rivers there were no means of communication; there were practically no roads, and the paths—often the sandy beds of rivers—were so narrow that the men marched in file through the jungles, where flank guards were wellnigh impossible. The theatre of war was as big as France, the British forces were split up into posts often not exceeding 2 officers and 40 men each, while the enemy was elusive and moved about in small parties, knowing the country and unhampered by transport and stores. Consequently there were no general engagements, and after the capture of Mandalay, no material to excite the imagination of any historian. Beyond the dry records of the Indian Frontier expeditions no one has attempted to write a connected narrative of this campaign.

The campaign has been rightly dubbed 'The Subalterns' War'. Their deeds are mostly unrecorded, but they marched and counter-marched with their small commands in pursuit of the enemy, rarely bringing him to action, but eventually they wore the enemy down, and brought the campaign to a successful conclusion. So scattered was the battalion in small columns that in December '86, all that remained at headquarters of the battalion at Mandalay was the Commanding Officer, the Adjutant, the Quartermaster, and one subaltern.

The campaign might almost be called a 'picnic', were it not for the fact that disease was more to be feared than the dacoit. Fever and ague especially were rife and exacted a heavy toll from the forces engaged, but it is time to return to the narrative.

At the same time that General Prendergast made his advance to Mandalay by river, four companies of the Regiment under Major Evans left Rangoon by rail for Tonghoo on the Sittang River, where they joined a column marching northwards into Upper Burma along the route now followed by the railway to Mandalay.

On 29th November the column crossed the frontier and, after several successful encounters with the enemy, arrived at Ningyan on 3rd December, where they captured 15 brass or bronze guns. During this advance the detachment of the Regiment lost 10 men from cholera.

On the 18th December General Prendergast, with 1,000 men, started for Bhamo near the Chinese border, 250 miles north of Mandalay. Proceeding by water he reached and occupied Bhamo on 28th December.

On 1st January the Viceroy of India, Lord Dufferin, issued a proclamation annexing King Theebaw's dominions to the British crown.

There now appears to have been a lull in the operations during which time the reorganization of the Army for jungle warfare was carried out.

On 18th February three companies of the Regiment under Major Bradshaw, forming part of the column that advanced to Ningyan, occupied Yamethin half-way between Tonghoo and Mandalay, being rather more than 100 miles distant from both these places.

On 21st March Lieutenant A. B. Fox was severely wounded in action at Kinyoirah, but no details of this encounter are recorded.

On 31st March Major-General White took over the command of the forces in Upper Burma when the general distribution of the troops was as follows: 1st Brigade at Mandalay, 2nd Brigade at Bhamo and two independent commands at Pyinmana and Taungdwingyi. Later on the Pyinmana command constituted the 3rd Brigade. The left half-battalion was in this latter command while the headquarters and right half-battalion a little later on joined the 1st Brigade headquarters at Mandalay.

At this time the half-battalion of the Regiment operating along the land route to Mandalay were distributed on the upper waters of the Sittang River. On 3rd April Colonel Dicken, commanding the Pyinmana column, hearing that Hlaingdet, 20 miles north of Yamethin, his headquarters, was threatened by the Minzaing Prince with 3,000 followers, started for Hlaingdet, which he reached on the afternoon of the 4th, when he learnt that the enemy were in force at Kyah Tun about one mile to the north. On the morning of the 5th Dicken moved out against them with the following troops:—

> 40 Rifles Liverpool Regiment,
> 73 Rifles Somersetshire Light Infantry,
> 15 Mounted Infantry,
> 70 Rifles Palamcottah Light Infantry,
> 47 Rifles Bengal Infantry,
> 13 Sabres 2nd Madras Lancers.

The enemy were located at Za-un; he attacked and completely defeated them, the enemy losing 12 killed and many wounded. Lieutenant Peacock of the Regiment was slightly wounded on this occasion. The column, after destroying some villages in the neighbourhood, returned to Yamethin on 11th April. While these operations were going on, Lieutenant Vallentin of the Regiment, with 20 Rifles Somersetshire Light Infantry and 30 Rifles Palamcotta Light Infantry, attacked and destroyed the dacoit villages of Libok and Shwemyo, 16 miles north-east of Pyinmana on 5th April.

Owing to the approaching rains all inland posts were filled up with six months' supplies, and river posts with four months' supplies.

On 16th April Major Bradshaw, with 60 rifles of the Regiment, 106 rifles of the Palamcotta Light Infantry, and 13 Mounted Infantry, proceeded to Thayetlin Bawhlaing, 13 miles south of Yamethin, and on the following day drove the enemy out of Kyauk Sahitkon and burnt it.

The headquarters and four companies of the Regiment were still at Rangoon, but on 1st May two companies under Captain Wilbraham started for Mandalay, being followed by the headquarters and remaining two companies ten days later.

On arrival at Mandalay the headquarters and half a company were left there, while the remainder of the half-battalion were sent out to occupy detached posts in the vicinity.

On 16th May Lieutenant Peacock, with a detachment of the Regiment, drove some of the followers of Buddha Yaza from the village of Pyingyi, 22 miles south-west of Yamethin, with the loss of one man wounded on our side, while eleven casualties were inflicted on the enemy.

On 20th May a new post was established with slight opposition at Yewun near Kyaukse, 40 miles south of Mandalay. The garrison consisted of one gun Royal Artillery, 12 sabres 2nd Madras Lancers, 50 rifles Somersetshire Light Infantry, 50 rifles Queen's Own Sappers and Miners, and 50 rifles Wallajahbad Light Infantry.

On 23rd June Captain J. Grant, 25th Bombay Light Infantry, started from Yewun with 120 rifles and marching south-west crossed the Paylaung River at Myithla, and then proceeded to Taligon, where he was attacked by a party of the enemy who were driven off by a detachment of the Regiment under Captain Wilbraham. The enemy retreated to Kume, and Grant followed them and drove them from some outer monastery buildings with a walled enclosure surrounding a pagoda. Here they made an obstinate resistance for an hour, when the place was stormed with the bayonet. On the following day the force returned to Yewun. Their casualties amounted to one corporal killed, Captain Wilbraham and seven men wounded. Captain Wilbraham died from the effects of his wound about a month later on 21st July.

On 24th June Lieutenant H. T. Shubrick marched with 2 guns and 30 men of the Regiment from Pyinmana to Theagon on the Yamethin Road about 6 miles distant. After destroying several villages near Theagon on the 26th, Shubrick occupied the hamlet of Quingyi, where, while halted for breakfast, he was attacked on all sides by dacoits. After some fighting the enemy were driven off, but Shubrick himself was killed, being struck in the neck by a bullet, while two men were wounded. The force then returned to Pyinmana under Lieutenant Coxhead, R.A. Serjt. E. A. Bath, who assumed command of the detachment of the Regiment on the death of Lieutenant Shubrick, was afterwards mentioned in dispatches for gallant conduct on this occasion and was awarded the silver medal for distinguished conduct.

On 28th July Major Persse of the Regiment commanding at Ava and Lieutenant Campbell, 25th Madras Infantry, commanding at Myinthi, made a successful combined attack on the village of Maygi, killing 13 of the enemy, of whom three were chiefs, and taking prisoner 2 chiefs and 33 others.

About this time, owing to the monsoon, operations became impossible. The number of troops now in Burma amounted to 24,000 men, and in addition there were 8,000 police. The wastage of the army had been considerable. From November 1885 to November 1886 over one thousand had died from disease and two thousand had been invalided, while the fatal casualties in action hardly exceeded one hundred. The Regiment suffered considerably from disease during this period, but the only officer to succumb was Major Bradshaw, who died at Ningyan on 31st July.

For the winter campaign of 1886–7 the Burma command was divided into eight military districts as follows:—

Upper Burma—
  1st Brigade   Mandalay   Brig.-General C. T. East.
  2nd   „   Bhamo   „ „ Griffith.
  3rd   „   Pyinmana   „ „ W. S. A. Lockhart.
  4th   „   Myingyan   „ „ H. S. Anderson.
  5th   „   Shewebo   „ „ R. C. Stewart.
  6th   „   Minbu   „ „ R. C. Low.

Detached forces in the Chindwin and Taungdwingyi districts.

Lieut.-General Sir Herbert Macpherson, K.C.B., K.C.S.I., V.C., was appointed to take over the chief command, but he died on his way to Mandalay on 20th October, and was shortly afterwards succeeded by Sir Frederick Roberts, then Commander-in-Chief in India.

The autumn campaign commenced with operations against a chief named Hla U in the area between the Mu and Chindwin Rivers north-west of Mandalay. Four columns were engaged in hunting him down, but the only column to include a detachment of the Regiment was No. 1 Column which started from Myinmu on the south of the theatre of operations. This column was composed of one troop 7th Bengal Cavalry, 25 rifles of the Regiment, 27 rifles Mounted Infantry and 95 rifles 5th Bombay Light Infantry.

Hla U was kept constantly on the move and by the end of the year his following was reduced to vanishing-point.

On the 13th November Lieutenant Eckersley was killed in action at Kyeetsayhyms, but no details of this action are recorded.

In the Pyinmana district (Brig.-General Lockhart) on 5th December Lieut.-Colonel Elton with 119 of the Queen's, 25 Somersetshire Light Infantry, 100 Biluch Light Infantry and 40 Mounted Infantry, marched for Yadan with the object of engaging Nga Hinat, who had a following of 700 men. The enemy were dispersed and the column returned to headquarters.

In December a concerted movement was made on the Hmawaing stronghold 50 miles south of Mandalay. Portions of the 1st, 3rd and 4th Brigades took part. The 1st Brigade column concentrated at Kumé on 11th December under the command of Major Aitken, R.A.; it consisted of 2 guns R.A., 50 rifles Somersetshire Light Infantry under Lieut. Braithwaite, 120 rifles Bombay Light Infantry and at the same time a small detachment of the Regiment under Lieutenant Elgar advanced to Kinle on the Natteck Pass 25 miles south-east of Kumé in rear of the enemy's position. The 3rd Brigade sent a column from Hlaingdet into the Upper Valley of the Paulaung River to prevent the enemy retiring south. The 4th Brigade column assembled at Wandwin, west of the Sittang River, under Captain Rose, 27th Punjaub Infantry. On 17th December Aitken's and Rose's columns marched on Hmawaing; Rose's column met with no opposition, but Aitken's column was fired at the whole way, their losses being two killed and eight wounded. Hmawaing was occupied at 2 p.m., and having burnt it the columns marched on to Kanswe, 5 miles to the north-west. On the 14th they occupied Yozun, after which the columns were broken up.

On 28th December the four companies which left headquarters on the 16th November 1885 rejoined at Mandalay and formed part of the 1st Brigade, having, while detached, been constantly and with unvarying success engaged against the enemy in thick jungle country. Several men were employed as Mounted Infantry under the command of Lieutenant Payne (who received the D.S.O. for his services with that Corps) and subsequently under Lieutenant Morse.

The following order was issued by the G.O.C. 3rd Brigade on the departure of the four companies for Mandalay:—

'YEMETHIN, 14th December 1886

The left wing Somersetshire Light Infantry is now virtually leaving this command.

In saying "Good-bye" to Capt. Cooper and his detachment, Brigadier-General Lockhart wishes to recognize the services rendered by them to this command during the present campaign.

Probably no detachment in the entire force has been more frequently engaged, and on every occasion the splendid reputation of the 13th has been maintained. The Brigadier-General wishes the Somersetshire Light Infantry good fortune and further renown in whatever fields they may find themselves in in the future.

signed P. D. JEFFREYS, Major
Brigade Major.'

Unfortunately Captain Cooper, the officer commanding the wing, died of fever at Yamethin on 27th December.

On 13th December three columns, under Lieut.-Colonel Cotton, Major Persse of the Regiment, and Captain Kenny respectively, marched from Myotha and Chaungwa and converged on Kané, south-east of Ava, on 22nd December, scouring the country in all directions, after which they returned to their stations.

On 1st January 1887 a detachment of the Regiment, under a subaltern, took part in an expedition to Mingzi, when they surprised the enemy's camp at Sabagin.

In the middle of January a column from Zagabin, 30 miles north-east of Mandalay, took part in an expedition to Mainglon, south-east of the Ruby Mines, in conjunction with a column from the Mines. The former column under the command of Lieut.-Colonel Deshon, R.A., consisted of two Gardner guns, 75 rifles Somerset L.I. and two companies 17th Madras Infantry. The object of the excursion was to settle the claims of two rival chiefs, which being accomplished, the columns returned to their respective stations.

The country was now becoming more peaceful, but there still remains one further action to be recorded, and that was the destruction of Hmawaing stronghold, which had on a previous occasion been burnt in December 1886. The forces employed were troops from the 1st and 3rd Brigades who assembled at Gonywa on 21st March. Here the troops were divided into three columns. The main column under Colonel Bance consisted of 2 guns, 2 Gardners, 74 rifles of the Regiment, under Lieutenant Cox, 40 rifles 15th Madras Infantry, 50 rifles 25th Bombay Light Infantry and 22 Mounted Infantry; the right column under Major Ilderton, 2/ Royal West Surrey Regiment, consisted of 50 rifles of that regiment and 34 rifles 27th Punjaub Infantry; the left column under Captain Presgrave, 15th Madras Infantry consisted of 75 rifles of that regiment and 30 rifles of the Regiment under Lieutenant Johnstone. The advance began at 6.30 a.m., and at 12 noon the main column was 100 yards from a stone barricade on the Hmawaing Height, which was immediately shelled. The troops then charged and carried the position at the point of the bayonet, the enemy flying in all directions. Lieutenant Cox and one man were slightly wounded.

It was now decided to reduce the forces in Burma and among the first regiments to go was the 2nd Battalion Somersetshire Light Infantry. The Battalion was concentrated at Mandalay on 31st March. On 2nd April Brig.-General East, commanding the 1st Brigade, published the following order:—

'On the departure of the "Prince Albert's" (2nd Bn. Somersetshire Light Infantry) from the Brigade under his command the G.O.C. desires to place on record his high appreciation of the services rendered by that Battalion whilst in Upper Burma.

'The Battalion has been marked no less by exemplary conduct and the smart performance of the duties required of it in quarters, than for its gallantry and endurance when actively engaged in the Field.

'Colonel Knox Leet and all ranks of the Battalion carry with them the Brigadier General's best wishes for their welfare in the future.

signed G. SIMPSON, Lt.-Col.
Brigade Major 1st Brigade
Burma Field Force.'

On 4th April the Battalion was inspected by General Sir George White, when he addressed them as follows:—

'Colonel Leet and Officers and Men of the 13th Light Infantry. I call you forth to-day not for the purpose of merely seeing you (I have had ample opportunities of doing that every day), but I wish to express to you the high estimation in which you are held both by the various Commanders-in-Chief and Senior Officers of this district. As I told the Hampshire Regiment when I had a similar parade two days ago, the Burma Campaign was not altogether

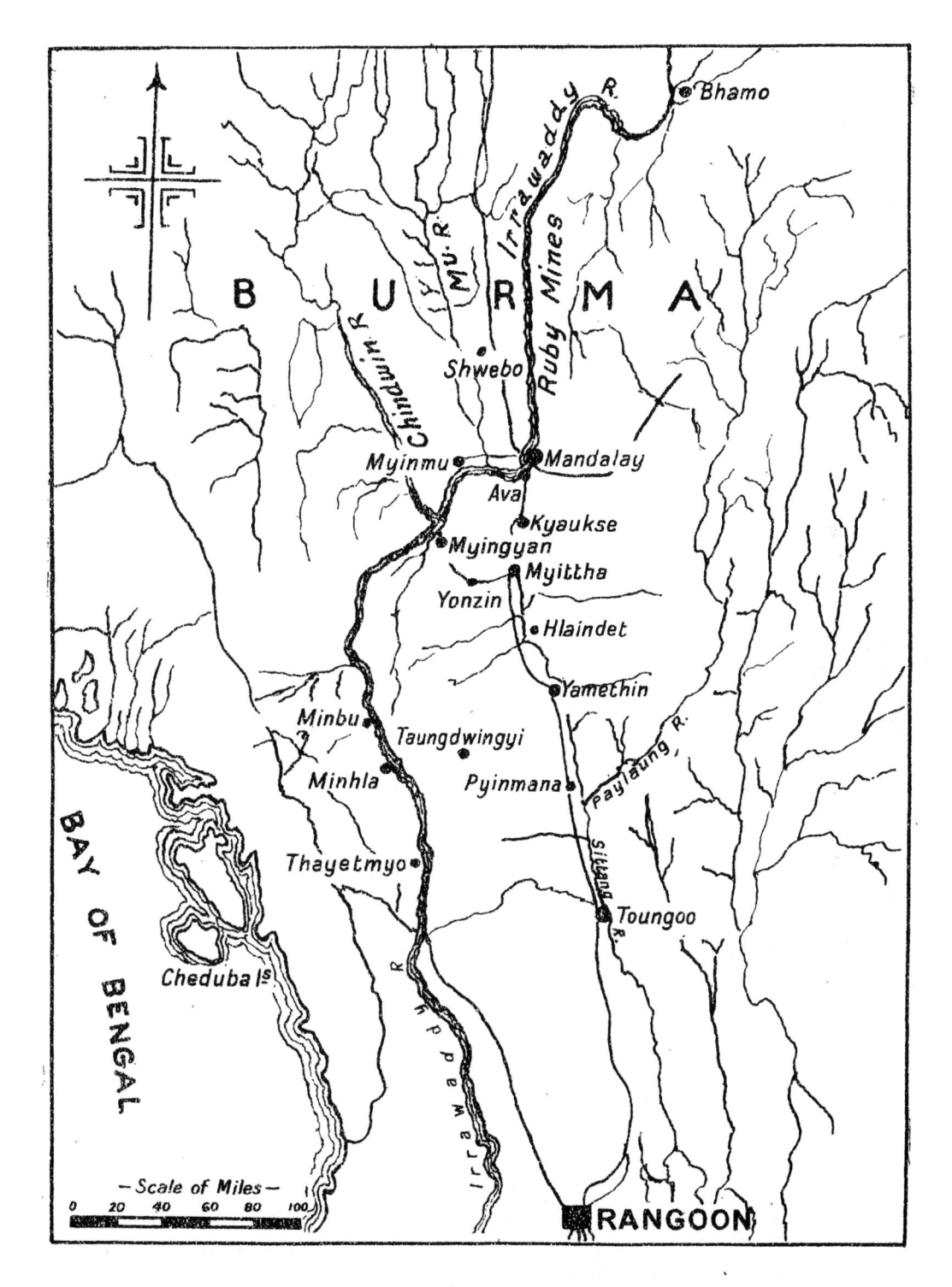

BURMA, 1885-7

a test of a soldier's fighting capacities, but that you have been harassed with jungle fighting, worn with marching, and afflicted with much sickness, all through which you have come with honours that will only increase the lustre of the regimental reputation.

'This is not the first chapter in your military chronicle, for as you sail down the river you will see to-day or to-morrow the town of Pagun and as you look upon the plain you will see the battlefield where those same Colours unfurled before me now, were fought for (possibly by your fathers), years ago.

'One Regiment has the proud distinction of calling themselves the "First in India", I would suggest that this Regiment the 13th having been in the First (and now the Third) Burmese War, should have added to its many distinguished honours "The First in Burma".

'Again I must specially mention the splendid disciplinary state of the Battalion, the value of which was strikingly apparent but a few days ago.[1]

'In saying farewell to you all, I wish you a pleasant voyage down the river, that you may like the Quarters for which you are bound, and that also when later on you meet your families, or leave the country and go to your homes, you may meet that reception that your distinguished services in this Campaign have fully entitled you. Good-bye.'

Immediately after the inspection the Battalion embarked on the ss. *Shoymyo* and proceeded down the River Irrawaddy to Rangoon. Lieutenant Cox and 108 other ranks were left behind to act as Mounted Infantry with the Burmese Field Force. After a short halt at Rangoon the Battalion embarked for Madras and on arrival there proceeded to Belgaum.

The losses of the Battalion during the war were as follows:—

Killed or died of wounds: 3 officers and 14 men. Wounded: 3 officers, 2 serjeants, 2 corporals and 28 men. Died from disease: 2 officers, 11 serjeants, 2 corporals, 2 buglers and 133 men.

The following officers were mentioned in dispatches:—

Colonel W. Knox Leet, V.C., Captain R. L. Payne, Lieutenants G. H. A. Couchman, F. M. Peacock, F. A. Morse, L. W. Fox, and W. P. Braithwaite and Serjeant E. A. Bath.

Captain R. L. Payne, Lieutenants G. H. H. Couchman and F. A. Morse were awarded the D.S.O.

Pte. Walter White was granted the D.C.M. for courageous conduct displayed by him during the operations against the rebels at Pyatoway on 23rd April 1886.

On 1st July Lieut.-Colonel W. Cox was appointed to the command of the 2nd Battalion in succession to Colonel W. Knox Leet, V.C., who retired.

In 1888, during the stay of the Battalion at Belgaum, medals for the Burmese Campaign of 1885–6–7 were presented to the Battalion by Brig.-General Cox.

---

[1] The General was referring to the attack on the Somersetshire Light Infantry by another Regiment; the former being well under control, considerable bloodshed was avoided.

On the 13th June 1890 the Battalion sustained a severe loss by the death at Belgaum of its Commanding Officer, Colonel William Cox, who succumbed at that station to an attack of peritonitis after a short illness. Lieut.-Colonel W. Cox had joined the 1st Battalion as a subaltern in July 1855 and had spent the whole of his service in the Regiment. He was succeeded in the command of the 2nd Battalion by Lieut.-Colonel W. C. F. Madden.

The Headquarters of the Battalion left Belgaum on the 30th October 1890 and proceeded by march route to Fort St. George, Madras, where it arrived on 6th January 1891, having been detained for several days, *en route*, at Dharwar.

The left wing left Belgaum on the 8th December 1890 and proceeded by march route to Bellary, where it arrived on the 30th December 1890.

On the 10th April 1891 the Mounted Infantry of the Battalion under Captain W. C. Cox, who had remained behind in Burma for one year after the Battalion had left, were presented with clasps to their medals inscribed 'Burma 1887-89'.

Mention must here be made of Lieutenant W. P. Braithwaite appointed adjutant of the Battalion on 15th November 1892. This officer, afterwards General Sir Walter Braithwaite, G.C.B., served with great distinction in the Great War first as Chief of the General Staff in the Gallipoli Campaign and subsequently as a divisional and corps commander in France. Later on he was Adjutant-General to the Forces and Colonel of the Regiment, and shortly after his retirement was appointed Governor of the Royal Hospital, Chelsea.

The 2nd Battalion's period of foreign service was now drawing to an end. On the 12th January 1894 the Headquarters and Right Wing left Fort St. George, Madras, by train for Poona *en route* for Bombay. Previous to departure a draft of 330 N.C.Os. and men was dispatched to Umballa to join the 1st Battalion, then *en route* to that station from England.

Previous to the departure of the right half of the Battalion from Madras, the following order was published by Brig.-General T. Van Straubenzee, C.B., R.A., commanding the Madras District.

'In bidding farewell to the H.Q. and Right Wing of the 2nd Battalion Prince Albert's Somersetshire Light Infantry, Brig.-General T. Van Straubenzee desires to convey to Lieut.-Colonel Madden, officers and men his appreciation of their good services during the three years they have been stationed at Madras. It is a matter of deep regret to him that their last year in India should have been exceptionally unhealthy and fatal to some of their number while many have suffered from abnormal sickness. The ordinary garrison duties, drill, and exercises have nevertheless during this, as in past seasons, been carried out by the Somersetshire Light Infantry with the same smartness and regularity and in the true soldierly spirit for which the Regiment was in previous years noted on Field Service in Burma, where as when opportunity offered for field movements, the work required of officers and men has ever been cheerfully and efficiently performed.

'The Regiment has been distinguished by being to the fore in manly sports of every description, whilst as citizens the men have proved themselves law-abiding and orderly. In leaving Madras all Ranks carry with them the best wishes of their comrades in arms and of the community generally.'

The left wing of the Battalion from Bellary, under Major Waddy, joined the right half Battalion at Guntakal on 13th January and on the 15th they reached Poona where they halted till the 19th, when they proceeded to Bombay and embarked on H.M.S. *Euphrates* for conveyance to England after over sixteen years' foreign service.

CHAPTER XXIV

SERVICE IN INDIA AND AT HOME. THE MOHMAND CAMPAIGN

1st BATTALION

ON the 19th December 1893 the Battalion, consisting of 22 officers and 641 other ranks, under the command of Colonel Hallam Parr, embarked at Gibraltar in H.M.S. *Euphrates* (receiving a draft from England of 108 rank and file by the same ship) for India, arriving at Bombay on the 9th January 1894 and leaving the same day for Deolali, arriving there on the 10th and leaving again on the 14th and 15th for Umballa, which latter place they reached on the 18th and 19th January, where they went under canvas. At Umballa a draft of 1 officer and 327 other ranks was received from the 2nd Battalion.

On the 21st March 1894 the Battalion left Umballa by march route for Sabathu and Jutogh in the Simla Hills, two companies under Major Gallwey being detached at the latter place. They arrived at Sabathu on the 26th March.

At the end of the hot weather the Battalion left its hill stations on 23rd October and marched to Umballa, arriving there on 28th October.

On the 7th November the Battalion, under the command of Major A. C. Borton, started on its march 190 miles to Lahore to attend the Vice-Regal Durbar, arriving there on the 24th November. The Durbar held by the Viceroy Lord Elgin was the occasion for holding a big concentration of troops at the capital of the Punjaub.

Colonel Hallam Parr's term of command came to an end on 8th November, when he was succeeded by Lieut.-Colonel A. C. Borton.

Of Hallam Parr it may be said that no commanding officer since the days of Sale ever made such a mark on the Regiment. To him we owe a notable revision of the Standing Orders in 1893, last undertaken by Lord Mark Kerr in 1859. The chief features of his system of command were to encourage the individual responsibility of officers commanding companies, and other subordinate commanders even down to squad and group leaders, to assimilate organization in the barrack-room to that in the field, and to revive as far as possible the old light infantry spirit by quickening movements all round. A stern disciplinarian and a good horseman, he was probably the best-turned-out officer in the Army. He revived or initiated green whistle cords, green pugarees on Indian helmets, and black sword knots.

Among other innovations were Regimental Calendars and *The Light Bob Gazette*, started in 1893 at Gibraltar, Captain H. J. Everett being the first editor. For the first year or so it was issued weekly and later on after arrival in India it

COLONEL HENRY HALLAM PARR, C.B., C.M.G.
afterwards
MAJOR-GENERAL SIR HENRY HALLAM PARR, K.C.B., C.M.G.
Colonel of the Regiment, 1910-1914

was issued monthly, but at the same time it was registered as a newspaper and a daily sheet containing Reuter's telegrams was issued, a great boon in up-country stations where the Indian newspapers arrived a day or two after publication. This news sheet during the South African War had such an enormous circulation that it was suppressed owing to pressure exerted by the daily press in India.

After a fortnight at Lahore the Battalion began its return march to Umballa on 6th December, arriving at that station on 23rd December.

The strength of the Battalion on 1st January 1895 was 26 officers and 1,031 other ranks. Of these totals no less than 1,025 were English by nationality, very different from former days when Irishmen very often predominated.

On the 20th March 1895 the Battalion left Umballa for its hill stations, Subathu and Jutogh, arriving at the former station on 26th March.

During the ensuing hot weather Lieutenant J. Thicknesse was attached for duty to the King's Own Scottish Borderers and Lieutenant J. E. Ubsdell and four other ranks to the transport taking part in the Chitral Relief Force.

The silver Field Service cap badge for the officers of the Regiment was approved with the substitution of 'P.A.' for 'XIII'—Horse Guards Authority 61002/4989 dated 27th August 1895. It may be mentioned that the Field Service cap replaced the Glengarry in the year 1887.

On the 7th November the Battalion, strength 19 officers and 805 other ranks, under the command of Lieut.-Colonel A. C. Borton, commenced its march to its new station at Meean Meer, all time-expired men being left behind for embarkation to England.

Meean Meer, at that time notorious as a fever trap, was reached on 3rd December when a company was detached to Fort Lahore.

A War Office letter dated 29th November 1895 approved of the cavalry pattern mess waistcoat which had been consistently worn by officers of the 1st Battalion contrary to regulations since the days of Lord Mark Kerr. This belated approval was due to the efforts of Colonel Hallam Parr, then employed at the War Office as Asst. Inspector-General of Ordnance, but a little later on in the next year the wearing of a whistle and chain on the sashes of warrant officers and serjeants and extra braiding on the serge frocks of band and buglers was ordered to be discontinued, and in like manner the green chevrons, and badges on white and khaki clothing.

On the 3rd April 1896 the Headquarters of the Battalion and four companies under the command of Lieut.-Colonel A. C. Borton moved by rail to Pathankote and thence by march route to Dalhousie, reaching that station on 8th April.

In June 1896 the officer commanding the 2nd Battalion received the following letters from the High Seneschal of Canterbury Cathedral:—

'The Precincts, Canterbury,
17th June 1896

My dear Sir,—

A piece of the old 13th Colours fell this morning from the poles in Canterbury Cathedral from rottenness; it is impossible to replace it. In the natural order of things it would be burnt so that it might not fall into improper hands, but some parts of the piece are so good that it has occurred to me that the Regiment might wish to have them to put under a glass case. They are—

The circle in the centre of the Queen's Color embroidered "13th Regt. First Somersetshire", and "Martinique". I have no right to offer them to the Regiment but if the Dean and Chapter had reason to believe that they would be acceptable, I think it very likely that they might order them to be handed over. (I mean the pieces above mentioned).

Yrs truly,
signed E. S. NEWTON DICKENSON, Lt.-Col.
High Seneschal.'

The O.C. 2nd Battalion sent an answer of which there is no record, to which Lieut.-Colonel S. Newton Dickenson replied:—

'The Precincts, Canterbury,
24th June 1896

DEAR SIR,—

In reply to your letter of 20th inst. to the Dean and Chapter, I have the pleasure by permission, and with the compliments of the Dean, to send you two pieces of the Colors of the 13th.: one the centre, and the other "Martinique" and also a detached piece.

The Colours as you know are in the Cathedral here, and these two pieces fell from off the poles, the silk having rotted away.

I am, dear Sir, truly yours,
signed E. S. NEWTON DICKENSON, Lt.-Col.
High Seneschal.'

The fragments of the Colours above referred to were forwarded to the O.C. 1st Battalion, who replied in the following terms:—

'Dalhousie, Punjaub, *25th July 1896*

MY DEAR SIR,—

Lt.-Colonel Waddy informs me that he has written to thank you for having forwarded to him the centre of the old Color (of this Battalion) which is deposited at the Cathedral.

I desire now to thank you, not only on my own account but on behalf of the officers whose predecessors fought under the old Color in Burma and at Jellalabad.

I need hardly tell an old soldier that it is a memento that will be most reverently cared for, and that in a glass case in our mess, it will be the means of keeping alive in the present generation the traditions of the past. I rejoice that the relic fell into the hands of a soldier who knew how to deal with it, and who was aware how highly it would be valued by the Regiment.

Pray accept my best thanks for what you have done for us. Will you add to your kindness by giving my compliments to the Dean and Chapter of the Cathedral and ask their acceptance of the grateful thanks of the Battalion I have the honour to command with the assurance that the fragment will be as religiously safeguarded by the present generation as it was by our predecessors who fought under it in the first Burmese War 1824 and in the Afghan Campaign 1838–42.

Believe me yours gratefully,
signed A. C. BORTON, Lt.-Colonel
Comg. 1/ The P. A. Somersetshire Light Infantry.'

The Colours referred to were deposited in Canterbury Cathedral in 1846.

In July 1896 the Colours of the regimental tie were changed from dark blue and red stripes to dark blue and dark green stripes separated by a thin line of feuille morte yellow. The dark blue to represent the existing facings, the dark green as distinctive of Light Infantry, and the feuille morte yellow the old facings of the Regiment.

On the 13th October Captain J. E. Ubsdell, employed as transport officer with the Chitral Relief Force, died at Drosh, Chitral, from enteric fever.

On the 20th October the headquarters of the Battalion, the Band with 'F', 'G', 'H' and 'L' Companies, left Dalhousie for Meean Meer, arriving there on the 26th October. The Wing marched from Dalhousie to Pathankote, and entrained at Pathankote for Meean Meer.

The strength of the Battalion on 1st January 1897 was 28 officers and 1,087 other ranks.

On the 1st February 1897 Captain C. M. R. Rycroft died at Meean Meer from enteric fever.

On the 13th April the headquarters of the Battalion, with 'C', 'D', 'I' and 'M' Companies, proceeded to the hill station of Dalhousie for the hot weather, arriving there on the 19th April.

On the 29th July, in consequence of trouble on the North-west frontier, orders were received by telegram for the Battalion to proceed immediately to Peshawar on 'relief scale'. The Meean Meer wing was ordered to proceed direct to Peshawar on relief by the Bedfordshire Regiment, and the headquarter wing at Dalhousie to proceed as soon as possible, halting at Meean Meer and Rawal Pindi *en route*. The married families were to remain in their present stations.

The headquarter wing marched from Dalhousie at 4 p.m. on 31st July and reached Pathankote (railhead) at daylight on 2nd August. There they entrained, halting by day at Meean Meer and Rawal Pindi on the 4th and 5th August respectively, and reached Peshawar on 6th August, at which station the Meean Meer wing had already arrived. The Battalion, strength 18 officers and 781 other ranks, here occupied the Right British Infantry Barracks.

THE MOHMAND CAMPAIGN

On the 7th August Brig.-General Elles, C.B., commanding the Peshawar district, received information that a gathering of Mohmand tribesmen under the Adda Mullah was threatening the village of Shunkargarh under the walls of Fort Shabkadr, about 20 miles to the north of Peshawar, then held by a detachment of Border Police.

A small column was immediately organized for the relief of Shabkadr. It consisted of 4 guns, 51st Field Battery, R.A., two squadrons 13th Bengal Lancers, two companies of the Somersetshire Light Infantry and the 20th Punjaub Infantry, the whole under the command of Lieut.-Colonel J. B. Woon, 20th Punjaub Infantry. Major A. Lumb commanded the two companies of the Regiment.

The column left Peshawar at 1 a.m. on the 8th, crossed the Kabul River by the ferry at Adizai, reached Shabkadr at 10 a.m. and found that the enemy had already burnt the village of Shunkargarh. Lieut.-Colonel Woon then, after a short halt, reconnoitred the enemy's position on some low hills covering the Gandab Pass to the West of the Fort, but owing to the intense heat and to the fact that the force was not yet concentrated, he retired to the shelter of the Fort for the night.

On the morning of the 9th at 5.30 a.m. Lieut.-Colonel Woon marched out with his force and found the enemy occupying a position on the same undulating plateau at the foot of the hills. His intention was to make a frontal attack with the infantry and to turn the enemy's left with his guns and cavalry. At 7.30 a.m. the force deployed, the two companies of the Regiment being on the left, the 20th Punjaub Infantry in the centre, while the guns and the greater part of the cavalry were on the right. One troop, however, of 13th Bengal Lancers was on the left rear of the Regiment.

The Infantry began the action shortly before 8 a.m., but the guns did not come into action owing to the difficulties of the ground till nearly an hour later. Meanwhile the enemy developed their attack on the left of the British force, which obliged Colonel Woon first of all to halt, and then to withdraw his line some 400 yards, at the same time reinforcing his left with one company of the 20th Punjaub Infantry from the centre.

At this juncture Brig.-General E. R. Elles arrived from Peshawar and assumed command. He ordered the 13th Bengal Lancers to make a detour to the right and make a charge along the whole length of the enemy's line. This charge was brilliantly and successfully carried out. The enemy retired after suffering heavy casualties along the whole front, and withdrew into the hills. The British force, after a short advance, finally withdrew to Shabkadr unmolested.

The British losses amounted to 4 officers wounded, 9 rank and file killed and 61 wounded. Of these numbers the regimental casualties were 2 officers wounded, Major A. Lumb and 2nd Lieutenant E. Drummond, 4 rank and file killed and 9 wounded. The enemy's strength was computed at 5,000 to 6,000 men, while their losses were estimated at 200 killed, besides a large number wounded.

Captain W. C. Cox, of the Regiment, who took over command from Major A. Lumb, wounded early in the action, was mentioned in dispatches, and so was Lieutenant G. B. Roney-Dougal, Orderly Officer.

THE MOHMAND CAMPAIGN

Reinforcements were now rushed up to Shabkadr and among them the remainder of the Regiment who left Peshawar on the evening of the 9th and arrived at Shabkadr at 12 noon on the 10th.

By the 12th the British force at Shabkadr was raised to 2,500 men. On the 14th a reconnaissance in force was made by the garrison, but no signs of the enemy were to be seen.

On the 18th the headquarters of the Battalion, with 'C', 'D', 'M' and 'I' Companies, returned to Peshawar and formed part of the Peshawar Reserve Column under Lieut.-Colonel A. C. Borton.

Owing to the hostile attitude of the Afridis in the neighbourhood of the Khyber Pass, this column bivouacked on the Jamrud road on the 24th, but returned to their lines on the 29th.

On the 31st August, owing to reports that the Mohmands were concentrating, 'I' Company and details under Major R. L. Payne, D.S.O., marched from Peshawar to Shabkadr and were followed by the headquarters of the Battalion on 2nd September.

On the 7th September orders were received for the formation of a field force for operations in the Mohmand country under the command of Brig.-General E. R. Elles, C.B., with the local rank of Major-General. The force consisted of two brigades and divisional troops. The Battalion was included in the 1st Brigade under the command of Brig.-General Westmacott, C.B., D.S.O., the other infantry battalions being the 20th Punjaub Infantry, and the 2nd Battalion 1st Gurkhas. On the 8th September the remaining three companies of the Battalion rejoined headquarters at Shabkadr from Peshawar.

The plan of operations was for the Malakand Field Force under Sir Bindon Blood to advance from the Swat Valley through Bajaur and to co-operate with the Mohmand Field Force advancing from Shabkadr.

On the 15th September the Mohmand Field Force advanced. The 1st Brigade, including the Regiment and Divisional headquarters, marching to Ghalanai 18 miles, the 2nd Brigade to Dand. Although no enemy was met with, the heat and the lack of water was very trying to the troops. The Kharappa Pass proved to be very difficult and quite impracticable for camels.

By the 18th the road had been sufficiently improved to enable the camel transport to reach Ghalanai.

Meanwhile on the 17th the 1st Brigade, with the exception of the Regiment, marched to Katsai, $2\frac{1}{2}$ miles south of the Nahaki Pass, where they were joined by the Regiment on the 20th, but the Battalion was rotten with fever, and had to leave behind at Ghalanai no less than 178 N.C.Os. and men.

On the same day the 2nd Brigade marched from Dand to Ghalanai. The enemy, about 1,000 strong, were reported to be holding the Bedmanai Pass, which it was proposed to attack by a combined operation on the part of Sir Bindon Blood's Field Force acting in co-operation with the Mohmand Field Force.

On 21st September the 1st Brigade marched to Lakarai (10 miles), constructed an entrenched camp, from which the camp of the 3rd Brigade (Woodhouse) Bindon Blood's force could be clearly seen distant about 6 miles. This latter camp had been attacked by the enemy on the 19th and 20th.

Sir Bindon Blood now placed the 3rd Brigade under General Elles's orders. In the meantime the 2nd Brigade had occupied the Nahaki Pass in rear. On the 22nd General Elles, with the 1st Brigade and Divisional Headquarters, marched to Khazina (6 miles), where he was joined by the 3rd Brigade from Nawagai.

THE ATTACK ON THE BEDMANAI PASS

The Pass was situated some 5 miles west south-west of the British position, and was now reported to be strongly held by the enemy. The plan of attack was for the 1st Brigade on the left with one battery to make a turning movement along the Yari Sar ridge, while the 3rd Brigade advanced along the pass road, and the Cavalry watched the approaches to the Mitai Pass.

Of the 1st Brigade the 20th Punjaub Infantry formed the first line of attack, supported by the Gurkhas with the Somersetshire Light Infantry in reserve. Very slight opposition was offered by the enemy, who were gradually driven from spur to spur, and the top of the pass was gained at 11 a.m. The losses on either side were very slight, the British loss being one killed and three wounded. It is probable that there were not more than 700 or 800 of the enemy holding the approaches to the Bedmanai Pass, though from the Cavalry reports the Mitai Pass to the north was more strongly held.

At the conclusion of the action the 1st Brigade advanced to Bedmanai village while the 3rd Brigade and Cavalry returned to their camp of the previous night.

On the 24th 'F', 'H', 'I' and 'M' Companies and 4 guns, under Major Lloyd Payne, D.S.O., marched back to the Bedmanai Pass to cover the advance of the transport, and the working parties of Sappers and Miners employed in demolishing the enemy villages, while the remainder of the Regiment still held Bedmanai village. The main body of the 1st Brigade had advanced down the Bedmanai Valley to Sarfaraz Kila. As soon as the transport had cleared the Bedmanai Pass, escorted by the Battalion they followed the main body to Sarfaraz Kila, which was not reached till 9.30 p.m.

On the 25th the 1st Brigade marched to Jarobi, the Adda Mullah's stronghold (12 miles), at the head of the Shindawa Valley. The Regiment found the advance guard with two maxims and No. 3 Mountain Battery. Such small parties of the enemy as were met with were easily dispersed, and having attained the heights commanding the Shindawa Valley, the covering troops remained in position while the Tor Kila and other fortified villages were being destroyed. The troops began to retire at 3.30 p.m. and reached Tor Khel at 6 p.m., where they bivouacked for the night. The casualties this day were one Native officer killed and 17 men wounded.

Jarobi was the farthest point reached by the 1st Brigade, and from now the Brigade moved back towards Nahaki by a different route to which the advance had been made. Hostile villages were destroyed by small columns sent out by the Brigade.

On the 26th the Brigade marched to Khwaria and on the 27th to Kung, where the Regiment was replaced in the 1st Brigade by the 2nd Battalion Oxfordshire Light Infantry from the 2nd Brigade.

On the 28th the Battalion, much weakened by fever and dysentery, commenced their return march to Peshawar in charge of a large convoy of sick and wounded men. Nahaki was reached that night, and Ghalanai the next day the 29th, where the sick and weakly men left behind on the 18th rejoined. The convoy, escorted by the Battalion, reached Dand on the 30th and Adizai on the Kabul River on 1st October after a four-hours' halt at Shabkadr. On 2nd October the Battalion marched into Peshawar, its strength being 20 officers and 558 other ranks.

The tribes in the Mohmand Valley having now submitted, the 1st and 2nd Brigades returned to Peshawar on the 6th and 7th October, when the Mohmand Field Force was broken up.

The Indian Medal 1895 with clasp inscribed 'Punjaub Frontier 1897–98' was granted to the troops employed in the action of Shabkadr and the subsequent operations in the Mohmand country.

The Mohmand and Malakand expeditions were, however, merely the prelude to more important operations to the west of Peshawar, namely the Tirah Expedition, but in this Expedition the Battalion took no part; they were reported by the medical authorities to be 'saturated with malaria and unfit for service'. Such was the result of nearly two years spent in Meean Meer, at that time notorious for its unhealthiness.

On the evening of 2nd October 'F', 'G', 'H' and 'L' Companies, strength 8 officers and 298 other ranks, under the command of Major R. L. Payne, D.S.O., proceeded by rail from Peshawar to Pubbi and thence by route march to Cherat, arriving at that station on 4th October. The headquarter wing occupied the Right British Infantry Barracks in Peshawar.

On the 4th November the left wing returned from Cherat to Peshawar, arriving there on the 7th.

On the 24th December the 1st Battalion, under the command of Major E. J. Gallwey, strength 16 officers and 699 other ranks, left Peshawar for Rawal Pindi, arriving there on the 25th December, and was located in West Ridge Barracks. 'C' Company, under Captain W. C. Cox, was detached to Fort Attock, while half a company under Lieutenant Chichester proceeded to Campbellpore.

On the 16th April 1898 the headquarters of the Battalion, with 'F', 'G', 'H' and 'L' Companies under the command of Major E. J. Gallwey, left Rawal Pindi by route march for Murree, arriving at that station on the 18th, when they were quartered at Kuldanna.

On the 28th and 30th May the remaining four companies of the Battalion left Rawal Pindi for Murree and were quartered at Kuldanna.

On the 23rd and 27th October the Battalion left Murree for Rawal Pindi by half-battalions and were quartered in the West Ridge Barracks.

On the 15th November Lieut.-Colonel A. C. Borton, having completed his period of service in command of the Battalion, was succeeded by Lieut.-Colonel H. A. Walsh.

On the 18th April 1899 the headquarters and 'C', 'D', 'I' and 'M' Companies proceeded to Murree and were quartered at Upper Topa, and on the 20th April a detachment of 50 N.C.Os. and men under 2nd Lieutenant J. S. N. Harrison proceeded on detachment to Campellpore, arriving there on the 23rd *idem*.

During the hot weather the companies at Murree returned to Rawal Pindi and were replaced by those who had been quartered in the latter station.

2ND BATTALION

To go back to the Records of the 2nd Battalion. It has been recorded that the Battalion left Bombay in H.M.S. *Euphrates* on the 19th January 1894 for conveyance to England.

They arrived at Plymouth Sound on the 15th February and were quartered at Fort Tregantle. Shortly after arrival the Battalion was rearmed with the Lee-Metford rifle.

On the 29th May the Battalion moved from Fort Tregantle to the South Raglan Barracks, Devonport.

On the 14th June Lieut.-Colonel W. C. F. Madden retired from the Service and was succeeded by Lieut.-Colonel J. M. E. Waddy.

On the 23rd May 1895 new Colours were presented to the Battalion by H.R.H. the Duke of Cambridge, Field-Marshal Commander-in-Chief, who was received with a Royal Salute by the Battalion drawn up in line, the Colonel of the Regiment, Lord Mark Kerr, being present on parade, after which the old Colours were trooped. Captain T.D'O. Snow commanded the escort while Lieutenants Boyle and Barry carried the Colours.

On the conclusion of the Troop the Battalion formed three sides of a square when the new Colours were consecrated by the Right Rev. Bishop Barry, D.D., assisted by the Rev. J. H. Foulkes, M.A. (Chaplain to the Forces).

The presentation then took place, Lieutenants Cooke-Hurle and Foord receiving the new Colours. The parade concluded with a March Past and Advance in Review Order.

His Royal Highness expressed himself as highly satisfied with the drill and appearance of the Battalion, the trooping of the old Colours and the reception of the new Colours being faultlessly performed.

H.R.H. made the following speech on this occasion:—

He had much pleasure in presenting those Colours or rather he should prefer to say a continuation of the old Colours to so distinguished and old a Regiment as that which had been so ably commanded for many years, especially under the immediate orders of the gallant General, their Colonel, Lord Mark Kerr, who at that moment was on his (the Duke's) right. He found on reference that the Corps was raised by the Earl of Huntingdon in 1685, and took part, under Lord Peterborough, in the Campaign in Spain and Portugal 1705–08.

It also took part in the Battle of Dettingen and in the taking and defence of Gibraltar. Those were some of the ancient actions of their distinguished Regiment, and he also found it took part, in 1809, in the capture of Martinique and the Burmese War of 1824, being present at the capture of Ava. Coming to more modern times he found that the Corps rendered great service during the Afghan War 1841–2 under Sir Robert Sale, whose name was a household word in the British Army, as also in the Regiment which he, Sir Robert Sale, had the honour to command. Those were difficult and troublesome times, and since then the Regiment had lost none of its former distinction or the confidence of a grateful country.

He also found that after the Afghan War, the Regiment was employed in the Crimea and Indian Mutiny under Lord Mark Kerr, so that altogether it had a very distinguished career, and still possessed in its honorary Colonel the highly distinguished officer who for many years commanded the Regiment, and was at its head at the relief of Azimghur. It also served in the South African Campaign in 1878–9. Looking at its past services he thought the Regiment was justified in feeling proud of its position, and he felt confident that should circumstances require it, the Regiment would try to emulate those great and distinguished services which were performed in olden days as well as in more modern times.

The object of such a ceremonial as that just carried out was to keep in the Regiment and in the Army the *esprit de corps* and soldierlike spirit which alone made the Army strong, powerful, and valuable to the country it served. Every officer, N.C.O. and man ought to feel that he belonged to a Regiment that had never disgraced itself, and never would disgrace itself, and that whilst they were connected with it no disgraceful sentiments should come into the hearts and feelings of any soldier connected with it.

They would, he felt sure, rather die for their Queen and country than that their Regiment should receive any discredit that might happen from any neglect of their own. They would never neglect their duty. Englishmen had always been proud of the Army and its reputation. It was a small army but a powerful one, inasmuch as it was composed of officers and men who would risk their lives in any part of the world for their Queen and country, and as long as that sentiment prevailed there would be no fear as to the result.

Personally he would do all he could on every occasion to bring to the minds of the young soldiers now in the Army the sentiments experienced in former days by their ancestors, and he hoped that such a sentiment would ever continue in the British Army.

He referred at the outset to the continuation as he called it of the old Colours. Personally he had always said he did not care if there was not much bunting on them, so long as there was the staff and the crowns that had been defended. New Colours did not add to the sentiment he had spoken of but rather made him wish that the old Colours could continue for ever and new ones not be required at all. But the Colours presented that day were the same as raised the Battalion, and as regarded their honour he had no doubt that they would be defended by the blood of every soldier in the Regiment should occasion require it.

H.R.H. then congratulated Lieut.-Colonel Waddy on being in command of such a distinguished regiment and he also congratulated the Regiment on the presence of that distinguished officer, General Lord Mark Kerr. It was a remarkable thing that an ancestor of Lord Mark commanded the Regiment from 1725 to 1732 and he hoped the present Colonel would live to see many days still and retain the pleasure of being the Colonel of the 13th Light Infantry.

Lieut.-Colonel Waddy, on behalf of the Battalion, replied in the following terms:—

'May it please your Royal Highness, on behalf of my comrades of the Prince Albert's Somersetshire Light Infantry I beg to tender my most sincere and heartfelt thanks for the distinguished honour you have conferred on us to-day by presenting new Colours. I feel confident that to-day will ever remain a day of pleasant memories to those who are now serving in the Battalion, saddened only by the regret we feel at parting with those old Colours which were presented to us on our formation in 1858 by that great and good Prince, the Prince Consort, whose name we cherish in our title, and are so proud to bear. Should it ever become our duty to defend these Colours in action I feel sure that as they fought of old, so again will there ever be found in our ranks brave and loyal hearts ready to shed their life blood for their Colours, their Country and their Queen.'

The following officers were present on the parade:—
Colonel: General Lord Mark Kerr, G.C.B.
Lieut.-Colonel J. M. E. Waddy, Commanding Battalion.
Major E. J. Fownes, 2nd in Command.
Majors E. M. Poynton and A. W. A. Pollock.
Captains C. H. Stisted, T. D'O. Snow, M. A. Foster, J. M. Vallentin, E. H. Swayne, W. P. Braithwaite (Adjutant) and E. C. Elger.
Lieutenants E. F. Cooke-Hurle, A. R. Foord, A. G. Boyle, W. J. Bowker, H. F. Hardman, A. P. Barry and J. B. C. Thomson.
2nd Lieutenants A. H. P. Luckhardt, C. B. Prowse, P. Mark-Wardlaw and A. H. Yatman.
Quarter-Master and Hon. Lieutenant L. Donnelly.

After the parade was dismissed, Lieut.-Colonel Waddy and the officers entertained about 400 guests at luncheon in a large marquee which was erected at the south end of the barrack square. On the 19th July the old Colours were deposited in St. Mary's Church, Taunton.

The escort, under the command of Lieut.-Colonel Waddy, consisted of 10 officers, Lieutenants Cooke-Hurle and Foord carrying the Colours, Serjt.-Major Bath, Bandmaster Ancliffe, 8 Colour-Serjeants, the Armourer Serjeant,

24 picked men wearing the Burma Medal, 24 picked marksmen and the Band and Buglers.

On arrival at Taunton Station the 3rd Battalion Somersetshire Light Infantry under Colonel Cornish Henley, and the 2nd Volunteer Battalion Somersetshire Light Infantry under Colonel Blake and the Regimental Depôt under Colonel Thompson, drawn up outside the station, presented arms as the Colour party and its escort marched off to St. Mary's Church.

As the troops passed the Memorial Cross in the centre of the town they saluted.

During the first part of the Service in the church the Colours, with an escort of officers, remained at the West Door. After the singing of a special hymn the Vicar, the Reverend Prebendary Askwith, took his place at the Altar, and the Colour party marched up the aisle to a slow march. On reaching the Chancel steps the Colours were handed to Lieut.-Colonel Waddy and Major Pollock, who advanced to the Altar rails and handed them to the Vicar, who in turn placed them on the Altar, the troops meanwhile presenting arms. After a prayer, the Vicar gave a short address and the Service concluded with the Hymn, 'Onward Christian Soldiers', followed by the Benediction.

On the 12th November, on change of station, the headquarters of the Battalion and four companies proceeded to Guernsey, followed on the 17th November by the remaining four companies who were stationed in Alderney.

The 2nd Battalion remained in the Channel Islands for eighteen months, when orders were received for their return to England. Prior to their departure the following testimonials of their good conduct were received:—

'From the High Constables of St. Peter's Port, Guernsey, to the O.C. 2/Somerset L.I., dated 20th May 1897.

Sir,—

We are authorized by the members of the Douzaine of this town and parish to convey to you their high appreciation of the exemplary and orderly conduct of the Prince Albert's Somersetshire Light Infantry while quartered in this island.

As High Constables of St. Peter's Port we can testify to the admirable conduct of the Corps and to the good relations which have always existed between the Regiment and the Police Force.

We heartily endorse the decision of the Douzaine and beg to convey to you, Sir, and through you to the officers and men the assurance that the conduct of the Regiment has won the admiration of all classes of the Community.

The gallant Prince Albert's Somersetshire Light Infantry will carry with them the best wishes of the inhabitants for their future welfare and prosperity in which none more cordially participate than, Sir,

Your obedient servants,
signed EDWARD VALPIED } High Constables of
„ R. H. PAYNE } St. Peter's Port.'

'From J. A. Le Cocq, Judge of Alderney, to the O.C. 2nd Somersetshire Light Infantry.

Sir,—

The members of the Court of the Island of Alderney desire me to write to you before the departure of the 2nd Battalion Prince Albert's Somersetshire Light Infantry under your command to express the esteem we entertain of the good and orderly conduct of all grades of the Regiment when quartered here.

The Regiment has been with us eighteen months and I am pleased to say that during that time not a single individual belonging to the Regiment has been produced before the Court for any offence.

Will you kindly convey to the officers and men that not only the Court but the inhabitants generally hold them in high esteem, and they also carry with them our best wishes for their future welfare.

I have the honour to be, Sir,
Your obedient servant,
signed J. A. Le Cocq, Judge of Alderney.'

Farewell order by Lieut.-General Stevenson, commanding Guernsey and Alderney District, on the departure of the 2nd Battalion Somersetshire Light Infantry from that Command.

'*20th May 1897*

On the approaching departure of the 2nd Battalion the Prince Albert's Somersetshire Light Infantry from the Guernsey and Alderney District, he, the G.O.C., desires to place on record his appreciation of the excellent conduct of the Battalion during its tour of service in the command.

Throughout a period of 18 months there has not been a single instance of a Somersetshire Light Infantry man having committed a civil offence, or misconducted himself in an unsoldierlike manner.

He is very sensible of the strong feeling of '*esprit de corps*' which pervades all ranks of the Battalion and congratulates them on their efficiency in shooting and marching.

signed W. Sitwell, Captain, D.A.A.G.'

On the 22nd May 1897 the headquarters and four companies, under the command of Lieut.-Colonel J. M. E. Waddy, embarked on the South-Western Railway Company's Steamer *Frederica* and proceeded to Alderney and there embarked the remaining four companies of the Battalion. The *Frederica* then proceeded to Southampton, where it arrived about 7 p.m. The Battalion passed the night at Southampton and left the following morning for Worthing, where it took part in the South-Eastern manœuvres, being encamped alongside the 4th (Militia) Battalion Somersetshire Light Infantry.

On the conclusion of the manœuvres the Battalion left for Aldershot, where it arrived on the 24th June and was encamped on Rushmore Hill, remaining there until 24th September, when it moved into Corunna Barracks.

In August of this year Captain W. Sitwell, D.A.A.G., Guernsey, presented to the officers of the Battalion a sword which originally belonged to Sir Robert Sale and said to have been worn by him at the Battle of Moodkee.

The sword was left by Sir Robert Sale to G. Sale Bedford, Esq., H.M. Woods and Forests, who presented it to his stepdaughter, Elizabeth Sitwell, the mother of Captain Sitwell.

On the 5th August 1898 Lieut.-Colonel E. J. Gallwey assumed command of the Battalion *vice* Lieut.-Colonel J. M. E. Waddy, whose period of service had expired.

CHAPTER XXV

THE SOUTH AFRICAN WAR

ON the 7th October 1899, in consequence of the strained relations between the British Government and the Boer Republics, orders were issued for the mobilization in Great Britain of an Army Corps consisting of three infantry Divisions, and Corps troops; a cavalry Division and certain lines of Communication troops.

The 2nd Battalion, originally destined to be one of the battalions on the Line of Communications, had already proceeded to Portland on 14th September. At this station the Battalion took over its mobilization equipment and received the large number of reservists, about 500, necessary to complete its war establishment. The calling up of the reserves, the great test of a short-service system, was an enormous success. Colonel Gallwey in his reminiscences states that 'not a man was absent'. On the other hand, there was some delay in the issue of khaki clothing which at that time was not the every-day working dress of the Army which it has since become.

On 11th October hostilities commenced, and here it will be convenient to give a brief review of the situation in South Africa at this time.

The Imperial troops in Natal consisted of some 16,000 men under Sir George White, in the Cape Colony 10,000, and in Rhodesia 1,500. The Boer Republics could put in the field some 50,000 men without counting a considerable number of their compatriots in the Cape Colony and Natal who, in the event of a successful invasion of the British Colonies, might be counted on to swell the enemy's ranks. As the seat of war was some 6,000 miles distant from Great Britain, and consequently any reinforcements from that country could not be available for hostilities for five or six weeks, it is apparent that the initiative lay with the enemy, and that the British forces would be reduced to the defensive made all the harder by the enormous length of the frontiers liable to invasion.

The Boer forces, with the exception of a small nucleus of artillery and police, might be termed, according to European ideas, irregulars; yet they had a system of peace-time organization not badly suited for active operations. The whole country was divided up into wards, and at the head of each ward was a field cornet, who was responsible for the assembly of his men at the appointed station in the case of an emergency. The wards in their turn were allotted to larger units termed commandos, generally designated by the name of the district they came from. The strength of a commando was, however, an uncertain factor: it might be anything between 300 and 3,000 men.

Their intermittent peace-time training was devoted entirely to rifle shooting, in which they took the greatest interest and acquired considerable skill, but their lack of training in other directions was made up by self-reliance and individuality engendered by generations of conflict with natives and wild beasts.

Armed with the latest German Mauser rifle, possessed of ample supplies of ammunition, and being all mounted, they were indeed a formidable foe, made more so by their extreme mobility: and in this connexion it may be observed that they were to be pitted mainly against British Infantry in the early stages of the war. With their ponies close at hand they could take as much or as little of the fight as it suited them, for it must be remembered that the Boer tactics were generally defensive. They acquired great skill in siting and constructing trenches, they relied on the British attacking, and they were not disappointed; they aimed at destroying the enemy by rifle fire before close quarters were reached. They were purposely not armed with a bayonet owing to their reluctance to come to close quarters.

When they did attack they never attacked in full strength; there were always some who kept back, and this may be accounted for by the lack of discipline. A popular or determined Boer Commandant could do much, but as punishment for disobedience was rarely enforced, decisive action could not always be relied on. Moreover, all great decisions were settled by Council of War when influential men would often reject by their votes the decisions of their appointed leaders.

Another rule or custom, which did not militate towards success, was the habit of 10 per cent of a commando being at liberty to go to their homes, no matter how urgent their presence at the front might be.

The initial deployment of their troops was, fortunately for the British, extremely faulty; instead of massing the major part of their forces for crushing the British in Natal or invading Cape Colony, no less than 9,000 men were sent to beleaguer Baden-Powell at Mafeking, and a somewhat similar force to invest Kimberley, where easy and comparatively bloodless successes might be expected.

Yet the Boers entered into the war with considerable confidence; had they not defeated the rooineks in the open field at Majuba in 1881? Even if the conduct of major operations of war was to a certain extent a closed book to them, did not they excel in partisan warfare, were not they fully acquainted with the nature of the theatre of war, with its rolling plains, its rocky kopjes, and its hidden river-beds?

Yes, the sequel of this war was to prove that Great Britain, and indeed the Empire, had to put into the field a larger army than it ever had before. Contingents from all the self-governing colonies were to take part. The British Army was to fight shoulder to shoulder with its comrades from overseas. It was indeed a fitting dress rehearsal on a small scale for the Great War drama which engulfed the world fifteen years later.

Sir Redvers Buller, designated as the Commander-in-Chief in South Africa, left Southampton on 14th October and reached Cape Town on 31st October, and was soon followed by the various units of the mobilized Army Corps and cavalry Division.

His original plan of campaign had been to invade the Orange Free State with the expeditionary force from home and advance over the open plains to Bloemfontein, while Sir George White in Natal and smaller forces in other parts of the Cape Colony guarding the main lines of railway were to act on the defensive, until the main army was ready to strike.

The news that reached Buller at Cape Town on 31st October was by no means reassuring. Mafeking and Kimberley were invested. In Natal Dundee had been evacuated, gallant actions had indeed been fought at Talana, Elandslaagte, and Rietfontein, but on 30th October Sir George White suffered a reverse at Lombard's Kop, and a few days later was closely invested in Ladysmith. Moreover, on 1st November the Boers seized Norvals Pont and invaded the Cape Colony.

It soon became apparent that the original plan of campaign would have to be postponed and that a great part of the troops arriving in South Africa would have to be diverted to Natal to relieve Ladysmith.

On 4th November the 2nd Battalion proceeded in two special trains from Portland to Southampton and there embarked on the Union liner ss. *Briton* for conveyance to Cape Town. Strength 28 officers, 1 warrant officer, 43 serjeants, 47 corporals, 14 buglers and 770 privates. Total 903 all ranks.

The names of the officers embarking were:—

Lieut.-Colonel E. J. Gallwey, Commanding.
Major R. B. Williams, 2nd in Command.
Major C. B. Little.
Captains F. M. Peacock, S. L. V. Crealock, L. G. T. Chandler, E. G. Elger, W. P. Braithwaite, A. B. Whatman, W. J. Bowker, D.S.O.
Lieutenants V. F. A. Keith-Falconer, J. B. C. Thomson, C. B. Prowse, P. M. Wardlaw, A. H. Yatman, F. B. Maddock, R. H. M. C. Miers.
2nd Lieutenants A. W. S. Paterson, H. G. R. Burges-Short, H. I. R. Allfrey, J. C. Parr, C. H. Little, W. H. M. Freestun, A. R. S. Sale-Hill, E. W. Worrall and G. B. Harrison.
Captain and Adjutant E. H. Swayne.
Lieutenant and Quartermaster P. Moran.
Attached, Captain R. E. H. E. Holt, R.A.M.C.

On the arrival of the ss. *Briton* at Cape Town on 20th November orders were received for the Battalion to proceed to De Aar, an important railway junction on the direct line to Kimberley. Half the Regiment had already entrained when fresh instructions were received changing the destination of the Battalion to Durban.

In fact the military situation had not improved since the departure of the Regiment from England. Although Sir George White had repulsed a general attack on Ladysmith on 9th November, he was so closely invested and Natal in such danger of being overrun, that more than one division of the Army Corps originally destined for the invasion of the Orange Free State had been directed to that Colony, while to replace them orders for the mobilization of the 5th Division at home were issued on 11th November.

The Battalion, having embarked on the ss. *Orcana* on 20th November, proceeded on the 21st to Durban and arrived there at daybreak on the 24th. After disembarkation the Regiment proceeded by train to Nottingham Road, 30 miles north-west of Maritzburg, where they encamped, and were equipped with 1st and 2nd Line transport.

Sir Redvers Buller had himself proceeded to Natal so as to be in close touch with the situation there.

The British forces now assembling at Frere consisted of four brigades of infantry, viz. 2nd (Hildyard), 6th (Barton), 4th (Lyttelton) and 5th (Hart), Lord Dundonald's Mounted Brigade, five batteries field artillery and naval guns (4·7 inch and 12-pounders), the whole under the command of Major-General Clery.

Thus a strong force was being concentrated for the relief of Ladysmith, while the action of Willow Grange on 23rd November, followed by the retirement of the Boers to the line of the Tugela, seemed for the moment to have stemmed the further advance of the enemy into Natal. In the western theatre of war Lord Methuen by his advance across the Orange River towards Kimberley, rendered notable by successful actions at Belmont, Enslin and Modder River on the 23rd, 25th and 28th November respectively, might be expected to relieve the pressure on the garrison of Ladysmith.

On the 6th December the Battalion moved towards the front, encamping at Mooi River on that day, at Willow Grange on the 7th, and at Estcourt on the 8th. At the latter place the Battalion in conjunction with the Natal Light Infantry, a newly raised colonial corps, relieved the 4th (Lyttelton's) Brigade, who proceeded towards the Tugela. Colonel Gallwey was appointed Commandant at Estcourt, and he had at his disposal besides the two battalions above noted, two naval 12-pounders, a mountain battery, and 100 irregular mounted men. Signalling communication by helio and lamp was daily maintained with the Ladysmith garrison.

Colonel Gallwey acted with considerable vigour as Commandant at Estcourt: he found all the public-houses open, and he forthwith closed them, he cleared the town of undesirables, and established a censorship. Yet these necessary proceedings called forth a remonstrance from the Attorney-General of Natal.

The week commencing 10th December, known as the 'Black Week', was ushered in by the defeat of Gatacre at Stormberg on that day, by Methuen's repulse at Magersfontein on the 11th and by Buller's failure to force the passages of the Tugela at Colenso on the 15th.

The Regiment at Estcourt was some 20 miles distant from the scene of action at Colenso and consequently took no part, but the continuous booming of the guns indicated that a considerable action was in progress. The British casualties on this occasion were over 1,100 killed, wounded, and missing. There was no immediate prospect of the relief of Ladysmith, but the cumulative disasters of the past week had opened the eyes of the authorities at home to the magnitude of the task they had to face.

Already on the 30th November the 6th Division had been mobilized at home, and on the 13th December orders for the mobilization of the 7th Division were issued. On the 18th December Lord Roberts was appointed Commander-in-Chief in South Africa with Kitchener as his Chief of the Staff. They left England for South Africa on 23rd December. In the meantime the 5th Division, under Sir Charles Warren, on its arrival in South Africa was diverted to Natal, where preparations for a further attempt to relieve Ladysmith were in progress.

Christmas and the New Year brought the following messages from Her Majesty the Queen to her troops in South Africa:—

25th December 1899. 'I wish you and all my brave soldiers a happy Christmas. God protect and bless you all. V.R.I.'

1st January 1900. 'Wish you all a bright and happy New Year. God bless you. V.R.I.'

On the 2nd January orders were issued for the 2nd Battalion to form part of the 10th Brigade, Commander, Major-General J. Talbot-Coke. The other battalions in the brigade were the 2nd Battalion Dorsetshire Regiment, the 2nd Battalion the Middlesex Regiment, and later on the Imperial Light Infantry. All the officers were given men's equipment and rifles.

On the 6th January the Boers made a determined attack on Caesar's Camp, Ladysmith, when they were repulsed after strenuous fighting.

Among those killed in this fighting was Lieutenant C. E. M. Walker of the 1st Battalion, who at the time was attached to the 1st Battalion Devonshire Regiment.

On the 9th January the Battalion marched in drenching rain with the other two battalions of the brigade from Estcourt to Frere (12 miles), crossing the Little Bushman's River *en route* which was in full flood. At Frere Camp a reinforcement of 174 N.C.Os. and men, including 130 Militia Reservists under the command of Lieutenant Hardman, joined the Battalion.

THE SPION KOP OPERATIONS

The River Tugela, roughly speaking, formed the general outline of the Boer front; the heights on the left bank nearly throughout its length commanded those on the right bank, with the exceptions of Hlangwane and Monte Cristo to the eastward of Colenso, both of which were occupied by the enemy, and 6 miles to the westward Spearman's Kop and Mount Alice covering Potgieter's Drift, and somewhat to the eastward Swaartz Kop covering Schiet Drift.

Sir Redvers' plan was to leave one brigade, the 6th (Barton), at Chieveley, and with the remainder of his force to march to Potgieter's Drift, cross the Tugela there, and having effected a lodgement on the opposing heights, to march on Ladysmith (16 miles) over ground which was considered less unfavourable for an advance than that of the railway line through Colenso.

Unfortunately the line of march through Springfield on the Little Tugela was in full view of the enemy, who, even if they had been less mobile than they actually were, could with ease transfer their troops, being on an inner circle, to the threatened point far quicker than could the British on the outer circumference.

On 10th January the march began. Dundonald's Mounted Brigade reached Springfield early in the afternoon and the same night seized Spearman's Hill and Mount Alice. The 4th, 10th and 11th Brigades followed at 5.30 p.m., reached Pretorius Farm at midnight and Springfield on the evening of the next day, the 11th. On this day Dundonald had occupied Potgieter's Drift, while Hildyard, with the 2nd Brigade, demonstrated towards Porrit's Drift, near which the Little Tugela joins the Tugela.

On 12th January the 4th Brigade occupied Spearman's Hill and Mount Alice and on the same day Sir Redvers Buller issued the following order:—

'The Field Force is now advancing to the relief of Ladysmith where, surrounded by superior forces, our comrades have gallantly defended themselves for the past ten weeks. The G.O.C. knows that every one in the force feels, as he does, we must be successful. We shall be stoutly opposed by an unscrupulous enemy—let no man be deceived by them. If a white flag is displayed it means nothing, unless the force displaying it halt, throw down their arms, and throw up their hands at the same time. If they get a chance the enemy will try and mislead us by false words of command and false bugle sounds, and every one must guard against being deceived by such conduct. Above all, if any are ever surprised by a sudden volley at close quarters, let there be no hesitation, and do not turn from it: rush at it, that is the road to victory and safety; a retreat is fatal. The one thing the enemy cannot stand is our being at close quarters with them. We are fighting for the health and safety of our comrades, we are fighting in defence of our flag against an enemy who has forced war on us for the worst and lowest motives by treachery, conspiracy, and deceit. Let us bear ourselves as our cause deserves.'

Springfield was now made the advanced base. On 14th January Sir Redvers, having fully reconnoitred from the commanding position of Mount Alice the Boer position in his immediate front, came to the conclusion that Potgieter's Drift was unfavourably situated for the main crossing of the Tugela. A glance at the map will make this apparent. On either side of the Drift at a distance of about 4 miles were two commanding features in the Boer position: to the westward Spion Kop, and to the eastward Vaal Krantz jutting out like bastions towards the Tugela and joined by a low range of hills forming a curtain of which Brakfontein was the centre. Between these two bastions the Tugela makes two deep bends towards the curtain, making lateral communications extremely difficult. Sir Redvers further decided to send his main body to cross at Trichardt's Drift, 5 miles farther up the Tugela and to turn Spion Kop from the westward.

In accordance with this plan Sir Charles Warren, who was in charge of the main operations, set out from Springfield at 5 p.m. on the 16th. Dundonald, with the mounted troops, led the way, and was followed by the 11th, 2nd and 5th Infantry Brigades, while the 4th and 10th Infantry Brigades moved on Potgieter's and Skiet Drifts. The 2nd Battalion, forming part of the 10th Brigade, moved to Spearman's Hill overlooking Potgieter's Drift.

Dundonald reached Trichardt's Drift at 2 a.m. on the 17th, and at 9 a.m. commenced crossing, followed in the first instance by the 11th and 5th Brigades.

On the 18th Dundonald moved up the right bank of Venter's Spruit towards Acton Holmes and defeated a party of 300 Boers, accounting for about 50.

On the 19th Hildyard, with the 2nd Brigade, marched to Venter's Spruit in support of Dundonald, the 11th Brigade to the neighbourhood of Fairview Farm, while the 5th Brigade moved in support of the 11th Brigade.

Warren now decided to attack Tabanyama, a large feature to the westward of Spion Kop, and as a preliminary measure to capture two important underfeatures, Bastion Hill and Three Tree Hill.

On 20th January Hart, with five battalions, occupied the first line of Boer trenches on Three Tree Hill, but found their main position 1,000 yards farther back. Dundonald captured Bastion Hill but was heavily shelled. The 2nd Brigade from Venter's Spruit moved to his support.

On 21st January the cavalry were withdrawn from Bastion Hill and replaced by the 2nd Brigade. The attempt to turn the enemy's right flank had failed. Warren now asked for the support of the 10th Brigade.

Already on the 20th, 'G' and 'H' Companies of the Regiment, under Whatman and Bowker, had moved from Spearman's Hill to Trichardt's Drift to hold the pontoon bridge over the river at that place, and they were followed by the rest of the brigade on the 22nd, who had received orders to join the 5th Divison under Sir Charles Warren.

January 22nd was spent in a general bombardment of the enemy's position, but during the day Sir Charles Warren came to the vital decision to attack Spion Kop. The attack was to be entrusted to the 11th Brigade (Woodgate), preceded by Thorneycroft's Mounted Infantry.

During the 23rd the 2nd Battalion moved to the lower slopes of Three Tree Hill, where they constituted the escort to the Field Artillery batteries shelling the enemy's position. As soon as it was dark the attacking column moved from its position west of Fairview Farm towards the southern slope of Spion Kop, and at 9 p.m. commenced the ascent in thick and drizzly weather. The summit was gained at 4 a.m. with unexpected ease, the Boer picquets offering little resistance. This success was signalled to the army below by the assaulting troops giving three cheers, as the thick mist prevented all signalling, and what was worse made it impossible for Woodgate and Thorneycroft to make out the extent and lay of the ground they had occupied. However, they proceeded to entrench themselves as best they could on ground which was hard and rocky. At 7 a.m. the mist rose slightly and then it was discovered that though the British were on the top of the hill they were not sufficiently forward to fire down the slopes on the far side; moreover, about an hour later it was discovered that the main line of trench was enfiladed from a spur called Aloe Knoll about 300 yards to the eastward. Between 8 a.m. and 8.30 a.m., the mist having finally cleared away, the Boers opened a heavy rifle and artillery fire, when it was realized what a terrible death-trap the British position had become. Woodgate was mortally wounded. At about 9 a.m. Warren, as yet unaware of the position on Spion Kop, ordered Talbot Coke to reinforce Spion Kop with one battalion, the Imperial Light Infantry, and a little later on another battalion, the 2nd Middlesex. It was not till 9.50 a.m. that Warren heard of the desperate situation on the top of Spion Kop when shortly afterwards he sent Talbot Coke with the 2nd Dorsets to Spion Kop. Thus all the battalions of the 10th Brigade were now on their way to Spion Kop with the exception of the 2nd Battalion, who had replaced the Middlesex Regiment in the outpost line 1,000 yards to the west of Spion Kop.

For several hours the fight had raged in ding-dong fashion on the summit of Spion Kop, but gradually the Boers forced back the British to the main trench line. About 12 noon Thorneycroft was informed that he was appointed to command the troops on Spion Kop. The arrival of the 2nd Middlesex and Imperial Light Infantry put new heart into the defence and at 2.30 p.m. Thorneycroft was enabled to send a written report to Buller asking for infantry reinforcements, pointing out the necessity of bringing artillery fire on to the enemy's guns, and demanding that water should be sent up.

Coke was now close to the summit and between 3.15 and 3.45 p.m. had sent the Scottish Rifles detached from Lyttelton's Brigade to reinforce the British left which was rendered secure for the rest of the day, but it was the British right flank where the danger was most pressing; here the Middlesex Regiment and the Imperial Light Infantry endeavoured to hold the enemy at bay.

Meanwhile, away to the east Lyttelton's Brigade had created a diversion. The 60th Rifles had crossed the Tugela at Kaffir's Drift at 1 p.m., and advancing northwards made for the Twin Peaks to the west of Brakfontein and east of Spion Kop. The advance was skilfully carried out and at 5 p.m. the Twin Peaks were captured. An effective lodgment had been made in the Boer position which, if exploited, might have altered the entire result of the battle.

The fighting on Spion Kop continued till nightfall, when the firing gradually died away. Late in the evening Warren gave orders for 200 men of the 2nd Battalion 'I' and 'G' Companies to proceed to Spion Kop with picks and shovels. Captain Braithwaite was in charge, but on ascending the hill he met Thorneycroft's men coming down. Thorneycroft, who had borne the heat and burden of the day, without instructions, and unaware of the preparations being made to continue the fight on the morrow, had decided to abandon Spion Kop. The retirement had commenced. It was too late.

Captain Braithwaite, afterwards General Sir Walter Braithwaite, has given the following interesting account of this incident:—

'When the two hundred men of the 2nd Battalion were sent up The Hill under Whatman and myself in order to dig trenches for the defenders, Jack

Hanwell, a very well-known Gunner, a Captain I think, and a R.E. Officer, whose name I forget, myself and Whatman started off. Jack Hanwell was the guide, as he had been up during the day. When we had got about half-way up we met Thorneycroft and Winston Churchill coming down. They had nobody else with them. Thorneycroft stopped us and asked us what we were doing. I handed him a note from Sir Charles Warren which explained our mission. There was not much light and Thoneycroft could not read Sir Charles's rather small handwriting; he was also rather excited, so Winston Churchill—I did not know it was Winston Churchill at the time—said: "Here, let me read it", and took the note and read it to Thorneycroft. It was to the effect that Thorneycroft was to hang on and my party was to dig trenches for his exhausted troops.

'However, Thorneycroft said: "I have done all I can and I am not going back, and my troops have been ordered to retire"—or words to that effect. He told us that we were not wanted and we had better go down again as there were no troops left to dig trenches for.

'Jack Hanwell and I sat down for a minute on a rock and discussed this novel situation, and got so far as to debate whether we should go and dig trenches for ourselves and try and hold the place, but, in the end, decided to do as the other troops had been ordered to do, and retire. And that is the story of that.'

Quite independently of Thorneycroft's decision to retire, Buller had issued orders earlier in the evening for the withdrawal of the 60th Rifles from the Twin Peaks, where indeed they were entirely unsupported.

These retirements were carried out without interference from the enemy, who, if we may believe the evidence of their own side, were already making preparations to retire, and were only induced to hang on till the morning by the determined action of Louis Botha.

Thus ended a day, remarkable for the gallantry displayed on both sides, but fraught with disaster to the British troops engaged in the struggle for the possession of Spion Kop.

Out of 4,500 men engaged on that ill-fated hill 68 officers and 976 other ranks were casualties.

As soon as it was light the next morning the Boers reoccupied Spion Kop. An armistice for twelve hours was concluded for the burial of the dead and the removal of the wounded, during which the troops on both sides remained in their respective positions. At nightfall the transport commenced its retirement across Trichardt's Drift, and they were all across by daybreak on the 26th.

The retirement of the army across the Tugela commenced from the left of the line on the afternoon of the 26th and continued till daybreak on the 27th, the 2nd Battalion being one of the last units to cross the Tugela. By the afternoon the army had reached Hattinge Farm between Trichardt's and Potgieter's Drift eighteen days after its departure from Frere and Chieveley, having suffered 1,750 casualties.

The 10th Brigade and Imperial Light Hourse remained at Hattinge Farm till 1st February when they marched to Spearman's Hill and encamped.

VAAL KRANTZ

Buller's next attempt to relieve Ladysmith was to capture Vaal Krantz, already referred to, and for this purpose the 11th Brigade, now commanded by Wynne (with Braithwaite as his Brigade Major appointed to fill the vacancy created by Vertue of the Buffs killed at Spion Kop), supported by six field batteries, were to cross at Potgieter's Drift and advance towards Brakfontein as a demonstration while the 4th Brigade, supported by the 2nd Division, were preparing to attack Vaal Krantz. As soon as the advance of the 11th Brigade had made itself felt, the main attack was to be launched, supported by the guns, 14 in number, on Swartz Kop, which feature completely commanded Vaal Krantz. The 10th Brigade were to remain in the vicinity of Potgieter's Drift.

At 6 a.m. on the 5th February the 11th Brigade advanced from Maconochie Kopjes, which position covered the crossing at Potgieter's Drift, and by noon had occupied a line roughly east and west of Vaal Krantz Farm and $2\frac{1}{2}$ miles north of their starting-point without evoking much opposition from the enemy.

At 9.15 a.m. a general bombardment of Vaal Krantz began, 50 guns taking part. A pontoon bridge was thrown across the Tugela about half a mile north-east of Swartz Kop, which was completed about 11.15, soon after which the 4th Brigade (Lyttelton) crossed and about 2 p.m. captured Mungers Farm, and a little later after some sharp fighting the southern edge of Vaal Krantz. In the course of the afternoon nearly the whole of that hill was in the possession of the British, but its value was extremely doubtful—it was commanded by a higher spur half a mile farther north, and was enfiladed by the enemy on Green Hill one mile to the east, also from Doorn Kop, a commanding feature still farther off in that direction.

Meanwhile the 11th Brigade, having fulfilled its mission, had retired to Maconochie Kopjes, while the greater part of the field artillery which had accompanied it had been withdrawn to support the main attack.

During the night of the 5th February the 4th Brigade entrenched themselves on Vaal Krantz. By the morning of the 6th the Boers had concentrated some 5,000 men and 10 guns north and east of Vaal Krantz and in the afternoon delivered a determined attack on the British position which was repulsed.

On the night of the 6th the 2nd Brigade (Hildyard) relieved the 4th Brigade on Vaal Krantz.

On the 7th Buller, judging it impossible to advance farther from Vaal Krantz, decided to retreat across the Tugela, which was carried out that night without molestation from the enemy. The 2nd Battalion of the Regiment and the 2nd Dorsets of the 10th Brigade occupied the Maconochie Kopjes on the 8th February and covered the retirement of the 11th Brigade.

Thus ended the third attempt to relieve Ladysmith. It had cost the British 350 casualties.

The army then marched to Chieveley. The 10th Brigade encamping at Springfield bridge on the 10th, Pretoria Farm on the 11th and Chieveley on the 12th.

Meanwhile the situation in Ladysmith was becoming daily more critical. The troops were on reduced rations, the sick rate was increasing alarmingly, and it became necessary to slaughter a large number of horses not only for the purpose of providing meat for the troops, but also because there was not sufficient forage to feed them. Consequently White's artillery was rendered more or less immobile. Should the enemy decide to attack Ladysmith again the result might well have been a terrible disaster to the British arms.

On the other hand, Buller's troops were in fine fettle, their losses had been made good by timely reinforcements, and they were determined to avenge their previous defeat.

Moreover, in the western theatre of war Lord Roberts was now ready with overwhelming numbers to deal the enemy a blow which was destined to alter the whole course of the campaign. His instructions to Buller were to keep the Boers fully occupied, but not to risk a general action unless he felt himself strong enough to force his way through to Ladysmith.

Some reorganization of Buller's army now took place. Lyttelton replaced Cleny (sick) in command of the 2nd Division, the infantry brigades being the 2nd (Hildyard) and 4th (Norcott). The 5th Division consisted of the 10th Brigade (Coke), 11th Brigade (Wynne) and attached 6th Brigade (Barton), while the 5th Brigade (Hart) was not attached to any Division.

It has already been mentioned that the enemy occupied strong positions on the right bank of the Tugela to the east of Colenso, notably the commanding features of Hlangwane, Monte Cristo and Cingolo. As a preliminary to a new attempt to cross the Tugela and relieve Ladysmith, Buller determined to capture these positions.

THE FINAL ATTEMPT TO RELIEVE LADYSMITH

Already on 11th February Dundonald had reconnoitred and occupied Hussar Hill situated 7 miles north-east of Chieveley, and separated from Hlangwane, Green Hill, Monte Cristo and Cingolo by the valley of the Gomba Spruit, but he was subsequently withdrawn.

On the 14th the army advanced, the 2nd and 5th Divisions occupying Hussar Hill without loss, the latter division, including the 2nd Battalion, being on the left. The artillery opened fire on Hlangwane and Green Hill.

On the following day the artillery action was continued; the 2nd Division occupied Moord Kraal Farm and rising ground to the north-west and reconnoitred across the Gomba Spruit towards Cingolo.

On the 16th orders were issued to attack Cingolo and Green Hill, which was carried out on the 17th and 18th. Advancing from the right, the 2nd

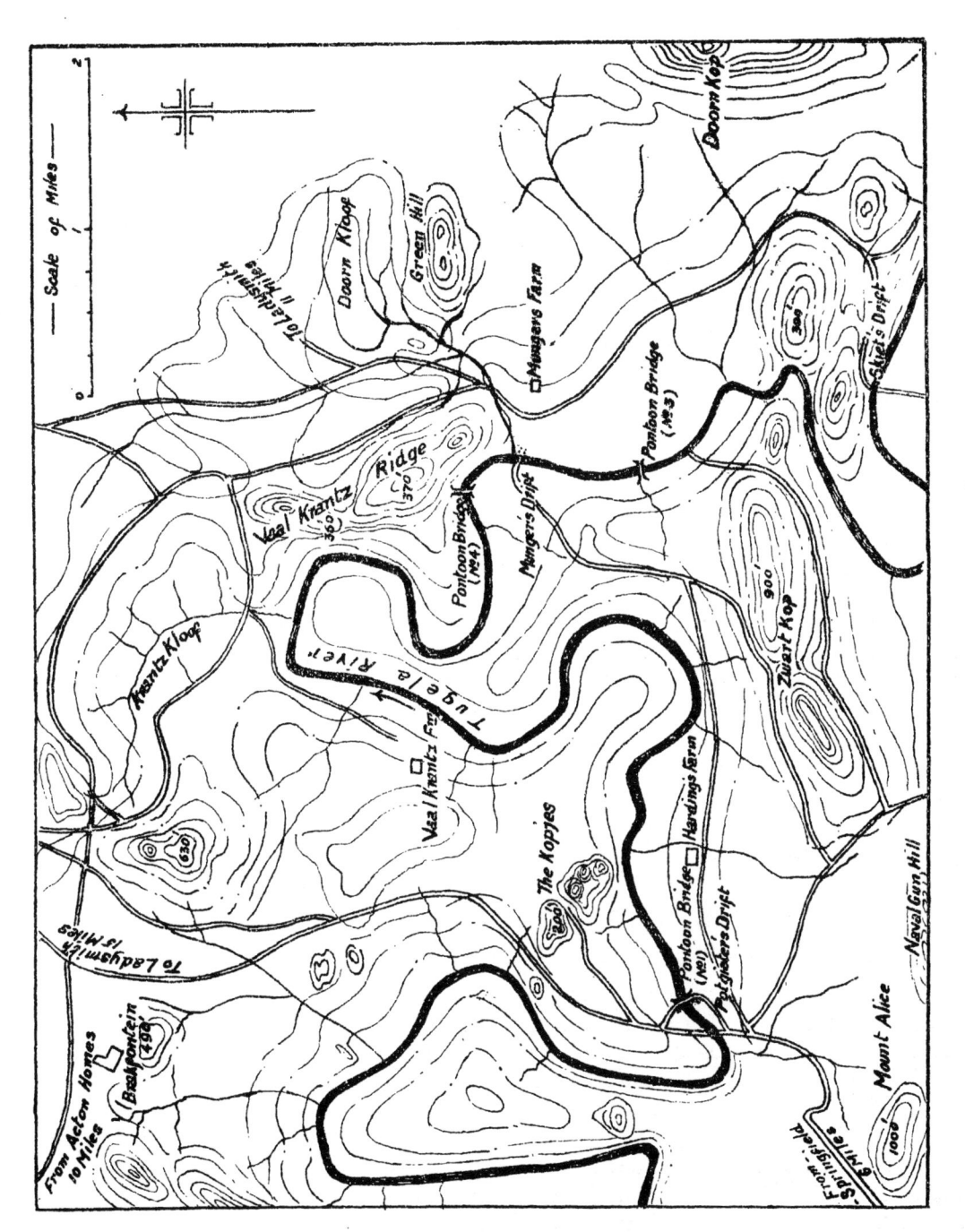

VAAL KRANTZ, FEBRUARY, 1900

Brigade captured Cingolo at 4 p.m. on the 17th, and on the 18th Monte Cristo, while on their left the 4th Brigade advanced to Bloy's Farm and the 6th Brigade captured Green Hill. The 10th and 11th Brigades were still on Hussar Hill and the 5th Brigade at Chieveley. The British casualties on the 17th and 18th numbered 242.

On the 19th Hlangwane was captured by the 6th Brigade, supported on the right by three battalions of the 4th Brigade; by the evening there were no Boers on the right bank of the Tugela.

On the 20th the 10th Brigade sent one battalion to Hlangwane, while the remainder occupied Green Hill with the exception of two companies, 'G' and 'C' of the 2nd Battalion under Captain Whatman and Lieutenant Keith-Falconer, who occupied Colenso. So far Buller's methodical advance had been attended with marked success.

While the news of the relief of Kimberly, the Boer evacuation of Magersfontein on the 16th, and the precarious situation of Cronje's army caused by the Battle of Paardeberg on the 18th, induced Sir Redvers Buller to believe that the enemy's opposition was crumbling, subsequent events belied these favourable forecasts.

At 6.30 a.m. on the 21st Coke received orders to concentrate his brigade behind Hlangwane in order to be ready to cross the pontoon bridge then being erected over the Tugela due west of Hlangwane mountain. At 7 a.m. the Brigade Commander informed Lieut.-Colonel Gallwey that the 2nd Battalion was to have the honour of leading the army across the pontoon bridge and that it would be the first to come into touch with the enemy. Soon afterwards the Battalion marched down to the Tugela, but owing to continuous shelling by the Boers the bridge was not ready until 1.30 p.m., when Talbot Coke issued the following orders:—

'Pontoon 1.30 p.m. *21st February 1900*

1. The enemy are thought to be in the Onderbrook Spruit parallel to the westerly Ladysmith road, and lower down towards the Tugela.

2. The 2nd Somerset L.I. will cross the bridge and advance in attack formation due west to the open ground marked "Tugela Drift" on the blue map. The 2nd Dorset will form second line, the 2nd Middlesex general reserve at the disposal of the Major-General Commanding.

3. On arrival at "Tugela Drift" the intention is to cover a position for our artillery to shell the enemy's position as supposed above.

4. The G.O.C. will follow the Somerset L.I.'

At 2 p.m. the 2nd Battalion crossed the pontoon bridge and deployed. 'F', 'B', 'H' and 'A' Companies formed the firing line (scouts under 2nd Lieutenant Allfrey), 'C', 'D', 'E' and 'G' Companies the reserve under Major Williams, 2nd in command. After crossing some low kopjes west of the railway at about 2.45 p.m., the Battalion advancing north-west towards Grobelaar's Hill came under heavy musketry and artillery fire especially from the right front, upon which Talbot Coke ordered two companies of the Regiment, 'D' and 'G', from the reserve, supported by four companies of the Dorsets, to capture two low kopjes 100 yards to the right front, which indeed they did, but the attempt to cross the Onderbrook Spruit south of Horseshoe Hills was unsuccessful. Meanwhile the main advance of the 2nd Battalion had come to a halt about one mile west and north-west of the low hills west of the railway, the two remaining companies of the reserve, 'C' and 'E', being now absorbed into the firing line. The Battalion now occupied a front of about one mile on a perfectly open plain devoid of all cover except anthills, and these of somewhat doubtful advantage. Some thousand yards in front of the line were the lower slopes of Grobelaar's Kloof, and there ensconced among the rocks and undulations of the ground were the enemy, unseen by our men, but pouring in a well-directed rifle fire against the widely extended British line.

To this fire our men replied, uncertain of the range, sometimes by volleys, at other times by independent fire, but always under control. No further advance was possible; the enemy had certainly been located, but they were not disposed to come out into the open, and indeed made no movement except on their extreme right. And so the day wore on till darkness put an end to the fighting.

About 3 p.m. the 11th Brigade had crossed the Tugela and taken up a position on the right of the reserves of the 10th Brigade, while on the left flank Thorneycroft's mounted infantry, after making various attempts to protect the left flank, retired about 6.30 p.m., when Gallwey had to throw back 'A' Company for the protection of the left flank of his line.

Still farther to the left rear the 5th Brigade (Hart) had occupied Colenso with two battalions, while one battalion had crossed the river.

At 7.15 p.m. Gallwey received orders to retire, which was skilfully carried out, commencing from the left, and covered by the reserve under Major Williams. By daybreak the next morning the Battalion had taken up a line of outposts on the low hills on the left of the 10th Brigade front. Part of 'A' Company on the extreme left did not come in till after daylight.

Colonel Gallwey in his account of this day's action concludes with these words:—

'The "roll call" added many names to those who had gone before in maintaining the name of the old 13th Light Infantry.

'I must put on record as Commanding Officer that nothing could exceed the discipline shown on the 21st February 1900. I have brought some names to the notice of the G.O.C., but they are only a few of the many who performed gallant duties on that occasion.

'General Talbot Coke was pleased to order a parade of the Battalion and personally thanked all for the manner in which his orders were carried out. He said he was aware of the fine reputation the Regiment bore, but he had never expected such steadiness and gallantry as the Somerset men exhibited on that occasion. Sir Charles Warren, he said, and other distinguished soldiers had witnessed the advance, which they declared was magnificent! He read

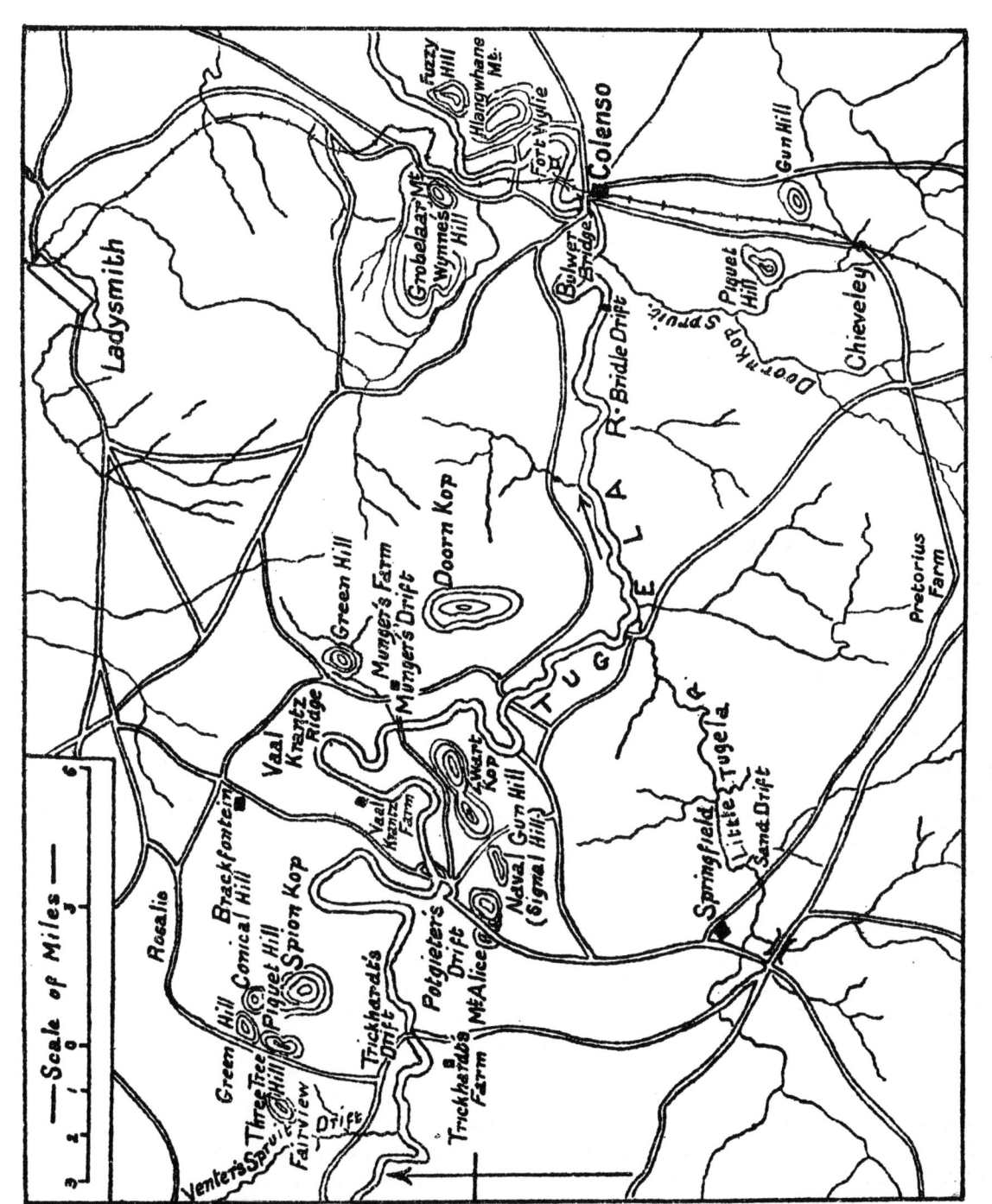

THE RELIEF OF LADYSMITH, 1900

out the names of officers, N.C.Os. and men who had been reported for distinguished conduct.

'On the 22nd we buried our comrades on the kopjes north of Colenso.'

The losses of the Battalion on this occasion were: killed, 4 officers, Captain Crealock, Lieutenant Keith-Falconer, 2nd Lieutenant Parr, and Captain Holt, R.A.M.C. attached; died of wounds, 5 N.C.Os. and men; wounded, 2 officers, Captain Elger and Lieutenant Prowse, and 72 N.C.Os. and men.

The casualties in the rest of the 10th Brigade amounted to 20.

During the night of the 21st–22nd, and the morning of the 22nd the 5th Division were reinforced by battalions of the 4th and 5th Brigades, while in addition 40 guns were available for operations on the left bank of the Tugela. Unfortunately the bridgehead occupied by the troops, $2\frac{1}{2}$ miles long and $1\frac{1}{2}$ to $\frac{1}{2}$ mile broad, was extremely congested for the number of troops. An advance across the open plain attempted on the previous day by the 2nd Battalion was clearly out of the question, so Buller decided to attack Wynne's Hill on the right front. At 2 p.m. the 11th Brigade advanced and succeeded in obtaining a lodgement on Wynne's Hill. Two battalions of the 4th Brigade (Norcott) were in support on the left rear. All that afternoon and indeed during part of the night desperate fighting took place for the possession of Wynne's Hill; the supports were absorbed in the firing line, while after dark two battalions of the 2nd Brigade (Hildyard) arrived as reinforcements. Notwithstanding this accession of strength, no further progress could be made.

On the morning of the 23rd most of the troops engaged on the 22nd were relieved by fresh troops, while the 5th Brigade (Hart), supported by two battalions of the 4th Brigade, were to attack Terrace Hill (Inniskilling Hill) still farther to the north-east. Late in the evening they succeeded in obtaining a lodgement on Terrace Hill.

On the night of the 23rd the position of the troops was as follows:—

Slopes of Terrace Hill: 5th Brigade and two battalions 4th Brigade.
Wynne's Hill: 2nd Brigade, two battalions 6th Brigade and two battalions 4th Brigade.
Behind Hill 244: 11th Brigade now commanded by Colonel Kitchener, who had temporarily replaced Wynne, wounded.
Colenso Kopjes: 10th Brigade.

On the morning of the 24th Hildyard, with the two remaining battalions, reinforced Hart. Further fighting took place, but there was no appreciable alteration in the positions of the opposing forces.

The British casualties in the last two days' fighting had amounted to 1,169 killed, wounded and missing.

There was a local armistice on the 25th for the purpose of removing the wounded. As the troops on the left bank of the Tugela had become very mixed up, Warren was given command of all troops east of the Langerwacht brook, and Lyttelton all those on the west of the Langerwacht brook with the exception of the 10th Brigade, who were still under Warren. At 8 p.m.

hostilities were resumed, when the enemy advanced to find out whether the British had retired, but they were easily repulsed.

Buller had now decided to widen the front of his attack and to include in his operations the capture of Pieters Hill to the east of the railway, and for this purpose it was necessary to shift the pontoon bridge from its position under Hlangwane to a new position lower down the Tugela just above Colenso Falls. During the 25th and the following night all the guns with the exception of one Battery were withdrawn to the right bank of the Tugela, and the next day 70 guns were in position downstream of the Falls. The 11th Brigade were also withdrawn to the right bank of the Tugela, where were also the 6th Brigade.

There was no serious fighting on the 26th, but orders for the attack on the 27th were issued. The 6th Brigade (Barton) were to attack Pieters Hill on the extreme right, next the 11th Brigade (Kitchener) were to make for Railway Hill, while the 4th Brigade (Norcott) were to attack Terrace Hill. The 5th Brigade (Hart) was in reserve near the pontoon bridge, while the remainder of the infantry occupied the positions previously held, the 10th Brigade (Coke), including the 2nd Battalion, occupying Colenso Kopjes.

The 27th February was the anniversary of the fight at Majuba Hill where the British had suffered defeat at the hands of the Boers nineteen years before, and in the course of the morning the news arrived of Cronje's surrender with 4,000 Boers at Paardeberg. Fitting omens indeed for the battle which was to decide the fate of the relief of Ladysmith. It may also be noted that in Warren's orders for the 27th the following telegram from the Secretary of State for War appears:—

'The whole country is watching with admiration your steady advance in the face of tremendous difficulties, the magnitude of which are fully understood here. The conduct of your troops is beyond all praise.'

At 8 a.m. a general bombardment of the enemy's position began. At 10.30 a.m. the 6th Brigade (Barton) crossed the pontoon bridge in its new position, followed a little later by the 11th Brigade (Kitchener). The attack was to be carried out in echelon from the right. The line of advance of the 6th Brigade was to creep along the sheltered left bank of the Tugela until opposite Pieters Hill, when turning northwards they deployed for the attack. After meeting with fierce opposition and varying fortune, Barton at 2 p.m. succeeded in establishing himself on the main ridge of Pieters Hill, though it was somewhat later that the most northerly feature of that hill fell into his hands.

Meanwhile Kitchener, following Barton's footsteps, until the donga which separates Pieters Hill from Kitchener's Hill was reached, turned northwards up the donga. At 1.30 p.m. he deployed and advanced and soon secured the railway cutting under Railway Hill and later on the eastern edge of that Hill also.

In accordance with the general plan, at 2.45 p.m. the 4th Brigade (Norcott) from its sheltered position near the pontoon bridge advanced north to the railway, and later on to the southern crest of Terrace Hill. About 5.30 p.m. the whole of Terrace Hill was captured, and about the same time Railway Hill was taken. A burst of cheering from the troops announced that the road to Ladysmith was open.

In the course of the day Lyttelton on the left had been holding the enemy in check. Musketry fire had at first been intermittent, but at 2 p.m. became very heavy and lasted for two hours.

The 10th Brigade had not moved from Colenso Kopjes with the exception of the Middlesex Regiment who had been sent to reinforce the 2nd Division.

The British casualties on the 27th amounted to 503, while from the 14th to the 27th they totalled 2,259.

At 6.30 a.m. on the 28th the Boers were reported to be in retreat both east and west of Ladysmith. The Mounted troops began to cross the Tugela at 7.30 a.m., Dundonald leading, followed an hour later by Burn Murdoch. In the course of the afternoon Dundonald, after some slight opposition, marched into Ladysmith with the Imperial Light Horse and Natal Carabineers.

On 1st March the army, with the exception of the 5th and 10th Brigades, marched to Nelthorpe, a station on the railway line about 7 miles from Ladysmith. The 5th Brigade were employed in making a road to connect the pontoon bridge with the Colenso–Pieters–Nelthorpe road, while the 10th Brigade were employed in protecting the rear and the Pioneers reconstructing the Colenso road bridge. A convoy of food was sent into Ladysmith and Buller himself rode in about 12 noon.

Thus ended the siege of Ladysmith which had lasted 118 days. The crisis of the campaign was past, actions entailing heavy casualties were not to recur, but the wearing down of the enemy's resistance was to engage the utmost efforts of the British Army for more than two years longer.

The 2nd Battalion, after the Battle of Pieters Hill, remained at Colenso till 7th March, when it received orders to join the 5th Brigade at Ladysmith on reorganization. On that day the Battalion, after parading to say farewell to General Talbot Coke and his Staff, marched to Pieters, and the following day to Observation Hill, passing through Ladysmith on the way and came under the orders of Major-General Fitzroy Hart, C.B.

On the 23rd March the 5th Brigade, including the 2nd Battalion, marched to Modder Spruit, and on the following day to Elandslaagte, where they pitched camp facing the battlefield. The 5th Brigade, together with the 6th Brigade (Barton), now formed part of the 10th Division under the command of General Hunter.

Early in April orders were received for the 10th Division to proceed to the Cape Colony. The 2nd Battalion marched to Modder Spruit on the 4th April, remained halted there till the 8th and then proceeded in three special trains to Durban, where they arrived on the following day. Here they were joined by the Volunteer Service Company of the Regiment under the command of Captain E. J. Whitting. The Battalion embarked on the ss. *Hawarden Castle* and proceeded to East London, arriving there on the 12th April.

S.L.I.—22

It is convenient to make mention here of the general situation in the western theatre of war in which the 2nd Battalion were about to take part.

Lord Roberts, with the main army advancing from Paardeberg, had captured Bloemfontein on the 13th March, and on the 15th Clements at Norvaals Pont and Gatacre at Bethulie had crossed the Orange River into the Orange Free State, when direct communication with Bloemfontein was established.

The Boers, however, recovering from the first effects of recent defeats, now began to give trouble. On 31st March Broadwood had suffered a somewhat serious reverse at Sannah's Post only 20 miles east of Bloemfontein and on the 4th April a British detachment near Reddersberg, 35 miles south of Bloemfontein, had been forced to surrender, while farther south-east on the 7th April Dalgety at Jammersberg Drift, on the Caledon River near Wepener, was surrounded by the enemy. The operations for the relief of Wepener will, however, form the subject-matter of the commencement of the next chapter.

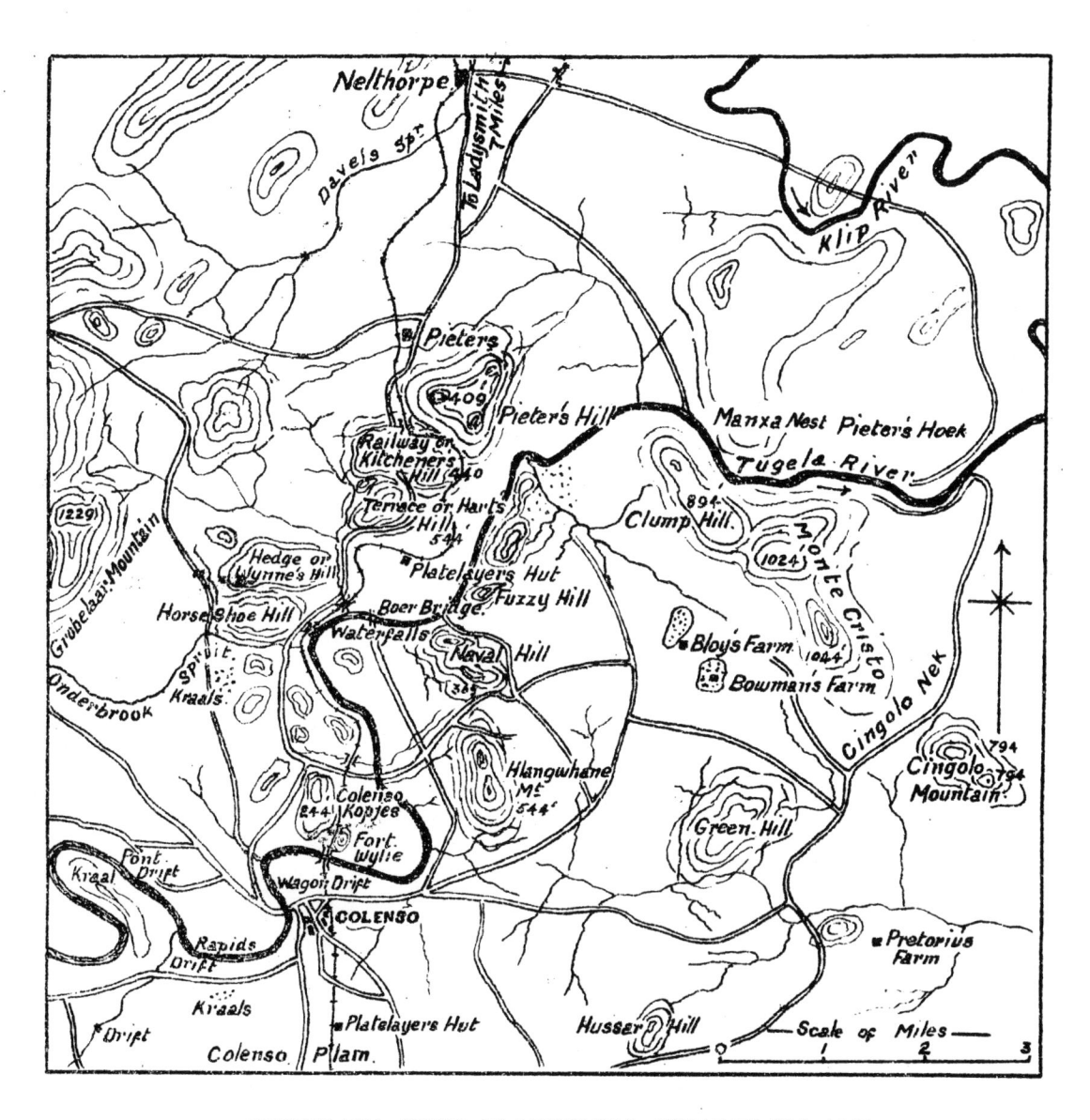

PIETER'S HILL (RELIEF OF LADYSMITH), FEBRUARY 27th, 1900

CHAPTER XXVI

THE SOUTH AFRICAN WAR (*continued*)

THE 2nd Battalion, after disembarkation at East London on 12th April 1900, where they met the 4th Battalion Somerset Light Infantry in garrison, proceeded by train to Aliwal North, arriving there on the 14th, and formed part of Major-General Hart's column. The other units of the column were the 1st Border Regiment, three companies of the 2nd Royal Irish Rifles, the 8th Battery R.F.A., at Aliwal North, and 20 miles northwards at Rouxville, Brabant's Horse and the Cape Mounted Rifles, 1,200 men with 2 guns.

On the evening of the 15th Hart marched to join Brabant at Rouxville, with whom he effected a junction on the 17th.

The object of the operations was the relief of Wepener, near which place Dalgety with some 1,800 mounted troops and 7 guns had been invested by 6,000 to 8,000 Boers under De Wet since 9th April.

Simultaneously with Hart's advance, Sir Leslie Rundle with the new 8th Division, one brigade 3rd Division and Brabason's Yeomanry, were to advance from Edenburg, on the main railway line to Bloemfontein, to Reddersburg and Dewetsdorp, while farther north large forces from the main army round Bloemfontein were directed to intercept the enemy's retreat northwards.

On the 19th and 20th Hart advanced without opposition, but on the 21st the enemy were reported to be in position at Bushman's Kop. The Infantry of the column, including 'B', 'C', 'E' and 'F' Companies under Captain E. H. Swayne, deployed for the attack, but the Boers, finding their retreat threatened by Brabant's Horse, withdrew after a slight skirmish.

On the 22nd the advance was continued and for the next few days the greater part of the mounted troops, together with three companies of each of the infantry regiments (those of the 2nd Battalion being under Captain E. G. Elger), marched well in advance, and were followed subsequently by the remainder of the force under Lieut.-Colonel E. J. Gallwey escorting the transport.

On the 24th April the advanced formation, as stated above, came into contact with the enemy posted on some kopjes 13 miles south of Wepener. Brabant's Horse and the artillery came into action and after some sharp fighting the enemy were driven from their position.

On 25th April the advance to Wepener was continued and the siege raised, but this fortunate outcome was largely the result of the pressure of other columns from the west and north-west. Already on the 20th Rundle had reached Dewetsdorp, where he was opposed by 2,500 Boers who had been detached from De Wet's force investing Dalgety some 25 miles distant. Farther to the north-west Pole-Carew and French were in contact with the enemy at Leeuwkop on the 23rd, and on the following day drove the enemy towards Thabanchu. The main body of the enemy under De Wet investing Dalgety now took alarm, and hastily retreating northwards after several engagements with British columns to the east of Bloemfontein, finally evaded them in the neighbourhood of Thabanchu on the 28th.

On the 27th April Hart's infantry, the 8th Battery R.F.A. with 400 of Brabant's Horse, marched to Caledon Bridge and crossed the river, and on the following day turning south-west they made for Smithfield, and entered that village on 1st May without opposition. The march was now continued and the railway reached at Bethulie on 3rd May, where the Battalion received six weeks' mails.

On the 5th May Gallwey, taking with him the 2nd Battalion, three companies of the Royal Irish Rifles and 2 guns of the 8th Battery R.F.A., was ordered to retrace his steps to Smithfield, which he reached on the 6th May and proceeded to place the village in a state of defence. The Battalion had marched 161 miles since leaving Aliwal North on 15th April.

The defence of Smithfield was easy as the high ground to the north and north-west provided good positions, but the chief difficulty was the absence of mounted men. This want was remedied by collecting some 30 ponies and mounting 30 men of the Regiment under Captain E. G. Elger. This detachment did useful work during the stay of the Battalion at Smithfield which lasted till the 22nd May, when they proceeded to Bethulie, reaching that place on the 25th.

On the 27th the Battalion entrained in two trains for Vryburg via Kimberley, which was reached on the 29th. New clothing for the whole Battalion was issued at Kimberley on the way.

It may here be useful to insert a short sketch of the progress of the campaign.

Lord Roberts with the main army commenced his march northwards into the Transvaal on 1st May and on the 27th crossed the Vaal at Vereeniging and on the 29th was at Germiston on the outskirts of Johannesburg.

Buller in Natal had occupied Newcastle on the 18th May.

Mahon had relieved Mafeking on 17th May. Hunter was operating in the Western Transvaal, Methuen in the Western Orange Free State, and Warren in Griqualand to the west of Kimberley.

On arrival at Vryburg, Colonel E. J. Gallwey took over command of the town and district and laid out the defences of the town which had a perimeter of 17,000 yards. The troops at his disposal were 'C', 'E', 'F' and the Volunteer Company of the Battalion, details of the 5th and 6th infantry Brigades, 4 guns of the 44th Brigade R.F.A., the Kimberley Light Horse and Royal Canadian Artillery. 'B' Company, under Captain H. F. Hardman and 2nd Lieutenant C. H. Little, proceeded up the railway line towards Mafeking, to Maribogo and Doornbult to act as guard to working parties repairing the line. Maribogo was then railhead.

On the 31st May 'A', 'D', 'G' and 'H' Companies, under Major R. B. Williams, together with the 1st Connaught Rangers, one troop Imperial Light Horse and the 22nd Company Field Hospital, marched to Devondale Siding, distance 15 miles, *en route* to join the column under the command of Major-General Hart.

The officers of this half-battalion the left wing were:—

'A' Company: Captain F. M. Peacock, Lieutenant H. G. Burges-Short, 2nd Lieutenant E. W. Worrall.
'D'   „   Major H. R. Lloyd and Lieutenant R. H. M. C. Miers.
'G'   „   Captain A. B. Whatman, 2nd Lieutenant G. B. Harrison and 2nd Lieutenant E. D. Bally.
'H'   „   Captain W. J. Bowker, D.S.O. and 2nd Lieutenant L. E. C. W. Wilmer.

Acting Adjutant and Quartermaster, Lieutenant P. M. Wardlaw.

The movements of this half-battalion will be referred to later.

HEADQUARTERS WING

In the main theatre of war Pretoria had been captured on 5th June and, in consequence of the Battle of Diamond Hill on 12th June, the main body of the Transvaal Boers had been driven farther eastward. Events in the Vryburg district do not call for much notice, but it is interesting to note that on 1st June Colonel Mahon and his Staff rode into Maribogo from Mafeking, and with them Major A. W. A. Pollock, a former officer of the Regiment who was acting as War Correspondent of *The Times*. On 4th June Lieutenant A. H. Yatman and half 'C' Company proceeded from Vryburg to Kraaipan, the new railhead, and on the 10th the first train ran through to Mafeking. Towards the end of the month Lieutenant C. H. Little and half 'B' Company moved from Doornbult to Maritsani, half-way between Kraaipan and Mafeking.

On the 26th August Lieutenant A. H. Yatman and half 'C' Company were engaged together with other troops (presumably at Kraaipan) against the Boers when four of the enemy were killed. In September Lieutenant Little and half 'B' Company rejoined Headquarters at Vryburg, while by the end of November Captain Hardman's and Lieutenant Yatman's detachments also returned to Vryburg. Amongst other posts in the Vryburg district was that of Schweizer Reneke, a small village 50 miles south-east of Vryburg, garrisoned by 80 men, mostly of the Royal Scots Fusiliers under Lieutenant A. P. Barry of the Regiment.

At the beginning of August reports from this post showed that the Boers were likely to give trouble, so Gallwey decided to reinforce the garrison by one company. Accordingly 'E' Company, under the command of Captain E. G. Elger, left Vryburg at 8 p.m. on 3rd August and arrived at Schweizer Reneke at 2 p.m. on 5th August. The main post was an isolated kopje outside the village. This was immediately strengthened and three additional works constructed on spurs of the hill to bring flanking fire on all approaches. On the

15th August the garrison was further reinforced by two 2·5 inch mountain guns and one maxim under Major Channier, Royal Artillery. Almost daily skirmishes with Boer patrols by the Mounted Infantry under Lieutenant A. P. Barry relieved the monotony of the little garrison. On 2nd September four Boers were killed, and again on 14th September Lieutenant Barry came across a party of 300 Boers, before whom he had to retire, having his horse shot under him and losing one man killed and one wounded, while three of the enemy were accounted for.

Meanwhile a new column was being organized at Vryburg; it consisted of three companies of the Battalion including the Volunteer Company, six companies Royal Munster Fusiliers, four companies 3rd Battalion King's Own Scottish Borderers, two howitzers 37th Battery R.F.A., four 12-pounders Royal Canadian Artillery and some 900 mounted troops from Paget's Horse, Cape Police, Cape Mounted Rifles, Yeomanry, Munster M.I. and Dennison's Scouts, the whole under the command of Major-General Settle. Sir Charles Parsons commanded the mounted troops and Lieut.-Colonel E. J. Gallwey the infantry. The following officers of the Battalion were present: Captain R. Brocklehurst, commanding, Captain and Adjutant E. J. Swayne, Lieutenant C. B. Prowse, 2nd Lieutenants C. H. Little, W. H. Freestun and A. R. Sale-Hill and Lieutenant and Quartermaster P. Moran. In addition there were Lieutenants J. R. Dawson and D. S. Watson of the Volunteer Company and Captain Ryder, K.O.Y.L.I. attached.

The column left Vryburg on the 19th September and arrived at Schweizer Reneke on the 23rd, having met with no opposition. Five days were spent at Schweizer Reneke, during which time the mounted troops scoured the country.

LEFT WING

It will be recalled that this half-battalion, accompanied by other units, under the command of Colonel Brooke, 1st Connaught Rangers, reached Devondale Siding on 31st May *en route* to join Major-General Hart's column in the Western Transvaal.

Brooke's column continuing their march on 1st June proceeded in successive stages to Doornbult Siding, Maribogo Pan, Geysdorp, Barber's Pan, Verdienne, Birges Vallei, Kalkespruit, to Lichtenburg, a distance of 104 miles, where on 8th June it joined the 10th Division under Lieut.-General Sir A. Hunter, of which the 5th (Hart's) Brigade formed a part.

On 10th June Hart, with the 5th Brigade, the 28th Battery R.F.A., one section Pom-poms, Balloon Section R.E., the 5th Divisional Ammunition Column, the Manchester troop Imperial Yeomanry, the 22nd Company Field Hospital and the 8th Bearer Company, set out eastwards, marching via Puttfontien, Kopjesfontein, Kraalfontein, Frederickstadt, Welverdienst, Bank Station and Randfontein to Krugersdorp, a distance of 128 miles, where they arrived on 19th June.

On 20th June the Union Jack was hoisted over the Public Buildings at Krugersdorp. 'H' Company, under Captain W. J. Bowker, D.S.O., attended the ceremony which was conducted by Lieut.-General Sir A. Hunter. On the 22nd the column resumed its march and on the 23rd Johannesburg was reached and on the 25th Heidelberg. During the above movements little or no opposition was encountered by Hunter and Hart, the Eastern Transvaal had become the main theatre of war, while the Free Staters were giving trouble on the lines of communication in the north-eastern portion of the Orange Free State.

At the end of June and beginning of July, the main army after the Battle of Diamond Hill was facing eastwards astride the railway line from Pretoria to Lourenço Marques, Buller was at Standerton, Methuen at Lindley, Baden-Powell at Rustenburg and Hunter at Frankfort in the north-eastern Orange Free State, the latter having left Hart with Williams's half-battalion and other troops at Heidelberg.

The disposition of the troops at and near Heidelberg was as follows: Hart held the railway from Zuikerbosch to Rietvlei: south-east of Zuikerbosch were the 2nd Division (Clery), and north-west of Rietvlei the 19th Bde. (Smith-Dorrien). On 28th June 'G' Company, under Captain A. B. Whatman, formed the garrison of a hill (afterwards known as Somerset Hill) 2 miles west of the town, the post on the crest being called Fort Whatman, and on 1st July 'D' Company, under Major H. R. Lloyd, and one troop of Marshall's Horse, were sent to garrison the Nigel Mines near Springs.

The real interest of the campaign at this time centres in the attempts to hem in the Free State Boers against the Basutoland border. The operations were under the control of Sir A. Hunter, and he had under him several columns based chiefly on the Bloemfontein–Vereeniging railway. The importance of the operations lay in the possibility of effecting a great coup by which it was hoped to capture not only the main forces of the Free State then in the field but also the Free State Government with its president Steyn. Hunter was at Bethlehem on 9th July and the other columns were gradually closing in on the Brandwater basin. All apparently appeared to be going well when on the 15th De Wet, with Steyn and the Free State Government, broke through the cordon and after various vicissitudes, passing by the rear of Hunter's columns, crossed the railway line south of Vereeniging at Honnings' Spruit on 21st July pursued by Broadwood.

On the same day the Boers attacked a post at Kraal Station, 8 miles east of Heidelberg, held by a detachment of the Royal Dublin Fusiliers under Major English. As soon as news of their attack reached Heidelberg, Hart set out with a detachment of the Regiment, 2 guns of the 28th Field Battery, Marshall's Horse, and some Yeomen to relieve the garrison. The enemy retired as soon as the guns opened fire and Hart's column returned to Heidelberg the same day.

THE FIRST DE WET HUNT

Troops were now gathering round for what has been termed the first De Wet Hunt. On the 27th June the detachment from the Nigel Mines and the garrison on Somerset Hill were withdrawn to Heidelberg, and on the following day Hart with the 2nd Battalion Royal Dublin Fusiliers, the wing of the Regiment, the 71st Company Imperial Yeomanry, 200 of Marshall's Horse commanded by Captain R. E. Corbett, late of the Regiment, the 28th Battery R.F.A. and 'G' Section Vicker's Maxims marched to Klip River Station, 21 miles, and entrained for Kopjes Station south of Vereeniging, where they arrived on the 30th July. On the same day Prinsloo, with 4,000 Boers, surrendered to Hunter in the Brandwater basin, while Olivier, who had broken out at the same time as De Wet, had been captured near Ventersdorp on the 27th.

On 31st July Hart marched to Kopje Allein on the Rhenoster Spruit, where he joined hands with the columns of Broadwood, Ridley and Little. On 3rd August the Colonial Division from Rundle's force arrived on the Rhenoster River. On 4th August Kitchener left Pretoria to take charge of the combined operations.

On this day De Wet was occupying the hills near Reitzburg. Methuen was watching the passages of the Vaal near Scandinavia Drift while Smith-Dorrien was in support at Frederickstadt. To the north-east of De Wet was Ridley, having under his command the Mounted Infantry of Legge, Dawson, and De Lisle, together with Roberts' and Kitchener's Horse. On the east and south were the 2nd Cavalry Brigade (Broadwood) and the 3rd Cavalry Brigade (Little), on their left Hart, Knox, and still farther to the west the Colonial Division (Dalgety). From these dispositions it seemed certain that De Wet would be driven north across the border into the Transvaal in which country it was considered that the Free Staters would be unwilling to follow him.

On 5th August Methuen learnt that De Wet was preparing to cross the Vaal at Rhenosterpoort; he accordingly marched towards Venterskroon. The Potchefstroom garrison were ordered to Roodekraal. Before daybreak on 6th August De Wet crossed the Vaal at Schoemann's Drift and divided his forces.

On 7th August Methuen attacked De Wet at Tygerfontein, and Kitchener on hearing the firing sent Broadwood and Little to De Wet's Drift, to be followed by Hart and Knox; the Colonial Division were ordered to Scandinavia Drift. Ridley's M.I. were ordered to proceed to Lindeque. In accordance with these orders Hart marched to Reitzburg.

On 8th August Methuen remained halted, which gave De Wet a start. Hart moved north-east of Vredefort. On the 9th Methuen marched to Leeuwfontein and attacked De Wet's rear-guard, while the 2nd and 3rd Cavalry Brigades reached Lindeque, which caused De Wet to move north.

Hart moved to Parys while Smith-Dorrien was ordered to move from Frederickstadt to Welverdiend and Bank Station. Meanwhile, farther north Ian Hamilton was at Grootplatz, 5 miles south-west of Commando Nek, watching the passes of the Magaliesberg.

On 10th August Methuen pushed on to Taaubosch Spruit, having got into touch with De Wet's rear-guard at Buffelsdoorn. Broadwood reached Bank Station, the Colonial Division, Frederickstadt, while Hart was 14 miles north of Lindeque Drift. That night the enemy crossed the railway between Welverdiend and Bank Stations.

On 11th August Methuen reached Frederickstadt, while Broadwood, Little and Ridley reached Welverdiend, where they met Smith-Dorrien with the 19th Brigade. Hart's troops were one day's march in rear. De Wet was supposed to be at Cyferbult.

On 12th August Methuen started with his mounted troops at 3 a.m., followed later by his infantry. When 6 miles south of Cyferbult he closed with the Boer rear-guard, capturing 16 wagons and releasing 60 British prisoners of war. Broadwood was 8 miles to the east, while Smith-Dorrien and Hart's Brigade were coming up from Welverdiend.

On 13th August Methuen was at Rietfontein, south of Tafel Kop, at noon, and made for the Selous River well to the west. Hart's Brigade marched to Cyferghat Mine and crossed the Mooi River. De Wet, however, skilfully eluded Ian Hamilton and crossed the Magaliesberg into comparative safety. Hart's Brigade, after another week of marching and counter-marching, finally reached Krugersdorp on 22nd August and halted for a week. Williams's half-battalion had marched 250 miles since leaving Kopjes Station on 31st July.

During this period Roberts, advancing along the railway to Komati Poort, had effected a junction with Buller advancing from the Natal railway in the neighbourhood of Belfast and on the 27th August had defeated the Boers at Bergendal, soon after which President Kruger fled to Lourenço Marques in Portuguese territory. On 1st September Lord Roberts proclaimed the annexation of the Transvaal, but the war was by no means at an end.

Although the Boer Governments had no permanent location, they still continued to exist; they moved about the country now with one commando and now with another. The commandos, mostly split up, alternating between despair caused by defeats and short-lived optimism caused by successful raids on the railways and British columns and posts, vanished into thin air when it suited their purpose, only to reappear in small concentrations when some unusually favourable opportunity occurred for the exercise of those guerrilla tactics which have made them famous in the world.

On the other hand, the British Army in occupation of all the chief towns and railways were only masters of the ground which they occupied: the theatre of operations was so vast and the lines of communication so long that the troops available for active operations were extremely limited. Moreover, Cape Colony was seething with rebellion. These circumstances may help to explain the long-drawn-out hostilities which ensued before the war was finally concluded.

Hart's column constituted as follows: 12th Battalion Imperial Yeomanry, Marshall's Horse, one 4·7-inch Naval gun, the 28th Battery R.F.A., one Vickers maxim, half-battalion of the Regiment, the 2nd Battalion South Wales Borderers, and the 2nd Battalion Royal Dublin Fusiliers left Krugersdorp on 30th August with orders to clear the country. On moving south-east towards the Johannesburg Waterworks whose garrison had been attacked, the enemy were discovered holding a high rocky ridge obstructing the advance of the mounted troops; this entailed the deployment of a detachment of the South Wales Borderers and the coming into action of the guns, upon which the enemy retired. The Yeomanry had 9 men wounded. The column reached Roodepoort on the 31st, Modderfontein on 1st September, Orange Grove on 2nd September, Nieupoort on 3rd September, near which place on the 4th the Yeomanry became involved with the enemy, when the half-battalion of the Regiment and guns were called upon to relieve them. On the following day the column moved towards Welverdiend and on the way in a small skirmish four Boers were killed by gunfire, including Commandant Daniel Thereon, a well-known leader of scouts.

On the 6th the column reached Welverdiend and Kleerskraal on the 7th. Orders were now received to make a surprise march on Potchefstroom. Starting at 6 p.m. on the 9th the column marched all night, the advanced parties arriving at 3.30 a.m., when all exits to the town were closed. As day broke some Boers ran the gauntlet and escaped, others were killed or wounded, while 78 prisoners were taken. On the night of the 10th Lieutenant T. B. Maddocks was shot by the enemy while going round his posts. He was subsequently buried in the civil cemetery at Potchefstroom.

On 12th September Hart, hoping to surprise a Boer commando in the neighbourhood, and having left a garrison including three companies of the Regiment in Potchefstroom, moved in two columns, the one towards Ventersdorp, which he commanded, and the other towards Frederickstadt, under Lieut.-Colonel Hicks. Although touch with the enemy resulted, nothing worthy of record occurred. On the 13th he reached Frederickstadt, where on the 16th he was joined by the garrison of Potchefstroom with all prisoners and refugees, it having been decided to evacuate the latter town.

On the 17th a convoy with the prisoners and refugees was sent to Welverdiend, while Hart advanced to Witpoortje and thence on the 20th to Bulskop, and on the 25th he was back again at Potchefstroom; finally after further marches he returned to Krugersdorp on 30th September, having marched 310 miles since 30th August, having collected large quantities of cattle, sheep and grain besides clearing the country of its inhabitants.

HEADQUARTERS WING

Major-General Settle's column, after spending five days at Schweizer Reneke, left that place with its little garrison on the 27th September and made for Christiana, at the extreme south-west corner of the Transvaal, where it arrived on the 30th and remained there till October 12th.

On 13th October Settle, who had been ordered to escort a convoy to Sir A. Hunter, then in the Bothaville district, marched up the valley of the Vaal. He reached Bloemhof on the 14th and, after crossing the Vaal there, made for Hoopstadt, where he arrived on the 17th. On the 19th he crossed the Vet River and made for Bothaville. On the 20th Settle's main body reached Elizabeth Rust, but the convoy, owing to heavy sandy roads, was only able to get as far as Wegdraai. On that night both camps were attacked by the Boers, the 3rd Munster Fusiliers escorting the convoy having 15 casualties. The enemy, however, were repulsed and the convoy rejoined the main body the next day

On the 22nd Settle, with the whole column, marched to Zandspruit, where he met the 3rd Cavalry Brigade and, having handed over supplies, commenced his return march at 2 p.m. on the 23rd, the headquarter wing of the Regiment forming the escort and rear-guard to the convoy. About 5 p.m. heavy firing broke out on the right and right rear of the convoy, the Cape Police and Cape Mounted Rifles under Major Berrange being heavily engaged. The infantry, however, showed a bold front and no loss to the convoy was incurred. On the other hand, the mounted troops had 36 casualties and lost 2 maxim guns. The convoy reached Hoopstadt safely at 11 p.m. that night. From Hoopstadt Settle marched south to Boshof, which he reached on the 31st without incident. Settle's column then proceeded to Kimberley, the infantry marching to Windsorton Road Station and thence by rail.

After a few days' halt at Kimberley, Settle's infantry marched to Modder River Station on the 7th, where they were joined by the remainder of the column. On the 8th Settle marched to Jacobsdaal, leaving a garrison there, and the following day towards Koffyfontein. On reaching Koffyfontein a garrison was left there and the force returned to Modder River on the 13th November.

On the 15th November Settle's column entrained for Graspan, a few stations down the line, and subsequently marched into the Orange Free State collecting cattle and refugees. On the 22nd they were at Rawah Springs and on the 26th at Volfein Kraal. On the 27th, on approaching Luckoff they were opposed by 150 Boers under Hertzog posted on a ridge commanding the approaches to the village. The 6th Lancashire Fusiliers, who had previously relieved the 3rd Munster Fusiliers, drove the enemy from their position. The enemy lost 3 killed and some wounded.

After remaining one day at Luckoff the march was resumed on the 29th and the railway at Jaggersfontein Station reached on 3rd December, where the captures of the trek were handed over, amounting to some 600 horses, 2,000 cattle and 15,000 sheep. The same evening the column started for Edenburg, and after trying marches with incessant rain, the oxen dying in large numbers, it reached Edenburg on 5th December. Here General Settle handed over the command of the column to Colonel Sir C. Parsons.

It is necessary now to revert to the doings of 'E' Company under Captain E. G. Elger at Schweizer Reneke. No sooner had Settle's column disappeared on 27th September than the Boers began to cluster round again, the garrison being summoned to surrender by Commandant Van Zyl on the 30th, and on 2nd October all communication with the outside world was cut, daily sniping on the part of the mounted troops under Lieutenant A. P. Barry with the enemy, and occasional captures of cattle by one side or the other varying the monotony of the garrison. On 28th October the garrison was again summoned to surrender, but on the 30th Lieutenant Barry, with 20 mounted men, attacked a party of Boers and killed nine of them with the loss of only three horses.

The garrison was now on very short commons, provisions were getting scarce and there was no tobacco. These conditions continued till 24th November, when gun-fire was heard in the direction of Vryburg, and on the following day Colonel Milne and a convoy arrived reporting a sharp engagement the day before.

On November 27th 'E' Company left Schweizer Reneke with the returning convoy for Vryburg, being relieved by two companies of the King's Own Scottish Borderers militia. Lieutenant A. P. Barry and his mounted infantry, however, remained in Schweizer Reneke.

On the 29th the convoy was attacked by a strong force of 700 Boers. 'E' Company was in the rear-guard, and during the fight, which lasted five hours, acquitted themselves right well, and eventually repulsed the Boers. Among the casualties of the force Captain E. G. Elger was wounded and one man of the Regiment was killed. On the 30th the convoy reached Vryburg, when Captain Elger and 'E' Company were congratulated on their spirited action of the previous day.

LEFT WING

Williams's half-battalion was back again in Krugersdorp on 30th September. For the next four weeks it formed part of the garrison of that town, but on the 27th October it received orders to join General Barton's column at Frederickstadt. This General had inflicted a sharp defeat on Christian de Wet only two days previously. On the 28th the half-battalion marched to Potchefstroom, a distance of 14 miles, and remained there till 3rd November, when they returned to Frederickstadt.

On 10th November Barton's column moved to Potchefstroom where they remained till the 16th, and then proceeded with a convoy for General Douglas at Klerksdorp. This operation they repeated on more than one occasion before the end of the month. Barton was now replaced by Colonel Babington in command at Potchefstroom.

Whilst Williams's half-battalion was there employed on convoy work, 'D' and 'H' Companies with 70 men of the New Zealand Mounted Infantry and one Elswick gun under Major Lloyd were dispatched under the orders of General Douglas on 25th November to Coal Mine Drift on the Vaal River about 10 miles south of Klerksdorp. Here they constructed a fortified post to command the Drift and to deny its use to the enemy. Beyond daily skirmishes with the enemy little of interest occurred, and on 12th December the detachment returned to Klerksdorp, where Williams's half-battalion was again reunited.

Towards the end of December Colonel Kekewich relieved General Douglas in command of his column, which was now composed as follows: Mounted troops, 550 of the 2nd Brigade Rhodesian Field Force, four companies of the Regiment, 2 guns 88th Battery R.F.A., 1 howitzer and 2 pom-poms.

Kekewich's column, acting in co-operation with those of Gordon, Babington and Pulteney, were to make a wide sweeping movement northwards against De la Rey and Beyers. Kekewich reached Ventersdorp on the 28th, where an advanced base was formed. On 2nd January 1901 the advance was resumed and on 3rd January Babington engaged De la Rey at Cyferfontein, where the Imperial Light Horse under Woolls-Sampson were roughly handled. The

Boers, under pressure from the combined columns, now broke up, De la Rey retreating north-west, while Beyers turned eastwards and eventually crossed the railway between Johannesburg and Pretoria on 12th January. On 9th January Kekewich was back again at Ventersdorp.

Williams's half-battalion remained at Ventersdorp till the 20th January, and afterwards were employed on convoy work. On 31st January they were at Krugersdorp and remained in the vicinity till 15th February, when they entrained for Potchefstroom where they formed part of the garrison. On 11th March Williams's headquarters, with 'A' and 'H' Companies, marched 10 miles south to Rooikraal, while 'D' and 'G' Companies, under Major H. R. Lloyd, joined General Benson's force.

On the 16th Benson's column started south for the Vaal River, reaching Reitpoort on the 18th, where during the next two days the column was engaged with the enemy, a Boer convoy being captured on the 21st. The column then turned northwards, and after taking over supplies from Bank Station on the 23rd, made a further circuit in the district and finally reached Krugersdorp on 4th April after capturing large quantities of stock, and having marched 153 miles. Williams's headquarters, with 'A' and 'H' Companies, arrived at Krugersdorp from Rooikraal on 10th April, when the wing took over the South Ridge Defences of the town. Williams's half-battalion remained at Krugersdorp till 1st May, when they entrained for Springs east of Johannesburg and rejoined the headquarters of the Battalion whose doings must now be recorded.

HEADQUARTERS WING

The headquarter wing reached Edenburg on 5th December 1900, and it so happened that it arrived in time to take part in the second De Wet hunt. De Wet, with 1,500 men and one Krupp gun, had left the Doornberg west of Senekal on 13th November and moved southwards. On the 16th he broke through the line of fortified posts between Thabanchu and Ladybrand, and then proceeded in more leisurely fashion towards Dewetsdorp, then garrisoned by British forces. This position De Wet invested on the 19th and captured on the 21st. Several columns were now hurried down by rail from the north and by the 24th, Pilcher, Herbert, and Barker, under General Knox, were in touch with the enemy in the neighbourhood of Helvetia. On the 5th December De Wet reached the Orange River which was in flood, and impassable, so turning northwards he made for the Caledon River, attempted to cross at Commissie Drift, but being baffled by a small British post, he turned up-stream, crossed the Caledon higher up, and reached Helvetia on the 10th, while Knox in pursuit arrived before Helvetia on the 11th.

Already on the 9th Sir C. Parsons, with his column including the headquarter wing of the Regiment, left Edenburg and reached Reddersburg on the 10th, just in time on the 11th to head De Wet retreating from Helvetia. De Wet then turned east and north, closely pursued by Knox, and finally broke through the Thabanchu-Ladybrand line of posts on the 14th.

Meanwhile, Sir C. Parsons had moved from Reddersburg to Dewetsdorp which he reached on the 14th, halted there till the 16th, and then marched to Thabanchu, where the column was broken up and the mounted troops sent to the Cape Colony.

On the 18th the headquarter wing marched to Sannah's Post in relief of the 2nd Gloucester Regiment. Here they proceeded to strengthen the defences, and a detachment of Mounted Infantry, 30 strong, was formed under the command of Lieutenant C. B. Prowse.

Very little occurred during December 1900 and early part of January 1901 to disturb the monotony of the garrison of Sannah's Post, but on the 25th Christian de Wet had again concentrated over 2,000 men in the Doornberg west of Senekal. With a view to invading the Colony and helping Kritzinger and Herzog, he set off south on the 27th, reached Tabaksberg on the 28th, where he was engaged by Knox on the 29th, and then made for the Thabanchu-Ladybrand line of posts which he crossed successfully at Israel's Poort on the 30th, on the same date that Bruce Hamilton, sent to forestall him, reached Sannah's Post from the railway at Bloemfontein. On the 30th and 31st small skirmishes took place between the mounted troops of the Sannah's Post garrison and the enemy, when one Boer was captured and three wounded.

De Wet and his pursuers now disappeared from the neighbourhood of Sannah's Post, when the usual routine of its garrison was resumed, only relieved by a raid on 14th February made by a party of Mounted Infantry, including Driscoll's Scouts, Bushmen and 5th Fusiliers M.I., under Lieutenant Prowse, on the Tabaksberg, when five horses were captured and a large quantity of forage destroyed.

On the 4th April the Volunteer Company (formed of men of the 4th and 5th Battalions) proceeded to Bloemfontein *en route* for England.

On the 6th April the headquarter wing of the Regiment being relieved by the 6th (Militia) Battalion Royal Warwick Regiment, proceeded from Sannah's Post to Bloemfontein and entrained there on the 9th for Springs, where they arrived on the 11th, and occupied the village and surrounding mines. Here, as previously narrated, 'A', 'D', 'G' and 'H' Companies, under Major H. R. Lloyd, rejoined the headquarters of the Battalion on 1st May.

The Battalion was now again concentrated with the exception of 'B', half-'C' and 'E' Companies.

In November 1900 'B' and half 'C' Company had been occupying posts on the railway in the neighbourhood of Vryburg, while 'E' Company had returned from Schweizer Reneke to Vryburg on the 30th.

On 2nd December, the posts on the railway having been withdrawn, the whole detachment, comprising 250 men under the command of Captain Hardman, proceeded by train to Kimberley.

Whilst in the Kimberley area, the detachment was again broken up, parties were found for the crew of the armoured train, and other duties, but the main body consisting of 100 other ranks under Captain Hardman formed part of the Kimberley column under Major Paris.

This column was employed in escorting convoys to the neighbouring garrisons. On the 13th December the column proceeded to Boshof, which they reached after some opposition on the 15th, and on the 16th they were back again in Kimberley.

On the 20th they marched to Modder River Station, where they halted till the 23rd, when they started for Koffyfontein, reaching that village on the 26th, and returned to Modder River on the 29th.

On 3rd January 1901 the column entrained at Modder River and moved to Fourteen Streams north of Kimberley, crossing the Vaal River. On the 10th the column re-crossed the Vaal River to Warrenton, and then marched back to Kimberley, arriving there on the 13th.

On the 16th the column again proceeded to Boshof, but were back again at Kimberley on the 21st.

Captain Hardman's party of 100 men were now relieved by a similar party under Lieutenant Yatman, but no records exist of their movements.

In February Captain Barry returned from Schweizer Reneke to Kimberley and assumed command of the Mounted Infantry there. At the end of that month 2nd Lieutenant Leveson-Gower was in command of an armoured train working under Captain Nanton, R.E. It was employed in patrolling the line at night between Belmont and Magersfontein with the object of preventing De Wet's cammandos, who had crossed the line at Houtkraal, from breaking back in small parties. On the night of the 27th, in conjunction with another armoured train, he opened fire from Belmont Station on a party of the enemy endeavouring to cross the line. After some firing the Boers retired.

The detachment of the Regiment at Kimberley continued to be employed as stated above until 20th May, when they proceeded by train to Springs in the Transvaal, where they arrived on the 26th and relieved a detachment of the King's Own Yorkshire Light Infantry. Captain H. F. Hardman now had under his command 150 other ranks and the following officers: Captain A. P. Barry, Lieutenant A. H. Yatman, 2nd Lieutenant Leveson-Gower and 2nd Lieutenant C. C. Wigram.

On 4th May the Battalion, less the Kimberley detachment, strength 13 officers and 474 other ranks, left Springs with the 2nd Cavalry Brigade under Colonel E. C. Knox and marched to Heidelberg. On the following days, the 5th and 6th, the column marched to the junction of the Vaal and Waterval Rivers where an enemy convoy of 80 wagons carrying many Boer families, 15 prisoners and several thousand head of cattle were captured. On the 11th the column was back again on the railway at Greylingstadt.

On the 12th, a Boer lager having been located at Platkop, a night raid was made by the 10th Hussars, 12th Lancers and 'D' and 'H' Companies of the Regiment, with the result that 35 wagons, 20 prisoners and a number of Boer families were captured. The congratulations of the G.O.C.-in-C. were received on the success of the operation.

At this time a number of British columns were ordered to converge on the high veldt between Bethel and Ermelo from the two railway lines, that in the north from Pretoria to Delagoa Bay, and that in the south from Johannesburg to Natal. For the purpose of this narrative it is only necessary to mention those of Plumer from the north, Rimington from Standerton and Knox from Greylingstadt. They were to converge on Bethel.

Knox, whose column included the headquarters and six companies of the Regiment, left Greylingstadt on 15th May and reached Bethel on the 20th, where after some skirmishing with the enemy, a junction with Plumer was effected and contact with Rimington established. The village of Bethel was destroyed.

Plumer then arranged a drive south with the three columns above mentioned from the line Bethel–Ermelo.

The convoys of these columns, consisting of 140 ox and mule wagons, a large number of Boer families, some prisoners of war, sick and wounded men, and 15,000 head of stock, were placed under the command of Colonel Gallwey and were to move on the right of the line of columns taking the main road to Standerton. Gallwey had for escort 'C', 'D', 'F', 'G' and 'H' Companies of the Regiment ('A' Company, Captain Peacock, remaining with Knox's column), four companies of the Royal Munster Fusiliers, 120 mounted men, and 2 guns R.H.A. under Lieutenant Furze. On 22nd May Gallwey's convoy moved out to a camp 3 miles south of Bethel. On the following days the march was continued, and on the 24th the rear-guard of the convoy moving through rolling country in a thick mist was attacked most persistently by the enemy under Commandant Viljoen. Major Lloyd, who commanded the rear-guard of two companies of the 1st Royal Munster Fusiliers and one gun of 'Q' Battery R.H.A., had a difficult task, as the stock, mostly sheep, were footsore, but eventually they got into camp at Goodehoop (according to the regimental diary) or Witbank (according to the official *History of the War*).

ACTION AT MOOIFONTEIN

On the morning of the 25th at 6 a.m. the convoy moved off towards Mooifontein when the advanced guard was at once attacked and almost simultaneously the right flank and rear of the convoy. 'C' Company (2nd Lieutenant E. G. L. Thurlow), 'H' Company (Captain W. J. Bowker, D.S.O.), with a few mounted men and 1 gun, 'Q' Battery R.H.A., formed the rear-guard under Major H. R. Lloyd.

'C' Company with one gun were established on a hill west of the camping ground, and 'H' Company on a ridge in support, while the mounted men covered the approaches on the east of the camping ground.

The task of the rear-guard was no light one, as they had to hold their positions until the whole of the convoy had left the camping ground and had got well out of rifle range. The wagons were marshalled five abreast and eventually got under way, but not before the Boers, who came on with great gallantry, had again and again endeavoured to dislodge 'C' Company by a direct attack and 'H' Company by an attack on its outer flank. This latter attack was rendered the more dangerous by the enemy having set fire to the dry grass, which under cover of the smoke he was enabled to come to quite close quarters. 'C' and 'H' Companies gallantly held their positions and eventually 'C' Company was able to retire on its support, 'H' Company.

In rear of the ridge, now held by 'H' and 'C' Companies, there was a spruit crossing the main road at right angles which afforded excellent cover. A fresh party of Boers advancing from the east now utilized this means of approach and if firmly established would have cut off the retreat of 'H' and 'C' Companies, Lieutenant Moran, the Quartermaster, seeing the impending danger, with great promptitude collected the cooks, wagon men, and such sick as were able to move, and kept off the enemy until 'H' and 'C' Companies were able to retire. Meanwhile the convoy, though attacked in front and on the flanks, continued to make steady progress and eventually reached Mooifontein after six hours' fighting, when the approach of Plumer's column caused the enemy to desist from their attacks. The losses sustained by Gallwey's force amounted to 31 killed and wounded. The Battalion casualties were 1 killed and 5 wounded.

The following were mentioned in dispatches: Major Lloyd, Captain W. J. Bowker, D.S.O., Lieutenant and Adjutant C. B. Prowse, 2nd Lieutenants E. G. L. Thurlow and E. D. Bally and Lieutenant and Quartermaster P. Moran.

No. 2310 Serjeant W. Miles was specially brought to the notice of the C.-in-C. for gallantry and good leading in action. The following N.C.Os. and men were promoted for distinguished conduct and gallantry in the field:—

No. 3385   L.-C. Hawes to be Corporal.
    4452   L.-C. Wilson   ,,   ,,

The above N.C.Os., seeing a man in danger of being burnt by a veldt fire, ran back and fetched him in, though the Boers were within 400 yards and firing hotly.

Again, No. 5809 Lance-Corporal Short was promoted to be Serjeant; when told off to obtain a few men to hold a kraal he did so in a most able and efficient manner. No. 5990 Lance-Corporal Willis and No. 2410 Pte. Vickery were promoted corporals for having displayed great dash and coolness.

The Boer strength was estimated at 600 men and 1 pom-pom under Commandants Viljoen, Brydenbach, De Villiers, Springt and Trichardt. Field Cornet Grobelaar came in afterwards to ask for assistance for their wounded. The Boers admitted 40 casualties.

On the 26th May Colonel Plumer joined Gallwey's column, when the whole proceeded to Standerton, where they arrived on the 27th and camped on the far side of the Vaal River to the east of the town. The following message was received from the Commander-in-Chief: 'Hearty congratulations on successful defence of convoy. Regret losses. Gallwey did well.'

On 30th May the Battalion moved camp 2 miles to the north-east of Standerton and rejoined Colonel Knox's column.

On 1st June Plumer, Rimington, and Knox, moving eastwards, made a wide sweep towards Piet Retief, where they arrived on 9th June after capturing some 34 Boers on the way. Piet Retief was destroyed. On the way to Piet Retief on 6th June, Major Lloyd, with 'D', 'G' and 'H' Companies of the

Regiment, two companies of the Royal Munster Fusiliers, 2 guns 28th Battery R.F.A., 50 Imperial Yeomanry, 100 Bushmen, one section Royal Engineers, having collected all empty wagons to the number of 168, together with the sick, prisoners, and Boer families, were dispatched to Wakkerstroom. On their way they were opposed by the enemy, especially at Mooipart Nek on the 8th, and they arrived at Wakkerstroom on the 10th, when they filled up with supplies ready to rejoin Plumer's columns.

On 11th June Gallwey at Piet Retief, with the remaining three companies of the Regiment, two companies 1st Royal Munster Fusiliers, 2 guns 'Q' Battery R.H.A., 250 Bushmen and 80 Imperial Yeomanry (Sharpshooters), having collected all empty wagons of the three columns, sick, and prisoners, proceeded towards Utrecht, crossing the Assegai River that day, the Intombi River on the 13th and the Pongola on the 14th.

On the 15th they were stoutly opposed at Elandsberg Nek and being unable to force the pass, encamped for the night. On the following morning Rimington, having heard of their plight, arrived with reinforcements, and together they forced the Nek. On the 17th they crossed the Pivaan River, and reached Utrecht on the 18th.

As before related, 'D', 'G' and 'H' Companies forming part of the escort of Major Lloyd's convoy were at Wakkerstroom on the 10th. On the 13th the escort having been increased by the addition of 120 of all ranks 10th Hussars, 86 Imperial Yeomanry, 34 New Zealanders, and 240 New South Wales Mounted Infantry marched via Castrels Nek to Zoekhoek, where they handed over supplies to General Plumer on the 14th. On the 15th they marched to Voverslaat, a Boer convoy with 22 men and families surrendering *en route*.

On the 16th Lloyd's convoy reached General Knox's column at Roodekraal, and having handed over supplies, and taken over empty wagons, set out for Utrecht, proceeding via Kliphoek, Elands Nek, and Pivaan River, and arrived there on the 23rd. Thus the six companies with Headquarters were once again concentrated. On the 25th orders were received for the Regiment to proceed to Springs where 'B' and 'E' Companies under Captain Hardman had been located since 26th May. 'C' and 'F' Companies, however, under Captain Brocklehurst were not immediately to accompany the Battalion. On the 25th June they joined General Knox's column. This column set out on the 28th, marching via Spitzkop and Kambula Hill of Zulu War fame to Paul Pietersburg, Piet Retief, and Amsterdam, which they reached on 5th July, thence to Carolina and Wonderfontein on the Pretoria–Lourenço Marques railway, where they arrived on the 14th. Proceeding westwards along the railway, they reached Middelburg on the 16th July, when the column was broken up, when 'C' and 'F' Companies entrained for Heidelberg on the 19th and reached that place the following day.

Meanwhile the headquarters of the Battalion, with 'A', 'D', 'G' and 'H' Companies, left Utrecht on the 26th, and, having crossed the Buffaloe River, reached Newcastle on the 27th. On the 28th they entrained for Springs. Soon after their arrival there, the Battalion was ordered to Heidelberg in relief of the 3rd Battalion King's Royal Rifle Corps; 'A', 'D', 'G' and 'H' Companies, under Major Lloyd, marched there on the 2nd July, followed by 'B' and 'E' Companies on the following day.

On 23rd July 'E' Company, under Captain E. G. Elger, relieved a company of the 3rd K.R.R. at the Nigel Mine. On 8th August the Battalion took over the Blockhouse line on the railway in relief of the 1st Battalion Rifle Brigade, 'A', 'C', 'E' and half 'F' Company occupying the blockhouses, while the other half of 'F' Company relieved 'E' Company at the Nigel Mines.

The 1st Battalion Duke of Cornwall's Light Infantry relieved 'F' Company at Heidelberg railway station and occupied it with their headquarters.

On 6th September 2nd Lieutenant Williams (son of Lieut.-Colonel R. B. Williams) was accidentally shot at the Nigel Mine and subsequently buried at Heidelberg—and yet another untoward fatality occurred on the 25th of that month, when Lieutenant Miers, who was attached to the South African Constabulary, holding a post near the Oceana Mine 12 miles from Heidelberg, was killed while out on patrol by Boers making treacherous use of the White Flag.

On 24th October the Battalion took over from the 1st Battalion Durham Light Infantry a line of blockhouses on the railway from Heidelberg to Zuikerbosch; these, with three previously held, covering a distance of 40 miles from Roodekop Station to Zuikerbosch.

Later in the year on 13th December the posts on the railway held by the Battalion were extended eastwards so as to include Greylingstadt and Waterval Bridge. Thus the Battalion was extended over a line 80 miles in length.

On 4th January 1902 Captain and Brevet Major J. M. Vallentin, then in command of the 5th Victorian Bushmen, who had previously established a reputation for gallantry and skilful leading in several engagements, was killed in a hard-fought action near the Oliphants Nek River. He was an officer of considerable promise and ability, and a graduate of the Staff College. On the 18th January the mounted Infantry Company serving with Colonel Open's column lost in a skirmish near Ermelo one man killed and two wounded.

In the middle of February a Boer commando, under Albert, Grobelaar and others, occupied the Zuikerbosch Rand near Heidelberg and commenced raiding the cattle in the vicinity of the town. These raids gave the Mounted Infantry under Lieutenant Freestun a good deal of trouble, especially on the 8th and 12th. About this time the Heidelberg garrison was reinforced by three companies of the Royal Inniskilling Fusiliers under the command of Lt.-Col. R. L. Payne, D.S.O., a former officer of the Regiment.

On the 13th February 'A', 'E', 'F' and 'H' Companies moved from Waterval Bridge and adjacent posts and doubled the blockhouse line from Zuikerbosch to Heidelberg.

On the 16th at 12.30 a.m. a party of 150 Boers attempted to cross the line held by posts of 'D' and 'E' Companies at Steinkraal. They charged the wire defences with a mob of cattle and some 50 men got across, leaving 150 cattle, some horses and a rifle in our hands. 'E' Company had one man dangerously wounded.

On the 18th the line held by the Battalion was again extended, 'A', 'F' and 'H' Companies taking over anew the line as far as Greylingstadt, which a few days later was extended to Waterval Bridge.

On the 16th March Lieut.-Colonel Gallwey, C.B., having completed his four years in command of the Battalion, proceeded to Cape Town *en route* for England to take over command of the 13th Regimental District, handing over temporary command to Major H. R. Lloyd during the absence on sick leave of Lieut.-Colonel R. B. Williams.

The following farewell order was published:—

'Officers, non-commissioned officers and men: You have well maintained the record of the 13th Light Infantry and I feel very much indebted to you for the loyal support you have given me in the field. I have served in the old Regiment continuously for the past thirty-one and a half years. My only consolation in leaving it is that I shall still wear the Regimental badge, and I hope to see you again in the Regimental District. Good-bye and good luck. I shall hope to welcome you on your arrival in England.'

On the 28th March a Boer patrol some 100 strong rushed some native Intelligence Scouts to the south-west of the town, killing two. The Mounted Infantry detachment, under Lieutenant Freestun, were engaged with the enemy and saved a party of the South African Constabulary from capture, covering their retirement with great coolness. Lieutenant Freestun was mentioned for the skilful way he led and handled his men. Four men of the S.A.C. were killed in this skirmish.

On 2nd April a draft of 150 men, under Lieutenant C. C. Maud, arrived from the 1st Battalion in India, and a few days later this officer started on his return journey to India with a similar draft of the 2nd Battalion.

Already in March the Boers were seriously considering the question of terminating hostilities, and on 12th April the Boer peace delegates met Lord Kitchener at Pretoria, after which they proceeded back to their commandos to consult them. On 15th May the Vereeniging conference was opened, and on the 18th the Boer delegates proceeded to Pretoria to confer with Lord Milner and Lord Kitchener. The conditions of the surrender were finally signed on 31st May.

On 1st June 1902 peace was proclaimed and two days later the following telegram was received from the Commander-in-Chief:—

'June 2nd. Please communicate to the troops the following gracious message that I have received from His Majesty the King and for which I have thanked him in the name of all concerned.' Begins. 'Heartiest congratulations on the termination of hostilities. I also congratulate my brave troops under your command for having brought the long and difficult campaign to so glorious and successful a conclusion.' Ends.

On 5th June 900 Boers of the Bethel, Heidelberg, Ermelo, Middelburg, Boksberg, Klip River, and Pretoria Commandos came into Kraal and laid down their arms.

Generals Bruce Hamilton and Louis Botha were present. Speeches were made and after laying down their arms in heaps and partaking of a substantial meal the Burghers were allowed to go where they liked. Much good fellowship ensued between the garrisons of posts and their late enemies and little bitterness was displayed by either side.

Before concluding the story of the South African War an act of retribution remains to be recorded. It will be remembered that Lieutenant Miers was treacherously murdered at Riversdrei on 25th September 1901. Among the Boers in the Burgher Camp at Heidelberg two of the men concerned were discovered, viz. Solomon Van Aas and Slabert. They were tried by Field General Court Martial, found guilty and sentenced, the former to death, and the latter to five years' penal servitude. The sentence of death was carried out by a firing party detailed from the Battalion.

THE REGIMENTAL MOUNTED INFANTRY DURING THE SOUTH AFRICAN WAR

Soon after the commencement of the War the want of sufficient mounted troops to cope with the mobile forces of the enemy necessitated the raising of many regular mounted infantry regiments. These regiments were, as a rule, composed of four companies, and generally speaking each regular battalion furnished sufficient officers and other ranks to form a company.

In the previous pages some mention has been made of small parties of the Battalion being mounted from time to time for reconnaissance work. If any officer can be said to be the father of the regimental mounted infantry it was Lieutenant A. P. Barry. It will be realized that in July 1900 this officer was in command of a company at Schweizer Reneke composed originally mostly of men of the Royal Scots Fusiliers, but later on replaced by details of other regiments, including some of the 2nd Battalion.

In January 1901 Methuen's column arrived and evacuated Schweizer Reneke, taking the garrison with him. Barry and his mounted infantry, after a short trek with Methuen, were sent in February 1901 with a convoy from Kuruman to Kimberley and there they established connexion with the detachment of the Regiment in the Kimberley column. Lieutenant Yatman now took over command of the Mounted Infantry, and they remained with the Kimberley column till 20th May 1901 when they proceeded by train with the rest of the Kimberley detachment to Springs as before related.

Meanwhile, towards the end of December 1900 another section of Mounted Infantry from the headquarter wing of the Regiment had been formed at Sannah's Post. In January 1901 this section, 30 strong, under Lieutenant C. H. Little, proceeded to Pretoria, and shortly afterwards joined the 13th Mounted Infantry, under the command of Major St. G. Pratt, Durham Light Infantry. The 13th and 14th Mounted Infantry formed a corps under Lieut.-

Colonel Jenner, D.S.O., Rifle Brigade. This corps again formed part of the command of Brig.-General Alderson, strength 2,000 of all ranks with 8 guns.

The 13th and 14th Mounted Infantry took part in the first great drive starting from a north and south line through Springs with the Delagoa Bay railway on the left and the Natal railway on the right towards the Swaziland and Zululand Borders. The drive started on 28th January 1901 and ended on 13th April, when the 13th Mounted Infantry reached Vryheid. From Vryheid they proceeded to Standerton, where another section of Mounted Infantry from the 2nd Battalion joined them under Lieutenant A. H. Yatman.

In September Botha's attempt to invade Natal caused large reinforcements to be sent there, and among them the 13th and 14th Mounted Infantry now under the command of Spens. On 24th September Spens was at Rorke's Drift. Botha, having abandoned his intention of marching on Dundee, made for Zululand and attacked Itala and Prospect on the 25th and 26th, being repulsed in each case.

On the news of these attacks reaching Natal, Bruce Hamilton, having collected 1,600 mounted men from the columns of Spens, Allenby and Pulteney, started at 10 a.m. on the 27th and marching via Isandhlwana, Fort Louis, and Babanago reached Itala at 9 a.m. on the 28th after a march of 48 miles. Botha eventually escaped northwards. In the course of these operations the 13th Mounted Infantry passed over the battlefield of Kambula.

In November 1901 the 13th Mounted Infantry, starting from Botha's Pass on the Natal border, took part in a drive in the North-Eastern Orange Free State, but the results were disappointing. On the conclusion of this drive they proceeded to Standerton, and were employed in the Eastern Transvaal till March, when the half-company of the Regiment with the 13th Mounted Infantry joined the half-company of the 26th Mounted Infantry on the Buffaloe River.

In May 1901 Lieutenants Barry and Bally with 50 men were sent from Heidelberg to Standerton, and these with a similar detachment of the Essex Regiment formed No. 4 Company of the 26th Mounted Infantry under the command of Major Wiggan, 13th Hussars. This battalion formed part of Colonel Colville's column. His column then consisted of the 26th Mounted Infantry, three companies of the Devonshire Regiment, 4 field guns, 2 pom-poms and some Colonial Mounted troops. Colville's column was for some time based on Standerton, taking part in several drives, but in September, in consequence of Botha's raid on Natal, Colville marched east to Amsterdam on the Swaziland border, but towards the end of the month he returned to the Natal Railway. In October Colville was covering the construction of a block-house line between Wakherstroom and Piet Retief and in the middle of November he was at Piet Retief. In the latter part of December 1901 and beginning of January 1902 Colville was based on Wakkerstroom and carried out a succession of night raids. Later on in March Colville was sent to guard the line of the Buffaloe River on the Natal border and there the half-company of the Regiment serving with the 13th Mounted Infantry joined the 26th Mounted

Infantry. Thus the Mounted Infantry of the Regiment was now concentrated in one company. Captain A. P. Barry was in command, with Lieutenants C. H. Little and E. D. Bally as his two subalterns. On the cessation of hostilities the 26th Mounted Infantry remained for some months on the Zululand border as the Zulus were giving trouble to the Boers, remembering, no doubt, old scores.

The total casualties incurred by the Regiment during the war were:—

Officers: Killed and died of wounds	8
,, Deaths from disease	1
,, Wounded	4
,, Missing and prisoners	Nil
Other ranks: Killed and died of wounds	21
,, Deaths from disease	84
,, Wounded	78
,, Missing and prisoners	Nil

The battle honours awarded to the Regiment were 'Relief of Ladysmith' and 'South Africa 1899–1902'. Two medals were awarded: the Queen's and King's South African War Medals.

SOUTH AFRICAN WAR, 1899–1902

Mentioned in Dispatches	Rewards
Lieut. A. P. Barry	
Quartermaster-Serjt. H. Barnes	
Pioneer Serjt. R. Basford	
Serjt.-Major E. W. Bath	
Capt. W. P. Braithwaite (3)	Brevet Major
Capt. R. Brocklehurst	
Pte. F. Cutland	D.C.M.
Pte. Day	
Capt. E. G. Elger	D.S.O.
Col.-Serjt. A. W. Ellis	D.C.M.
Capt. H. J. Everett	Brevet Major
Capt. M. A. Foster (4th Batt.)	D.S.O.
Col.-Serjt. H. French	D.C.M.
Col.-Serjt. J. Galbraith	D.C.M.
Lieut.-Colonel E. J. Gallwey (2)	C.B.
Col.-Serjt. J. Hackett (4th Batt.)	
Serjt. S. Hannam	
Lance-Corpl. C. Hawes (Promoted Corporal by C.-in-C.)	D.C.M.
Serjt. P. Hewlett	D.C.M.
Serjt. G. Hill (4th Batt.)	
Serjt. J. Hillier (4th Batt.)	
Col.-Serjt. Hills	
Serjt. M. Hiscock	D.C.M.

Mentioned in Dispatches	Rewards
Pte. H. Hutchins	D.C.M.
Lieut. V. F. A. Keith-Falconer (Killed in action)	
Quartermaster-Serjt. G. Kemp (4th Batt.) . .	D.C.M.
2nd Lieut. C. H. Little (2)	
Major H. R. Lloyd (2)	Brevet Lieut.-Colonel
Lieut.-Colonel W. Long (4th Batt.) . . .	C.M.G.
Col.-Serjt. C. Mace	
Capt. R. H. Manley (4th Batt.)	
Pte. F. Marsh	D.C.M.
Lieut.-Quartermaster P. Moran (2)	
Col.-Serjt. H. Norton	
Serjt. J. Oates	D.C.M.
Capt. S. E. Owen Swaffield (3rd Batt.)	
Capt. E. H. R. C. Platt	Brevet Major
Lieut. C. B. Prowse (3)	
Lance-Corpl. F. J. Short (Promoted Serjeant by C.-in-C.)	
Col.-Serjt. F. J. Stephens (4th Batt.)	
Capt. E. H. Swayne	Brevet Major
Serjt. E. Taylor	
Serjt.-Major T. Tobias (4th Batt.) . . .	D.C.M.
Capt. J. M. Vallentin (3) (Killed in action) . .	Brevet Major
Pte. Vickery	
Lieut. C. E. M. Walker (Killed in action)	
Lieut. P. M. Wardlaw	
Col.-Serjt. W. C. Watson	
Capt. A. B. Whatman	D.S.O.
Major R. B. Williams	Brevet Lieut.-Colonel
Lance-Corpl. Wills	
Lance-Corpl. J. Wilson (Promoted Corporal by C.-in-C.)	
Capt. S. H. Woodhouse (4th Batt.)	
Pte. C. Woods	D.C.M.

OFFICERS OF THE REGIMENT EXTRA-REGIMENTALLY EMPLOYED DURING THE SOUTH AFRICAN WAR

Captain A. G. Boyle employed successively on Special Service in South Africa from 8th March 1900 to 27th February 1902 as Station Staff Officer, District Commandant, Area Commandant, and Administrator Martial Law in the Cape Colony.

*Captain and Bt. Major W. P. Braithwaite. Brigade Major 11th Infantry Bde. from 29th January 1900 to 31st October 1900 and as D.A.A.G. from 1st November 1900 to 9th September 1902; took part in the action at Vaal Krantz 5th to 7th February 1900; operations on Tugela Heights

---

* This officer also served in the 2nd Battalion.

SUND...

TVeasy MOVIES

Sky MOVIES **Premiere**
Sky 301 Virgin 401/431

10.30am Nanny McPhee & The Big Bang As 8.00pm.
12.20pm Fireflies in the Garden Melodrama starring Ryan Reynolds. (S, D) (2008, 15) ★★★★
2.10 Astro Boy Animation with the voice of Nicolas Cage and Freddie Highmore. (S, D) (2009, PG) ★★★
3.45 The Greatest Melodrama starring Carey Mulligan and Susan Sarandon. (2009, 15) ★★★
5.30 Leap Year See 9.50pm.

PRIME-TIME

8.00 Nanny McPhee & The Big Bang Fantasy sequel. The nanny helps the mum of three unruly children. Stars Emma Thompson and Rhys Ifans. (D) (2010, U) ★★

9.50 Leap Year Romantic comedy. A American woman go a journey across Ir with a laid-back Iri publican. Stars M Goode and Amy (S, D) (2009, P

11.30 Oscars Re Live Coverage (D) See featu
1.30–5.00am Annual Aca Coverage hosted b and Ann

Sky MOVIES S

6.20am histor (1934
8.10 St (195
10.25
Se
11.
A

SOUTH AFRICA, 1899–1902

14th to 27th February 1900; operations in Natal March to June 1900, including action at Laings Nek (6th to 9th June); operations in the Transvaal east of Pretoria, July to 29th November 1900; operations in the Transvaal 30th November 1900 to April 1901, and in operations in Cape Colony April 1901 to 31st May 1902.

Captain and Bt. Major H. J. Everett. Special Service Officer, served as Adjutant 4th Regiment Mounted Infantry 7th February to 6th April 1900, and as Staff Officer (D.A.A.G.) to the 4th Mounted Infantry Corps from 7th April 1900 to 31st May 1902; took part in the Relief of Kimberley; operations in the Orange Free State February to May 1900, including operations at Paardeberg (17th to 26th February), action at Poplar Grove, Vet River (5th and 6th May) and Zand River; operations in the Transvaal in May and June 1900, including actions near Johannesburg, Pretoria, and at Diamond Hill; operations in the Transvaal east of Pretoria July to 29th November 1900, including actions at Belfast (26th to 27th August); operations in the Transvaal January to April 1901, July 1901, March 1902, and May 1902; operations in the Orange River Colony, June 1901 to January 1902, February 1902 to May 1902; operations in Cape Colony January to February 1902.

Lieut.-Colonel and Bt. Colonel R. L. Payne, D.S.O., commanding 1st Battalion Royal Inniskilling Fusiliers; took part in operations in Natal March to June 1900; operations in Transvaal east of Pretoria July to 29th November 1900, including actions at Belfast (26th to 27th August) and Lydenburg (5th to 8th September). Afterwards Colonel of the Regiment.

Captain and Bt. Major E. H. Platt. Special Service Officer Mounted Infantry. Took part in operations in Orange River Colony, April 1901 to 31st May 1902. Commanded 15th Regiment Mounted Infantry from October 1901 to May 1902.

*Lieutenant C. B. Prowse employed as railway Staff Officer 16th June 1900 to 15th November 1900.

*Lieutenant E. G. L. Thurlow employed as railway Staff Officer from 19th December 1901 to 16th January 1903.

Captain and Bt. Major J. M. Vallentin served as Brigade Major 7th Infantry Brigade during the Siege of Ladysmith and subsequently in Natal and Transvaal. At one time he was Commandant at Heidelberg and in October 1900 he was employed with the South African Constabulary. At the end of 1901 he took over the command of a column, and was killed at the hard-fought action of Bankkop on 4th January 1902.

*Lieutenant A. B. Whatman was employed as Brigade Signalling Officer from 11th September 1900 to 11th June 1901.

* These officers also served with the 2nd Battalion.

CHAPTER XXVII

PEACE SERVICE AT HOME AND ABROAD

1st BATTALION

It will be recalled that at the beginning of the hot weather of 1899 the 1st Battalion was quartered as follows: Headquarters and four companies at Murree, remaining four companies at Rawal Pindi with a detachment at Campbellpore.

The headquarter wing under the command of Lieut.-Colonel H. A. Walsh took part in the Abbottabad manœuvres at the end of October and subsequently proceeded to Rawal Pindi, arriving there on 15th November. On the 8th December the Campbellpore detachment rejoined headquarters, when the Battalion was once more concentrated.

In May 1900 the whole Battalion proceeded to the hills and were quartered at Gharial (Murree). At the end of the hot weather in October the Battalion again proceeded to Rawal Pindi, taking part in manœuvres on the way and reaching their destination on 10th November.

On the 17th May 1900 the Colonel of the Regiment, General Lord Mark Kerr, K.C.B., died at the age of 83. He had been Colonel of the Regiment since 1880 and was the second officer of that name to command the Regiment, his predecessor having been Colonel from 1725 to 1732. His career in command of the 1st Battalion has been fully dealt with in these pages, and it only remains to add that after commanding the Battalion he continued to take the most lively interest in the Regiment until the time of his death.

He was succeeded in the command of the Regiment by Lieut.-General Sir John Cox, K.C.B., at that time 79 years of age, a grand old veteran, who had served in the 1st Battalion in the Afghan War 1840–2, in the Crimean War, and also in the Indian Mutiny.

On 14th November the Battalion again found the Campbellpore detachment, strength 56 of all ranks, under 2nd Lieutenant Hagger.

In February 1901 the Battalion took part in the Attock-Hutti manœuvres, and subsequently in March formed part of the Rawal Pindi Movable Column, Lieut.-Colonel H. A. Walsh being in command with Captain E. F. Cooke-Hurle as his staff officer.

In April the Battalion again proceeded to Gharial (Murree) for the hot weather, and returned to Rawal Pindi at the end of October.

Lieut.-General Sir John Cox, K.C.B., did not live long to enjoy the command of the Regiment, as he died on the 2nd October 1901 and was succeeded in command of the Regiment by Major-General E. L. England, C.B., who joined the 1st Battalion in 1855 and served in the Indian Mutiny and South African Campaigns 1878-9, when he commanded the Battalion at the Battle of Ulundi.

Manœuvres were carried out from the 15th to 31st January 1902, and on the 13th February a draft of 4 serjeants, 6 corporals and 140 men under the command of Lieutenant C. C. Maud left Rawal Pindi *en route* to join the 2nd Battalion in South Africa. This draft was subsequently replaced by a similar party from the 2nd Battalion who arrived on 22nd May, by which time the Battalion was again quartered in the Murree Hills, the barracks being at Kuldanna.

At the end of the hot weather the Battalion returned to Rawal Pindi on 8th October and then marched to Peshawar on change of stations, arriving there on 17th October.

The following is an extract from the Rawal Pindi District Orders, dated 8th October 1902:—

'On the departure of the 1st Battalion Somerset Light Infantry the Officer Commanding the District has great pleasure in announcing his entire satisfaction in the discipline and good feeling which has prevailed in all ranks during the time they have been quartered in the district. The Somerset Light Infantry has been four years continuously at Rawal Pindi and the Murree Hills and during the whole of this period the conduct of this Regiment has been all that could be desired. In bidding farewell, the officer commanding Rawal Pindi District wishes all ranks the best of good luck in every way.'

Soon after arrival at Peshawar Lieut.-Colonel H. A. Walsh's term of a command came to an end, when he was succeeded by Lieut.-Colonel C. W. Napier-Clavering.

Lieut.-Colonel H. A. Walsh had a distinguished career in the Regiment, having joined the 13th Light Infantry on the 28th February 1874. He was Adjutant of the 1st Battalion from 1880 to 1884 and subsequently was Adjutant of the 3rd Battalion from 1885 to 1890. During the campaign against Sekukuni in 1878 and during the Zulu War 1879 he served with the Mounted Infantry, taking part in the actions of Kambula and Ulundi. He served with the Camel Corps in the Soudan Expedition 1884-5 being present at the action of Abu Klea, where he was dangerously wounded; he was mentioned in dispatches and received the Brevet of Major.

His farewell order dated 28th October 1902 is as follows:—

'In bidding farewell to the Battalion Lieut.-Colonel Walsh thanks all ranks for the truly loyal and soldier-like support they have always given him, a support that has enabled him to command with confidence, and which has brought the Battalion to the excellent state it now is in.

'In leaving the dear old Regiment in which he has served for nearly thirty years it is a great consolation to him to know he leaves it in able hands, and he knows the same support will be accorded to Major Napier-Clavering as has ever been shown him.

'Before leaving, Lieut.-Colonel Walsh would have liked to have shaken the hand of every dear old comrade in the Battalion, but his feelings make it impossible, and he feels sure all will take the will for the deed.'

During the hot weather of 1903 two companies, 'F' and 'L', under Captain F. G. Thoyts, proceeded to the Murree Hills, and two companies, 'G' and 'D', under Major F. M. Peacock, to Cherat, both detachments returning to Peshawar in the following October.

In the following year 1904 the headquarters of the Battalion with 'C', 'H', 'I' and 'M' Companies under the command of Lieut.-Colonel C. W. Napier-Clavering proceeded to Cherat in April, returning to Peshawar in October. In September 'H' Company and other details under Captain A. H. Yatman, 120 strong, proceeded from Cherat to Fatehgarh. A month later the Battalion less the Fatehgarh detachment left Peshawar and proceeded by train to Cawnpore, where they arrived on the 29th November.

The following is an extract from the 1st (Peshawar) division orders dated 25th November 1904:—

'The G.O.C. 1st Division cannot allow the 1st Battalion Queen's and 1st Battalion Somerset Light Infantry to leave Peshawar without expressing his appreciation of their good behaviour whilst under his command. There have been few Courts Martial and but little drunkenness. These two fine Regiments have well sustained the character of the British Army and by their discipline done honour to their own great Regimental traditions.

'In bidding farewell Major-General Sir E. G. Barrow desires to thank the Commanding Officers for their loyal assistance and to wish all ranks Godspeed.'

As a result of the inspection of the Regimental Signallers during the training season 1904–5 the Battalion stood first in the whole of India and were specially commended by the Commander-in-Chief. On the 8th July the Fatehgarh detachment arrived at Cawnpore.

In October 1905 an outbreak of beri-beri occurred which necessitated the Battalion vacating barracks and going under canvas. They returned to barracks in January 1906.

In April 1906 a party of 3 officers and 51 other ranks, afterwards increased to 130 other ranks, under Lieutenant Alexander, proceeded to Kailana in the hills, returning to Cawnpore on 1st November.

On the 9th November 1906 Lieut.-Colonel and Brevet Colonel C. W. Napier-Clavering, on completing his period of command of the Battalion, retired on retired pay and was succeeded by Major C. H. Stisted.

The following is an extract from Battalion Orders dated 7th November 1906:—

'Colonel Napier-Clavering in taking leave of the Battalion wishes every one serving with it health, happiness and success. He is confident that the high standard of conduct and efficiency which has distinguished the Battalion hitherto will always be maintained in the future.'

On the 1st January 1907 the companies of the Battalion were re-lettered as follows:—

'A' and 'B' Depôt Companies at Taunton.

'C', 'D', 'E' (late 'L'), 'F', 'G', 'H', 'I', 'K' (late 'M') Service Companies.

For many years prior to 1881, the year in which the Depôt at Taunton was formed, the Depôt companies moved about with the Battalion when quartered at home, but it is difficult to account for two companies lettered 'L' and 'M'. In the eighteenth century, especially in the early part, it was quite a common thing for a battalion to have ten or even twelve companies, but at that time, the companies, like the regiments to which they belonged, were known by the names of their commanding officers.[1]

The letters 'L' and 'M' were always a source of irritation to the babus in the pay offices in India as they could not understand why the Battalion should occupy more of the alphabet than other regiments.

On the 6th January 1907 the Battalion, strength 20 officers, 702 warrant officers, N.C.Os. and men, proceeded from Cawnpore to Agra to take part in the Durbar on the occasion of the visit of His Majesty the Ameer of Afghanistan.

They formed part of the 22nd Infantry Brigade, the remaining battalions being the 1st Battalion Oxford Light Infantry, the 1st Battalion Durham Light Infantry and the 2nd Battalion Royal Welch Fusiliers.

The following order was published at the request of the Ameer on the 9th January:—

'His Majesty the Ameer has requested the General Officer Commanding the Eastern Command to express to the troops who paraded this morning in honour of his arrival his regret that they got wet. His Majesty desiring to show his appreciation of the soldier-like manner in which the troops turned out, and at the same time to share their discomfort, refrained from cloaking himself during the processions, as they were not cloaked.'

The G.O.C. Agra Concentration issued the following order on 15th January 1907:—

'The General Officer Commanding Agra Concentration desires to express to all officers, non-commissioned officers and men his thanks for the way in which all duties during the Ameer's visit have been performed. The high appreciation of His Excellency the Viceroy and of His Excellency the Commander-in-Chief has already been conveyed to the troops.

'Both at the review and on all ceremonial occasions all ranks showed the keenest interest in assuring success. Sir Alfred Gaselee has much pleasure in noticing the exemplary conduct of the men during their stay in Agra and its vicinity.'

---

[1] Since writing the above I am reminded that Havelock in 1843 writes of his company as number 4, which proves that the companies were designated by numbers at that time. Just prior to the Crimean War in 1854 the 1st Battalion was augmented to twelve companies, and it is possible that the designations 'L' and 'M' date from that period.—Author.

The Battalion returned to Cawnpore on the 19th January.

On the 10th April 3 officers, the headquarters of 'G' Company and details made up to 171 strong under the command of Captain C. W. Compton proceeded to Kailana in the hills for location during the summer months. The detachment returned to Cawnpore on the 28th October.

A slight alteration in the honorary distinctions of the Regiment was made by Army Order 208 dated 1st September 1907:

'His Majesty the King has been graciously pleased to approve of the date being added to the honorary distinction already awarded, as enumerated below:

'The Prince Albert's (Somersetshire Light Infantry) "Ghuznee 1839".'

On the 14th December 1907 the Battalion left Cawnpore in two trains for Poona where they arrived on the 16th December, being stationed in the Wanowrie Barracks. 'G' and 'K' Companies on arrival proceeded to Kirkee, a few miles distant, on detachment. They returned to headquarters in the following March.

In February 1908 Captain A. B. Whatman, D.S.O., was appointed Chief Signalling Officer to the force under Major-General Sir James Willcocks, K.C.M.G., C.B., D.S.O., which operated in the Bazar Valley against the Zakka Khel Afridis.

The following is an extract from Sir James Willcocks's dispatch which appeared in the *Gazette* of India, Army Department, dated Fort William, 20th March 1908:—

'Captain A. B. Whatman, D.S.O., Somersetshire Light Infantry, Chief Signalling Officer.

'No officer in the force did better work. The signalling to and from India and tactically in the field was of a very high order. His energy, perseverance under trying conditions, and his coolness in all circumstances are remarkable and I strongly recommend him for advancement.'

Captain A. B. Whatman, D.S.O., was subsequently awarded a Brevet Majority.

In the autumn of 1908, the tour of the Battalion abroad came to an end. 'G' and 'I' Companies, consisting of Captain C. W. Compton (in command), Captain R. A. Currie, Lieutenant I. M. Smith, 2nd Lieutenant G. E. M. Whittuck and 182 N.C.Os. and men preceded the Battalion, and embarked at Bombay on the Hired Transport *Dongola* on the 15th October and reached Southampton on the 5th November.

The remainder of the Battalion, consisting of Lieut.-Colonel C. H. Stisted in command, Majors M. A. Foster, D.S.O., H. C. Johnstone, and A. B. Whatman, D.S.O., Captains H. M. Martin, J. B. Thomson and A. H. Yatman, Lieutenants W. Watson, N. H. Stone, G. Fleming, H. C. Dickinson and W. M. Sutton, 2nd Lieutenants F. G. Mills, and R. A. B. P. Watts, Captain and Adjutant A. W. S. Paterson, Lieutenant and Quartermaster D. J. Owens, Serjt.-Major A. W. Phillips, Bandmaster T. A. Mitchell and 751 N.C.Os. and men, left Poona for Bombay on the 29th October and embarked the following day in H.M. Hired Transport *Plassy* for Southampton.

The 1st Battalion reached Malta on 12th November, when Major A. B. Whatman, D.S.O., Captain H. M. Martin, 2nd Lieutenant F. S. Mills and R. A. P. B. Watts and 369 N.C.Os. and men disembarked and joined the 2nd Battalion, who had arrived the same day from England. Facilities were given for landing, and a number availed themselves of the offer, while several officers and N.C.Os. of the 2nd Battalion came on board. This was one of the rare occasions on which linked battalions met.

The voyage to England was continued the same evening and Southampton reached on the 20th November, when the Battalion disembarked and proceeded to Portland, arriving there the same evening. At their new station they were joined by Major E. F. Cooke-Hurle, Captains F. G. Thoyts, L. A. Jones-Mortimer and T. F. Ritchie, 2nd Lieutenants F. D. Bellew, R. H. E. Bennett, R. V. Montgomery, J. B. Taylor and 321 N.C.Os. and men left behind by the 2nd Battalion.

THE 2ND BATTALION

At the conclusion of hostilities in South Africa on 1st June 1902 the 2nd Battalion, with the exception of the Mounted Infantry, was concentrated at Heidelberg. They remained there till 11th September, when they marched to Elandsfontein on the outskirts of Johannesburg, arriving there the following day. On the 25th October they set off again on the march to Potchefstroom, arriving there on 1st November. On the 22nd December the Battalion moved into cantonments after over three years in tents and bivouacs.

On 22nd January 1903 Mr. Joseph Chamberlain, M.P., accompanied by Lord Milner, Sir A. Lawley and General the Hon. N. G. Lyttelton, G.O.C. South Africa, arrived at Potchefstroom at 4.30 p.m. to inspect the district and meet burghers' deputations.

A Guard of Honour was furnished at the station consisting of Captain A. R. Foord, Lieutenant P. M. Wardlaw, Lieutenant W. H. M. Freestun, and 100 rank and file with band and buglers. The Guard was specially complimented on their fine appearance.

On 23rd January General the Hon. N. G. Lyttelton inspected the Potchefstroom garrison on parade. The troops were drawn up in line and received Lord Milner with a Royal Salute. The Brigade then marched past. The following troops were present on parade: 1st King's Dragoon Guards, 85th Battery R.F.A., 8th Pom-pom Section, 8th Battalion Mounted Infantry and the 2nd Battalion. A general order was published congratulating the troops on their appearance.

A few words about the Mounted Infantry Company of the Regiment forming part of the 26th Battalion Mounted Infantry. For some months after the declaration of peace the 26th Mounted Infantry remained on the Zululand border, but later on in the autumn the Battalion was broken up, when the company of the Regiment was transferred to the 3rd Battalion Mounted

Infantry at Pretoria, and later on in January 1903 to the 8th Battalion at Potchefstroom.

Orders were soon after received for the 2nd Battalion to proceed to England when the Mounted Infantry rejoined the Battalion.

The 1st Battalion left Potchefstroom for Cape Town on April 2nd, arriving there on the 7th, when they embarked on board the s.s. *Staffordshire* which left Cape Town on the 9th, and proceeding via St. Helena and Las Palmas arrived at Southampton on 30th April.

The following officers embarked with the Battalions: Lieut.-Colonel R. B. Williams, Major and Bt. Lieut.-Colonel H. R. Lloyd; Captains A. R. Foord, T. A. Thicknesse, and C. B. Prowse (Adjutant); Lieutenants P. M. Wardlaw, C. H. Little, W. H. M. Freestun, L. E. C. W. Wilmer, E. P. Bally and C. M. A. Samuda, 2nd Lieutenants W. W. Llewellyn, C. C. Wigram, P. E. Bradney, H. L. Skrine, N. A. H. Campbell, H. B. Popham, M. C. Miers, J. M. Smith, A. G. Williamson, W. M. A. Foster and Lieutenant and Quartermaster P. Moran.

The Battalion disembarked on 1st May, and proceeded by train to Bentley *en route* to Bordon Camp near Aldershot, where they took over hutments. The Battalion now formed part of the 5th Brigade 3rd Division.

On arrival a congratulatory telegram was received from the Mayor of Taunton: 'Please express to 2nd Battalion the town's and my hearty congratulations on safe return and admiration of their service to their country.'

On 5th May the Queen's Medals for the South African Campaign were presented to the Battalion on parade by Major-General Bruce Hamilton commanding 3rd Division 1st Army Corps.

On 6th May the Battalion left on two months' furlough on return from active service.

It is not out of place to insert here a letter from Field-Marshal Sir Evelyn Wood, G.C.B., G.C.M.G., V.C., in reply to a telegram from the O.C. 13th Regimental District congratulating him on his promotion to Field-Marshal.

'Salisbury, *21st April 1903*

MY DEAR GALLWEY,—

I am indeed grateful to you for your kind telegram. Please convey to all concerned in it my sincere appreciation of the compliment paid to me. I admire the Regiment so much and indeed have done so for many years that it is all the more gratifying to have received such a message. I have been on the move ever since I was sent off, which is the cause of so many days' delay in my being able to express my thanks. I often recall to mind that morning, the 29th March 1879, when I saw some 23,000 Zulus advancing on my position and the confidence I felt in your Battalion.

I am yours very sincerely
signed EVELYN WOOD.
Comg. 13th R.D.

'To Colonel Gallwey, C.B.'

On 6th April 1904 the Battalion moved to Devonport and was quartered in the hutments at Crown Hill.

In the following year 1905 the Battalion proceeded to Salisbury Plain (Perham Down) for Brigade and divisional training, returning to Devonport on 31st August.

On 21st September H.R.H. the Duke of Connaught inspected all the recruits who had joined the Battalion since the 1st January (178 men).

On the 8th March 1906 2nd Lieutenant S. V. Wasborough was awarded the Royal Humane Society Bronze Medal and Certificate for saving the life of Private Lee of the Battalion who was carried out to sea by an undercurrent when bathing near Fort Tregantle on the 13th July 1905.

On the 8th August the Battalion proceeded to Salisbury Plain for brigade and divisional training, returning to Devonport on the 31st August.

On the 21st February 1907 the Battalion took part in lining the streets of Devonport on the occasion of their Royal Highnesses the Prince and Princess of Wales opening the Keyham Dock Extension Works. In the evening there was a Naval and Military Tattoo in the grounds of Admiralty House. Bandmaster J. Ancliffe of the Battalion conducted the massed bands of the Garrison. H.R.H. expressed to the Major-General Commanding his appreciation of the able manner in which Mr. Ancliffe performed this duty.

On the following day a Guard of Honour consisting of Major R. Brocklehurst, Lieutenants W. H. M. Freestun and L. E. C. W. Wilmer, with 100 other ranks, was furnished at Millbay Station on the departure of Their Royal Highnesses the Prince and Princess of Wales. H.R.H. expressed himself as very pleased with the smart appearance of the Guard of Honour.

The new pattern mess kit, rolled collar and open waistcoat, approved in 1904, was finally taken into wear this year.

On 1st August the Battalion proceeded to Salisbury Plain for brigade and divisional training, followed by manœuvres. They returned to Devonport on 9th September.

On 1st April 1908 the provisions of 'The Territorial and Reserve Forces Act 1907' came into force and the Militia ceased to exist. Under this Act the 4th (Militia) Battalion was disbanded, and the 3rd (Militia) Battalion was converted into the 3rd (Reserve) Battalion.

The 1st, 2nd and 3rd Volunteer Battalions Somerset Light Infantry were divided into two territorial battalions of eight companies each, and became known as the 4th and 5th Battalions Prince Albert's Somersetshire Light Infantry.

In 1908 the 2nd Battalion proceeded to Willsworthy Camp, Dartmoor, for battalion and brigade training, and subsequently on 3rd August proceeded by march route to Exeter, and thence by train to Gillingham, Dorset, where they detrained, and marched to Parkhouse, Salisbury Plain, via Mere, Fonthill Bishop, and Wylye, arriving at their destination on 11th August. Here brigade training was completed, and was followed by divisional training at West Down. The Battalion returned to Devonport on 5th September.

In the autumn the Battalion was placed under orders to proceed abroad, and embarked at Devonport on 5th November in the Hired Transport *Rohilla* for Malta, where they arrived on 11th November and disembarked the following day, having met the 1st Battalion returning home from India as before related.

The following officers accompanied the Battalion to Malta: Bt. Colonel C. H. H. Couchman, D.S.O.; Majors W. C. Cox, H. C. Frith, and E. H. Platt; Captains W. J. Bowker, D.S.O., C. J. Troyte-Bullock, H. G. R. Burges-Short, H. I. R. Allfrey (Adjutant) and P. Moran (Quartermaster); Lieutenants L. E. C. Willmer, E. D. Bally, C. M. A. Samuda, S. V. Wasborough, and G. N. Atkinson; 2nd Lieutenants R. H. Waddy and D. Kenworthy.

On 22nd April 1909 the Battalion attended a review by His Majesty the King, at which Her Majesty the Queen and H.I.M. the Dowager Empress of Russia were present. H.R.H. the Duke of Connaught commanded the parade.

On 10th May the Battalion lined the streets on the occasion of the visit of Their Imperial Majesties the German Emperor and Empress. The Battalion furnished the Guard of Honour at Valetta Palace, consisting of Major E. H. Swayne in command, with Lieutenants L. E. C. Wilmer and E. D. Bally and 100 rank and file.

On 13th May the following order was issued on the departure of Their Imperial Majesties the German Emperor and Empress:—

'His Royal Highness the Field-Marshal Commanding-in-Chief and High Commissioner Mediterranean has been requested by Field-Marshal His Imperial Majesty the German Emperor to express his appreciation of the smart appearance and steadiness of the troops who lined the streets on the 10th instant and of the Guard of Honour in attendance on His Imperial Majesty. It was a great satisfaction to the German Emperor to see the British Army so well represented.'

His Imperial Majesty the German Emperor was pleased to confer on Major E. H. Swayne the 3rd Class of the Order of the Red Eagle and on Lieutenants L. E. C. W. Wilmer and E. D. Bally the 4th Class of the same Order on the occasion of their being on the Guard of Honour at Valetta Palace.

His Majesty King Edward VII granted these officers private permission to wear the decoration whenever they are in the presence of Their Majesties or the Prince of Wales, or the German Emperor or Empress (King and Queen of Prussia) or any member of the Prussian Royal Family, and when invited on State occasions to meet any other members of the English Royal Family, the German Ambassador, or the Ambassador of King Edward VII in Germany. In the event of any doubt arising as to the occasion on which a member of His Majesty's Service should wear a Foreign Order the question shall be decided by the Chief of the Department under which the officer concerned is serving. The above was intimated in a letter from Lord Knollys, the King's Private Secretary, to each of the officers concerned.

On 31st July H.R.H. The Duke of Connaught relinquished the command of the British Troops in the Mediterranean when the following General Order was issued on 6th August:—

'Field-Marshal H.R.H. the Duke of Connaught bids all ranks farewell and wishes to assure them of his deep interest in their welfare and of his constant concern for their future efficiency in peace and war.

'It has been a great pleasure to H.R.H. to be so closely associated with an important command of the Royal Navy, and he takes this opportunity to express to Admiral the Hon. Sir Assheton Curzon-Howe and the Mediterranean Fleet his warm thanks for all they have done to assist him in his endeavours to promote the efficiency of his command.

'H.R.H. attaches very great importance to the development of a close sympathy between the two Services, and hopes that whenever portions of the Royal Navy and Army are in the same station opportunity will be taken of working together.'

An act of gallantry may here be recorded. On 2nd September No. 8069 Lance-Corporal L. Barnes was awarded the Royal Humane Society's Testimonial for his gallant conduct in attempting to save Private J. Shean of the Battalion from drowning whilst bathing in the harbour at Malta on 1st July.

In 1910 on 29th January His Majesty the King was graciously pleased to approve of the 13th Royal Regiment of Canadian Militia, Hamilton, Canada (subsequently known as The Royal Hamilton Light Infantry) being affiliated to the Regiment. This was the first case of a Regimental alliance connected with the Regiment.

On 22nd February 2nd Lieutenant A. H. H. Parr, eldest son of Major-General Henry Hallam Parr, C.B., C.M.G., died in hospital at Malta of enteric fever.

On 7th March the Battalion proceeded to the neighbouring island of Gozo for battalion training, returning to Valetta on 2nd April.

On 4th April Major-General E. L. England, C.B., Colonel of the Regiment, died. He was succeeded by Major-General Henry Hallam Parr, C.B., C.M.G.

On 21st April Colonel G. H. H. Couchman, D.S.O., vacated command of the Battalion when the following order was published:—

'On the completion of his period of command Colonel Couchman desires to thank all ranks of the Battalion for their loyal and willing support which has made his command such a pleasant one. The Battalion has always risen to the occasion when necessary and Colonel Couchman feels wherever it may go it will keep up the high reputation which it has always borne both in peace and war. He wishes all the best of luck, prosperity, and good-bye.'

He was succeeded in the command by Lieut.-Colonel H. J. Everett.

On 20th May on the occasion of the funeral of His late Majesty, King Edward VII, a special memorial service was held in St. Paul's, Valetta, at 5 p.m., when H.E. The Governor, the Lieut.-Governor, the Naval Commander-in-Chief, and representatives of all regiments and ships were present.

The King's Colour, which was draped with black crepe, and a Colour Party of the Prince Albert's (Somersetshire Light Infantry) were present in the Church during the service, the Battalion being specially selected for this duty by His Excellency owing to its bearing the name of His late Majesty's father. At 'Retreat' the Bugles, together with those of the 3rd Battalion King's Royal Rifle Corps, sounded the 'Last Post' on the Valetta Palace Square.

On the 22nd June, the occasion of the Coronation of H. M. King George V, Major-General Henry Hallam Parr was created a K.C.B.

In 1911 the Battalion was placed under orders to proceed to Tientsin and Peking, North China, and embarked on 17th September in the Hired Transport *Somali*, when the following officers accompanied the Battalion: Lieut.-Colonel H. J. Everett, Majors E. H. Platt, W. J. Bowker, D.S.O. and H. F. Hardman, Captains H. G. R. Burges-Short and A. R. S. Sale-Hill, Lieutenants T. A. Walsh (Adjutant), G. W. Lawson, S. V. Wasborough, G. N. Atkinson, R. H. Waddy, F. S. Mills, R. A. P. B. Watts, G. P. Steer and C. A. Williams, 2nd Lieutenants V. W. Roche, R. B. Denny, G. N. Molesworth, and R. L. Moore, Lieutenant and Quartermaster D. J. Owens, while Captain P. M. Wardlaw and Lieutenants N. H. Stone and W. Kenworthy were already on board the ship with a draft from the 1st Battalion.

His Excellency the Governor and Commander-in-Chief, Sir Leslie Rundle, in bidding farewell to the Commanding Officer, expressed himself as being very sorry to lose the Regiment from his command; he wished them the best of luck in future and felt confident that they would do well whether in peace or war.

Brigadier-General G. G. A. Egerton, commanding the Infantry Brigade at Malta, wrote to the Commanding Officer as follows:—

'I write a line to bid you and your Battalion farewell before you commence your long journey to the East. I very much regret that I shall not be at Malta to see you before you embark and I need hardly say how much I feel losing personally both you and your Battalion from the Brigade under my command. I shall always look with the greatest pleasure to my two years' association with the Regiment and hope to meet again the many friends I have made in its ranks.'

The Battalion reached Port Said on the 21st September and left again the same day for Colombo, where they arrived on 4th October. Calls were made at Singapore on 10th October and Hong-Kong on the 17th, and the port of disembarkation, Chingwangtao, was reached on 23rd October. Having dispatched advance parties to Tientsin and Peking, the remainder disembarked on the 25th and proceeded by rail to Tientsin and Peking, the headquarters and six companies proceeding to the former station, while 'C' and 'D' Companies made up the Legation Guard at Peking.

Ever since the Boxer troubles in 1900 the foreign Concessions at Tientsin had been garrisoned by contingents furnished by the Great Powers. Besides Great Britain, Austria, France, Germany, Japan, Russia and the United States all furnished troops with a view to guarding the railway to Peking and being at hand in case of further trouble threatening the Legations at the Capital.

At the time of the arrival of the 2nd Battalion North China was in a more disturbed state than usual, not so much on account of any anti-foreign feeling, but rather owing to the rival ambitions of various Chinese generals who were constantly warring among themselves. In consequence of this state of affairs the 1st Battalion Royal Inniskilling Fusiliers, whom the 2nd Battalion were to have relieved, were retained in China for an extra year.

In January 1912 the Battalion had six detachments on the railway, viz. at Fengtai, an important railway junction outside Peking, Lin-Hsi, Leichuang, Kaiping, Wali, and Kuyeh. The last four were relieved by the 15th Regiment American Army at the end of the month.

On the evening of 29th February some Chinese troops in Peking mutinied, and a good deal of indiscriminate shooting, looting, and burning took place. The Legation Guards were constantly under arms, while Peking continued in a disturbed state for several days afterwards.

On the following day, 1st March, at 12.30 a.m. the Chinese 3rd Division quartered in and around Fengtai where 'E' and half 'B' Company were stationed, got out of hand and commenced shooting and looting round the railway station. The European women and children were with some difficulty brought into the fortified post, and dispatched in the afternoon by train to Tientsin.

On 2nd March there was again trouble at Fengtai owing to a conflict between the Chinese mutineers and the loyal troops under General Chen, railway traffic being stopped for a time, but eventually the latter got the upper hand. On the same evening the Chinese troops in the city of Tientsin mutinied, part of the town was burnt down and indiscriminate shooting continued all night. The European troops stood to arms, while 'H' Company occupied the railway station, being relieved by French troops the following day.

On 3rd March six companies of the Royal Inniskilling Fusiliers were sent by train to Fengtai and an ultimatum delivered to the Chinese military authorities demanding their withdrawal from the railway station by 8 a.m. on the 4th. This ultimatum was complied with. The detachment of the Regiment at Fengtai were sent to reinforce the Legation Guard at Peking, being relieved by two companies of the Royal Inniskilling Fusiliers.

On 5th March Lieutenant N. H. Stone, with 8 Mounted Infantry and 30 Chinese Cavalry, was sent from Peking to Tungchow, 30 miles south of Paotingfu, to bring in the Bishop of Peking, one missionary, and the body of another who had been murdered. The party was accompanied by Lieut.-Colonel Willoughby, military attaché at Peking, and Major Barton of the Legation. Lieutenant Stone's party returned to Peking on the 9th, having successfully accomplished their task.

The disturbances now gradually died down, though for some days mounted infantry patrols continued to watch the Chinese troops in the neighbourhood of Tientsin.

On 10th June 'G' Company proceeded to Shan-hai-Kwan, which is situated on the Gulf of Liaotang, where the Great Wall of China meets the sea. There the company carried out musketry and field training and also formed the headquarters of a convalescent camp.

During this year the title of the Regiment was changed in two minor respects in order to make it shorter—viz. the omission of 'The' before 'Prince Albert's' and the omission of the suffix 'shire' in 'Somersetshire'. The new title then read 'Prince Albert's (Somerset Light Infantry)'.

On 3rd September 'A' Company proceeded on detachment to Wei-hai-Wei in relief of a company of the Royal Inniskilling Fusiliers.

During September and October battalion training was carried out at Huang Tsun about 20 miles south-east of Peking.

Towards the end of the year the privilege of wearing the Regimental tie, &c., was extended to the officers of the 13th Royal Regiment (Canadian Militia) as set forth in the following letter from the Colonel of the Regiment to the officer commanding 13th Royal Regiment (Canadian Militia):—

'DEAR COLONEL NEWBURN,—

Colonel Frith commanding the 1st Battalion has told me of the wish of your Regiment to wear the Officers' Colours of the Somersets.

The officers of the 2nd Battalion Somersets in China have now been communicated with, and the officers of both battalions are in favour of the proposal, and are quite willing that the officers of your Regiment should adopt the Colours.

Of this, as Colonel of the Regiment, I cordially approve.

My brother officers and I hope that it will be an additional link between the two regiments.

I am sorry that when you paid your visit to the 1st Battalion I was not in the neighbourhood of Bordon, as it would have given me great pleasure to have made your acquaintance.

I trust that I may do so at some future visit of yours to England.

With my best compliments to you and your Regiment,
  Believe me, dear Colonel Newburn,
    Yours very truly,
    HENRY HALLAM PARR, Major-General.
Colonel, Prince Albert's (Somerset Light Infantry).'

On 7th April 1913 'A' Company returned to Tientsin from Wei-hai-Wei. The movements of the other detachments do not call for detailed enumeration, but it may suffice to say that detachments were normally relieved every six months, the Legation Guard at Peking taking two companies, Fengtai one and sometimes two companies, and Shan-hai-kwan or Pei-tai-ho one company in the summer months only; thus the headquarters at Tientsin rarely exceeded half a battalion.

On 7th October the detachments were withdrawn to Tientsin and on the 20th the Battalion left Tientsin by rail for Chingwangtao, where they embarked on the Hired Transport *Soudan* for service in India.

On arrival at Hong-Kong on 27th October, the Battalion disembarked and went into camp on the mainland as the transport had to be painted. After a week on shore the voyage was continued on 3rd November, Singapore was reached on the 9th, Colombo on the 15th and finally Karachi on the 21st. The Battalion, having disembarked, proceeded in two trains to Quetta on the 22nd, arriving at their destination on the 23rd, where they relieved the 1st Battalion, Essex Regiment. A pleasing incident of their arrival was the welcome accorded to the Battalion by Brigadier-General W. P. Braithwaite, C.B., Commandant of the Staff College, Quetta, and an old officer of the Regiment.

In March 1914 the old eight-company organization of the Battalion came to an end, and was replaced by the four-company organization. 'A' and 'B' Companies became No. 1 Company, 'C' and 'D' No. 2, 'E' and 'F' No. 3 and 'G' and 'H' No. 4. No appreciable difference in the establishment of the Battalion was caused by this change.

On 4th April Major-General Sir Henry Hallam Parr, K.C.B., C.M.G., Colonel of the Regiment, died, a most distinguished officer whose regimental career has been recorded on these pages, while his extra regimental services will be found in Appendix A.

He was succeeded in the command of the Regiment by Major-General R. L. Payne, C.B., D.S.O., at that time commanding the 5th (Mhow) Division in India. General Payne joined the Regiment in 1876, and served in the Sekukini and Zulu Campaigns, South Africa in 1878–9, the Burma Campaign of 1885–6 and in the Mohmand Campaign, North-West Frontier, in 1897.

On 21st April Lieut.-Colonel H. J. Everett vacated the command of the Battalion and was succeeded by Lieut.-Colonel E. H. R. C. Platt.

The following farewell order was published by Lieut.-Colonel H. J. Everett on vacating the command:—

'The Commanding Officer, in bidding farewell, wishes to thank all ranks for the way in which they have backed him up in his responsible duties.

'He feels convinced that the 2nd Battalion will maintain and increase the high reputation of the Regiment both in sports and on manœuvres, in peace and in war.

'He wishes all ranks the best of luck in the future.'

Colonel H. J. Everett joined the Regiment in 1885, was Adjutant of the 1st Battalion from 1890 to 1894, saw active service in the South African War 1899 to 1902 as already described in the previous chapter, and was a graduate of the Staff College.

A few months later in August 1914 the Great War broke out. The 2nd Battalion, having recently arrived in India, was one of the few British battalions to remain in the country and consequently had not the same opportunities as its sister regular battalion to prove its mettle and to add its share to the Regimental Honours which its efficiency and high reputation had every promise of doing.

1st BATTALION

It remains to complete the record of the 1st Battalion who arrived at Portland from India on 20th November 1908. When the rank and file of the Battalion had returned to Portland from furlough in January 1909, the barrack accommodation at the Verne Barracks proving insufficient to house all the men, 'E', 'F', 'H' and 'K' Companies, strength 8 officers and 380 other ranks, were sent to Crown Hill Barracks, Devonport, and remained there till the 30th April, when they rejoined the Battalion at Bovington Camp, Wool.

During the late summer the Battalion proceeded to Victoria Barracks, Windsor, in relief of the 1st Battalion Irish Guards for duty at Windsor Castle for a few weeks. This was the first time since 1882 that a line battalion had been on duty at Windsor. On completion of this duty the Battalion returned to Portland, and after the furlough season in the following winter 'C' and 'D' Companies, under Captain L. A. Jones-Mortimer, proceeded to Dorchester, where they occupied the old Royal Horse Artillery barracks.

On the 27th November 1909 Lieut.-Colonel C. H. Stisted relinquished the command of the Battalion and was succeeded by Lieut.-Colonel H. C. Frith.

In the summer of 1910 company training was again carried out at Bovington Camp, Wool, and battalion training at Bulford, Salisbury Plain, at the conclusion of which the Battalion received special praise from General Sir C. W. M. Douglas, K.C.B., Commander-in-Chief Southern Command, and also from Brig.-General H. H. Burney, C.B., commanding the 9th Infantry Brigade, for the way in which their training had been carried out.

In June 'The Old Comrades' Association' of the Regiment was founded under the Presidency of the Colonel of the Regiment. The objects of the Association being—

(1) To assist those who, owing to poverty, are in need of pecuniary assistance and who have served in the Somerset Light Infantry (Prince Albert's) or are the dependants, widows, or orphans of persons who have served in the said Regiment.

(2) To promote *esprit de corps*, and to keep in touch with old comrades.

(3) To assist in obtaining civil employment.

On the 23rd August, for the second year in succession, the Battalion proceeded to Windsor for duty and this time in relief of the Scots Guards. The Battalion returned to Portland and Dorchester on the 13th September.

In March 1911, on the occasion of the great strike in the coal industry, 'C', 'D' and 'E' Companies, each of a strength of 3 officers and 60 other ranks, proceeded to South Wales to help preserve order. Major J. B. Thomson was first of all in command, but was later relieved by Major J. A. Thicknesse. The

MAJOR-GENERAL R. L. PAYNE, C.B., D.S.O.
Colonel of the Regiment, 1914-1919

detachment returned to Portland, after nearly six months' absence, on the 14th September.

Lieut.-Colonel Freeth, D.S.O., Lancashire Fusiliers, commanding Troops, Strike Area, South Wales, wrote as follows on the conclusion of this duty:—

'Your detachment is leaving to-morrow. They have been so long under my command that I cannot let them go without writing to you to say how very thoroughly they have all, officers and men, done their work down here. I am not merely giving my own opinion, but that of everybody who has come in contact with them. So far as I am concerned I hope I shall never have anything to do with the strike again, but if I do, I hope I shall be backed by officers and men reliable and trustworthy as those under the command of Thicknesse.'

On the occasion of the coronation of His Majesty King George V on 22nd June, the Battalion furnished a contingent to 'D' Composite Battalion, 19th Provisional Brigade, consisting of the Battalion Staff, Lieut.-Colonel H. C. Frith being in command, and one company of 3 officers and 50 other ranks. The other companies were furnished respectively by the 1st Battalion East Yorkshire Regiment, 1st Battalion Leicester Regiment, 1st Battalion East Lancashire Regiment, 2nd Battalion Border Regiment, 1st Battalion Hampshire Regiment, 1st Battalion Dorset Regiment and 2nd Battalion Middlesex Regiment.

On Coronation Day the Provisional Battalion lined the streets at Whitehall and on the following day during the Royal procession they did similar duty in Trafalgar Square.

During their stay in London they were encamped in Regent's Park near the south entrance to the Zoological Gardens.

On the 3rd October 1911 the 1st Battalion changed quarters, moving from Portland and Dorchester to Bordon (Quebec Barracks).

On the 18th May 1912 Bordon Camp was visited by Their Majesties the King and Queen. The 1st Battalion carried out in the presence of Their Majesties an attack on a flagged position concluding with a bayonet charge. An account in *The Times* of this attack concludes with the following words:—

'The keenness of all ranks was remarkable. It wanted no Silver Light Infantry Bugles to put nerve into the attack, though they added to the effect of the final phase.

'Whatever the faults in method that the critical eye of an inspecting General might discover, nothing could extinguish the buoyant fitness of a very remarkable Battalion. They must have pleased the King greatly.'

From the 8th to the 30th July the Battalion was encamped at Rushmore near Aldershot for brigade and divisional training, and again from the 8th to the 21st September took part in inter-divisional and army manœuvres in Cambridgeshire and neighbouring counties.

In the following year 1913 the Battalion was again encamped at Rushmore from 29th June to 26th July for brigade and divisional training and subsequently on the 12th September took part in Command and Army Exercises.

On the 28th September the Battalion moved from Bordon and proceeded to Colchester, where they were quartered in the Goojerat Barracks.

On the 27th November 1913 Lieut.-Colonel H. C. Frith relinquished the command of the Battalion and was succeeded by Lieut.-Colonel E. H. Swayne. Colonel Frith joined the Regiment in 1882 and was employed with the Egyptian Army from 1885 to 1905, during which time he saw much active service in the Soudan, in 1885 when he was present at the action of Giniss, and again in 1889 when he was present at the action of Toski. From 1897 to 1902 he was Station Staff Officer, 1st Class, in India.

The following is a copy of his farewell order:—

'Lieut.-Colonel Frith on relinquishing the command of the Battalion wishes to place on record his grateful appreciation of the loyal support he has always received from the Officers, Warrant Officers, N.C.Os. and men during the period of his command, and he feels confident that the same support will be extended to his successor.

'He desires to express his best wishes for the future success of the Battalion, and of all belonging to it.'

At Colchester the Battalion formed part of the 11th Infantry Brigade (Brig.-General A. Hunter-Weston) of the 4th Division (Major-General T. D'O. Snow, commanding).

This latter officer, afterwards Colonel of the Regiment, had seen active service with the 1st Battalion during the Zulu War, and with the Camel Corps in the Gordon Relief Expedition in 1885, had been Adjutant of the 1st Battalion from 1886–90, and was a graduate of the Staff College.

The important point to note is that the Battalion now, for the first time in its history in peace-time, formed part of fighting formations (brigade and division) in which it was destined to fight in war. It is difficult to exaggerate the importance of this period of training—January to July 1914. Supervision by the same commanders and the same staff that were to function in war, the opportunities for the co-operation of the different arms, and the personal relations engendered between officers and men of all units were advantages which left their mark on the 1st Battalion in the forthcoming ordeal.

CONCLUSION

THE preceding pages show that the Thirteenth, now The Somerset Light Infantry (Prince Albert's), has gained laurels in Europe, Asia, Africa and America over a period of 229 years. From the time of its declaration in favour of the Protestant interest at the Revolution, it has run a career of glory, at the commencement of which was the Battle of Killiecrankie, followed soon after by the Battle of the Boyne and the Siege of Cork. Leaving the Army in Flanders in 1703, after a short campaign under the renowned Duke of Marlborough, it next formed part of the force in the Peninsula, and highly distinguished itself in the first defence of Gibraltar in 1704–5, a few months after the capture of that fortress from the Spaniards. While serving in Spain, the chivalrous Earl of Peterborough formed the greater portion of the corps into a cavalry regiment—an event unprecedented in the military history of the British Army—in which character it proved its bravery at the disastrous Battle of Almanza.

The second defence of Gibraltar in 1727, the battlefields of Dettingen, Fontenoy, Falkirk, Culloden, Roncoux and Val all attest its valour; subsequently the expedition against St. Domingo, the campaign in Egypt under the immortal Abercromby, the capture of Martinique and Guadaloupe and the campaigns on the Canadian frontier in 1813–14 added to its ancient renown.

Constituted a corps of Light Infantry in 1822, the Regiment next took part in the 1st Burmese War, in which it sustained a prominent part. Then follow the campaigns in Afghanistan 1839–42, the capture of the stronghold of Ghazni, the advance on Kabul, the Defence of Jellalabad and subsequent recapture of Kabul.

Even after the lapse of many years the Defence of Jellalabad, associated as it is with the name of 'The Illustrious Garrison' and the Royal title of 'Prince Albert's', still holds the pride of place in the Records of the Regiment, while the names of Sale and Havelock have obtained a distinguished niche in their country's history.

The Siege of Sevastopol in the Crimean War and the Relief of Azimghur in the Indian Mutiny will ever be treasured as precious memories in the Regiment.

Coming down to more recent times, the campaigns of 1878–9 in South Africa, when the Regiment greatly distinguished itself at the critical Action of Kambula and at the Battle of Ulundi, are additional battle honours on the Colours of the Regiment. Then follows the 3rd Burmese War of 1885–6, when the Regiment renewed the high reputation it had gained in that country some sixty years previously.

A short campaign on the North-West Frontier of India in 1897 and the long-drawn-out South African War 1899–1902, when the Regiment took a prominent part in the Relief of Ladysmith and the subsequent operations for the pacification of the country, form a fitting and glorious conclusion to the distinguished war records of the Regiment prior to the Great War.

Such were the traditions that the Regiment handed over to the various units that bore its name during the Great War and nobly did these units fulfil the trust they inherited, as is described in the next volume.

APPENDIX A

SUCCESSION OF COLONELS OF THE THIRTEENTH
SUBSEQUENTLY
THE SOMERSET LIGHT INFANTRY (PRINCE ALBERT'S)

	Appointed	
Theophilus Earl of Huntingdon	20th June	1685
Ferdinando Hastings	December	1688
Sir John Jacob, Bart.	13th March	1695
James Earl of Barrymore	15th March	1702
Stanhope Cotton	8th July	1715
Lord Mark Kerr	25th December	1725
Lord Middleton	29th May	1732
The Honourable Henry Pulteney	5th July	1739
His Royal Highness William Henry, Duke of Gloucester, K.G.	25th June	1766
The Honourable James Murray	16th December	1767
George Ainslie	5th June	1789
Alexander Campbell	11th July	1804
Edward Morrison	15th February	1813
Sir Robert Henry Sale, G.C.B.	15th December	1843
Sir William Maynard Gomm, G.C.B.	10th March	1846
Philip M'Pherson, C.B.	15th August	1863
Philip Spencer Stanhope	3rd February	1864
Lord Mark Kerr, G.C.B.	22nd February	1880
Sir John William Cox, K.C.B.	18th May	1900
Edward Lutwyche England, C.B.	3rd October	1901
Sir Henry Hallam Parr, K.C.B., C.M.G.	5th April	1910
Richard Lloyd Payne, C.B., D.S.O.	5th April	1914

THEOPHILUS, seventh Earl of Huntingdon, succeeded to that dignity on the decease of his father in 1655. In the reign of King Charles II he was attached to the principles entertained by James Duke of Monmouth, who was at the head of a political party in the kingdom, but quitted it upon seeing that the views of those with whom he was connected were destructive of the Constitution; and in 1683 he was appointed a member of the Privy Council. He held several appointments in the reign of King James II; was captain of the band of gentlemen pensioners, now the Honourable Corps of Gentlemen-at-Arms; and on the breaking out of the Duke of Monmouth's rebellion in June 1685 he exerted himself in raising men for the King's service, and was appointed Colonel of one of the regiments embodied on that occasion, now the Somerset Light Infantry. At the Revolution in 1688, he adhered to King James II, and being with his regiment in garrison at Plymouth was arrested by Colonel the Earl of Bath, Lieut.-Colonel Hastings, and other officers, who declared for the Prince of Orange. Continuing firm in his adherence to the Roman Catholic cause, he was removed from his appointments by King William; was excluded from the benefit of the Act of Indemnity passed on the 23rd May 1690, and upon the receipt of advice of the intended descent in favour of the exiled Sovereign from La Hogue, in 1692, was sent a prisoner to the Tower of London; but was not long detained in confinement. The Earl of Huntington was one of the peers who protested against the Act of Settlement in 1701. His lordship died suddenly at his house in Charles Street, St. James's, on the 30th May 1701.

FERDINANDO HASTINGS, cousin of the former colonel, entered the Army in the reign of King Charles II, and was promoted to the command of a company in the 1st Foot Guards; in 1686 he was appointed Lieutenant-Colonel of the Regiment which is now the Somerset Light Infantry. At the Revolution in 1688, he united with the Earl of Bath in bringing over the garrison of Plymouth to the interest of the Prince of Orange, and was rewarded with the colonelcy of his Regiment. He served in Scotland under Major-General Hugh Mackay against the clans under Viscount Dundee, and distinguished himself at the Battle of Killiecrankie on the 27th July 1689. He afterwards proceeded with his regiment to Ireland, and served at the Battle of the Boyne, and at the reduction of Cork and Kinsale, in 1690; he evinced ability and personal bravery in several detached services in 1691, and served in the expedition under Lieut.-General Meinhard Duke of Leinster in 1692. He was afterwards found guilty of extortion in his regiment, and was cashiered on the 4th of March 1695.

SIR JOHN JACOB, Bart., of Bromley, in the County of Middlesex, commenced his military career in the summer of 1685, and was for many years an officer in the Regiment which is now the Somerset Light Infantry, in which corps he rose to the rank of Lieutenant-Colonel. He evinced great courage, and received a severe wound at the Battle of Killiecrankie, where Viscount Dundee was killed; also behaved with signal gallantry, under the eye of his Sovereign, at the Battle of the Boyne in 1690; and served under the Earl of Marlborough at the capture of Cork and Kinsale. King William III highly approved of his conduct, and promoted him to the colonelcy of his Regiment in 1695. Being afterwards desirous of retiring from the service, he obtained permission to sell the colonelcy for fourteen hundred guineas to his brother-in-law, James Earl of Barrymore. He died in 1739.

JAMES, fourth EARL of BARRYMORE, embraced the interests of the Prince of Orange at the Revolution in 1688, and was nominated Lieutenant-Colonel in the Army on the 31st December of that year. He subsequently held the commission of Captain in the 17th Foot, and purchased the colonelcy of the

APPENDIX A

13th Regiment in March 1702. He was promoted to the rank of Brigadier-General in 1706, and to that of Major-General in 1708. He served in Portugal in the War of the Spanish Succession, and gallantly led his regiment to the charge at the Battle of the Caya, on the 7th May 1709, overcoming all opposition, and recapturing the Portuguese guns; but not being supported by the Portuguese horse of the left wing, his regiment became insulated, and he was taken prisoner. In 1710 he was promoted to the rank of Lieutenant-General; and in 1713 was sworn a Member of the Privy Council. He was elected a Member of Parliament for the borough of Stockbridge in 1713, and afterwards for Wigan in Lancashire. He retired from the colonelcy in 1715. His decease occurred on the 5th January 1747, at Castlelyons, where a magnificent marble monument has been erected to his memory.

STANHOPE COTTON served with reputation in the wars of Queen Anne, as Captain, Major, and Lieut.-Colonel of Foot; he was several years in Bowles's Regiment, which was disbanded at the Peace of Utrecht; and he was rewarded with the rank of Colonel, and the appointment of Lieutenant-Governor of Gibraltar. In 1715 he obtained the colonelcy of the present Somerset Light Infantry, then in garrison at Gibraltar, and under his care that Regiment became celebrated for its efficiency and orderly conduct. He died on the 7th December 1725.

LORD MARK KERR, fourth son of Robert fourth Earl and first Marquis of Lothian, choosing the profession of arms, was appointed Captain of a company of infantry on the 1st January 1694, and served in Flanders under King William III. He was at this period of delicate appearance, seemingly quiet and without much spirit. It is related that during these early campaigns the following incident occurred: One evening at a large party, a foreign officer grossly insulted his lordship, who apparently took no notice of his conduct. The tent was crowded, and the festivities continued. After several of the guests had retired, Lord Mark Kerr was reminded that it was incumbent upon him to call out the offender, whereupon he replied: 'It is too late for that; they are burying him outside now.' He had, in fact, slipped out unperceived, except by his antagonist and second, and killed his insulter in a duel, and the grave had been dug in the camping ground. On the breaking out of the war in Queen Anne's reign, he obtained the lieutenant-colonelcy of General Macartney's newly raised regiment (disbanded at the Peace of Utrecht), with which he embarked from Scotland in the spring of 1704, and served the campaign of that year on the Dutch frontier. On the 1st January 1706 he was promoted to the colonelcy of a newly raised regiment of foot, with which he served in the expedition under the Earl of Rivers in the same year, and when the projected descent on the coast of France was abandoned, he proceeded to Portugal, and afterwards to Spain. He commanded his regiment at the Battle of Almanza, on the 25th April 1707, which was formed between two brigades of Portuguese cavalry; these quitted the field at the first attack. It was afterwards fiercely engaged with very superior numbers, and literally cut to pieces; his lordship was wounded in the arm, his lieutenant-colonel and major were both killed and his regiment lost twenty-three officers killed, wounded and prisoners. In February 1711 he was promoted to the rank of Brigadier-General, and in 1712 he was nominated Colonel of the 29th Foot. He commanded a brigade of infantry in the expedition to Spain, under Lord (afterwards Viscount) Cobham, in 1719, and served at the capture of Vigo, Rondendella, and Pont-a-Vedra. In 1725 he obtained the colonelcy of the 13th Regiment, and was promoted to the rank of Major-General in 1727. In 1732 King George II removed him to the 11th Dragoons, which, under his lordship's command, became the crack regiment of the day; he was advanced to the rank of Lieutenant-General in 1735, and in 1740 His Majesty conferred on him the governorship of Guernsey; in the same year he was appointed General of the Ordnance in Ireland, and in 1743 he was promoted General of Foot. On the 30th July 1745 he was constituted Constable and Governor of Edinburgh Castle. After the defeat of Lieut.-General Sir John Cope at Prestonpans on the 21st September of that year, some of the dragoons, who had fled from the field of battle, galloped up to the castle, but the Governor refused to admit them, and threatened to open fire upon them, as cowards who had deserted their Colours. They afterwards sought shelter at Berwick. Lord Mark Kerr, on meeting Sir John, is reported to have observed, that he was 'the first general who had ever brought the news of his own defeat', a sarcasm which has been perpetuated in the well-known Scotch song of 'Johnnie Cope'. His lordship, in 1751, was placed on the staff of Ireland. It is recorded in Douglas's *Peerage of Scotland* that—'He was a man of marked and decided character; with the strictest notions of honour and good-breeding; he retained, perhaps, too punctilious an observance of etiquette, as it gave him an air of frivolity. He was soldier-like in his appearance; formal in his deportment; whimsical, even finical in his dress; but he commanded respect wherever he went, for none dared to laugh at his singularities. Manners, which in foreign courts (where they had been acquired) would have passed unobserved, were considered as fantastic in his own country, and were apt to lead his impatient spirit into rencontres too often fatal to his antagonists. Naturally of a good temper, his frequent appeals to the sword on trivial occasions drew on him the imputation of being a quarrelsome man; but he was inoffensive unless provoked; and never meddled with any one, but such as chose to meddle with him.' His lordship, there is no doubt, although a great dandy and somewhat of a duellist, was the pink and type of the military gallantry and pluck of his time, and was a popular character in his day. He died in London on the 2nd February 1752, and was interred during the evening of the 6th in Kensington Church.

JOHN MIDDLETON was granted a commission in the Army in the reign of King William III, and was promoted to the rank of Captain in 1706; he served in Spain during the War of the Spanish Succession, and also on board the fleet, where his company was employed as Marines. He was for many years an officer in the regiment now known as the King's Own Scottish Borderers, in which corps he rose to the rank of Lieutenant-Colonel, and was promoted to the rank of Colonel in 1711. He commanded the 25th in Scotland, under the Duke of Argyle, during the rebellion of the Earl of Mar; and in 1721 was rewarded with the colonelcy of that corps, which he held until 1732, when he was removed to the 13th Regiment. He was promoted to the rank of Brigadier-General in 1735. His decease occurred on the 4th May 1739, at which period he was member of Parliament for Aberdeen.

THE HONOURABLE HENRY PULTENEY was appointed Ensign in a regiment of foot on the 10th January 1703, and served during Queen Anne's wars, under the celebrated John Duke of Marlborough. He was for several years in the 1st Foot Guards, and was promoted in July 1715 to the command of the grenadier company in the 2nd Foot Guards, with the rank of Lieutenant-Colonel. In 1733 he was promoted to the commission of second Major, with the rank of Colonel, and in 1734 to that of first Major in the same regiment, from which he was removed, in 1739, to the colonelcy of the present Somerset Light Infantry; at the same time he was appointed Governor of Hull. He was promoted to the rank of Brigadier-General in 1742, and accompanied the Army to Flanders, under the Earl of Stair. On the 3rd July 1743 he was advanced to the rank of Major-General; on the 8th August 1747 to that of Lieutenant-General; and on the 22nd February 1765 to that of General. On the elevation of his brother to the dignity of Earl of Bath, he was distinguished by the style of Honourable; and upon his brother's decease, in 1764, when the title became extinct, he succeeded to the paternal estate. He afterwards resigned his commissions. He died on the 26th October 1767.

WILLIAM HENRY DUKE OF GLOUCESTER, K.G. His Royal Highness was the third son of Frederick Prince of Wales (who died 20th March 1751), and was elected a Knight of the most noble Order of the Garter in 1762, and a few days before he was of age, viz. on the 17th November 1764, his brother, King George III, conferred on him the dignity of Duke of Gloucester and Edinburgh, and Earl of Connaught; in December following he took his seat in the Privy Council. In 1766 His Royal Highness was appointed Colonel of the 13th Regiment; and on the decease of his brother, Edward Duke of York, in the autumn of 1767, he received a grant from the King of Cranbourne Chase Lodge, Windsor Forest. In December of the same year he was promoted to the rank of Major-General, and appointed Colonel of the 3rd Foot Guards. In April 1770 he was advanced to the rank of Lieutenant-General, and nominated to the colonelcy of the 1st Foot Guards. He was promoted to the rank of General in 1772, and to that of Field-Marshal in 1793. His Royal Highness was distinguished as a polite scholar and an accomplished gentleman, engaging in his manners, respectful to his Sovereign, affable to his acquaintance, and generous and condescending to his inferiors; a liberal supporter of every institution calculated to promote the interests of society, accompanied by a modest serenity of conduct which kept many instances of his generosity out of public view; and a meekness of disposition pervaded every feature of his character, which ensured for him the love of all ranks. He died on the 25th August 1805.

THE HONOURABLE JAMES MURRAY, son of the Duke of Atholl, served several years in the 15th Foot, of which regiment he was appointed Lieutenant-Colonel on the 15th January 1751. He served with his corps in North America in the early part of the Seven Years War; had the local rank of Colonel in that country on the 7th January 1758, and was appointed Colonel-Commandant in the 60th Royal American Regiment on the 24th October 1759. He also served in Germany, under Prince Ferdinand of Brunswick, and was wounded in the breast by a musket-ball, which could not be extracted, and he was never afterwards able to sleep in a recumbent posture. He was promoted to the rank of Major-General in 1762; appointed Colonel of the 13th Regiment in 1767, in succession to His Royal Highness the Duke of Gloucester; was advanced to the rank of Lieutenant-General in 1772, and to that of General in 1783. In 1789 he was removed to the 21st or Royal North British Fusiliers. He also held the appointment of Governor of Hull. His decease occurred in 1794, and he was buried in Westminster Abbey.

GEORGE AINSLIE was appointed, in 1755, Sub-Lieutenant in the 2nd or Scots troops of Horse Grenadier Guards, of which General Eliott, afterwards Lord Heathfield, the celebrated Governor of Gibraltar, was lieutenant-colonel; and when Colonel Eliott raised his famed regiment of 'Light Horse', now the 15th, or King's Hussars, Lieutenant Ainslie was appointed Captain of the first troop therein. He proceeded with the 15th Light Dragoons to Germany in 1760, and distinguished himself in the memorable action at Emsdorf on the 16th July in that year, the first enterprise in which that regiment was engaged, and where it acquired great honour. He was also present at numerous other actions, where 'Eliott's Light Horse' availed themselves of every opportunity to acquire additional laurels; and on the 29th March 1762 he was promoted to the majority of the regiment. At the engagement near Homburg, on the 1st July 1762 he highly distinguished himself, and was commended in the public dispatch of Prince Ferdinand of Brunswick. In the action near Friedberg, on the 30th August following, he was attacked by three French Hussars, and received a dangerous wound in the head. He was promoted to the lieutenant-colonelcy of the 15th Light Dragoons in 1770; to the rank of Colonel in the Army in 1779; and to that of Major-General in 1782. In 1789 King George III rewarded him with the colonelcy of the 13th Regiment, His Majesty having frequently witnessed, and expressed his high approbation of the condition of the 15th Light Dragoons under Colonel Ainslie's command. He was afterwards appointed Lieutenant-Governor of Scilly Island; was promoted to the rank of Lieutenant-General in 1796, and to that of General in 1801. He died in 1804.

ALEXANDER CAMPBELL was appointed, on the 21st April 1769, Ensign in the 42nd, Royal Highland Regiment, then in Ireland; and in December 1770 was promoted to a lieutenancy in the 2nd Battalion of the Royals, which he joined at the Island of Minorca. In September 1772 he obtained a company in the 50th, from which he exchanged to the 62nd Regiment in November following. He embarked for Canada with the 62nd on the breaking out of the American War, and served the campaign of 1776, under General Carleton,

APPENDIX A

afterwards Lord Dorchester. In 1777 he served under Lieut.-General Burgoyne, in the desperate attempt to advance from Canada through the country, in a state of rebellion, to Albany, sharing in the toils and fighting of that enterprise, and being included in the convention at Saratoga. On the 26th December 1777 he was promoted Major in the 74th Regiment, and proceeding to New York was appointed to act as Major of the 1st Battalion of Light Infantry, with which he served two campaigns, and at the termination of the war he commanded at Penobscot. On the 31st December 1782 he was promoted to the lieutenant-colonelcy of the 62nd, with which regiment he served in Scotland and Ireland until June 1789, when he exchanged to Captain and Lieutenant-Colonel in the 3rd Foot Guards. He served in the campaign of 1793, and part of that of 1794, in Flanders, under His Royal Highness the Duke of York; in the meantime he had been promoted to the rank of Colonel (12th October 1793), and commissioned to raise the late 116th Regiment, when he withdrew from Flanders. He subsequently commanded a brigade in the forces under Lieut.-General the Earl of Moira, and was promoted to the rank of Major-General on the 26th February 1795. In 1796 he served under Lieut.-General Sir Ralph Abercromby in the West Indies, and was appointed Colonel of the 7th West India Regiment in November of that year. He served on the staff at Newcastle in 1797; in Ireland in 1798; and afterwards in Scotland. In 1802 his regiment was disbanded; he was promoted to the rank of Lieutenant-General in April of that year, and placed on the staff of Ireland, and subsequently on that of Scotland, where he served five years. In 1804 he was appointed Colonel of the 13th Regiment; in 1812 he was promoted to the rank of General, and was removed to the 32nd Regiment in 1813. He died on the 24th February 1832.

EDWARD MORRISON entered the Army as Ensign in the Coldstream Guards, on the 20th January 1777; was shortly after employed as Assistant Quartermaster-General; and on the 15th September 1780 succeeded to a lieutenancy with the rank of Captain. From November 1781 to June he served as aide-de-camp to the Commander-in-Chief in the West Indies. He was promoted to a company, with the rank of Lieutenant-Colonel, on the 13th January 1790, and in 1793 was appointed Deputy Quartermaster-General; but obtained permission to join the 1st Battalion of the Coldstream Guards in Flanders, in 1794. He was appointed Governor of Chester on the 2nd November 1796. On the 26th February 1795 he received the brevet rank of Colonel; and on the 19th of November 1800 was appointed Colonel of the Leicester Fencibles, and on the 1st January 1805, of a battalion in the 60th Regiment. He was advanced to the rank of Major-General on the 1st January 1798; and in April following was appointed to the staff in Ireland, where he commanded the Limerick District during the rebellion. He was removed to the staff in England in July 1803, and on the 1st January 1805 was advanced to the rank of Lieutenant-General; in May 1809 was appointed Lieutenant-General and commander of the forces in Jamaica, and was promoted to the rank of General on the 4th June 1814. On the 15th February of the previous year King George III conferred on him the colonelcy of the 13th Regiment, which he held to the period of his decease, which occurred on the 3rd December 1843.

Sir Robert Henry Sale at the early age of fourteen had the honour of carrying his Sovereign's colours as Ensign in the 36th Regiment, to which he was gazetted on the 19th January 1795; he was promoted to a lieutenancy on the 12th April 1797 and on the 8th January following exchanged into the 12th Foot, with which regiment he served at the Battle of Mallavelly, gained by Lieut.-General (afterwards Lord) Harris on the 27th March 1799. In less than two months occurred the siege of Seringapatam, where Lieutenant Sale's services were rewarded by a medal. He served throughout the campaign of 1801, in the Wynaud country, and on the 23rd March 1806 obtained his company. Captain Sale took part in the storming of the Travancore lines in 1809; and was at the capture of the Mauritius in 1810. On the 30th December 1813 he was promoted to the rank of Major; and the 2nd Battalion of the 12th being reduced in January 1818, Major Sale was placed on half-pay. On the 28th June 1821 he exchanged to the 13th Regiment, with which he proceeded to India, joined the expedition under Major-General Sir Archibald Campbell, and served throughout the Burmese War, being present at the capture of Rangoon and the storming of the stockades near Kemmendine, on both occasions displaying such heroism that he received the thanks of the commanding officer on the field of battle, and particular notice in general orders. He also stormed the seven stockades near Kumaroot and Pagoda Point. On the 1st December of the same year (1824) he stormed the enemy's lines, and on the 5th of that month led a body of sixteen hundred men in the engagement which resulted in the utter defeat of the Burmese, who were driven from all their positions. These successes were followed up, and on the 15th December the entrenchments at Kokien were stormed; here Major Sale was severely wounded in the head. In the following year he commanded a brigade at the reduction of Bassein, and subsequent operations from the 10th of February to the 2nd May 1825. On the 2nd June he attained the rank of Lieutenant-Colonel; on the 1st December he commanded the first brigade and repulsed the Shaans and Burmese at Prome, and the next day stormed the adjacent lines and heights. He was again severely wounded at the storming of Melloon on the 19th January 1826. For these services he was constituted a Companion of the Order of the Bath. He became Colonel by brevet on the 28th June 1838, and in the following October was appointed to the command of the first Bengal brigade of the Army of the Indus, which formed the advance throughout the campaign in Afghanistan: he commanded the force sent to Girishk in May 1839, and on the 23rd July headed the storming party which captured the fortress of Ghazni, deemed by the Afghans impregnable. A sabre-wound in the chin and contusions on the chest and shoulder from musket-shots were the results of the formidable conflict; but not the only ones, for his services were acknowledged by Sir John Keane, and Her Majesty nominated him a Knight Commander of the Bath, his name was enrolled in the list of

Eastern Knights constituting the order of the Dooranee Empire, which had been founded by Shah Shoojah, and he was advanced to the local rank of Major-General in Afghanistan, his promotion bearing the date of the capture of Ghazni. In September 1840 the forces sent to subdue the Kohistan country were entrusted to his command; and after storming the towns and forts of Tootumdurra, Julgar, Babookoosghur, Khandurrah, and Purwan, Dost Mahomed was compelled to surrender to the authorities at Kabul. In forcing the Khoord-Kabul Pass on the 12th of October 1841, he was shot through the leg. His gallant defence of Jellalabad, his daring sorties, and final defeat of the besieging army under Akbar Khan, for which services he received the thanks of Parliament, and was made a Knight Grand Cross of the Order of the Bath, are detailed in the Regimental Record, and completely identify Sir Robert Sale's name with the 13th Light Infantry, the connexion being rendered more intimate by Her Majesty, who conferred on him the colonelcy of the Regiment in December 1843, on the decease of General Edward Morrison. On the 29th March 1844 he was appointed Quartermaster-General to the Queen's troops serving in the East Indies. Advancing with the army to repel the Sikh invasion, Sir Robert Sale, G.C.B., had his left thigh so dreadfully shattered by a grapeshot at the Battle of Moodkee on the 18th December 1845, that he did not long survive the wound, but, after a distinguished career, fell like Wolfe, Sir John Moore, and other heroes, in the hour of victory.

SIR WILLIAM MAYNARD GOMM was appointed Ensign in the 9th Foot on the 24th May 1794, and on the 16th November following was promoted Lieutenant therein. His first service was with the expedition to the Helder, in 1799, and he was present in the actions at Bergen on the 19th September and the 2nd October. He proceeded with the expedition which embarked, in August 1800, for the coast of France and Spain, under Lieut.-General Sir James Pulteney, Bart.; on the 25th June 1803 he obtained his company in the 9th, and received the brevet of Major on the 1st January 1805, in which year he proceeded to Hanover. He shared in the expedition to Stralsund and siege of Copenhagen, in 1807. Brevet Major Gomm proceeded to Portugal in 1808, and was present at the battles of Roleia and Vimiera, on the 17th and 21st August; served during the retreat, under Lieut.-General Sir John Moore, and Battle of Corunna on the 16th January 1809. He next proceeded with the expedition to Walcheren, and was present at the siege of Flushing in that year. Again embarked for the Peninsula in 1810, and was appointed a Deputy-Assistant in the Quartermaster-General's Department on the 31st August. Was present at the Battle of Busaco on the 27th September, and in that of Fuentes d'Onor on the 3rd and 5th May 1811. On the 10th October he was promoted Major in the 9th, and appointed Assistant-Quartermaster-General on the 6th December following, in which capacity he served in the Peninsula until the end of the war. Major Gomm was present at the assault and capture of Badajoz, the siege of which lasted from the 17th March to the 6th April 1812; was at the Battle of Salamanca on the 22nd July, and received the brevet of Lieutenant-Colonel on the 17th August; was at the action of Villa Muriel on the 25th October; Battle of Vittoria on the 21st June 1813; siege of San Sebastian, and the battles of the Nivelle and Nive, in November and December. During the night preceding the latter action the 9th drove back the French posts, on which occasion Lieut.-Colonel Gomm was wounded. In 1814 he was at the investment of Bayonne, and on the 25th July, of that year, was appointed Captain and Lieutenant-Colonel in the Coldstream Guards. In January 1815 he was constituted a Knight Commander of the Order of the Bath, and as Quartermaster-General of the Fifth Division, Sir William Gomm was present at Quatre Bras and the ever-memorable Battle of Waterloo.

Sir William Gomm has received the gold cross and one clasp for Badajoz, Salamanca, Vittoria, San Sebastian, and Nive; the silver war medal with six clasps for Roleia, Vimiera, Corunna, Busaco, Fuentes d'Onor and Nivelle; the Waterloo medal, and the insignia of a Knight of the 2nd Class of S. Anne of Russia. On the 16th May 1829 he was promoted Major in the Coldstream Guards, and Lieutenant-Colonel therein on the 23rd June 1836; was promoted to the rank of Major-General on the 10th January 1837, and in 1839 was appointed to the command of the forces in Jamaica. While serving in that island as Lieutenant-Governor and Member of Council, Sir William devised measures for the improvement of the health of the troops, and established the Mountain Barrack of Newcastle. In March 1842 he entered on the command of the northern district of England, and in the same year was appointed Governor and Commander-in-Chief of the Mauritius. On the 10th March 1846 Her Majesty conferred on him the colonelcy of the 13th Light Infantry, and on the 9th November following he was advanced to the rank of Lieutenant-General. He quitted his command at the Mauritius in May 1849 and in January 1851 commenced his duties as Commander-in-Chief in India and an Extraordinary Member of the Council. He was promoted General on the 20th June 1854, and held the command in India until the end of 1855, in which year (20th June) he had been made a Knight Grand Cross of the Bath. General Sir William Maynard Gomm, G.C.B., was removed to the Coldstream Guards on the 15th August 1863.

PHILIP M'PHERSON embarked for the Peninsula in May 1809, as a volunteer in the 52nd Light Infantry, and served as such in the advance to Talavera and the retreat thence to Campo Mayor. On the 2nd November 1809 he was promoted to an ensigncy in the 43rd, from which time he served with the light division until the year 1814, and was present at the following battles, affairs, sieges, and skirmishes, viz. the combat of the Coa, on the 24th July 1810; affair of Martiago; skirmish near and Battle of Busaco on the 26th and 27th September; capture of Coimbra, on the 8th October; and affair of Alemquer, on the 10th of that month. In 1811 was present in the skirmishes at Pombal, Redinha, Casal Nova, and Foz d'Arouce, on the 11th, 12th, 14th and 15th March; the action at Sabugal, on the 3rd, and affair at the bridge of Marealva, on the 23rd April; battles of Fuentes d'Onor, on the 3rd and 5th May; and the affairs at Espeja and Soita. On the 13th June of this year he was promoted Lieutenant in the 43rd. In 1812 Lieutenant M'Pher-

APPENDIX A

son served at the sieges and storming of Ciudad Rodrigo and Badajoz—the former from the 8th to the 19th January, and the latter (where he was contused on the head in the trenches by the bursting of a shell) from the 17th March to the 6th April; affair at Carvellejo; action at Castrajon, on the 18th July; skirmish at Petiegua; the Battle of Salamanca on the 22nd July; the subsequent occupation of Madrid, on the 12th, and capture of Fort Retiro two days afterwards, and skirmish at San Munos in November. In 1813 was in the actions of the Pyrenees from the 28th July to the 2nd August, and those consequent on the passage of the Nivelle on the 10th November; affair at Bayonne and passage of the Nive, from the 9th to the 13th December. In 1814 shared in the affairs at Tarbes and Tournefeuille in March, and the Battle of Toulouse on the 10th April. For these services he received the war medal with eight clasps, for Busaco, Fuentes d'Onor, Ciudad Rodrigo, Badajoz, Salamanca, Nivelle, Nive, and Toulouse.

Lieutenant M'Pherson exchanged to half-pay of the 28th Regiment on the 20th April 1815, and to full pay of the 30th on the 25th April 1816, but reverted to half-pay of the latter corps on the 25th March 1817. He was appointed lieutenant on full pay of the 46th on the 19th May 1825, and removed to the 35th on the 12th October 1826; was promoted Captain unattached on the 13th March 1827, and appointed to the 17th Foot on the 26th November 1829. Captain M'Pherson embarked with a detachment of his regiment for New South Wales in April 1830, and served with it in that country, and afterwards at Bombay. He received the brevet rank of Major on the 23rd November 1841. In the following month Brevet-Major M'Pherson was appointed aide-de-camp to Sir Charles Napier, and served in that capacity and as military secretary during the campaign in Scinde; was present at the destruction of the fort of Emaum Ghur, on the 14th and 15th January 1843; shared also in the battles of Meeanee and Hyderabad, on the 17th February and 24th March following. He was twice mentioned in dispatches, and for his services received the Scinde medal and was nominated a Companion of the Order of the Bath. He received the brevet of Lieutenant-Colonel on the 4th July 1843, and attained the rank of Major in the 17th Foot on the 1st August 1844. He was promoted Lieutenant-Colonel of the 17th on the 3rd December 1852, and embarked in command of that regiment for Gibraltar in April 1854; on the 20th June of that year he received the brevet rank of Colonel, and proceeded in December following with the 17th to the Crimea, and on the 18th of that month was appointed to the command of the first brigade of the fourth division, and served during the siege of Sevastopol from that date to the 15th June 1855, when he was compelled to return home on account of ill health brought on from over fatigue in the trenches. Colonel M'Pherson was general of the day in the trenches in command of the attack on the occasion of several sorties by the Russians, and for his services on the night of the 11th May 1855, when the enemy was repulsed with considerable loss, was personally thanked by Lord Raglan. He received the Crimean medal and clasps, also that given by the Sultan, together with the insignia of the 4th Class of the Order of the

Medjidie, and of a Knight of the Legion of Honour. In September 1855 Colonel M'Pherson was appointed inspecting field officer of a recruiting district, and promoted to the rank of Major-General on the 21st December 1858. The colonelcy of the 13th Prince Albert's Light Infantry was conferred upon him on the 15th August 1863. Major-General M'Pherson, C.B., died on the 2nd February 1864.

PHILIP SPENCER STANHOPE, Lieutenant-General, appointed Colonel of the 13th Prince Albert's Light Infantry, on the 3rd February 1864. This officer joined the Grenadier Guards as Ensign on the 30th of March 1815; he was promoted Captain on the 17th July 1823; Lieutenant-Colonel on the 16th March 1832; Colonel on the 9th November 1846; Major-General on the 20th June 1854; Lieutenant-General on the 20th April 1861, and General on the 22nd November 1868. According to Harts' *Army List*, he saw no active service. He died in 1880.

GENERAL LORD MARK KERR, G.C.B., a son of the sixth Marquis of Lothian by his second wife Harriet, daughter of the third Duke of Buccleuch, was born in 1817 and entered the Army when 18 years of age. He was appointed to command the 1st Battalion then at Gibraltar in 1854 from the 28th Regiment. He first saw service in the Crimea and was present at the Battle of the Tchernaya, and the siege and fall of Sevastopol. Lord Mark took a distinguished part in the suppression of the Indian Mutiny, while in command of the 1st Battalion and on 6th April 1858 with a field force consisting of artillery, cavalry, and infantry he effected the relief of Azimghur. For this service he received the Companionship of the Bath, and was thanked by the Governor-General for 'the gallantry and skilful management which met and broke through a very formidable opposition'. Subsequently he took a leading part in hunting down the mutineer bands in Oudh.

Lord Mark Kerr afterwards acted as Brigadier-General at Delhi, and from 1874 to 1877 he commanded the Poona Division of the Bombay Army. He was promoted Major-General in 1868 and General in 1878. In 1893 he received the Grand Cross of the Bath. He was appointed Colonel of the Regiment on the 22nd February 1880, which appointment he retained till his death on 19th May 1900.

LIEUT.-GENERAL SIR JOHN WILLIAM COX began his career as Ensign in the 13th Light Infantry, 26th June 1838; Lieutenant, 22nd April 1840; Captain, 9th April 1847; Major, 15th December 1854; Lieutenant-Colonel, 20th July 1858; Colonel, 4th September 1863; Major-General, 23rd March 1869; and Lieutenant-General, 1st September 1882. Appointed Colonel, the Bedfordshire Regiment, 15th June 1893.

General Cox served in the 13th Light Infantry in the Campaigns of 1840, 1841, and 1842 in Afghanistan, and was present at the assault and capture of the town and fort of Tootumdurra, storm of Julgar, night attack of Babookhooshghur, attack on Khandurrah, storming the Khoord-Kabul Pass, affair of Tezin, forcing the Jagdalak pass, reduction of the fort of Mamoo Khail, heroic defence of Jellalabad and sorties on the 14th Nov ember (mentioned in dispatch), 1st December 1841, 11th March, 24th March and 1st April 1842, the general action with and defeat of the besieging force under Akbar Khan before Jellalabad on the 7th April 1842 (mentioned in dispatches for gallant conduct throughout the day, and as being in the forefront of a party which captured two of the enemy's cannons); the storming of the Jagdalak heights, general action at Tezin, and recapture of Cabool for which he has the medal, and also another for Jellalabad. Served in the Crimea from 30th June 1855, and was at the Battle of the Tchernaya, siege and fall of Sevastopol (medal with clasp, 5th class of the Medjidie, and Turkish medal). Served in the Indian Mutiny Campaign, and commanded the left wing of the 13th Light Infantry from August 1857 to October 1858, and was actively employed in the Azimghur and Gorakhpur Districts and southern borders of Oudh, present in eight engagements, in three of which he commanded the whole force, in three others he commanded a separate column, and in the remaining two he acted as principal staff officer to the force (repeatedly mentioned in dispatches, Brevet of Lieutenant-Colonel, C.B. and medal). He was appointed Colonel of the Regiment on 18th May 1900. He died on 3rd October 1901. Served twenty-seven years in the Regiment. Captain W. C. Cox of the Regiment was his son.

MAJOR-GENERAL EDWARD LUTWYCHE ENGLAND joined the 13th Light Infantry on 5th July 1855. He was promoted Lieutenant in 1858, Captain in 1864, Major in 1877, Lieutenant-Colonel in 1879, Colonel in 1883, and Major-General in 1894. He served in the Indian Mutiny Campaign in 1858, and was present at the actions at Amorah on 17th and 25th April (medal). He served in the operations against Sekukini in the Transvaal in 1878, including the storming of Tolyana's Stadt. Also throughout the Zulu war of 1879, taking part in the engagements of Zunguin Nek and Kambula Hill, and, in command of the 1st Battalion in the action at Ulundi. (Mentioned in dispatches, Brevet of Lieutenant-Colonel, medal with clasp.) He was a Graduate of the Staff College and served on the staff in Canada as Brigade-Major 1876–8. He commanded the Regimental District at Taunton from 1886 to 1891. He was appointed Colonel of the Regiment on 3rd October 1901. He died on the 4th April 1910.

MAJOR-GENERAL SIR HENRY HALLAM PARR, K.C.B., C.M.G., born on the 24th July 1847, was the younger son of Thomas Clements Parr, Barrister-at-law, and Julia, eldest daughter of Sir Charles Elton, Bart., of Clevedon Court, Somerset. He was educated at Eton and Sandhurst and was gazetted to the 13th Light Infantry in 1865. He served as Adjutant to the 1st Battalion 1873–4. In 1877 he obtained his first staff appointment, that of Military Secretary to Sir Bartle Frere, Governor of the Cape Colony, South Africa. Promoted Captain in 1878, he served in the Kaffir and Zulu Wars 1878–9, when he was mentioned in dispatches, later created a C.M.G., and received the medal with clasp. During this period he served as staff officer to Colonel Glyn, commanding No. 3 column, which was the first to arrive on the scene of the disaster at Isandhlwana.

In 1881 he was appointed to General Sir George Colley's staff but arrived after the disaster of Majuba. Subsequently he was made Commandant of the Remount Depôt in Natal and afterwards organized and trained a battalion of Mounted Infantry. In 1882 he was promoted Captain and then saw service in Egypt under Sir Garnet Wolseley, where he commanded a battalion of Mounted Infantry and was severely wounded at the action of Tel-el-Mahuta. This earned him a mention in dispatches, Brevet of Major, the award of a medal and the Khedive's star. In 1883 he was appointed Provost Marshal in Cairo and in the following year Commandant of Suakin with the Brevet of Lieutenant-Colonel. He took part in the action of Tamai, was mentioned in dispatches and awarded the 4th class of the Order of the Medjidie. He took part in the Nile Expedition of 1884–5 in the attempt to relieve General Gordon. He was then made Adjutant-General of the Egyptian Army with the rank of Pasha. In 1886 he was promoted Brevet Colonel and appointed A.D.C. to the Queen. Owing to indifferent health he left Egypt in 1887. In 1889 he was appointed A.A.G., Southern district, at Portsmouth, but when the command of the 1st Battalion fell vacant in 1890, he gladly sacrificed the substantive rank of Colonel to which he had been promoted and accepted the Command of the Battalion. With this battalion he served in Aldershot, Gibraltar and Umballa in India. On completion of his command he returned home, and served as A.A.G. and A.I.G. Ordnance at the War Office, 1895–8. Promoted to Major-General in 1898, he was appointed to command the troops at Shorncliffe. Shortly after the outbreak of the South African War in 1899 he took over the command of the South-Eastern District, his ill health preventing him from serving abroad. In 1902 he was given the command of the North-Western District with headquarters at Chester, and retired from the Army in 1906.

On the 5th April 1904, on the death of Major-General E. L. England, he was appointed Colonel of the Somerset Light Infantry, which appointment he held till his death on 4th April 1914. He was created a K.C.B. in 1910.

In 1888 he married Lilian Mary, daughter of George Monck Gibbs, by whom he had two sons, Hallam and George. Both in after years served in the Regiment. The former died in Malta in 1910, and the latter was killed in France in 1914.

MAJOR-GENERAL R. L. PAYNE, C.B., D.S.O., joined the Regiment from the Militia on the 19th January 1876. He was promoted Captain 8th May 1885, Major 8th November 1894, Lieut.-Colonel Commanding the Royal Inniskilling Fusiliers 27th January 1900, Brevet Colonel 29th November 1900, Colonel 18th July 1905, Major-General 7th November 1907. He was Adjutant of Volunteers from 15th September 1887 to 14th September 1892, and commanded the 10th Brigade Irish Command 18th July 1905 to 6th February 1908. He commanded the Karachi Brigade 14th April 1909 and the 5th Mhow Division, 30th October 1912, and was appointed Colonel of the Regiment on the 5th April 1914. He retired from the Army on the 23rd June 1917. He served in the South African War 1878–9; expedition against Sekukini, Zulu Campaign, engagement of Zunguin Nek, action of Kambula

APPENDIX A

and Battle of Ulundi (medal with clasp); Burmese expedition, 1885–6, mentioned in dispatches, D.S.O., medal; N.W. Frontier, India, 1897–8; with the Mohmand Field Force (medal with clasp); South African War 1899–02, including actions at Belfast and Lydenburg. Mentioned in dispatches; Brevet of Colonel; Queen's Medal (three clasps), King's Medal (two clasps).

APPENDIX B

SUCCESSION OF LIEUTENANT-COLONELS

Francis Villiers	1685
Ferdinando Hastings	1686
Sir John Jacob, Bart.	1688
Edward Pidow	1695
Edward Pearce	1704
Mark Anthony Moncal	1706
Thomas Jones	1711
Francis Bowes	1715
William Hargreave	1720
Francis Farquhar	1731
Moses Moreau	1736
Thomas Cockayne	1744
John Crawford	1749
David Chapeau	1759
Samuel Edhouse	1761
David Ogilvie	1765
Andrew Edhouse	1781
Coppinger Moyle	1783
George Nugent	1787
John Francis Cradock	1789
John Whitelock	1791
Jonas Watson	1795
Laurence Bradshaw	1796
Hon. Charles Colville	1803
William Williams	1812
Michael McCreagh	1821
Robert Henry Sale	1830
Tristram Charnley Squire	1843
A. A. T Cunynghame	1846
Charles Stuart	1846
Lord Mark Kerr	1854
William Forbes MacBean	1865
Robert Blackall Montgomery	1873
Philip Edward Victor Gilbert	1878
Edward Lutwyche England	1880
Thomas Alphonso Cary	1885
Irving Stening Allfrey	1887
George Herbert Anchite Kinloch	1889
Henry Hallam Parr	1890
Arthur Close Borton	1894
Henry Alfred Walsh	1898
Charles Warren Napier-Clavering	1902
Courtney Heathcote Stisted	1906
Herbert Cockayne Frith	1909
Edward Hopton Swayne	1913

2ND BATTALION

Arthur Home	1858
William Forbes MacBean	1865
Peter Macdonald	1865
Thomas Maunsell	1868
Arthur Bainbrigge	1875
William Edward Brown	1878
Philip Edward Victor Gilbert	1880
William Knox Leet	1883
William Cox	1887
William Charles Frederick Madden	1890
John Miller Elgee Waddy	1894
Edmond Joseph Gallwey	1898
Raymond Burlton Williams	1902
George Henry Couchman	1906
Henry Joseph Everett	1910
Ernest Henderson Platt	1914

NOTE.—It will be observed that Lt.-Colonel W. F. MacBean and Lt.-Colonel F. E. V. Gilbert commanded both battalions at different periods.

APPENDIX C

SUCCESSION OF ADJUTANTS

Lieut. Talbott Lascells	. .	1685
,, Henry Cartwright	. .	1691
,, Edward Booth	. .	1695
Captain-Lieut. Josias Clarke	.	1706
,, ,, Matthew Draper		1715
Lieut. J. Crump	. . .	1715
,, Theophilus Lucy	. .	1718
,, Thomas Cockayne	. .	1725
,, Edward Scott	. .	1739
Ensign John Crawford	. .	1751
Lieut. Daniel Daniel	. .	1751
,, Thomas Weldon	. .	1751
,, John Braithwaite	. .	1756
,, William Bannatine	. .	1760
,, William Taylor	. .	1766
,, Thomas Daniel Black	.	1769
,, James Montgomery	.	1775
,, John Hemming	. .	1780
Captain James Lowrey	. .	1783
Lieut. George Parsons	. .	1796
,, James Blake	. . .	1804
Ensign William Bell	. .	1806
,, John Kemple	. .	1811
Lieut. Thomas Eden Kelly	.	1820
,, Michael Fenton	. .	1822
Ensign William James Hutchins	. . .	1825
Lieut. William Meadows Brownrigg	. . .	1828
,, Henry Havelock	. .	1834
,, Hamlet Wade	. . .	1838
,, John Stuart Wood	.	1840
,, Thomas Beckwith Speedy	. . .	1844
,, George Wade	. .	1846
,, Gerald Fitzgerald King		1865
,, George Kemmis	. .	1870
,, Henry Hallam Parr	.	1873
,, Frank Boyd Bradshaw	.	1874
Lieut. Edmund Joseph Gallwey		1879
,, Henry Alfred Walsh	.	1880
,, John Jervis Palmer	.	1884
,, Thomas D'Oyly Snow	.	1885
,, Henry Joseph Everett	.	1890
,, Victor Keith Falconer	.	1894
Captain Edward Forbes Cooke-Hurle	. .	1898
,, Amhurst Blunt Whatman, D.S.O.	. .	1902
,, Rynes Alexander Mark Currie	. .	1904
,, Arthur William Sibald Paterson	. . .	1907
,, John Sandbach Noel Harrison	. . .	1910
Lieut. William Moxhay Sutton		1913

2ND BATTALION

Lieut. John Bond	. . . .	1858
,, Edward Lutwyche England	. . . .	1860
,, John Paterson Fox	. .	1860
,, Robert Stuart Clarke	.	1862
,, Arthur Close Borton	.	1874
,, Anthony Lumb	. .	1878
,, Charles Blakeway Little		1883
,, Robert Brocklehurst	.	1888
,, Walter Pipon Braithwaite	. . . .	1892
Captain Edward Hopton Swayne	. . .	1896
Lieut. Charles Bertie Prowse	.	1900
Captain Cecil Hunter Little	.	1904
,, Henry Irving Rodney Allfrey	. . .	1907
Lieut. Theobald Alfred Walsh		1910
,, Victor Wellesley Roche		1913

APPENDIX D

MEDALS

CULLODEN, 16TH APRIL 1746

Gold medals were bestowed by command of George II on the senior officers.

Obverse: Bust of the Duke of Cumberland to right, 'Cumberland' above.

Reverse: A nude figure (Apollo) stands in front of a dragon pierced through the neck by an arrow. Above, 'Actum est ilicet Periit' (the deed is done, it is all over, he has perished). Below in the exergue, Prod: Colod: Ap: 16, 1746.

The medal is oval in shape, has an ornamental border and a loop for suspension.

Commemorative medals for Culloden, in copper, bronze, etc., are numerous, about thirty different dies being known.

EGYPT 1801

As a reward for the British operations in Egypt in 1801 resulting in the expulsion of the French, the Turkish 'Order of the Crescent' was considerably extended, and the officers who had served with this expedition received a gold medal, which was given in four different sizes, according to the recipient's rank.

Obverse: The Sultan's cypher within an ornamental border of roses and leaves which contains the date 1801 at the base.

Reverse: Within a similar border the Crescent and Star.

An orange ribbon was worn with the medal, attached by a short gold hook and chain, and several other varieties of suspension.

The rank and file received no decoration for this campaign until 1850, when a clasp for 'Egypt' was added to the Military General Service Medal of 1848. By this time (forty-nine years after the event) most of those entitled to be decorated were dead.

There was an issue of gold medals in 1810 to commemorate the victories of Rolica, Vimiero, Corunna, and Talavera; the grant of these medals was afterwards extended to embrace victories in the Peninsula, Java, West Indies and North America. They were given in a large size for General Officers, and a similar size for Colonels and Field Officers, or to others who had commanded a battalion in action owing to the death or removal of the original commanding officer. Both medals were of similar design.

Brigadier Colville received the large medal and Lieut.-Colonel Keane the small one for 'Martinique'.

APPENDIX D

Obverse: Britannia seated on a globe, a wreath of laurel in her extended right hand, a palm branch in her left, the lion of England on the right, and a shield with the Crosses of the Union on the left.

Reverse: The name of the battle for which the medal was given within a wreath of laurel.

The recipient's rank and name is engraved on the edge, and the medal is covered with glass to preserve it.

The ribbon was crimson with blue edges. This was for many years the only recognized official ribbon, and was considered to be the Military Ribbon of England.

MILITARY GENERAL SERVICE MEDAL 1793–1814

This medal was granted by G.O. dated 1st June 1847. It was a retrospective medal to commemorate victories in Egypt, Sicily, The Peninsula, Java, N. America and W. Indies; one was presented to every surviving officer and soldier who had been present at any action for which the gold medals had previously been granted. The medals and clasps were issued in 1848, but the clasp for Egypt was not granted till 1850.

Obverse: Head of Queen Victoria, 'Victoria Regina' above and date 1848 below.

Reverse: Queen Victoria crowning with a wreath of laurel the Duke of Wellington, who kneels before her; date 1793–1814 in the exergue.

The recipient's name, rank and regiment, is indented on the edge of the medal, which was worn on the left breast from a crimson ribbon with blue edges.

Twenty-nine clasps were issued, of which the survivors of the Regiment were entitled to three, viz. 'Egypt', 'Martinique' and 'Guadaloupe'.

APPENDIX D

Nominal List of Officers, Non-Commissioned Officers and Men of the 13th Foot who were awarded the Army General Service Medal granted under General Order dated 12th February 1850

Rank	Name	Martinique	Guadaloupe	Egypt
Ensign	Andrews, A. *	—	—	Yes
Asst. Surg.	Ayton, R.	Yes	—	—
Ensign	Barrett, K.	Yes	Yes	—
Lieut.-Col.	Bradshaw, L.	—	—	Yes
Lieut.	Colclough, B.	—	Yes	—
Captain	Holgate, B.	Yes	—	—
Lieut.	Handcock, R. B.	Yes	Yes	Yes
,,	Holbrooke, F.	—	—	Yes
,,	Kelly, F. P.	Yes	Yes	—
Ensign	Pattison, R.	Yes	Yes	—
Captain	Staunton, J.	Yes	Yes	—
Lieut.	Tronson, E. J.	Yes	Yes	—
Major	Turner, C.	Yes	—	—
Serjt.	Anderson, W. (later Lieut.)	—	—	Yes
Private	Andrews, T.	Yes	Yes	—
,,	Byrnes, W.	Yes	—	—
,,	Burke, U.	Yes	—	Yes
,,	Birmingham, P.	Yes	Yes	Yes
,,	Barrett, M.	Yes	Yes	—
,,	Bradley, J.	Yes	Yes	—
Corpl.	Burrows, E.	Yes	Yes	—
Private	Burke, J.	Yes	Yes	—
,,	Baker, J.	—	Yes	—
,,	Carter, B.	Yes	Yes	—
,,	Clarke, R.	Yes	Yes	—
,,	Clow, M.	Yes	—	—
,,	Conroy, H.	Yes	Yes	—
,,	Cornick, J.	Yes	—	—
,,	Cosgrove, W.	Yes	—	—
,,	Cooper, W.	—	—	Yes
,,	Davis, W.	Yes	Yes	—
Bugler	Davies, W.	Yes	—	—
Private	Dowling, O.	—	—	Yes
,,	Donahoe, M.	Yes	Yes	—
Serjt.	Dennehy, M.	Yes	Yes	—
Private	Donnelly, P.	Yes	Yes	—
,,	Egan, W.	—	—	Yes
,,	Gilmore, W.	Yes	Yes	—
,,	Gillespie, J.	Yes	Yes	—
,,	Gillispie, N.	—	—	Yes

* Ensign A. Andrews afterwards served as Captain 95th Foot (now Rifle Brigade) and was awarded clasps 'Vittoria', 'St. Sebastion', 'Nivelle', 'Nive', 'Orthes', 'Toulouse' and 'Pyrenees'.

APPENDIX D

Rank	Name	Clasps awarded		
		Martinique	Guadaloupe	Egypt
Private	Gillett, T.	—	Yes	—
,,	Gillett, H.	—	Yes	—
,,	Gibbons, M.	Yes	—	—
,,	Holloway, G.	Yes	Yes	—
,,	Howley, A.	Yes	Yes	Yes
,,	Hudson, J.	Yes	Yes	Yes
,,	Hennessey, D.	Yes	Yes	—
,,	Hynes, G.	Yes	Yes	—
,,	Jennings, L.	Yes	Yes	—
,,	Keally, J.	Yes	—	—
,,	Kelly, W.	Yes	Yes	Yes
,,	Kenshella, E.	—	Yes	—
,,	Kyle, W.	Yes	Yes	—
,,	Lally, W.	Yes	Yes	—
,,	Long, W.	Yes	Yes	—
,,	Loomes, T.	Yes	Yes	—
,,	McDonough, M.	Yes	Yes	—
,,	McCoole, H.	—	—	Yes
,,	McCormick, J.	Yes	—	—
,,	McKone, C.	Yes	Yes	—
,,	McLaughlin, J.	Yes	Yes	—
,,	McGrogan, J.	Yes	—	—
,,	Mahony, M.	Yes	Yes	—
,,	Matthews, J.	—	—	Yes
Serjt.	Matheson, A.	Yes	Yes	Yes
Private	Merrifield, J.	Yes	—	Yes
,,	Miles, W.	Yes	Yes	—
,,	Moran, P.	Yes	Yes	—
,,	Nickle, R.	Yes	Yes	—
,,	O'Hara, P.	Yes	Yes	—
Serjt.	O'Melea, G.	Yes	Yes	Yes
Private	Pearce, R.	Yes	Yes	—
,,	Rush, P.	Yes	Yes	—
,,	Rooney, T.	Yes	Yes	—
,,	Rice, G.	Yes	Yes	—
Corpl.	Rogers, J.	Yes	—	Yes
Private	Rodgers, J.	—	—	Yes
,,	Roach, E.	—	—	Yes
Serjt.	Rochford, W.	—	—	Yes
,,	Sherridan, C.	Yes	Yes	—
Private	Shirkey, D.	—	Yes	—
,,	Scadding, T.	Yes	Yes	—
,,	Simpson, D.	Yes	Yes	—
,,	Smith, W.	Yes	Yes	—
,,	Stewart, J.	Yes	Yes	—
,,	Wooley, W.	Yes	Yes	—

S.L.I.—26

APPENDIX D

ARMY OF INDIA MEDAL, 1799–26

A retrospective medal granted in 1851 by the H.E.I.C.

Obverse: Head of Queen Victoria crowned 'Victoria Regina' above.

Reverse: A seated figure of Victory, a laurel wreath in her left hand, an olive branch in her right; a trophy of Oriental arms and a palm tree in the background. Above 'To the Army of India'. In the exergue 1799–1826. Ribbon pale blue.

This medal had twenty-one battle honours, but the 13th were only entitled to one battle honour, viz. 'Ava'.

I. Office

RETURN OF OFFICERS NOW OR LATELY SERVING IN THE ARMY WHOSE CLAIMS TO RECEIVE MEDALS UNDER THE GENERAL ORDER DATED 21ST MARCH 1851 HAVE BEEN EXAMINED AND ALLOWED BY THE BOARD OF GENERAL OFFICERS

Names and present Rank	Regiment and Rank in which the claimant formerly served	Occasions on which the presence of each Claimant has been verified by the Board
Flood, Warden, late Captain 51st Foot	Lieut. 13th Foot	Ava
Fenton, Michael	Captain, 13th Foot	,,
Grimes, Charles, Depôt Paymaster, H.-Pay.	Paymaster, 13th Foot, and Judge Advocate to Bengal Division	,,
Havelock, Henry, C.B., Lieut.-Col.	Lieut., 13th Foot and Dept. Asst-Adjutt-General	,,
Moorhouse, Henry, late Lieut., 56th Foot	Ensign, 13th Foot	,,
Pattison, R., Lieut.Col1, Major Retd full pay 13th Foot	Captain, 13th Foot	,,
Squire, T. C., late Lieut.-Col. 13th Foot	Captain, 13th Foot	,,
Stehelin, Fras Willm, late Capt. 13th Foot	Lieut., 13th Foot	,,
Tronson, Edwd Thomas	Captain, 13th Foot	,,
Tinling, C. H. L., Major unattd	Lieut., 13th Foot	,,
Wilkinson, Arthr P. S., late Major 13th Foot	Lieut., 13th Foot	,,

APPENDIX D

Further Return of Officers ... whose claims to receive Medals under the General Order dated 21st March 1851 have been examined and allowed

Barrett, Knox, Capt., H.-P., unatt^d	Brevet Capt., 13th Foot Ava
Croker, R. W., late Lieut. 13th Foot	Lieut. 13th Foot ,,
Meredith, R. M., late Major 13th Foot	Lieut., 13th Foot ,,
Sibley, Charles W., Capt., 64th Foot	Ensign, 13th Foot ,,

Return of Non-Commissioned Officers and Men now or lately serving in the Army whose claims to receive Medals under the General Order dated 21st March 1851 have been examined and allowed by the Board of General Officers

13th Foot at Ava

Acott, Job	Private	Humphries, Robert	Private
Atkinson, Patrick	,,	Lack, John	,,
Bowden, William	,,	Lloyd, James	,,
Bartlett, Henry	,,	Miller, Richard	,,
Brice, Thomas	,,	McBride, John	,,
Brown, James	,,	Matthews, James	,,
Burns, James	,,	Moran, Danl	,,
Barrett, Philip	,,	Martin, Thos	,,
Cooke, Thomas	,,	McImally, Rich^d	,,
Coulton, Patrick	,,	McLea, James	,,
Connolly, James	,,	Meahan, Hugh	,,
Conroy, Henry	,,	McCarthy, Patrick	Serj^t
Costello, Dennis	,,	Murphy, Edwd	Private
Cummings, William	,,	Morgan, Richard	,,
Crowley, James	,,	McDowall, Thos	,,
Carey, Michael	,,	McQuade, John	,,
Conway, Thomas	,,	O'Hara, James (Duplicate issued 1858)	,,
Davitt, James	,,		
Dane, Robert	Bugler	Pyke, Isaac	Color-Serj^t.
Dalton, Mark	Private	Pitcher, Willm	Private
Durkin, Patrick	,,	Pepper, John	,,
Doutch, William	,,	Pyke, Isaac	,,
Doyle, Francis	,,	Rourke, Patrick	,,
Davis, William	,,	Ross, George	,,
Fahey, Patrick	,,	Reed, Thos	,,
Guitar, James	,,	Simpson, Rich^d	,,
Gilmore, Bernard	,,	Tracey, Willm	,,
Gom, John	,,	Vaisey, Thos	,,
Hunter, Alexander	,,	West, Hugh	,,
Hughes, John	,,	Webber, William	,,
Hennessy, Daniel	,,	White, Luke	Bugler (now serving)

(FURTHER LIST OF N.C.OS. AND MEN—GENERAL ORDER OF 21ST MARCH 1851)

13TH FOOT AT AVA

Cooke, Thomas	. .	Private
Hawthorn, William	. .	,,
Lingham, James	. .	,,
Pryor, William	. .	,,

Do. 3rd List

Burns, John	. .	Private
Dunphy, John	. .	,,
Evans, William	. .	,,
Knight, George	. .	,,
Milburn, Thomas	. .	,,
Naysmith, Cumming	. .	,,
Smith, William	. .	,,

Do. 4th List

Burke, John
Beatson, Fred[k.]

Do. 5th List

Aston, Joseph	. .	Private
Moran, Andrew	. .	,,
O'Brien, Thomas (Auckland)		,,
Stone, James	. .	,,

Do. 6th List

Atkinson, Christ[n.] . . Private

Do. 7th List

Curd, Thomas
Leary, John

Do. 8th List

Lynch, Ja[s.], Corporal (F[t.] William, E. Indies)
Wells, Thomas, Private (F[t.] William, E. Indies)

Further List

Beeson, William	. .	Private
McIntyre, John	. .	,,

'GHUZNEE 1839'

This medal was originally intended as the gift of Shah Shoojah, but owing to his death those entitled to it did not receive the decoration till 1842, when it was given in the name of the Government of India.

Obverse: A view of the fortress; 'Ghuznee', on a scroll below.

Reverse: Two branches of laurel enclosing a space intended for the recipient's rank, name, and regiment. Above '23rd July', a mural crown, and '1839' below.

A crimson and yellow ribbon, halved, was originally ordered to be worn with the medal, but it was afterwards changed to crimson and green halved; the reason of the change is not known.

Many of the 13th medals seem to have had the recipient's name, &c., indented on the edge of the medal, and the same applies to the medals for Jellalabad (1st) and Cabool.

This was the first occasion in India in which a silver medal was given to all ranks engaged, European and Native; previously the Native troops had been the lucky ones. It was also the first time that an Indian medal was issued with a bar for suspension, the bar being of silver.

APPENDIX D

FIRST JELLALABAD MEDAL

General Order, Allahabad, 30th April 1842.

'The Governor-General is pleased to direct that a Silver Medal be made for every Officer, Non-commissioned officer and Private, European or Native, who belonged to the garrison of Jellalabad on the 7th April 1842.'

Obverse: A mural crown superscribed 'Jellalabad'.

Reverse: VII. April, 1842.

The ribbon is crimson, yellow and blue shaded; and Lord Ellenborough in a letter on the subject states that the idea was to represent the colours of the Eastern sky when the sun rises without a cloud, crimson falling into yellow, and yellow into blue'. It was Lord Ellenborough's intention that this should be henceforth the military ribbon of India, and it was worn with all the Indian medals for 1842, as well as with the stars for the Gwalior Campaign, the Scinde Campaign medals and in later times with the Kabul to Kandahar Star of 1880.

Though usually called the rainbow ribbon, it will be seen from the above extract that the ribbon did not owe its design to the rainbow.

This medal was struck and issued by Lord Ellenborough on his own authority, and he was dissatisfied with his production after having seen the English-made Cabool Medal. He was not the only one who did not approve of it. Soon after its issue unfavourable remarks regarding the design were made in certain high quarters. 'It was even whispered that Her Majesty was not quite pleased at the absence of her head and titles from the obverse of a medal struck for services in which a Royal Regiment took the most distinguished part.'

The second Jellalabad medal was the result of this.

SECOND JELLALABAD MEDAL

General Order. Commander-in-Chief, 13th March 1845, stated:—

'That the New Medals had arrived from England and would be issued to officers and men on their returning those originally presented to them.'

Obverse: Head of Queen Victoria crowned, 'Victoria Vindex.'

Reverse: A figure of Victory flying over Jellalabad, a laurel wreath in her right hand, a Union Jack in her left; surrounded by the words, 'Jellalabad, VII. April.' In the exergue MDCCCXLII.

This was a most unpopular medal; the majority of those entitled to it never claimed it, preferring to retain their original medal.

A list exists at the India Office of those officers and men of the 13th Light Infantry in India entitled to exchange their medals. It contains the names of 16 officers and 174 N.C.Os. and men. Only two officers and less than 50 N.C.Os. and men claimed the new medal.

The G.O. of 1845 makes no mention of a new ribbon for the new medal, nor is any official notification on the subject known to exist. The evidence of recipients goes to prove that a half-crimson, half-blue ribbon either accompanied the second medal or was issued soon after.

The fact of there being two different Jellalabad medals and two different ribbons led to some confusion, as though the majority of officers and men retained the first medal and rainbow ribbon, there were some who wore the first medal with the crimson and blue ribbon; while of the few who applied for the second medal, some wore it with the rainbow ribbon.

It is thought that those who wore the crimson and blue ribbon were few in number. Sir Robert Sale received the second medal, but he wore it with the rainbow ribbon. Most of the Jellalabad medals which come up for sale have the rainbow ribbon.

The policy of using the rainbow ribbon for several different medals granted for the same and subsequent campaigns was extremely confusing, as a man might be entitled to two or more medals all of which had the same ribbon.

This was obviated in 1846 when clasps were first introduced.

THE CABOOL MEDAL 1842

Awarded for the re-occupation of Cabool.

Obverse: Head of Queen Victoria crowned, to left 'Victoria Vindex.'

Reverse: 'Cabool 1842' within a laurel wreath surmounted by a crown. The ribbon for this medal is the military ribbon of India.

CRIMEA 1854–5

The grant of a medal for services in the Crimea was notified in December 1854.

Obverse: Head of Queen Victoria crowned 'Victoria Regina' 1854.

Reverse: A figure of Victory crowning with laurel a Roman soldier, who bears a shield with a lion in its centre. 'Crimea' on the left. Five clasps were issued, but the 13th Light Infantry only received one, 'Sevastopol'.

The ribbon is pale blue with yellow edges.

The recipient's name, rank, &c., is either indented or engraved in square capitals on the edge.

As regards British decorations, the V.C., the Medal for Distinguished Conduct in the Field, and the rare Naval Medal for Conspicuous Gallantry owe their origin to this campaign.

FRENCH WAR MEDAL (CRIMEA)

This medal was given to about 500 selected N.C.Os. and men of the British Army.

Obverse: The Emperor's head, surrounded by a blue enamelled circle on which in gilt letters are the words 'Louis Napoleon'; a silver laurel wreath surrounds the enamelled circle.

Reverse: 'Valeur et Discipline' on a gold ground.

The medal is surmounted by an eagle to which is attached a ring for the ribbon orange with green edges.

APPENDIX D

INDIAN MUTINY

This medal was granted to all who had borne arms in suppressing the Mutiny.

Obverse: Head of Queen Victoria. 'Victoria Regina.'

Reverse: A figure of Britannia standing in front of a lion; in her outstretched right hand is a laurel wreath, on her left arm a shield, which bears the crosses of the union banner. Date 1857-58 in the exergue.

Ribbon. Scarlet and white in alternate stripes.

SOUTH AFRICA, 1878-79

For the various campaigns in South Africa during the years 1877-78-79 a medal was authorized in August 1880.

This medal is similar to the one granted in 1853, with the exception of the exergue, which in the first medal contains the date 1853, and in the later medal four assegais and a shield.

Obverse: Head of Queen Victoria to left, 'Victoria Regina.'

Reverse: A lion crouching beside a bush. Above 'South Africa.'

Ribbon orange, with two broad and two narrow purple stripes.

A clasp was granted with the medal, such clasp bearing the date of the year or years during which the recipient was engaged. Troops employed in Natal, but who did not cross the border received no clasp.

THE INDIA MEDAL, 1854

First issued for the Burmese War of 1852-3 and subsequently for various frontier campaigns between 1852 and 1895. Twenty-three clasps were issued with this medal.

The Regiment is only concerned with Burma 1885-7, and Burma 1887-9. The latter is confined to the M.I. Company who remained behind after the 2nd Battalion had left Burma.

Obverse: Head of Queen Victoria to left, 'Victoria Regina.'

Reverse: A figure of Victory crowning a seated warrior, in the exergue the lotus flowers.

Ribbon red with two dark blue stripes.

The Distinguished Service Order was instituted on 6th September 1886.

THE INDIA MEDAL, 1895

This medal was granted in 1896 to commemorate the Chitral Campaign of 1895.

Obverse: Bust of Queen Victoria to left, legend 'Victoria Regina et Imperatrix'.

Reverse: The figures of a British and Indian soldier standing supporting the Royal Standard. The word 'India' on the left of the field, the date '1895' on the right.

Ribbon, crimson with two green stripes.
This medal has six clasps.
The Regiment only received the clasp Punjab Frontier 1897-98.

THE SOUTH AFRICAN WAR, 1899-1902

Two medals were awarded for this war.
(1) The Queen's South Africa Medal.
Obverse: The bust of Her Majesty Queen Victoria to the left, crowned and veiled, and wearing the ribbon of the Order of the Garter, surrounded by the legend, 'Victoria Regina et Imperatrix'.

Reverse: A figure of Britannia, with a shield, trident, and palm branch at her feet, holding in her left hand a flag, and extending her right hand and a laurel wreath towards a company of advancing soldiers. On the left is shown the sea, and a man of war, and above it, is the legend, 'South Africa'.

Ribbon: Two outer red stripes, two blue stripes, and a central stripe of orange.

Twenty-six bars were authorized for this medal.
The 2nd Battalion earned the following bars: Relief of Ladysmith, Cape Colony, Transvaal, Orange Free State, as well as two bars South Africa 1901 and South Africa 1902 if not eligible for the King's Medal.

(2) The King's South African Medal in recognition of the services of the troops in the later phases of the war, issued to all those serving in South Africa on or after 1st January 1902, and who on that date had completed 18 months war service or subsequently completed such service before 1st June 1902.

Obverse: The bust of the King to the left in uniform with medals and order; legend, 'Edwardus VII., Rex, Imperator'.
Reverse: The same as the Queen's Medal previously described.
Ribbon: Orange, white, and green, in three equal stripes.
Bars. Two. South Africa 1901, South Africa 1902.

REGIMENTAL MEDAL, 1825

(1) The introduction of the Order of Merit to reward deserving soldiers was confirmed in 1825 by Colonel McCreagh, commanding the Regiment.

The medal was bestowed in gold for 20 years' service and good conduct, in silver for 14, 10 and 7 years. The design in each case being similar, with the exception of the number of years' service for which the decoration was granted.

Obverse: A suspended bugle with 'Ava', 'Martinique' upon it, the regimental No. XIII within the bugle cords. A sphinx with 'Egypt' above the bugle. Legend, 'Medal of Merit for (14) years' good conduct'.

Reverse: Blank.

APPENDIX D

The ribbon, which is really more of the nature of braid, is yellow with red edges. The yellow was adopted in reference to the regimental facings, a common custom with regimental medals.

These medals were entirely of a regimental nature, the expenses being borne by the officers, and it is hardly necessary to add that the gift of the medal was an honour greatly valued. With the issue in 1833 of the Medal for Long Service and Good Conduct by order of the King (William IV) all these regimental medals gradually died out, much to the regret of those to whom it had been a regimental custom.

(2) A regimental Prize for Ball Firing.

Obverse: A bugle horn with cords in relief; surmounting it is an engraved garter on which are the words 'Ball Firing Prize 100 yards'. The Badge is suspended from a crown, to which a clasp is attached.

The reverse is all engraved. Above in Roman Numerals 'XIII' in the centre, the recipient's name, W. Webber, surmounted by Sphinx and underneath two branches tied together. This rare badge is in Colonel Murray's collection.

(3) Badge consisting of a bugle horn attached by cords to a Sphinx bearing the word 'Egypt', between the cords '13' and on the bugle 'Martinique' 'Ava'.

Reverse: N. Gillespie seven years efficient.' In the Murray collection.

The above information is taken from the *Historical Record of Medals and Honorary Distinctions conferred on the British Army, Navy and Auxiliary Forces from the earliest period*, by George Tanred, late Captain Royal Scots. It is a pity that no date is given on the badge for Ball Firing.

THE LONG SERVICE AND GOOD CONDUCT MEDAL, 1833

'Discharged soldiers receiving a gratuity for meritorious conduct shall be entitled to wear a silver medal.'

To be eligible for this medal men must have served 21 years in the Infantry, or 24 years in the Cavalry, have no convictions by C.M., have borne an irreproachable character, or have particularly distinguished themselves in the service.

Obverse: A military trophy surrounding an oval shield, bearing the Arms of the United Kingdom, having in the centre the Arms of Hanover.

Reverse: 'For Long Service and Good Conduct', with an ornamentation below.

This medal was suspended from a small steel bar and clip, a steel bar being sometimes used in place of the bar.

The recipient's name, &c., is indented in large letters on the edge of the medal, also the year of discharge.

On the accession of Queen Victoria a similar medal was issued, but the Hanoverian Arms were omitted. A silver bar for suspension was introduced about 1851 and the date of discharge omitted.

By R.W. of 1875 the previous rules regarding the granting of these medals on discharge were cancelled, and the medal was bestowed with a gratuity, not exceeding £5, on N.C.Os. and men who had 18 years' service of an irreproachable character. The medal is now given with or without a gratuity according to War Office decision.

Since 1874 the recipient's name, &c., has been engraved on the edge.

With the accession of King Edward VII a new medal was issued, having on the obverse the bust of the King in Field-Marshal's uniform, the reverse remaining as previously.

The ribbon in all three cases is a red ribbed one.

On the accession of King George V his bust takes the place of King Edward and the legend as regards the name is altered accordingly.

The Meritorious Service Medal was instituted on 19th December 1845.

Obverse: Diademed head of Queen Victoria with the legend 'Victoria Regina'.

Reverse, Inscription 'For Meritorious Service', surmounted by a crown and encircled by a broad wreath of laurel.

Ribbon red.

APPENDIX E

COMMENDATORY DOCUMENTS ISSUED IN THE CHANNEL ISLANDS, 1817

Aux Etats de l'Ile de Jersey. L'an mil huit cent dixsept, le vingtième jour d'Août. Sensibles aux soins que le Lieut.-Colonel Messire William Williams, et tous les autres officiers du triezième Régiment d'infanterie de sa Majesté, ont apporté durant leur séjour dans ce pays à ce concilier l'estime des habitans, et à y entretenir une heureuse harmonie, et pleinement satisfaits du haut dégré de discipline dont lequel ils ont constamment gardé et maintenu le dit Régiment, et leur attention à prévenir tous sujets de plaintes et de disputes, à fair observer l'ordre et respecter les lois, du zèle avec lequel ils se sont toujours prêtes à soutenir et à appuyer les autorités constituées, Les Etats saisissent cette occasion de leur première séance depuis que le dit Régiment a été rapellé hors du service de cette île, où il a été en quartier pendant deux ans, pour leur rendre par ce présente Acte, le témoignage de leur approbation et leur exprimer leur vive reconnaissance. Et les Etats prient le Lieut.-Colonel Messire William Williams, Chevalier Commandeur de l'honorable Ordre du Bain, le Lieut-Colonel Weller, et le Lieut-Colonel Handcock, qui ont chacun d'eux, l'un après l'autre, eu le commandement du dit Régiment, et tous les autres officers de ce corps, d'en accepter leurs sincères et unanimes remercîments. Les Etats ont requis Son Excellence Monsieur le Lieutenant-Gouvernour de vouloir bien transmettre, de leur part, le présent Acte au Lieut.-Colonel Messire William Williams, lequel est prié de le communiquer à Lieut.-Colonel Weller, à Lieut.-Colonel Handcock, et à tous les autres officiers du treizième Régiment, auquel effet le Greffier est chargé de le transcrire sur parchemin, afin qu'il soit mis sous le sceau de l'île et de le remettre à Son Excellence.

Frs. Godfray, Greffier

In acknowledging the receipt of the Act of the States, Colonel Sir William Williams observed:—

'To possess the good wishes of those with whom a soldier resides must ever be the most pleasing reflection, but particularly where, in the performance of his duty, approval emanates from so high and so respectable an assembly as the States of Jersey; it thence becomes a source of the most heartfelt and lasting gratification, and will be recorded, and handed down, as one of their dearest memorials. In communicating the contents to the officers of the 13th Regiment, I am to request that you will accept their thanks; they being actuated with the most fervent wishes for the prosperity of the island.'

On quitting the island of Guernsey the following letter was received dated 4th May 1819:—

'SIR,—The Royal Court of this island have desired me, as their president, to express the high regard which they in common with its inhabitants entertain for the officers of His Majesty's 13th Regiment of Foot; as well as their approbation and admiration of the general conduct of the men of that corps while quartered among us; and I feel much pleasure in being thus enabled to assure you, Sir, that from all classes I have heard no other sentiments but those of regret, at the approaching departure of the Regiment, which under your command, and that of Lieut.-Colonel Sir William Williams, has shown itself throughout so orderly, and worthy of the esteem of this and the neighbouring islands; and the officers in particular by their gentlemanly and social manners, have so thoroughly gained the good will of those who had the pleasure of their acquaintance, that one and all unite in the best wishes for the happiness and prosperity of the whole corps, in which none is more sincere than he who has the honour to be,

Sir, yours etc.
PETER DE HAVILLAND,
Bailiff of Guernsey.'

In acknowledging the receipt of this letter, Lieut.-Colonel Richard Butler Handcock stated:—

'It will, no doubt, be extremely gratifying to Sir William Williams, as it is to all ranks of the Regiment now here, to find that their conduct has been thought deserving of so great an honour. Penetrated by the repeated proofs of esteem and affection, which they have received from the inhabitants of Guernsey, the officers request me to offer their sincere wishes for the general prosperity of the island, and for the individual happiness and welfare of those friends to whose polite and marked attention they are so deeply indebted.'

APPENDIX F

MEMORANDUM ON THE METHOD OF WEARING THE SASH

From 1661 to 1700 there seemed to be no special rules about the wearing or colour of officers' sashes; they were worn both round the waist and from the shoulder.

From about 1730, however, it had become a general custom to wear a crimson sash from the right shoulder to the left side—and this was undoubtedly the custom at the time of Culloden. If the serjeants wore sashes at all, they probably conformed to the method of wearing adopted by the officers, for from 1770 to 1857 there is ample evidence that the sash was worn round the waist and tied on the left side both by officers and serjeants, the only difference being that the colour of the officers' sash was crimson and the serjeants' crimson with a stripe of the colour of the regimental facing in the centre.

In 1857, when the tunic took the place of the coatee, the sash once more was worn from the shoulder to the side, but this time the officers wore it from left to right and the serjeants from right to left.

Lord Mark Kerr joined the Regiment in 1854, and it is quite clear that then and for a number of years previously the serjeants of the Regiment had been wearing their sashes round the waist differently from serjeants of other regiments—that is to say, tied on the right side.

When did the practice commence, and what is its origin?

Lord Mark attributed the origin to a distinction awarded to the Regiment at the Battle of Culloden, but there is no evidence in support of this theory, or of another theory that the distinction was gained at the Pass of Killiecrankie.

In the eighteenth century Colonels of Regiments did very much as they pleased in odd methods of clothing—the colours, facings, and lace of uniforms were laid down by regulation, but petty variations were very much according to the Colonel's caprice. It is probable that the method of the wearing of the sash in the Regiment originated in some such way as this.

Another interesting fact arises from the statement on page 40 of Carter's Records that the privilege of wearing the sash differently from other regiments was granted to both officers and serjeants of the 13th.

The extension of this privilege to the officers was eventually confirmed by Regulation in 1931, as will be seen by the following correspondence:—

APPENDIX F

'The War Office,
London, S.W.1.
18th February 1931

His Royal Highness the Duke of York, K.G., K.T., G.C.M.G., G.C.V.O.,
 Colonel-in-Chief, The Somerset Light Infantry (Prince Albert's).

SIR,—

The Regiment is very anxious to have the custom of Officers knotting the sash on the right side confirmed to them in regulations, and have pressed me to get this done before I leave the War Office. I think the attached correspondence will give Your Royal Highness all the information on the subject, and if you would be pleased to approve of my sending this letter to the Army Council, perhaps you would give me permission to add at the bottom that Your Royal Highness, as Colonel-in-Chief, approves of this application being submitted.

I have the honour to be, Sir,
Your Royal Highness' obedient and
humble Servant,
(Sd.) WALTER BRAITHWAITE,
General,
Colonel, The Somerset Light Infantry,
(Prince Albert's)'

'H.R.H. The Duke of York's Office,
11, Grosvenor Crescent, S.W.1.
February 18th 1931

DEAR GENERAL,—

The Duke of York has received your letter of February 18th and read the correspondence, which I return.

He fully approves of the proposal with regard to knotting the sash, and is very glad to give you permission to state this fact in your letter to the Army Council.

Yours sincerely,
(Sgd.) PATRICK HODGSON

General Sir Walter Braithwaite, G.C.B., A.D.C.,
 The War Office, S.W.1.'

'War Office,
London, S.W.1.
17th February 1931

The Under Secretary of State,
 War Office,
  London, S.W.1.

SIR,—

I have the honour to request that the Army Council may be pleased to recommend to His Majesty that the long-established custom in The Somerset

APPENDIX F

Light Infantry of wearing the sash tied on the right side in full dress may be further regularized by the inclusion in King's Regulations, paragraph 964, of a note extending this privilege to the officers.

2. As the Army Council are undoubtedly aware, the custom was in 1865 officially recognized in the case of Warrant Officers and Serjeants of the Regiment, and this recognition in the present edition of King's Regulations appears as a note in paragraph 971. That official recognition was not then accorded to officers also was apparently due to the fact that at that time officers of all regiments wore the sash over the left shoulder and knotted on the right side. There was, therefore, no point in including the officers of The Somerset Light Infantry in the official sanction then given.

3. Subsequently, however, in 1898, the Dress Regulations were changed so that officers wore the sash round the waist and Warrant Officers and Serjeants wore it over the right shoulder, the knot in both cases being tied on the left. The privilege of tying the knot on the right was, in the case of Warrant Officers and Serjeants of The Somerset Light Infantry, still covered by King's Regulations but, unfortunately, no application was then made by the Regiment for an amendment of the Regulations as regards officers, though the custom of wearing the sash knotted on the right side in the case of Officers, as well as Warrant Officers and Serjeants, has persisted up to the present time, properly by regulation in the latter case, and improperly—by tradition and custom—in the former.

4. As evidence that the custom applied to Officers as well as to Warrant Officers and Serjeants, I attach copies of letters dated 1865, the originals of which are preserved in the 1st Battalion, The Somerset Light Infantry. The letter from Colonel Wade shows the custom to have been in existence for many years prior to 1865, and that of Major Wilkinson carried the date back to 1792, when his father joined the Regiment. At these periods, by previous dress regulations, both officers and serjeants of other regiments wore the sashes knotted on the left side.

5. I hope, therefore, that the Army Council will agree to recommend that the old established custom of officers being allowed to tie the knot of the sash on the right side, so highly prized by all ranks of the Regiment, should now be regularized by King's Regulations.

I attach the concurrence of H.R.H. The Colonel in Chief.

I have the honour to be, Sir,
Your obedient Servant,
(Sgd.) WALTER BRAITHWAITE,
General,
Colonel, The Somerset Light Infantry,
(Prince Albert's)'

APPENDIX F

Copy

'Hangwell Hall, Bedale.
March 25th, 1865

My Lord,—

In reply to your letter of the 23rd instant. I beg to state that I have a distinct recollection that in the records of the 13th Regiment, the privilege of wearing the Sash tied on the Right side was accorded to the Regiment for distinguished conduct, (I believe at the Pass of Killiecrankie) and during my twenty years' service in the Regiment, both Officers and Serjeants invariably tied the Sash on the Right side.

I may add that having been Adjutant of the Regiment for some years, these records were in my custody and were frequently perused by me.

Hoping my testimony may be instrumental in maintaining the distinction for my old Regiment.

I remain, My Lord,
Your very obedient Servant,
(Sgd.) Hamlet C. Wade, Col.
late 13th P.A. Light Infy.

To Lord Mark Kerr, C.B.,
    Cmdg. 13th P.A. Lt. Infy.'

Copy

'Drumbrae, Bantry.
March 25th 1865.

Sir,—

I have the honour to acknowledge receipt of your letter of the 23rd inst. and beg leave to state for the information of Colonel Lord Kerr, C.B., that the *Officers* and *Serjeants* always used to wear their sashes tied on the Right side, even previous to the Regiment being made Light Infantry. This I can answer for having been born in the Regiment. My father, Lieut.-Colonel Wilkinson, served in the Regiment many years before me, having joined about 1792, and the tradition I always heard was that the Duke of Cumberland granted the Regiment this distinction on the field of Culloden.

I never saw the Records which are said to have been lost at Azimghur in 1858 and cannot answer for their contents, but believe any allusion to the above circumstance must have been mentioned in former records, which I have heard were lost many years before that period.

I have the honour to be, Sir,
Your obedient Servant,
(Sd.) R. B. Wilkinson, Major,
late of 13th Light Infy.'

APPENDIX F

'54/Misc./2846 (M.G.O.7.B.)

The War Office,
London, S.W.1.
26th February 1931

Sir,—

With reference to your letter of the 17th instant, I am commanded by the Army Council to acquaint you that His Majesty The King has approved of officers of The Somerset Light Infantry (Prince Albert's) wearing their sash tied on the right side in full dress.

I am to add that King's Regulations and Dress Regulations will be amended in due course.

I am, Sir,
Your obedient Servant,
(Sgd.) A. E. WIDDOWS.

General Sir Walter P. Braithwaite, G.C.B., A.D.C.,
   Colonel of The Somerset Light Infantry (Prince Albert's),
      Adjutant-General to the Forces,
         War Office, S.W.1.'

INDEX

(Besides battles, actions and matters of general interest only officers of the Regiment are mentioned in this index, and they are described by their highest rank or title.)

Aboukir, Bay of, 116
Afghan War, 165–208
African, South, War, 322–361
Ainslie, General, 107, 122, 381, 386
Alexandria, 116–119
Allfrey, I. S., Colonel, 294, 296, 396
Almanza, Battle of, 65, 66, 67
Ava, 156–158
Azimghur, 237–241, 257

Bainbrigge, A., Lieut.-Colonel, 273, 274, 297, 396
Band, 97, 125
Barcelona, Siege of, 53–56, 61, 62
Barry, D., Chaplain, 77, 78
Barrymore, Earl of, 42, 43, 47–49, 51, 53, 54, 56, 61, 64, 68–72, 75, 76, 381, 382
Baskerville, Lieut., 109
Bassein, 154, 155
Blockhouse Lines, 355
Borton, A. C., Colonel, 308, 309, 313, 316, 396, 397
Bowes, F., Lieut.-Colonel, 76, 396
Boyne, Battle of, 21–23
Bradshaw, L., Lieut.-Colonel, 110, 112, 113, 115, 118, 120, 396
Braithwaite, W. P., Brig.-General, 302, 305, 306, 318, 324, 329, 331, 359, 360, 375, 379
Brown, W. E., Lieut.-Colonel, 292, 297, 298, 396
Burmese War (1824–26), 146–158
Burmese War (1885–87), 298–305

Camarett Bay, 30, 31
Campbell, A., General, 122, 137, 381, 386
Canada, 137–140
Cary, T. A., Colonel, 295, 296, 396
Catalonia, Campaign in, 67
Caya, Action on the, 70
Champlain, Lake, 138
Charlton, W., Captain, 75
Cheduba, 146–148
Chetwynd-Stapylton, Lieut., 181, 202
Cloghessy, Private, 124

Colours, 9, 45, 68, 87, 97, 98, 121, 141, 158, 221, 222, 253–255, 262–264, 293, 294, 309–311, 316, 319, 366
Colville, Hon. Charles, Major-General, 109, 114, 115, 118, 120, 126, 129, 130, 133, 396
Cork, Siege of, 25, 26
Cotton, Colonel, 75–78, 381, 383
Couchman, G. H. A., Colonel, 305, 370, 371, 396
Courts Martial, 98
Cox, Lieut.-General Sir John, 194, 230, 231, 234, 236, 242–246, 252, 260, 362, 381, 392
Cox, W., Lieut.-Colonel, 277, 279, 280, 286, 287, 305, 306, 396
Crimean War, 227–232
Culloden, Battle of, 92, 93

Dana, G., Lieut.-Colonel, 122
Dennie, W. H., Lieut.-Colonel, 148–150, 152–154, 158, 161, 166, 167, 169, 171–178, 182, 184, 185, 187, 193, 195–197, 201, 202, 208, 210
Deserters, 10
Dettingen, Battle of, 85, 86, 294

Earthquake, 192, 193
Egypt, 115–121, 225
England, E. L., Major-General, 277, 278, 280, 287, 288, 290–293, 295, 298, 362, 371, 381, 393, 396, 397
Everett, H. J., Colonel, 308, 359, 361, 371, 372, 375, 396, 397

Falkirk Muir, Action of, 91
Fontenoy, Battle of, 87–89
Frith, H. C., Colonel, 370, 374, 376–378, 396

Gallwey, E. J., Colonel, 287, 291, 308, 315, 321, 324, 325, 333, 334, 339–342, 352, 354, 356, 359, 368, 396, 397
Ghazni, 170–176
Gibraltar, Sieges of, 49–52, 79–81

419

INDEX

Gilbert, P. E. V., Colonel, 250–252, 276, 279, 280, 282, 287, 288, 292, 293, 298, 396
Gloucester, Duke of, 99, 100, 381, 385
Gomm, Sir William, 220, 254, 258, 381, 389
Grobelaar's Kloof, Attack on, 333–335
Guadaloupe, 131, 225

Handcock, Lieut.-Colonel, 123, 139, 142
Hargrave, W., Lieut.-Colonel, 81, 396
Hastings, F., Colonel, 10, 11, 13, 14, 16–20, 22–29, 32–35, 381, 382, 396
Havelock, Sir Henry, 145–147, 149, 155, 157, 159, 160, 162, 164, 166, 168, 171, 172, 185, 188, 191, 192, 195, 196, 202, 203, 205, 213, 214, 219, 234, 235, 397
Hoban, Sergt., 184, 187, 206, 266, 267
Horne, A., Colonel, 253, 257, 259, 260
Hounslow Heath Camp, 4, 5, 10, 12
Howard, Lieut., 149
Huntingdon, Earl of, 4, 9, 12, 13, 381
Huy, Surrender of, 46

Illustrious Garrison, 198
Inspections, 37, 99, 101, 102, 103, 104, 106, 107, 114, 125–127, 133–137, 141, 159, 160–163, 177, 220, 222–226, 256

Jacob, Sir John, 11, 36–39, 381, 382, 396
Jellalabad, Siege of, 186–203
Jones, John, Lieut.-Colonel, 56–59

Kabul, 166, 175, 180, 181, 188–190, 206–208
Kambula, 284–288
Kandahar, 166, 169, 170, 176
Keane, Lord (of Ghazni), 129–133, 166, 167, 169–171, 173–176
Kerr, Lord Mark, General, 78, 80, 82, 381, 383
Kerr, Lord Mark, General (G.C.B.), 227, 229–231, 233–242, 244, 246–252, 255, 257, 258, 260–265, 316–318, 362, 381, 392, 396
Kershaw, Major, 179, 189, 190, 210
Khoord-Kabul Pass, 182, 183, 188
Killiekrankie, Battle of, 16–19
Kinloch, Colonel, 287, 291, 296, 297, 396
Kinsale, capture of, 27

La Cole Mill, 139
Ladysmith, Relief of, 325–337
Leet, W. K., Colonel, 270, 284, 285, 287, 298, 304, 305, 396
Liége, Siege of, 45
Light Bob Gazette, 308, 309

Light Infantry, 104, 143, 144
Loches, Captain de, 31, 40, 66

Macbean, Colonel, 266, 269, 270, 396
Macdonald, Lieut.-Colonel, 260, 266, 268, 271, 396
Madden, Colonel, 298, 306, 316, 396
Martinique, Capture of, 127–130, 225
Maunsell, T., Lieut.-Colonel, 271, 273, 396
M'Creagh, Colonel, 145–147, 150, 151, 157, 159, 396
M'Pherson, Major-General, 258, 381, 390
Medals, 120, 158, 160, 202, 203, 209, 225, 231, 305, 368, 388–410
Mein, Lieut., 182, 183, 190, 207
Middleton, Lord, 83, 381, 384
Miers, Lieut., 355, 357
Mohmand Campaign, 311–315
Moncal, Lieut.-Colonel, 40, 42, 51, 396
Montgomery, Colonel, 270, 276, 293, 396
Mooifontein, Action of, 352
Moreau, Lieut.-Colonel, 83, 396
Morrison, Lieut.-General, 137, 144, 381, 387
Mounted Infantry, 295, 357, 358, 367
Moyle, Lieut.-Colonel, 106, 396
Murray, The Hon. James, General, 100, 381, 385
Mutiny, Indian, 233–253

Napier-Clavering, Colonel, 363, 364, 396
Nimequen, Action of, 43

Officers, List of, 4, 11, 38, 42, 71, 76, 77, 81, 83, 120, 167, 176, 177, 209, 230, 231, 252, 280, 287, 291, 318, 324, 341, 342, 366, 367, 368, 370, 372
Ogilvy, Lieut.-Colonel, 104
Origin of the Regiment, 3

Parr, Sir Henry Hallam, 270, 292, 297, 308, 371, 374, 375, 381, 393, 396, 397
Pay, Rates of, 8
Payne, Major-General, 279, 280, 287, 291, 303, 305, 313–315, 355, 361, 375, 381, 394
Pearce, Lieut.-Colonel, 38, 60, 396
Pearce's Dragoons, 60–67, 69, 71
Pieters Hill, Battle of, 336, 337
Platt, Lieut.-Colonel, 370, 372, 375, 396
Port au Prince, 110
Portugal, Expeditions to, 48, 49, 68
Pulteney, General, 83, 96, 381, 385

Regimental Dinner, 271
Rorne, Lieut.-Colonel, 36

INDEX

Sale, Sir Robert, 145–147, 149–163, 166, 168, 170–189, 192–209, 211–215, 218, 219, 321, 381, 388, 396
Sale, Lady, 189, 190, 204, 206–208, 214
San Mateo, Siege of, 56–59
Sashes, 264, 265, 413–417
Schweizer Reneke, 341, 342, 347, 348
Sekukini Campaign, 277–280
Sevastopol, Siege of, 229–232
Shipwreck, 47
Snow, Major-General, 295, 296, 316, 318, 378, 397
Somerset, County of, 105
Somerset Militia, 130, 272, 292, 369
Spencer, Lieut.-Colonel, 109, 110, 111, 116
Spion Kop, Battle of, 326–330
Squire, Lieut.-Colonel, 211, 212, 214, 215, 220–222, 396
Standing Orders, 106, 160, 308
Stanhope, Lieut.-General, 381, 392
St. Domingo, 108
Stisted, Lieut.-Colonel, 364, 366, 376, 396
Stuart, Lieut.-Colonel, 222–227, 396
Swayne, Lieut.-Colonel, 318, 324, 339, 342, 360, 370, 378, 396, 397

Territorial System, 369
Tezin, 183
Thornhill, Major, 148, 153, 154, 156, 158
Tiburon, Cape, 109
Title of Regiment, 33, 105, 201, 292, 369, 374

Tolyana Stadt, 279–280
Tronson, Lieut.-Colonel, 178, 201
Truckee, Heights of, 215–218

Ulyett, Armourer Sergt., 196
Ulundi, Battle of, 290–291
Uniform, 8, 9, 97, 112, 113, 132, 254, 256, 272, 273, 308, 309

Vaal Krantz, Battle of, 331
Val, Battle of, 95, 96
Vallentin, Major, 300, 318, 355, 360, 361
Venloo, Siege of, 44
Victoria Cross, 239, 284, 285
Villiers, Lieut.-Colonel, 4, 396

Waddy, Colonel, 277–280, 286, 287, 291, 307, 316, 318, 321, 396
Walsh, Colonel, 280, 287, 291, 295, 316, 318, 362–364, 396, 397
Weller, Lieut.-Colonel, 133, 137, 140
Wepener, Relief of, 339, 340
Whitelocke, Colonel, 108–111, 396
Williams, R. B., Colonel, 280, 287, 291, 324, 333, 334, 341, 345, 348, 349, 356, 360, 368, 396
Williams, Sir William, 137, 138, 139, 141, 142, 145, 396
Wilson, Bugler, 172

Zulu War, 281, 288

Printed and Bound by Antony Rowe Ltd